The Life and Literary Works of
Alfred John Brown

Walker, Writer and
Passionate Yorkshireman

by

John A. White

First published by **John A. White** in 2016 in a limited edition of 500 copies
of which this is copy number   144

A CIP catalogue record for this book is available from the British Library.

ISBN 978-1-5262-0511-7

Typeset in Arno Pro by SpiffyMap Ltd.

Printed, bound and distributed by
SMITH SETTLE
Gateway Drive, Yeadon, LS19 7XY

Contents

Index of Photographs

Index of Maps

Foreword

For almost 40 years, between his first book *Four Boon Fellows: a Yorkshire Tramping Odyssey*, in 1928, and his death in 1969, A.J. Brown was one of the most popular, and most widely read authors about the Dales and indeed the whole of Yorkshire.

This was well before Alfred Wainwright was to monopolise walkers' bookshelves. Alfred Brown probably helped to pave the way for that later author's success, through his books and articles – especially in *The Dalesman* – by popularising many now famous walks or as he would call them hikes or 'tramps' through the fells, moors and dales, often covering huge mileages in a day, in an area extending from Calderdale to Teesdale, from the high Pennine summits to the rugged Yorkshire coast, including that still neglected yet fascinating area of chalk upland, the Yorkshire Wolds.

It is impossible to overemphasise the influence of 'AJB' on a whole generation of Dales lovers and walkers at a time when access to the Dales was mainly by steam train, foot and tram, and country lanes were not monopolised by cars. He writes in an energetic, masculine prose style, rich in anecdotes and personal reminiscence, a style no longer fashionable, but very much of its time and highly readable. His work is rich in humour with a zest for life – including a love of Yorkshire ale and inns – and he had what was rightly described as an encyclopaedic knowledge of England's greatest county as it was in the 1930s, 40s and 50s.

Not only have AJB's many books been unjustly neglected (and surely it is high time to reprint at least one of his Yorkshire classics such as *Striding Through Yorkshire* or *Broad Acres*) but too little is known about Brown's complex personality. He was, at various times, and despite initial serious health problems to a considerable degree cured by a love of walking and the hills, a soldier with a distinguished military career in two World Wars, in both the Royal Field Artillery and the Royal Air Force, an entrepreneur in the Bradford wool industry, a capable linguist, a journalist, and a poet. But above all, through his popular walking books and topography, he was a champion not just of the Yorkshire Dales, but of the whole of what he would surely claim to be God's Own County.

If that was not enough, he was also one of the founding fathers of the modern countryside movement (he was the first President of the West Riding Ramblers Association), a tireless campaigner for rights of way and the freedom to roam the open fells, a man with a passion for the best possible way of experiencing Yorkshire's rich heritage – on our own two feet.

Doubly welcome, therefore, is John White's excellent, thoughtful biography of this remarkable, and highly influential Yorkshireman, who contributed so much to our ability to understand and appreciate what lies all around us. In reminding us of AJB's remarkable personality and many achievements, John has done us a great service.

Colin Speakman, Hon. D. Lit.

Writer
Chairman, Dales Way Association
Vice President, West Riding Ramblers Association
Vice President, Yorkshire Dales Society

1. A.J. Brown's early tramping days

Preface

I first became aware of Alfred John Brown or 'A.J.' as he was known to his readers, but 'Alfred' as I refer to him, after a short account of his life appeared in the November 2008 issue of the Yorkshire *Dalesman* magazine and realised that I had much in common with him. I grew up in Bradford, I attended the same school and I developed a love of moorland walking in my youth, and recalled that I had one of Alfred's the early 'tramping' books, although ashamedly unread at the time!

I then discovered via the *Dalesman* that there was a long-standing interest in Alfred's life and works, after an earlier account of his life had appeared in the August 1981 issue of the magazine. Indeed, a regular contribution of letters and articles in the magazine relating to his popular 'tramping' routes with references to his writings, suggested a continued interest in him long after his death in 1969. I also found that Alfred was a regular contributor to the magazine, ever since his Yorkshire Three Peaks Walk was published in the inaugural issue of the *Yorkshire Dalesman* in April 1939.

So with my interest aroused, I began my investigations, not just to satisfy my own curiosity, but to interest others who also recognised there was more to Alfred than his literary work. My enquiries took me in many directions, both literally and metaphorically, sometimes haphazardly, often fortuitously, but always rewardingly, in the manner described by Halliwell Sutcliffe, that other great Yorkshire writer and friend of Alfred: 'it is odd how constant zeal in any cause is served by what seems chance'.

A search of my old school St. Bede's library archives led to an 'Old Boy' contact who referred me to Tom Scott Burns, an established writer who had begun a biography of Alfred. Unfortunately Tom's life was cut short by a degenerative disease, otherwise the story might have appeared 30 years ago, but Tom's contacts allowed me to trace all five of Alfred's offspring. However I realised this was only just the beginning of my quest!

By now I was familiar with most of Alfred's literary works and I began to form a reasonable overview of his life from those who knew him well and, importantly, I had the tacit agreement of his family to attempt to write his life story. Subsequently I was made aware of a voluminous archive of published and unpublished material which a member of the family had deposited with the Special Collections Department of the West Yorkshire Archive Service at the Bradford Central Library. Although this collection was catalogued in detail, it still required considerable review and analysis.

More dauntingly, there then came to light many detailed diary journals, personal notes and jottings, along with private, family and business letters written by Alfred during his life, most of which had been stored in the loft of a family member and had literally not seen the light of day for many years. This invaluable find necessitated the reading of many hundreds of thousands of words in Alfred's own inimitable, almost undecipherable handwriting, which proved a formidable challenge, as exemplified by this personal dedication to his wife from one of his early books:

This wealth of information was then used to provide a different kind biographical account of Alfred's life by integrating the two major strands of his life story – his working life and his literary life. The interdependent and sometimes conflicting nature of these strands might therefore be best illustrated in a textile analogy. The 'fabric' of Alfred's life is made up from the 'warp' of his working life, 'woven' together with the 'weft' of his literary life, by the 'shuttle' of the biographer's pen, to create the rich 'pattern' of 'cloth' that represents the life story of Alfred John Brown – a comparison which Alfred might have found apposite as a former textile agent in the Bradford Wool Trade.

I intended to write only a short account of Alfred's life and literary works, however the work took on a life of its own to become an in-depth biography. I remain cautious about the reception of this book since I am aware of those wise words of warning to potential authors by the writer and literary critic Christopher Hitchens: 'Everyone has a book in them, but in most cases that's where it should stay.' I sincerely hope that the present book does not belong in this category, but only you, the reader, can judge whether or not I should have kept the story to myself.

John A. White, Liverpool, 2016.

Acknowledgements

I want to begin by thanking all the members of the Brown family: Felicity, Barbara, Rosemary, Christopher and Adrian, who individually provided the encouragement which facilitated this definitive biographical account of Alfred John Brown's life and literary achievements, and collectively for their financial support towards the production costs of the book.

I am also grateful to many people who helped to put me on the trail of the story including: Dr. James Hagerty, former Headmaster of St. Bede's RC Grammar School, Bradford, Professor Graham Mulley, Old Boy of St. Bede's RCGS, Bradford, Denise Burns, widow of writer Tom Scott Burns and Steve Goodier, freelance writer, all of whom directed me to sources of information for the biography.

I would also like to thank key individuals who provided access to historical source materials for the work including: Jill Crowther, Librarian, St. Bede's and St. Joseph's Catholic College, Bradford, Robert Finnigan, Diocesan Archivist, Hinsley Hall, Leeds, Letisha Lawson and Anthony Hughes, Archivists, West Riding Archive Service, Bradford Central Library and the West Riding Archive Service, WW1 Servicemen's Health Records, Wakefield.

Acknowledgements for illustrative work are also due to the following people: Ingrid Arnot, Technical Illustrator, Gary Richardson Freelance Writer/Photographer for maps and Sheena Richardson, Artist for the dust cover design. In addition I acknowledge the sources of some map illustrations from Alfred John Brown's former publishers.

Finally I would like to thank my '*rédacteur en chef*', Margaret Harley, for her sterling work as editor of the book. Her expert guidance and suggestions helped transform the text from a loose narrative into a recognisable biography. Additionally, I thank Dr. Jonathan Harley of Spiffymap Ltd., for the type scripting and layout design of the text in readiness for the production of the book by Smith Settle, Printing & Bookbinding Ltd., who have also kindly agreed to act as distributors.

There are many other people to whom I owe a debt of gratitude although space does not allow a mention. Suffice to say they are all gratefully appreciated and they know who they are.

Introduction

The book provides an insight into the many facets of the Alfred John Brown story in a comprehensive account of his life. The memoir is also about his many vicissitudes, which often bordered on the edge of adversity, his repeated bouts of ill-health, occasions of economic crisis and several changes of career. And yet despite these frequent shifts in fortune, he managed to secure an orderly family life and always provided for his wife and children, primarily as a textile salesman.

However Alfred was driven by an overriding writing ambition and his literary output was rooted in his life experiences. It found expression mainly in topographical works, an anthology, in personal stories, two novels and a book of verse (see Appendix). He was at his best when he walked and wrote about his beloved county of Yorkshire for others to enjoy, but he derived satisfaction in writing for his own pleasure. Even so he harboured a desire to become a successful novelist, which remained an unfulfilled dream, in spite of an attempt to become a full-time writer.

The story of his life is told through a series of generically titled chapters that reflect key periods during Alfred's eventful existence. The text is illustrated by photographs and maps selected to elaborate the story line, and liberally sprinkled with references and notes to provide source material and supplementary information.

The book portrays Alfred's life story in a series of themes which correspond to various phases of his life. These are elaborated in a timescale of life and literary events which were often related to contemporary historical episodes associated with his life. The narrative unfolds through a consideration of some twelve key periods, each one a story within the story line, which comprised his life.

In order to illustrate this story line a diagrammatic timeline synopsis is presented overleaf which provides a chronological guide to the story. This timeline also offers a convenient series of reference points in the life and literary works of Alfred John Brown, and the portrayal of this intriguing individual as a prodigious walker, prolific writer and passionate Yorkshireman.

John A. White, June 2016

Timeline: Alfred John Brown Life and Literary Works

Life Events

1894
Born Bradford
Attended St.
Bede's G.S.,
Bradford in 1905

1909
Began career in
Bradford wool trade

1915-1916
WW1: Gunner RFA.
Discharged 1916.
Returned to wool
trade in 1922

1927
Married Marie Eugénie Bull,
settled in Burley-in-Wharfedale

1930-1939
Extensive business
travel across Europe

1940-1945
WW2: Officer RAF
Intelligence Branch

A.J.Brown: Walker, Writer & Passionate Yorkshireman

1923
First book *A Joyous
Entry into Brighter
Belgium*

1926
First novel
*The Lean
Years*

1928
First Yorkshire
book *Four
Boon Fellows*

1931
First tramping book
*Moorland Tramping
in West Yorkshire*

1932
Second tramping book
*Tramping in Yorkshire
North & East*

1938
Third tramping book
*Striding Through
Yorkshire*

1943
RAF book *Ground
Staff - A Personal
Record*

Literary Events

Timeline: Alfred John Brown Life and Literary Works

Life Events

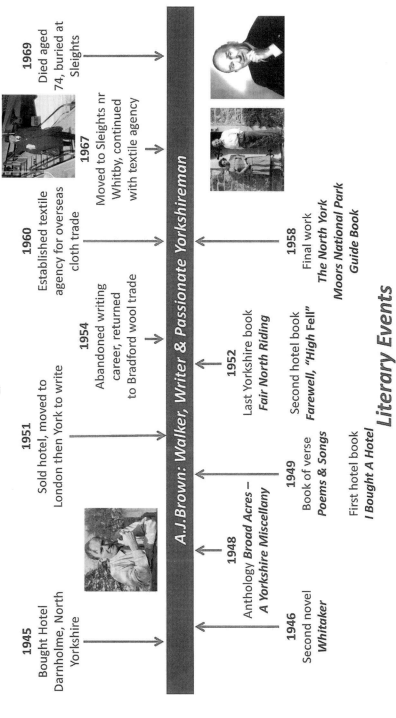

1945
Bought Hotel Darnholme, North Yorkshire

1951
Sold hotel, moved to London then York to write

1954
Abandoned writing career, returned to Bradford wool trade

1960
Established textile agency for overseas cloth trade

1967
Moved to Sleights nr Whitby, continued with textile agency

1969
Died aged 74, buried at Sleights

A.J. Brown: Walker, Writer & Passionate Yorkshireman

1946
Second novel *Whitaker*

1948
Anthology *Broad Acres – A Yorkshire Miscellany*

1949
Book of verse *Poems & Songs*

First hotel book *I Bought A Hotel*

1952
Last Yorkshire book *Fair North Riding*

Second hotel book *Farewell, "High Fell"*

1958
Final work *The North York Moors National Park Guide Book*

Literary Events

To: Jill,

I sincerely hope you find this biography to be interesting and a good read

Love from Leslie

CHAPTER 1

Bradford Born and Bred

'Doy' Boy to Office Boy

Alfred John Brown was born in Bradford, in the West Riding of Yorkshire on 21st August 1894, the second son of a family of five children which included an elder brother Edwin (b. 1889) and sister Gertrude (b. 1892), together with younger twin brother and sister, Thomas and Vera (b. 1902). His father, Alfred John Brown Snr., had relatives from the Kildwick area of the Aire Valley in the West Riding, while his mother, Mary Anne Brown (née Geoghegan), was a descendent of a family who were originally from Mountmellick, County Laoise, in the Republic of Ireland. Alfred John Brown Snr. was an electrical engineer working for the Bradford Electric Company, while his wife Mary kept house in a modest Victorian terraced home at 98 Paisley Road (now demolished) in the expanding middle class suburb of Little Horton Green, less than a mile southwest of Bradford city centre. All the children were brought up as devout Catholics and attended the local St Joseph's RC Elementary School, next to St Joseph's Catholic Church in Manchester Road. The church was founded in 1881 as a part of the expansion of churches in the late 19th century to cope with the growing population of Catholics, largely as a result of Irish immigration in the late 1840s following the famine years in Ireland.

During these early childhood years Alfred, along with his brothers and sisters, became familiar with the countryside around his industrialised home city, especially the moorland area a few miles north of Bradford, where the family often spent holidays and occasional weekends at a stone cottage in the village of Low Hill, near the hilltop township of Baildon. The old village was on the edge of the moors and was built to house miners and quarrymen who worked at the surface coal pits and quarries in the mid to late 19th century.[1] It was here as a young child that Alfred became very puzzled when the local shopkeeper addressed him as 'doy', which he took to mean 'boy', until it was explained to him that locals still used many dialect words and that the term was one of endearment and meant 'darling', which he found embarrassing, although it suggests that he was a bonny little boy at the time. Alfred and his family were fortunate to be able take such holidays since paid time off work was not available

1

to the majority of the working population at this time, and although the family also took holidays in Scarborough on the east coast of Yorkshire, it was these moors and subsequent experiences of other local moorland areas in his youth, which made the greatest impression on Alfred's young mind, and which eventually led to his lifelong interest and passion for the Yorkshire moorland and dales countryside.

Meanwhile Alfred's more urgent activity was his secondary education, and in this regard he followed in the footsteps of his elder brother Edwin, and in turn was followed by his younger brother Thomas, to the newly-established St. Bede's RC Grammar School in the centre of Bradford, which was only a short walk away from home.[2] The school had been founded in 1900 and was housed in Houghton House, the former cancer hospital of St Catherine's Home, at the corner of Drewton Street and Houghton Place,[3] just to the north of the city centre off the busy route of Manningham Lane which served the largest middle-class suburban development in Bradford of the late 19th century. The early years of the school were fraught with financial difficulties and it was not until just after the time of Alfred's entry in 1905 on a part scholarship provided by the Education Authority, that the Governors had secured its future by the establishment of a trust to manage its own affairs.[3] This was fortunate since St. Bede's was the only Catholic boys' grammar school in the West Riding of Yorkshire and was the first one founded in Yorkshire for nearly 400 years.

It was Alfred's elder brother Edwin, later dubbed 'Eddie' by his siblings, who first entered this hallowed institution on the opening day of Tuesday 12th June 1900. The headmaster was Fr. Arthur Hinsley, who was to become Cardinal Archbishop of Westminster, and his deputy was Fr. John O'Connor, on whom the fictional character 'Fr. Brown' was based in G.K. Chesterton's novels. There were two other members of staff, but only 37 boys of varying age who made up the first complement of pupils,[3] and Eddie recalled his experience many years later in a short article written for the school magazine:

> I was one of those funny little fellows in the lace collars and white waistcoats... We dressed of course in those days, not in pullovers, blazers and flannels, but in white ruffles, velvet suits, lace collars and, on special occasions white waistcoats... I was too young to appreciate the historic significance of that first day. What did impress me was that on my way home I could meander through the open market. I can still recall the chalky smell of Dr. Hinsley's gown.[4]

But at least Eddie did not suffer the same embarrassment as one of his contemporaries and namesake, though no relation, John Brown, the first boy entered on the school register, who arrived at the school earlier in June and found the iron gates locked shut but a side door open. Then in answer to the school caretaker Pat Riley's call: *'oow's thee'ar?'* replied that he was told to attend school for the first time that day, but was firmly told: *'Tha's a week t' sooan at least lad! Tha' mun cum back nex' week!'*[5]

Fr. Arthur Hinsley

Edwin J. Brown

2. First staff and boys at the school

It was soon Alfred's turn to follow his brother to the school in 1905 at the age of eleven and he became roll number 41 on the register of boys. By now the school was beginning to expand and when the total number of pupils reached over one hundred in 1906 the Governors responded by giving the boys a holiday! There were now three divisions in the school; the junior department for boys between 8-11 years old, the senior school for boys aged 11-15 years, and the supplementary school which prepared those aged 16 years and above for entry to university and professional examinations. Some of the boys were boarders and were accommodated in residence in premises at St. Patrick's Preparatory School in Westgate, before moving temporarily to the splendid Rose Mount Villa about a mile and a half away in Queens Road, Manningham.[3] Alfred however was a day pupil in the senior school during his three short years of attendance, until he left at the somewhat premature age of almost 14 years in 1908, since the leaving age was not raised to 14 until the Education Act of 1918.

Alfred's reminiscences of the school were like those of many other boys at the time. He was somewhat in awe of the great institution that he had joined, which in every aspect was seen as being both foreign and formidable to the young impressionable mind. He later recounted some of his early experiences of the place in a special edition of the St. Bede's School Magazine which celebrated the school's silver jubilee in 1925:

> Curiously enough, it was the vastness rather than the smallness of Drewton Street which impressed me the most. Coming, as I did – young, small and innocent from the one-roomed desert of an elementary school, the many passages, stairways and box rooms bewildered me. Inside, I associated the school with a number of powerful odours. The smell of cedar wood in my own classroom, and the learned reek of the textbooks stacked in my own desk quite appalled me. I always associated Latin with a foisty smell. The smell of the Chemy. Lab. never lost its magic savour. To me Mr. Taviner was the grand alchemist par excellence. At any moment I was aware that something might blow up, possibly, somebody.[6]

Two other prophetic instances also stand out in Alfred's account of his early recollections of his St. Bede's experiences, one in which he first attempted to write a poem, and the second which led him towards his eventually successful linguistic endeavours as he explained:

> I remember, too, with some vividness, writing my first 'poem'. Mr. Touhey set the subject, which was, I think, 'Newcastle' (his native city). I cannot forgive him for that, but I am sure that my verses were quite condign punishment for him.

> Lastly, I remember one tremendous triumph. A moment came in my school life when my one ambition was to remember, guess, create or crib the German equivalent of the word 'Grandfather'. I can still see Mr. Kreling careering up and down the room waiting for some small voice to utter the noble word. The whole class was stumped. And then, quite suddenly, out of the void it came... to ME! Even now I can hear myself spluttering that simple yet how precious word, 'Grossvater!' Frankly I expected to be wrong. I expected it to mean grand-duke or grand-uncle, with the peculiar cussedness of German words for meaning something else. I also expected a fat dictionary round my head! But it was right! He beamed. The class was saved. I think it was the proudest moment of my life. [6]

During this youthful period of his life Alfred continued to develop his love for the great outdoors, although unlike his younger brother Thomas, it was not via the opportunities afforded by the boy scouts. Thomas was destined to join the St. Bede's, 1st Bradford Central Scout Troop, when he arrived at the school on 9th September

1913. The troop had been formed shortly after Robert Baden-Powell had founded the scout movement in the summer of 1907, and he had begun the publication in six fortnightly parts of his handbook *Scouting for Boys* in the early months of 1908. This publication had fired the imagination of a group of pupils at the school who formed the 'Bloodhound' Patrol and later cajoled a teacher, Fr. Charles Tindall, to become the first scoutmaster. The school scout troop was founded in 1908 and became not only the first Catholic scout troop, but also the first school scout troop in the world as well.[7,8]

3. St. Bede's School, 1900-1919

Three of the founding boys of the 'Bloodhound' Patrol, Joseph Bennett, Peter Nicholson and William Rogers, who were boarding pupils at Rose Mount Villa, the residence of the then headmaster, Fr. John H. Brennan, were classmates of Alfred, although there is no evidence that Alfred was a member of the scout troop, which given the orientation of scouting towards outdoor experiences seems somewhat at odds with his developing interest in the countryside. Perhaps it was because of the discipline involved in the organisation, or he did not want to be part of a highly organised group for the purpose of his leisure activities, which had already been influenced by walks with his father and elder brother over the moors to Ilkley, that he just continued to enjoy his family rambles.

A favourite route for these walks involved taking the tram from Bradford to the outskirts of the city, alighting at Saltaire before proceeding through Shipley Glen, then via footpaths past outlying farms to the famous near-halfway house of Dick Hudsons pub on the edge of the moor.[9] This was the traditional stopping off point for all ramblers, where they would eat their sandwiches and drink tea outside, before continuing over Rombalds Moor connecting industrial urban Airedale with scenic rural Wharfedale. The path took them via the Twelve Apostles stone circle to the white house of White Wells overlooking the spa town of Ilkley, with views of the impressive hill of Beamsley Beacon and mid Wharfedale in the distance. Then in the late afternoon, having had tea in Ilkley, the family would start their 8 mile return trail home, often in the dark, ending in a moonlight dash in order to catch the last tram home to Bradford. It was during these youthful moorland wanderings, when no doubt Alfred got his first taste of the pure, invigorating air of the rolling uplands, which formed the basis for his subsequent moorland 'tramping', and the close affinity which he developed for the dales and moors of Yorkshire that was to last a lifetime.

By now the family were living in a larger Victorian terraced house at 13 Spring Place in the westerly Shearbridge suburb of Lister Hills overlooking the city, but still only a short distance from the centre of Bradford. However holidays were still taken in moorland areas, but now to the west of Bradford in an old stone cottage on the edge of the Ogden moors in the village of Mountain, close to the Old Raggalds Inn, near Queensbury. Alfred later acknowledged that it was in this area where he learned to love the moors more deeply, with a curious intensity and to grow familiar with that most sombre, mournful tract of wild moorland known as the 'Brontë country'.

It was also about this time that Alfred met another young lad of the same age, one George Coulehan Heseltine, the son of a Hull dentist, Arthur Heseltine, whose wife had died when George was still a child. George had been brought up by his maternal aunt following the death of his father when George was still a youth. He was studying hard for a scholarship to university and had a keen interest in walking and bird watching on the Wolds of the East Riding of Yorkshire, but his aunt was not able to support his outdoor interests in the long school holidays. Fortunately her cousin, Alfred's mother, suggested in an exchange of letters, that it would be possible for George to spend time with Alfred during the family's regular holidays to the cottage on the moors, and that the boys with similar interests may get along well with each other. This was something of an understatement, since Alfred and George went on to become life-long friends, fellow walkers and writers, and George would be Alfred's best man at his wedding some years later.

The two young lads enjoyed their visits to the Ogden Moors between Queensbury and Denholme to the west of Bradford, even though the cottage was very primitive with flagstone floors, oil lamps for lighting and water drawn from a nearby well which served the local community, but since they only spent their nights there, they enjoyed their days exploring the local moors. Alfred already knew his way around the locality, but George was fascinated by the contrasts of the more rugged scenery with that to which he was accustomed in the East Riding. Together they roamed over to Oxenhope and Haworth, to the lonely ruined farmstead of Top Withins, which they assumed was the site of Wuthering Heights of the Emily Brontë story, even though it remained unclear as to whether the site was the inspiration for the location. What did this matter to two youths who were enamoured of the literature of this bygone era and their daily rambles through the countryside in which the classic novel was set?

However it was not all easy going for the pair at first. Alfred was several inches taller than George with a longer stride and more accustomed to the terrain, which meant that George was always struggling to keep the pace set, although he made up his lack of stature with his more powerful physique and associated strength and endurance, which would match the two admirably in their subsequent exploration of the Yorkshire Dales in later life. Meanwhile, these holiday rambles soon came to an end when George had to return to his academic studies and Alfred had already left school to start a new life in the world of work, although from this time onward they began to correspond with each other and meet up on every possible occasion. However as it will be seen, Alfred's associations with his old school 'alma mater' were far from over.

Off to Work He Went

It remains unclear why Alfred left school so young. It is unlikely that additional money was needed to support the family like many other households at the time, since his father had a reasonably well-paid job and Alfred was being supported by a part scholarship in lieu of school fees. Moreover, both his elder brother Eddie and his younger brother Thomas were able to take full advantage of the secondary education years available to them. It may have been that the world of learning was not so compelling to Alfred or that he did not realize the importance of academic qualifications at the time, since he later returned to his studies at evening class while at work. Whatever the reason, young Alfred left secondary education a short time before his fourteenth birthday, and started a very different daily routine indeed.

His day now began at 5.00 a.m. when he had breakfast with his father, then he often left home in the dark, and stumbled upon the local 'knocker-up' who did his rounds of tapping with his bamboo rod on the bedroom windows of the mill-hands who worked in the many woollen mills of Bradford. At times Alfred counted himself lucky to be going to his 'office job' as he passed other, often younger, pale-faced boys and girls, who clattered along the streets in their clogs on the way to those dark satanic mills. Even so he was careful not to let his former schoolmates know exactly what his work entailed.

His new 'office job' consisted of working for a firm of traders in the St. James's Wholesale Fruit and Vegetable Market, which also housed the city's Abattoir at the rear, only half a mile east of the city centre. It was close to the Great Northern Railway Goods Station which handled most of the produce needed to supply the four major markets, two wholesale and two retail, that Bradford had at that time. His job mainly involved dealing with the bill payments and transactions of the retail buyers of fruit and vegetables from behind a pay desk (a ledger stand) in the corner of the vast goods area. But he was often required to help out with the manual labour of moving produce, as well as the inevitable role given to the new-comer, that of errand-boy, who brought the tea and sandwiches from the market café for his boss and other workers. Alfred enjoyed the noisy, hustle-bustle and brusque banter of the market traders and their use of colourful language, even though he was often ridiculed for not swearing himself, although this did not concern him since he thought that this was a fine way of life, and even hoped eventually to become a market trader himself.

However, all this was in contrast to what his father had in mind. He had hoped that his son would obtain a job in which he used his head not his hands, one that started at a reasonable time and meant that he came home clean instead of dirty, which provided a salary not a wage, and would lead to greater opportunities than had been available to himself in his younger days. This ambition for Alfred became even more pronounced when his father just happened to pass through the market one day and found his son not at his 'desk', but staggering under the weight of great sacks of potatoes from a recently-arrived consignment which needed to be stored urgently. To his chagrin, Alfred tried to explain that he had just been helping out because things were so busy, but his father was not impressed, neither with the situation nor the pay of six shillings per week, and especially not with the foul language used by most workers in the market. He demanded that Alfred only stayed long enough to obtain a letter of recommendation from his present employer, and that he should immediately start to write letters of application for a more suitable new job. He did so in spite of an offer by his boss to raise his wage by an extra one shilling per week, but his father would hear none of it and Alfred bowed to his demands.

And so it was that just one month later Alfred started a new job, on trial, as a temporary supernumerary clerk in the Superintendent's Office of the Exchange Railway Station with the Great Northern Railway Company in Bradford, at the rate of eight shillings per week, with the opportunity of a permanent appointment subject to passing the necessary examinations in due course. His new office was on top of the booking office which occupied a central position in the concourse close to the platforms above the throng of all the passenger crowds who used the station. He was somewhat daunted initially by trying to master the complexities of dealing with all the detailed train journals which train guards were required to keep of all their journeys and the arithmetical challenge of totting up the many waybills of carriage accurately, which he was required to do. However, Alfred convinced his boss that although he was not quite fifteen years old and looked somewhat younger, this well-dressed, slightly built, shy, round-faced cherub, with clear blue eyes and closely-cropped brown hair, parted and plastered down with brilliantine, was not without intelligence, and would most likely respond well to the opportunity afforded by a secure and successful career in the railway company.

Alfred found the idea of going to the railway station to work exciting, since for him it was associated with annual holidays to the seaside. He was also pleased by the friendly reception from his fellow office workers, and especially to learn of the availability of privileged travel tickets which entitled not only him, but also immediate members of his family to travel at the company's expense. The glamour of his new situation soon lost its attraction though, especially on Saturday afternoons, when he would otherwise be playing football or cricket. Similarly the scenes of the departing excursion trains to the nearby Dales, to which he had become so attached from his early days, no doubt took the shine off his new job, that not even the thrill of issuing tickets in the booking office, the most exciting place in the station, could assuage.

This apparent ambivalence to Alfred's new role may have been detected in his demeanour by one of the senior ticketing staff who confided to him that there was no future in 'clerking', and that even with hard work and passing of examinations, the best he could hope for in future was eventually a station master's job in a small station. He also suggested that Alfred should take a chance in the world of work and get into a more exciting occupation such as sales, preferably wool sales, in London if possible, where the biggest wool transactions were conducted and fortunes were to be made by enterprising young men. He further intimated that Alfred should ask his father to get him out of the railway company before it was too late and he became trapped there for ever. However it was an uncle on his mother's side of the family, Thomas Geoghegan, a successful businessman in the printing trade, through personal contacts, who found him a job at one of the most reputable and successful firms of wool merchants in Bradford, and ended his brief period of employment with the railway company.

Start of a Wool Trade Career

Alfred had now made a very positive career move that would become almost a life-long occupation and one in which from the beginning he would be more than a just an apprentice. He became a specifically selected trainee who was expected to learn the rudiments of the wool trade gained from time spent in the various departments of the firm, in order to achieve success in whatever direction he could best employ his talents through hard work, tenacity and initiative. Therefore in order to be able to make the most of this unique opportunity and his place in this newly adopted trade, he had to come to terms with the scale of the industrial might of his home city, which had spawned one of the largest manufacturing enterprises of the Victorian era, and continued to lead the world in its field at the start of the 20th century.

Bradford had grown from a small market town with a population of less than 13,000 people at the beginning of the 19th century into a rich industrial city of over 225,000 at the end of the century. It was known throughout the world for its specialisation in worsted cloth, a fine, lightweight, smooth cloth prized for its excellent quality, from the city which justified its title and accolade of 'Worstedopolis',[10] a term coined by the Bradford historian William Cudworth (1830-1906). The yarn was made from wool which had its short fibres removed by combing and the long fibres laid parallel to provide a very smooth yarn quite distinct from the intermingled variety produced in other parts of the West Riding woollen industry. The manufacture involved the combined processes of combing, spinning, weaving, dyeing and finishing, and produced a hard-wearing cloth which was in demand globally.

By the time Bradford's population reached almost 290,000 in 1911 nearly 70,000 workers were employed directly in worsted manufacture, with many thousands more indirectly in the engineering, transport and commercial sectors of the support services which were dependent on the industry. It is little wonder then that the skyline of Bradford resembled a forest of blackened chimneys,[11] belching out smoke across the great geographical 'bowl' in which the city is located, contributing to the levels of air pollution, ill-health and shortened life expectancy unknown at any time since. However even by the early 20th century 'Worstedopolis' was showing the early signs of industrial decline due to a worldwide depression of product prices and hence profits, along with strong foreign competition and the introduction of softer fabrics, which Bradford tried to counter by a shift towards newer fibres and materials in an attempt to hold its premier position as a worldwide cloth distributor.

It was this dynamic, rapidly changing industrial environment that Alfred entered in

1909, so it was hardly surprising that he contemplated with trepidation his own future under such circumstances. Many years later he reflected on his initial step into the wool trade during a speech he delivered to the attendees of the St. Bede's Old Boys' Dinner, in which he intimated that he had almost come full circle in his first career appointment, in that the office of the wool firm in which he worked was directly opposite his old school at 21 Drewton Street, Bradford:

> It has been my fate to be placed in a cell in that gloomy building opposite, and stare across at the old school whenever I lift my head from the desk. I regard myself as the ghost of St. Bede's...
>
> > Doomed for a certain time to walk the earth
> > And for the day confined to waste in offices
> > Till the foul crimes done in my schoolboy days
> > Are burnt and purged away. [12]

This was in contrast to the vague memory he had of the view of the wool firm's warehouse from the opposite side of the road during his school days which

> ...was through its association with visits made for non-too pleasant 'interviews' in the Headmaster's room [*usually involving punishment via 'six of the best' delivered to his rear end*] on which occasions I got an upside-down view of the warehouse through the Headmaster's window.[13]

However, Alfred applied himself to the task required, starting on the ground floor of the firm of Woolley and Wensley, Agents and Merchants (Shipping and Forwarding). Initially he helped the warehousemen to weigh, pack, load and blend wool, marking, craning and piling bales of wool, and joined in their games of football in the mill yard during the short lunch break. This activity together with the physical demands of the job helped him to gain weight and grow taller as befitted a rather late developer. Then after six months he was transferred to the sorting room to begin his wool education in earnest, since wool-sorters were a class apart from other workers, and were greatly respected for their keenness of perception and highly-developed sense of touch required to be able to separate, class, 'rig' and sort the different grades of wool.

It was also at this time that Alfred must have recognised the inadequacies of his education so far, since he registered for evening classes at the Bradford Commercial College during 1909/1910 to continue his studies in the groundwork subjects of the day including: arithmetic, handwriting, essay writing, orthography, dictation, and English. Geography was also studied mainly from the standpoint of trade with various countries, while History was studied from its economic aspects, and all subjects required both class work and regular homework exercises in his notebook.[14] One interesting homework topic involved writing an essay on the likely impact that the aeroplane might have on travel in the future, and this in the same year that the Frenchman Blériot had only just managed to fly across the English Channel!

It was evident from his night school notebook that his hand writing was beginning to change from a somewhat simplistic style to a more sophisticated script which began to resemble that of his tutor, whose comments liberally annotated the marked homework exercises. Furthermore, Alfred went on to study commercial French and German languages in his night school curriculum, since these were extensively used by wool traders in their dealings with the overseas markets in Continental Europe. Indeed it was often said that Bradford businessmen were among the best linguists of any group of merchants in the country at this time.

4. A young A.J. Brown

While work and study became more important in Alfred's life, escape during the occasional holidays was even more necessary now and he explored all the moors within walking distance surrounding Bradford. A favourite area was to the west of the city, leading to the so-called 'Brontë moors', which were much less frequented than the more popular tracks around Ilkley Moor. Tramping over these desolate uplands, past abandoned and ruined farms where people had fought but given up the struggle of attempting to wring a livelihood from the land in despair, he naturally contemplated his own manner of trying to earn a living, and sometimes had doubts about the progress of his career in the work in which he was engaged. But it was with growing strength and stature, as well as the sense of boundless energy derived from tramping for hours over these rough moorlands, that he became uplifted, but also occasionally downcast at the thought of what he had left behind in his workaday world. In his later years he summed up some of his feelings of the importance of these brief interludes of escape in a short poem:

ONE WEEK

On Sunday through the fields I walk,
And with the Higher Spirits talk.
On Monday to the office-stool
I go, and scribble for a fool.
For six week days, I earn my wage:
He only asks my soul in pledge.
On Saturday, I take it out,
A little soiled and knocked about.
What though it be a little shrunk?
I gladly take it from its bunk.
On Sunday through the fields I walk,
And with the Higher Spirits talk.[15]

Alfred continued with the firm for six years and worked his way through various departments of the business, until at the age of 21, he was given the chance to work as an understudy to the chief buyer of the company on '*t'Change*', as the Bradford Wool Exchange was known in the local vernacular by those who did business in this great Gothic Revivalist style building. Everyone of importance in the wool trade could be found at the Wool Exchange, it was the 'Mecca' of the textile industry, where all the real business was transacted under the great white marble statue of Sir Richard Cobden (1804-1865), who had been known as the 'Apostle of Free Trade', and was a doyen in the cause of international peace and goodwill.

Alfred must have been very impressed by the imposing, larger than life-sized figure of Cobden, mounted on a polished red granite pedestal, which overlooked the scene (and still does in this well-preserved building), since he later wrote a poem about what the great man might have thought about the activity going on the trading floor. The lines seem to capture both Alfred's, and perhaps Cobden's, bemusement and the bewilderment of the trade, as well as a sense of exasperation and longing to be out on the moors where the business really began:

LINES TO THE STATUE OF COBDEN IN THE BRADFORD EXCHANGE

Here Cobden, with a carven face,
Stares on the traffic of this place:
Transfix'd with wonder to behold
Such very golden fleeces sold:
Clearly astonished to hear
The curious fables whisper'd near
Frankly discomfited to be
Watchdog to such company.

But Cobden, is it not a bore
Always to stand upon this floor,
Always to hear within this room
Tales of booming – of the Boom:
Always to see from that high steep
Soft hats and bowlers – never sheep?

Don't you get weary now and then
Of tending flocks of stupid men,
Are you not tempted once for all
To step down from your pedestal,
And stamp out thro' the swinging doors
To find real sheep upon real moors:
To hear real shepherds talk of wool
Till it seems almost beautiful?

Sometimes when I look up, I think
Your carven eyes relax – and wink! [16]

5. *The statue of Sir Richard Cobden*

The men who formed the clientèle of '*t'Change*', for this was an exclusively male business, would no doubt have had little time for such esoteric reflections. They were wealthy businessmen, often self-made millionaires, who had sometimes won and lost fortunes, old 'dyed in the wool' Yorkshiremen, whose motto was the Bradford saying: '*wee'ar tha's muck, tha's brass*'. They had been brought up in '*t'mill*' and what they did not know about wool manipulation was not worth knowing, although mixed with these old hands was a sprinkling of more cultured men of good education, who had inherited their father's mill and money, whose sons in turn were now Alfred's colleagues. These newcomers had progressed from universities as gentlemen of the third generation, with little trace of an accent, but well-dressed in their Bond Street clothes and their old school ties. Thus even *'t'Change'* was changing. It was into this milieu that Alfred was suddenly immersed and gained a glimpse of the opportunities that his new career might bring. But alas this was only short-lived, and for him at least, it was temporarily interrupted by the events of the First World War, whereas for many others of his generation, it was terminated for ever.

References and Notes

1. Joyce W. Percy, 'The lost Villages of Baildon Moor', The Bradford Antiquary, *Journal of the Bradford Historical and Antiquarian Society*, Third Series, 1999, Vol. 7, pp. 19-46.

2. **Note**: Alfred's sisters Gertrude and Vera later attended St. Joseph's Catholic Girls' Grammar School, which was founded in 1908 in Bradford.

3. James M. Hagerty, *St. Bede's Grammar School 1900-2000: Celebrating 100 Years of Catholic Education*, Section 6, 'Drewton Street', pp. 8-12.

4. E.J. Brown, St. Bede's School Magazine, Summer, 1950, Vol. 4, No. 4, p. 52.

5. John Brown (no relation), St. Bede's School Magazine, Summer, 1950, Vol. 4, No. 4, p. 53. **Note:** John Brown became Headmaster of St. Patrick's RC School, Leeds.

6. Alfred John Brown, St. Bede's School Magazine, Jubilee Number, 1925, pp. 175-176.

7. James M. Hagerty, *op.cit.*, Section 15, 'The Scouts', pp. 66-75.

8. **Note:** St. Bede's Scout Troop disbanded in 1986, but some former scout members celebrated the centenary of its formation in 2008.

9. **Note:** The pub was originally called the Fleece Inn, but got its present name from Dick Hudson (Landlord 1850-1878).

10. William Cudworth, *Worstedopolis: A Sketch the Development of the Worsted Trade in Bradford*, Old Bradford Press, 1888.

11. **Note:** Even by the mid 1950s the biographer could count almost 300 mill chimneys from his home in the Bradford Moor area which had a panoramic view of the city.

12. Alfred John Brown, St. Bede's School Magazine, Spring, 1936, Vol., iv, No. 50, pp. 365. **Note:** Unfortunately both of these fine buildings have been demolished.

13. Alfred John Brown, 'An Author Looks Back', short article in the *Yorkshire Evening Post*, 5th January, 1936.

14. Alfred's night school notebook, In: Alfred John Brown, Catalogue No. 69D90, Section 12, Items 1-4, The West Yorkshire Archive Service, Bradford Central Library.

15. Alfred John Brown, 'One Week' in *Poems and Songs*, Horne and Son Ltd., Abbey Press, Whitby, 1949, p. 34.

16. Alfred John Brown, *ibid.*, 'Lines to the Statue of Cobden in the Bradford Exchange' p. 42.

CHAPTER 2

Alfred's Great W.A.R.: War, Affliction, Recovery

Alfred's Great War

When the First World War was declared on Tuesday 4th August 1914 the Territorial Battalions throughout the country had already received orders to mobilise, and at the Belle Vue Barracks in Bradford, Alfred's elder brother Edwin reported for duty since he was already a member of the Royal Field Artillery Territorial Force, while Alfred followed him the following year and enlisted in May 1915 in the Royal Field Artillery. Alfred had waited almost nine months to join up because his employers had pressed him to stay at work when the first new battalions were being formed, since they had already released a generous proportion of their staff for war service. Both Edwin's and Alfred's service in their respective units are recorded in the index of the City of Bradford Roll of Honour dedicated to all the men from the city who served in the war.[1]

6. Gunner A.J. Brown

7. 2ⁿᵈ Lieutenant E.J. Brown

Edwin became part of the 1/2 and Alfred the 2/2 West Riding Brigades of the Royal Field Artillery, with their headquarters based at Belle Vue Barracks in Manningham Lane in west Bradford. Each of the Brigades had three batteries with an ammunition column, and they were equipped with 15 pounder horse-drawn guns and support vehicles. Both Brigades were part of the 49th West Riding Division during the war, in which the 'first line' 49th Division, including the 1/2 WRB RFA (Edwin's Brigade) embarked for France on 15th April 1915. The 'second line' 49th Division, including the 2/2 WRB RFA (Alfred's Brigade), remained in England for almost a year to continue training, before being sent to France in January 1916, and then remained at the Western Front for the rest of the war.[2,3]

During the early period of the war Edwin saw action in France, while Alfred continued training as a gunner with the newly-established Brigade in the north of England throughout 1915, before his last posting to Salisbury Plain in early 1916 to complete final artillery training. Like many of their school friends from St. Bede's, both Edwin and Alfred were keen to do their duty for King and Country in the great conflict, although their respective fortunes were to differ markedly from each other and for that matter, from so many of their school contemporaries. Edwin was a forward signaller with the RFA which involved directing fire on enemy targets and he was one of the first artillery men from his old school to be wounded. The very nature of his role exposed him to many risks, and resulted in a shrapnel wound to his foot in 1915 at Ypres in Belgium, which led to a short stay in hospital before he returned to duty at the front.

About this time there was also an unwritten duty for old boys of St. Bede's who were serving in the armed services to convey their experiences of the war to pupils still at school, and Edwin often wrote to the Headmaster, Fr. Charles Tindall, to describe both the serious and the humorous day to day events of his life on the front line, as extracts from his communications published in the school magazine indicate. In a letter sent shortly after his promotion to 2nd Lieutenant, he recounted one of his most dreadful experiences:

> ...being hunted by 'whizz-bangs' (small calibre, but deadly German shells) as my companion and I were attempting to join up broken wire, when suddenly we found ourselves enveloped in flames, and tried to run to safety from the shells which pursued us just dropping in each spot as we left it, before collapsing exhausted in a shell hole, at which point providentially the guns ceased for a moment, and we were at last able to find a trench in which to shelter, up to our necks in water, until darkness fell and we were then able to return to our posts...[4]

In another letter from the front Edwin described the conditions he was living in as well as an occasion of off-duty 'sport':

> ...we had a real bending as regards rain during the last few days and every
> dug-out, including the officers' is full of water. The country here is very flat
> and the water rises very quickly with some of the trenches 5-6 feet deep in
> water. The water is up to our gun muzzles in the gun pits and today when
> we fired the gunners were waist deep in water...

and continued:

> ...the rats are getting a bit familiar, of course we feed them too well. We had
> a rat hunt last night, just imagine, 20 or 30 fellows in a dark dug-out, all
> trying to 'norp' Jimmy rat [to 'naup': a Yorkshire dialect term to 'hit on the head']. It
> was a real bombardment, tins of jam, lumps of hard cheese, and boots, but
> it was the remains of a fancy pudding which the cooks had been trying out
> on us, which ultimately knocked the rat out...[5]

Unlike his brother Edwin, whose only respite from the front line was his recuperation from war wounds, Alfred was able to benefit from a break in training in 1915
and astonished members of his unit when he told them he intended to take his first
leave at Easter enjoying a walking holiday in Yorkshire. This plan seemed quite mad-
ness to them having spent weeks 'drilling' in marching practice. Of course as he tried
to explain to them, there was a whole world of difference between 'route-marching'
and walking for the sheer pleasure of it, and that the love of walking for the sake of it
was in his blood, but they still did not understand. So following a couple of days to
visit his parents, Alfred was joined by his boyhood friend, George C. Heseltine, who
although serving in a different army unit, also was a kindred spirit when it came to
walking and had shared many moorland rambles with him previously. Their walking
route took them from Ilkley to Kettlewell in Wharfedale, then over Great Whernside
into and along Nidderdale, and finished back at the large army camp where they were
based in Harrogate, a distance of some 60 miles. Alfred later revealed that this walk
had influenced the whole of his life and opened his eyes to the glory of Yorkshire.[6]
Henceforth he set himself the task of climbing every hill, crossing every moor and
exploring every dale in the county – a feat which he eventually not only succeeded in
doing, but also wrote about in his most popular topographical books. A key moment
on this walk came at the top of Great Whernside on Easter Day 1915, when George
handed Alfred his own Ordnance Survey map, upon which they both signed their
names on the cover, and Alfred kept as a gift that sealed a friendship which was to
endure a lifetime.

Meanwhile, Alfred was still undergoing training as a gunner and learning how to transport gun carriages and their supporting equipment using horses, but at this time, unlike his brother, he did not appear to be in regular communication with his old school, although later he was to contribute extensively to the school magazine. In one such article he detailed several aspects of his army life which could not have been more of a contrast to that of his brother Edwin. Alfred was often engaged in manoeuvres across the north midlands of England with his artillery brigade in preparation for what was still envisaged to be a dynamic war, unlike the static war which it became in reality. Alfred recalled one of the many transfers of his Brigade in 1915, in which they moved their base from Southwell in Nottinghamshire to Grimsby in north Lincolnshire, with an overnight halt in Caistor on the north Lincolnshire Wolds.[7] The article provides a vivid description of this experience and his obvious enjoyment of the life of soldiering:

> A two day trek across England, by (say) a full Bgde [Brigade] of Artillery – with nightly bivouacs, en route, offers an interesting subject for contemplation. To the soldier born, it is a thing to remember; the Reveille in the half light, the delicious dip in the river, the mad endeavour to be ready for 'Boot and Saddle', the entrancing whiff of frazzling rashers, prepared by an indescribably dirty cook over an evil smelling fire – are but a promise of what is to follow.
>
> From the first ring of the bugle, the camp is a confusion; apparently an inextricable one, hundreds of horses are led hither and thither, a thousand men are doing a thousand different things, a hundred orders by a like number of irascible directors are heard by all and heeded by none, the guns, alone, are stolid and impassable. And yet, in perhaps half an hour's time, the bugles ring out their strident summonses; horses are 'hooked-in' to guns, limbers etc., gunners stand impatiently at their posts, drivers put one foot in the stirrup and ache to mount, horses chafe at the bits and snaffles; a whistle's shrill note momentarily petrifies all – and we are off! Gun follows gun in stately notation, wagons, forage vehicles slip into their appointed places, and soon the long mobile column stretches far down the quiet country road on a perfect summer morning, the march is begun.
>
> Mile succeeds mile, the sun is ever fiercer. Now through placid meadow lands, where yokels greet us cheerily, now past great, old farmhouses where jovial farmers eye amazedly or buxom, kind-hearted wenches rush out with ripe apples and kindred commodities; now creeping along at the tortuous

'Walk March', now jogging at the comfortable trot. Orderlies and outriders in the rear are impatient for a canter and will steal one if not carefully watched. To mount the crest of a hill at the rear of such a cavalcade and look down the long mobile column, reaching to the valley below – with sun glinting on burnished steel and saddle, with team after team of horse and man, interspersed with gun, limber, firing battery wagon – all offering a startling contrast with the tranquil scenery, is indeed an arresting and imposing spectacle.

The horses are watered at midday, 'horses first' always in the army – a charitable precept – and when they are browsing over nosebags of corn and the like, the men may make the most of their unsubstantial ration of bully & bread or bread & bully (the palate occasionally relishing the variation). None the less, this noontide reflection is the choicest pleasure of the day and he is a poor philosopher who cannot lunch with avidity, and take his wine from the river – assured that he has finally attained his 'El Dorado'.

By evening, if we are fortunate, we clatter into some straggling old world village (like an Algerian Caravan approaching a monstrous 'Caravanserai') whose serene setting might lead us to suppose we are intruders – marauders in a peaceful land – did we not know that many a troop of horse, and rascally horse into the bargain, had thundered over the same solid cobbles three centuries ago. When we have leisure to do so, we may see the yet extant ruins of the old church, the havoc of Cromwell's cannon balls.

The village folk are all out to welcome us and their whimsical comments afford much amusement in the ranks. To our delight, the order runs along that we are to rest here for the night. The guns are manoeuvred into careful alignment on the village square, the villager wiseacres make profound estimates of their calibre, boys and girls are in high glee and wonder 'which end the "bullet" comes from?'. Horses are installed in the commodious stabling of the eight or nine inns (no unusual number for a sober village); the rest are tethered to piquet-lines – and when all have been watered and fed, when guards and piquets have been posted for the night – the weary saddle-sore troopers may sit down to their evening collation. It is strange if the unambitious issue of the QMS [Quarter Masters Stores] is not considerably augmented by the open hearted villagers. They cannot do enough for us, and were we to accept the measure of their hospitality, we should be hard beset to answer the 'Reveille' on the morrow.

To be sure, we must give them a little in return; regale them with anecdote, banter and song, but this we do gladly, for there are few better 'talkers' than a well-fed trooper, and for 'one crowded hour of glorious life' – he lords it over the simple rustics, good humouredly. Village-folk, however, retire betimes and when the Last Post's sonorous note strikes the echoing hills, the sentries alone are there, languid, weary-eyed to greet it, and they, alas! are too engrossed in the practical to realize its poetic significance.

Tomorrow's march will bring to each, he knows not what; a not far tomorrow will find him in less-peaceful company; that day is always dimly present in perspective; never forgotten, it is seldom spoken of; but it is a surprising thing if the philosopher who has transformed a weary round of routine into a passable cycle of delight, will not, at least, extract from this promised, unexplored vineyard – a fair mead of wine, mixed, it is true, with yet unknown quantity of bitterness.

The advent of that day was the magnet which attracted him irresistibly at the onset: it will not fail him when he enters the last stages of the Great Adventure.[8]

In early 1916 Alfred's training came towards the final stages of preparation when his Brigade was posted to Larkhill Camp near Durrington on the Salisbury Plain in Wiltshire, before eventually embarking for France later that year. The camp was close to the Lark Hill Firing Range, a site specifically set aside for live artillery firing practice for the batteries of the Royal Field Artillery, initially as a tented camp for summer training, it was then based in huts, although the situation there was far from ideal for year-round training. While the conditions were overcrowded and none too sanitary, they must have seemed like a paradise compared with those the troops would have to endure in France. Nevertheless one inspired 'wag' serviceman, Private Ernest Osborne, wryly summed up the men's feelings about the place in a poem entitled 'The Joys of Lark Hill', which ended with the lines:

> Now when this war is over and we've captured Kaiser Billy,
> To shoot him would be merciful and absolutely silly.
> Just send him down to Lark Hill Camp amongst the rats and clay,
> And I'll bet it won't be long before he drops and fades away.[9]

In Alfred's case the sentiments in this verse were to be somewhat prophetic. One day he reported sick with a sore throat to the Camp Medical Officer, but since his condition was not considered serious at the time he was told to return to his duties. Some days later he went home on leave again back to his family in Bradford where his condition worsened considerably, he became hospitalised, was diagnosed with diphtheria and was never able to return to his unit. For Alfred this was the end of his war before it had really begun, and while he never had to live through the horrors which many of his compatriots had to endure, he had to face his own nightmare of an illness which would lead to almost total incapacitation. This was also compounded by his own perverse sense of guilt that he had been unable to 'do his bit' while many of his friends fought valiantly, suffered physical wounds and psychological damage, and often died bravely in the war which was supposed to end all wars.

The scale of personal loss to the Bradford community in general, and to those families whom Edwin and Alfred knew in particular, can be judged from the sheer numbers who were involved directly in the conflict. The Bradford Council Roll of Honour, which was drawn up in 1922 when the city war memorial was unveiled, contains the names of some 37,000 men all of whom served, were wounded and died during the war. The 1911 census recorded a Bradford population of 288,458, and while this figure would have risen naturally by 1914, the number of men between 18 and 30 years of age (the age range of almost all the men who served), was probably not more than about 55,000. Therefore the Roll of Honour represents something like two thirds of all the eligible men who were actually involved in the war.

While these figures provide some indication of the city-wide involvement in the war, the records from Edwin and Alfred's old school reflect a similar commitment made by the families of those with whom they both grew up and went to school. A total of over 200 former pupils who attended the school in its early days between 1900 and 1910 (dates which covered all those of required age to serve from the start to the end of the war), served in some 37 different units of the British and Commonwealth Countries, with 34 in the Royal Field Artillery and 33 in the West Yorkshire Regiment, which included the two famous Bradford 'Pals' Battalions.[10] The school Roll of Honour lists 41 former pupils killed in action (with 6 missing in action presumed killed), and a similar number of wounded, or in a few cases discharged unfit for service on medical grounds, which represents an overall 'casualty' rate of some 40%. Moreover, all those killed or missing in action, as well as the wounded, would have been known personally to Edwin or Alfred.

It is also worthwhile to reflect upon the known outcomes of some of the 25 members listed in Alfred's school year group of 1906-1907 (Table 1), which indicates that five were killed in action, one seriously wounded, one discharged as unfit for further

Name	War Service Details and Other Notes
Appleton, Samuel	
Bennett, Joseph	(First Scout Group Member, 'Bloodhound' Patrol, 1907/1908).
Brooks, Joseph	
Brown, Alfred	2/2 West Riding Brigade, the Royal Field Artillery, Illness and medical discharge 1916.
Cash, George	
Connolly, Stephen	
Corry, Gilbert	2nd Bn. Canadian Infantry, lost right leg at Battle of Lens 1917, medical discharge 1918.
Dalby, Harold	
Hall, William	West Yorkshire Regiment, killed in action, France, 26th August 1916, aged 22 years.
Hanly, Joseph	Served with the Australian Light Horse Corps.
Henegan, Kevin	West Yorkshire Regiment, killed in action, Flanders, 20th November, 1917, aged 25 years.
Hoban, Bernard	
Hynes, Richard	(Married Alfred John Brown's elder sister, Gertrude).
Jobson, Joseph	23rd field Company, Royal Engineers, killed in action, Flanders, 21st September, 1918, aged 25 years.
Maher, John	1st Battalion Irish Guards, missing, presumed killed in action, 6th November 1914, aged 21 years.
McShee, Thomas	Served with the Royal Field Artillery.
McWeeny, Austin	Served with the West Yorkshire Brigade, the Royal Field Artillery
Moore, Stanley	2nd Battalion, Durham Light Infantry, killed in action, Flanders, 10th July 1917, aged 22 years.
Nicholson, Peter	Served with Royal Army Service Corps (First Scout Group Member, 'Bloodhound' Patrol 1907/1908).
O'Neill, Frederick	Served with the Royal Navy, HMS Marlborough.
Owens, Leonard	
Quinn, Francis	Served with the West Yorkshire Brigade, the Royal Field Artillery.
Riordan, Francis	
Rogers, William	Served with the 5th West Yorkshires (First Scout Group Member, 'Bloodhound' Patrol, 1907/1908).
Sweeny, Alfred	Served with the West Yorkshire Brigade, the Royal Field Artillery, awarded the Military Medal.

Table 1. World War One Service of the 1906-1907 Year Group, St. Bede's Grammar School, Bradford

service on medical grounds (*'hors de combat'*, namely Alfred himself), along with five others who served in various branches of the services and one who was awarded the Military Medal. Interestingly, another former classmate of Alfred's from his previous elementary school of St. Joseph's, Corporal Samuel Meekosha, was awarded Bradford's first Victoria Cross, and unlikely though it seems, both he and Alfred were the only ones from their respective schools' era who volunteered and served again in the Second World War of 1939-1945.

The final note on this subject deserves to be left to Alfred, who while developing his literary and poetical talents later in the First World War, penned a short poem asking pupils and old boys of his former school to remember and pray for all those who served in the most bitter conflict of the 20th century. The poem is often included as part of the Remembrance Day Service held each year in November at St. Bede's, and is inscribed on a plaque on the War Memorial in the School grounds:

BEDESMEN, IN ARMS!

For Faith and Right and Liberty
O bear yourselves right gallantly
               Regina Coeli!
O thou befriend them daily
And steel their hearts most gaily.
           While those hang back
And shun the hero's track
Keep thou the truer track
       And remember Bedesmen!
Your motto shall be DEEDSMEN!
And ye who cannot fight
O pray with all your might
           That they who can
May come home man for man
But mourn the brave who die
O mourn their loss most bitterly
And pray thou most earnestly
That God may bless them for eternity! [11]

8. St. Bede's War Memorial, Bradford

Alfred's Great Affliction

In early February 1916 when Alfred went back home to Bradford on 'draft' leave and he thought he had overcome the sore throat he had reported to the Medical Officer at Larkhill Training Camp on Salisbury Plain, and recalled that he had never had a day's illness before and never felt better than he did when he returned home on leave. However it soon became apparent that he had brought an infection with him and his condition deteriorated, which required him to be sent for observation to St. Luke's Hospital, which later that year became the principal Bradford War Hospital. After three days he was transferred with suspected diphtheria to the Bradford Fever Hospital in Leeds Road, which later became one of several Auxiliary War Hospitals in Bradford. The fact that Alfred was admitted to the Fever Hospital indicated that he was considered to be highly infectious, therefore needed to be isolated, and spent over two months there before he was discharged with a questionable discharge record.[12] However he was one of many cases, since during 1916 there were 512 admissions to this hospital for infectious diseases, mainly for diphtheria, and mostly children and teenagers amongst whom it was common, but only a few adults, including six other soldiers admitted during this time.

9. Bradford Fever Hospital

What Alfred's hospital record does not show is that early in his hospital stay, he received an unauthorised visit from his brother Edwin, who was on extended leave while recovering at Ripon Hospital in North Yorkshire from a second more serious wound received in France in late 1915. This visit was against all the regulations of the

Isolation Hospital and was probably due to an error made by one of the junior members of staff, who could have been dealt with very severely and possibly dismissed as a result. When the error was discovered it led to Edwin himself being isolated for several days to make sure that he had not contracted the disease. Furthermore, while the outcome of Alfred's hospitalisation suggested that he had recovered from the diphtheria infection, the long term effects of the disease were still tó manifest themselves in some particularly debilitating ways.

Diphtheria is an upper respiratory tract infection caused by *corynebacterium diphtheriae*, and is characterised by symptoms of a sore throat causing swallowing difficulties, a low fever state and an adherent grey-white membrane covering the tonsils, pharynx and/or nasal cavities. It was common in young children before widespread vaccination became available in the 1920s, with sometimes fatal consequences, and therefore it was at the time often referred to as the 'strangling angel of children'. The immediate effects of this disease could be devastating for the patient and also very disconcerting for others who witnessed their plight. Later in his recuperative phase in an Ilkley Convalescent Home, Alfred had been so moved by his previous observations in this regard, that he wrote a lengthy moving poem 'Diphtheria Ode', which expressed the intense emotion about the fear surrounding the condition and its impact on those children afflicted by its worst symptoms, as the following selected powerful lines demonstrate:

> Thou who art bland Respect of Age
> The puniest babe resistent not thy rage.
> One I have known, and he a tender child
> (Lord! Still I marvel how in death he smil'd).
> A ravenous eagle, thou hast swooped adown
> Clawing with eager talons through the gown
> Of this sweet innocent, tearing his heart
> With fiendish cruelty's, for fiend thou surely art
> Till I, myself, fast failing 'neath the blast
> Have, hapless watched him choking. Thou hast past
> Seeking a grosser prey; the while he sobbed
> Piteously for aid. His life so robbed
> Fast ebbed and fast his agonies increast
> (Such are the horrors of thy daily feast)
> Long thro' the night his sobbing murmur made
> Till impotent to soothe, I anguished prayed

'Take him! Take him O Lord! for it is time'
And God received an angel; thou – a crime...[13]

The symptoms of the disease which Alfred was to suffer could have been caused by a toxin released by the diphtheria bacterium, and since there were few effective anti-toxin drugs available when he contracted the condition, it is likely that the longer term effects of the illness began to appear several weeks after the initial infection. The effects of the diphtheria toxin are known to affect heart muscle function and the loss of muscular function in the limbs, resulting in weakness due to wastage of these muscles, which in some cases can progress over several months. In Alfred's case the long term effects resulted in the whole left side of his body being partially paralysed (post-diphtheric paresis), along with some paralysis around his left eye resulting in blurred vision, but it was unclear whether these effects were brought about by the diphtheria toxin itself or even by the anti-toxin injections he had received. The doctors treating Alfred were in disagreement on this point, which was perhaps unsurprising given the scant availability of evidence concerning the diagnosis and treatment of the condition in the medical literature in the early 20th century. More recent medical opinion suggests that Alfred may have suffered the hemi-paresis (the paralysis of his left side) due to a stroke, which could have been brought about by the cardiac complications resulting from the diphtheria infection.

Whatever the cause may have been, the outcome was that Alfred's expectations of an early recovery from the original disease were dashed, and he became progressively weaker with time, so that after a year he considered himself to be a total wreck from the paralysis which had set in. He eventually became so weak and helpless that he was unable to walk without assistance and had to be wheeled about in a 'bath-chair'. It was at this point that he also probably began to believe in the most pessimistic prognosis that he received from his own doctor: 'you should write seven years out of your life!' which as circumstances were to prove, was not very far off the mark.

Patient No.	76 (order of patients in 1916)	Name	Alfred John Brown
Age	21 yrs	Residence	St. Luke's Hospital (previous location)
Occupation	Soldier, 2892, 2/2 WR Bgde	Admitted	12th February 1916
Vaccination	None	Prior illness duration	3 days
Disease	'said to be' Diphtheria	Final Diagnosis	'none made'
Result	'R' ('Recovered')	Discharged	15th April 1916

Table 2. A.J. Brown Hospital Discharge Notes

Alfred's Great Recovery

It is unclear what happened to Alfred immediately following his discharge from two months stay in the Leeds Road Fever Hospital in Bradford after his supposed recovery, but undoubtedly his condition worsened, and even though his family was very supportive, further periods of hospitalisation and convalescence ensued. He was also subsequently discharged from the army on the 19th September 1916 as unfit for further military service on medical grounds ('*hors de combat*'), and in the following July 1917, he received a reference from his former Commanding Officer which stated:

> This is to certify that No. 2892, Gunner, A. J. Brown has served in the 2/2 WRB, RFA for one year and 122 days. He is sober, industrious and used to horses. Character: Very Good.[14]

However what Alfred desperately wanted at this time was not just a character reference and some compensation, but if possible, a cure for his ills. In the event little was forthcoming. From 1916 onwards he received a partial military pension during the period of his illness of 12 shillings and six pence per week out of a possible maximum of 25 shillings per week. Furthermore, the amount that he received progressively declined to 5 shillings and 6 pence per week by 1922, when his degree of disablement was judged to be reduced by only 15-20% of normal capability, so that Alfred became more dependent on his meagre savings during this time.[15]

Furthermore, there was to be no miracle cure, nor it seems some slow but effective medical treatment to improve his physical disability. Instead what he was to experience was a number of clinical placements in a series of attempts to discover the best ways to manage his condition, probably in the hope that time would be the great healer. During 1916-1917 Alfred spent a considerable amount of time in number of hospitals and convalescent homes and received whatever care was deemed to be appropriate for the range of disorders from which he was suffering. He also underwent various assessments by the local Health Board in Bradford and the Board of Military Medical Officers at the Royal Hospital in Chelsea, London. At this time his left leg dragged like a dead limb when he walked, his left eye showed astigmatism resulting in blurred vision, he had lost all desire to eat ordinary food, which often caused him acute indigestion, and as a result he was beginning to waste away and looked like a shadow of his former self. He was also beginning to suffer psychologically from the spectre of the terrible reality of his condition.

Unfortunately no medical records exist after Alfred's diphtheria infection, although the details of the various institutions where he received care around this time are known,[15,16] and these were interspersed with periods of time spent at home with his family. Most of these institutions were in his local area, but some were further afield and included: the Field House Auxiliary Military Hospital, Daisy Hill, Bradford, Mount Vernon Military Hospital, Hampstead, London, the Semon Convalescent Home, Ilkley, the Meathop Sanitorium, Grange-over-Sands and the Royal Northern Sea-Bathing Infirmary, Scarborough. The variety of such institutions may be taken as an indication of the serious attempts that were made to find a solution to Alfred's ongoing problems. But his own doctor, who had previously delivered the most pessimistic prognosis, remained of the opinion that Alfred's best chance for recovery was likely to come from a simple diet, with massage and a routine of regular fresh air, and indeed, as before, he was not very far off the mark once more with this new prognosis.

It was during these periods of hospitalisation and convalescence that Alfred began to develop an interest in classical literature and poetry, and indeed he often quipped that his real education took place in hospital. However, in between these times at home, he was especially grateful to his friends who regularly came to read to him in the evenings, since the aftermath of his illness had affected his eyes in a curious way that prevented him from reading more than a page or two at a time. Many years later he acknowledged the valuable reading contributions of his friends in a short poem:

IN THE COMPANY OF BOOKS: UNABLE TO READ

Let me have the poets all around,
That, spirit-wise, with them I may commune;
Around me, let the whisp'ring leaves be strewn:

I cannot read – my tortured eyes are bound,
But I can hear the sweet-engender'd sound,
Disposed like a Heaven-wafted tune.[17]

Poetry became Alfred's standby during his illness and he particularly enjoyed Shakespeare, Milton and Keats, and was able to memorise poems very well. However his enjoyment of poetry was not merely in passive appreciation, since he spent considerable time writing his own verse, as is evident from an unpublished journal of poems, written in longhand, between April and September 1917.[18] It contains almost fifty poems, along with a few other short pieces of prose, although only six have any reference to the First World War, and a similar number to his own illness, while most concern the natural world and the human experience. This was followed by a second unpublished journal of poems that contains a further twenty-four poems, also written in longhand, between September 1917 and February 1918, which followed similar themes.[19] Both of these works also contain many strange topics along with some poignant lyrics that might be said to have been wrung from his soul, and probably represent the formative period in his creative writing of verse. However, only four of these pieces of verse were to appear in his later book *Poems and Songs* which was published in 1949, including a verse which, somewhat perversely but humorously, reflected on the possibility of his own early demise:

EPITAPH: FOR MYSELF, SHOULD I NOT RECOVER MY PRISTINE VIGOUR

Here in this quiet congregation
Of Laity and Prelates sad -
Lies one (at least) who quit creation
Unfeign'dly glad.
And felt his love could never flag
But when his boyish jubilation
Was blighted by disease (the Hag)
He thought it time to make the station
(Death!)
And packed his bag.

Among these bones and old headstone
You'll chance to find a vagrant
His Virtues are discussed with groans
His Vices are too flagrant
But whose Chance chance may direct here
For pity's sake will shed a tear
And be not over proud or prudent
To pause and pity -
His poor ditty,
And chuckle with the jesting vagrant.

Weep not for my frail corpse – nor mourn
When it shall pass beyond your ken –
Death is but Life Eternal born
And Love triumphant over Sin.[20]

Parts of the two unpublished journals of poems were written in identifiable locations, on specified dates, in and around the Ilkley and Bradford areas, and therefore, together with other related information, they provide an indication of Alfred's particular situation during the period in question. For example, in March 1917, Alfred wrote a letter to Fr. Charles Tindall, Headmaster of his former school and editor of the St. Bede's School Magazine, in which he offered a contribution towards the magazine that commented on his health:

> The composition of the enclosed article *['Warfare in England'*[7]*]* has whiled away a couple of pleasant hours for as you know, I am still restlessly obliged to husband my strength (or weakness) at the fireside... the pleasure of musing over those glorious days when I was astride

something more fiery than an Astrachan cushion is of ample reward for the labour expended... As to my health, I fear I cannot report great strides but I hope to travel to Grange-over-Sands next week and remain there six to eight weeks. A whiff of sea-air, and a breath o' the moors may effect a desirable transformation, Deo Volente.[21]

Subsequently, while Alfred was convalescing at the Sanatorium in Meathop, near Grange-over-Sands on Morecambe Bay, during the late spring and early summer of 1917, he wrote a short poem in early June entitled 'Texts at Cartmel Priory',[22] about the works of a scholarly monk who lived at the nearby former Augustinian Priory founded in 1189 in the picturesque village of Cartmel in south Cumbria (then in Lancashire). It was here also that one of the few photographs of Alfred was taken during his long period of rehabilitation, and it provides some indication of the slow process of his recovery.

10. A.J. Brown at Meathop Sanatorium   11. The Silver War Badge

The badge in Alfred's right lapel in the photograph is the Silver War Badge, which was issued in the UK to service personnel who had been honourably discharged due to wounds or sickness during the First World War. The badge was instituted from 12th September under Army Order 316, and was accompanied by a King's Certificate under separate regulations. Approximately 1,150,000 badges were awarded and had to be claimed from and approved of by the authorities. The badge was issued to all those who served at home or overseas during the war, and who had been discharged from the Army under King's Regulations, most commonly K.R. 392 (xvi), which indicated that the soldier had been released on account of being permanently physically unfit. To qualify for the badge, a recipient had to have served for at least seven days between 4th August 1914 and 31st December 1918, and his incapacity had to be caused by military service. The sterling silver badge had a pin for wearing as a brooch and was intended to be worn on the right breast while in civilian dress (it was forbidden to wear it on a military uniform), since it had become the practice of some women to present a white feather for cowardice or lack of patriotism to apparently able-bodied men who were not wearing the King's uniform during the Great War. In addition Alfred's 'Medal Card' from the Silver War Badge List, is kept at the National Archives (23) (List TO/180), and indicates his full name, service corps, service number, rank, dates of discharge and enlistment, as well as his cause of discharge, namely 'sickness' under paragraph 392, section xvi, King's Regulations. Unfortunately neither Alfred's Silver War Badge nor King's Certificate have been located.

During the spring and summer of 1917 he would often find a quiet spot such as the library, or more often the local churchyard or park where he could benefit from the fresh air and continue to experiment with writing verse in his journal. It was clear however that his condition had not improved a great deal and that he was still suffering from his debilities as he noted in what he termed 'a soliloquy provoked by pain after experiencing some pleasure in the completion of a sonnet':

IN PAIN

Give me one, – just one, whole hour of Happiness,
Of Ease, of Health – one cycle – be it
never fleeting - if intoxicating, exhilarating
Energy – one boyish scapegoat scamper
on the Moors – one – (the very prototype of
which we have squandered so many times in
the past) – one glorious buffeting in a wild
Nor' Easter – with the harebells flying,
the curlews screaming, the ling all blowing,
the heather blooming, the sky in benediction,
and Earth a paradise – give me
this, just one, inspiring hour –
and I would have none of thee![23]

Later that year, in November and December 1917, Alfred spent about three to four weeks in further recuperation at the Semon Convalescent Home in Ilkley, before he returned home to Bradford for the rest of the winter. While at home, Alfred was desperate to overcome his ongoing physical limitations and was prepared to try any form of intervention which might be beneficial, and thus he followed up his doctor's previous advice of massage treatment. This was readily available at the Windsor Public swimming baths in Morley Street in the centre of Bradford, where specialities of 'Turkish' and 'Russian' baths were available, that also included whole body massage manipulation to promote muscular relaxation and release of tension. Whether or not this type of complementary treatment had any effect on Alfred is unknown, but he also followed up his doctor's advice with a routine of regular fresh air.

Later in his convalescence Alfred spent part of the winter of 1918/1919 at Gibbiter Farm, close to the village of Beamsley, near Ilkley in Wharfedale, and attempted to build up his stamina once more. At first, his daily walk in the bracing air took him no further than the gate of his lodgings, but after a few weeks of perseverance he was able to walk along the lane to the River Wharfe where he could rest and appreciate the views. In order to record his achievement, he would mark the distance made each day with a stone placed on the wall at the side of the lane, although progress was sporadic and sometimes the next day he would have a relapse and not be able to walk at all. Then after a few days of rest, a new spirit of strength came and he gradually extended the distance walked, although it was never greater than half a mile at most during his first visit to Beamsley. It may have been from one of these experiences that Alfred was subsequently inspired to write the short poem in which he expressed his hope for a new beginning:

MORE THAN FOR WEALTH

More than for wealth, or the applause of men:
I pray my health will bloom again.
To walk the fields, with strength assured,
And tread the paths in youth explored:
To march o'er moors, at eventide,
With bouyant zest, and easy stride:
More than for gold in lavish measure,
More than for Fame's deceiving pleasure:
This I do crave, and this I would treasure![24]

In the spring of 1919 Alfred went back to Scarborough again for a second time during April, since his previously-attempted 'cure' in the summer of 1918 had been a failure. This former visit had involved a stay at the famous Sea Bathing Institute in Scarborough, which had been noted for its use of medicinal seawater baths in the treatment and rehabilitation of muscular problems since the early Victorian era. This time Alfred went back again with his own rehabilitation regimen in mind, one that was based on daily walking exercise. However there were the usual disappointments and relapses as before, but Alfred again persevered and on one fine spring day, he took his first 'long' walk along Marine Drive and made it as far as Peaseholme Park at the farthest end of the Promenade, where he promptly collapsed and had to take a taxi cab back to his lodgings. Nevertheless he had walked well over a mile, which led him to the conclusion that this was the turning point in time, that his cure had really begun, and from this occasion he never looked back.

In the spring of 1920 Alfred returned to Beamsley once more, where he found that he could easily manage the short walks that he had struggled to cope with on his first visit, and since the winter of 1919 he had begun to explore the footpaths and woodlands along the River Wharfe, where he also started to take a keen interest in country life matters which would become a lifelong passion. However, he was not satisfied with these gentle walks, and his ambition turned to the ascent of the hill Beamsley Beacon, which at a modest height of 1,250 feet overlooks the village of Beamsley, and was then, and still is, a popular 4 to 5 mile moorland trek. This he achieved on Whit Sunday of 1920, and thus he completed his first 'conquest' since his climb of Great Whernside, with his friend George C. Heseltine in the spring of 1915. He was at last beginning to feel young again and thirsted for new challenges, which ultimately became the driving force for his subsequent explorations of 'God's Own Country' on foot and the basis for much of his topographical writing.

Alfred's initial attempts at writing were undoubtedly associated with his long spells of hospitalisation, convalescence and self-directed rehabilitation, and although he was somewhat dismissive about his early verses and prose sketches, he acknowledged that he experienced for the first time the essential joy of creating these pieces, and that fact, in itself, was sufficient reward for his efforts. He also became aware of the possibility of exposing his literary work to a wider audience, as an undated note towards the end of his journal of unpublished poems of 1917 indicates, in which he suggested in the item below, that the work may be a 'Prologue to a Melody of (Projected) Verse by a Yorkshire Bard':

The author desires, in the first place, to proffer <u>his greeting</u> to the public. At the same time, though expressing the natural hope that the collection of random poems submitted will not be found entirely devoid of merit, but feels it incumbent upon him to offer a slight explanation, or apology, for the sombre atmosphere pervading several of the pieces included. He would point out that these were composed at a time of great physical distress, while though adversely affecting the beginning of production, may be at least extemporised with, on the grounds that this very suffering was the apparent impetus which set the whole mechanism of inspiration in motion. Finally, the author, having doubtless by his initial verbosity already forwearied the patient reader – and bearing in mind, the first law of Syntax which allows that brevity is the mark of Genius – begs respectfully to make his temporary Adieu.[25]

However the project was never fulfilled, and both the 1917 journal[18] together with the 1917/1918 journal[19] were to languish mostly unread for nearly one hundred years. And yet even if this project had come about, it would not have been Alfred's first foray into the realm of publishing, since during his incapacitation he became involved in the production of the St. Bede's School Magazine, which was then published at regular intervals during the academic year. An embryonic version had begun as a small annual magazine shortly after the opening of the school in 1900, but unfortunately it did not survive for long, and sadly no copies exist today.

Then in 1914 a revitalised version of the magazine came into existence, with the object of recording the many aspects of the school's life and to act as a focus for activities of the Old Boys of the school. Alfred had already made a contribution to the magazine towards the end of the First World War with a long article entitled 'Warfare in England' in 1917,[7] which he later acknowledged had given him much pleasure at seeing his own contribution in print, even though at the time he had modestly requested that the Editor omit his name at the end of the piece. Then in subsequent issues of the magazine he wrote further pieces of prose, before being co-opted in 1921, by the headmaster, Fr. Charles Tindall, to the Editorial Board, together with his cousin, Laurence Geoghegan, whose father, Thomas Geoghegan, printed the magazine on behalf of the school. It was concerning this new role which he had been given that Alfred later commented:

Only those who are afflicted with writing fever can appreciate the thrill of having a whole magazine and printing press to play with... It gave me personally, just the kind of stimulus I needed at a difficult time, and in due course I began to get articles accepted by other misguided editors. It is of course, altogether more satisfactory to launch into the wider world of letters, but I doubt if one ever quite recaptures the thrill of seeing one's early efforts, and particularly one's first poem, printed in the School Magazine.[26]

Alfred's first published poem was appropriately about the joys of walking and life's destiny:

A ROAD SONG

When day went by with scarce a sigh,
Under a clear and serene sky,
O then I strode along the road
That twists and turns about the downs.
O then I trod the springy sod,
And turned my back upon the towns.

When day goes out with howling shout,
And madcap winds are hurled about,
O then I chose my stoutest shoes,
And turn me out to the flaming West –
O then I use my eager thews
And march along with joyous zest.

When night draws nigh, with plaintive sigh,
Under a dread and solemn sky –
When lowering cloud-racks in the West
Shall tell me that my time is near, -

Then for that road- of all, the best!
I'll clothe me with especial care,
So to be called – all unappalled
To walk into Death's nobler air.[27]

Alfred continued to make further regular contributions to the St. Bede's School Magazine, and supplemented his role as a member of the Editorial Board with a series of short poems, which included his seasonal observations: 'Late Autumn'[28], the robust verse in defence of the criticism of his hometown of Bradford: 'This Town'[29], the joy of watching a bird bathe in the River Wharfe: 'Ring Ousel'[30], the delights of stargazing: 'Starlight'[31] and the varieties of delicious English apples: 'November Apples'.[32]

Subsequently all of these poems were to be included in his much later published book *Poems and Songs* (1949). He also later commented on the valuable contributions made by others to the magazine, particularly the schoolboys, who, in his opinion, brought a special vitality to the publication:

> I have just been looking over some old school magazines and, as usual, I have been astonished at their wit, wisdom and fecundity, not to mention their style. Indeed it is enough to make a man foreswear the practice of literature forever and leave it in the hands of those blithe alumni who prank it so captivatingly before they are fairly in or out of their teens. For, it is the youngest scribblers who carry it off with the lightest ease. How readily wit flows from their wild pens! How gracefully they soar over the impediments of syntax and style![33]

This was a particularly important period in Alfred's life, since it was during this time that he began to lay the foundations of his writing career, which accompanied the self-directed restoration of his own health. He readily acknowledged that, had he not been afflicted by his illness, and undergone such a long painful recovery process, he may never have had the time nor the inclination to embark on such an alternative career possibility. However he was realistic enough to reflect on the difficulties involved, and in a short article he wrote for the school magazine, concerning his first tentative steps: 'On First Appearing In Print', he encouraged others to follow in his footsteps into publication, although he put the process into perspective for the would-be writer:

> The correct title of this article should perhaps be 'On First being Paid for Appearing in Print'. The writer had, in truth, already fluttered with a fledgling wing over the pages of the 'St. Bede's Magazine' before essaying flight in the larger world. But the honour of capering across the columns of the magazine is adequate reward without the degrading accompaniment of a £ cheque...
>
> When an unknown writer sends an article to the Editor of the 'St. Bede's Magazine' he receives a very courteous hearing; and it will have to be a very appalling article if the Editor does not reward him with a generous eulogy...
>
> The London Editors, alas, were not educated in the same school. When one sends an article of outstanding merit to a London Editor he usually

returns it by the next post. Enclosed with it, is a contemptuous slip of paper on which is compressed the very essence of irony...

Every one who sends articles to the papers is at first like Noah sending out his doves. They come back with deplorable regularity, but eventually, they find a resting place, and – miracle of miracles – appear in print.[34]

Fortunately for Alfred, he was able to keep these wise words of advice firmly in his mind during the difficult periods ahead, when he would often struggle against the onslaughts of ruthless newspaper and magazine editors, as well as hard-headed book publishers.

References and Notes

1. Documents relating to the First World War, Bradford Council Roll of Honour (1914-1918), Document 7D91 (Alphabetical Index Cards), The West Yorkshire Archive Service, Bradford Central Library.

2. The West Yorkshire Archive Service, Bradford Central Library, Document No. 6D95, The Bradford Volunteer Artillery, 1914-1938.

3. **Note**: The biographer's father served as a gunner with the 277th Battery, 70th West Riding Field Brigade, The Royal Artillery - Territorial Army, in the late 1920s and was based at Thornbury Barracks in Bradford Moor.

4. E.J. Brown, Jottings from the School Magazine, A letter to the Headmaster, In *Book of Remembrance 1914-1918, 1939-1945*, St. Bede's Grammar School, Bradford, by Terence Larkin, 1999, p. 43.

5. E.J. Brown, 'Life in the Trenches', St. Bede's School Magazine, December 1915, No. 4, pp. 101-102

6. Alfred John Brown, *Broad Acres – A Yorkshire Miscellany*, Country Life Limited, London, 1948, Chapter 18, 'In Praise of Maps', pp. 127-128.

7. A.J. Brown, article entitled: 'Warfare in England', a personal communication to Fr. Tindall, Headmaster, St. Bede's RC Grammar School, Bradford, 26th March 1917, In: St. Bede's Archive, Box 9/3, Hinsley Hall Pastoral and Conference Centre, Leeds.

8. **Note**: The article probably appeared in the summer 1917 edition of the St. Bede's School Magazine, but the bound volume set 1916-1920 (Numbers 1-10) is missing from the School Archives. Alfred's handwritten copy, together with the Editor's note of the title change from 'Training Days' to 'Warfare in England', is located in **7** above.

9. Ernest Osborne, In: papers belonging to Private E. Osborne, the Bradford Industrial Museum, Moorside Mills, Moorside Road, Eccleshill, Bradford.

10. Terence Larkin, *Book of Remembrance, 1914-1918, 1939-1945*, St. Bede's RC Grammar School, Bradford, 1999.

11. Alfred John Brown, A Journal of Unpublished Poems, 1917, 'Bedesmen, In Arms!' p. 21.

12. Health Records of the Bradford Leeds Road Hospital, Collection Reference C800, Admission and Discharge Registers, 1887-1972 (year 1916), The West Yorkshire Archive Service, Wakefield.

13. Alfred John Brown ibid., 1917, 'Diphtheria Ode', pp. 37-40.

14. Julian Laverack, *The Lean Years*, Methuen & Co. Ltd., London, 1926, p. 21. (Julian Laverack was the pen name used by Alfred John Brown for his novels).

15. AJB Correspondence File: Health and War Pension Letters (1915-1922).

16. Notes on 'Hospital Tom' (1916-1917), In: Alfred John Brown, Catalogue No. 69D90, Section 7/2, The West Riding Archive Service, Bradford Central Library.

17. Alfred John Brown, 'In the Company of Books: Unable to Read, In: *Poems and Songs*, Horne and Son, Ltd., Abbey Press, Whitby, 1949, p. 8.

18. Alfred John Brown, *A Journal of Unpublished Poems*, 1917.

19. Alfred John Brown, *A Journal of Unpublished Poems* 1917/1918.

20. Alfred John Brown, op. cit., 1917/1918, 'Epithalamium (to GCH)' [George Coulehan Heseltine], p. 16, 'Dust To Dust', p. 19, 'My Home' ('Fain Would I Dally'), p. 23, 'Epitaph', pp. 21-22.

21. A.J. Brown, letter 26th March, 1917, In: Private Letters to Fr. Tindall, Box 9/3, St. Bede's RC Grammar School Archive, Hinsley Hall Pastoral and Conference Centre, Leeds.

22. Ibid., Alfred John Brown 1917, 'Texts at Cartmel Priory', p. 37.

23. Alfred John Brown, ibid., 1917, 'In Pain', p. 82.

24. Alfred John Brown, ibid., 1917, 'More than for Wealth', p. 9.

25. Alfred John Brown . ibid., 1917, 'Prologue to a Melody of (Projected) Verse by a Yorkshire Bard', p. 36

26. A. J. Brown, 'Memories of the Magazine', St. Bede's School Magazine, Summer 1950, Vol. vi, No. 4, p. 54.

27. A.J.B., 'A Road Song', St. Bede's School Magazine, June 1921, No. 9, p. 26.

28. A.J.B., 'Late Autumn', St. Bede's School Magazine, October 1921, No. 10, p. 272.

29. A.J.B., 'This Town', St. Bede's School Magazine, June, 1922 Vol. ii, No. 12, p. 36.

30. A.J.B., 'Ring Ousel', In: St. Bede's School Magazine, October 1922, Vol. ii, No. 13, p. 52.

31. A.J.B., Poem: 'Starlight', St. Bede's School Magazine, February 1923, Vol. ii, No. 14, p. 66.

32. A.J.B., 'November Apples', St. Bede's School Magazine, November 1923, Vol. ii, No. 16, p. 107.

33. Alfred John Brown, 'On School Magazines', In: A.J.B. Journal, May 25th 1925 – November 27th 1927, June 1925, p. 28.

34. A.J.B., 'On First Appearing In Print', St. Bede's School Magazine, June 1922, Vol. ii, No. 12, p. 27.

CHAPTER 3

Return to Reality, Roaming and Writing

Back to the 'Old Firm'

Alfred spent over six years of slow recuperation and rehabilitation, and had recovered sufficiently well to make an attempt to re-establish a 'normal life', so he returned to work in the worsted trade in Bradford. He was fortunate to be able to take up his former employment, since many soldiers who returned from the war, especially those who were incapacitated, were often denied the opportunity of a return to their previous jobs. In a world where the nature of work had changed, including the role of women, who had found emancipation in the outlets for employment, men who had returned to live in a land 'fit for heroes', often found that they now had to become heroic once more in order to survive the new harsh economic conditions. Before the war, Alfred had become almost indispensable in the offices of the old firm of Benjamin Wensley and Robert Woolley, who were now ageing principals of the successful worsted yarn export company with a staff of over twenty workers. However after such a lengthy recovery, Alfred was still something of a ghost of his former self, but he returned to work on light duties only, and often started his day later in the morning, took a longer than normal lunch period and sometimes finished work early to help him cope with the slow pace of his return to normality.

This relatively relaxed routine was not just magnanimously agreed by the two company directors, since Alfred's previous training and experience saw him rise through the company to take charge of the overseas worsted yarn dealing activities, at a time when the wool trade in general was faced with increasing competition from abroad. As a result, Alfred's promotion in 1922, after only one year back with the old firm, was a testament to his powers of recovery, and he was rewarded with a new salaried position of £350 p.a. instead of his previous wage of £200 p.a., and he became a manager at last.[1] This new position might have spelled the end of any thoughts of roaming and writing which Alfred harboured at this time, but this was certainly not the case. During his first year of return to work, he often wandered around his old moorland haunts of Oxenhope and Haworth to the west of Bradford, and began short sketches and notes about his walking exploits in the hope that he might find some appropriate outlets for his work in both the local and national press. Then as part of his promotional package, he had also been given some holiday time by the company in 1922, and Alfred decided to continue to foster his physical recovery by a return to Beamsley in Wharfedale. It was here that the routine of fresh air and moorland walking again stimulated his mind and body, as it had done previously in his early recovery phase, and brought about his return to full health.

It was also about this time that Alfred assumed further responsibilities in his new managerial position, which involved business travel in France and Germany, as part of his new and important role in export sales, with the overall remit for the continued development of the overseas worsted yarn trade. This may have been the stimulus which spurred Alfred to take his first holiday abroad in August 1922, when he spent two weeks on a tour of Belgium. It is not clear why he chose Belgium for this excursion, but as he reflected later upon the venture: 'I had not forgiven the doctors and the fever for denying me the "pleasure" of a campaign in Flanders in 1916, but now I had my reward'.[2] However this holiday was not intended as a substitute for the experience he had missed as a result of being unable to serve his King and Country fully during the Great War. Indeed, far from it, since his itinerary largely avoided the former areas of conflict, with the intention of dispelling the idea that Belgium was utterly devastated by the war, to the extent that most people were deterred from visiting such a delightful country. It is also likely that he used this opportunity to develop the travelogue writing skills which would serve him well in his future walking adventures. The degree to which he achieved this end can be judged in the splendidly entertaining book he wrote about his visit: *A Joyous Entry into Brighter Belgium*.[3] Alfred had carefully made copious notes during his tour and recorded his observations of people, places and events in the kind of detail which was to become the hallmark of his future writing style. Therefore it seems appropriate to offer a series of précis in order to provide an insight into the experiences recounted by Alfred in his first book, which was produced in very limited numbers and has become a rare find indeed.

The Brighter Side of Belgium

Alfred suggested that his text constituted: 'A Little Book about A Little Country with Big Ideas', and prefaced his work with a short introduction recounting some previous historic 'Joyous Entries' of great men in Belgian history, which unfortunately were often followed by 'Doleful Departures'. The impression made by this opening may also describe Alfred's own experiences of his brief tour, which started out as an adventure and finished in somewhat mundane circumstances.

In keeping with Alfred's exploratory nature, instead of choosing the short cross channel route to the continent, he chose the alternative of a 24-hour North Sea crossing on a cargo steamer from Goole to Antwerp, with only ten passengers, soon to be friends, for company. After the ship had slipped down the Humber estuary late at night, they were invited to the bridge by the friendly captain, who regaled them with anecdotes of his WW1 experiences in the Channel. Then in complete contrast, a tour of the engine room allowed the more ambitious among them to try their hands, literally, alongside the stokers who fired the boilers continuously. But all too soon, fatigue and the need for fresh air, enticed these 'land-lubbers' to view the night sky from deck side, before two bells sounded 1.00 a.m. of the middle watch, and sent the weary travellers to their cabins. Then on waking, the mill-pond sea had turned into a heavy swell, and the stomach-churning, rocking and reeling of the ship sent most seasick passengers fleeing from their breakfasts for a return visit to the deck rails! However following further

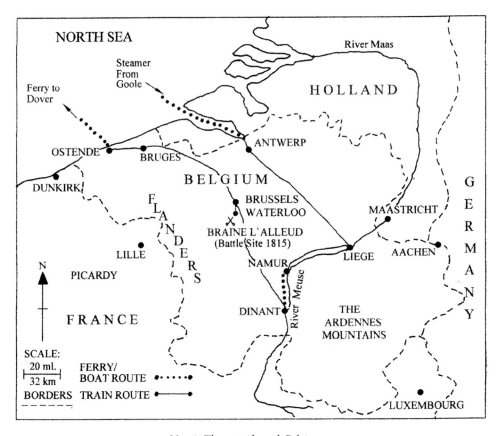

Map 1. The route through Belgium

cabin-based recuperations, and a thoughtful delay by the captain to save dinner until entry into calmer waters, most were able to enjoy their entry into a Brighter Belgium.

The immediate impression which Alfred gained of the country was that it seemed a curious thing that:

> In one of the smallest countries they insist upon having the biggest of everything. Cathedrals, grottoes, citadels, carillons, museums, paintings (some of which cover half a church side): where else would you find them so enormous and so numerous? And, aptly enough, in a country which has been the biggest battlefield in the world, there is a constant battle for supremacy between Canton and Canton.

It was in Antwerp where Alfred and his friends also gained an insight into the Belgian passion for feasts, when they arrived on the feast of *Kermesse*, which in recent times equated with a fair, although originally it designated the anniversary of the foundation of a church or parish on behalf of a patron (origin: '*Kirk*'-church, '*Mis*'-mass). This was just one of 36 special feasts celebrated locally each year, with many more minor ones, but being close to the feast of Our Lady of the Assumption on 15th August, the event slipped seamlessly into the 'Fêtes Marie', in which Belgian husbands paid homage to their wives called Marie, hence the preponderance of 'Maries' in Belgium. It was here also that Alfred experienced the full impact of the 'carillon' bells that chimed on the hour and remarked that they 'resembled a hundred delicate and exquisitely-attuned cymbals clashing together'. The only things which spoiled the ambience of the city for the English visitors was the inability to obtain English tea, or an English cooked breakfast, and the avalanche of American tourists, who, having arrived from Bruges before lunch, were anxious to leave for the Bernese Oberland that evening, having 'done' Belgium.

Soon Alfred's party moved to Liège but not without incident. They had been arrested on the train for illegal occupancy of a reserved compartment and spent time explaining to the authorities in Brussels their unintended transgression. The result of this misdemeanor was a late arrival at their destination, and the wrath of an impudent official at their hotel, who not only demanded advanced payment for their stay, but also an inflated gratuity for services which had yet to be rendered! Little wonder that the once noble city of Liège left little room for sentiment among the visitors for a place which could not quite bridge the gap between scenic splendour and industrial activity. However, Alfred in a more munificent mood, acknowledged one of the great edifices not mentioned in the guidebooks at the time, namely the famous Fort de Loncin, which saw the dour Belgian defenders resist for twelve days the massed German artillery onslaught and held up the colossal army's advance in the early days of August 1914.

The next stop was Namur, but again not without incident. On a tour of the citadel by tramcar, Alfred's party was accosted by an irate Frenchman, who recalled the former historical English transgressions, and verbally attacked the tourists, surprisingly, much to the applause of the other Belgian passengers. But he was repelled by that peculiar patriotism which makes an Englishmen abroad defend his kind, to such an extent, that upon arrival at their destination, the adversary, having exhausted his venom, insisted upon cultivating their acquaintance and showed them courteously the features thereabouts. The next day the party boarded a River Meuse steamer to see the Ardennes between Namur and Dinant, where the hilly mountain scenery allows a river passage via numerous locks through a landscape of little villages nestling in wooded ravines, which enchanted the tour party further as they also explored one of the many flooded underground caves by boat. Dinant also provided the opportunity to explore the citadel fortress on the limestone cliffs above the city, which over the centuries had acted as a bastion of resistance. The last time, unfortunately, it resulted in its partial destruction on 23rd August 1914, in which many of the civilian inhabitants were killed in the German advance and occupation.

A tour of Belgium would have been scarcely complete without a visit to Brussels, but as Alfred suggested it was a place to avoid in the heat of summer, so much so that upon arrival in the capital the party's collective desire was to leave it again quickly. Nevertheless they tried to enjoy the café culture, albeit enervated by the climate, rather than the intoxication of the beer, which Alfred described in somewhat derogatory terms: 'Bock Belgica is to Bass Beer, as Lemonade is to Champagne'. Nor was the local food *pièce de resistance* of '*Roseboeuf au Cheval*' [sic] appealing to their appetites, until it was ascertained that it was not horse-beef at all, but ox-beef instead. It was in the capital that the party attempted to come to terms with the finer 'points' of the famous Belgian lace making industry, and the many locally-characterised forms of lace '*points*' or varieties, which signified either the particular pattern or ground work of the lace from different regions, while the only thing which they all appeared to have in common was a high price. Then the most baffling memory the group took with them from Brussels was the number, variety and extensiveness of the museums that Alfred could only describe as a form of 'National Museumania', which defied the endurance of even the most ardent enthusiasts for such institutions.

It would also have been remiss not to have visited Waterloo a few miles south of

Brussels, so the tour group arrived at the station of Braine-l'Alleud three miles away from where the battle was fought in 1815. In his wisdom Wellington, who wrote his dispatches from Waterloo, considered it to be the only local name which posterity would be able to pronounce properly, and thus it took its place in history. Alfred was less inspired by the relatively small scale of the battlefield compared with the western front of the Great War, but more by its significance in the history of warfare, particularly at nearby Hougoumont. It was here in 1815 that the then allies of British, German, Dutch and Belgians faced the French led by Napoleon, on what should have been the last great battle of all, and should have sounded the death-knell of war. Instead Alfred suggested:

> Here, it might well have ended, but it did not end. The armies were reshuffled; allies became enemies, and enemies became friends, and the mechanical carnage in France and Flanders followed... And all the portents are that the cards will be re-shuffled again. How many futile anti-climaxes will follow?

How very prophetic this assessment of the situation turned out to be at the time 16 years before the next conflict of World War Two.

It was out of this despondency that Alfred's spirits were lifted once more with a visit to the penultimate place of the tour, the Grand-Place of Bruges, and under a beautiful starry sky listened to the most captivating carillon of all from the towering Belfry which looked down on the square. There in the crowded cafés he and his fellow listeners were entranced by the rhythmic, throbbing bells that echoed their silvery notes from on high, delivering a 'Concert de Carillon', which included works by both classic and contemporary composers each night between 9.00 and 10.00 p.m. But as Alfred concluded, Bruges was much more than a belfry, it was a reliquary of famous antiques contained in its many churches and guild halls, whilst outside its architecture was matched only by its canals, with an odour, if not splendour, to compete with those of the Venetian waterways.

Alfred's final observations concerning Belgium were reserved for Ostend, which he suggested had not quite picked up the pace with the rest of the country's revival. In his opinion it had: 'lost its gaiety... has all the breezes of Blackpool without having the breeziness... instead all of the jolly, if gaudy, glitter of Brighton, there was only a thin line of pale lights culminating in the light-house beam', and that most of the townsfolk took excursions along the coast to other resorts for their leisure activities. Soon after it was time to conduct the doleful departure from the Digue of Ostend on the conventional channel crossing to Dover. In Alfred's opinion this was conducted according to a precise, perfect plan, within a strict schedule, but it totally lacked the adventure and camaraderie of the outgoing journey, and everyone behaved in a typically restrained English fashion. It was not until the party reached home shores that the feelings of euphoria returned. But for Alfred, even this response was delayed until he had: 'returned to the North and the moors... Home – what a perfect place'.

Upon his return home Alfred quickly organised his 72-page handwritten travelogue of his trip[4] into the draft of the book which was published in the following year 1923. Then in later years he reflected upon the motivation to write it, and the significance he placed upon this, his first book:

> I enjoyed the trip so much that I wrote my first book on the strength of it. Looking back it seems rather impertinent to write a book about a country after a two weeks' acquaintance, but it was only a little book, and it was entirely adulatory; and nobody paid the slightest attention to it anyhow... [and] I paid for its production... That little book was a landmark in my life; it commemorated my cure and my entry into literature and it was worth every penny it cost me. But, of course, being a Yorkshireman, I didn't intend to pay for any more books being printed![2]

And yet, despite Alfred's pessimistic view about the book's reception by the public at large, it received almost uniformly good reviews in a number of press notices of the day, including the following:

'A pleasant little book about Belgium and its people... There is not a dull page...' – *Daily News*

'A capital book to take on a tour... The spirit of pleasure pervades it and invests even contretemps of various kinds with humour' – *The Month* (the English Jesuit Journal)

'Written with a delightful naïveté... The personal touch of a man who is not to be led by the nose round rows of masterpieces. A very jolly little book' – *Leeds Mercury*

'Unexpected pleasure lies beneath... this volume... Written with wit, humour and liveliness' – *Christian World*

'Eminently readable' – *Liverpool Courier*

'A series of impressions sketched with the lightest of pens... We heartily recommend Mr. Brown as a most entertaining travelling companion' – *Catholic Book Notes*

Further recognition and support for the book came from Alfred's Alma Mater in the form of a glowing tribute published in the St. Bede's School Magazine which stated:

> Several Old Boys have distinguished themselves in the literary world by writing descriptions and articles for papers, but it is left to Mr. Brown to be the first to bring out a book, We congratulate him on his achievement, and heartily recommend to our readers to peruse the book themselves. *A Joyous Entry into Brighter Belgium* is a brightly written account of a trip through some Belgian towns, we recommend all our readers who have been to Belgium to read it; and all those who have not, to read it also – and then go to Belgium. We look forward to other important works from his pen.[5]

Finally, it is worthwhile to note that St. Bede's had a special relationship with Belgium during the First World War. Many Belgian refugees who fled Belgium during the German invasion and occupation arrived in Bradford, and since St. Bede's was the only Catholic Boys' Secondary School in the city, the School Governors opened its doors to all Belgian boys of relevant school age who wished to be admitted.[6] A total of 59 Belgian boys were enrolled between 1914 and 1917 and they were soon integrated into the life of the school, with language difficulties overcome by the appointment of a Belgian refugee, Mr. M. Wiedershoven, as an assistant teacher. The School's Roll of Honour includes the names of those Belgian boys who attended the school and who also served in the forces during WW1. After the war most of the refugees returned home to Belgium, and some retained the links with their former classmates who had become close friends during their school years.

Alma Mater, Semper Fidelis

During the early to mid 1920s Alfred became closely aligned with his old school via the St. Bede's Old Boys' Association, which had a large membership involved in a variety of sporting, social and religious activities, as well as an annual religious retreat which began in 1922. Alfred attended the second retreat, held during the weekend of 14th-16th July 1923 at the school's Heaton Hall, along with a mixture of older pupils of the school, as well as 'Old Boys' and members of staff.[7] One of the highlights of the retreat was the contribution made by the renowned Catholic convert, priest, writer and philosopher, Fr. Cyril Charles Martindale, S.J., M.A. (1879-1963), from the Jesuit Academic Community of Campion Hall, Oxford University. He particularly impressed Alfred with his entertaining readings at mealtimes from his recent novel *Mr. Francis Newnes* (1921), and perhaps further stimulated Alfred's growing desire to write.

Alfred had met Fr. Martindale on a previous occasion during his attendance as a representative of the St. Bede's Religious Study Circle, at the Oxford Summer School held during the week of 14th-19th August 1921, which was a special event organised for the Catholic Study Circles throughout England.[8] The Summer School involved a series of lectures and seminars delivered by leading religious scholars of the time, and was attended by an eclectic audience of church leaders, military figures, legal authorities and representatives of the public, who not only studied together, but lived, dined and relaxed informally in an atmosphere which Alfred declared: 'If this was not the Christian idea of State, one could feel that it was eminently desirable... the Socialist only preaches "Communism", while the Catholic practises it.'[8] Alfred's own faith had been severely challenged, but strengthened by the trials and tribulations of his previous long-standing illness, so it seemed appropriate that he should have been selected to attend this auspicious event. He was very impressed by the experience, and he may have been instrumental in securing the eminent Oxford Scholar, Fr. Martindale, to be a leading participant in the St. Bede's Annual Religious Retreats in subsequent years.

12. The old Heaton Hall

13. The new school

Alfred also became closely involved with the new developments at his old school during the summer of 1925 when the Silver Jubilee of its foundation was celebrated, along with the opening of a new wing to the old Heaton Hall building, which had been acquired in 1919, after the school had moved from its founding premises in the centre of Bradford, to a new location in the hilltop village of Heaton on the outskirts of the city. This landmark event in the history of the school was reported in a special Jubilee Edition of the School Magazine,[9] which recorded the official opening of the new extension on 12th June 1925 by the English Cardinal Francis Bourne, and the newly-written 'Hymn to St. Bede' by 'A.J.B.', which was sung by the schoolboys at the Jubilee Day Celebrations on 12th June 1925. Alfred later humbly reported the impact that this ceremony had upon him at the time in his journal:

> During the Jubilee Celebration, the boys sang a little Hymn to St. Bede which had been written for the occasion, splendidly, so that it about sounded like a real Hymn...! But I confess I was quite distraught while listening. It seems almost indecent to hear one's own Hymn being sung in public! I suppose when one has done as many as thirty or forty one gets over it; but the first time is quite an ordeal... The tune was one of Stainer's and suited it admirably.[10]

Hymn to St. Bede.

BAEDA, on this great day, we greet
  Thee on thy throne!
And beg thy presence where we meet
  In this thy home!

Thou who didst plant the tiny seed
  Whence sprang the Tree:
Attend us in our present need
  And hear our plea.

Grant that our School, like thine, may grow
  Strong with the years:
Hold thou the torch that we may know
  When danger nears!

We are thy children, and our School
  Bears thy great name:
We are most proud to learn thy Rule
  And spread thy fame!

Under thy banner and thy shield,
  Clad in thy mail:
We shall not shrink: we shall not yield:
  We shall not fail!   A. J. B.

The original musical score to the hymn entitled 'Exsurgat Deus' ('Let God Arise') was written in 1885 by Sir John Stainer (1840-1901), the popular Victorian composer, who had been the organist at St. Paul's Cathedral, London, then Professor of Music at Magdalen College, Oxford University, and composed over 150 hymns during his career. Later in 1899, the Victorian music lyricist, Mr. Arthur C. Ainger (1841-1919), a master at Eton College, Windsor, wrote a stimulating set of verses for the music under the title 'Let God Arise', which was often used in times of war, not surprisingly, since the first verse proclaims:

> Let God arise to lead those
> who march to war!
> Let God arise and all his foes
> be scattered far!

It then continues the theme of exalting the cause of holy righteousness in times of adversity. It is likely that Alfred had been influenced by this impressive hymn, since there are some striking similarities between its first verse and that of the last verse of Alfred's School Hymn to St. Bede, which subsequently became known as 'Baeda', and continues to be sung as the school song.[10a]

Notwithstanding these esoteric contributions, Alfred had also to provided material for the School Magazine during the early part of 1925, with a lengthy but amusing article entitled 'Shoe Leather and Salvation'[11] which emphasised the need to look after one's footwear properly by the employment of a good cobbler and the avoidance of cheap shoddily-made shoes . This was followed in the same edition by 'Quacks!'[12] which was an appreciation of the entertainment provided by the talkative sellers of the indoor Yorkshire 'Quack' Market in Bradford on Saturday evenings. These now long-gone colourful characters would try to out-talk, out-banter and even 'out-quack' one another with their sales pitch, in a bid to sell off their wares at the end of the day. Then in an attempt to almost completely fill this edition of the magazine, Alfred included another poem entitled 'Rain'[13] which confirmed his appreciation of even the most inclement weather while out walking, and one which would also appear in his later book *Poems and Songs* (1949).[14]

A Pilgrimage to Rome

The 1920s represented a prolonged and periodically intensive phase of Alfred's faithful involvement with his old school and culminated in the Old Boys' Pilgrimage to Rome in August 1925. However this was not the first Pilgrimage to Rome made by the school, as there had been an earlier one by the Scout Troop in June 1925, as part of the School's Silver Jubilee Celebrations, which also included a public audience of almost jamboree proportions with the Pope in St. Peter's Square, since it was attended by almost 10,000 scouts from all over the world.[15]

The Old Boys' Pilgrimage Group, made up of some 45 former pupils and their specially-invited friends, left Bradford by rail for Italy on Friday, 14th August 1925, for the option of a 10 day trip of £18, or 16 day trip of £23. It was led by the headmaster of the School, Fr. Charles Tindall, and incorporated not only the Rome pilgrimage on the shorter visit, but Naples, Capri, Pompeii, Florence and Venice on the longer visit. The highlight of the pilgrimage was a private audience with Pope Pius XI, at which a personal address on behalf of the pilgrims was delivered to the Pope by Monsignor Arthur Hinsley, the first Headmaster of St. Bede's School (1900-1904), who was at this time Rector of The Venerabile, the English College in Rome, where selected English students were trained for the priesthood for service in England.

Alfred later recalled this meeting with the Pope[16] and commented on the contrast between the quiet reverence shown by the English Pilgrims and the exuberance dis-played by their Italian counterparts:

> The most significant feature of our audience with the Pope was the silence with which we received him. When he at last appeared, not a word passed our lips; not a man so far forgot himself as to give utterance to the terrible profanity of cheer. After his speech we did give him stiffly and self-consciously three rousing cheers. He then passed into the great hall beyond, whence the crash of cheers burst on our ears: 'Viva il Papa!' [*Long Live the Pope!*] from a thousand mainly Italian throats which signalled his appearance. How cold we must have seemed by comparison!

After the formalities of the papal audience, the Old Boys' stay in Rome was some-what more relaxed as they embarked on various sightseeing tours of the Eternal City. Furthermore, their comfort was enhanced by the generous hospitality provided by Dr. Hinsley at the English College, who kindly provided them with the opportunity of relaxed recreation in the only swimming pool in Rome at that time, which had recently been constructed in the peaceful college garden. The group photograph of the pilgrimage party in the garden shows most of the men casually dressed, with the women in more formal attire, but all appeared to be relaxed among their clerical col-leagues and their Rector host.

A comprehensive report of the pilgrimage was published subsequently in the School

Magazine.[17] This included an account of the journey to Rome by Alfred's cousin, Laurence Geoghegan, a description of the stay in Rome by Alfred's friend, John McWeeney, and, as might be expected, an entertaining travelogue of the extended holiday visit to Naples by Alfred. His description of the escapades of the pilgrimage party's division into three natural sub-groups: the 'Irrepressibles' – who were always up at dawn, the 'Intellectuals' – who were always hoping to be up at dawn, and the 'Irresponsibles' – who were just dropping to sleep at dawn, brought Alfred unaccustomed praise by a fellow Old Boy who 'had laughed his sides sore when he read the article.'[18]

Laurence Geoghegan   Alfred John Brown   Marie-Eugénie Bull (?)

Fr. C. Tindall   Mgr. A. Hinsley

Headmaster, St. Bede's RC Grammar School   Rector, the Venerable English School, Rome

14. St. Bede's Old Boys Association, Rome Pilgrimage Group, 1925

However Alfred later came to judge this pilgrimage in rather a circumspect summary fashion, which led him to a less than satisfactory conclusion about the experiences he associated with the trip: 'Rome... Naples... Capri... Pompeii... Florence... Venice. I am richer by all these and poorer by about £40... I hope it was worth it... In short I behaved like a condemned tourist, which, *malgré moi, [in spite of myself]* I was. Not an ideal holiday, not the best circumstances for me.'[19]

It was perhaps significant that there was more than a tinge of regret in this melancholic view by Alfred, who had invested considerable time, energy and expense in taking part in the pilgrimage. In spite of his close ties with his old school, the trip had been somewhat uncharacteristic of his holiday activities to date. Furthermore Alfred was also at a crossroads in the conflict between his business career and that of his literary aspirations, in which he became more focused in the use of his preciously limited leisure time. However there was a personal development associated with this latest adventure which would have the most profound impact on Alfred's life in future.

The Waywardness of Wanderlust

Alfred's vacations in Europe in the early 1920s developed into an altogether more demanding leisure activity, when he and his cousin Laurence Geoghegan, decided on a walking holiday in Brittany and the Pyrenees in the summer of 1924. Although Alfred was seven years older than Laurence, they had become good friends through their involvement with the social events provided by the Old Boys' Association, and enjoyed outdoor activities together, but this new adventure was to present a much more challenging experience. The initial idea was to spend a week walking parts of the undulating coast of Brittany as a prelude to the more demanding heights of the mountains of the Pyrenees, which on reflection was probably not the ideal form of preparation for what was to come. Even their previous walking experiences in the Yorkshire Dales would have hardly been sufficient preparation for the demands of the Pyrenean peaks to follow.

Bumbling around Brittany

The journey began after a channel ferry crossing when they arrived in Châtres by train during the second week of August 1924. After an overnight stay they viewed the magnificent cathedral, before they entrained once more to Quimper on the coast of Brittany from where their 'walk' began. It was on this train journey that the inadequacy of their preparations became apparent, when Alfred enviously espied the large scale map of Brittany, which their American compartment companions had compared with their own generalised map of France. Moreover, when they arrived in Quimper, they found all the hotels were full, and with few francs between them it seemed like a night under the stars was likely, until they found a shared, single-bed room above a wine shop, which they endured rather than enjoyed.

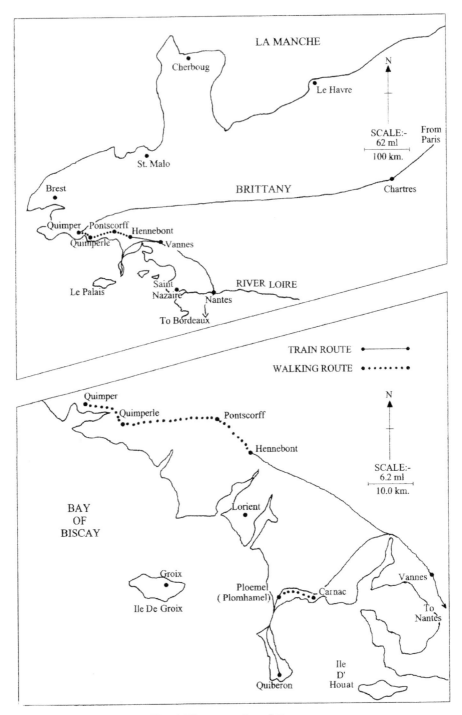

Map 2. The journey through Brittany

When they left next day their footslogging began, but they halted after a couple of miles to quench their thirsts from a bottle of local wine, before they drowsed in the heat of the day to make up for the lack of sleep from the night before. After a brief respite, temptation took over shortly after when a local farmer offered them a lift, and upon asking where they were going, was bemused by Alfred's response: 'to Spain', to which he replied that he hoped they were not going to walk all the way! He suggested a more realistic objective was the next town of Quimperlé, and recommended a hotel which would allow them to plan the next phase of their Brittany tour. However his suggestion was ignored as Alfred and Laurence pressed on, but unwisely stopped at a couple of the innumerable inns which lined these Breton roads, before they had to spend a night in a field and used their mackintoshes as ground sheets.

On waking their they realised they had nowhere to wash, until they stumbled across a small village, where a benevolent innkeeper allowed them to use the water pump for washing in the yard and provided a washbowl with soap and towels. They also availed themselves of the kind offer of breakfast with coffee, bread and butter, before they once more felt respectable enough to join the throngs of well-dressed local people who streamed to church for the 7.00 a.m. mass to celebrate one of the greatest holy days in France, the Feast of the Assumption of Our Lady on the 15th August, 1924.

By now they felt they were beginning to get into their stride as they headed to Pontscorff, where Alfred suggested they make themselves more presentable still by bathing and shaving in a lake, before they continued to Hennebont, where they lunched at the most pretentious hotel they could find to celebrate the feast day. Then in a return to the coast, they boarded a train with a change at Vannes and arrived at the little fishing port and pleasure resort of Quiberon, at the end of a peninsula connected by a narrow causeway to the mainland. At this point Alfred and Laurence halted their pedestrian progress to take the opportunity of a proper bath, sleep in a proper bed and enjoy the extravagance of hotel meals taken on the terrace that overlooked the sea. So much for the rustic, simple approach which they had espoused at the outset as the guiding principle for their adventure!

The next day Alfred suggested a visit to the ancient Celtic monoliths at nearby Carnac. So it was back on the coastal railway once again with a change to the mainline to arrive at Ploemel, where they sat upon one of the fallen flat druid stones and gazed back over the bay to Quiberon to the site of their recent restful sojourn. In the heat of the day thirst drove them to seek sustenance at a nearby farm, where they were overwhelmed by the hospitality of a farmer, who served them with warm milk and strong local cider, and they reciprocated with a toast to his bountiful harvest, before they caught the train back to Vannes.

It was in Vannes where an argument took place, which concerned Alfred's perceived merits of seeing more of this ancient city and Laurence's desire to push south to Bordeaux and the Pyrenees. Indeed they had not done justice to the sights of Vannes that evening as they wandered around the city and struggled to find an inn for the night. Further disappointment came the next day when they boarded a primitive 'omnibus' train from Nantes to Bordeaux, without corridors let alone a food salon. As the prospect of a difficult 10-hour journey dawned upon them, they bundled themselves and their baggage off the moving train, to discover that there was not another Bordeaux train until 10.30 p.m. that night.

Thus they were fated to see the sights of Nantes as a substitute for those of Vannes, but they enjoyed their visit to the ancient cathedral and castle of this busy port on the outlet of the River Loire. In compensation they even managed to find a tea shop, which not only served something close to English tea, but delicious cakes which they consumed in great quantities as well as buying supplies for their next train journey. Their other significant purchase was two maps: 'one of Brittany to see where we had been and one of the Pyrenees to see where we were going!' Then later that evening, Alfred and Laurence settled into a comfortable second class carriage for the overnight journey en route for Bordeaux, the Pyrenees and Spain.

Peril in the Pyrenees

On arrival in Lourdes, Alfred and Laurence changed trains for Pau and on to Laruns, where the narrow valley of the Gave D'Ossau opens on to the plain below the mountains. The plan was to buy the essentials needed for the Pyrenees in Laruns, including a gourd or goatskin container for wine, some food supplies and a blanket to sleep on, if and when required. However the temptation of a three mile ride in the soon departing old motor bus to Les Eaux Chaudes higher up the valley, postponed the purchase of provisions, a decision which they were soon to regret. Upon arrival they found there were no gourds available and little in the way of food except bread, so they continued up the Gave D'Ossau valley towards Gabas. En route they followed the older track instead of the new road because although it was much steeper it shortened the distance considerably.

At this point Alfred and Laurence gained their first views of the rocky pinnacles of the Pyrenees with bare rugged peaks which reached to the sky, typified by the Pic du Midi at 9,462 ft. that towered above their intended route along the lower grassy slopes and forests. This awesome impression led them to contemplate the enormity of their undertaking as they arrived at nightfall in tiny Gabas, the last village on the French side of the frontier, where they were glad of the excellent food and lodgings offered by the Hôtel des Pyrénées. Among the other guests were some intrepid French climbers who planned to tackle the Pic du Midi, and an English family on a cycling holiday bound for Spain the following day. In the friendly conversation which ensued at supper, Alfred and Laurence challenged the family to a race to the Hôtel Mur in Jaca on the Spanish side of the frontier, where they were all due to stay. The amicable bet without stakes was duly accepted before both parties retired to bed to be ready for the race.

It was an inauspicious start for Alfred and Laurence next morning to find that the cycling family had already left by the time they arrived for a meagre breakfast of coffee and bread, with no possibility of any substantial English style fare. Moreover, the local shop offered little in the form of suitable food, not even bread, with only a kilo of saucisson and cheese available, and since they had no gourd, they had to beg an old bottle and cork from the shopkeeper, which he filled with red wine from a large cask. Back at the hotel Alfred obtained a kilo of bread as the last contribution to their provisions, before they set off on the most challenging and eventful part of the entire expedition.

They followed a route that left the tree line behind and kept to an old track which diverged from the new road, until the track disappeared and they had to rejoin the road over a mile away after a struggle across an intervening knee-deep torrent which tumbled down the valley. Further up the road they hoped for an inn stop at the hamlet of Soques, which was marked on the map as the last habitation before the frontier. However hopes were dashed when they asked a passing mule train drover how far it was to Socque [*sic*], only to be told: 'Soque? Soque is here, this is Soque!', as they gazed in disbelief at the barren, rock-strewn, grassy wastes leading up towards the stony peaks towering above them.

So with gritted teeth they trudged the last few miles to the frontier under the fierce heat of the sun from which there was no shelter. They planned to leave the road just before the frontier to find a watershed crossing point at the Col de Peyreget, then proceed into the valley of the Canal Roya, which runs parallel with the Pyrenean range, and follow its watercourse to the Aragon River as a direct route to Jaca. If they failed to find this route, at least another day's journey would be required via Sallent and the Rio Gallego valley, to arrive at their destination. They left the road to try to find the Col and tracked a stream for almost a mile before it split into two tributaries, but their map gave no indication of the likely route to follow. For over an hour they searched

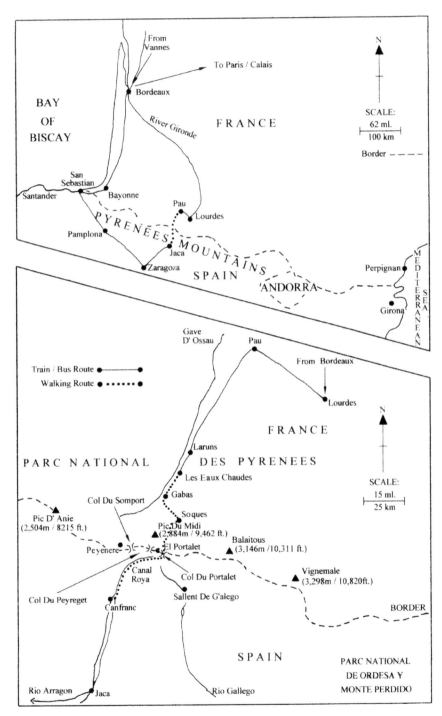

Map 3. The journey over the Pyrenees

for the break in the mountain range, before they asked directions from two local men passing with a donkey, and were told that they had never heard of the Canal Roya and knew of no Col in the vicinity. Now there was no alternative but to return to the road and to cross the frontier at the Col du Pourtalet, but not before a brief stop at the head of the valley of the Gallego for some refreshment from their meagre, but now dwindling food supplies – the distasteful saucisson, the cheese finished, the bread rock-hard – and only water from the mountain stream to revive their sinking spirits.

They then questioned the value of the only available map of the Pyrenees which they had bought, because the scale and features were more appropriate for motoring than walking and concluded: 'map-less in Brittany is one thing, but map-less in the Pyrenees is another'. According to their map there was a way into the Canal Roya via the first tributary that fed into the Rio Gallego on the right bank of the river, but the problem was there were several tributaries that joined the river, so which one would lead to the desired Col or just a dead end? They passed several unlikely streams then selected one, almost at random, near a derelict Spanish customs post, but as they descended towards the river they became aware of yet another inadequacy in their preparations. Their leather-soled shoes became polished by the slippery grass slopes which made it almost impossible for them to keep a foothold. The only solution was to remove their shoes and put on an extra pair of thick socks over their stockings to gain purchase until they reached the river at the confluence of their chosen tributary. They hoped that they had chosen the right watercourse, because without help from the map only the compass gave any reassurance, since it confirmed that the stream ran in the right direction, due west, from a well-defined little valley running up into the mountains.

Alfred and Laurence left the bed of the stream and climbed a narrow cleft in the rocks from which the water emanated between two sheer walls of rock to the right and left, which had begun to reflect the now setting sun. As the climb grew steeper they often returned to the stream to soak their burning feet and top up their dwindling wine bottle water supply to slake their powerful thirsts. After about two hours it seemed they were nearing the end of the narrow valley as the ground rose precipitously and became closed in by rocky walls on both sides, which partially hid the enormous peaks around them. But doubts still persisted about this chosen route as they scrambled on hands and knees under the weight of their packs, with the going only made easier when the blinding sun dropped below the valley head. But the view of the aptly-named Pics d'Enfer (Peaks of Hell), which towered over the Rio Gallego valley to the south east, provided no inspiration if they had to return to the alternative route.

However, when Laurence took his turn to lead up through the distant gap in the rocky walls he made a joyful discovery, the outcrops of rock were streaked with a dull red hue, the sign of the Canal Roya, from which the magnificent rocky valley got its name. He stood on the summit of the Col which was only a yard or two wide and gazed into the deep trench of the impressive valley that stretched out westwards, and was soon joined by an elated Alfred in a frenzy of self-congratulation at their achievement. Then almost at once the realization came that it was now 7.30 p.m., and with their food almost gone, they would have to spend the night high in the mountains.

Undeterred, they scrambled down the steep slope of the Col, often slithering and sliding over the grassy spikes which penetrated their clothing and their flesh, until they reached a stream in a canyon below the valley head. But the going became progressively more difficult, since the torrent plunged beneath the precipitous sides of rock, and as darkness fell it made further progress more dangerous, so a halt was called beneath the shadow of a large boulder near the stream, where they prepared to camp for the night. But they were still concerned that this may not be the Canal Roya, since all of the rocks in this region were tinged red, including those in other adjacent valleys. Moreover their plight was further aggravated by the thought that bad weather or a sprained ankle suffered by either of them at this stage would result in a trek of another day or more without food, and in such a fatigued state could leave them in dire straits.

These gloomy thoughts did little to help their restive state and they could not light a fire for warmth, since they were well above the tree line with no wood available, so in dropping temperatures they donned every garment available, spread out the mackintosh groundsheet and covered themselves with their lightweight raincoats. As they looked up at the cold, starry night, there was not even the respite of a pipe full of tobacco between them, as the moon eerily lit the surrounding peaks, the nearby torrent became deafening and the temperature plummeted to freezing point. However Alfred brought some light relief later when he declared it was now Thursday, 21st August 1924, his 30th birthday, and he proposed to celebrate the occasion with a drink to their good health from the stream at 2.00 a.m. precisely, the hour of his birth! When this ceremony was over they returned to their resting place, huddled together for warmth, abandoned all hope of sleep and waited for dawn.

Unsurprising at first light, lack of sleep and sustenance, as well as stiffness, fatigue and the chilled mountain air made progress painfully slow in the difficult terrain, before a phantom path which appeared and disappeared gave them some hope of escape. Even so, huge mountains loomed in front and crags rose all around them hiding the secret of any outlet, and it was not until Alfred led the way this time, along the path which rose upward avoiding the torrent below that a clear view became a welcome sight. Far below, winding through the narrow valley ahead was the thin white line of a road which ran at right angles to the valley. This road, the only one within twenty miles, turned out to be the Somport road leading up to the Col du Somport, and more importantly for them, leading southward to Jaca, their intended destination some 12 miles away. Their good fortune continued when they came across a bus in the small village of San Antonio, which provided them with a much-welcomed ride to arrive at the Hôtel Mur later that morning.

On arrival at the hotel they were greeted by a friendly patron who empathized with their story of being lost in the mountains, since he had suffered similar problems trying to follow routes advocated by the English writer Hilaire Belloc in his walking book entitled *The Pyrenees* (1909). They were immediately shown to the breakfast table while their rooms were prepared, but being unable to use the dysfunctional bath, they later retired to bed with the promise of being woken again for lunch. Laurence however woke early and went off to explore Jaca, then returned to the still recumbent Alfred with the good news that he had bought him a belated birthday present: a gourd!

Later that evening, while Alfred and Laurence waited patiently for supper, they were made aware of their previous night's good fortune, when the rumblings of a thunderstorm in the distance soon became one of the worst storms which either could remember. The electrifying flashes, shuddering clashes and torrential rain lasted for over four hours, and they reflected on how lucky they had been. If they had been caught in these terrible conditions the night before, their chances of survival would have been very slim indeed. Then their thoughts turned to their fellow travellers, the English family of cyclists, who had not yet arrived at the hotel. However, a pleasant surprise awaited them next morning at breakfast, when the family greeted them with incredulity with the realization that the 'foot-sloggers' had won the race by some twelve hours over the 'pedal-pushers', who had arrived late at night during the storm, albeit after a much longer route via Sallent.

Their perilous adventure was over and all that remained was to make the long arduous journey homeward. This began on a packed horse-bus to the local station where they boarded a train for Zaragoza, where an overnight stop was required due to their misinterpretation of the confusing Spanish railway timetable. Their travel situation did not improve next day either, when the 6.00 a.m. train from Zaragoza steamed leisurely into San Sebastian at 12.00 midnight, having taken 18 hours for a very roundabout trip of some 250 miles and called at every station on the way. The only respite from the tedious journey was the opportunity which Alfred and Laurence had to improve their respective Spanish and French conversational skills by chatting with a number of interesting characters along the way. So it was with some regret that they arrived in the small hours of the morning in Bayonne before beginning the final stages of their trip back to England, but it was not the end of the Pyrenean story.

A full account of their holiday exploits was published in an entertaining book produced by Laurence in 1925.[20] However Alfred and Laurence's trek over the Pyrenees had been preceded by another party of former St. Bede's Old Boys, including J.J. Brannigan, who reported a similar three day adventure, over an almost identical route from France into Spain in the summer of 1923.[21] He had also commented on the pitfalls and problems of such a demanding walk during an era when the Pyrenees area was beginning to become popular with walkers. Moreover Alfred had later endorsed this cautionary approach in a lengthy article about the dangers of wandering in the Pyrenees without adequate preparation.[22a] 'Jim' Brannigan was a younger contemporary of Alfred's at school and had also served with the Royal Field Artillery during the First World War. He was an active member of the Old Boys' Association and subsequently was a teacher at the school. He also married a cousin of Alfred's and eventually became the Deputy Headmaster of St. Bede's.

A Career Crossroad – *The Lean Years*

Alfred's holiday journeys to Europe came to an end during the mid 1920s, although he had European responsibilities at work which required frequent travel abroad. It was during this period when the growing demands of his employment caused him to think seriously about the impact this was having upon his fledgling writing career. Whilst it was possible for Alfred to indulge himself in writing for the enjoyment gained and the challenge of having modest contributions accepted by newspapers and magazines, he now began to contemplate a new a direction for his literary aspirations. This was illustrated in a discussion which took place in the summer of 1925, between Alfred and the editor of the north of England newspaper, the Yorkshire Observer, which had published several short articles by Alfred. He explained that the reason why he had ceased to send further work for consideration was: 'I seem to get no further *forrade [forward]* with it... no scope, and that I had to choose between doing a lot of little things, and one or two big ones...'[23] However the editor kindly asked Alfred to send the occasional article from time to time.

One of the larger pieces of work in which Alfred was busily engaged was the drafting of his first novel about the life of 'Ambrose Gildersome'. This was a semi-autobio-graphical story which describes Alfred's recovery from illness after the war and the early years of employment with a West Riding wool firm, leading to Ambrose's sub-sequent success as a writer. Alfred had started writing two years earlier in July 1923 and by December he had produced some 200 pages of handwritten draft for a possible book.[24] However the novel had not been completed at the time, probably because of Alfred's work demands, and also because of the need to secure the interest of a poten-tial publisher before he could commit further time to the project, but none-the-less he continued to make revisions to the work throughout 1924 and 1925.[25]

Then in January of 1926, Alfred received the good news that Methuen and Company, London, had accepted his new novel, now called *The Lean Years*, which was to be pub-lished under his newly-adopted pseudonym 'Julian Laverack'[26a] with an initial print run of 2,000 copies. Alfred wrote about this momentous news in his journal with obvious elation:

> The incredible has happened, Methuen has accepted my novel *The Lean Years!!!* Such luck after all the years! I was frantically excited (thank god) and even now am scarcely sober... Already the agreement is signed and sealed – and there are no flies in the amber of success. Indeed they want the option of my next two novels – 'on the same terms'. Well the terms to me seem generous enough for an income, and they shall have 'em, bless 'em.[27]

It is not entirely clear what the next two novels were likely to be, but Alfred was already working on a couple of draft manuscripts at that time. The first one entitled *Whitaker*[28] was another semi-autobiographical story of a young man's rise to success in the wool trade, which was subsequently abandoned for a more rustic life in the country, but this novel was not to see the light of day for nearly twenty more years! The second one entitled *Two on a Tour*[29] was a travel story about two friends on hol-iday in the Alps in 1924, which was based on a train journey to Switzerland, Austria and Italy, by Alfred and his cousin Laurence Geoghegan, and included a trek over the Austrian-Italian Alps, but the novel was never completed. What is clear however is that Alfred now considered that a writing career was possible as an author. Meanwhile when *The Lean Years* by Julian Laverack was finally published on 9th September 1926, it was dedicated by Alfred: 'To my mother with affection and gratitude' and he wrote the disclaimer: 'The characters, names and places in this book are purely fictitious. No reference to any living person is intended'. Even so, the novel moves from a reason-ably accurate account of Alfred's return to work in the wool trade after his World War

One illness, into a fictional romantic adventure story of Ambrose Gildersome, which is paralleled by his ever-growing literary aspirations, culminating in his success in both endeavours. Nonetheless, the mix of fact and fiction makes compelling reading and the work represented a successful entry into the world of novel writing for Alfred.

The book received both acclaim and some criticism from the local press, which became intrigued by the identity of this 'new author' on the literary scene. A review by the *Yorkshire Observer* commented:

> We have not previously noticed the name of Mr. Julian Laverack among our novelists. Indeed, we strongly suspect that it is merely a nom de guerre, and that when it is discovered, if ever, we shall find that it hides the identity of some clever and gifted Bradford man who has been living in the West Riding with shrewd and far-seeing eyes, and has now broken into the ranks of our younger fiction writers with great effect.[30]

In contrast, the *Yorkshire Evening Post* took a more balanced stand in its review and stated:

> Mr. Julian Laverack has written a Yorkshire romance of the kind that proves a temptation to the reviewer to label 'wholesome', and more so when the paper wrapper informs us truly... 'The wind from the moors blows across its pages'. Sometimes, indeed, Mr. Laverack's enthusiasm for the moors would appear to run away with him.[31]

There was also a note of intrigue expressed in the *Yorkshire Evening Argus* by the critic 'Mistress Page', who stated:

> There seems to be a much more than facile imagination brought into the spinning of *[the yarn] The Lean Years*. Julian Laverack is merely a singularly euphonious pen-name; it hides the identity of a man who knows his setting from intimate personal experience... Mr. Laverack should find plenty of appreciative readers in the West Riding; and one hopes that in future he may be added to the list of notable Yorkshire writers.[32]

Finally, there was the disclosure of the identity of the 'new author' in the *Yorkshire Evening Argus*, by the columnist 'Merlin', who asked the question:

> Who is Julian Laverack? Who is it that under the cover of this euphemistic pen-name has given us in *The Lean Years* a fascinating story with an intimate local flavour?

Then Merlin reported on a meeting with this illusive novelist:

> I have met Julian Laverack in the flesh: a pleasant, modest young man
> in the early thirties, with the kindly eyes and face of one who has fought
> his way through the waters of tribulation... it was Mr. Alfred John Brown,
> who lives in the Horton district of Bradford... Evidently one of us, but to
> make sure I asked him if he were a Yorkshireman... 'Violently Yorkshire' he
> replied... More satisfactory still he is a Bradfordian... yet another recruit to
> the Bradford school of novelists.[33]

In the year before the publication of *The Lean Years*, Alfred had also received the
good news from his employers that he was to receive a salary increase of about £4.00
per month, which was a substantial annual increase of about 15%.[34] Even so, in early
1926, Alfred applied for another job with a new firm and was offered the management
of their yarn department in February 1926.[35] This new post also offered a considerable promotion with the likelihood of foreign travel, including business trips to the Far
East and beyond. However even with this better offer in mind, Alfred was still torn
between trying to balance the demands of his commercial life with that of his love of
writing as he stated:

> If I am to be a businessman always from 9.00 a.m. to 6.00 p.m., I may as
> well get as much from it or at least experience out of it, as possible; and it is
> up to me to see that I am not gradually transformed into a 'whole-hogger'.
> From 6.00 p.m. to 9.00 a.m., I should still be able to be an artist, if not a
> poet; and I still intend to write many books. If my 'hog book' is a best seller
> [*Alfred was already working on his next book about a walk through the Yorkshire Dales*]
> then I may be able to cast myself loose; but until such time, I think my first
> duty is to earn a decent living and save a little money, else I shall never be
> free to do anything at all... until then I must flirt with the two hostile forces
> of commerce and literature.[35]

In addition to this dilemma, Alfred had qualms about how his old firm would react to
the news of his impending departure, especially since the principal of the new firm,
Mr. D. Hamilton, was a business friend of his old boss Mr. Woolley. However, he was
assured by Hamilton's ethical declaration: 'there are certain decencies to be observed
even in business', and that he would take on Alfred only if he was released by his old
firm so that the two business friends would not be estranged by the arrangement.[35]
Alfred need not have had any concerns, Woolley released him at once, but he was
heartily sorry, while the rest of his colleagues were almost dumbfounded and seemed

genuinely grieved. Then in a final gesture Alfred went to the Wool Exchange once more, bought his last lot of mohair at a bargain price for his old firm, and although feeling a little down in the mouth, he then went straight to his new firm later that day with the notion that he had it 'all to do again, my lad!'[36]

In his new job there was no doubt in Alfred's mind that he was now higher in the commercial world than ever before, quite literally, since he occupied the top floor of a six storey warehouse with windows on all three sides, which had magnificent views.[37] The building, now sadly demolished, was situated at 6 Canal Road, the only flat road out of Bradford, which had followed the line of the old Bradford Beck and the now-declined Bradford Canal, northwestwards towards the River Aire Valley, and was now a main transport route for both road and railway. One of the views Alfred had was over the passenger and railway goods termini of the Midland Station on the perimeter of Forster Square, towards his former drab office in Drewton Street about half a mile away. The other, and more important view as far as Alfred was concerned, was over the impressive expanse of Forster Square and along busy commercial Market Street, in which the Wool Exchange with its medieval Flemish Cloth Hall style was situated. Then into Town Hall Square, with its magnificent Town Hall modelled on the Palazzo Vecchio in Florence topped with a two hundred feet high clock tower[38a] with a glimpse of the three domed Moorish-styled Alhambra Theatre. Finally the view extended over his home district of Little Horton, up to the hilltop village of Wibsey, with his beloved moors of Queensbury beyond. It might be suggested that with such a view Alfred would have some difficulty in concentrating on the new job in hand.

However Alfred commented that such pleasant distractions were little enjoyed, since he hardly had time to lift his eyes up to enjoy the scenery.[37] He now worked at a large flat desk, which was considered then an unmistakable mark of importance, with his own telephone, in a semi-private office, or 'cage' as he referred to it. He was also in charge of forty-seven foreign agents in every conceivable corner of the world, and while he got on well with the rest of the staff he lamented:

> I miss the friendliness of the old faces. I feel somehow to have been 'amputated'. Some very precious part of me has been lopped off and I am still rather sore – or perhaps I just forgot to bring my heart with me? ... My room is full of sunshine in fitful spasms, but I bite my lip and get on with the job.[37]

He also mused about the present lamentable state of his literary output:

> My writing has suffered a sharp setback, and for a fortnight I have done
> next to nothing, but I must finish my 'Yorkshire Book' somehow [a Yorkshire
> Dales tramping book]. I feel the desire as keenly as before. The consciousness
> of the County being all around me is always upon me, and when that goes, I
> may be a partner in the firm perhaps; but a slave none-the-less.[37]

Perhaps it was at times like this present career crisis that he looked back upon a previous entry in his journal, which knowingly or not, had set him on a track which would lead to a successful way forward in terms of his future writing career. In the autumn of 1925 Alfred had reflected upon the emigration of two of his friends[39], and wondered whether he should consider such a bold move himself in the light of his perceived humdrum existence, but he rejected the idea on the grounds:

> I have such a passionate love for England, and such an overmastering love
> for my own green Shire, that I would be miserable were I out of it for more
> than a month at most... Here in England – in my own vast County – there
> are open spaces enough in all conscience to satisfy any reasonable man...
> For myself, I find it is less and less the foreign lands, and more and more my
> own moors and fells which call me, and which conceal the more surprises...
> Life is too short to explore intimately more than one country – or indeed
> – one County; and I would rather know all the secret paths and tracks over
> my own moors, than hack my way across the world... Travel – it is a cant
> saying – broadens the mind; but the only effect it has had on mine, has been
> to make my own country and my own people seem the most desirable in
> the world.[39]

Clearly with this statement Alfred appeared to have nailed his colours to the mast, and it seemed that with a start already made on his first 'Yorkshire Book' about tramping through the Dales, he had established the basis of what was to follow in his subsequent topographical writing about Yorkshire, while he set aside any immediate possibility of a future novel.

And yet with hindsight, this was perhaps a wise decision, since considering the outcome of his first novel *The Lean Years*, the future of a writing career did not look very promising. The sales of the book did not live up to the expectations of the publisher, nor for that matter those expressed by the local press, who had reviewed the work favourably. This was probably due to the combination of the book not having received more widespread reviews by the national press, the paucity of publicity and promotion and the reluctance of the publisher to offer a reprint. In addition, the economic circumstances at the time, following the General Strike of May 1926, had left the retail market depressed, with the result that the book languished without any real prospect of any upturn in sales in the foreseeable future.

It was therefore fortunate that Alfred's situation at work had improved considerably otherwise he might have come to regret any rash decision to opt for an alternative writing career instead, in the hope that it could become the mainstay of his financial support. In the climate of uncertainty which existed at the time, life was going to be difficult enough for Alfred to be successful at work, given the harsh economic realities of depressed commercial markets, let alone to make any attempt to derive a living from the relatively moribund state of publishing. There was no real alternative for Alfred except to continue as 'a business man by adoption and force of circumstance, and a writer by choice of heart.'[39] In addition, there were other personal developments which occurred that would have the most profound impact on him for the rest of his life.

References and Notes

1.   Julian Laverack, *The Lean Years*, Methuen & Co, Ltd., London, 1926, pp. 132-133.
     Note: Julian Laverack was the pseudonym adopted by Alfred John Brown for his novels.

2.   A. J. Brown, *I Bought a Hotel*, William Norgate Ltd., London, 1949, Chapter: 'Books and Authorship' iii, Autobiographical, p. 147.

3.   Alfred J. Brown, *A Joyous Entry into Brighter Belgium*, Simpkin, Marshall, Hamilton, Kent & Co., Ltd., London, 1923, p. 128.

4.   Alfred John Brown, West Yorkshire Archives Service, Bradford Central Library, Document No. 69D90, Section 1, 'Travel Guides', item 1/2, 'Holiday Adventures', (no date) August 1922.

5.   A.J.B., St. Bede's School Magazine, November, 1923, Vol. ii, No. 16, Old Boys' Corner, Notes, p. 101.

6.   J. M. Hagerty, Centenary History of St. Bede's Grammar School, Bradford, (Bradford 2000), Chapter 7, 'The First World War', pp. 13-14.

7.   St. Bede's School Magazine, July, 1923, Vol. ii, No.15, Editor's Report, p. 90.

8.   A.J.B., St. Bede's School Magazine, October 1921, No. 10, 'Oxford Summer School', p. 283.

9.   St. Bede's School Magazine, Jubilee Number, 1900-1925, Vol. ii, No. 20, Editorial, pp. 166-168.

10. AJB Journal, May 1925 - November 1927, (no date), June 1925, p. 36, 'On Hearing One's Own Hymn'.
     10a. Note: St. Bede's Boys School integrated with St. Joseph's Girls College to become St. Bede's and St. Joseph's Catholic College in September 2014.

11. A.J.B., St. Bede's School Magazine, 'Shoe Leather and Salvation', January, 1925, Vol. ii, No. 19, pp. 157-159.

12. 'Tom O'Bedlam' (A.J.B.), St. Bede's School Magazine, 'Quacks', January, 1925, Vol. ii, No. 19, pp. 162-163.

13. A.J.B., St. Bede's School Magazine, 'Rain', January, 1925, Vol. ii, No. 19, p. 163.

14. Alfred J. Brown, 'Rain', Poems and Songs, Horne and Son Ltd., Abbey Press, Whitby, 1949, p. 20.

15. J. M. Hagerty, op. cit., Chapter 15, 'The Scouts', p. 67.

16. AJB Journal, op. cit., 'An Audience with the Pope', 18th August 1925, pp. 55-56.

17. A.J.B., St. Bede's School Magazine, 'The Old Boys' Pilgrimage to Rome, Southward to Naples', Autumn 1926, Vol. ii, No.22, pp. 210-217.

18. AJB Journal, op. cit., 'Alfred's Reaction to Praise', 12th March 1926, p. 118.

19. AJB Journal, op. cit., 'Home Again', 1st September, 1925, pp. 48-50.

20. Laurence Geoghegan, *A Furious Fortnight in Brittany and the Pyrenees*, 1925, A Book for Private Circulation.

21. J.J. Brannigan, 'Across the Pyrenees', In: St. Bede's Magazine, Vol. ii, No. 16, November

1923, pp. 104-105.

22. Alfred J. Brown, 'Perils of the Pyrenees – Experiences of a Mountaineer', a report in the Yorkshire Post, 13th May, 1930.
22a. Note: The biographer and a friend made the same trans-Pyrenean trek in 2011 and can affirm the dangers and demands.

23. AJB Journal, op. cit., 'On Talking to an Editor', (no date), July 1925 pp. 37-38.

24. Alfred John Brown, West Yorkshire Archives Service, Bradford Central Library, Document No. DB38, Case 4, Section No. 3, a short story: 'Ambrose Gildersome', 1923.

25. Alfred John Brown, West Yorkshire Archives Service, Bradford Central library, Document No. 69D90, Sections No. 2.1.1 – 2.1.3, an unpublished manuscript: 'Ambrose Gildersome', 1924 -1925.

26. Julian Laverack, op.cit. The Lean Years, Methuen and Company Ltd., London, 1926.
26a. Note: The pseudonym was derived from Alfred's maternal grandmother's Christian name Julia Geoghegan, and 'Laverack' a northern surname of mediaeval origin, as well as a Yorkshire dialect word for the Lark songbird, It was also often used as nickname for someone who was an early riser with a cheerful disposition.

27. AJB Journal, op. cit., 'Notes on Publishing The Lean Years', January 1926, pp. 100-101.

28. Alfred John Brown, West Riding Archive Service, Bradford Central Library, Document No. 69D90, Section 2/2/1, an unpublished manuscript: 'Whitaker', 1924-1927.

29. Alfred John Brown, ibid., Document No. 69D90, Section 7/1, a short story: 'Two on a Tour', 1924.

30. 'New Bradford Author - The Lean Years by Julian Laverack', Yorkshire Observer, 21st September 1926.

31. 'Our Books of the Week: Yorkshire Moors and a Yorkshire Town', Yorkshire Evening Post, 23rd September 1926.

32. 'The Lean Years: The Human Document of a Wool Merchant's Shipping Clerk', 'Mistress Page', *Yorkshire Evening Argus*, 18th September 1926.

33. 'Julian Laverack: Identity of New Bradford Author Disclosed', 'Merlin', *Yorkshire Evening Argus*, 22nd September 1926.

34. AJB Journal, op.cit., 'Notes on a salary Increase', 15th September 1925, p. 70.

35. AJB Journal, op. cit., 'Full Circle', 16t February 1926, pp. 103-110.

36. AJB Journal, op. cit., 'Burnt my Boats and Crossed the Rubicon', 1st March 1926, p. 111.

37. AJB Journal, op. cit., 'Reflections of My New Job, Conflict with Writing Activities', 1st March 1926, pp. 114-117.

38. George Sheeran, *The Buildings of Bradford–An Illustrated Architectural History*, Tempus Publishing Ltd., Stroud, 2005, pp. 75-77.
38a. Note: As a boy the biographer can remember being able to tell the time from the huge Town Hall clock, which had a face of 10 feet 6 inches in diameter, from his home in Bradford Moor, at a distance of over 1.5 miles with the unaided eye.

39. AJB Journal, op. cit., 'On Emigration', (no date) October/November 1925, pp. 78-79.

CHAPTER 4

'Needles and Pins, Needles and Pins...'

Needles and pins, needles and pins,[1]
when a man marries his trouble begins...
– Old Nursery Rhyme

An Unromantic Beginning?

Whenever Alfred was at a crossroads in his life, he often returned to his journal to reflect upon his circumstances and consider events with some degree of objective detachment. This process was applied in the Spring of 1926, when the three demanding strands of his life developed in parallel which he neatly summarised:

> I am so busy living that I have no time for scribbling, least of all to myself in this sort of diary. And yet, if only to jog my own treacherous memory, I will jot down some of the momentous things which have happened to me within the last few weeks: (i) *The Lean Years* accepted, (ii) Wensley, Wooley & Co. left behind & a new career begun at Woolley's without the Wensley & Co., (iii) I became engaged.

> People keep rushing up to me to congratulate me and I am compelled to ask 'what for?' – I mean which of these sensational events? This is always the engagement... A man might write a thousand books, secure a hundred directorships; but not one, nor all of these things would so ring from pole to pole as would the announcement of his engagement... This, of course, is natural and right.[2]

The first two of these events in Alfred's life appeared to develop out of his ongoing literary and occupational efforts, but the third, and most important event to him, his engagement, appeared to have emerged from almost nowhere, since there was little indication of any emotional involvement until this time. Indeed, since Alfred had returned to full-time work after the physical recovery from his protracted illness, there appeared to have been little female social interaction, especially at work, where he found it psychologically difficult to enter into any close relationships. However there were some hints of a previous special friendship that he enjoyed with a female colleague, which had come to an end and caused him some regret[3], but it seems likely that this was not a serious relationship, since the girl was already engaged at this time.

Alfred had preferred to socialise mainly with his more long-standing friends and family acquaintances, largely through his involvement in the many activities of the St. Bede's Old Boys' Association, and it may have been through such an outlet that Alfred had come to meet his fiancée in the first instance. It was noted earlier that Alfred had taken part in the pilgrimage to Rome in August 1925, in which the Old Boys enjoyed a hectic holiday experience in Italy. The touring group also included a number of specially invited friends and acquaintances, among whom one young woman in particular subsequently became Alfred's fiancée, since it was established that she was indeed a member of the party.[4]

It is also more than likely that Alfred's friendship with his future fiancée had been established through close family connections. He had always enjoyed sporting social occasions and often joined a group of young tennis players who played regularly on courts adjacent to the house of his cousin, Laurence Geoghegan, who lived at 'Vermont', a large Victorian house at 20 Cunliffe Villas, in the fashionable Manningham district of Bradford. The tennis courts had no facilities attached so the Geoghegan's house became a centre for tennis parties, along with many other social, cultural and musical events which were also held there. It was at one of these tennis parties that Alfred subsequently confirmed he had met his bride to be, when they played in a scratch mixed doubles match, which when asked about their first meeting he reportedly said 'You can hardly call it romantic,'[5] but thereafter they had met at every opportunity.

Moreover, it became evident that their friendship had progressed beyond something of a casual relationship by the end of 1925, when Alfred presented a little hand-held mirror as a seasonal gift to his intended, along with a short but evocative poem of endearment entitled:

TO M.E.B. WITH A MIRROR

This tiny glass, so limpid now and still
As a pale forest pool in Lyonesse:
How it will dance when your sweet features fill
Its depth with their rich loveliness!

How it will quiver when your flashing eyes
Wink like keen stars in its sphere!

15. Marie-Eugénie Bull

How it will glory when it doth comprise
Within itself a Face without compeer!

Yet, still unsatisfied, will then conspire
To filch your very breath to cool its fire.[6a]

As 1926 progressed the demands on Alfred to balance the three major aspects of his life; work, writing and romance, became ever more intense, but never to the point where his growing love for his fiancée did not find expression and provide him with a release from the conflicting elements of work and writing, as he confided: 'The truth is I am committing literary suicide; and at the same time developing into a strenuous, restless, horribly successful businessman.'[7]

Alfred also began to count on the support that he received from his fiancée to help him in these difficult times, as he noted: 'M. has been quite splendid... and she is not quite twenty yet. I have bought her a gorgeous kimono for her birthday.'[8] However one year on, Alfred was still struggling to balance work demands with his love of writing: 'Every now and then I am seized with the desire to journalise again. It is the only kind of writing (apart from letters) that comes easily to me – without effort. Apart from this, I think it helps me clear my mind and certainly facilitates my other writing.'[9] It is also probable that his journal provided him with an outlet for the growing demands of his job about which he lamented: 'the job has proved an undoubted success, so far as it goes. It goes, alas, much too far into my roots. It engulfs me. It sucks me in.'[9]

These feelings may be judged in the light of the excessive travel demands which were placed on Alfred at this time: 'I have been twice abroad with the bags already [*large sample bags of cloth pieces of made up yarns*]. Berlin, Vienna, Warsaw, Paris, Amsterdam, Prague; all these and a host of other towns I have also visited,' which led him to conclude ruefully: 'Make no mistake about it, commerce will never win me, though it may beat me,' then further to pose the question to himself: 'will marriage make me or complete the strangulation?'[9] But Alfred need not have worried, since these concerns probably reflected the last minute anxieties that pass through the mind of many a prospective bridegroom in the lead up to such an important event as marriage.

Wedding Preparations and Problems

Notwithstanding the competing demands upon his time, Alfred now turned his attention to the important preparations which needed to be completed before the forthcoming wedding could take place, and he was in a reflective mood on the occasion of his thirty-third birthday when he noted: 'the first I have spent at home for about ten years.'[10] Alfred had often been away on his birthday during the previous ten years, in convalescence during his prolonged recovery period, then on various holiday and walking tours and most recently on business trips. He then reflected:

> Today the banns were called for the first time. On September 19th we are to be married... and although Marie is twenty-one the day before the wedding, the Registrar would not accept the banns without the written 'consent to the marriage of a minor' by a parent or guardian being formally completed. Then he entered them as AJB, Bachelor, 32, MEB, Spinster, 20, – by the way, her full name is Marie-Eugénie Marguerite Michel Bull. Rather a mouthful for such a tiny lass! She insisted on Michel at confirmation because she thought it was the best of all, and after admitted that she had chosen this name since she would have liked to have been born a boy! The wedding announcement will read 'Brown-Bull'

which although Alfred amusingly thought sounded like the name of a public house he further noted:

> This is noble; of the earth, earthy; of the dales, daley, and of the pastures.[10]

Marie-Eugénie Bull was born in Bradford on 18th September 1906, the youngest of the five children, including brothers Gaston, Willie, Pierre and sister Marguerite, of Mr. Charles Alfred and Mrs. Félicité Marie Bull (née Messe). The family resided at 54 Peel Square, then a fashionable 1850s Victorian terrace designed by the architect William Metcalfe,[11] in the Westgate area of the Manningham district of Bradford. Charles Bull was a successful Bradford wool merchant, while Félicité Marie Messe was from a French family who resided in the Calais area, and among her ancestors was one J.B.P. Martin de Grandsire, who had been the Paymaster General of the French Army under Napoleon I (1769-1821). Unfortunately Marie-Eugénie's mother had died when she was only seven years old, and later she had spent some of her teenage years aged 12 to 15 in France, where she helped to look after her brother Gaston's twin daughters, her nieces Edwina and Patricia. She then returned to England as a young lady schooled in the French custom and style, and spent a year at a Convent Boarding School in Sanderstead in Surrey.

In this regard it was perhaps inevitable that an erroneous conclusion was drawn by readers that the character of Julian Laverack's half-French heroine, Miss Miranda Manners, partner of Ambrose Gildersome, was based upon Marie-Eugénie Bull in Alfred's book *The Lean Years* (1926). Nevertheless, it was true that she possessed some of the attractive physical attributes of the said character which were detailed in the book, and since Alfred had known Marie-Eugénie before he had written the book, it is likely that his bride-to-be had much to do with the formation of the character in the novel.

In order to celebrate Marie-Eugénie's forthcoming birthday and their imminent wedding, Alfred bought her a present for these occasions, and related an amusing incident which took place, which nevertheless also revealed some of the hidden tensions underlying preparations leading up to such an important event:

> Yesterday I bought Marie a combined 21st birthday and wedding present. The present (a real moleskin coat) caused some comedy and commotion. After hesitating between a sham 'squirreline' and this, we took the moleskin. On arriving home, bursting with news, Marie-Eugénie rushed in to show 'Papa' and Mrs. Gibson (her father's housekeeper). How cruel people can be; or how unthinking. Not a word was said when she put it on – only the blasted dog – the pet of Mrs. 'Doings' [Mrs. Gibson] discovered a sudden loathing for it and snapped, barked, howled and ran about the room in a panic. Even when Marie went upstairs (near tears) to take it off, it went on barking and beldering; but of course nobody controlled it and only after some demur was it taken to the kitchen. And then it raved, and still they stared glumly about, and still Marie stayed upstairs in tears. After a while it was brought in again and it continued louder than ever! Marie's headache, my nerves… nobody moving, I lost my temper, and gave it a good kick up the backside and went in search of Marie-Eugénie.[10]

However Alfred did regret his actions later and checked to make sure the animal was unhurt, but hoped that it had learned its lesson. Meanwhile time was now getting short and there were still lots of other arrangements to complete before the wedding. They had already rented a small house in a village near Bradford and were hurriedly buying enough furniture and fittings so that it would be ready to live in after the honeymoon. Their ambitious plans of buying Jacobean-style furniture had to be abandoned for the more practical and less costly, second-hand, but good value furnishings, except for the odd rare item such as a 300 year old oak kist, which Alfred surprised himself having been tempted to buy against his own better, Yorkshire, more frugal judgement: 'I have been splashing money about like water in my own way. I think in fivers, who hesitated to spend half a sovereign before.'[12]

There were all the fittings required including curtains, carpets, linen and kitchen utensils and crockery, not to mention the services needed of decorators, chimney sweeps and other odd job men in order to make the house habitable. There was also the little matter of the remaining wedding arrangements to complete, including the sending out of the daunting formal wedding invitations in the French, silver gilt 'Faire-Part' style to the many French relatives of Marie-Eugénie, along with Alfred's own family and friends, as well as the appointment of best man, groomsmen and brides maids, not to mention details of the ceremony itself. Then, if the problem of the Registrar's parental consent requirement was not enough, and had caused Alfred to feel 'as if I were eloping with a schoolgirl,'[13] a further problem arose. This time it was the need to assure the Church that Marie-Eugénie's religious credentials were in order i.e. the requirement to produce her baptismal certificate. Normally this would not have been a problem, but it was not readily available, since Marie-Eugénie had been baptised in France in the private chapel of the Château de Bourg, which was owned by an aristocratic friend of her mother, who had been a Governess to the family, and an original copy was now required. The chapel was in the Parish of Saint-Servan, in lower Normandy in the Diocese of Rennes , and it was necessary to request a copy of the document in question,[14] which fortunately was quickly forthcoming, or the whole event would have had to be postponed even at this late stage!

'A Wedding of Unusual Interest'[17]

Finally everything appeared to be in place for the big day, except perhaps for the matter of Alfred coming to terms with this momentous event in his life, and like all prospective bridegrooms, he thought deeply about the implications: 'A man said to me on t'Change today [Bradford Wool Exchange] – apropos my marriage – "Well I suppose that you are living on air just now, in the clouds so to speak." I smiled. For wherever I am living it is not there. Never, as I hastened to assure him, had I been so face to face with the hard realities of life.'[15]

Alfred John Brown and Marie-Eugénie Marguerite Bull were married on Monday, 19th September, 1927, at St. Patrick's Catholic Church in Sedgefield Terrace, off Westgate, in Bradford. The Bull family resided in St. Patrick's Parish which was the second oldest in Bradford, the church having been opened in 1853. They not only worshipped there, but lived a mere 200 yards away from the church, separated only by the grounds of the old Bradford Infirmary building, at the junction of Westgate and Lumb Lane, on the edge of the Manningham district of Bradford, about three quarters of a mile north of the city centre.

16. & 17. Alfred J. Brown & Marie-Eugénie Brown

Although the wedding was not unduly large, it nevertheless attracted widespread interest and notification by the local and regional press, which reported extensively on the lead up to the event[5,16] and the wedding itself,[17,18,19,20,21,22] in which the following most fulsome description occurred in the Telegraph and Argus newspaper:

A wedding of unusual interest took place this morning at St. Patrick's Church, Bradford, the bridegroom being Mr. Alfred J. Brown, youngest son of Mr. and Mrs. A.J. Brown, Spring Place, Bradford, and the bride Miss Marie-Eugénie Bull, the youngest daughter of Mr. Charles Bull and the late Mrs. Bull. The bridegroom is better known as Julian Laverack, the novelist. He is a Yorkshireman, devoted to his county and particularly fond of her moorlands. For this reason sprays of white heather were included in the bride's bouquet of Madonna lilies. *[The flower of this plant is said to be the basis of the 'fleur-de-lis', which signifies purity for Roman Catholics.]* Miss Bull made a charming bride in her gown of white Chantilly lace adorned with a white satin sash. Her veil of Brussels net was bound by a simple wreath of orange blossom. *[The wearing of orange blossom was introduced from France in 1820, and symbolised innocence, while the tree from which the bloom is derived, denoted abundance and prosperity, and the chaplet of flowers worn on the bride's head, together with the bouquet represented fruitfulness.]* Although the bride is English *[in fact half-French]*, many of her relatives are French, and the two small bridesmaids who attended her came over from Versailles for the wedding. They were Miss Edwina and Miss Patricia Bull (nieces of the bride). Both were dressed in shell-pink crêpe-de-chine trimmed with net frills. They wore Dutch caps of lace and carried bouquets of red roses. *[This was strange given Alfred's passionate affinity with Yorkshire and its white rose emblem, not the rival red rose emblem of Lancashire!]*

Mr. Charles Bull gave away his daughter. Captain G.C. Heseltine of London was best man *[Alfred's long-standing friend, fellow walker, author and journalist]* and the groomsmen were Mr. Tom A. Brown *[Alfred's younger brother]* and Mr. John P. Mullarkey *[Alfred's cousin on his mother's side]*.

Nuptial mass was celebrated by Father Charles Tindall *[Headmaster of St. Bede's Grammar School]*, assisted by Canon John Earnshaw *[Parish Priest of St. Patrick's Church]* and Father Thomas Blessing *[Parish Priest of St. Joseph's Church, where the Brown family worshipped]*. The organist was Mr.Richard

BRADFORD NOVELIST'S MARRIAGE.

INTERESTING CEREMONY AT ST. PATRICK'S.

HONEYMOON SECRET.

The Bride and Bridegroom leaving Church.
" Telegraph and Argus " Copyright.

18. The Brown Wedding press item

Hynes, brother-in-law of the bridegroom *[Richard was a former school friend of Alfred and had married his elder sister Gertrude]*. The music included Gounod's 'Ave Maria', Mozart's 'Aria' and Mendelssohn's 'Wedding March'.

After the ceremony a reception was held at the Trevelyan Hotel, Bradford *[formerly at 92 Godwin Street, now demolished]*, and later in the day Mr. and Mrs. A.J. Brown left for their honeymoon, though where it is to be spent has been kept a close secret. The bride travelled in a mauve crêpe-de-chine dress, with mauve velvet hat and moleskin fur coat *[the very same one which had caused the comical commotion earlier!]*. On their return the bride and groom will reside at Burley-in-Wharfedale.[17]

Alfred John Brown snr.

Mary Anne Brown

Alfred John Brown

Marie-Eugénie Brown

John Mullarkey

Thomas Brown

Richard Hynes

Gertrude Hynes

Vera Brown

Renée Dixon

Capt. G.C. Heseltine

Andrée Ratcliffe

19. The Brown Wedding group

'A Honeymoon in Arcady'[5]

There had already been some speculation in the press about where the couple were likely to spent their honeymoon,[5,17,19,20] but the only conclusion arrived at was that it was to be spent 'somewhere in Yorkshire', which in turn, it was also suggested, was likely to be the setting for the next 'Julian Laverack' novel[20]. It was hardly surprising then that the assumed general location for their honeymoon was correct, but most surprisingly that Alfred and Marie-Eugénie spent some time roving from place to place in the dales, and beyond, then as Alfred noted: 'before settling down for a week at one of the tiniest and most remote inns in the north, which to me will always remain the most romantic inn in Christendom.'[13]

After a short train journey the honeymoon started in the historic city of York, where they stayed a night at the Black Swan Hotel which was one of the oldest and most famous inns in the city, but has since been converted into offices.[23] They then proceeded to the east coast of Yorkshire, to an unspecified location in the old fishing port and popular holiday resort of Whitby, with its early Christian connections dating back to the seventh century, before moving yet again, this time to the Yorkshire Dales.[24] Perhaps Alfred was keen to show Marie-Eugénie the splendour of this magnificent countryside, which although familiar to him would have been almost unknown to her, if so, he could not have chosen a more impressive location.

They spent a short time at the now famous Tan Hill Inn, the highest at 1,732 ft. and arguably one of the most remote inns in England, which sits alone on the windswept moors overlooking Stainmore to the north, Arkengarthdale, an offshoot of Swaledale to the east, the ridges of the northern Yorkshire Dales to the south and views towards the Eden Valley to the west. The inn, which dates back to the 17th century, known as the 'King's Pit' until the 1930s, was named after the main mine nearby, since it supported a local coal mining community in the early 19th century. It then became a prime location for sheep fairs in the mid 20th century, when it was still relatively inaccessible, especially in winter, because it was often cut off by drifting snow. Most recently it has made its mark as a stopping off point for walkers on the Pennine Way long distance footpath, and as a popular venue for television commercials which advertise double glazing, as well the many celebrities who patronize the ideals of rural living. But perhaps its real claim to fame resides in one of its most interesting characters, the late inn-keeper from 1903 to 1937, Mrs. Susan Peacock, whom Alfred described in this encounter in one of his later literary works:

> To enter the old inn when Susan Peacock was in her prime was quite an experience, for she had a sharp tongue and a caustic wit; and woe betide anyone who crossed swords with her. I remember the keen glance she gave me when I took my young wife to see her on our honeymoon tour. '*Eey lad, a' thowt it wor thi daughter!*' she exclaimed to my amusement, and when my wife in her excitement signed her name in the Visitors' Book, Susan looked still more dubious. When my wife corrected her mistake and wrote my own surname (which had of course the same the same initial letter 'B' as her maiden name), Susan instantly quoted the old saw: 'The woman that changes her name and not the first letter; Is all for the worse and none for the better.'[25]

Finally, Alfred and Marie-Eugénie spent the last week of their honeymoon at one of Alfred's favourite inns, the Cat Hole Inn, near Keld, in upper Swaledale, where the River Swale branches into the becks of Birkdale and West Stones Dale. Alfred had spent many a hard-won night here after a day's fierce buffetings on the surrounding 'tops', and this little inn always had a special place in his affections: 'for it is here that I have set forth on some of my happiest tramps, and to its hospitable door I have returned at all hours of the night, never to be refused a bed, and always to be fed like a Lord.'[26] Where better then to complete a 'Honeymoon in Arcady' as the newspaper had proclaimed earlier?[5]

20. & 21. The Cat Hole Inn, Keld, c. 1930 and c. 1935

Alfred and Marie-Eugénie stayed for the week of the 23rd to 30th September, 1927, and were warmly hosted by Mr. and Mrs. W. G. Hutchinson, the proprietors of the cosy inn, where Susan Peacock, later landlady of the Tan Hill Inn, had earlier been married to the former Cat Hole inn-keeper Richard Parrington. During their visit they wandered around the hamlet of Keld, which lies at the head of one of the most picturesque and enchanting of all the Yorkshire Dales, and often described as the wildest and most beautiful dale in England. In the late 19th century, Keld had a population of over 6,000 at the height of the lead mining boom in Swaledale, but following its decline, only the Grade II listed buildings of the Congregational and Methodist Chapels, the School and the Literary Institute, remain as a testament to its former illustrious past. Nevertheless Keld, which nestles below Kisdon Hill at 1640 ft., continues to be an attractive location at the crossing point of both the Pennine Way and the Coast to Coast long-distance footpaths, and has some of the most scenic waterfalls nearby including the 'Forces' of Wainwath, Currack, Catrake and Kisdon, along with many other smaller falls. However, the well-known Cat Hole Inn public house on the edge of Keld, called 'time' for the last time in 1954, and it is now a private house. The local Temperance Movement bought it at auction, which would have both amused and dismayed Alfred in equal measure, especially since the hamlet then remained 'dry' for over 50 years!

When Alfred and Marie-Eugénie's idyllic sojourn in this Arcadian paradise came to an end, they would probably have been more than satisfied and somewhat surprised to know that the generous hospitality which they received came at a most frugal price. The receipted bill of 7s/6d per day, per person for seven days full board and lodgings was £5. 5s. 0d, with an even more abstemious drinks bill of only 3s/6d, and a car hire charge of the return transport to and from Hawes of 12s/0d[27]. The taxicab hire was necessary to take them over the 10 miles of moorland road via the famous Buttertubs Pass, which connects Swaledale with Wensleydale, where they caught the train at Hawes on the Wensleydale railway. The Wensleydale line, which was closed in the 1960s and is now partially re-opened, was a 40 mile route connecting the East Coast mainline at Northallerton, with the West Coast mainline via Garsdale, on the now famous Settle to Carlisle line, which has been reprieved twice from closure and is now one of the most popular tourist lines in the country.

This journey southwards provided a suitable finale to Alfred and Marie-Eugénie's honeymoon tour, since the route took them through some of the most impressive scenery offered by any railway in the country. The line passes through Dent, the highest station in England at 1,150 ft., over the quarter mile long, 24 arch, 100 feet high viaduct to Ribblehead, with spectacular views of the Yorkshire Three Peaks of Whernside (2,425 ft.), Ingleborough (2,372 ft.) and Penyghent (2,277 ft.), on the journey to Horton-in-Ribblesdale and Settle, before it continues to the West Riding of Yorkshire. Then after a final change of trains again at Shipley to the Ilkley branch line, Alfred and Marie at long last alighted at their destination of Burley-in-Wharfedale, where they would begin their new life together.

The First Place to call Home

Alfred and Marie-Eugénie had already made arrangements to establish their temporary new home life in a house which they rented for a year in Burley-in-Wharfedale, near Ilkley. They had chosen this area since the small village was located in Wharfedale, one of Alfred's favourite dales, about 12 miles northwest of Bradford, and was a relatively easy daily commute by bus or train to Alfred's office in Bradford. During their courtship, they had been determined to rent a country cottage with gardens in a more rural location further up the dale, but a combination of higher costs and a longer distance for Alfred to travel to work, had made this impossible. Instead they opted for a terraced house, which although rarely available for rent, Marie-Eugénie had been lucky to find at a reasonable charge of 15 shillings per week, plus 3s/6d for rates, and was located at 33 Grangefield Avenue, close to the centre of the village.

Burley-in-Wharfedale was originally an agricultural community of likely Roman and Anglo-Saxon origins, and had developed in the late 18th and early 19th centuries into an industrial village with many of its residents employed in the cotton mills at Greenholme Mills, which were powered by a goit (an artificial water channel) from the River Wharfe. Then with the decline of its own textile industry, and the rise of industry and commerce in nearby Leeds and Bradford during the later industrial period, it became a dormitory settlement for the two large cities nearby, especially in the early 20th century, which saw an influx of middle class, socially mobile people who were employed in both of the nearby centres of business. It was into this newly-developing community that Alfred and Marie-Eugénie were to become immersed during the coming years of their residence in the village.

Their modest little stone-fronted, terraced house was in a relatively new street in the village, with a square bay window front, plain bedroom window above, but only a small backyard, which served as a tiny garden, surrounded by a high back wall. The interior was comprised of a sitting room, dining-cum-kitchen room, a scullery for general food preparation and washing, two bedrooms and an attic.

It was Alfred's intention to convert the small second bedroom into his 'den' in which all the books and paraphernalia from his bachelor days might serve as a stimulus for his writing activities, since he maintained that the nature of one's surroundings was critical to creative writing:

> The smaller a man's room, the better book he will produce. For the less room there will be for boring Books of Reference, Encyclopaedias, Fudge, Facts and Year Books; and the more he will be compelled to draw on himself… The ideal room would be just big enough for his desk, his chair and himself; and then he would spin a cocoon of a book out of his own mind and bury his very soul in it – coming out with wings immortal!… Dump a genius in a learned man's library with polished mahogany desk, polished mahogany shelves galore, lined with polished books, and he will produce a polished piece of pedantry and no more![28]

Indeed it proved to be, and this tiny little room, his so-called 'den', provided him with the kind of stimulation needed to complete by Easter 1928, what is often regarded as one of his finest pieces of writing: *Four Boon Fellows – A Yorkshire Tramping Odyssey.*

When Alfred and Marie-Eugénie arrived at their new home after their return journey from honeymoon, they left their luggage temporarily at the railway station in order to arrive casually at the new abode, without attracting the unwanted attention of all the neighbours in the street, since they were still somewhat self-conscious about their new status. They were naturally thrilled again at the sight of their first home but they left it immediately, since in spite of all the help they had received from family and friends to make the house hospitable for their return, the larder was not stocked yet, so instead they celebrated their new home-coming with a meal out at one of the local village inns. This was the kind of special treat to which they had become recently accustomed on holiday, but one which would have to be pared back if they were going to make ends meet in future. Later that evening however, they were able to sit down in front of the fire, with the curtains drawn, remote from the outside world and enjoy their own little world of married life together.[13]

References and Notes

1. 'Alan Dale', 'Needles and Pins', unpublished manuscript written under another pseudonym of Alfred John Brown (no date) circa 1930s, The West Yorkshire Archive Service, Bradford Central Library, Document No. 69D90, Item 7/14.

2. AJB Journal, May 1925 – November 1927, 'Crowded Hours', 15th April 1926, pp. 123-125.

3. AJB Journal, ibid., 'Dreams', 14th April 1926, p. 120, 'Now my dreams', 6th May 1926, pp. 131-132, 'Full Circle', 28th February 1927, (Untitled entry), 10th March 1927, p. 117, 'Beautiful Bits', (no date), p. 153.

4. Mrs. R. Sturrup (née Brown), identification from the Rome Pilgrimage Group photograph, August 1925, in Chapter 3.

5. 'A Honeymoon in Arcady', 'Bradford Author to Marry', an interview reported in the Leeds Mercury, 16th September 1927.

6. Alfred J. Brown, 'To a Lady with a Gift of a Miniature Mirror', Poems and Songs, Horne

and Son Ltd., Abbey Press, Whitby, 1949, p. 95.

6a. Note: the original hand-written copy, dated 30th December 1925, was found among drafts of early poems by AJB.

7. AJB Journal, op. cit, Untitled Entry, 15th May 1926, pp. 133-135.

8. AJB Journal, op. cit., Untitled Entry, 8th September 1926, pp. 139-140.

9. AJB Journal, op. cit., 'Resume', 24th July 1927, pp. 144-147.

10. AJB Journal, op. cit., '33rd Birthday', 21st August 1927, pp. 148-152.

11. George Sheeran, *The Buildings of Bradford – An Illustrated Architectural History*, Tempus Publishing Limited, Stroud, Gloucestershire, Chapter 5: 'Building a Victorian City': 1850-1914, pp. 102-103.

12. AJB Journal, op. cit., 'On Getting Married', 30th August, 1927 pp. 156-161.

13. 'Alan Dale', op. cit., 'Prologue', pp. 1-12.

14. Marie-Eugénie Marguerite Bull, Extract of the Registers of Baptism in the parish of Saint-Servan, Diocese of Rennes, 20th August 1907.

15. AJB Journal, op. cit., Untitled Entry, 8th September 1927, p. 162.

16. 'Marriage of a Catholic Novelist', *The Universe and Catholic Weekly*, 9th September 1927.

17. 'Bradford Novelist's Marriage: Interesting Ceremony at St. Patrick's', *Bradford Telegraph and Argus*, 19th September 1927.

18. 'Bradford Novelist: Mr. A.J. Brown Married to Miss M.E. Bull', *Yorkshire Evening News*, 19th September 1927.

19. 'Bradford Novelist Married: Mr. A.J. Brown and Miss M. E. Bull', *Yorkshire Observer*, 20th September 1927.

20. 'Novelist Weds: Mr. A.J. Brown of Bradford and Miss M.E. Bull', *Yorkshire Post*, 20th September 1927.

21. 'Novelist Married at Bradford', *Sheffield Daily Telegraph*, 20th September 1927.

22. 'Yorks Novelist Married', *Daily Chronicle*, Northern Edition, 20th September 1927.

23. Alfred John Brown, 'Going Private or A Family Story', unpublished manuscript, 1951-1957, The West Yorkshire Archive Service, Bradford Central Library, Document No. 69D90, Item 7/11/1, Chapter 10, 'Ancient York" (i) p. 309.

24. Alfred John Brown, A short biographical account by AJB, The West Yorkshire Archive Service, Bradford Central Library, Document No. 69D90, Item 3/4/9, 1947.

25. Alfred J. Brown, *Broad Acres - A Yorkshire Miscellany*, Country Life Limited, London, 1948, Chapter 20, 'Keld', pp. 136-138.

26. Alfred J. Brown, *Moorland Tramping in West Yorkshire*, Country Life limited, London, 1931, Section XX1X, 'Yorkshire Inns – And Ale', p. 165.

27. Receipted bill, the Cat Hole Inn, Keld, Richmond, Yorkshire, 30th September 1927.

28. AJB Journal, op. cit., 'In Praise of Little Rooms', p. 47, (no date), circa 1925.

CHAPTER 5

A Change in Literary Direction

If the years preceding Alfred's marriage to Marie-Eugénie in 1927 may be summed up by the title of his first novel as 'the lean years', the next five years, following his change of marital status, may be described as one of his most prolific periods of productivity, in terms of his personal circumstances, family life and literary output, with a continued commitment to the textile industry. The latter was by no means an easy achievement in view of the economic pressures which the industry had endured following the General Strike of 1926, and the need to develop new products in order to counter the growing competition from cheaper overseas markets. There was also the need to respond to the financial crises which the General Depression of the 1930s had brought about in the economy of this country and that of the western world, all of which placed Alfred under considerable strain at work.

It may have been these prospects of such a gloomy economic scenario that stimulated Alfred to develop his literary talents further, and thus create the possibility of an alternative future career in writing, which would allow him to provide the additional financial support for his subsequent family. Whatever the reasons, this period of time saw Alfred settling down to the demands of a new life as a married man after his bachelor years, the birth of three of his five children, a second house move to cope with the pressures of his rapidly growing family and a complete change of literary direction. This resulted in the publication of not only a major tramping odyssey, but a series of seminal topographical walking books on Yorkshire, which were to establish Alfred's reputation as a leading authority in this field, as well as producing several other important works, and all of this whilst maintaining his day job.

Alfred's 'Magnum Opus': *Four Boon Fellows*[1a]

Alfred's literary output had been growing steadily during the 1920s and had culminated in the reasonably successful novel *The Lean Years* in 1926, but he had already started to lay the foundations for a series of walking books which would become the hallmark of his subsequent successful writings in future. Initially, Alfred's deep affinity with Yorkshire really began with his next book as he recounted:

Two years later, I gave expression to my love of Yorkshire and walking in my first book *Four Boon Fellows [1928]*... I wrote this book to please myself and thoroughly enjoyed the task. It was an unusual book and not to everybody's taste: a kind of rollicking extravaganza concerning the adventures of four men called Wharfe, Aire, Ouse and Swale, who wander about the Shire at Easter time. It is essentially an Easter book and should be read at that joyful season.[2]

However the book had been in preparation for quite some time and the background material came from a 100 mile tramp from Barnard Castle to Ilkley, which Alfred and his cousin Laurence Geoghegan had made in the early 1920s[3], when Alfred had probably started drafting notes for the book. Furthermore, Alfred had made frequent references to his so-called 'Hog' book in his daily journal during the period in question[4], as well as the doubts and despair he was having about ever bringing it to a successful conclusion:

If my novel does well *[The Lean Years, 1926]*, and if my Hog book is a best seller, then I may be able to cut myself loose.[5] ...My writing has suffered a sharp set back and for a fortnight I have done next to nothing, but I must finish my Yorkshire (Hog) book somehow.[6] ...And my book. How it suffers. My Iliad (Hog book) that is never to be published... Inwardly I weep.[7]

Then continued the following year:

Will my Hog book ever be published[8] ... Dent *[the London Publishers]* are still nibbling at the Hog book.[9]

Alfred had first made a hand-written draft of the book in a foolscap ledger of some 400 pages with many inserts during 1926.[10a] He then had a 484 page type scripted draft manuscript prepared entitled 'Four Boon Fellows – On Foot Through Yorkshire' ready for consideration by potential publishers in 1927.[10b] However this draft had only one positive response as Alfred recalled with pleasure, but also with some concern that:

After the book had been rejected by most of the publishers in London, Mr. Hugh Dent, of J.M. Dent & Sons, wrote me a charming letter to say that as a Yorkshireman he felt the book ought to be published but as a publisher he had grave doubts. To my everlasting delight, he finally decided to publish and be damned.[11]

Subsequently, an agreement was duly signed for the book by the publisher and Alfred on 29th December 1927, with the intended publication date of 31st May 1928, initially for 2,000 copies, with a possible further print run of up to 5,000 copies, dependent upon sales.[12] The contract entitled Alfred to receive royalties of 12.5% of the profits on the first print run, rising to 15% on the second and 20% on any possible sales thereafter. However, whilst this contract seemed to be very reasonable, even with the most successful sales figures envisaged, the amount that Alfred was likely to receive would only have netted him less than half of his annual salary at the time, and therefore would not have allowed him to make the break from his job as he had previously hoped.

Structure, Style and Scope of the Book

The structure of the book was very ambitious for its day in terms of its format, which makes it somewhat difficult to follow, since unlike the table of contents, which suggests merely an account of the actual journey made by these four 'boon fellows' i.e. close, congenial friends, what transpires is not so simple or so straightforward. In fact the journey itself only represents the framework on which the narrative is constructed and the complex storyline proceeds on three separate yet interactive levels, which at times can be confusing to the reader.

The first and major level, involves the discursive discussions among these four fine 'bullyrocks', or just 'impudent villains' as Alfred referred to them, nicknamed respectively as 'Wharfe' (Alfred), 'Ouse' (George Heseltine, Alfred's best man and closest friend), 'Aire' (Laurence Geoghegan, Alfred's cousin) and 'Swale' (Alfred Sclater, Alfred's friend from the West Riding Ramblers' Federation). They represent the many-faceted sides of the complex and sometimes truculent Yorkshire 'character', and accordingly, they constantly argue with each other about the relative merits of their own Dales districts. Each of them is adamant in the belief that theirs is the one, true 'Janua Coeli' or entrance to heaven, even though they concede unanimity in all matters concerned with the integrity of Yorkshire as a whole.

The second and subsidiary level, which involves a totally different quality of discourse, is introduced by a lengthy prelude to the book, and concerns that of the 'Scribe', namely the writer, Alfred, and the 'Pater', who is a fatherly figure and confidant of the 'Scribe'. The 'Pater' represents an abstract figure to whom the 'Scribe' can refer and seek advice from in times of frequent conflict among the aforesaid protagonists, and therefore appears regularly throughout the text. This figure was just as real as the other four characters, and appropriately enough, was another friend of Alfred's, Father Maurice McEvoy, a Mill Hill missionary priest, whom Alfred referred to as the 'certain foreign missioner – somewhere in the bush'. He was in the 'British

Cameroons', West Africa at the time, and to him Alfred 'heartily dedicated' the book, along with: 'all men who have not yet lost the use of their legs.'[10a]

The third and minor level introduces a nebulous figure into the storyline at a very early stage of the prelude, that of the 'Hog', and explains why Alfred had often referred to this particular piece of writing as his 'Hog' book. The 'Hog' character is represented by the motorised road user who had begun to commandeer the open roads through some of Yorkshire's most scenic areas, almost to the exclusion of the walker and indeed the cyclist, who once had free, unfettered rein of those beloved byways. This final character pervades the storyline in an insidious fashion and may explain why the book was sometimes taken at face value to be a counterblast to the increase in motorised transport which would eventually threaten to ravage the countryside at large.

The text is written in a 'picaresque' style, a popular sub-genre of prose fiction (from the Spanish 'picaro': a rogue or rascal), which is usually satirical and depicts in realistic and often humorous detail the adventures of a roguish hero who lives by his wits in a corrupt society. Thus the 'picaresque' in this case refers to the narrative account of a series of loosely-linked episodes, which records in embellished detail, the adventures of these four rogues during their odyssey, or long wandering journey through the great Shire. It is often delivered with a 'pasquinade' or satirical emphasis, and frequently displays combinations of prose and verse, sometimes in the French 'Aucassin' or 'sung-story' style. Little wonder that the resultant product was in Alfred's words: 'not to everybody's taste.'

The style is further enriched by the use of an extensive range of locality-specific words, phrases and terminologies, which are used to support and illustrate the themes being described. However this puts even more demands on the reader, in terms of the knowledge and understanding needed to readily appreciate the relevance of such usage in the dialogue among the characters portrayed in the storyline.

Therefore in order to be able to make the most of these exchanges, the reader requires either a working knowledge of, or access to sources of information on, a variety of Yorkshire Dialect terms, and also many older English words which are no longer in common usage. In addition, a familiarity with some Greek mythology would also help, along with English historical events relevant to the region, as well as the local history of the Shire, in both prose and poetic forms. Finally, if all this were not enough, the translation of some classical and ecclesiastical Latin words and phrases which are sprinkled in the text is also needed. This may seem somewhat daunting to the potential reader, but it is well worth the effort to extend one's knowledge of such material in order to more fully appreciate the work, if only to become acquainted with some 'tyke speyk' or Yorkshire Dialect Speech.

The scope of the book is described by Alfred's intentions at the outset in which he stated:

> I will set down the story of the Easter pilgrimage of Wharfe, Aire, Ouse and Swale. I will relate how in spite of all perils they accomplished their noble resolve: I will tell how they circumvented the Hogs for the space of three whole days and nights: I will trace their splendid track from beginning to end: I will most faithfully record their adventures, their rencontres; their conversations and silences; their fasts and their carouses; their brawls and barneys and (above all) their modest eulogies of the Shire... Furthermore, I will certainly include an account of some of the greatest Walkers who have gone before; of the lost Fellowship of the Road which they endeavoured so manfully and so vainly to revive; and the rebuffs they met with in the attempt. I will paint, too, a picture of the Inns which they visited and the Hotels which they fled. But above all I will mention only such places as I have visited on foot. *[pp. 6-7]*

In order to achieve these ambitious intentions, it is not surprising that the scope is very extensive and covers a multitude of topics, which are not listed, since they occur naturally as the storyline progresses and are not indexed. Originally Alfred had been badgered by his publisher to compile an index for the book, but he steadfastly refused to accede to this pressure and indicated that there was so much contained in the book that any index would occupy as much space as the text itself, and commented: 'this modest little book is not a Guide Book, and heaven forbid that I should make it easier for a Hog to find his way to any blessed place mentioned that he has not already found.' *[p. 322]*

Instead it was Alfred's view that the book would appeal to all those who would plod diligently through the pages and in doing so read for their own delight about everything it contained. However, as a compromise, he did provide at the top of nearly every page a 'finger post' clue to its general orientation, and the topic being described, discussed or discerned therein, from the 'Abuse of Ale' to a 'Yorkshire Litany'; a total of 293 topics in 310 pages, almost one for each page. In doing so, Alfred also displayed a vast knowledge of local folk lore and legends and a comprehensive familiarity with the geography of the County. Moreover, he is able to enliven his treatment of the subject matter with an extensive range of over 60 traditional song and ballad lyrics, as well as poetic stanzas, of which more than a quarter were taken from his earlier works[13,14] and many of which were subsequently to be published,[15] although one in particular, 'There Must be Dales in Paradise', first appeared in the book and would assume special significance in the fullness of time.

Finally, the essential scope of the book is best summed up by Alfred's reflections about his deep feelings for his beloved County of Yorkshire:

> How rich is our County in rivers; in little dales and mighty dales; in crumbling castles. In abbeys and priories; in inns and sturdy villages; in scrambling walls and rugged roads; in boulders, screes and scars; in noble halls and pleasances; in lonely tarns in moor and mountain; in wild birds; in tumbling ghylls; in gnarled oaks and ash and thorns; in firs and pines; in generous food; in lusty lads and lasses – in short – for my breath fails me! – in every decent thing the heart of man could desire, so much so, that to particularise them all would exhaust the patience and the credulity of all unfortunate exiles and foreigners! [p. 120]

Then subsequently, as if to qualify this seemingly unbridled glorification of the County, he went on to declare:

> Even so, I am a great believer in foreign travel, for until a man has done the tour of the world how can he satisfy himself of the supreme glory of his own beloved lands? [p. 145]

Impact of the Book

It was a great disappointment to Alfred that even though the first edition in 1928 priced at 7s/6d received excellent press reviews, and also had the distinction of being reprinted once in 1930 priced at 3s/6d, it was never well advertised and marketed and sales fell after the first edition, which meant that it had to be remaindered i.e. sold off at cost price, thus ending any hope of Alfred's dream of becoming a full-time writer at this stage. Moreover, as Alfred later reflected: 'I never made a penny piece on it. Actually I lost on it, as I never recouped even the expenses of typing it, let alone the beer I consumed in walking across Yorkshire in writing it.'[11] Nevertheless, he felt that if it had been the success which the press reviews suggested could be expected, his whole career might have been completely different. However, it did not alter Alfred's subsequent view: 'In my opinion, it is the best book I have ever written.'[11] Most importantly, this view was also shared by Marie-Eugénie, who continued to encourage Alfred's writing.

The popular press reception that the first edition of the book enjoyed may be judged by the following brief notices,[16] which represent a sample of the most favourable local, regional and national press reviews that appeared at the time:

'A brilliant exception... The most original and amusing book about Yorkshire... we have read.' – *Yorkshire Weekly Post*

'This epoch-making book... racy, unconventional, exhilarating. A convincing dissertation on the superior advantage of legs over wheels...' – *Bookfinder Illustrated*

'A lusty cursing of motor cars and all their ways. The talk has a sort of rombustious swagger.' – *Times Literary Supplement*

'A roistering, go as you please walking tour... full of genuine high spirits... good songs.' – Beachcomber (D.B. Wyndham Lewis), *Daily Express*

'Intensely interesting work which will be quoted long after we are dead... Unlike anything we have seen. Fresh, new, novel.' – J. Fairfax-Blakeborough, *Yorkshire Herald*

'One of the most brilliant writers Yorkshire has produced this generation... Fine rhetorical arguments... Drinking songs that Falstaff might have chanted.' – *Yorkshire Evening Post*

'Lively, blustering, dialogue; cheerful songs and laughter. A declaration of the rights of walking men.' – *The Universe* (Catholic National Weekly Newspaper)

'A book of strange ideas... here is the pedestrian's friend.' – *Daily Chronicle*

'A glorification of legs over wheels' – *Leeds Mercury*

'In a fairly extensive acquaintance with the literature of the Tankard, we hardly remember anything better than the praise of Yorkshire Ale.' – *Birmingham Post*

'The jolliest and most original book about a walking tour published for a long time.' – *Liverpool Daily Courier*

'Racy dialogue, legend lore... mirth provoking.' – *Yorkshire Observer*

Whilst no doubt Alfred was pleased with, and maybe even surprised by, the widespread distribution and the virtual unanimity among these reviews, he was most impressed by one particular review in the Yorkshire Evening Post, which gave the book nearly a whole middle page of coverage, with two full columns and more than any other it captured the very essence of the book. Therefore a shortened excerpt is presented:

> After all the books that have been written in praise of the charms and other characteristics of Yorkshire and Yorkshiremen by travellers, scientists, antiquarians, essayists and impulsive amateurs who – following a great example afar off – write because they must, one would have said it was impossible to discover in the broad acres *[Yorkshire]* any scope for originality. This only goes to show how dangerous it is to generalise without leaving ample room for exception.
>
> *Four Boon Fellows* is a brilliant exception. Its author, Mr. Alfred J. Brown, is to be congratulated upon having written the most original and in parts the most amusing book about Yorkshire it has been our good fortune to read. At first glance it is almost repellant. It is for the most part thrown into the form of a dialogue between four representative Yorkshire characters – Aire, Swale, Wharfe and Ouse – who set out in a spirit of good-humoured rivalry to discover the charms of the county and to pull the legs off the orthodox and the ultra-modern. As a rule nothing is more stilted, more boring than formal dialogue. Mr. Brown, however, is not stilted, and he is entertainingly informal. In style he has parodied very cleverly the grotesque piled up exaggerations of Rabelais, and the whimsical discoveries of Sterne; and these are so wilfully and withal so neatly blended that instead of pausing to criticise, one reads right on, sharing the jolly fun...
>
> ...To think of treating adequately such a book of 300 pages in a brief review is hopeless. It is full of racy fun and vigour, relieved again and again by touches of sincerity. There is also an abundance of poetry and other verse, rattling song and humour. Aire, Swale, Wharfe and Ouse are exuberantly representative of Yorkshire and Yorkshiremen, as they see themselves, if not invariably as others see them.[17]

There was a further set of reviews however, which were far less favourable and appeared in *The Tablet*, a National Catholic Weekly Journal that prided itself on the in-depth coverage and treatment of religious, political, social and current affairs, as well as the arts and literature, with a special emphasis on Roman Catholicism. These more critical appraisals of both the first and second editions of the book also made some interesting comparisons with a previous work by Hilaire Belloc (1870-1953) entitled *The Four Men – A Farrago*,[18] in terms of both style and content.

In the first review the book critic confided:

> Gladly we have made a fifth, with 'Four Boon Fellows', whose adventures
> on the road with Mr. Alfred J. Brown entertainingly relates; for we, too,
> in better times have tramped English Highways and are ready as the boon
> fellows themselves to curse the Hogs and the Hoggetts [*motorcyclists*] by
> whose petrol-driven wheels pedestrianism now spells peril. But such
> companionship the four would have scorned, they are A, and O, and W, and
> S, boasters all, in unison or in rivalry, of the merits of their own Yorkshire,
> and none but a fellow-countryman dare have intruded himself into the
> company. At first we feared that these four good fellows – all of them of
> the Household of the Faith, with Mass at St. Wilfrid's, York, to fortify them
> for their pilgrimage – would find nothing more to talk about than ale and
> ale-houses, of which matters, to tell the truth, their conversation became
> somewhat wearisome; but after a while copious refreshment loosened their
> tongues on other subjects, and those who follow them will be gladdened
> with Yorkshire verse and the praises of pudding, with legends, anecdotes
> and an occasional serious reflection. These four boon fellows are not so
> interesting as a quartette as Sailor and his companions whom Mr. Belloc
> sent striding some years ago along the lanes of his loved county [*Sussex*];
> their range is narrower, and the hogs get rather more frequent curses than
> are needful for literary proportion. Yet we think we may be grateful to Sailor
> and company for having probably set these other four men upon the way. In
> the manner of treating his theme, Mr. Brown writes with a Bellocian touch
> and with something of the Bellocian skill. He has produced a jolly book,
> the better for being read a bit at a time.[19]

This somewhat condescending review, with its conservatively Catholic view of the
'demon drink', suggested that discourse among the four lads only came to life after
they had imbibed, was prefaced by the almost back-handed compliment that at least
they were Catholics. The reviewer then appeared to surreptitiously suggest that Alfred
had borrowed the Belloc story for the idea, and indeed, that he had utilised some of
the Bellocian approach and technique in pursuing his theme, when in fact Alfred had
already developed what might be called his own, unique 'Brownian' style of writing,
mixed with his own, typically, dry-witted Yorkshire humour, which underpinned the
exchanges of a more interesting set of characters, with a much wider range of interests,

in a far more challenging rural landscape and time frame. Then in a second review, presumably by the same reviewer, a further comparative nuance is also made, but this time in a more positively redeemingly Catholic note, in which the reviewer almost warmed to his task.

> On its first appearance, about two years ago, we welcomed Mr. A.J. Brown's *Four Boon Fellows*, the story of a tramp in Yorkshire by the quartette W. A. O. and S., whose pride in their native county was exceeded in intensity only by their hatred of 'Hogs', that is to say motorists. A wider public can now enjoy the book in a cheaper version. Re-reading this lively and amusing volume, we are convinced that during their journey, the boon fellows must have raised a tankard to another four: Sailor and his companions, whose tramp through Sussex many years previously hailing them as true comrades in the kinship of the road. Mr. Brown dedicates his book to a foreign missionary priest, and more than once in the course of the odyssey sounds a note of the Catholic Faith.[20]

It is worth commenting that in fact the analogy between the two books in question is somewhat disingenuous, in that it focuses upon a somewhat superficial comparison, rather than a more discerning contrast between them, and does not do justice to either book in its own right. At the outset there is a clear distinction between the two texts, which is evident from their respective sub-titles; Alfred's 'A Tramping Odyssey', may be defined as a long, wandering journey involving a series of loosely-linked episodes which embellish the adventure, whereas Belloc's 'A Farrago' may be defined as a confused collection, or hotch-potch, involving a mixture of unrelated parts.

Moreover, Belloc's story is told in a mythical or allegorical fashion, and his characters, 'Myself, Grizzlebeard, The Sailor and The Poet', are taken to be aspects of his own personality and represent his solemnity, irony, optimism and sadness respectively, whereas Alfred's story is told in a satirical style and the characters, 'Wharfe, Aire, Ouse and Swale', are real people who represent various aspects of the Yorkshire personality, and are associated with specific Dales areas of the County. Furthermore, while Belloc's characters are taken on an imaginary four day 60-70 mile journey across Sussex, Alfred and his friends completed an arduous three day 100 mile tramp down through the West Yorkshire Dales.

While it is true to say that both books portray a humorous discourse among the respective characters, which is related to a wide range of social, philosophical and religious issues, as well as the topics of landscape, food and drink, not to mention 'hogs', both reflect upon a disappearing lifestyle associated with unspoiled rural England. Moreover the contrast between the gentle, rolling uplands of the South Downs of Sussex in the late Victorian era (Belloc's book was almost ten years in gestation from 1902), and that of the mountainous, moorland fells and deep valleys of the West Riding Dales of Yorkshire during the post World War One era, could not be more starkly portrayed.

In summary, there is a subtle distinction in the purposes and intentions of the two writers with regard to the approach in their respective books. It was Belloc's purpose at the outset to record the image of his adopted county as it was then, before the inevitable changes associated with the dawning of a new century came about, as his melancholic statement suggests in the preface: 'For I know very well in my mind that a day will come when the holy place shall perish and all the people of it and never more be what they were'. Whereas it was Alfred's intention in the beginning to celebrate the good fortunes of his own County, albeit in the face of the envisaged onslaught of 20th century progress, as his optimistic first sentence suggests: 'Why should I not – however unworthily – sing the praise of our County that we have tramped together?'

Finally, in practical terms, there is one more important and fundamental distinction to be made between the two books. Whilst there is a reasonably straight forward descriptive account of Belloc's route in the text, which makes it relatively simple for the modern traveller to follow, Alfred's route is not very easy to discern. It is often deeply hidden within the textual account which makes it very difficult for the would-be walker of today to follow, and hence the reason for the elaboration with the maps and details of the route which follows. In doing so, it is hoped that anyone interested in tramping in the footsteps of these 'Four Boon Fellows' in future, will have a reasonably well illustrated description of the way, which together with the relevant O.S. maps, provides the necessary guidance for the walk to be completed.

However the final word should be left to Alfred in bringing the 'Yorkshire Tramping Odyssey', which he and his companions had completed, to a suitably symbolic conclusion at the end of their journey:

> These Four Lads were scattered to the four corners of the earth... Swale to the North; Wharfe to the South; Ouse to the East, and Aire to the West; so that, taking the Priory [*Bolton Priory*] as their centre-point, they made the Sign of the Cross over the whole Shire with their footprints, and so followed their guiding stars.' [*p. 308*]

The 'Yorkshire Tramping Odyssey' Route

The route taken by the 'Four Boon Fellows' went from Barnard Castle on the River Tees southward through the main West Yorkshire Dales of Arkengarthdale, Swaledale, Wensleydale, Langstrothdale, and Wharfedale, (see map), to Ilkley on the River Wharfe, a journey of almost 100 miles, during the Easter Holiday of 1926. Since these Dales are aligned in a northwest to southeast direction, a traverse of the intervening mountain moorlands was required, so the trampers passed through some of the most beautiful scenery of the North and West Ridings of the County.[21a]

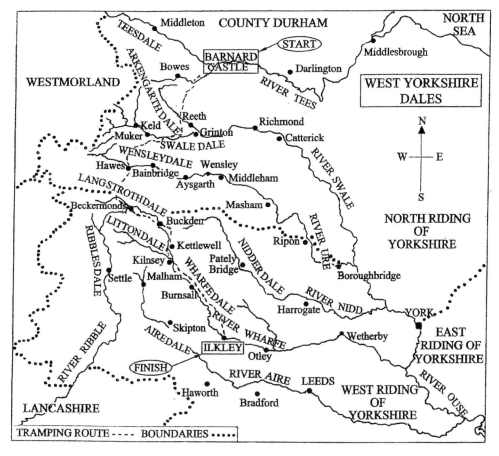

Map 4. Route taken by the Four Boon Fellows

The route was divided into three long, albeit arduous stages (and a fourth short, easy one), in order to make the journey manageable within the time available, but since it is enmeshed within the storyline, the precise way followed by the group is often difficult to establish without a great deal of searching and sifting out carefully the possible alternatives some-times suggested. Therefore a day-by-day map is also provided, along with a brief account of each day's tramp and additional descriptive material concern-ing some related items of interest associated with the places which the party visited on the journey.

Day 1: Holy Saturday, 3rd April 1926 (23 miles)

The 'Four Boon Fellows' assembled early at York and boarded trains, first to Darlington and then to Barnard Castle, where their epic tramp began. But with no time to view the 12th century castle built by Bernard Balliol, they crossed the footbridge at the bottom of the steep main street over the River Tees near the old mill from County Durham into North Yorkshire.

They followed the road along the riverside past the ruined 12th century Egglestone Abbey and Rokeby Park, where Sir Walter Scott found the inspiration for some of his great writings. On arrival at the confluence of the River Tees and River Greta, near Greta Bridge, they paused for refreshments at the Morritt Arms Hotel, an old coaching inn on the old A66. Their journey continued via the medi-aeval village of Brignall, with its derelict 13th cen-tury Church of St. Mary, which was abandoned in 1833, along with most of the village, to another site nearby.

The route then followed the deep wooded gorge of Brignall Banks and forded the River Greta near Thwaite, before the group ascended Barningham Moor, via the hamlet of East Hope. Here they fol-lowed Hope Edge and joined a minor road on Hope Moor at the top of the broad ridge of The Stang. There a brief halt for sustenance was taken at the

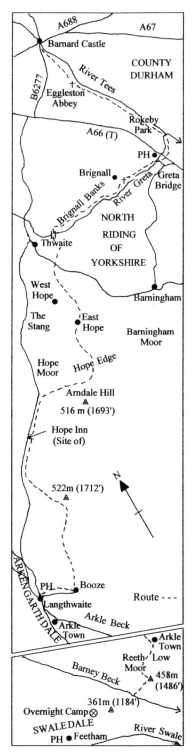

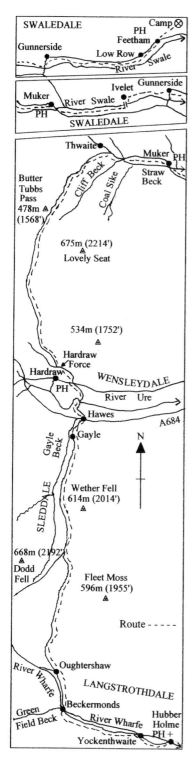

Hope Inn (no longer in existence) on the road down into Arkengarthdale.

Instead of taking the steep road into the dale, they followed an old path along the side of Booze Moor and Low Moor, but resisted the temptation to detour to the hamlet of Booze, which in spite of its name has no public house. So they found hospitality at Langthwaite's cosy Red Lion Inn, before they crossed the Arkle Beck into Arkle Town. These small settlements later found fame when they featured in the BBC television series about the country veterinarian James Herriot, *All Creatures Great and Small.*

As the daylight began to fade, the group set out over Reeth Low Moor, and after a descent into Swaledale, the weary walkers decided to spend the night on the fellside, under the stars, with their groundsheet spread over the soft *ling* (heather). Then despite the pain of aching limbs and 'skinned heels and blistered toes' they all slept very soundly indeed.

Day 2: Easter Sunday, 4th April 1926 (30 miles)

On Easter Day, these devout Catholics considered fulfilling their 'Easter Duties', but the nearest church meant a 10 miles detour to Richmond. Therefore they deferred their obligations on this occasion, said their morning prayers and took a purifying plunge into the cold River Swale instead.

Then to prepare for the long day ahead, they called into the Punchbowle Inn at Feetham, where they enjoyed a hearty breakfast of porridge, ham, pace eggs, sausages, havercakes, bread, marmalade, jam and cheese, all washed down with tea in pint pots.

The now satiated group continued along Swaledale, via Long Row and Gunnerside, crossed the River Swale at Ivelet Bridge and went on to Muker. Here they stopped again, this time to chat over ale with the famous Nancy Peacock at the Farmer's Arms, before they tackled the spectacular road over Butter Tubs Pass. The pass was so named for the cool limestone pot-holes where farmers once stored their butter on the way to market on hot days.

The group continued down into Wensleydale, past England's highest unbroken waterfall of 90 feet at Hardraw Force. This feature has provided a natural acoustic amphitheatre for the annual brass band competition held there since 1884, with access gained by a small fee paid at the Green Dragon pub at nearby Hardraw.

The route then took them via the ancient market town of Hawes, then ascended from Wensleydale over into picturesque Sleddale, and descended once more into Langstrothdale, an extension of Upper Wharfedale. They passed through the quaint villages of Oughtershaw, Beckermonds, Yockenthwaite and finally Hubberholme, where they found splendid food and lodgings for the night at the George Inn.

The old inn faces the 12th century church of St. Michael and All Angels and is often referred to as the 'Cathedral of the Dales'. It is noted for its rare 16th century rood loft and Robert Thompson's oak pews, each with his own trademark of a mouse emblem.

The churchyard also contains the ashes of the Bradford-born writer and playwright, J.B. Priestley, who chose this spot as his final resting place, since it was in his opinion: 'one of the smallest and most pleasant places in the world'.

Day 3: Easter Monday, 5th April 1926 (39 miles)

After another early start the group set out along one of the most scenic dales, following the River Wharfe through Upper, Middle and Lower Wharfedale. They passed through Buckden, with its famous Buck Inn, and ascended Buckden Pike to observe some of the finest views of most of the major dales' summits in the western area.

The descent into the hamlet of Starbotton however proved a disappointment, since the Fox and Hounds Inn was closed for repairs, so the party pressed on to Kettlewell for refreshment at the Racehorses Hotel, one of three hostelries available at the time.

After lunch they continued along the river footpath, past Skirfare Bridge where the River Skirfare joins the Wharfe from Littondale, and arrived at Kilnsey. Its famous 170 feet Crag was carved by glacial action, is now a popular venue for the climbing fraternity.

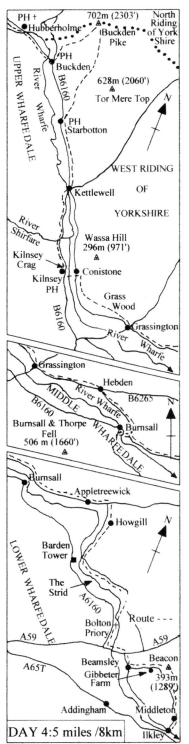

Having crossed the Wharfe, they proceded via Conistone through Grass Wood and reached the 7th century market town of Grassington. Then they detoured along the old drover's road to Hebden, before a return to the River Wharfe at Burnsall, famous for its seven arch bridge and the annual fell race.

They then pressed on via Appletreewick to see the breathtaking view of the 'Strid', where the Wharfe is forced through a deep narrow channel only 6.5 feet wide. This has often tempted the unwary to try to leap across, mostly with disastrous results, as the victim slips into the maelstrom, is sucked down into underwater caves, and there is no record of any survival.

In contrast, the route then passed the tranquility of Bolton Priory, the ruined 12th century Augustinian Abbey, immortalised by the artists Landseer and Turner, and the poet Wordsworth, and now part of the Bolton Abbey Estate formerly owned by the Dukes of Devonshire.

The end of this long day's tramp was Beamsley and a night's rest, most probably at Gibbeter Farm, where Alfred had spent some of his post WW1 convalescence in 1920. Finally, the following day the party walked wearily the last few miles via Beamsley Beacon and Middleton down to Ilkley, where they each entrained once more for their respective journeys home.

References and Notes

1. Alfred John Brown, *Four Boon Fellows – A Tramping Odyssey*, J. M. Dent and Sons Ltd., London, 1928, re-issued 1930.
    1a. Note: Alfred chose this whimsical book title from a line in the great Yorkshire Ode: 'In Praise of Yorkshire Ale', p. 91.

2. A. J. Brown, *I Bought a Hotel*, Williams and Norgate, London, 1949, Chapter: 'Books and Authorship' iii, 'Autobiographical' pp. 144-152.

3. Thomas Burns, 'Alfred John Brown: Yorkshire's Tramping Author', *The Dalesman Magazine*, Vol. 42, No. 5, August 1981, pp. 358-361.

4. Alfred John Brown, Journal, May 1925 – November 1927.

5. Ibid., 'Full Circle', 28th February 1926, p. 105.

6. Ibid., (No Title), 10th April 1926, pp. 115-116.

7. Ibid., 'Crowded hours', 15th April 1926, pp. 123 -125.

8. Ibid., 'Résumé', 22nd July 1927, p. 146.

9. Ibid., 'On Leisure', (No Date) November 1927, p. 165.

10. Alfred John Brown, West Riding Archive Service, Bradford Central Library, Document No. 69D90,
    10a. Section 3/1/1 and **10b**. Section 3/1/2, the 'Four Boon Fellows' manuscripts.

11. Ibid., Section 3/4/9, 'Biographical' – a short summary by AJB, pp. 150-151.

12. Literary Agreement Contract, AJB Literary Agreements File (1923-1959).

13. Alfred John Brown, Journal of Unpublished Poems, 1917.

14. Alfred John Brown, Journal of Unpublished Poems, 1917-1918.

15. Alfred J. Brown, *Poems and Songs*, Horne and Son Ltd., Abbey Press, Whitby, 1949.

16. A selected sample of some 25 press reviews of *Four Boon Fellows*, AJB Literary Agreements File (1923-1959).

17. 'Four Boon Fellows: A Book For Yorkshiremen', the Yorkshire Weekly Post, Saturday, May 26th 1928, p.4.

18. Hilaire Belloc, *The Four Men – A Farrago*, Thomas Nelson and Sons Ltd., London, 1911.

19. *The Tablet*, Saturday, July 28th 1928, Vol. 152, No. 4603, 'New Books and Music to Buy, Borrow or Leave Alone'.

20. *The Tablet*, Saturday, March 29th 1930, Vol. 155. No. 4690, 'New Books and Music to Buy, Borrow or Leave Alone'.

21. Michael Bradford, *The Fight for Yorkshire*, Hutton Press, Beverley, 1988, pp. 40-42.
    21a. Note: This map of Yorkshire shows the three County Ridings which had existed for over a thousand years, and despite the boundary changes of 1974 they were never abolished, only supplemented by other local government divisions at the time.

CHAPTER 6

New Life, New Family, New Challenges

The full impact of Alfred and Marie-Eugénie's new life together began to dawn upon them, like all other newly-weds, after their return from honeymoon to their first rented house in Burley-in-Wharfedale. At the time Alfred had promised himself that he would keep a regular journal, although not like the daily one which he had found himself unable to maintain previously, but a general account of the ordinary life of everyday people like themselves. However he was somewhat disappointed after the first six months of marriage to note that the journal was little more than a collection of mainly blank pages, interspersed with odd pages of hastily scribbled notes, to be written up when he had more time.[1]

In his first entry he noted the observation made by others about the problems associated with settling into a marriage, and the subsequent challenge which he had set himself to test their prognostications: 'So many "Dismal Jimmies" have warned us that marriage will open our eyes that I have decided to keep a journal of the first year or two to see how their jeremiads are justified.'[2]

He then continued with the subsequent realistically honest, but nevertheless hopeful entry:

> Here we are, about to start a joint partnership as Man and Wife and neither
> of us has the least idea of what we are in for... We met in a tennis tournament
> in a scratch 'mixed doubles'. Perhaps tennis is not the best introduction to
> matrimony, but no more is it the worst. For what is marriage but a perpetual
> Mixed Double involving the usual amount of give and take? Even the
> 'Dismal Jimmies' seem to agree on that point.[2]

However, the new journal which Alfred envisaged was to be quite unlike the previous one which he kept, since it was not just an attempt to record the day to day activities, but the impressions and experiences of early married life, although there is only very limited evidence of any original hand-written material.[1a] Nevertheless, whatever records Alfred kept at the time, were eventually to become an extensive draft document for a potential book, and although this was never published, it formed an extraordinarily detailed account of the first three years of Alfred and Marie-Eugénie's life together.[1] What follows therefore, is a précis of this lengthy piece of work, which portrays only the salient features of the events that occurred during this time.

'Adam and Eveness'

One of the first impressions of settling down together was the notion of loneliness, which before his marriage Alfred had regarded only 'Adam and Eve' as creatures of legendary loneliness, but he began to realise that every newly married couple had a lot in common with these primordial parents. He reflected on the incredible gulf which surrounded any young couple who had taken a house in a strange neighbourhood. Even after six months, Alfred and Marie-Eugénie had not quite lost the illusion of 'aloneness', or 'Adam and Eveness' as Marie-Eugénie called it,[2] especially when they were indoors on the long winter evenings, and sometimes even in the company of others for example at the cinema, which seemed to emphasise their isolation.

These feelings of 'aloneness' may have also been reinforced by the fact that they had made little progress in getting to know the neighbours in their terrace, with the exception of the lady next door, so that even gregarious Alfred had almost given up the task. But this situation could be partly explained by that entrenched Yorkshire tradition of not acknowledging people who had not been brought up in the neighbourhood, and even then it was often jokingly said that '*off comed 'uns*', as they were called, did not usually get spoken to until they had been around for twenty years at least! However Alfred suspected that it was not just this anecdotal position which isolated them, but the fact that they were seen to belong to the 'better class' as it was known thereabouts, and they did not conform to the local standards of their neighbours' behaviour.

For example, Alfred dressed in a suit every day to go to work, but refused such dress formality on Sundays, and usually spent the whole weekend in old tweeds, whilst his neighbours donned their Sunday best outfits to go to Chapel. Marie-Eugénie in particular found it difficult to overcome her innate shyness and speak to people easily. She came from a relatively sheltered, genteel background, and was somewhat daunted by the formidably forthright, gossipy band of brawny Northern women neighbours, no matter how well-intentioned they were! It was perhaps not surprising that neither of them were taken into the bosom of the terrace neighbourhood. Even Alfred experienced some unease with social stratification on his daily rail commute to work in Bradford, whereby there existed three clear social distinctions on the 8.20 a.m. train, and although these commuting acquaintances met on the common ground of the platform, the passengers appeared to fall naturally into their respective stratified social groups. Alfred amusingly described them as the 'Mansion-ites' or upper middle class passengers, with an air of superiority, the 'Villa-ites' or middle class passengers, with a forlorn air of 'in-between-ness', and the 'Terrace-ites' or lower middle class passengers, with an air of jolly, hobnobbing friendliness. Typically Alfred occasionally mixed his groups of travelling companions, much to the annoyance of some of the established social order, but most often veered towards the more sociable 'Terrace-ites', with whom he found some kindred spirit and close fellowship.[2]

A New Arrival

It was not long before Alfred and Marie-Eugénie were house hunting once more, since they had only taken their rented house for one year until they were able to establish themselves financially, having passed up the opportunity of renting a traditional country cottage higher up the dale on the grounds that it needed costly repairs and updating. Now there was even more urgency, since Marie-Eugénie was expecting their first baby, which was due in the first week of August 1928. This anticipated event gave much pleasure to both of them, and perhaps even more to the over-friendly, middle-aged, self-appointed village mid-wife and next door neighbour, Mrs. Heaviside, who unusually had befriended both of them.[2] But in July of 1928 Alfred had secured a place in a maternity nursing home in Ilkley for the birth of the new baby, and also engaged someone to help around the house, since he was often away travelling abroad with his job. Then with the lease about to expire on the property in September, they had to find an alternative place to live which they could afford. Although Alfred's salary had increased to £450 p.a., the extra amount had been absorbed by the additional costs of the baby's arrival, the hire of the home helper, along with furnishings and fittings, which left very little money for house rental and especially for house purchase.[2]

However the great occasion was soon upon them, and Marie-Eugénie was admitted to the Belle Vue Maternity Nursing Home, in Cowpasture Road, Ilkley, on the Saturday of the August bank holiday weekend. Meanwhile Alfred spent the night at the house of friends George and Renee Dixon, who lived across the valley about half a mile away within sight of the nursing home. But by next day it was obvious that the baby was in no hurry to arrive and Alfred was duly dismissed, only to spend the afternoon cooling off from the late summer heat with a dip in the River Wharfe. He then returned once more to the nursing home, where this time he was refused entry and told to go home and to telephone later for any news. Therefore Alfred returned to his friend's house again and after several phone calls to the home he was told in no uncertain terms not to trouble them again that night, since they were far too busy, and that a member of staff would call him when there was any news to report.

Then on the Monday, 6th August 1928, at 12.25 a.m. Alfred received the call with the good news that a healthy, six and one half pound girl had been born at 12.15 a.m., and with this joyful news he stayed up for the rest of the night staring across the magic dale waiting for the opportunity to visit the next morning, at which time he was allowed to see his wife and lovely new child but only for a minute.[2] Subsequently, Alfred's almost delirious delight and heartfelt happiness at their new family member's arrival, may be judged from the letter which he wrote to his old friend, best man and walking companion, 'Ouse', namely, George Heseltine:

My Dear Ouse,

Enfin! Félicité Anne Marie and Marie-Eugénie are home! Call out the court poets: Let us sing Tra la la la la long live the king! And Queen of the fairies! Anoint the Muse! I must go seek some dew-drops for her. And hang a pearl in every cowslips ear! Our queen and all her elves came here anon.

We call her Fay for short and Fay *[fairy-like]* she surely is. You tell me to describe her! As if I dare – or daring could! In the bath she is like an exquisite piece of Dresden China – alive. In her cups she is like Titania. She is like Arthur Rackham's inspiration, a pure dream child. Some say a love-child. Howbeit she is certainly a lass with a delicate air...

Yesterday, in her triumphal progress, she called at church in Ilkley to be baptised. She likes the Creature Water, and has a pretty taste for salt (wit and wisdom are surely hers), but she hates the chrism oil – and this pleases me as it looks as if she will eschew hair oil...

Does one dare to dissect a flower, a moonbeam, or a masterpiece? Well then, she has little dark beads for eyes. Candid, lovely eyes that frighten me when she turns them on me in fits and starts. A frail, yet exquisitely shaped head with a mass of dark brown or is it black hair. Her hands are like petals; her toes coral pink and quite the daintiest pair of feet you ever saw. If you know Francis Thompson's 'Snowflake', you know her far better than I can describe her. Of one point only I am in doubt: they say she has her father's nose!... Well at least it is an admission that her father contributed something to her make-up – if only the nose!

Do not think I exaggerate lest you should see for yourself. Lord, what a fortnight it has been. Couriers from France, Argentine, England... Holy commotion everywhere... Finally a new fledged maid who breaks down and wants to go home... *Figurez-vous, mon vieux!*

Thine, 'Wharfe' [*Alfred*] **3**

Felicity Anne Marie Brown was baptised at The Sacred Heart of Jesus Church in Stockeld Road, Ilkley, since Burley-in Wharfedale did not have its own Catholic Church until 1932. The service was conducted by Fr. James Bradley on Sunday, 18th August 1928, and Mr. Thomas Brown, Alfred's younger brother, was Godfather, and Mrs. Marguerite Owen, Marie-Eugénie's older sister, Godmother. However the homecoming was not without problems, since neither new parent had any experience of dealing with a new baby. Even the new home help Ethel, who had been hired to assist Marie-Eugénie with domestic chores was only used to infants not babies, and was so homesick that she was almost unable to carry out her duties. However, the knowledgeable Mrs. Heaviside came to the rescue, and helped to organise the daily routine of the household. Then within a few weeks Marie-Eugénie and Alfred had to cope with the baby's nightly crying episodes, albeit with the administration of a dose of 'dill water' for her colic, but just when everything appeared to be going smoothly, a minor disaster happened. A tap which had been left running in the bathroom resulted in an overflow and the flood brought down the kitchen ceiling just as they were eating dinner, which together with the need for more space, and the imminent end of their lease, caused them to think seriously about their domestic situation.**4**

On the Move Again

Later that year after much searching, Alfred and Marie-Eugénie found a house which suited their requirements, although it was quite unlike their ideal country cottage that they had in mind previously. Instead it was a one year old, suburban-style, half brick, half pebble-dashed, large semi-detached property on the outskirts of Burley-in-Wharfedale, on the Bradford Road at the edge of the village. It had much more space than their rented terrace house and included a large dining room, sitting room, large hallway, kitchen and scullery, with three bedrooms and bathroom, as well as a fine attic bedroom which would serve as Alfred's new 'den'. It also had uninterrupted views at the front which looked over wooded green pastures leading down to the River Wharfe nearby, hence the reason for naming the house Wharfegate, whilst the rear looked up towards Burley Moor and Rombalds Moor beyond. It also had large as yet unfinished gardens to the front and rear, and was separated from the other five pairs of neighbouring houses by fencing. Furthermore it was only a short walk to the railway station for Alfred's daily commute to work, with the alternative of taking the Bradford bus which stopped outside on the main road.

22. Wharfegate, Burley-in-Wharfedale

The asking price of the property was £950 and since Alfred could raise a deposit of up to £200, he secured a mortgage from the building society for the remaining capital required at a 5% interest rate. Alfred also negotiated with the builder to reduce the price by a further £50 in order to compensate for the several improvements needed in order to make the house more habitable. The deal was finally secured by a deposit of £90, with an agreement to pay off the rest of the mortgage over 16 years before they could truly say the house was theirs, but at the time they were both very pleased with their new acquisition.[4]

It was with great pleasure that the family finally moved into the new house, although not for one of the moving men whose task it was to struggle with the many boxes of Alfred's books up to his attic 'den', and was overheard to say that *'this 'aint no hattic – it's a bloomin libery!'* However the inspirational views of the moors afforded by the dormer-windowed 'den', which became Alfred's secluded sanctuary, would provide him with the stimulus to write some of his fabled Yorkshire tramping books in the future. That is, of course, when he had attended to the many domestic jobs that were required to bring the house into order, which proved to be quite an unequal challenge to Alfred's abilities. He readily admitted that his talents were quite limited to the basic tasks of painting, decorating and simple joinery, although the more demanding work of gardening and vegetable growing proved to be a rewarding, if somewhat unaccustomed form of exercise, which he eventually began to relish. Nevertheless there were some jobs quite beyond his enthusiastic capabilities, such as the leaky roof which required expensive repairs by a roofer to fix a major problem that should have been done by the builder.[4]

The year 1928 seemed to draw swiftly to a close and the new Brown family was looking forward to their first Christmas together in their new home, to which they invited Marie-Eugénie's widower father, Charles, to join them for their special festive meal, before spending the rest of Christmas week with their friends the Dicksons in Ilkley. However upon their return home they had to forgo the services of their home help Ethel by mutual consent, since she had not only overstayed her Christmas leave, but also overstretched her welcome in the household by insisting on being treated as a member of the family as well.[4] The New Year therefore saw her replacement by Jennie from County Durham, a big strong, happy, easy-going girl who unfortunately did not last too long either, since she appeared to be more interested in reading her 'penny dreadfuls' than doing the housework. She was also released in the spring and replaced this time with Kate, another pleasant young maid this time from Tyneside in the northeast, with the hope that she would settle in well where others had failed.[4]

These minor domestic difficulties were soon overshadowed by more serious matters that summer, when Alfred who was quietly mowing his lawn one evening, was accosted by an aggressive bailiff with a County Court Summons brought about by an outstanding bill of £8. 2s. 0d. by the rascal builder for the cost of various extra repairs needed to the house since the previous summer. Unfortunately, while Alfred had agreed to pay for these over and above the purchase price, he had no recourse to recover the expensive leaking roof repair bill of some £20, of which he believed he had every moral right to expect to be offset against these so-called extras. Nevertheless he was advised by his solicitor to accede to the demand since he could not afford the long expensive process of contesting the issue,[4] and in any case he had more important family matters to occupy his attentions at this time.

A Second New Arrival

When Felicity Anne approached her first birthday in August 1929, and was beginning to walk, there was more celebration in the Brown household with the expectation of the arrival of a second baby which was due in September. This time though Marie-Eugénie and Alfred were hoping that with the help of a maternity nurse, the baby would be born at home, and notwithstanding the extra sense of security the maternity home would bring, they were planning for such an event. Unfortunately this was not possible because the maternity nurse was recalled to the hospital and there was no replacement available, so Marie-Eugénie returned to the Belle Vue Maternity Nursing Home in Ilkley once more for the birth, while Alfred waited nervously again at his friend's house in Ilkley for the outcome. Once more he received the good news by telephone of the birth of a chubby little daughter of seven and one quarter pounds, with chestnut brown hair, and that mother and baby were both very well indeed.[4] This time he immediately announced the glorious event in the local *Bradford Telegraph & Argus* newspaper on the same day, Thursday, 26th September 1929.

It was also significant at this time that Alfred contracted another cold-like infection, similar to the one he had suffered earlier in the year, which had kept him off work for a few days. There was also a pattern beginning to emerge in the onset of these symptoms, since they appeared to be triggered at times of minor crises and may have been stress-related, or perhaps more likely due to an ongoing reduced resistance to infections, which had resulted from the prolonged illness he had suffered during and after the war years previously. The effects of these bouts of illness usually lasted between ten days and three weeks, during which time he was always significantly below par even by his own estimation. Furthermore he suspected that these cold-like effects were similar to the fevers which he had suffered during his previous post-diphtheric illness, although no medical evidence had been able to confirm this suspicion, and Alfred continued to live life as normal as possible during these temporary bouts of illness.[4]

Six weeks following her birth, the new baby was baptised with the name of Eugénie Elizabeth Barbara Brown at the Sacred Heart of Jesus Church in Ilkley, on the 10th November 1929, with Fr. James Bradley once more officiating, but this time Alfred's life-long friend George Heseltine from London was Godfather, while Marie-Eugénie's cousin, Simone West, who was visiting from France, was Godmother. Alfred and Marie-Eugénie went through almost every name possible for their new daughter before they agreed on Eugénie after Marie herself, then Elizabeth after Alfred's grandmother Brown, and thirdly on Barbara after no one in particular. However, Alfred had forgotten to check the name with his parents, and only later discovered that his grandmother, whom he had never met, had in fact been called Adelaide, not Elizabeth, whence Adelaide Mary Dunne of Norfolk married Lot Michael Brown of Kildwick, Yorkshire, in 1840. In fact both Alfred and Marie-Eugénie thought Adelaide was the loveliest and most desirable of names, and would have preferred it to Elizabeth, but by then of course it was too late.

Meanwhile there were other comings and goings in the Brown household during that year. Kate who had been the model home help so far, had left later in the year, but had returned temporarily until a replacement was found.[4] She was followed by Maud in the New Year, but she had the shortest reign of all, less than one month, after it was discovered that she was not only a liar and a thief, but had numerous male callers visiting at night. She then had the temerity to leave without working her notice, but not without taking some more of Marie-Eugénie's possessions. Then it was Ada's turn in the long line of home helps, and she appeared to be the best maid by far, so far, but of course only time would tell.[4] However, with the approach of their third wedding anniversary, Alfred and Marie-Eugénie's finances were over-stretched, and they considered not only going without the services of a maid, but possibly the need to move to another house to save on running costs, before later that Summer an unexpected turn of events came to their rescue.

Reflections on Marriage

On the day after Alfred and Marie-Eugénie celebrated the third anniversary of their wedding, Alfred's journal told its own story, and although he had never set out to record a treatise on marriage, he offered some insight into what marriage seemed to him, and suggested that it could be described in three distinct phases: firstly the 'Romance', secondly the 'Game' and thirdly the 'Partnership'.[4]

In their 'Partnership', Alfred concluded that they had been very successful, especially since the first few years were notoriously difficult for many couples, since they had achieved much satisfaction from their first three years together in which they had two jolly children, a furnished house in the country, a well-stocked garden which produced some of their food, and lots of friends, albeit with the usual problems of a growing overdraft and an outstanding hefty mortgage with thirteen years left to repay. However even these financial concerns were soon to suddenly disappear, with the exceedingly generous legacy provided by Marie-Eugénie's father, Mr. Charles Bull, who decided that they should benefit sooner rather than later from his good fortune. As a result they received an advance on their inheritance, which would allow them not only to pay off their overdraft, but also to clear their mortgage as well and become the outright owners of 'Wharfegate' immediately.[4]

In their 'Game' of homemaking, Alfred considered that it resulted in their gaining an infinite variety of experiences, which required them to fulfill the many roles needed, but only at the expense of work, leisure and other personal interests, which he admitted that sometimes he regretted. Finally, with respect to their 'Romance', Alfred made the analogy that marriage was like a voyage through unknown seas in a new ship, which was full of surprises and perils, especially for any ill-matched pair, but recognised that their match was not of this type, since like any good captain he had chosen his mate carefully and vice-versa. Nevertheless he acknowledged that his irregularly-kept 'logbook' had not given a complete account of their voyage, as it had not paid much attention to the 'perilous seas' because they had been weathered successfully, and that such squalls were only 'storms in a teacup' which could easily be overcome. In conclusion, while Alfred shied away from any prescriptive list of things that may go to make up a happy marriage, he offered the good old-fashioned recommendation of marrying for love, along with the guiding principles embodied in the two famous 'bears' – to 'bear' meaning to support, and to 'forbear' meaning to be patient, in equal measure, to help the matrimonial voyage steer a successful course through life.[4]

Recurrent Conundrum of Career Choice

It might be assumed at this time that Alfred had been able to allocate his time equitably across the range of his family, work and literary activities, but any simple balance needed to keep all three of these aspects of his life in equilibrium, belied the reality which these respective demands made upon his precious time. This was best illustrated in a poignant letter that Alfred wrote to Marie-Eugénie while she was still at the maternity nursing home in Ilkley recovering from the birth of their second daughter Barbara in late August 1929. In a hurried note written late at night, Alfred summed up the many problems he was attempting to deal with simultaneously:

10.30 p.m. (no date)

Darlingest,

Terribly sorry I could not come to see you today. I had been working over at the office and only came home at 8.30 (no tea). I have had the expected letter from Methuen – refused. [*He was referring to his new novel: 'Whitaker', which he had recently submitted as a manuscript to his London Publisher who published his previous novel*].

Disappointing of course, but I was in two minds about publishing, so perhaps it is as well. Of course I am put out, knowing it to be much better than *The Lean Years* – but their standard is commercial evidently – hence the brilliant detective novels.

I have written to Walpole [*Sir Hugh Walpole, the successful novelist, whom he had met recently at a lecture in Bradford*] and enclose a copy [*of the letter in which Alfred had sought advice from Walpole on a writing career*]. Don't take it too seriously. I am not done yet by a long way, though I begin to fear I shall not do many more books. Business gets too exacting and of course I cannot afford to drop it can I?

Don't worry about money. I don't want you to leave the home [*maternity home*] until you are absolutely well – a week or two walking about and finding your feet.

I will come tonight for a short while, but I have all to pack and arrange [*Alfred was due to depart on a business trip to the continent*]. It is an awful rush – please give Mary [*the home help*] my bags. I will bring one home – Dixons will lend you some,

Good night, lovely one, your lonely Alfred.[5]

It was evident from this letter that Alfred had become fearful of his potential to fulfil a writing career in view of the demands which continued to be placed upon him by his business activities. In this regard he had written to Hugh Walpole, in which he explained his circumstances in the hope of some help to resolve the conflicts which he faced at the time:

1ˢᵗ October 1929

Dear Mr. Walpole,

You bore with me (the distraught fellow who you met outside the Bradford Lecture Hall) so patiently the other night, that I feel that I must tell you the sequel to the night's entertainment. In short: a girl – born at 7.15 a.m. next morning... we have a saying that a lad can get a lad, but it takes a man to get a lass!

The other sequel is not so consoling. Methuen have turned down the novel ('Whitaker') quoting; 'It is a most carefully written and conscientious study, but I doubt if it would interest a large public and we could not publish it with any hope of commercial success'...

This, as I think I explained, was my second novel (I am under contract with Methuen to submit the next two), and I had naturally worked hard on it... I fancy if it had been published I should lose my job as it resolves itself into a 'j'accuse' – the Industrialists, especially the wool Lords.

Having been a writer now for over ten years I am used to such disappointments but it seems damnably hard to get serious consideration by the critics who count. The financial reward has been so negligible that I almost (not quite) despair of ever making a living with my pen alone – much as I hate being half and half... Even so, I must write something or I am miserable.

My days are devoted to wool (I am a yarn manager and foreign traveller) and my nights to literature, wife and babies. I am just on the point of leaving home for a month in Europe with the horrid bags *[of yarn samples]*. I may just have enough leisure to write an essay a week or a fortnight and still contrive to do bits on trains, for the rest is all rush and tumble. Business becomes more exacting every year; the struggle is fiercer and there is precious little time for anything except the job in hand.

I have written on impulse and hope you are not bored. I can assure you that I am not in the habit of writing to successful authors: I once wrote to J.B. Priestley – but tore my letter up – I may very likely tear this up *[fortunately he did not!]*.

Finally Alfred concluded with this revealing and honest summary of himself at this stage of his life:

I am 35 years old; a catholic; introspective; realist; a great walker (or was before my responsibilities grew heavily upon me); a Yorkshireman too fond of the County to leave it (London does not tempt me); very proud, very shy, very sensitive; intensely interested in writing, not a great reader (no time); in love with life; often unwell (war legacy: eyes and innards); just beginning to despair and to grow old and to wonder whether I am a writer at all. I was a poet up to three years ago but he died, business worries killed him. Financial worries are strangling what little of an artist in me remains.

Alfred then signed off with the plea:

Jube domine benedicere! [*Pray master, speak well of me!*]

Ever yours sincerely A.J.B.[6]

While Alfred received a supportive response to this letter,[7] no evidence of it has been found in his files, although subsequently he wrote to J.B. Priestley and sought further advice about his writing career. But it was also about this time that Alfred began to take stock of his present situation, though not directly through the medium of his detailed journal, but instead in the form of a short sketch in which he reflected upon his journal, and he drew some interesting comparisons between himself and another very successful writer of the time, Robert Graves. Thus he attempted a summary of their respective lives to date:

I have just been reading Robert Graves' *Goodbye To All That* [1929] and found it fascinating in parts... Relatively his ways have been pleasant ways, and moneyed relatives and influential friends there to rescue him and his family when all else failed. Still there are similarities and I read his book with fellow feeling.

I, too, am (or was) a poet, whether he would admit it or not; I, too, had a bad war (though I was invalided as early as 1916): I, too, dreamed of living by the pen, having nearly perished by the Sword – or rather the Germ.

What I admired most about him was his audacious marriage and his courage in taking a real cottage in the country, and attempting to live on about £200 a year with little windfalls which make all the difference, but we had nobody to come to the rescue if we failed and I had no influential friends to sponsor my manuscripts in the lean years, and M (Marie-Eugénie) far from being a land girl had come straight from a French Convent School. Even so, I am full of admiration for his 'adaptability' especially the cheerful way in which he faced eight years of napkins and all that they imply.

The thing that interested me most was the similarity between his essential life and mine, despite the fact that we are poles apart to outward view. Like him, I spent my post war years fighting ill-health and keeping myself alive by writing poetry which nobody wanted, and at that time I was kicked about from pillar to post (or from one hospital to the next). Long before I had found my feet, I married and had a baby before the first year was out; and a second within two years.

All the time I have pursued a commercial career by day rising from errand boy at one shilling per week to manager at £500 per annum. I have travelled on business to Poland, Austria, Germany, Scandinavia, Bohemia, Holland, France, Italy, and Switzerland, and still contrived to write seven books... out of which three have been published, and the rest are still doing the rounds (except the poetry, which long ago I put aside out of despair)... I have contributed to the *Spectator*, the *Saturday Review*, *Chambers*, *The Window*, *Country Life* etc. etc... and still not made anything like a clear £20 on the lot!

Hence I suppose this chronicle *[a reference to his journal 'Needles and Pins']*... with which I hope to pay off all debts and make enough capital to lead the sort of life Graves and his friends live and start all over again. But not of course without M *[Marie-Eugénie]* and the children with all their frailties... for heaven knows I have more than enough of my own to counterbalance theirs.[8]

Whilst Alfred admired other successful writers who had overcome many similar difficulties to those which he faced in trying to establish himself in the highly competitive literary world, he was also keen to get the benefit of some more practical advice from such a personage, in order to help him decide upon a possible suitable pathway for his own future writing career. It was to this end therefore, after some considerable delay in making such a bold move, Alfred finally decided to write to another of his successful contemporaries, the journalist, playwright and novelist, J.B. Priestley, with whom Alfred had a great deal more in common than some of the other literary icons of the time:

Dear J.B. Priestley,

I hope you will not mind the familiarity, but I always think of you as 'JBP' and after all, we are both Bradford lads... A few years back, I was introduced to you at a meeting of the Bradford English Society, but you will have forgotten about that. Actually I have been on the point of writing to you dozens of times, but held back for fear of making myself a nuisance.

However, my bosom-friend, G.C. Hesletine, tells me that he met you at the Press Club dinner and I was astonished to learn that that you did know me after all.

Alfred then proceeded to detail at some length his writing career so far, before he made an apology and came to the point of his letter:

You must be heartily sick of this long screed but I have nearly done... In spite of all this stuff, I am still only a 'spare-time' writer though I have been trying to make myself independent since 1918. By day, I have an exacting job in Bradford and do a lot of foreign travelling which eats up my time. Now that I am getting literary contracts, I find it increasingly difficult to hold both jobs down and soon will have to decide to chuck one or other. You can guess how difficult it is to work at high pressure all day (and Bradford offices are hell-upon-earth these days) and write all night – apart from the strain on my wife.

So far, alas, I have failed woefully to make more than 'bacca money with my pen, though I may do better this year if I can hold out. I have two small daughters (and a third in the offing!), so it means a terrific risk to resign my job, much as I want to. However, that is my little problem and I fancy I shall have to hang on for a bit longer.

Perhaps some day when you are in the north again, we can meet for a short chat – in a bar in Bradford, or better still, here. Don't be misled by the name of the house [Wharfegate], it is conveniently placed on the main road to Ilkley,

Now you know all about me – 'appen,

Yours sincerely, A.J. Brown.[9]

It seemed unlikely that, given the speculative nature of Alfred's letter, he was expecting to receive a reply to his letter to Priestley, however only three days later, he received a most supportive response, even though it was prefaced by a piece of literary criticism of one of Alfred's previous books, which nonetheless he probably valued as much as the sound advice which followed in Priestley's response:

Dear A.J. Brown,

Your letter was not in the least bumptious and I was glad to have it. Let me say that I remember Four Boon Fellows very well, and I thought that there was a lot of very good stuff in it, but that the Belloc-out of Rabelais manner was all against it. It is a manner I am heartily tired of, anyhow, for it has been worked hard by Belloc himself, and then by my friends D.B. Wyndham-Lewis and J.B. Morton. And I was glad to see in the West Riding hiking book *[Moorland Tramping in West Yorkshire, 1931]*, which has some very pleasant things in it, you have modified it a good deal.

You have been rather unlucky so far, though most of us are with our first books. My first books had colossal presses and gave me some sort of reputation, but to this day the money I have made out of them has been trifling. I sympathise with you in your desire to escape this double life of Bradford trade and authorship, but I must point out that if you were a professional author – unless you happen to be enormously successful – you would still have a double life of hack jobs and things you wanted to write. For years, I toiled away at reviews of stupid books and little articles, in order to be able to write the books I wanted to write, and it is just as bad – perhaps worse – to be tired out with actual writing as office work. A lot depends on how little you can live on. I would suggest this, that you do not give up your job until you've made enough out of one book – or a commissioned series of articles – to give you at least a year's income in advance.

You have to remember that books are not doing as well as they did, and that journalism offers a rapidly narrowing field to an intelligent writer. On the other hand, if one were suddenly plunged into an era of prosperity again (and I am very pessimistic on this subject) it would, I fancy, be quite safe to take the plunge, but with a wife and family, you might find struggling along as a freelance journalist the most wretched business, far more soul-destroying than the Bradford trade.

Next time I am in Bradford, I will try to get in touch with you, and if I do find myself getting out Ilkley way, you may depend on it that I will come to see you,

With very best wishes, whatever you decide to do,

Yours sincerely, J.B. Priestley

p.s. I have kept the little book (*Moorland Tramping in West Yorkshire*). I hope to make use of it before I'm too old an' daft to tak' onny notice.[10]

Alfred, of course, must have been delighted to receive such a down-to-earth appraisal of his current work/literary dilemma, along with the offer to meet with his latest distinguished literary correspondent, and wrote immediately to express his gratitude for the advice and support by Priestley, together with his intended course of action:

Dear J.B. Priestley,

It was really good of you to reply to my letter so promptly, and devote so much time to the pros and cons of my personal problem. I cannot dispute your arguments against resignation, since I have turned most of them over (or had them turned for me!) more than once in the past few years. Actually my own cautious idea is to get two year's income in hand before taking the plunge, though so far I have failed to get half a one! Indeed the main case against my job (and any commercial job) in these grim years is that it just keeps one and no more.

I quite agree that one is no worse off doing a commercial job than in hack journalism. In any case, that kind of writing never appealed to me and I am too old to take it up. The chief 'snag' of my trade is that it is a full-steam-ahead-all-day sort of job; and that I am liable at any time to be ordered off to Poland or God knows where! On another full-time job. Meanwhile I must stick to my last.

I do so hope that you will drop in here some day this year and hope I have the luck to be in England. There is a little pub called the Hermit on the edge of the moors just above our house: but you probably know it already.

Again thanking you for your sympathetic letter and encouragement, and with all best wishes,

I am yours sincerely, A.J. Brown.

p.s. Don't bother to acknowledge this.[11]

While there is no evidence that Priestley acknowledged this letter, nor entered into any further correspondence with Alfred, it is likely that Alfred often pondered his literary future, and the advice he had been given, over a pint of ale in his favourite local pub, The Hermit in Burley Woodhead, less than a mile from his Wharfegate home. The pub, previously known as The Woolpack, had been renamed after Job Senior (1770-1857), a recluse who had fallen on hard times and lived as a hermit in a self-made hovel on nearby Burley Moor, but earned his keep by odd jobbing and as a story teller and entertainer at the pub. Alfred often called there after tramping over the moor, and it was in this friendly hostelry that he formulated ideas for his subsequent books on tramping in Yorkshire.

23. The Hermit pub, Burley Woodhead

References and Notes

1. Alan Dale, 'Needles and Pins', written by Alfred John Brown under this pseudonym, an unpublished type scripted manuscript, which tells the story about the trials and tribulations of early married life, West Yorkshire Archive Service, Bradford Central Library, Document No.69D90, Section 7/14.
    1a. **Note**: there is only very limited evidence of Alfred's written account of this journal in a short item entitled: 'Retrospect', Document No. 69D90, Section 8/2.

2. Alan Dale, Ibid., pp. 1-57, passim.

3. AJB letter to GCH, 20th August 1928, AJB Personal Correspondence File, 1926-1932.

4. 'Alan Dale', op.cit., pp. 71-276, passim.

5. AJB letter to MEB, (no date) late September 1929, AJB Personal Correspondence File, 1926-1932.

6. AJB letter to Hugh Walpole, 1st October 1929, AJB Personal Correspondence File, 1926-1932.

7. AJB letter to MEB, 12th October 1929, AJB Personal Correspondence File, 1926-1932.

8. Alfred John Brown, 'Goodbye to All That', West Yorkshire Archive Service, Bradford Central Library, Document No. 69D90, Section 8/3 (circa 1930).

9. AJB letter to JBP, 16th February 1932, AJB - J. B. Priestley Correspondence File 1932.

10. JBP letter to AJB, 19th February 1932, AJB - J. B. Priestley Correspondence File, 1932.

11. AJB letter to JBP, 22nd February 1932, AJB – J. B. Priestley Correspondence File, 1932.

Chapter 7

The Yorkshire Tramping Trilogy

A Yorkshire Topographical Writing Tradition

Alfred always maintained: 'rough walking was my cure and salvation' and 'I must write something or I am miserable,' so that these activities were as much a part of his life as the day to day demands of his job and the attention he devoted to his growing family. Furthermore his leisure pursuits of walking and writing were not only physically and psychologically important to him, but actually enhanced each other, and together they provided a means of escape from the demands of his family and working life. Therefore Alfred not only maintained his involvement in these two vital interests, but increased his commitments to both of them during this time, which ultimately resulted in a new style in his literary work, namely that of topographical writing. This new orientation not only allowed him to develop a different approach to his writing, but also to concentrate his efforts to become as efficient as possible in fulfilling both his walking and writing ambitions simultaneously.

Alfred was well aware of the works of former and contemporary Yorkshire writers who had developed topographical writing into a fine art form, and not only created vivid descriptions of landscape with its natural and man-made features, but extended the boundaries of traditional topographical limits. These now encompassed many other aspects of the wider landscape setting including the human and natural history of the surroundings, the economic activities of agriculture and industry, as well as architectural styles, modes of transport and even the character of the people and the social institutions found in particular localities. Moreover, the localities chosen for description by these writers were mostly rural rather than urban, and often reflected a way of life which was slow to change compared with the rapid progress made in urban areas. Such writing often extolled the virtues of the countryside and was therefore very appealing to town and city-based dwellers, who found in these literary works a chance to escape the drudgery of urban life, especially if such writing provided easy access to, and guidance around, desirable places of simple rural recreation, even if for some, it was solely from an armchair.

Some of the early topographical writers of the nineteenth century had been drawn into writing in their spare time, often as a result of their professional activities, for example Canon John Christopher Atkinson (1814-1900), who had spent most of his life ministering to the parishioners of Danby in the North Yorkshire Moors, and wrote of his experiences in the classic book *Forty Years in a Moorland Parish*. Canon Arthur Neville Cooper of Filey (1850-1943), the so-called 'Walking Parson', also devoted some of his time keeping contact with his wider fold by exploring of the county's highways and described them in his works: *Tramps of the Walking Parson*, *Across the Broad Acres* and *With Knapsack and Notebook*. Similarly Dr. Reginald William Snowden Bishop (1864-1921) described his experiences of medical practice in the remote areas of the county in *My Moorland Patients* and was credited with the first reference to Yorkshire as being 'God's own Country'.

Other early topographical writers were often in public service, such as Charles Joshua Atkinson (1869-1943), a town planner from Burley-in-Wharfedale, who described his beloved Wharfedale in *Recollections of a Yorkshire Dale*, and William Grainge (1861-1913), the town clerk of Grimsby who wrote memorable historical and topographical works such as *Nidderdale*. The former businessman William Riley (1866-1969) became one of the most popular of Yorkshire character writers after his initial success with his first book *Windyridge*, and the Leeds artists supplies shop owner, Edmund Bogg (1850-1931), devoted himself almost exclusively to the descriptions of Wharfedale in his works: *A Thousand Miles in Wharfedale*, *Higher Wharfedale – The Dale of Romance*, *Lower Wharfedale*, and *In the Bosom of the Wharfe*.

Many of the early Yorkshire topographical writers, who became the forerunners of the later so-called 'vagabond' writers, were authors in their own right and had pursued writing careers from an early age. One of the most learned and scholarly was Harry Speight (1835-1915), whose books on a variety of Yorkshire themes were models of scholarship, research and patient exploration, while Joseph Smith Fletcher (1863-1935), the Halifax born writer, was one of the most prolific writers that Yorkshire has produced. Later Richard Blakeborough (1850-1918) and his son, John Fairfax-Blakeborough (1883-1978), together produced valuable chronicles of the North and East Ridings of Yorkshire. However it was the Haworth-born writer, Halliwell Sutcliffe (1870-1932), who devoted almost his whole life to acquiring a deep knowledge of dalesfolk and their countryside, who best described the essence of what characterised Yorkshire at the time.

Yorkshire topographical writing was of course not an exclusively male preserve, and the Brontë novelist sisters, Charlotte (1816-1855), Emily (1818-1848) and Anne (1820-1849), had incorporated many landscape descriptions into their works, albeit under the guise of their male pseudonyms. Other female novelists had also managed to capture the character of various Yorkshire landscapes including: the West Riding of Yorkshire by Phyllis Bentley (1894-1977), the East Riding of Yorkshire by Winifred Holtby (1899-1935), and to a lesser extent the dialect poet and writer Dorothy Una Ratcliffe (1887-1967). Later it was those indefatigable authors Marie Hartley (1905-2006) and Ella Pontefract (1896-1945) who focused their attention on the Yorkshire Dales, and subsequently Joan Ingleby (1918-2000) who joined Marie in the quest to account for most of the uplands and lowlands of Yorkshire with vivid descriptions of the landscape and its peoples.

It was into this well-established genre of Yorkshire topographical writing that Alfred bravely decided to immerse himself, albeit using a different approach to those of his predecessors and of some of his contemporaries, who were also seeking alternative ways to express the glories of the Yorkshire landscape. He was also keen to develop a new expression to his own style of writing after his first attempt with *Four Boon Fellows – A Yorkshire Tramping Odyssey*. Now there was a new focus on 'tramping' *per se*, and one which would take him and his readers off the beaten track, over the previously untramped moorland ridges, and away from the congested moorland byways. He had often complained that one could not appreciate the fragrances of the moors because of the smell of the petrol fumes which had been the *bête noire* of his previous book. Thus he did not simply continue in the traditional footsteps of the well-established Yorkshire topographical writers, he developed his own unique style, which became the hallmark of the 'Yorkshire Tramping' book series.

Tramping New Moorland Trails: 'Ower T'Tops'

Nowhere else in the world does a man realise how small
and inarticulate he is as on a high and lonely moor
– A.J. Brown

Alfred had been disappointed with the sales of his previous book *Four Boon Fellows*, but with a downturn in the retail economy, most writers, even successful ones, were going through difficult times with little prospect of an upturn in the near future. Nonetheless, because of his need to walk and his passionate desire to write, he continued to participate fully in these activities, insofar as his spare time would allow. During his many weekend rambles he was constantly seeking novel routes to explore the vast tracts of his beloved County, and he carried a pocket-sized notebook to record his exploits, including the routes taken and any special features encountered, as well as unusual incidents which occurred along the way. Sadly almost none of these note-books have survived.

When Alfred got home, he reviewed the field notes and subsequently re-worked them as short sketches about the experiences on the moorland ridges he had traversed, or 'ower t'tops' as he referred to them, with a view to publishing them as brief articles in popular periodicals. But none of these sketches met with any interest from most publishing editors, until one day, more in hope than expectation, he sent a couple of items to the prestigious *Country Life* Magazine in London. Then much to his surprise and delight, the editor and founder of the magazine, Edward Hudson, replied by return of post, accepted both articles and even asked for more.[1] This was to be just the start of a long and pleasant association that Alfred enjoyed with this publisher, which within the first year, resulted in him being requested to write a book about Yorkshire, along the same lines as his brief sketches, but with maps and footpaths identified to assist the readers.

Alfred was most taken aback by this suggestion, and for him, the offer was somewhat of a teaser as he reflected:

> I had been tramping roughshod about Yorkshire for several years – 'trespassing' if you like – ignoring footpaths and tracks, so now I had to begin all over again. Not, of course from the very beginning, for I had learned a lot about tracks and roads even if I did not use them; but it meant a good deal of re-discovery. Still it was a joy. It meant more walking – but with a purpose instead of just walking for fun. The result was Moorland Tramping (West Yorkshire) – a new kind of walking book.[1]

The elation this good news brought about was perhaps somewhat reduced by the contractual terms for the work in question. He signed a publishing agreement with Country Life Ltd., on 29th April 1931 to deliver the complete manuscript along with twelve maps, by the deadline of 15th August 1931, and in return the publisher agreed to publish the work within six months of the receipt of these items.[2] Under the terms he received an advance of £50 on delivery of a 'ready for press manuscript', and royalties of 10% on the retail selling price when the initial print-run of 6,000 copies had been sold. However if the book did not sell the full print run and had to be remaindered, then the royalties were to be paid only on the shortfall, although the license right for printing and publishing was retained by Alfred. Finally, he was entitled to six free copies of the book, and to buy further copies, but not for sale, at a one third discount price i.e. the publication cost of the book. Nevertheless Alfred no doubt considered that he had obtained a good deal given his circumstances at the time.

He was now left with the problem of the twelve maps needed for the book, and since his cartographical skills were limited to making rough sketch maps of the routes he had tramped, someone with considerable graphical talent was needed to produce the required maps. Fortuitously, one day Alfred came across a passenger on his bus journey to work who was reading one of his previous books, and in his naturally affable style he struck up a conversation with this fellow traveller.[3] This chance acquaintance turned out to be William Littlewood (1893-1985), who was also living in Burley-in-Wharfedale and working as an advertising agent in Bradford. William had studied art at evening classes in the local art school of his home town Scarborough, and eventually became a freelance artist in the realistic style. Subsequently he was the illustrator of the updated children's classical books series *What Katy Did...*, originally by the American authoress, Susan Coolidge (1835-1905). Alfred had met a most valuable contact who not only illustrated his subsequent books, but he and his wife Kathleen and their daughter Katie, also became lifelong friends of the Brown family. Curiously though, William's name never appeared as a contributor to Alfred's books, and only his diminutive signature can be found tucked away on the illustrated dust jackets. This may have reflected William's reluctance to display his own work, except rarely at the Royal Academy of Artists and the Royal Society of British Artists, although in 1989 Scarborough Art Gallery displayed a retrospective of his work, and currently holds fifteen of his originals, while his daughter Katie Sowter (1944-2003) also became a notable artist.

Moorland Tramping in West Yorkshire[4]

The book was printed and released by Country Life before the end of 1931, which in itself was some kind of achievement. It was a reasonably-priced (3s. 0d.), hard-backed, pocket-sized book of 200 pages, ideal for walkers to carry with them when exploring the tramping routes it contained. Alfred dedicated the book: 'to G.C. Heseltine, Esq., Prince of Walkers; Boon Companion on Many Tramps', since George had shared many of Alfred's walks since they were teenagers, and as his best friend had kept in close contact with him in later years, even though he was now based in London working in the legal profession. In the frontispiece, there was a shortened version of Alfred's poem: 'There must be Dales in Paradise' which had appeared in his previous book *Four Boon Fellows* perhaps as an inspiring message to what may be expected from this new approach to tramping.

In the Forward, Alfred explained how this book was 'a new kind of book... the main purpose is to lead walkers to the unexplored moorland tracks, and show the delights of rough moorland tramping as distinct from road walking'. This statement of intent was justified when he indicated that during the previous decade main-road walking had become more of a trial than a pleasure, on account of the ubiquitous petrol engine. He also suggested that the day of the old-fashioned 'open-road' walking tour had passed, and that a new style of cross-country tramping had taken over. He noted that since the First World War, ever-increasing numbers had sought solace in walking, and that Ramblers Federations had been established all over the country, with local Commons and Footpaths Preservation Societies that sprang up locally. New tramping journals had been established to cater for the needs of this new breed of walkers, or 'hikers' as dubbed by the press. In the North of England in particular, Alfred commented that the 'walking movement' was particularly virile, and that it was estimated that up to 20,000 ramblers left Manchester by train every Sunday morning for the surrounding moors. There had also been large demonstrations at the Winnats Pass near Castleton in Derbyshire, and on Ilkley Moor in Yorkshire, by ramblers who lobbied in support of the speedy passing of the Access to Mountains Bill in Parliament. The Act was seen ambitiously as a 'Charter for Walkers' at the time, and although finally enacted in 1939, it was largely ineffectual and was later repealed.

Meanwhile Alfred's prediction was that the time would come when the vast army of walkers would be powerful enough to insist on repeal of the out-of-date laws that restricted the right of free access to the moors and commons of Great Britain. Later the Countryside Act of 1949 followed, which although it defined the areas of open country, had little effect on access. Some further impetus was gained however in 1951 with the creation of the first National Park in Great Britain in the Peak District of Derbyshire, whereby access arrangements were made with local landowners to allow ramblers to roam on previously forbidden moors. Subsequently the Ramblers' Association launched the 'Forbidden Britain' campaign in 1985 to try to secure the statutory right of access to open countryside, which led to an annual 'Forbidden Britain Day', again in the Peak District of Derbyshire, and mass trespasses in the 1990s on a scale not seen since the 1930s. Finally, further successful lobbying by a variety of interested groups eventually resulted in the Countryside Rights of Way Act of 2000, which allowed the 'right to roam' on all uncultivated open country in England and Wales, which was finally fully implemented on 31st October 2005.

Alfred would no doubt have been delighted with these developments, but also dismayed that it took so long to bring about the changes when he was writing his 'new kind of walking book', which he hoped would not only meet the needs of the grow-ing band of walkers, but also would be a prelude to a series of books. It was envis-aged that this book would be followed by with a companion volume on East and North-East Yorkshire, with additional volumes added by other writers on Derbyshire, Northumberland, Durham, Westmorland, and the Lake District in due course, subject to the availability of the necessary financial support.

Finally Alfred ended the Foreword to the book with a terse note on the style, structure and content of the proposed series: 'There will be nothing hackneyed or "guide-bookish" about these books. The ground covered will be largely new, and the subject will be approached in an original way, attention being concentrated on the mountains, moors, and fells; on ridge-to-ridge "crossings"; on upland villages and out-of-the-way inns, rather than on motor-haunted show places.'

In the Preface of the book Alfred wrote a mini-treatise on the subject of 'hiking', and outlined his perspective on this recently-introduced term by the press, to describe the already popular activity of simply walking. He disliked the term 'hike', still more 'hik-ing' and most of all 'hiker', even though it was used by enthusiastic journalists who described this new trend, and that all these American terms supposedly sprang from the same old Saxon root: 'hyke' – 'to walk vigorously'. Even so he indicated that there was much to be said for the odious word 'hike', since it drew attention to the rapidly growing army of walkers, and the consequent publicity which had helped to swell the ranks still more, although he wondered for how long these new recruits to the activ-ity would continue to pursue their interest, and whether or not this trend was just another popular but passing fad. Hence to his own astonishment he found himself actually writing a Preface about 'hiking for hikers'. But he reassured his friends and readers: 'as a rose by any other name would still smell as sweet, so walking is still walk-ing, even though it be mis-called "hiking". And it will not be called "hiking" again in this book!'

The book was not set out in a standard chapter format, but divided instead into three main parts, with each part further subdivided into many numbered sections, each in turn related to the themes of the three main parts. In addition there was an Appendix which provided summary information on further tramping routes, which were not included in the main text, and a comprehensive index to help the reader cross reference items of interest. The overall structure of the book resembled a cata-logued collection of recommended walking routes with supplementary information, rather than a guide book *per se*, which had been Alfred's original intention.

If the preface might be described as a minor discourse on the subject of walking, then what follows in Part One of the book *Moorland Tramping*[5] is a major discourse of some thirty-six pages which contains information, guidance and advice with respect to walking-related themes. Here Alfred expresses his own philosophy with regard to the practices of walking relevant to moorland tramping, before he embarks on a detailed description of the many routes covered in later sections of the book.

At the outset Alfred describes in his view the characteristics of three groups of perambulists: 'walkers', 'professional walkers' and 'real walkers', which covered the range of walking patterns: 'sauntering', 'race walking' and 'tramping' respectively. He even suggests: 'Tramping is to walking what poetry is to prose', since he maintains that tramping provided a kind of lyrical thrill gained from the poetic movement of this type of walking, which provides its own rapturous reward. However he emphasises that it is not necessary to be skilled in the art of walking to achieve the simple enjoyment of man's most natural activity. Nevertheless he is adamant about the equipment needed to get the most out of tramping and suggests that the reader follows his example. The items he prefers include: sturdy shoes not boots, breeches not long trousers and a long hacking jacket with large poaching pockets for maps and sandwiches, not for illegal game. On longer tramps he advocates a light rucksack with a minimalist approach to its contents to include: personal spare clothes, emergency rations and rainwear, but never to be without a stout walking staff for support and self defence in a tight spot. But he is more blasé when it comes to accommodation on extensive tramps, and holds the dated but optimistic view: 'one of the great joys of tramping is the uncertainty about a night's lodging, and the subsequent arrival at an unknown inn under the benign stars'. In this regard he was fortunate to live at a time when such expectations were often fulfilled by most dales inns, and if not he was almost sure to benefit from the renowned hospitality available at remote dales farms.

However, to find these places of refuge he insists that the reader should be able to navigate using a map and compass and never set out without some basic training in their use, as well as have some familiarity with the terrain to be encountered. These were fundamental requirements if the reader intends to follow Alfred's advice about getting off the beaten tracks and being able to negotiate the demanding routes that he proposes, where few roads, no roads or only ancient tracks are the norm. Furthermore he suggests that the ability to read the landscape from a relief map allows enjoyment of the best kind of tramping by going *'oer t'tops'* and concludes: 'Happy is the man who has discovered the tops!... Pity the poor wretch to whom the shepherd's phrase strikes no accord'. Indeed the tops are very special places to him: 'the last secret places of England... for centuries they have not changed, and perhaps they never will change until man disappears from the face of this earth'.

In the achievement of tramping rewards, Alfred describes the joys to be had during such endeavours:

> The joy of setting out at early morning with a whole day ahead; the keen bite of frosty air as one strides along with the rime still on the fields: the joy of a sudden sprint down a green hillside on some bridle path with the dew sparkling on the sunlit grass, the joy of breasting a hill on boisterous days; the fun of being swept off one's feet and hurled forward over the high moor by leaps and bounds; the beauty of easy rhythmical movement, mile after mile, when the body has become properly attuned; the sudden sight and smell of the sea, bursting into view from a mountain top in the Pennines; or moments when the track is no longer a thing of earth and rocks and stones, but a golden glory high above the common world, trailing off westward through an enchanting land... Rest assured, you will not experience these ecstasies in an easy chair by the fireside! Tramping is an active delight that only those who practise it can rightly apprehend... And every man who tramps will find his own crock of gold.

Then in an aside from the main theme of the book, Alfred also suggests an alternative tramping experience which he describes as 'river rambling' and comments: 'second only to the joy of tramping over the high moors, I would recommend the thrill of exploring rivers...'[5,5a] Inevitably such expeditions require familiarity with the tops, since he suggests that the 'river pilgrimage' should start as near as possible to the source, with a descent down the watercourse following the formative stages including: 'sikes' – tiny streams, 'becks' – larger mountain streams and 'ghylls' – becks between high banks. Thus the ramble follows a route from the high watershed above to the dale below, and often demands a gruelling transition in the early stages where: 'every mile counts as four; every waterfall is a milestone passed, but such milestones as you will never find on the wayside!'

In Part One the reader is also introduced to the first of twelve maps in the book, but curiously Map 1, like the other eleven maps, is listed in the index and not identified in the text, although all the maps are presented at the appropriate points as sketch relief illustrations. The exceptions to this rule are the maps associated with the 'additional routes from dale to dale', which are outlined in the Appendix. In the case of Map 1, it provides the reader with a sketch map of the major mountains and rivers of West Yorkshire, along with two suggested tramping routes along the Pennines, which traverse the main dales and rivers of the area. The first from High Force in Teesdale to Malham in Airedale, a distance of some 42 miles, the second from Barnard Castle in Teesdale to Buckden in Wharfedale, a distance of some 26 miles. It was most likely that these suggested routes were chosen to represent the typical topographical landscape of the West Riding Dales to the uninitiated reader.

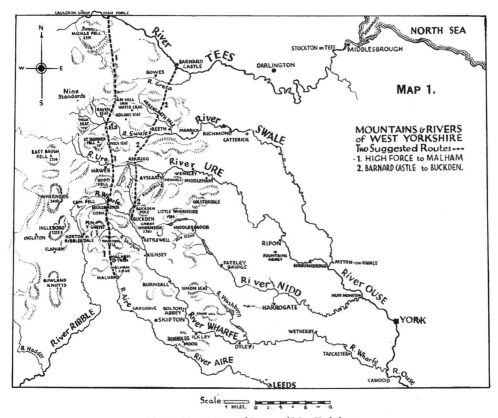

Map 8. Mountains and Rivers of West Yorkshire

To complete this extensive introductory section, Alfred then sets out the terms of reference for the book and why it should not be considered as just a 'guide book'. Even then he admits being fond of little two-penny guidebooks, but not larger ones costing up to 'half a guinea' (10s/6d), that are too big for his rucksack and also 'too meticulous and eulogistic by far'. Then he declares that the purpose of his pocket-sized book is to lead the reader away from the main roads, on to the moorland tracks, although wherever a track goes nearby a famous abbey, hall or village, it is acknowledged, but anyone who expects a compendium of the sights and curiosities of the West Riding is going be very disappointed. Instead the book shows how the moors can be best explored, and in the subsequent chapters Alfred describes selected moorland "crossings" in detail, starting with the dales which are the natural approaches to the moors.

In Part Two of the book: 'The Dales',[6,6a] Alfred admits that while many books have already been written about the Yorkshire Dales, he explains that the dales are not all alike, each has its own distinctive features, folklore and legends, so that each needs to be explored individually to appreciate them fully. However for the purpose of this book he comments: 'fortunately for me, the dales are only anecdotal to my main theme – the moors – so I will not attempt to deal with them in detail'. Even so, he is careful to acknowledge that a tramping book on Yorkshire without some reference to the dales would be inappropriate, and therefore the book concentrates on their main features and tramping possibilities rather than their individual characteristics. In the accompanying Map 2, Alfred outlines the basic geographical distribution of the main dales and rivers of West Yorkshire, which with the exception of the River Ribble, all spring from the Pennine uplands and eventually find their way to the River Ouse and then to the North Sea.

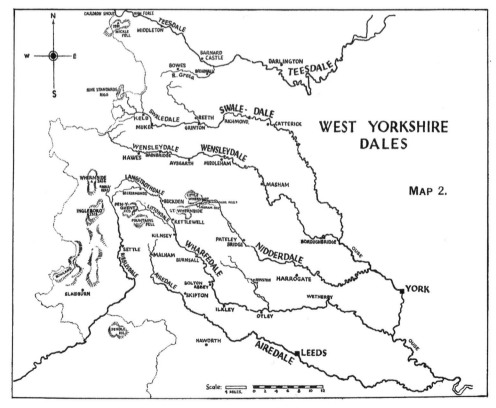

Map 9. The West Yorkshire Dales

While Alfred acknowledges the benefits of the exploration of the individual dales for those with sufficient time, he outlines some of the more important cross-dale routes which not only provide excellent cross-country tramping , but also cover good stretches of the the dales country without the reliance on roads. He also suggests that those who normally keep to the well-beaten tracks of Airedale and Wharfedale should explore the more northerly dales and their tributary dales. All of these were then easily accessible by good rail and bus services, and could be readily covered at weekends without much expense. He then provides a description of suitable routes and his own impressions of the dales, starting with Teeesdale in the north, followed by Swaledale, Wensleydale, Ribblesdale, Nidderdale, Wharfedale and finishing with Airedale in the south.

In Part Three of the book: 'Random Tramps and Adventures',[7] Alfred details a few well-chosen examples of tramping in the Walden Beck, Malhamdale, High Craven and Bowland areas. He also provides some accounts of a few memorable tramps, along with amusing observations and guidance on matters relevant to moorland tramping in general. To begin with though he could not have chosen a better example than one which surely represents the type of tramping which he enjoyed most, and was possibly one of his favourite routes among those presented. It is for this reason that this particular route has been selected for presentation in more detail.

Three Peaks in One Day[7a]

The three peaks route of Whernside, Ingleborough and Pen-y-Ghent has come to represent one of the classical walking challenges in Yorkshire today. The walk covers a distance of some 24 miles and requires nearly 5,250 ft. of ascent. The challenge is to cover the route in 12 hours and so become a member of the 'Three Peaks Club'. The established route is a circuit of the three mountains, anticlockwise in sequence, with a start and finish at Horton-in-Ribblesdale (see map – standard circuit). However for the purpose of his tramp, Alfred chose a non-circuitous, but still sequential route, which includes a little more walking variation, with increased distance and with slightly greater ascent and descent, but arguably offers a more enjoyable, if somewhat more challenging, but nevertheless interesting day out.

This linear route might even be given the alternative name: 'The Six Peaks, Dales and Inns Walk'. It tops six summits: Whernside, Ingleborough, the subsidiary peaks Little Ingleborough and Simon Fell, Pen-y-Ghent and the subsidiary peak Plover Hill. The walk passes through parts of six dales: Dentdale, Deepdale, Chapel-le-Dale,

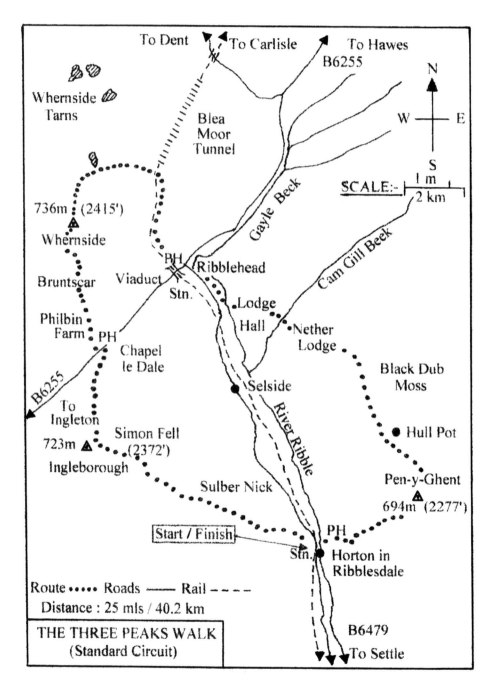

Map 10. The standard 'Three Peaks' circuit

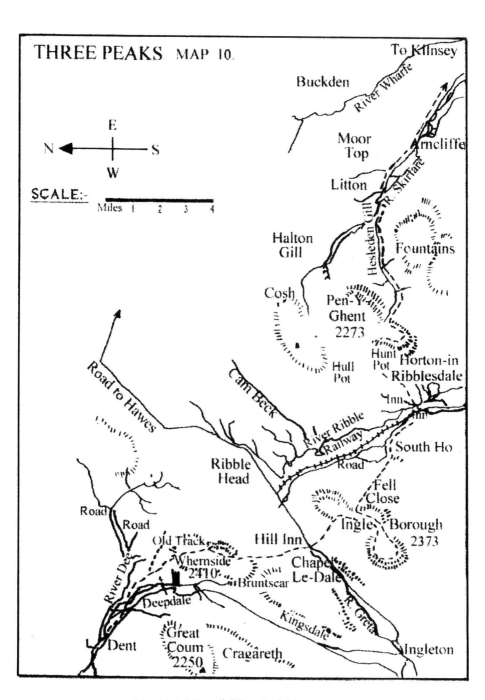

Map 11. A.J. Brown's 'Three Peaks' Linear Route

Ribblesdale, Littondale and Wharfedale. Furthermore it can include six inns, starting in Dent after an overnight stay at the Sun Inn, with refreshment breaks at the Station Inn, Ribblesdale, the Hill Inn, Chapel-le-Dale, the Golden Lion Inn, Horton-in-Ribblesdale and the Queen's Arms, Litton, before finishing at the Tennant Arms in Kilnsey for a well-earned overnight's rest.

Alfred's alternative route covered a distance of some 30 miles, with over 6,350 ft. of ascent and with rest breaks he completed the route in 12 hours walking time, at a pace of about 2.5 mph, and he reassured the reader of its feasibility:

'And lest anyone should question any word of this *[tramp]*, I append my timetable – not because I claim to have established a record or care a jot for such things – but simply to confound the sceptical and to encourage the adventurous.'[7a]

Left Dent	7.00 a.m.
Whernside Pikes	8.10 a.m.
Whernside Summit	9.00 to 9.30 a.m.
Philpin Farm	10.00 a.m.
Weathercote Cave	10.15 a.m.
Hill Inn, Chapel-le-Dale	10.30 to 10.45 a.m.
Ingleborough Summit	12.00 to 12.15 p.m.
South House Farm	1.25 p.m.
Crown Inn, Horton-in-Ribblesdale	2.00 to 3.00 p.m. lunch
Hull Pot	3.45 p.m.
Pen-y-ghent Summit	4.50 p.m.
Hesleden Beck Bridge	5.15 p.m.
Litton	6.15 to 6.45 p.m.
Kilnsey (Wharfedale)	9.15 p.m.

Finally, in summary of the allure of the 'Three Peaks' Alfred states:

In fascinating alignment they stand, this noble triumvirate, daring any man of spirit to take them one after another in his stride between sunrise and sunset!

before he reservedly adds a qualified endorsement:

On the whole I am no great lover of freak tramping and mountain-scamping of this sort... but this challenge is not so easily to be resisted once a man has stepped within its magic circle, and I commend it to the attention of all tramping men.

Towards the end of part three of the book, Alfred turns his attention to one of his favourite topics included in all his tramping books that of 'Yorkshire Inns and Ale', since he believed in the intrinsic benefits that these hostelries provide: 'my own inclination, when I enter any of these dales villages is to spend a week in each inn to drink my fill – not only of ale, but lore and legend and friendliness in which they all abound.' He also has the temerity to mention particular inns and praise their ales and food, and comments on the kind of welcome which the traveller on foot always expects and receives at the list of chosen inns: 'refuge in a storm, comfort in distress, solace at eventide, and veritable fountains of hospitality', and therefore shows how great his indebtedness is to such places.

He then enters into the 'tea versus ale' drinking debate, and while he admits that tea was a good stimulant when one came in frozen from the fells in the afternoon, in his opinion, the best thirst quencher after a hard day's tramping in the heat or cold was ale, but offers the maxim: 'Tea in reason is good, ale in reason is better, and either in excess is an offence unworthy of true trampers and equally reprehensible.' However, in order to fully appreciate the value of good Yorkshire 'Stingo' (Ale), he was in no doubt that it should be taken with sustenance, and that there were: 'four elemental things – bread, cheese, onion and ale which have to be taken together to be rightly savoured.' Finally, he expresses his regret in not being able to mention all the many inns which he has enjoyed on his tramps, but offers the consolatory appreciation: 'for all that have warmed the cockles of my heart, made new friends, and sent me to sleep in a feather bed, I render my heartfelt thanks'. But eventually he tries to correct this anomaly in the subsequent volume.

In the final section of part three of the book, Alfred provides sound advice and strategies on coming to terms with the then complicated issue of Right of Way. He outlines the problem with the law which governs access controlled by Urban and District Councils, but warns that as with all other legal regulations: 'there are so many "ifs and buts" about it that it is hopeless to attempt to lay down any rules'. In practical terms, he gives sound advice on how to deal with irate landowners, game keepers or farmers when challenged in such circumstances, with amusing examples of how he has overcome personal, often hostile rebuke for supposed trespass, in which his modus operandi has always been: 'in such moments it is well to remember that a little tact will open far more gates and paths than a display of temper', and therefore he suggested others should adopt this non-confrontational stance. Alfred was an advocate of open access to the countryside, and a keen supporter of the Access to Mountains Bill legislation that was then being considered by Parliament, and as an affirmed activist he declares: 'I, for one, will not rest in my shoes until all walkers have free and unfettered access to every moor and common in England, Scotland and Wales'. However it was nearly seventy years before future legislation actually achieved the desired success, and Alfred's dream, along with that of countless others of a right to roam, became the reality that is enjoyed today.

Finally in the Appendix there appears a catalogue of 'Additional Routes from Dale to Dale'[8,8a] which Alfred was unable to include in the text. These are listed under each of the seven West Yorkshire Dales covered, along with further tramping routes recommended and reference to the particular maps included in the text, which were intended for use in conjunction with the relevant OS maps. Furthermore there are three additional districts added that cover areas outside the classic dales districts that include the Haworth Moors, the Calderdale countryside and the South Pennines.

Impact of the Book

The sales of this first tramping book undoubtedly achieved the expectations of the publisher, and as on previous occasions, Alfred received an early congratulatory note for the publication of this new book from his *'Alma Mater'*,[9] which subsequently noted:

> Mr. Brown's *Moorland Tramping* has had a significant sale. It is a book we can recommend with confidence to anyone who has never thought of setting foot on the moors. The book is unique in its way, indispensible to 'hikers', though this word is one that Mr. Brown bans absolutely from the pages of his book'[10]

While the popular press reception the book received was evident in the following brief reviews which represented some of the most favourable opinions:

> 'This little book tells us how the real walker may enjoy rambles in the Pennine Country and the Yorkshire dales' – *The Yorkshire Herald*

> 'Sufficiently topographical to enable one to follow the routes described... A book every lover of moors should possess' – *Hiker & Camper*

> 'No man is in a better position to give advice to trampers than Mr. A.J. Brown... He knows every moor and dale-land path, every inn, and every trick of the weather' – *Yorkshire Weekly Post*

> 'Mr. A.J. Brown is a well-known figure in Yorkshire. His recent book on

Moorland Tramping is compiled from experiences of many years of walking' – *Radio Times* (North Regional Programme)

'To those who want to walk on the Yorkshire moors... Like freemen – I recommend *Moorland Tramping* – 'Beachcomber', *Daily Express*

'*Moorland Tramping* is the jolliest walking book I have read since Belloc's Path to Rome... The wind of the open road roars through the pages' – Stanley R. Baron, *News Chronicle*

'Moorland Tramping is the best thing of its kind on the West Riding of Yorkshire' – *The Yorkshire Observer*

'A real tramper's companion for the fireside – and that rarer thing – a book for the rucksack too' *Out-o'-Doors*

Meanwhile the influential and popular National Catholic Weekly Journal *The Tablet* provided another very supportive review in its critically conservative literary and arts section:

Mr. A.J. Brown has a great deal to say on the art of tramping. His book *Moorland Tramping* is just right for a real tramper – not a stroller or a professional walker – to tuck in his rucksack when he sets out to explore the lovely dales and peaks of West Yorkshire. The twelve excellent maps, the suggested routes, and the author's many comments on inns, cobblers, shoes and equipment, are very helpful to the novice; and especially valuable is Mr. Brown's advice on the proper things to say to keepers, farmers, and property owners, etc., on the laws of right-of-way. We note with pleasure that he believes courtesy to be the best password.[11]

However, not all the reviews were so positive, and in a generally very supportive evaluation of the book by the Yorkshire Observer newspaper, there was a sting in the tail of a detailed review concerning Alfred's style of writing and his prose:

This chummy little book by Alfred Brown, who will be remembered as the author of *Four Boon Fellows*, should be sure of a good sale. Certainly it deserves one. First as a guide to the moor country of the West Riding. Secondly, as a volume of flavoursome essays on the wonder of the hills and the joys of walking. Thirdly, as a handy companion – just right to drop in your side-pocket or the pouch in your rucksack before setting forth in the brightness of the tramper's morning.

Mr. Brown advises the true lover of moorlands and fell country to include in his equipment a book of verse. This advice should be revised in favour of the present volume. If there is room only for one book, let poetry wait and take *Moorland Tramping* instead. Mr. Brown's book is in large part a compilation of carefully-mapped tramping routes in the seven dales, and therefore deserves preference on utilitarian grounds. Many of the itineraries will be virgin soil for most walkers. The writer tells, for example, of an unfrequented quarter of Bowland country. For such unhackneyed territory the walker is always thirsty, and Mr. Brown writes with gusto of hills, rivers, villages, old inns and good ale.

Sometimes, I fear, his gusto has a bookish flavour, and Mr. Brown should rid his style of such excrescences such as 'haply', 'withal' ' waxing', 'vouchsafed' and 'by this token'. But Mr. Brown's writing at best has a lucid beauty which comes out notably in his description of the River Nidd. However, if Mr. Brown were to do a little weeding his prose would be more telling.[12]

Nevertheless, the book seemed to have found a niche in the growing market of popular walking publications, and following its uptake among the increasing numbers of walkers, the publishers decided to follow up its success quickly with another companion edition. Alfred was then asked to produce a similar-styled book to include those other areas of the county that had not so far received much attention, namely North and East Yorkshire.

Tramping in Yorkshire – North and East[13]

It may seem surprising that within a few months of the publication of *Moorland Tramping in West Yorkshire*,[4] Alfred signed another contract with his publishers for the delivery of his second book in the 'Yorkshire Tramping' series. Although he had been working on a draft of the new book while he was completing the first one, it remains a mystery how he had found the time to complete the exploration needed for this new piece of work. While West Yorkshire was almost on his doorstep, North and East Yorkshire were far from his home, and would have necessitated considerable time and expenditure in order to complete all the fieldwork that was required. This would have presented a much more formidable challenge in terms of the logistics involved to accomplish a detailed description of other tramping routes among the more remote uplands of the largest county in England.

Moorland Tramping was sold out at almost once, but instead of a reprint, the Country Life editor persuaded Alfred to write a companion volume which covered the North and East of the county. As already stated, Alfred was originally given a roving commission to write about any county in England, but he never had any ambition to write about any other county than Yorkshire. Therefore he signed another agreement with Country Life on 9th March 1932, to deliver the completed manuscript originally titled 'Tramping in East Yorkshire', along with an unspecified number of maps, by 30th June 1932. In return the publishers agreed to publish the book within six months of receipt of the finished manuscript.[14] The terms and conditions for the new book were almost identical to the previous contract in terms of Alfred's advance of £50 with payment of 10% royalties, although a lower print-run of 5,000 copies was agreed initially, along with the usual paltry provision of his six free copies and an option to buy further copies at cost price but not for resale by him, as well as the now-established clause of selling off the 'remaindered' stock if sales failed to achieve the initial print-run. Once more Alfred happily accepted this arrangement, although it seemed that the likely returns for the outlay of his time, effort and expenditure were meagre given the recent success of the previous book, especially compared with the rewards that other more established writers were receiving for comparable works at this time.

Once again Country Life produced another hard-backed, reasonably-priced (3s/6d), pocket-sized book of some 224 pages, which was in print before the end of 1932 with the final title *Tramping in Yorkshire – North and East*. This time Alfred dedicated his book to Charles Joshua Frederick Atkinson, a town planner from Burley-in-Wharfedale, in recognition of his work in connection with the 'Commons, Open Spaces and Footpaths Preservation Society'. Then in a note of acknowledgement, Alfred indicated that some of the passages of the book had also been used for broadcasting purposes,[15,15a] as well as a few extracts that had appeared in serial form in the local press, for which he gave thanks for permission to use this material to the BBC and the Editor of the Yorkshire Post respectively. Alfred had earlier broadcast a weekly series on the topic 'Unknown Yorkshire' on the BBC Radio North Service, Leeds, and also published a weekly series on 'Yorkshire Byways' in the Leeds-based *Yorkshire Post* newspaper during the spring of 1932. Unfortunately none of these broadcast scripts have been located among the archives, although the series of newspaper articles are available on microfiche in the Yorkshire Post Archive at Leeds Central Library.

Scope, Style and Structure of the Book

In the Foreword Alfred outlined the scope of what was intended by the book compared with its companion volume *Moorland Tramping in West Yorkshire*, which had dealt exclusively with West Yorkshire in a line extended from Sheffield northwards to the River Tees. This included the main Pennine Ridge and the Western Dales and Moors of the North and West Ridings of Yorkshire, whereas the new volume *Tramping in Yorkshire – North and East* covered the rest of the County of Yorkshire east of a line which stretched roughly from Northallerton to York and Selby. Thus it included not merely the East Riding of the county, but all of the easterly region of the North Riding, as well as the length of the Yorkshire coastline from Redcar in the north to Spurn Head in the south, as outlined on the frontispiece Map 1.

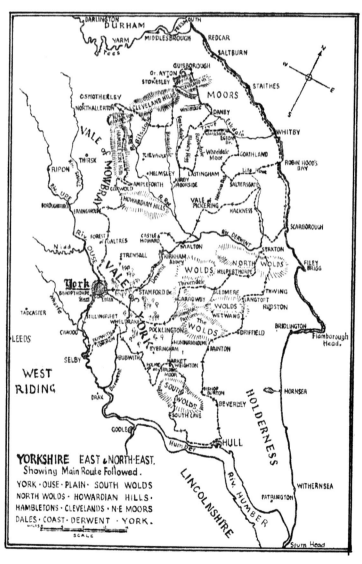

Map 12. Yorkshire East and North-East

This region of course represented a very diverse countryside that included a vast area which Alfred readily acknowledged could not be covered completely in such a small volume, and therefore he set limits on its scope. He set out: 'to discover the best tramping routes in East and North Yorkshire in a series of expeditions across the Vale of York, the Wolds, the Howardian, the Hambleton, and the Cleveland Hills, the North-East Yorkshire Moors and Dales, the Derwent Country and down the coast' (see Map 12). And if that was not difficult enough, in keeping with the former companion book, his main objective is to: 'avoid motoring-roads and seek footpaths, bridle-paths, old "drove-roads" over the hills, and moorland tracks', whilst at the same time he includes information on the famous abbeys, villages and inns on the line of his tramps.

However in a slight deviation from the earlier companion volume, Alfred indicates that while his various expeditions form a somewhat ambitious and almost continuous pilgrimage, that begins and ends in York, these routes can be subdivided into a series of weekend tramps. He also acknowledges that the length of the routes cited might be too long or too arduous for everyone, even though he had personally accomplished them all in one day. He therefore he indicates in the text as many inns on the wayside as possible, so that the stranger to the districts concerned may be able to take a break for the night in a suitable hostelry. Then as in the companion volume Alfred includes an extensive appendix of alternative routes for exploration as well as a detailed index for easy reference. Finally Alfred sums up his primary reason for extending the tramping series to cover the rest of Yorkshire when he states: 'East and North East Yorkshire is not nearly as well-known as it should be and one of the chief objects of this little book is to induce the growing legion of walkers to get into their seven-league boots and explore it. They will not be disappointed.'

The writing style used this time was something of a 'travelogue' approach and not dissimilar to that which he had used previously in *Four Boon Fellows*, without the literary embellishments, but most unlike the former companion book on West Yorkshire, which was a very matter of fact account of the tramping routes recommended in the western dales. This time the text recounts a series of tramping expeditions of varying durations, ranging from a weekend to a full week, and thus it reads almost a like a story which makes for very entertaining reading.

The overall structure to some extent reflects the scope of the book, which covers large and very varied areas of the county, and it is divided into eleven major geographical parts in an attempt to best exemplify the many varied landscapes of these other areas of Yorkshire. Each part is then further subdivided into a series of sections that follow successively and provide the detailed tramping routes selected to represent the particular geographical part under consideration. In addition there are further tramping routes provided for each part and section suggested in the Appendix, and quite the most detailed index is provided at the end of the book to help the reader sift through the extensive contents.

Then without detracting from the tramping routes outlined, the detailed contents of the book also provide a useful insight into many aspects of the topographical landscape. These include: its history, ancient monuments, classical buildings, towns, villages and inns, as well as local legends and folklore, along with the interesting characters that Alfred occasionally meets on his journeys, which often give rise to the amusing incidents during his tramping exploits. All these reinforce the impression of an underlying storyline, which, whether intended or not, provides an appealing, almost thematic approach to the book. This in turn is assisted by the detailed 'finger posts' at the top of each page to indicate clearly the topic under consideration, and thus helps the reader deal with the multi-faceted material covered, in the same successful way that this technique had been used in Alfred's earlier book the *Four Boon Fellows*.

Overall the text is illustrated with eleven sketch maps including the first which is a general one of the whole geographical region covered by the book (see above), followed by ten most detailed sketch maps of each specific part of the book in which the best tramping routes of each sub-section are displayed. However, Alfred warns the reader that these sketch maps, which identified his recommended tramping routes, are not intended as a substitute for the list of OS maps that he also provides, and he advises that these are to be used with his own maps to fill in the important details along the way.

The eleven detailed tramping sections of the book accompanied by their respective maps include the countryside to the north and south of an imaginary line which runs approximately north-east to south west across the country through the city of York. After beginning a tour of 'York',[16] Alfred describes six routes around the East Riding areas to the south of the imaginary line that include: 'The Ouse',[17] 'The Vale of York',[18] 'The Wolds Way South',[19] 'The Wolds Way North 1'[20] and 'The Wolds Way North 2'.[21,21a] However he admits that he is no great lover of the flat country that surrounds York: 'It may be alright for sauntering, but not for tramping as I understand it.' Nevertheless the Wolds Way has a special appeal for him:

> There is a quietness about the Wold Country and a benignity not found anywhere in Yorkshire... a pastoral peace. The scattered villages seem to have

escaped the tumult and notice of the modern world... little communities of people living natural sheltered lives.

But in a note of sad realism he comments: '...that the older, more leisurely England, will soon be no more than a memory.'

Alfred's descriptive account then moves to the uplands to the north of the imaginary line as he describes five routes around the North Riding areas that include: 'Over the hills',[22] (The Howardian and Hambleton Hills), 'The Cleveland Hills',[23] and 'The North East Moors and Dales'.[24] He then turns his attention to 'The Yorkshire Coast',[25] which he finds particularly attractive: 'The coast with its crazy indentations, kaleidoscope changes of colour and scene, enchanting little bays, superb cliffs and abbey walls, unspoiled fishing hamlets, surprise creeks, caves and moorland hinterland can challenge the comparison with any stretch of coastline in England.' He finally turns inland and describes a three day tramp along 'The Derwent Way'[26,26a] to return to York at the heart of the county, where the three Ridings meet and his opinion: 'If there is a better place than York to finish a pilgrimage I have yet to find it.'

In the Appendix[27] Alfred lists 'Some Additional Routes and Suggestions' and he also summarises many extra tramping routes in each of the sections since there has not been sufficient opportunity to provide all the details of these well chosen alternatives. In a selective bibliography he lists a number of other books which although useful are not essential and he recommends some background reading for the North and East Regions of Yorkshire. Finally in a comprehensive Index Alfred not only provides a further detailed cross-reference list of topics covered in the text, but also a separate Index of Inns of which there are 88 listed that are described in the text and recommended for lodging, food, ale and good hospitality on the routes outlined.

Impact of the Book

This companion book was also well received in press reviews, particularly by the *Times Literary Supplement*, which acknowledged the contribution of his previous book, made a recommendation for an additional item of inclusion, and complimented Alfred on his writing style:

> Mr. Brown describes certain walks in the county which lies between Humber and Tees, and as he showed in his companion volume on the Pennines, *Moorland Tramping in West Yorkshire* (a review of which appeared in the Literary Supplement of December 17th 1931), he is most at home on

the high moors; but he gives their due to the dales, which to many form the chief attraction of North East Yorkshire.

He makes no claim to the comprehensiveness of a standard guide book, but the ground is well covered. The only omission of importance is no mention of the pleasant walk over the detached Eston Hills (a lowland heath just south of Middlesbrough), which would be useful to people living on Tees-side or visiting Redcar and Saltburn.

Mr. Brown's book fills a gap in the numerous literature on the subject. He writes in a pleasant, easy style and varies his narrative with an occasional anecdote. His descriptions are based on personal experience, just as are his recommendations of inns, which walkers will find suitable; and although mainly occupied with the joys of walking, he does not neglect to mention places of historical interest. The book is well supplied with good sketch maps.[28]

However, as in the case of the previous book, not all critics were happy with Alfred's style of writing, and once more after receiving the appropriate acclamation for his work, there was some criticism probably by the same reviewer, this time in the *Yorkshire Observer*:

The publication of A. J. Brown's new book – *Tramping in Yorkshire, North and East* – gives me another opportunity of repeating what very good and how very little appreciated walking country there is beyond the Ouse, across the plain *[of York]* and up on the Yorkshire Wolds. Go. You would be surprised. A.J. Brown has been; and returned to write a whole-hearted, companionable invitation that slips easily into the pocket, has two hundred odd pages, and costs three bob *[three shillings]*. He has made several good bee-lines across the country, and dozens of others wherever there is a green track riding the dales, or the thought of an inn in the next village.

He has a hearty way with him. He takes the day's troubles in his stride. He has what I suppose is called an objective rather than a subjective attitude towards the countryside. The country is there for his walking; the inn for food and lodging. The villages live for a day in his books and then are left again until called for.

Then in a contrasting mode the reviewer was critical of Alfred's treatment of historical notes in which he stated: 'there is A.J. Brown at his worst: completely egoistic, slightly bombastic, and psuedo-Bellocian: beating the big drum...' followed by the almost complimentary comment on Alfred's description of his welcome at an inn: 'there is A.J. Brown at his best (almost): genial, unaffected and refreshingly free from his rather tiresome convention,' before finishing with the back-handed compliment: 'Mr. Brown would tell you he walks over hill and dale – actually he rides the high horse most of the time. But one thing I know: when I next go to the Wolds, I shall take this book with me.'[29]

Striding Through Yorkshire[30]

After the publication of the two companion books on tramping in Yorkshire, which had both achieved their projected sales targets, Alfred had hoped that these would subsequently be reprinted in order to meet the obvious demand for this new kind of walking book, but unfortunately his publishers were reluctant to follow up these initial successes. This was most probably due to the economic circumstances at the time, in which the 'Great Depression' of the early 1930s was having an enormous impact on the country resulting in declining production, rising unemployment and a devastated retail market. As a result the printing industry was also hit hard by the fall in imports of paper products, and therefore publishing companies in general reduced their output to conserve their precious resources, which in turn resulted in far fewer books being published during this period.

This situation persisted until the late 1930s, so that it was not surprising that Alfred's two companion tramping books did not see a revival for over five years, but even then this did not result in reprinted versions, and instead the two volumes were issued in a combined edition under the title *Striding Through Yorkshire*. Accordingly, Alfred signed another agreement with Country Life on 3rd November 1937 to deliver the complete manuscript with material for illustrations (maps) by 15th January 1938, with the usual, by now, meagre royalties, but with no specific publication date agreed, although the book was released later that year. Under the circumstances it is not surprising that Alfred declared that as far as 'Yorkshire' was concerned this book was going to be his swan song, partly because of his horror of being repetitive, partly because he preferred to be walking much more than writing about it, but undoubtedly also because of the poor prospects for writers during the foreseeable future. However in the interim, he now redirected himself to the production of a further book:

> The combined edition which could fairly claim to embrace all of Yorkshire
> – certainly all of the wildest walking country in the three Ridings – so that

anyone wishing to undertake a circular tour from any starting point such as York, need only put the one book in his rucksack and be sure of having the broad acres at his feet.[31]

While the new book still retains the original division between the previous companion books, Alfred revises and rearranges the chapters, as well as adding in total about 50 new 'additional routes' immediately after the relevant sections to which they belonged, instead of at the end in an appendix. He also adds several new chapters, including ones on the 'Sedbergh – Dent country' and 'The Three Counties' border route (Durham, Yorkshire and Westmorland) on the extreme north-western edges of Yorkshire, as well as the 'Sheffield – Derwent' country in the south of the county. In addition, there is an expansion of Alfred's beloved Wharfedale section with a considerable number of new routes added, many of which had not been published before, together with a separate section on the adjoining 'Littondale' as well as many other minor improvements.

In order to be able to include this new material Alfred sacrifices some of the text from the *Moorland Tramping in West Yorkshire* volume, especially the lengthy introductory chapters and extraneous material under the subtitle of 'Random Tramps and Adventures'. Even so, the new book contains nearly 400 pages and 23 maps, but he hopes the revisions make it textually more concise and practical than the previous separate volumes, and appealing to the more discerning readers 'who liked to "cut out the cackle" and get on with the walking'. This attempt to concentrate more on the actual tramping routes is also aided by the orientation of the so-called 'finger post' headings at the top of each page, which coincide with each of the sub-section titles which described the routes.

There are also other important modifications in the new book, which include an Appendix update on the 'Right of Way' legislation and its implications for walkers, although such developments were then still far short of the 'right to roam' benefits enjoyed today. In addition, Alfred includes another Appendix which listed some 35 Youth Hostels in Yorkshire for the benefit of the many younger walkers who do not wish to, or could not afford to stay at a village inn. Then for the benefit of the more mature walker who prefers 'home comforts', he sprinkles the text liberally again with reliable inns which offer room and board at reasonable prices, and these are the subject of yet another separate 'Index of Inns' which totals almost 150. Clearly Alfred was something of an authority on inns, as he explained to J.B. Priestley in a letter to him earlier in the year, and although not knowing it at the time, this fascination with these hostelries would eventually lead to a major shift in his career later in life. It would be satisfying for Alfred to know that during the present time of the apparent demise of the country pub, most of the inns identified in the text are still in business today, albeit offering some interesting variations on their traditional services, but thriving none-the-less. Furthermore, pubs have become a focus for a more recent trend in walking fashions – that of the 'pub walk' variety, whereby the pub is the centre for a circular walk in the surrounding countryside.[32]

Finally, in a revised acknowledgement page, Alfred shows his appreciation to those who had helped inspire him to write this series of books, with accreditations to George C. Heseltine and Charles Joshua Fearnside Atkinson, both of whom he recognised in the earlier companion books, along with A.J.M. Sclater. Alfred Sclater, also of *Four Boon Fellows* notoriety, was the President of the West Riding Ramblers Federation at the time, and a veritable fount of information on the tracks around the Washburn Valley area of the West Riding. In addition Alfred acknowledges the input of George Herbert Bridges Ward (1876-1957), a Labour Party politician, activist for walkers' rights, and the founder of the Sheffield Clarion Ramblers Club in 1900, and William Shaw, for their suggestions of some of the additional new routes contained in this combined volume.

This final combined book in the tramping trilogy received advanced notice for its publication from the local press in somewhat muted anticipation expressed by the formerly critical *Yorkshire Observer*:

> Another of the Country Life books in the Tramping Series entitled *Striding Through Yorkshire*, by A.J. Brown, is promised from early June. Mr. Brown is familiar to Yorkshire ramblers and explorers through his previous books. His new book covers the whole of Yorkshire in one volume and is much more than a guide book since his knowledge of the district includes matters of historic interest. His writing is in itself an incitement to tramp over the country. The book contains several maps.[33]

Later the *Yorkshire Evening Post* gave the book a much more supportive review, albeit somewhat tempered by the now familiar, local press critique of Alfred's style:

> Mr. Alfred J. Brown, the West Riding rambler who has added to the new literature of Yorkshire walks and walking with *Moorland Tramping [in West Yorkshire]* and *Tramping in Yorkshire [North and East]*, has brought the best of these two volumes together with additions in *Striding Through Yorkshire*.
>
> Mr. Brown is rather too determinedly hearty – about, say, a pint of ale – and he seems to have no word for motorists but road-hogs. In short, he wears

his studded boots a little self-consciously, but he knows all the man-sized walks in Yorkshire, and, along with his excellent maps, is a complete guide to the moors and the tops from Teesdale down to the Aire, and from the Pennines across to the Whitby moors and the coast.

The variety to be obtained in so much walking is enormous, and the book is an entertaining record of direct observation and personal experience as well as a guide through widely different country and moorland scenes. The book is as up-to-date as can be about rights of way and so on. It has a long list of inns that can be recommended, and has some interesting references to the Pennine Way which is now engaging the attention of the rambling brotherhood.[34]

However, the most comprehensive and certainly the most complimentary review of the book came from an even more locally-based press source, that of the somewhat parochial, but nevertheless knowledgeable, *Shipley Times*, which recognised the true value of the book to the growing band of tramping aficionados:

Striding Through Yorkshire contains the essence of Mr. Brown's two earlier books. *Moorland Tramping [in West Yorkshire]* and *Tramping in Yorkshire [North and East]*, both now out of print. It incorporates the delightful descriptive commentary that the made the earlier volumes so deservedly popular, with a good deal of new and carefully arranged data and some excellent and easy-to-follow maps.

In combining the two books, the chapters have been revised and rearranged and several new chapters as well as 'additional routes' have been inserted. In the Wharfedale and Washburn Valley area alone, about 50 new routes have been included. The book claims with considerable justice to embrace all Yorkshire and certainly all the wildest walking country in the three Ridings.

Mr. Brown has a breezy style of writing that is as refreshing as the country with which he is dealing. He is not content to indicate a path. He comments on it. He will turn from the unravelling of an intricate route to put in an aside on the merits of an inn that takes his fancy. He will leave the signposts to take care of themselves, while he writes of the wind and the heather and the rain that lashes the face like a flail. He will leave his woodland path for a moment to lean on a gate and chat with the oldest inhabitant. His book gains immensely from these vagaries. It is not only a guide book, but a volume for lovers of Yorkshire wherever they may be.

It is difficult to give an adequate idea of the scope of this compact little book which runs to nearly 400 pages and yet slips easily and comfortably into a jacket pocket. Mr. Brown deals in detail with the Dales of West Yorkshire, and has parts on York, the Ouse, the Vale of York, the Wolds Moors and Dales, the Yorkshire Coast and the Derwent Way to York. There are separate chapters on rights-of-way, inns and Youth Hostels, and a comprehensive index. There are 23 maps.[35]

Epilogue: The Yorkshire Tramping Trilogy

The trilogy was a very popular among walkers of the day and sales easily achieved the projected publishing targets that had been agreed at the outset for each of the three books. The publishers acknowledged that they could have sold many times over the initial print-run of *Striding Through Yorkshire*, although it was reprinted and revised in the 1943, 1945 and 1949 editions, and sold over 20,000 copies in total. So what went wrong? Perhaps the 'Big Slump' associated with the post 1933 'Great Depression' was partly to blame, since only limited supplies of raw materials such as paper were available and restricted further reprints even of this most successful edition. However this may not account for the book not achieving its full potential. Alfred had by now established himself as one of the leading writers of walking books on Yorkshire, alongside other more well-established topographical writers, but the competition for this specialised niche in the market was probably another factor in the limited sales.

Halliwell Sutcliffe, who was by then approaching the end of his writing career, had recently published his narrative historiography *The Striding Dales* in 1929,[36] one of a long line of popular books on Yorkshire life and times. William Riley, who was at the peak of his popularity, had likewise published his novel account of the open roads of the Yorkshire highlands *The Yorkshire Pennines of the North-West* in 1934,[37] and had also built up a huge following for his Yorkshire-based works. Then there was also a new cadre of writers who were beginning to enter the specialised walking book market, such as Donald Boyd who had published his walking guidebook account entitled *On Foot in Yorkshire* in 1932,[38] and followed this up with his co-author Patrick Monkhouse in a book *Walking in the Pennines* in 1937.[39]

Alfred meanwhile had demonstrated a unique, if an ill-timed ability to capture the essence of the free spirit of tramping, which had immediately drawn the attention of the new recruits to this form of walking and fired their enthusiasm to explore unknown landscapes. Unfortunately, much of this captive new audience would become recruits of another variety in the looming crises that would unfold towards the end of the

1930s, and would overshadow the leisure pursuits of many for the duration of yet another world conflict, the Second World War.

In retrospect however, Alfred's works probably helped lay the foundations for other popular writers on walking in Yorkshire for example Alfred Wainright[40,41] to explore this magnificent county and bring the area, as well as the activity of walking, into the realm of a popular leisure activity, which has seen a most remarkable resurgence in modern times. Furthermore, there is now a plethora of long distance pathways available to all walkers via the internet, which crisscross Yorkshire and incorporate many of the routes which Alfred embarked upon all those years ago.

Alternatively, for the traditionalist, who likes the feel of a book, it is still possible to obtain copies of each book in the Yorkshire Tramping Trilogy, especially if one is prepared to delve into the dark recesses of the now ever-shrinking numbers of second-hand book shops, or rummage through the piles of older books at country book fairs, and even search the internet for obscure sources of these once mighty tomes. The internet also provides a valuable source of 'out of print books' which are often available through the 'print to order' services of book dealers who supply new facsimile copies of the original texts. But once one of these rare treasures has been found or a new online copy obtained, the pleasure to be gained from it is not just in its possession, but in its use, since one will not get to know 'God's Own Country' by merely reading the book. Only by tramping off into the sunset on one's own feet, with the book in one's pocket, will one ever discover the forgotten joy of walking – a sentiment that Alfred would have wholeheartedly endorsed.

References and Notes

1. Alfred John Brown, *I Bought a Hotel*, Williams and Norgate Ltd., London, 1949, Chapter: 'Books and Authorship', Section III: 'Autobiographical', pp. 150-151.

2. Memorandum of Agreement, Country Life Ltd., London, 29th July 1931, AJB Literary Agreements File.

3. Personal communication: Mrs. R. Sturrup (née Brown).
   Note: the Brown children referred to William Littlewood affectionately as 'uncle'.

4. Alfred J. Brown, *Moorland Tramping in West Yorkshire*, Country Life Ltd. and George Newnes Ltd., London, 1931.

5. Ibid., Part One: 'Moorland Tramping', pp. 5-40.
   5a. Note: AJB's related article: 'The Sources of Rivers' was published in *The Yorkshire Post*, 20th August 1929.

6. Ibid., Part Two: 'The Dales', pp. 41-88.
   6a. Note: The term 'dale' is of Scandinavian origin 'dal' meaning valley and almost exclusively applied to Yorkshire, while the total number of all major and minor dales has been estimated at 562: *The Dalesman* Magazine, June 2008, p. 48.

7. Ibid., Part Three: 'Random Tramps and Adventures', pp. 89-182.
   7a. Note: A full account of AJB's 'Three Peaks' route was published in the *Yorkshire Post*, 10th May 1930, and the timetable was later published in the inaugural edition of *The Yorkshire Dalesman* Magazine, April 1939, p. 21.

8. Ibid., Appendix: 'Additional Routes from Dale to Dale' pp. 183-192.
   8a. Note: A full description of a route from 'Coverdale to Colsterdale' later appeared in *The Yorkshire Dalesman* Magazine, Vol. ii, April 1939, pp. 6-7.

9. St. Bede's School Magazine, Autumn, 1931, Vol. iv, No. 36, p. 86.

10. St. Bede's School Magazine, Spring, 1932, Vol. v, No. 38, p. 10.

11. *The Tablet*, Saturday, January 2, 1932, Vol. 159, No. 4782, p. 10, 'New Books and Music – To Buy or Borrow or Leave Alone'.

12. 'Moorland Tramping in Yorkshire: A Delightful Guide To The Moor Country', *Yorkshire Observer*, 17th November 1931.

13. Alfred J. Brown, *Tramping in Yorkshire – North and East*, Country Life Ltd., London, 1932.

14. Memorandum of Agreement, Country Life Ltd., 9th March 1932, AJB Literary Agreements File.

15. Alfred J. Brown op. cit., 'Acknowledgement'.
   15a. Note: A short extract and details of the broadcast series appeared in the St. Bede's School Magazine, Summer, 1932, Vol. v, No. 39, p. 129.

16. Ibid., Part One: 'York', pp. 1-13.

17. Ibid., Part Two: 'The Ouse', pp. 14-39.

18. Ibid., Part Three: 'The Vale of York', pp. 41-57.

19. Ibid., Part Four: 'The Wolds Way South', pp. 59-80.

20. Ibid., Part Five: 'The Wolds Way – North (1)', pp. 81-91.

21. Ibid., Part Six: 'The Way of the Wolds – North (2)', pp. 92-101.
    21a. **Note**: AJB was later credited with the term, if not the concept of the Wolds Way Walk by David Rubinstein: *The Wolds Way*, Dalesman Books, 1932, Introduction, p. 7.

22. Ibid., Part Seven: 'Over the Hills', pp.102-134.

23. Ibid., Part Eight: 'The Cleveland Hills', pp.135-158.

24. Ibid., Part Nine: 'The North East Moors and Dales', pp. 159-186.

25. Ibid., Part Ten: 'The Yorkshire Coast', pp. 187-197. .

26. Ibid., Part Eleven: 'The Derwent Way to York', pgs. 198-208.
    26a. **Note**: An account of the route: 'A.J. Brown's Derwent Way' was published by Malcolm Boyes and Hazel Chesters, *The Yorkshire Journal*, Issue No.1, Spring 2010, pp. 74-79.

27. Ibid., Appendix: 'Some Additional Routes and Suggestions', pp. 209-215.

28. 'Tramping in Yorkshire (North and East)', *Times Literary Supplement*, 28th July 1932.

29. 'Go To The Wolds', *Yorkshire Post*, 24th September 1932.

30. Alfred J. Brown, *Striding Through Yorkshire*, Country Life Ltd., London, 1938.

31. Ibid., 'Forward', p.2.

32. The 'Pub Walk' series of books of North, South and West Yorkshire, Countryside Books, Newbury, Berkshire.

33. 'New A.J. Brown Book', *Yorkshire Observer*, 22nd May 1938.

34. 'Rambling in Yorkshire', *Yorkshire Evening Post*, 3rd June 1938.

35. 'Striding Through Yorkshire, Mr. Alfred J. Brown's New Book', *Shipley Times*, 11th June 1938.

36. Halliwell Sutcliffe, *The Striding Dales*, Frederick Warne & Co., London, 1929.

37. William Riley, *The Yorkshire Pennines of the North-West*, Herbert Jenkins Ltd., London, 1934.

38. Donald Boyd, *On Foot in Yorkshire*, Alexander Maclehose & Co., London, 1932.

39. Donald Boyd and Patrick Monkhouse, *Walking in the Pennines*, Alexander Maclehose & Co., London, 1937.

40. Alfred Wainwright, *A Pennine Journey*, The story of a long distance walk made in 1938, Michael Joseph, London, 1986,

41. David and Helen Pitt Eds., *A Pennine Journey*, Fances Lincoln Ltd., London, 2004.

CHAPTER 8

Celebrations of Contemporary Civic and County Culture

It might be assumed that Alfred had devoted all of his attention to the time-consuming production of the 'Yorkshire Tramping Trilogy' in the early 1930s, but this was not the case. He was able to undertake concurrent forms of writing in spite of his busy work load, which included long spells of foreign travel and the ever-increasing demands of his growing family. Indeed, as on previous occasions, he also demonstrated a remarkable ability to change the direction of his literary work and deliver alternative material for the appreciation of different audiences, and this change of direction was manifested once more. When Alfred was called upon to make an important contribution to the greatest civic celebration since the award of Bradford's City Charter in 1847, namely that of a colourful spectacle in the history of Bradford, which was presented as the Pageant of Bradford in 1931, he readily responded.

The Bradford Pageant of 1931[1]

The Historical Pageant of Bradford of 1931 was an extravagant celebration of civic pride held during the week of Monday 13th to Saturday 18th July in Peel Park, the first public park opened in Bradford in 1852. It was named after Sir Robert Peel (1788-1850), the politician, Prime Minister and advocate of free trade, and was set in 56 acres of rolling landscape less than a mile from the city centre. The purpose of the Pageant was to remind the city's population of their great heritage, born of much sacrifice and labour, hence the city's motto: *Labor Omnia Vincit* (Work Conquers All), and also to inspire future generations with the enthusiasm of their forefathers in order to promote the continued evolution of the city at a time of considerable austerity and hardship. It was intended that the spectacular display would be a means of advertising and promoting the city in conjunction with the Imperial Wool Industries Fair, which was also being held in Bradford in July of that year.

These ambitious expressions of belief in business and society were only exceeded by the sheer size and scale of the event, which assumed truly monumental proportions, and occupied the attention of a legion of planners and producers for many months in preparation of a programme of activities to be performed by an even greater number of participants. An indication of the immensity of the Pageant can be gained from the fact that 30,000 people were involved altogether or 10% of the city's population, with 7,500 as actual Pageant performers, 16,000 in other types of displays, and 9,000 in various administrative, organisational and practical support activities. It was estimated that a majority of the city's almost 300,000 residents attended the events, with many more attracted from outside the city. Indeed, such was the strength of spirited public support that the Pageant was extended over a further three days, and many of the performers gave up part of their holidays to prolong the activities. It was perhaps more remarkable that given the vagaries of the English summer, with some of this open air Pageant spoiled a little by rain, this apparently did nothing to dampen the spirits of the performers and audiences alike. Undoubtedly, it also seems that much of the success was attributable to the organiser of the Pageant, Frank Lascelles (1895-1934), who had earned himself the epithet: 'the man who staged the Empire' for his imperial pageantry works throughout the British Empire, as well as many local Pageants in England during the period 1907-1932.[2]

Alfred's Role in the Pageant

The Pageant's Book of Words[3] told the story of Bradford's glory during six time periods, from Roman times through to the Industrial Revolution, and Alfred was one of six authors of the so-called 'Episodes' that portrayed significant periods in the city's history, including: Episode (i) 'The Coming of the Romans' by Herbert L. Wright, Episode (ii) 'Paulinus in Bradford Dale' by the Rev. E.A. Alban, Episode (iii) 'Bradford in Norman Times' by Phyllis Bentley, Episode (iv) 'Bradford in Plantagenet Times' by Phyllis Hambledon, Episode (v) 'Bradford in Stuart Times' by Alfred J. Brown and Episode (vi) 'Bradford in the Industrial Revolution' by Elizabeth Southwart. Each Episode had a large performing staff including adult principals, other supporting performers and children, and was under the management of a group of officials who carried out chairman, marshal, stage management, treasury, wardrobe, music and property organisation roles. Each management group was supported by a system of members' committees, which organised and integrated all the events of the Pageant.

Alfred's responsibility was to put together one of these six main historical sequences that represented a significant era during Bradford's history, specifically during the period of the First Civil War (1642-1646) and its aftermath. This included: Scene (i) The Battle of Adwalton Moor (1643), Scene (ii) The Second Siege of Bradford (1648),

24. *Episode Authors of the Bradford Pageant of 1931*

Scene (iii) The Bolling Hall Ghost and Scene (iv), Part (i) Entry of Cromwell into Bradford (1644) and Part (ii) The Return of The Monarchy (1662). In order to perform these scenes, Alfred had at his disposal some 450 adults and 80 children, many of whom were teachers and their school children, as well as local dramatic society members. In addition there were 50 horse infantry and foot soldiers, all fully replete in costumes of the period with simulated armaments of the times, all of which were manufactured by an army of volunteers who provided all the necessary props for each scene. It was perhaps the sheer number of performers involved, the wardrobe and weaponry authenticity, together with magnificent open scenery of the park, which no doubt gave the wondrous and appreciative audiences a true sense of reality of the performances that were so vividly portrayed in this and each of the other episodes of the Pageant.

However Alfred's role was not only in the script-writing for the production of the fifth Episode of the Pageant, since he, along with other well-known authors and poets, also made an important contribution to the literary contents of the Souvenir Book of the Pageant.[1] In his book a series of short articles and poetry were intended to capture some of the themes associated with Bradford and its local context in relation to the Pageant's main focus. A summary of these contributions included the following works: J.B. Priestley (1894-1984): 'Jess Oakroyd's Homecoming', Halliwell Sutcliffe (1870-1932): 'The Bolling Ghost: A Fantasy', William Riley (1866-1969): 'The Message of the Moors', Phyllis Bentley (1894-1977): 'One Night in Bradford: A True Story', Alfred J. Brown (1894-1969): 'Saturday Night in Town', Elizabeth Southwart (1874-1947): 'Heyday of the Handloom', Humbert Wolfe (1885-1940): 'Labor Omnia Vincit', James A. Mackereth (1872-1952): 'Pageantry' and Austin Priestman (1883-1953): 'The Brontë Sisters'.

'Saturday Night in Town' – Alfred's Appreciation of Bradford

This short abridged version of the article by Alfred in the Pageant Souvenir Book[1] was the only one to reflect on the simple attractions which Bradford had to offer its ordinary residents, who mostly viewed their own city through the narrowly-focused prism of their own neighbourhood. Other districts were perceived to be inhabited by 'strange' residents and consequently this was reflected by the idiosyncratic point of view held by many Bradfordians. Alfred suggested this apparent tendency for attachment to one's own neighbourhood and locally-held prejudices, which was almost 'clannish' in nature, was only broken down when individuals travelled abroad, and that only in these circumstances did it resemble anything like a true 'Bradford Brotherhood'. As an example of this tendency, he recounted a recent meeting in a remote Baltic town with a man speaking perfectly good German with a pronounced Bradford accent, whom he had not met before, even though he was in the same trade as Alfred, since he hailed from another 'foreign' district across the city. However they became instant friends and spent an enjoyable evening together talking 'Bradfordiana'.

While Alfred conceded that travel broadened the mind, he also recognised that it was not necessary to indulge in foreign travel to view such an old-fashioned provincial city as Bradford with any less regard than its continental counterparts. On the contrary, to Alfred the streets of Bradford seemed to be every bit as lively and amusing as any other streets in Europe, so that even after a surfeit of splendid sites in the capitals of Europe, he was only too delighted to see the familiar streets and lovely buildings of his home city. Even the rain did not dampen his enthusiasm for the old place.

On return from his lengthy continental travels, Alfred often stated that his only concern was that the 'Street Improvements Committee' might have pulled down more familiar landmarks, since he was quite satisfied with Bradford as it is – or as it was, and was often was dismayed to see it change before his very eyes. However, he took some solace in the fact that there was still enough left of old Bradford to make it different from any other city on earth, and that its crazy pattern of hilly streets in the centre of the city would defeat the attempts of even the cleverest modern architects to improve its appearance. Even the ubiquitous assembly of some 300 mill chimneys pouring out their black clouds of smoke would dazzle the stranger when seen from one of the many surrounding hilly vantage points of the city. Furthermore he suggested there were: 'few more enchanting night-scenes as that of Bradford viewed from a local hill-top on a winter's night, when all the bright lamps of the twisting streets make shining necklaces like earthy Pleiades, and electric trams glide up and down the dark hills like majestic galleons on turbulent seas'.

Nevertheless, it was on Saturday night in particular, especially rainy, wintry Saturday nights, when the streets were gleaming beneath the brilliant street arc-lamps and the shops were shining like radiant palaces that Alfred suggested was the best time to come down from the heights of the surrounding hills. It was at this time the streets were at their most interesting with crowds swarming to the theatres and 'pictures', parents laden with shopping trailing small children, the bustle of the General Market where crowds were often the thickest and appeared like a beleaguered city within a city. But for those who could not stand the crush, there was always an escape into a bookshop, or especially the City Library and the cloisteral calm of an upper reading room, where the recluse could retire from the roaring life outside. In Alfred's view there was as much drama in a library as in the seething streets, if only one could get behind the masks of the readers. Then when he had his fill of these Saturday night imaginary 'thrills', he proceeded into the rain-swept streets once more to find every-one hurrying home to bed in Bradford – while in Madrid folks would be just thinking about dinner, in Paris or Berlin the all-night shows had just begun, in Warsaw par-ty-goers would dance until morning: 'But all good Bradfordians are making for home like the sensible folk they are. And what can one do but follow the trail, marvelling at their virtues?'

Postscript to the Bradford Pageant

The Bradford Pageant finished with a memorable closing scene which produced a powerfully dramatic and symbolic finale to the whole event. When the last Episode of the evening came to an end, the large amphitheatre was cleared and suddenly filled with light. Then the cast of performers emerged from the shadows and moved slowly down the slopes to fill the arena once more. They all stood together to sing 'Land of Hope and Glory' and then raised their hands skywards to sing the hymn often sung on such festive occasions: 'O God Our Help in Ages Past'. Finally, as the first verse ended, they lowered their arms, turned and gradually retraced their steps, and allowed their voices to fade away as they moved back into the shadows of the night.

The Pageant had been an enormous success in which the city's educational and cultural resources, civic leaders and businessmen were brought together to produce remarkable results, which excited the imagination of the public at large and fulfilled many of the expectations of the organisers. This was in stark contrast to the subsequent attempt to stage a similar Pageant, held in conjunction with the civic exhibition to celebrate the centenary of the award of the City's Charter in 1947, which did not receive the same public support and, because it was poorly attended, the Corporation suffered a heavy financial loss. However, times had changed during the intervening period, and while the problems which had been faced by the local community in the early 1930s were no less daunting in the post World War Two era, the same community spirit, which had been present in the earlier days, had somehow disappeared, and with it the likelihood of ever staging another civic celebration of the same order of magnitude in the future. The Souvenir Book of the Bradford Pageant thus remains a unique historical document of this most memorable event.[1]

The Heaton Review

Alfred's involvement with the celebrations associated with the Bradford Pageant of 1931 was not the only literary activity he was engaged in during the early 1930s, since he was a also a regular contributor to the local press as well as to some other popular regional and national magazines and journals. He also made a few contributions to a local literary and arts initiative which, even though it had only modest beginnings, was to have a major cultural impact not only in Bradford, but throughout the County of Yorkshire, the rest of the country, and indeed the Empire and beyond – the journal *The Heaton Review*. This literary enterprise began as little more than a Parish Magazine in 1927, but flourished rapidly to become 'A Northern Miscellany of Arts and Literature' by 1932.[4] A subsequent editorial claimed that it achieved the status of an annual review: 'which speaks for Yorkshire and the North Country to readers throughout Great Britain and those living abroad.'[5] Indeed, it had by this time attracted a wide range of gifted writers, artists, poets, essayists and critical commentators of contemporary society, from both local and national talent available, to support these claims.[6]

The original 1927 *Heaton Review* was guided by its founding editor, Reverend Reginald Henry Britton Butler, a curate at St. Barnabas C. of E. Church in the Heaton suburb of Bradford. Butler had the altruistic vision for a journal to be more than just a traditional 'church magazine'. He wanted one that would re-establish the Church among a wider audience and stimulate the spirit of cooperation and tolerance in the public at large, in a rapidly changing society after the First World War. To establish such an ambitious journal, Butler had an editorial committee of ten members who were drawn mainly from the middle-classes that represented the residents of the district. In addition the senior Anglican Vicar of the Parish, Reverend Canon Richard Whincup, MC, MA (1874-1944), a distinguished and decorated World War One field chaplain, retained an ex-officio role and the right to scrutinise material submitted for publication and also to appoint the editor.

In 1929, the key role of editor passed to Mr. George Green Hopkinson, a local somewhat philanthropic businessman, who was largely responsible for the *Heaton Review*'s subsequent development into an even more ambitious journal of literature and the arts, although it continued to be published annually between 1927 and 1934. During this period it had only modest circulation figures of a few hundreds to a couple of thousand copies per issue, mainly to local readers, but also to significant numbers of expatriates abroad.[6] Moreover none of the distinguished contributors received payment for their work which helped keep the costs down, and any small profits supported the church funds so that it retained its philanthropic status.

The early editions of the journal were focused on local topics, general interest items along with a strong element of religious material, which were gradually reduced in later editions as the journal developed a primary literary and arts dimension to reach a wider readership. This expansion included contributors not only from locally-recognised talent, but also from regional and national literary and arts figures of eminence. Thus the *Heaton Review* now reflected its subtitle: 'A Northern Miscellany of Art and Literature', and was now aimed at the more discerning 'middlebrow' sector of the population. In just eight brief years the review not only promoted local literary and artistic endeavours, it established the status of 'Northern', or more rightly 'Yorkshire' contemporary culture, class and county identity firmly within the national awareness of developments outside London.[7]

The *Heaton Review*'s self-proclaimed identity as a miscellany of high quality literary and artistic production was exemplified by an impressive catalogue of contributors, all of whom gave their time and effort freely to help achieve the ambitious ideals to which the journal had aspired.

Among the notable essayists and 'general interest' contributors were: Sir Michael Sadler (1861-1943), the Barnsley-born former Vice Chancellor of Leeds University and Master of University College, Oxford, Professor Edward Victor Appleton (1892-1975), the Bradford-born scientist and later Nobel Prize winner for Physics in 1947, Sir Neville Cardus (1889-1975), the renowned cricket commentator, journalist and author, Sir Eugene Ramsden (1883-1955) the Gomersal-born Conservative Politician, Geoffrey Woledge (1901-1998), the pioneer of Librarian Management Practice and Amy Mollison (née Johnson, 1903-1941), the pioneering woman aviator, who was tragically killed on active duty with the Air Transport Auxiliary Service in World War Two.

Leading writer contributors to the *Heaton Review* included: John Galsworthy (1867-1933), Hugh Walpole (1884-1941), who together with John Galsworthy, held the post of President of the Bradford English Society for a time, Gilbert Keith Chesterton (1874-1936), John Boynton Priestley (1894-1984), George Bernard Shaw (1856-1950), Sir Herbert Read DSO, MC (1893-1968), Julian Huxley (1887-1975), Dorothy Una Ratcliffe (1887-1967), Phyllis Bentley (1894-1977), Phyllis Hambledon (1892-1976), Malachi Whitaker (Margaret Olive Taylor, 1895-1976), Winifred Holtby (1892-1935), Margaret Storm Jameson (1891-1986), William Riley (1866-1961) and Oliver Onions (1871-1961).

There were also two distinct groups of artist contributors to the *Heaton Review*, 'well-established' artists included: Sir William Rothenstein (1872-1945), Jacob Kramer (1892-1962), Augustus John (1978-1961) and Fred Lawson (1888-1968) and those deemed 'new generation' artists at the time. These included: Henry Moore (1896-1986), Edna Ginesi (1902-2000), who was married to Raymond Coxon (1896-1997), Philip Naviasky (1894-1983) and Roland Pitchforth (1895-1962).

Finally, those well-established poets who also contributed to the *Heaton Review* included: Rabindranath Tagore (1861-1941), who had won the Nobel Prize for Literature in 1913, Humbert Wolfe (1885-1940), Wilfrid Childe (1890-1980), Alberta Vickridge (1890-1963), James A. Mackereth, (1872-1952), and Wilfrid Gibson (1878-1962). Other less well-known poets included: William Kerr, J. Malham-Dumbleby, Tom Turner, Harriet Raspin, Marguerite Buisson, Francis Watson, Henry Ainley, Hilda Brierley and Alfred John Brown.

Alfred's Contributions to the Heaton Review

Alfred was one of the few contributors to the journal who had little exposure of his poetry to expert criticism, so it seemed surprising that four of the five contributions which he made were poems that he had written during his early writing career. Nevertheless it is perhaps a measure of the quality of these four poems that they were accepted. His remaining contribution was a short story, a piece of prose of the type that he often submitted to popular journals at the time.

The first poem Alfred had published in the *Heaton Review*, entitled: 'Old Raggalds' Inn', was a ballad-like set of six verses which acknowledged the well-known attributes of this old institution.[8] The Raggalds, near Queensbury, whose name was derived from the Old Norse term *'raggald'* meaning a villain or ruffian, was very familiar to Alfred. He had often passed it during his youthful explorations with his best friend George Heseltine on their early tramps to the 'Brontë Country', and it was also a stopping-off point for Alfred during his post World War One recuperative walks around Bradford. But this was not the first time the poem had been published, since it appeared as one of the many verses and songs which were contained in Alfred's previous book *Four Boon Fellows*.[9]

OLD RAGGALDS' INN

Now, here's to the Inn with the rollicking name
And the stiffest of Sack and the fattest of game,
O here's to the Inn that is hoary with fame -
Old Raggalds'! Old Raggalds'!

And where be this Inn and O where can it stand?
Why it stands on my moors and its Stingo is grand;
For it clings to the heart like a clasp of the hand -
At Raggalds'! Old Raggalds'!

You can't see the ceiling; it's one mighty flitch,
And the oak's from the bog and it's blacker than pitch;
And the cellars are deep and the barrels full rich -
At Raggalds'! Old Raggalds'!

And who be the landlord: be he jocund or wroth?
And be he a rascal, or scoundrel, or both?
Why Coggan's a man that will keep to his troth -
Old Coggans! Of Raggalds'!

Then fill up the glasses and give us a toast
In season and reason without any boast.
"Oh I'll give you the toast," quoth the jovial host -
" 'Tis Raggalds'! Old Raggalds'!"

So here's to the Inn with the rollicking name,
And the stiffest of Sack and the fattest of game,
O here's to the Inn that is hoary with fame -
Old Raggalds'! Old Raggalds'!

In the poem Alfred celebrates the old name of the familiar moorland roadside inn, which has a reputation for its comfort, fine food and strong ales. He also pays tribute to the current innkeeper who, unlike his predecessors, can be trusted to deliver the services and hospitality for which it is famous. In the Review, the poem is also illustrated by three finely-dressed, old Victorian gentlemen, seen enjoying smoking their long clay pipes while engaged in friendly conversation, but with no evidence of any drinks being consumed. The sketch is by a little-known artist, R. James Williams, who may have been employed as an illustrator by the printers and publishers of the *Heaton Review*.

Alfred also had a second contribution to the *Heaton Review* in the same edition of the journal entitled 'November Apples',[10] which was a four verse celebration of the types of apples that are on sale in the fruit and vegetable market in Bradford, and describes apple varieties from the major apple growing areas of the country including: Baldwins (Somerset), Jonathans (Kent), Snows (a hardy northern variety), Permains (Worcestershire), Russets (Sussex), Keswicks (Cumberland) and Cox's Pips (Buckinghamshire). The poem was probably written when Alfred was convalescing from his illness during WW1 and perhaps recalls his first job working in the fruit and vegetable market in Bradford before the war. However this was not the first time that the poem had appeared in print, since it was published in the St. Bede's School Magazine in 1923.[11] But it was the first time that Alfred's artist friend William Littlewood had illustrated any of Alfred's poems with sketches of a busy market stall and customers, a barrel and basket of apples and a traditional scene of apple-picking.

It was interesting that the 1932 edition of the *Heaton Review* also contained a series of a short reviews about the life and works of 'Yorkshire Authors' by a member of the editorial team,[12] which no doubt helped to promote the work of the writers featured, and fulfilled one of the aims of the journal. Each review provides an appreciation of the recently-published works of six authors including: Marjorie Astin, Alfred J. Brown,

Rutherford Crockett, Winifred Holtby, Beverley Nichols, and Alberta Vickridge, most of whom made contributions to the *Heaton Review* during its short lifetime.

NOVEMBER APPLES

Now apples bloom on every stall,
This is no month of gloom at all!

Buxom Baldwins in fours and fives,
Gay as gossiping farmers' wives;
Jostle now cheek by jowl, perchance
With plump and jovial Jonathans.

And modest Snows of aspect meek
Fairly freak'd like a maiden's cheek,
With Permains stand in pyramid piles,
Rosily shining and wreath'd in smiles!

Superior Russets of gorgeous hue
Deign now to nod and wink at you;
Rollicking Keswicks with bulging hips
Are nudging the sides of Cox's Pips.

Here is a choice of England's bounties,
Apples from half a score of counties.
Shining and laughing on every stall;
This is no month for gloom at all!

In the following year's edition of the *Heaton Review*, Alfred also contributed two further poems, the first entitled: 'These Fields',[13] which appeared to have been written specifically for the journal, since there is no record of publication previously, nor was it among the poems from the journals which Alfred had written during 1917 and 1918. Furthermore, it is unusual since the poem is unlike any he had written before, and focuses upon an appreciation of the natural world of fields, farm animals and trees, features that are largely excluded from his previously published and unpublished poems. The impetus for this piece may have come from the rural location of Alfred's 'Wharfegate' home with fields nearby that were part of an active pastoral farming community on the edge of Burley-in-Wharfedale. This poem, like others in the Review, was illustrated by William Littlewood with accompanying sketches of a rural scene and farm animals also depicted.

THESE FIELDS

These fields:
These still, green English fields, I love,
And the quiet river,

And the dim lark above,

Winging and singing:

Scornful of praise, and the dull ways of earth,

Sharing with angels his music and mirth.

And cows –

That scarcely move,

But browse

Daylong, dew-lapped in the lush meadow grass,

Stolid: unheeding, stubbornly feeding,

Though the world pass.

Horses at evening

When the day closes,

Neighing and whinnying

Through high-lifted noses...

These trees:

These great, green English trees, I love,

This oak, beech, ash, and thorn

Standing solemnly in the grove,

As they have stood since my forbears were born.

Alfred's final poetry contribution to the *Heaton Review* was a celebration of the attributes of his home town and was simply entitled 'Bradford',[14] although it appeared earlier entitled 'This Town' in the St. Bede's School Magazine.[15] However the earlier version of the poem has been modified by the addition of some slightly different verses, but it continues to represent a spirited defence of the beloved city of Alfred's birth in the face of some criticism which it had received by those who were less than enamoured by its image and the impression which it presents to visitors. It may have been revived by Alfred as a riposte to some of the earlier criticism by J.B. Priestley in this same journal, that portrays the city as 'a dark ugly place where you can take a three-penny tram to Arcadia',[16] which suggests the town's only merit was that one could easily escape from the gloomy place to the surrounding pleasant countryside. It was just the sort of back-handed compliment for which he had become notoriously despised by many of Bradford's resident loyal population, and was one of the reasons why the London-based, 'expat' writer had been refused his 'Freedom of the City' status until very late in his life.

Alfred on the other hand, who never received any accolade from his home city, always retained a love of Bradford and a deep affection for its people. This was expressed in his Bradford poem that in style is similar to his prose in terms of a broader topographical nuance in his writing. The geography of the city's landscape is reflected by its streets which follow the undulations of topographical features. He suggests that the locality has been transformed from a rural pastoral setting to an urban industrial one that has produced the city's wealth, although the wool that was once derived locally is now supplied globally to provide the raw material. Indeed it was once said that all the sheep in the UK could not supply the wool needed to keep the looms of Bradford's mills busy even for one day.

BRADFORD

I have heard men speak ill of this town,
   this neighbourly town
   with its crazy old streets

   that go uP
   and as suddenly down

This town with its mansions and mills
   not like Rome on *seven* hills
   but on hundreds of hillocks that climb
   by yards at a time

   With dizzy street freaks

   Pursuing the peaks

This town that is chock-a-blockful
   of the world's finest wool
though you won't see a sheep
   or a frisky lamb leap—
with nice civic pride—
   as they creep side by side
past the warehouse walls,
   But a million bales
   will be wagging their tails
   when a customer calls!

This town with its Fine Lady Row
   (where the dawn-sirens blow!)
its A l d e r m a n b u r y
   (not found in a hurry!)

   its Tumbling Hill Street

(where the lambs used to bleat)
its Tennysons, Brownings, street-poets galore
big Pots by the score!
   What could one want more?

This town that is wash'd by a stream
which—for modesty's sake—
we hide: lest its pellucid gleam
should make pilgrims mistake—
it—for Tiber in teem!

This town with its crowds and its cherubs!
   some call them street-arabs!
     sweet arabs!

If I were a millionaire
with a flair
for the fame—
of philanthropist's name:
I would go
when the lamps
are aglow

   uP and down

   Ivegate
on Saturday night
scattering largesse
to each pinch't-faced mite
And bring them delight
with a marvellous toy
and a bathbun to bite.
That were paradise quite!

And still men speak ill of this town
   This friendly old town!

With its seven hundred hills
its mansions and mills,
its crystalline rills,
its frocks and its frills,
its tatters and drills,
its vanishing valley
its shipless Ship Alley
its crowds and its cherubs
and laughing street arabs . . .

How *dare* they speak ill of this town!

Furthermore on the subject of the city's quaint streets, Alfred comments that while some may be relatively obscure and others reflect their former pastoral glory, even the finest streets echo to the sounds of an industry that pervades the whole place. Alternatively some have the appealing quality of being named after famous poetical characters which had even given rise to the quirky naming of one district in the eastern suburb of Undercliffe as 'Poets Corner'. In fact in this area there were nine famous poets identified on the Bradford street map of this period.

However Alfred admits that other features of the city are not so endearing, such as the infamously polluted Bradford Beck, or '*T'mucky Beck*' as it was known, which collected, but could hardly cope with, the run-off from the many streams that drain the vast natural bowl-like depression in which Bradford is located. This watercourse flows northwards along the valley containing the major transport links of road, rail and the former canal, and the only level route out of the city which was vital to its economy.

Alternatively Alfred turns his attention to another more pleasing aspect of the city, namely its residents. In this regard he especially finds the appeal of the street-children bring out the sentimental side of his character and stimulate an urge to reward these urchins for their attempts to hustle crowds of adults on their nights out. Then in a final flurry Alfred provides a lyrical litany of some candid qualities of the city which are served up as a rhythmical rhyming riposte to those who dare to decry his beloved Bradford.

Alfred's only prose contribution to the *Heaton Review* was a short story entitled 'Toyland',[17] which tells the story of the gift of a rocking-horse to his daughter and the resultant effect the new toy has on the little girl as well as himself, together with the impact that toys can have of on the family home, and the importance of toys for children. Alfred's young daughter Barbara has been given a monster-sized rocking horse which is big enough for him to sit on. Naturally she is afraid of the large creature but gradually warms to it, gives it pet names and even sits on it when held securely in place as it is rocked. But Alfred admits that he is slightly envious of his daughter's good fortune since he never had a rocking horse and only 'rode' on one that belonged to a friend. He also recalls that at the time he believed the horse to be 'alive', not in the sense of a pet, but in an imaginative way, and even reminisces about his horse experiences of World War One when he had 'ridden far fiercer steeds – but never with the same raptures I felt for that wild, wooden mare of long ago.'

Alfred also reflects on how children's toys, like pets, become part of an extended family and characterise the home by confirming the presence of children in an otherwise adult world. He suggests that they create a new dimension to a household that is often lacking in childless couples' homes or those parents too house-proud to allow their unfettered presence. He also contends that 'Toyland' is not only part of the real world for children but an equally important part of their imaginary world that allows their creative imagination to come to the fore. Thus Alfred's short story of 'Toyland' perhaps emphasises the importance that his young family has assumed in his life, which until this point has been dominated by adult matters.

Alfred's last contributions to the *Heaton Review* were in 1933,[13,14] and the following year this once prestigious journal came to the end of its short but very productive life, for unknown reasons, and was not replaced by a similar publication. In a detailed review of the journal,[6] it was suggested that it was very much a product of the culture, class and sense of purpose of Yorkshire portrayed during the inter-war years, and as such, therefore, it may have come to a natural ending with the rapidly-changing structure of society and reading interests in this period. It has also been suggested that there were attempts to launch another similar literary magazine called 'The North Country' in 1936, by one of the most regular contributors to the *Heaton Review*, Dorothy Una Ratcliffe,[6] but this never came to fruition, although a number of other regular contributors to the *Heaton Review*, including Alfred, found an outlet for some of their future work in *The Yorkshire Dalesman* which was established in 1939. This magazine was a more commercially-oriented, topical publication which was purposely aimed at a much wider, primarily Yorkshire, readership, and did not set out to be a narrowly-focused literary and arts journal. Nevertheless it tapped into a new readership market which still exists today and became one of the most successful regional magazines of its time. What is clear is that the *Heaton Review* stimulated an awareness and interest in Yorkshire Literature and its many accomplished writers, and this was evident by an event which brought together many of the best exponents of twentieth-century Yorkshire literature: the Yorkshire Authors' Dinner.

A Celebration of Yorkshire in Literature:
The Yorkshire Authors' Dinner 1938

On Saturday 8th October 1938, the first Yorkshire Authors' Dinner was held in Leeds, but precisely how this event came about remains unclear. It may have been due to a collective initiative by a number of vested-interest organisations such as the Yorkshire Branch of the 'PEN' Club of the UK, the Association of Yorkshire Bookmen, The Leeds 'Savage' Club of writers and artists, the Bradford English Society, along with support from publishers and the local press and radio. Whatever the origin, the context of this glorious event was probably best described by Alfred when he writes about

'Yorkshire in Literature' in which he declares:

> Anyone wishing to make a pilgrimage to the birthplaces of twentieth
> century Yorkshire authors, and to their particular county, will have no lack
> of choice. At a Yorkshire Authors' Dinner held in Leeds in 1938, about
> one hundred writers accepted invitations, and about as many more sent
> apologies for absence. A mere list of names is impressive evidence that
> Yorkshire is still most fruitful literary soil, for many of these writers have
> made international reputations.[18]

The event had a specific Yorkshire orientation, since it was held at the Great Northern
Hotel in Leeds, one of the large railway hotels of the era, and was attended by 113
guests,[19] probably the greatest congregation of Yorkshire writers assembled at the
time, and certainly since then.[20] The menu was distinctly Yorkshire in flavour, and
several classic dishes famed throughout the county and beyond were offered, especially Yorkshire Pudding, served traditionally as a separate course, of course![20] Even
the table decorations had been specially chosen to represent the county. Two of its
distinguished authors, Phyllis Bentley and Lettice Cooper, had picked arms-full of
heather from the hillsides around Middlesmoor, near Ramsgill, up-dale from Pateley
Bridge in Nidderdale,[21] to which were added white roses, the emblematic flower of
the county. Finally the design motif on the guest list consisted of a writer's quill pen
overlaid by a white rose.

The list of toasts made at the dinner was also interesting,[20] in which the order
of precedence was naturally to 'The King' (George VI), followed by the evening
chairman's introduction made by J.B. Priestley, then toasts to 'Literature' (presumably Yorkshire literature) proposed by Sir Herbert Read, Lettice Cooper and Roger
Dataller, with a reply by Humbert Wolfe. Then followed toasts to 'Yorkshire' proposed
by Margaret Storm Jameson, James Keighley Snowden and Sir Edward Bairstow, with
the final reply by Phyllis Bentley. While there is no record of the content of these
toasts and replies, it is likely that they formed the major part of the evening's proceedings, although it was unlikely that any awards were conferred on any of the guests present, since the occasion was essentially a celebration of the contributions to Yorkshire
literature made by the collective efforts of all those in attendance at the dinner.

The guest list for the evening remains a testament to the widespread talent of
Yorkshire writers that was prevalent both locally and nationally at the time. Even
though only slightly more than half of the 182 writers listed alphabetically on the
programme were actually present at the dinner, the event was a resounding success.

Yorkshire Authors' Dinner

John Redwood Anderson
W. L. Andrews
Lorna Armistead
E. C. Bairstow
Nigel Balchin
William Barrow
Dorothy Bartlam
Margaret Bauman
Phyllis Bentley
S. E. J. Best
J. Fairfax Blakeborough
Florence Bone
E. C. Booth
Joseph Boothroyd
Dennis Botterill
Gordon Bottomley
Benjamin Bowker
M. M. Brash
Bernard Brett
Alfred Brown
Elizabeth Burgoyne
Montague Burton
Barbara Callow
F. Brunton Carmichael
F. A. Carter
Wilfrid Childe
J. M. Clark
G. N. Clark
E. Kitson Clark
George Kitson Clark
Ina Kitson Clark
Mary Kitson Clark
Arthur Coe
Percival Hale Cook
Barbara Cooper
Leonard Cooper
Lettice Cooper
Dorothy Crisp
Rutherford Crockett
Lydia Crowe
W. B. Crump
Roger Dataller
Geoffrey Dennis
I. W. Dicks
Ebeneezer Downing
Alfred Dunning
Watson Dyke
James Eaton
Caroline Eccles
C. Mabel Edgerley
W. Thompson Elliott
G. Bramwell Evans
Carl Fallas
L. F. Feaver
A. Fieldhouse
Margaret Fox
Shamus Fraser
Percy Frudd
David Garnett
Eleanor Gaukroger
H. L. Gee

M. A. Gibb
R. H. Goodyear
Edward Green
Russell Green
T. Green
G. R. A. Greenwood
J. R. Gregson
Ronald Gurner
Alan Hadfield
Eleanor Dunbar Hall
Wilfrid Halliday
Phyllis Hambledon
George Hardwick
Oswald Harland
T. W. Harrison
Marie Hartley
H. W. Harwood
Gordon Heller
Rayner Heppenstall
G. S. Heseltine
Robert Hield
Norman Hillas
John Hind
Rose Marie Hodgson
George Holroyd
William Holt
J. M. Hopper
Maurice A. Horspool
F. Austin Hyde
Cutcliffe Hyne
George Jackson
Ernest Jacob
Naomi Jacob
Muriel Jaeger
Storm Jameson
Phyllis Kelway
Frank King
C. H. Kitson
Clifford Lees
F. L. Lucas
James Mackreth
Arthur Mann
John Marsh
Sidney Matthewman
Alfred Mattison
Mary McClure
Humphrey Metcalfe
William Moffat
Doris Langley Moore
June Moore
Sidney Moorhouse
F. J. Morris
G. F. Morton
Maboth Moseley
James Mosey
John Walker Myers
Kathleen Nesbit
Ben Norton
John O'Connor
Oliver Onions
J. W. Parratt

R. W. Parsons
Diana Patrick
Ronald Peacock
Frederic Peaker
John Percival
Alan Peters
Ernest Phillips
W. Carter Platts
Ella Pontefract
H. E. Priestley
J. B. Priestley
V. S. Pritchett
C. B. Pulman
Nancy Quennell
Bertrand Ratcliffe
Dorothy Una Ratcliffe
Herbert Read
Kathlyn Rhodes
W. Riley
John Rothenstein
William Rothenstein
Michael Sadlier
Guy Schofield
Percy Scholes
R. C. Sheldon
Edward Shillito
Edith Sitwell
Osbert Sitwell
Sacheverel Sitwell
Naomi Royde Smith
Keighley Snowden
Elizabeth Southwart
Gordon Stowell
W. Stanley Sykes
G. Taylor
A. A. Thompson
Leonora Thornber
Dorothy Tinker
Leonard Townsend
Walter Townsend
Ben Turner
Tom Turner
Mary Tyreman
Alberta Vickridge
B. Wade
G. Wade
Leo Walmsley
S. H. Waters
Francis Watson
D. E. Webb
E. V. Westwood
Frank Whitaker
Malachi Whitaker
Winifred Williams
Cecilia Willoughby
Humbert Wolfe
Walter Wood
Winifred Woodcock
Catherine Wright
Ammon Wrigley

GREAT NORTHERN HOTEL, LEEDS

on Saturday, 8th October :: 1938

It is also interesting is to compare that list with the other detailed list of Yorkshire authors that Alfred documents in his later book *Broad Acres* (1948),[18] in which there are 205 authors identified. Mysteriously, though, he leaves his own name from this list, although he did include his cousin Laurence Geoghegan and his friend George C. Heseltine. This personal exclusion may have been a measure of the modesty of the man in not including his own name among such an exalted group of writers, although perhaps by way of substitution he did include his name-sake Howard B. Browne (1875-1960) the Headmaster of Morley Grammar School and a locally well-known writer on Yorkshire. Another relatively unsung writer and promoter of literary activity, the Reverend Monsignor John O'Connor, of G.K. Chesterton's 'Father Brown' fame, is also rightly included in both lists.

In summary of his own Yorkshire authors list, Alfred does not claim it to be comprehensive, and he thus apologises to anyone whom he inadvertently omits from it, and comments that even the largest banqueting hall in one of the largest hotels in Leeds was not big enough to hold them all.[18] He also raises the interesting questions of why Bradford, for example, has been so prolific in terms of literary and artistic talents. Is it true he asks that Leeds, Halifax, Keighley, Sheffield, York and Hull have contributed their quota, but no other Yorkshire city could boast such a galaxy of distinguished writers and artists as Bradford? He acknowledges that while some of its gifted writers and artists were of foreign descent, they were all born and bred near Bradford and have spent most of their impressionable years in that industrial city, so that most of these brilliant men and women are as Yorkshire as the surrounding hills and dales. Perhaps only they could explain it, but whatever it was, the question remained unanswered then as it does today.

A Yorkshire Advocacy: Another Tyke 'Went Up To Cambridge'

It may seem unusual for someone like Alfred, who had left school not having matriculated, to attend such a prestigious institution as Cambridge University, but it happened, although not under the usual circumstances of 'going up to Cambridge'. Instead, Alfred was invited to attend a meeting of the 'Cambridge University Yorkshire Society', as the guest speaker at one of its early meetings, following the foundation of the Society by William Cowley (1913-1994) and a group of undergraduate Yorkshire exiles who had banded together to honour their County of origin. Due to a confusion of dates, Alfred had missed the first meeting of the Society, which included a 'Bump Supper' (a riotous celebration by a college of the type normally associated with rowing events) and bonfire, not to mention lashings of good old Ramsden's Yorkshire ale.

He therefore duly responded to a subsequent invitation in order to provide the inaugural lecture to the Society on Friday, 6th March 1936.

Alfred 'On Yorkshire'

The 'lecture' really was more of an informal 'after-dinner' address to the gathered assembly, and it covered a widespread range of topics related to the theme appropriately entitled: 'On Yorkshire'. It was delivered in a decidedly jocular, sometimes satirical fashion, with much anecdotal reference to the main theme, as well as abstracts of Yorkshire verse written by Alfred in his recently-published works, but it also included more serious matters related to the image and status of 'God's Own Country'. The notes of Alfred's address are recorded in a 48-page, type-scripted document, which also contains some of his penciled 'prompts' in the margins.[22]

25. Alfred J. Brown with A.A. Dent and Bill Cowley (left to right) at Cambridge in 1936

Alfred begins his address to 'Friends, Yokels and Gentlemen' firstly with an apology for having rushed to attend the meeting such that he had not yet had time to find his feet in such a rarified academic atmosphere, before congratulating the organisers of the event for their endeavours, with the hope that the new Society will be a roaring success in the future. He then reflects upon the fact that the world is in such a sad mess at the time, with the Spanish Civil War, the Abyssinian crisis, the rise of Hitler's Third

Reich and the 'Slump' in world trade all standing between the country and the abyss. It therefore seems to him that the more Yorkshire Societies and Yorkshire members, the sooner the country would regain its sanity and a strong foreign policy that will make the rest of England a land fit for Yorkshiremen to live in again. Moreover, he welcomes the possibility of the proposed formation of a 'Yorkshire Dales Folk Society' – a Society for the promotion of Yorkshire Folklore – and suggests: 'the League of Nations is all very well in its own way, but a League of Yorkshiremen is far more likely to restore the peace and goodwill among men'.

At this point Alfred explores the influence of a 'foreign air' whereby he has doubts that a 'Yorkshire Society' can flourish so far south as Cambridge, but he is comforted by the fact that even in London a great 'Society of Yorkshiremen' has contrived to exist, and indeed this appears to continue to flourish in spite of the 'air'. Thus the co-founder and first Chairman of the 'Society of Yorkshiremen in London', Sir Richard Robinson (1849-1928), has been convinced of the fundamental principle that, wherever two Yorkshiremen are gathered together, there is a 'Yorkshire Society' – the only essential condition is Yorkshire birth – and given that distinction, all Yorkshiremen are brothers, and are proud to recognise each other, even in the close confined formality of railway carriages, after of course, the usual protracted period of suitable scrutiny. In such proscribed circumstances though, Alfred says he is always glad to break the potential impasse with the dialect phrase: '*Ezn'tonnyonyironnyeron*' (isn't any of you here on your own?), after which it is only necessary to mention some obscure out-of-the-way place in the County, to stimulate a miraculous effect whereby: 'babel has broken loose and before many minutes have passed we have been fratching furiously in defence of our own pet village or inn'. He then concedes that this seemingly fierce rivalry between people often from the different Ridings is merely a superficial thing, and that the further away from the County they were, these fevered differences are forgotten, and the only thing that matters is Yorkshire.

Since his commercial travels take him the length and breadth of Europe, he notes that he is not only in a position to comment on the proliferation of 'Tykes' in the most remote corners of these lands, but also feels able to comment on their preferences for their own 'Nappy Ale'. In this regard he recalls one of the characters to whom he had made reference in his book *Four Boon Fellows*, with the marvellous Ode 'In Praise of Yorkshire Ale',[23] which recounts the many places that he has visited, and the wines and liquors he has consumed. He says that nowhere has he found the equal to the aforementioned brew. Then Alfred recites suitable extracts from the poem to substantiate the claim, and comments that unfortunately the parity in quality of Yorkshire's noble ale is not matched by samples he has imbibed in southern England while tramping in Sussex. Here the ale appears to him flatter than the scenery, to the extent that he is driven to describe his distaste for it in his rhyme: 'The Malediction of the Wharfe', [24] parts of which he also recites to convince his audience of the veracity of his claim. But, after all he is preaching to the converted!

In a return to his main theme once more, Alfred propounds Yorkshire's superiority over all the other counties in the country, in which the County could be considered:

> One vast homogenous whole: a great sprawling County, or (even) a great nation on its own, populated by a unique race of men called Yorkshiremen... a race to be feared and admired, but especially to be feared whether it be on the battlefield, the cricket field, the rugby field or the field of politics – particularly the field of politics... a County in short, that towers over all counties of England, and in a further apposite analogy: the three Whernsides seem to typify Yorkshiremen best – just as there is a Little Whernside, a Whernside and a Great Whernside, so there are also little Yorkshiremen, Yorkshiremen and Great Yorkshiremen; and even the little Yorkshiremen are as giants among the pigmies over the border.

Furthermore, Alfred proposes that the character of its inhabitants has changed little over hundreds of years, especially during times of conflict, so that whenever tyranny has threatened, Yorkshiremen are up in arms and excel each other in the defence of their County. This is evident, he suggests, by the number of castles which have never been conquered, the extent of the county which has never been altered by others, the foreign chieftains who have been laid to rest, and the number of their own 'Ancients' who have apparently lived on through these conflicts. Moreover he points out that:

> when the Old Squires sallied out to war, the yeomen went with them. Each crisis called forth a man, Fairfax in the Civil Wars, Clifford in the Scottish Rebellion, Norton in the Rising of the North – and always a Metcalfe in the vanguard of the fight...

Alfred then sums up the attributes of the Yorkshire character with which many others concur:

> And through all this, Yorkshire folk have remained what they always were, grimly determined, obstinate, steadfast, shrewd, level-headed, witty and wise... and withal kindly and hospitable. If they turn their attention to money (as they do in the industrial West Riding), they make money – hand over

fist, though they never admit to it. If they cultivate the land, they stick to it until they have beaten it. If they go in for politics they make considerable noise. If they rove the seas like Captain Cook, they leave an imperishable name. You can take any profession you please and you find a Yorkshireman near the top of the list... a Bentley *[1662-1742, Classical Scholar]*, a Wright *[1855-1932, Philologist]* a Marvell *[1621-1678, Poet]*, a Snowden *[1864-1937, Politician and Pacifist]*, an Asquith *[1852-1928, Prime Minister]* and so on. But underneath all this struggle and fret, lies their intense love of the homeland and of kith and kin which is expressed so persistently by the dialect poets. And coupled with this love of home is a tenderness, a pathos and a humour.

He also provides examples of some of these attributes, and recites extracts from the poems *'T'First o't'Sooart'*, by the Halifax poet John Hartley (1839-1915), and *'Owd Moxy'* and *'Ah nivver can call her mi wife'*, by the so-called 'Burns of Bradford Dialect' poet Ben Preston (1819-1902).

However, even though Alfred lauds the many admirable qualities possessed by his Yorkshire kinsmen, he admits that there is one rather less-endearing trait that they almost all universally display, which is summed up by the old adage: 'You can always tell a Yorkshireman, but you can't tell him much!' He exemplifies this by the reactions which are often generated by some of his public broadcasting activities, whereby he has tried to convince his fellow Yorkshiremen that he has something worthwhile to say about matters relating to Yorkshire. Typically, following his series of radio broadcasts about 'Unknown Yorkshire' on the BBC Northern Service from Leeds in the early 1930s, he received letters of complaint from members of the Yorkshire listening public because he fails to mention 'this or that', or has not described some obscure hamlet, church or inn. Even the mention of the word 'beer' has resulted in his receipt of a pamphlet by the 'British Society for the Prevention of Inebriety' by one irate listener! Undaunted, Alfred still proclaims that, thirst apart, the inn is an 'Open Sesame' source to village life, where he often gets a fund of local gossip and information while toying with a tankard of ale. He has also developed a personal philosophy in dealing with this undeniable, but indefensible Yorkshire trait of being resistant to any knowledge being imparted by others, and states:

I have long since ceased to convince any Yorkshireman that I know anything at all about Yorkshire when talking to him, and when I see the customary gleam in his eye, I know that he is not even listening; he is only waiting for me to stop so that he can start and tell me of some place he knows better – or that I don't know anything at all.

Obviously, while Alfred does not hold his present audience in such contemptibly low esteem, he comes to the conclusion that they would nevertheless realise the impossibility of his attempt to talk about Yorkshire comprehensively in the short time available and suggests that: 'when one thinks of Yorkshire, one does not think of it in any great detail. It is too immense and diversified for that'. As a result he explains that, when he dreams about Yorkshire while far away on his travels abroad, he often thinks of those odd bits and pieces, which for that moment sum up for him the whole beauty and magic of the great Shire. He then describes the over-riding impression of the Yorkshire scenes which often spring to mind on such occasions including:

> The ridge of moor flung up against the sky; an old track trailing away westwards, a shepherd rounding up his flock on the tops; a remote farmstead in the high dales; an outpost on a moor, a lonely inn; a wild ghyll tumbling down the Pennines; the feel of the wind on the tops; a few green pastures cut out of the moor – and as a West Riding man – a jostling mass of men, women, boys and girls, pouring from a mill at evening...

Nonetheless he says he always tries to analyse the concept of the County a little more closely by the thought of those particular parts which impress him most, and briefly describes a list of examples to which he has drawn attention in his two recent books: *Moorland Tramping in West Yorkshire* (1931) and *Tramping in Yorkshire – North and East* (1932). The list of his special scenery includes the Black Pennines, the dales' 'Three Peaks', Malham Cove and Gordale Scar, the Hambledon and Cleveland Hills, the Wolds, and the varied coastline form Saltburn to Spurn Head, as well as his own beloved Wharfedale. But Alfred is not merely a 'moorsman' at heart, and his list also includes some of the famous people he is proud to claim as Yorkshiremen for whom he expresses deep appreciation, and he briefly comments on the likes of the father and son writers, Richard Blakeborough (1850-1918) and Fairfax Blakeborough (1887-1976), the late dialect poet of Leeds University, Professor Frederick William Moorman (1872-1919), the self-taught Oxford Scholar of Comparative Philology, Professor Joseph Wright (1855-1930), the road builder and great pedestrian Blind Jack Metcalfe (1717-1810), the 'Ancient' Henry Jenkins (1500-1670), and the rebellious nobleman Richard Norton (1494-1585), as well as the members of the Skipton Clifford Dynasty that lasted for over 500 years. However, while he indicates that he could continue with his litany of iconic Yorkshire figures, he moves quickly and somewhat tangentially toward the termination of this part of the presentation with a brief consideration of two notorious nutritional Yorkshire icons namely: 'Yorkshire Pudding' and 'Yorkshire Parkin', before a final flourish with a review of the esoteric eleven verse Yorkshire anthem: '*Ilkla Moor baht 'at*', albeit with 14 'impromptus' supressed.[25]

At this point, even though he is clearly running out of time, Alfred is still not finished with his topic, and he now turns his attention to two positive suggestions for the academic promotion of 'Yorkshire' when he asks the question of this prestigious institution: 'what about a Yorkshire Chair?' after all, he continues: 'People seem to endow Chairs at Universities for all sorts of dull subjects; here is a chance for somebody with a few thousand pounds to spare to endow a Chair on a really engrossing topic – Yorkshire'. This suggestion for an academic basis for the promotion and study of 'Yorkshire' may not seem so bizarre today, given that in the new millennium, three University Yorkshire-related courses have been established: Hull University's BA Yorkshire Studies, Leeds Metropolitan University's MA Northern Studies and Bradford University's BA Combined Honours Local and Regional Studies. However, the radical sort of Chair that Alfred envisages was not at all like a conventional Chair, fixed and immovable, but rather a travelling Chair, in the charge of a Peripatetic Professor, who would have the complete freedom to wander about the County wherever he fancied. Alfred also proposes some duties which might be expected of the endowed scholar to promote his subject, which will include a return to Cambridge at least once a year in order to give account of his stewardship. But why stop there, he continues on a related theme: 'Why not establish a "Yorkshire Press" at the University?' In Alfred's view it is high time that publishing got away from the domination of London and Fleet Street, and established a 'Yorkshire Press' as the sole arbiter of Yorkshire literature. He suggests that there were many noteworthy Yorkshire writers of prose and poetry who have not had their just reward because of the ridiculous fetish for London, and that the only Yorkshire authors that most people recognise are the Brontës, and, excellent though they are, even the 'Brontë Cult' has been overdone.

Now it really is time to end his discourse, and Alfred does so by stating that it has not been his intention to lecture to his audience, far from it, only to throw out a few ideas about the County of Yorkshire as he perceives it, and he brings the talk to a close by a final reflection on his own passionate relationship with his beloved County:

> My first love was and is to tramp about the dales and moors especially '*ower t'ops*' in wild weather and associate with kindred spirits; and my only regret is that I shall one day have to cross the '*Brig O' Dread*' and leave them behind.[26] Perhaps, then, you will let me end by quoting a few verses I once wrote to hearten myself for the crossing.

Alfred then proceeds with the delivery of his six verse poem 'Dales in Paradise'[27] in which the second verse perhaps best captures the overall theme of the poem:

> There must be dales in Paradise,
> Else what will dalesmen do
> Throughout the long eternities,
> And none to wander through!
> Where we'll walk and sing and laugh and laike,
> Before the rest of heaven's awake?

But even now Alfred is still not done and he finally finishes off his presentation with a recitation of the traditional poem: 'The Song of the Yorkshireman',[28] which explores the genealogical origins of the Yorkshireman's ancestry, and thus leaves his audience to ponder the question begged by the chorus:

> Am I a Roman: am I a Dane   Am I a True-Blue Englishman?
> Am I a Saxon: am I a Celt?   By your leave – if you please,
> Am I a Norseman: am I a Thane?   I am better than these:
> Am I a Percy – minus a belt?   For I am a Home-Fed Yorkshireman!

Following Alfred's address to the Cambridge University Yorkshire Society (CUYS), it was reported that members of the Society were delighted with his talk and according to one correspondent: 'he impressed the guests with his deep knowledge of Yorkshire and his general breezy genius.'[29] It was also suggested that Alfred should have been 'on form', since he had been well-entertained at supper in the Vice-President's room at Jesus College before the address, and afterwards by Sir Arthur Gray (1852-1940), Master of the College and first president of the CUYS. Moreover, Alfred had also acknowledged how much he had enjoyed the occasion in his subsequent letter to Stanley Umpleby in which he stated: 'I shall always count my Cambridge trip worth-while if only for the new friendships formed thereby, especially the two Middlesbrough lads yourself (Stanley Umpleby) and Bill Cowley. I had heard of you before but only vaguely. Now I seem to know a good deal about you and your splendid work.'[30] Furthermore, it was apparent that one of Alfred's suggestions which he made during his address had already been taken up by members of the Society when they started the foundations of a 'Yorkshire Press'. Subsequently, several Yorkshire Dialect Poems by members of the Society had been published by the CUYS in what was an embryonic development to foster and promote Yorkshire Literature, although Alfred's proposal for a 'Yorkshire Chair' remained an unfulfilled dream.

Envoi

The meeting of the Cambridge University Yorkshire Society in March 1936 was not the only one which Alfred was invited to attend in the role as a guest speaker; he was also requested to make another address at the Society's Dinner to celebrate the first anniversary of its foundation later that year,[31] which suggested that the Society had been formed in late 1935. On this occasion Alfred was accompanied by his friend, walking companion and East Yorkshireman, George C. Heseltine, and once again he spoke on his favourite topic of 'Yorkshire', as well as proposed the toast: '*T'County*'. It seemed that George Heseltine was also invited to speak about one of the principal characters who featured in his earlier book: 'Great Yorkshiremen' (1932), namely the self-assured, presumptuous and somewhat 'prickly' Yorkshireman, Dr. Richard Bentley (1662-1742), the renowned Classical Scholar, Doctor of Divinity, Fellow of the Royal Society, controversial Master of Trinity College and one-time Vice Chancellor of Cambridge University. Furthermore, Alfred was once again in attendance during his war time service with the RAF, at an 'Informal Gathering of Yorkshiremen' of the Cambridge University Yorkshire Society, which was held on 18th October 1941 at King's College,[32] which also suggested that the Society continued its activities in to the war years and probably beyond.

The original Society had been started in 1935 by William (Bill) Cowley (1913-1994), who was born in Middleton, North Yorkshire. After his Cambridge studies he worked in India for several years as a civil servant and magistrate, during which time he was instrumental in setting up the 'Tara Devi' project near Simla, in the Himalayan foothills of Northern India. This was the Indian equivalent of the Scout Association's landmark leadership training camp, which had been established in 1919 at Gilwell Park in Epping Forest, England. Following his return to England, Bill took up farming in North Yorkshire, and wrote several books about the North and East Ridings of Yorkshire and Yorkshire Dialect Poetry as a member of the Yorkshire Dialect Society. He is probably best remembered for the foundation of the North York Moors Lyke Wake Walk Club for those able to complete the 40 miles trek from Osmotherley to Ravenscar in less than 24 hours and his guide book *The Lyke Wake Walk* (1964).[26]

It is uncertain however, for how long the Cambridge University Yorkshire Society continued to exist in its original form after the Second World War, and apparently no such Society exists today at the University. Nevertheless, in subsequent years, other Yorkshire-related Societies came into existence, namely the York Cambridge Society towards the end of 1930s, founded by the late Mr. John Dronfield, headmaster of St.

Peter's School, York (1937-1967), which was an association of Yorkshire Alumni who had attended Cambridge University during the war.[33] This Society continued to meet regularly after the war and held formal dinners with invited guest speakers, but unfortunately no records of its earlier activity remained after the death of Mr. Dronfield. Even so, this Society, together with another now combined branch of the Yorkshire Cambridge Society of North and West Yorkshire, still flourishes today. What is not certain is whether or not the original 'Cambridge University Yorkshire Society' was the forerunner of today's branches of the 'Yorkshire Cambridge Society'.

References and Notes

1. *Historical Pageant of Bradford (The Souvenir Book)*, Percy Lund, Humphries & Co, Ltd., the County Press, Bradford, 1931, Mechanics' Institute Library, Bradford, Reference Number: 942.817.

2. Frank Lascelles, see: www.thesibfords.org.uk/sibipedia/frank-lascelles

3. Historical Pageant of Bradford, Book of Words: 'The Living Story of Bradford's Glory', Peel Park, Bradford, July 13th -18th 1931, Mechanics' Institute Library, Bradford, Reference Number: 942.8D.

4. A Report in the *Bradford Telegraph and Argus*, 8th December 1932.

5. Editorial, *Heaton Review*, Vol. vi, 1933.

6. David Russell, 'The Heaton Review 1927-1934: culture, class and a sense of place in inter-war Yorkshire', Journal: *Twentieth Century British History*, 2008, Vol. 17, no. 3, pp. 323-349.

7. *Heaton Review* (Editions 1927-1934), Local Studies Department, Bradford Central Library, File Ref. No. LSS-R B052 HEA.

8. Alfred J. Brown, 'Old Raggles Inn', *Heaton Review*, Vol. v, 1932, facing p. 25.

9. Alfred J. Brown, *Four Boon Fellows – A Yorkshire Tramping Odyssey*, J.M. Dent and Sons Ltd., London, 1928, p. 141.

10. Alfred J. Brown, 'November Apples', *Heaton Review*, Vol. v, 1932, p. 32.

11. Alfred J. Brown, 'November Apples', St. Bede's School Magazine, November, 1923, Vol. ii, No. 16, p. 107.

12. 'Yorkshire Authors' by R.W.P., *Heaton Review*, 1932. Vol. v, pp. 63-65

13. Alfred J. Brown, 'These Fields', *Heaton Review*, 1933, Vol. vi, p. 9.

14. Alfred J. Brown, 'Bradford', *Heaton Review*, 1933, Vol. vi, p. 54.

15. Alfred J. Brown, 'This Town', St. Bede's School Magazine, June, 1922, Vol. ii, No. 12, p. 36.

16. J.B. Priestley, 'Bradford', *Heaton Review*, 1931, pp. 7-9.

17. Alfred J. Brown, 'Toyland', *Heaton Review*, 1932, Vol. v, pp. 51-52.

18. Alfred J. Brown, *Broad Acres – A Yorkshire Miscellany*, Country Life Limited, London, 1948, chapter 26, 'Yorkshire in Literature', (iii), pp. 198-201.

19. 'Yorkshire Authors', a report of the Yorkshire Authors' Dinner, *Yorkshire Post*, 11th October 1938.

20. Alfred John Brown, West Yorkshire Archives Service, Bradford Central Library, Document No. 69D90, Section DB 38/4.

21. Lettice Cooper, *The Yorkshire West Riding*, The County Book Series, Robert Hale Ltd., London, 1950, p. 256.

22. Alfred John Brown, 'On Yorkshire', A Lecture to the Cambridge University Yorkshire Society, Cambridge, March 6th 1936.

23. Alfred John Brown, *Four Boon Fellows*, J. M. Dent and Sons Ltd., London (1928), p. 98.

24. Ibid., Poem: 'Malediction of the Wharfe', pp. 143-144.

25. Ibid., Song: '*On Ilkla Moor baht 'at*', pp. 303-306.

26. Ibid., Poem: 'The Cleveland Lyke Wake Dirge', pp. 148-149.

27. Ibid., Poem: 'Dales in Paradise', pp. 307-308.

28. Ibid., Poem: 'The Song of the Yorkshireman', pp. 71-74.

29. 'Tykes at Cambridge University', a short unaccredited report, *Yorkshire Gazette & Herald*, 3rd April 1936.

30. Alfred John Brown, letter to Stanley Umpleby, 15th March 1937, AJB Yorkshire Dialect Society File, 1930s-1950s.

31. 'Tykes at Cambridge', a short unaccredited report, *Yorkshire Observer*, 1st December 1936.

32. Alfred John Brown, West Yorkshire Archive Service, Bradford Central Library, Document No. 69D90, Section DB38/C4.

33. Personal Communication, Mrs. Patricia Cook, Secretary of the York Cambridge Society.

CHAPTER 9

The Pre-War Brown Family Fortunes

The decade of 1930-1940 was a period of prolific literary productivity for Alfred during which he published extensively. Over this time he established his credentials as one of Yorkshire's leading contemporary writers with a major focus on the County's image and status as a noteworthy location in the landscape of England. This alone could be seen as a significant achievement, but it was accomplished along with his ever-demanding role as a textile agent for a major Bradford Worsted Company, which required long periods of travel in Europe. All of this was accompanied by rapidly-changing circumstances in Alfred's personal life, in which his family doubled in size, his young children embarked on their school careers and domestic upheavals resulted in dramatic changes in both home and school lives. Together with the looming international crisis at the end of the decade, these presented additional challenges to the family's fortunes in the lead-up to the second major conflict of the twentieth century, namely the Second World War, in which Alfred would once more take up the call to serve his country.

Alfred, Marie-Eugénie and their two young children, Felicity and Barbara, had settled into their new life at 'Wharfegate', one of the three named pairs of recently-built, large semi-detached houses that were situated on the main Bradford Road leading out of the village of Burley-in-Wharfedale. They had got to know their new neighbours, the Harrisons at 'Chelmer', which shared an adjacent driveway, and the Normingtons at 'Sandholme', which was the adjoining house, and in both cases, each set of neighbours had their own young families, so there was no shortage of children to play with in the neighbourhood.[1] Since Alfred's busy work schedule continued almost unabated, social interaction with their neighbours, like that with their other friends and relatives, was mainly confined to the weekends, and even then time was short for the completion of the many unfinished jobs needed in the new house, not to mention work on the extensive front and rear gardens after the house building.

These domestic jobs inevitably presented problems for Alfred since, by his own admission, he had neither the skills nor the motivation to carry out the odd jobs around the house. He preferred to delegate such work to skilled workmen available locally, while he was content to concentrate on the heavy garden work, a task for which he was more temperamentally suited, because he enjoyed outdoor physical labour as a means of winding down from the pressures of his hectic commercial life. This type of activity, together with a ramble over the nearby Burley Moor, also put him in the right frame of mind for some of his more challenging literary work, which inevitably had to be done either late at night or very early in the morning, when the household was peaceful and quiet. However, even these times of relative tranquility did not last very long.

And Then There Were Three

In the spring of 1932 it was confirmed that Marie-Eugénie and Alfred were expecting their third child, and this time they both agreed that, notwithstanding the valuable services provided previously at the Belle Vue Maternity Home in Ilkley, they were determined to arrange for a home birth for their new offspring, since they were now in much better circumstances and had the support they needed to manage the imminent event. It was therefore with great joy and some relief that another baby girl was delivered safely at home on 31st August 1932, with the arrival of Rosemary, much to the pleasure of her two inquisitive sisters, who were no doubt looking forward to the times when they could take part in the daily care of their new sister.

Once more there was little delay in the arrangement for the reception of the new baby into the Catholic Church, and Rosemary Marguerite Ella Brown was baptised by Father Frederick W. Le Fevre on 19th September 1932,[2] with Frederick Reynolds, a friend of her parents as Godfather, and Vera Brown, Alfred's younger sister as Godmother, and the middle names chosen included 'Marguerite' from her mother and 'Ella' from a distant relative of her father. This time it was possible to conduct the baptismal service in the newly-constructed Roman Catholic Church of Blesseds, later Saints, John Fisher and Thomas More, which was just a few yards along the road from the family home in Burley-in-Wharfedale, instead of the RC Church of the Sacred Heart of Jesus in Ilkley, where Felicity and Barbara had been baptised. The new church had been consecrated by Bishop Cowgill of Leeds on 12th June 1932, and Rosemary was only the sixth child on the baptismal register of the church, which had been established to meet the rising number of Catholics in the Burley-in-Wharfedale and Menston areas. The church had the remarkable distinction of having most of the funding for the purchase of the land required in 1930 donated by a retired civil servant and late convert to Catholicism, Frederick W. Le Fevre, who was later ordained Father Le Fevre and became its first parish priest. He trained for the priesthood following a late vocation after the death of his wife Ethel, and subsequently provided the adjacent Memorial Parish Hall, named after his only son Eric Le Fevre. Father Le Fevre became a good friend of the Browns and he had some communality with Marie-Eugénie in that they both had a strong French family heritage.

In the early years of family life Alfred had deemed it necessary to provide a helper for Marie-Eugénie in coping with the demands of new parenthood, and this became even more important with the new addition to the young family, especially since Alfred's work took him abroad more often, with extended periods of travel during the early to mid 1930s. He often made repeated journeys of up to two to three weeks to countries throughout continental Europe including Estonia, Latvia, Lithuania, Poland, Hungary, Romania, Germany and even as far as Turkey.[3] These necessitated long-distance boat and train travel, since he was invariably weighed down by bulky bags of sample materials from his company. He had once tried more expedient air travel on a trip to France in 1929, which involved a flight from the small airfield of the then Great West Aerodrome near the West London village of Heathrow to Le Bourget airport in the Saint-Denis suburb of Paris. But he had mixed feelings about this new form of transport and reported that it was: 'exciting, but I was very sick for the last half hour. In future I prefer to be sick in comfort. However it was good fun, but I was rather bored after an hour; we were over the clouds and couldn't see anything – 6000 feet and 100 mph.'[4] It was not surprising that his future business travel was mainly by train, since travel by air to the more remote parts of Europe was not possible at the time, and also rail travel offered him the advantage of being able to write on the long journeys involved and thus keep up his literary output.

The Sisters' Early School Life

The elder sisters, Felicity and Barbara, began their school life at a local state infant and junior school in the village of Menston, about two miles from home that required a bus journey each way. Unfortunately neither of them had settled down since they were considered as outsiders to the district, and during their time there they were subjected to some degree of bullying, so their parents were unhappy with their education in such an unfriendly environment. Therefore when it was time for Rosemary to start nursery school, Alfred and Marie-Eugénie opted for a change of school, and all three sisters began attendance at the Littleburn Home School, a privately-run educational establishment on the edge of the village of Burley-in-Wharfedale. This had the advantages of being only about a quarter of a mile away from home, and could easily be reached via a public footpath that led through the farm fields at the back of Wharfegate, and also meant an interesting and enjoyable walk to and from school each day.[1]

The Littleburn Home School was located in a large detached private house at the corner of Old Menston Lane and Endor Crescent, just off the main Bradford Road leading out of Burley-in-Wharfedale. It had been established by two traditional educationalists in the early 1930s, Miss Little and Miss Burns, hence the name of the school, and catered for boys and girls from nursery age to eleven years of age. The two Principals were aided by several assistants who provided educational support for the relatively small mixed-aged classes at the time. The school was situated in a pleasant rural setting at the edge of the village, and although it did not have a large playground of its own, there was an area of additional land on the opposite side of the road which was used as a play area. This had the advantage of having the small stream Mickle Ing Beck flowing alongside, which was a wonderful source of entertainment and pleasure for the pupils at the school.

The general ethos of the school was far from being that of a quirky little country school and unlike many of the state-run urban counterparts of the time, since it was a 'PNEU' school, that is affiliated to the 'Parents' National Education Union', an organisation which was established in 1892, which adhered to the principle that education should be focused on the child as a person, and advocated the use of the very broadest curriculum, not merely concentration on the three 'R's', so that the talents of the individual child could be fostered and developed. The roots of this sometimes discredited, but often lamented, 'child-centred' learning approach to education, now often used by the 'Home Schoolers' movement today, lay in the philosophy expounded by the Victorian educationalist, Miss Charlotte Mason (1842-1923). She had founded the House of Education Training School in Ambleside, Cumbria, for the training of her protégées, originally as governesses and later as teachers. It subsequently became the Charlotte Mason College of Education and is now part of the University of Cumbria.

It is not surprising that the three young Brown sisters thrived in such a liberated educational environment, which together with their parents' support and progressive ideas at home, was largely responsible for laying the foundations for the rounded development of their intellects and talents. Alfred probably regarded the education of his children as especially important, possibly because of leaving school early without completing his own secondary school studies, even though it was his own choice to leave school early and start work as soon as possible. He may have ruefully remembered the additional years of night school study which he had to complete to round off at least the formal part of his education. He therefore wished to ensure that his own children began their school careers in the best possible circumstances, which would then lead them along a continuous and complete pathway to their own educational fulfilment.

It was not just on the subject of education that Alfred held some strong views, he also had some radical, if somewhat risky, ideas about the health and well being of his daughters, especially concerning the normal vaccination procedures which were required in the early years of childrens' lives. He was firmly of the opinion that childhood vaccinations against the communicable diseases of the time were not always in the best interest of the child's health. This attitude may have reflected his own experiences of the injections for post-diphtheric paralysis that he received in early adulthood, which as far as he could discern, had led to some complicated side effects that he continued to suffer in later life, without conferring any of the intended benefits. His attitude and belief on this subject was best summed up by his previously-stated abhorrence of the principles involved in this form of medical intervention:

> Vaccination rouses my passions; I hate and loathe the beastliness of it all. The idea of injecting calf-pox into the body of a perfectly healthy and helpless infant with the avowed intention of giving it a mild dose of smallpox and causing agonising and pain and sickness for days with the object of fortifying it against a possible epidemic of this much over-rated disease months or years hence, strikes me as a crime.[5]

This view may also have been reinforced by his own experiences of never having been vaccinated as a child, but having to submit to such procedures upon joining the army in the First World War. Afterwards he felt his arm stiffen, but not knowing about the side effects of injections, off he went immediately to try to relieve these normal effects by a vigorous row on the river, and promptly fainted when he returned to his barracks and was ill for a week afterwards.[5]

While Alfred's view on vaccinations raised a few eyebrows among his friends with young children, it also caused further problems for Alfred. The law required compulsory vaccination for every child unless its parents applied for an exemption on 'conscientious grounds' and he had to obtain such an exemption from a local magistrate to satisfy the regulations. Moreover, he experienced even greater difficulties when the family had earlier travelled on holiday to visit relatives in France. He had not completed the necessary special form required and after he reported in person to town hall officials to declare his own vaccination status, he was visited by the local gendarmerie and was then required to convince an appointed doctor of his own risk-free health status.[5]

Notwithstanding these challenges, Alfred held on tenaciously to his own lack of belief in both the principle and the practice of all forms of inoculations, and with some good evidence to back his belief. He continued to suffer repeated, regular infections of influenza-type illnesses that often laid him low, and even with his relatively robust constitution, these attacks often required him to either work 'below par' or take time off work to recover. In this regard, even his own doctor was of the opinion that the injections of the mild toxins he had undergone in an attempt to cure his post-diphtheric paralysis, which resulted in his medical discharge in the First World War, could now be responsible for his lowered resistance to infections, a condition which would subsequently affect him for the rest of his life. It was with some justification that Alfred took this stand on the issue of health protection, and he remained an advocate of the natural benefits of good food, fresh air and plenty of exercise as a means of promoting better health, after all, this approach had worked in his own case.

A Further Addition to the Family

The early family life of the three young sisters in the early 1930s was somewhat idyllic in the pleasant semi-rural setting of Burley-in-Wharfedale, since they not only had other children to play with, especially the Harrison children, Shirley, John and Margaret, in the next door house, 'Chelmer', but they also had school friends, including Angela, the daughter of two of Alfred and Marie-Eugénie's close friends Teddy and Mildred Harper, who also lived in the village. Furthermore, they were soon joined in the locality by members of their extended family, including their twin cousins, Patricia and Edwina, and younger sister, Odette, who were the daughters of Marie-Eugénie's brother Gaston Bull. He had returned to England from France to live nearby in Guiseley, after the tragic death of his wife Hélène, so that Wharfegate had become something of a social centre for both family and friends.[1]

The Brown family itself had not yet achieved its full complement and in the summer of 1935, Alfred and Marie-Eugénie were blessed with another addition, to the delight of Alfred, with the arrival of their first son, Christopher, who was born at home on 25th August 1935. Once more, as was the custom of the day, the new baby was baptised shortly afterwards by the family friend, Father Le Fevre, on 8th September 1935, as Christopher Charles Pierre Brown, with the middle names chosen from Marie-Eugénie's father and brother respectively, in a ceremony at the local RC Church of St. John Fisher and St. Thomas More, where Christopher became the 32nd child on the parish baptismal register.[2] This time the close friend of the family, Edwin 'Teddy'

Harper acted as Godfather, with Marguerite Owen (née Bull), Marie-Eugénie's elder sister, as Godmother.

It was also about this time that Alfred and Marie-Eugénie secured the services of possibly the best home-helper that they ever had during the early days, when a local girl named Mia, the daughter of a German immigrant family, came into their employment as a part-time assistant and took over the duties of the many previous helpers.[1] However, unlike most of the former assistants, Mia, who was only in her late teens, became not only a domestic helper, but also a close friend of the family to whom the children became especially attached. She had a delightful sense of fun and actively joined in the many childhood games and activities which they enjoyed so much. This was in spite of the fact that Mia had been born with a deformity of a lower leg, which resulted in a type of 'club foot' condition, and required a considerably built up shoe to overcome the problem of the deformity of the foot and lower leg.

The lifestyle enjoyed by the Brown family during the mid to late 1930s began to improve steadily after the Great Depression of the early to mid-part of the decade, although economic hard times still persisted among the more important industries. This affected Alfred's own textile trade, and only by sheer hard work and through vigorously-pursued export initiatives, was he able to provide adequately for his growing family. It was understandable that during this time Alfred's literary output went into something of a decline compared with his previous highly productive period, although he was also now more focused on the needs of his young family, and as a result spent less time on his own interests and more on those of the family. Nevertheless, he continued to be involved with the West Riding Ramblers' Federation, of which he had been Vice President for some time, and was subsequently made President in 1933.[6] This was after the death of his close colleague, the well-known Yorkshire author, Halliwell Sutcliffe (1870-1932), about whom Alfred wrote a moving memorial in the Federation's official handbook.[7] The WRRF was at the forefront of the campaign to open up and preserve access to areas of moorland, and Alfred played a major role in this campaign by representing the organisation in disputes about rights of way in Upper Wharfedale,[8] routes over the famous Ilkey Moors,[9] as well as his own local Rombalds Moor.[10]

The young Brown children were able to enjoy the freedom which the large rear garden provided, and via a gate at the end, were able to explore the wide open fields of the local farmland beneath the Burley Moors beyond. The little stream Wood Head Beck, which flowed through the farmland at the back of Wharfegate, provided many happy hours of fun in making dams and paddling pools. During the summer harvest time, the children were often involved in making small 'stooks' of the conically-stacked barley, and helped gather hay that the farmer used as fodder for his animals.[1] Weekends and short holiday periods were often spent outdoors, with family adventures taken down the nearby lane of Iron Row which led past Greenholme Mills along the river Wharfe to Greenholme Farm, where a series of stepping stones beneath a large weir allowed crossing of the river to the extensive footpaths beyond. However Alfred was always careful not to impose his own tramping enthusiasm on walks with the children, while Marie-Eugénie was a firm advocate of cycling both as a means of recreational activity and as a form of transport to and from the local shops.

Traditional family holidays were often taken at the seaside, with the Yorkshire coast being a particularly favourite location, and the small Victorian seaside resort of Filey was the preferred venue chosen for summer holidays.[1] Initially the family would often stay in a bed and breakfast boarding house in the town itself, before subsequently taking a rented cottage in the quiet picturesque hamlet of Flat Cliffs, near Primrose Valley, about two miles south of Filey, where extensive sandy beaches provided the ideal location for a family seaside holiday. The Brown family would hardly recognise the transformation of this tranquil place today. The surrounding area has become one of the most popular holiday parks on the east coast of Yorkshire, with luxurious static caravans and holiday homes, complete with extensive recreational and social amenities, provided for the many thousands of holiday makers who arrive from all over the UK throughout the year.[11]

Dark Clouds Begin to Gather

Towards the end of the 1930s, life in the Brown household like many others had gradually changed for the better after the austerity years of the earlier part of the decade, but already there were signs of the disturbing developments in Europe. There was a gradual slide towards another major conflict, only twenty years since the end of the last Great War, and this time the rise of the Nazis in Germany threatened peaceful coexistence with its neighbours. The results of the expansionist policy by Germany were to have a major impact on Britain, Europe and indeed the rest of the world, and in the beginning Alfred was in a prime location to observe the initial moves which would ultimately lead to the Second World War of the twentieth century.

During early March 1938, Alfred was in Austria as part of his roving commission to travel throughout Europe as sales director of his company, David Hamilton & Co., Exporters of Wools, Yarns and Wastes, and he was engaged as part of a major export drive to sell products and establish contacts with expanding markets abroad.[12] While he stayed at the Grand Hotel in Vienna, he witnessed the events that led up to the proposed 'Schuschnigg Plebiscite', a proposal by the Austrian Federal Chancellor, Karl Schuschnigg (1897-1977) for a snap vote 'for' or 'against' Austrian Independence, which was due to take place on Sunday, 13th March 1938. On the Thursday evening prior to the vote, Alfred observed the preponderance of the boisterous, but peaceful Schuschnigg supporters, over the younger, but more rebellious and threatening Nazi Party supporters, who paraded in the Kärtnerstrasse, the main shopping thorough-fare, and he realised that the atmosphere was somewhat electric and potentially highly dangerous. But he was assured by his Austrian hosts that the majority of people would vote 'for' the proposal and thereby proscribe the growing menace of the Nazi Party in the country, and that all the rival political posturing would be over by the weekend.

Imagine Alfred's surprise the next day, Friday, as he walked back to his hotel on a balmy spring evening before getting ready to depart for home, when he heard a noisy news-vendor who shouted some astounding news to the passers-by. Hitler had just announced on the radio that the plebiscite was cancelled, and that the German Army was marching on Vienna to establish the '*Anschluss Österreichs*', literally the 'link-up with Austria', but in reality the occupation and annexation of Austria into Germany. This news had an immediate impact and soon afterwards the streets were filled with hysterical supporters of the Nazi Regime, backed up by bands of stormtroopers and 'Brownshirts', who then advanced on the Grand Hotel to raise a large German flag, before they moved on to the Imperial Hotel further down the street and claimed both buildings for Germany. Importantly there was no sign whatsoever of the Austrian police who should have kept some sort of public order. This left Alfred and his fellow English colleague 'Smith' bemused, especially later when they were accosted by young men when they refused the 'Heil Hitler' demands made by noisy intruders who entered their hotel. Instead the two friends continued to talk very loudly in English, even though they were both fluent in German, and ignored the baying mob, and 'Smith' at one point politely requested their leader, in that ingratiating and injured air of a well-bred English gentleman: 'I say, do tell your people to go away. We can't hear ourselves talk in here!'

However, in view of the rapidly changed situation which they now faced, Alfred and his colleague telephoned the British Consul to ask his advice about what they should do, and were told to take a taxi at once and head for the border, which was likely to be closed at any time. Even so Alfred decided to stick to his plans and depart the next day, but spent a sleepless night due to the tumult of the crowds outside and the arrival of German armoured vehicles. He rose early, had breakfast and prepared to leave his colleague behind in Vienna, since he had further personal business to complete elsewhere. Alfred was pleased to learn that the borders were still open for bona-fide travellers and he took his seat on the Orient Express which left at noon on Saturday. But he still had to run the gauntlet of the Nazi Customs Officers at the Austro-German border, although his passport and supporting documents ensured his continued safe passage, unlike some of the other mainly Jewish passengers, who were ordered to leave the train, strip-searched and detained.

It was only during this rail journey which ran alongside the main road into Austria that Alfred became fully aware of the new mechanised German Army which advanced on Vienna, as well as the many goods trains loaded with the weaponry of war. This left a marked impression upon him with regard to the might of the Third Reich and filled him with a sense of foreboding of what was to come. Although Alfred's greater surprise occurred when he arrived back in England, where he expected to find that the nation had been roused to the dangers, and that the Government might have at least declared a state of emergency, only to discover that the annexation of Austria by Germany had left most of the population quite unmoved, and that the country had not even begun to think about the possibility of war, let alone prepare for it.

This occasion was not the only time that Alfred had come face to face with the future enemy.[12] Later in July of 1938 during a visit to Greece on business, he had the dubious distinction of spending a week in the same Athens hotel as Joseph Goebbels (1897-1945), Hitler's propaganda minister, who attempted to solicit support from the Greek Government for Germany's expansionist designs, fortunately without success. In this encounter Alfred gained the distinct impression that Goebbels was a furtive, little rat of a man, who used to limp along at the head of his outrageous entourage, quite unlike his host, the honest and friendly General Ioannis Metaxas (1871-1941), who although also small in stature, was big in personality, and impressed Alfred greatly when he used to arrive at the hotel for meetings, without escort or ceremony, dressed soberly, carrying an umbrella and looking every bit like an English country solicitor. It was this unassuming, intelligent and outspoken Prime Minister of Greece, who won immortal fame and the admiration of the nation, by his subsequent stand against Italian and German aggression towards his country.

This time on his return from Athens, Alfred broke his journey in Vienna in response to an urgent appeal from some old Jewish business friends, who were trying to leave the country, and during his brief stay at the Grand Hotel once more, he reflected on the changes since his last visit. The carefree cosmopolitan character of this elegant meeting place for foreign visitors had gone, and was replaced instead by groups of German businessmen of the 'bullet-headed' variety, greeting each other with flashing arms of the Hitler salute and loud 'Heils', which made for a very dreary and depressing ambience. Alfred then accompanied his Jewish friends to the British Consular Offices in an attempt to secure a visa for them to come to England en route to Australia, but he found himself in a sea of refugees who pressed their case for exit visas. Fortunately he was recognised by the Consul whom he knew and gained private access to him with a request to have his friends' cases considered officially, provided that their papers were in order. It was only many months later that Alfred learned that his friends were able to flee the country, although much to his chagrin, he found that they were unwilling to show their appreciation by considering joining the British Armed Services in the fight against Hitler. Their only priority was to get to Australia to start a 'new life' i.e. a new business, and they seemed to think that the war was of no concern to them once they were free of Vienna.

Alfred visited Vienna several more times on his business journeys around Europe during 1938-1939, and each time he found the city more depressing and lifeless compared with its former days. Although the 'Hitlerite salutes' and the 'Heils' were less conspicuous, the Grand Hotel was less prosperous and the Viennese had become more and more disillusioned with the '*Anschluss Österreichs*', and the majority of the people were only too pleased to see the back of the hated invaders. However, Alfred now had to consider his own situation, that of his family and indeed that of his country, in the lead up to the conflict of World War Two, a period which would be characterised by many changes in circumstances for everyone concerned.

Another Brush with 'The Boche'

Alfred had another close call with German officialdom during the lead up to the Second World War, when, on the eve of the war, he was on his final trip to Europe during the last week of August 1939, but this time unusually, he was accompanied by his wife.[13] Marie-Eugénie had never been with Alfred on one of his European business trips before, but she had been invited to stay with friends in Poland, and although retrospectively it seemed to have been a somewhat rash decision at the time, the uncertainties of the political crisis did not dissuade Alfred and Marie-Eugénie from making the journey. They arranged the temporary services of an experienced child-carer, Mrs. Pickard, to look after the children, when Mia the home-help had unfortunately decided to visit her relatives in Germany during the late summer of 1939.

All the travel arrangements had gone according to plan, when Alfred and Marie-Eugénie travelled by boat-train from Harwich to the Hook of Holland, then on to Berlin where they stopped briefly so that Alfred could show his wife round the city, which by now he knew so well, but they found that the gloomy, melancholic ambience only matched the poor weather conditions at the time. The women Berliners in particular looked anxious and miserable, as well they might have been, as most of their menfolk had already been mobilised and sent away, since the German Army was already under arms with the Polish crisis about to be dramatically exploited.

As a result, Alfred and Marie-Eugénie left Berlin the day after they had arrived and entrained for Riga in Latvia, where the next day, Sunday 20th August, they found the delightful contrast of a city bathed in sunshine, and later joined friends on a nearby Baltic beach, with any thoughts of a serious clash with Germany dismissed by their Latvian hosts who believed that 'appeasement' would succeed and war would be averted. Nevertheless before Alfred conducted his business in Riga, he called on the British Consul whom he knew well to discuss the current political situation, and found that the Consul was not only surprised to see him, but even more shocked to hear of his plans to visit Poland towards the end of the week. He advised Alfred and his wife to return to England immediately 'before it was too late', since in his opinion war between Germany and Poland was imminent, and in that case England would inevitably become involved because of the undertaking given to Poland by both England and France to stand by Poland in such an event. However when Alfred explained his wife's desire to visit her friends in Poland, the Consul agreed to defer a decision to ask them to leave officially for a couple more days while Alfred completed his intended business arrangements in Riga.

Two days later Alfred called on the Consul once more and found him to be more emphatic than ever about them leaving, and only agreed to their stay for one more day, until Thursday 24th August, by which time a debate in the House of Commons in London would have brought matters to a head. He further advised Alfred to listen to the BBC news that evening for more information about the quickly worsening situation. The BBC news later was as bad as it could have been, and the statement by Viscount Halifax (Edward Frederick Wood, 1885-1959), the then Foreign Secretary who was a supporter of 'appeasement', convinced Alfred that there was no room for hesitation and that they must return home at once.

Finally, Alfred met the Consul one more time on the morning of Friday 25th August, and against his advice he indicated that he had booked seats on the Riga-Berlin-Paris express train which left that afternoon. Instead the Consul suggested that the most sensible route was by boat to Sweden and then by sea to England, but Alfred explained that he preferred the riskier but quicker overland journey by rail. By this time the bad news had spread rapidly, and when Alfred and Marie-Eugénie arrived at the station, it seemed as if all the foreigners in Riga were trying to leave on the same train. Nevertheless they eventually found themselves aboard the train in the company of a happy band of fellow-travellers in such high spirits, which not even the gloomy, taciturn but not quite truculent German officials at the border were able to dispel, as they crossed the 'Polish Corridor' before they arrived in Berlin early next morning. Here they found the situation more desperate, with even bigger crowds waiting on the platform, where notices had been posted warning that this train was likely to be the last one leaving Germany.

The remainder of the now-crowded train journey across Germany was largely uneventful until they reached the German-Belgian frontier, where all the passengers had to undergo the most rigorous of customs examinations by a squad of brusque and quite hostile German officials who scrutinised everything most assiduously. Then after all their luggage had been turned inside out by these officials, a squad of SS men entered the train and ordered everyone to stand in the corridors while they searched the passengers' belongings, which resulted in several unfortunate people being taken in charge and detained.

It was not surprising that relief was mixed with celebration on the part of those passengers, who like Alfred and Marie-Eugénie, eventually reached and crossed over the Belgian frontier. Here they were greeted with friendly smiles by the Belgian sentries before they proceeded to Paris, where there was yet another warm welcome by their French allies. It was on the morning of Saturday 26th August, that Alfred and Marie-Eugénie were at last able to relax after their long journey before they caught the train at noon on Sunday morning to London, where they found themselves among a new exodus at Kings Cross station. This time it was among the many children evacuees who were being sent away from the dangers of the likely bombing of the capital. The fateful declaration of war did not come until the following Sunday 3rd September 1939 at 11.00 a.m., by which time Alfred and Marie-Eugénie had arrived safely home to their family, unlike their close family friend and house-keeper Mia. She had been detained in Germany with the outbreak of the war and was unable to return to England until after the war, though happily for her, then as Mrs. Mia Ruermünd in the company of her new husband![1]

Evacuation – A Family on the Move[14]

Following the outbreak of World War Two in September 1939, Alfred and Marie-Eugénie wasted no time and decided to move the family out of the West Riding of Yorkshire which, like any other industrialised region of the country, was likely to be a target for the anticipated bombing offensive to be mounted by the German Luftwaffe. This situation was expected, given that Burley-in-Wharfedale was close to the nearby RAF station at Yeadon, where the 609 Bomber Squadron was based, and was also the site of the 'AVRO' factory, which produced Lancaster bombers during the war. Even though the factory had been heavily disguised by sloping earth banks to hide any shadow effects from its walls detectable by aerial photography, along with a camouflaged roof to look like the nearby Yeadon Tarn which was drained and its image repainted on its roof to confuse enemy bombers, it was likely to be known to German intelligence and therefore a target along with the surrounding area. The decision to evacuate the family was not made entirely upon this perceived threat to safety, but also with regard to the health problems that Marie-Eugénie had experienced since Christopher's birth, as well as the likely health-promoting benefits for the children which might be had in a location devoid of pollution from local industry. Thus the decision was made to move the family to the West Lancashire coastal holiday resort of Blackpool, while Alfred remained at work in Bradford. It was also decided to carry out structural alterations at their Wharfegate home with a view to selling the house, so Alfred took temporary accommodation in a hotel close to his office, and he then made occasional weekend visits by car to be with the family.

Towards the end of September Alfred rented a house at 91 Newton Drive for £120 per year in the pleasant suburb of the Layton Hill area of Blackpool, about one and a half miles from the pleasure beach and the famous Blackpool Tower, but close to the extensive Stanley Park and Gardens on the eastern outskirts of the town. The house was a well-proportioned detached property which easily accommodated a large family, as evidenced by the fact that it is now converted into several apartments. The choice of location was close to the well-known RC Convent School for Girls operated by the Sisters of the Holy Child Jesus, now St. Mary's Catholic College, which was situated only about a mile away on St. Walburga's Road and therefore within easy walking distance for Felicity, Barbara and Rosemary to attend.[14] It was the second time that all three girls were together in the same school, albeit that Felicity attended the upper school, although she had been a weekly border together with her cousin Odette at St. Joseph's RC College for Girls in Bradford, but now like her two younger sisters she had the advantage of becoming a day pupil once more.

Meanwhile Alfred took a businessman's room at the modest rate of £1 17s 6d per week at the Eldon Lodge Hotel in Eldon Place, off Manningham Lane in Bradford,[14] which had the advantage of being only a two minute walk from his office in Drewton Street. This location must have been something of a *déjà vu* situation since he was then in close proximity to the old building which housed the St. Bede's RC Grammar School of his schooldays, and it would no doubt have reminded him of his fateful decision to opt out of formal education as he walked past his old 'Alma Mater' on his way to work every day. Furthermore Alfred's ownership of a private motor car must have also caused him some consternation at that time, given his hostile views on the detested road 'Hogs', whom he criticised so vehemently in his earlier writings about the Yorkshire dales. Yet this new asset not only allowed to him visit his family in Blackpool occasionally, but also to make regular trips to oversee the now 'mothballed' family home of Wharfegate, since he had become a member of the growing band of motorists before the war.

The children settled down well in Blackpool and became adjusted to their new life and new school, but Marie-Eugénie continued to suffer ill-health, with dizzy spells, headaches and a lack of energy, which may have been associated with another difficult early pregnancy.[14] This necessitated the hire of a daily home help for cooking and housekeeping, as well as to assist with the demands of the three sisters at school and to look after the infant Christopher at home.[14] In addition, further strains were placed on the household when their close friends, Teddy and Mildred Harper together with their daughters Selma and Angela, who had also moved to Blackpool from Burley-in-Wharfedale, took temporary accommodation with the Brown Family, until they were able to move into their own house nearby.[14] However, even when these welcomed friends moved out at last, the situation did not improve when all the children contracted measles just before Christmas. The only relief came when Alfred spent an extended period of time with his family during the festive season instead of the brief weekend visits.[14]

When the New Year brought some respite from the family's health problems, these were replaced by a bout of food poisoning which affected everyone including Alfred, who also suffered from his now common condition of combined influenza symptoms and catarrh.[15] As a result Alfred spent a few days with his younger brother Tom and wife Cicely and their children in Bradford, and left his Spartan hotel room for the home comforts of hot baths, heated rooms, extra blankets and hot whisky 'toddies'.[15] Meanwhile the health situation continued to deteriorate in Blackpool when Alfred received news that Marie-Eugénie had now also contracted measles, though not from the children's earlier infection according to the local doctor, this was of great concern, given the already fragile state of her early stage of pregnancy.[15] This latest health crisis was further complicated by the travel difficulties that Alfred experienced as a result of the adverse weather conditions associated with one of the worst winters of the time, which made the drive to and from Blackpool at the weekends almost impossible.

Then, just as it seemed things could not get any worse, there came the news that Alfred had to appear in court as a result of being involved a road accident on a recent risky journey to visit the family one weekend, and while Marie-Eugénie expressed the hope that a favourable outcome would ensue,[15] this was not to be the case, and it was reported in the local press:

> Alfred John Brown (45), company director, whose address was given as Eldon Lodge Hotel, Eldon Place, Bradford, was at Skipton Court fined £2, together with £2.3s. costs, and his license endorsed and suspended for one month, for driving a motor-car without due care and attention at Broughton [near Skipton] when it was alleged that he cut out from behind another car and collided with a car coming in the opposite direction.[16]

Alfred and the other driver had both been extremely lucky not to have been seriously injured in the collision. He must have regretted the enforced interruption of his weekend visits to Blackpool, and perhaps considered the wisdom of the evacuation his family, given the series of problems which had beset them all during the first six months of this arrangement. Nevertheless, Marie-Eugénie offered her love and support once more during these depressing times, when they exchanged Valentine's Cards in February 1940, as evidenced by a rare piece of verse which she wrote in an accompanying letter:

> On Valentine's day
> Romance holds sway,
> For those who love
> The flight of the dove.
> The first days of Spring
> Walking on heath and ling.
> The scent of the flowers,
> The dream filled hours.
> Verse on the lyre
> Of one's heart desire.

> Marie-Eugénie Marguerite Brown, from one who loves you.[15]

It was about this time however, that Alfred and Marie-Eugénie began to consider a return to Burley-in-Wharfedale, and Alfred had searched for the possibilities of other properties in his favourite dale of Wharfedale. The local estate agent had identified the large detached property of Beacon Hill House, in the hamlet of Langbar, near the village of Beamsley, beneath the spectacular hill of Beamsley Beacon, as suitable for the family's needs, but the size, cost and relative remoteness were prohibitive.[15] Perhaps this place would have been the ideal location for a successful writer to find continued inspiration, but Alfred had not been able to aspire to this level of literary success, although he continued to dream that this would be the case some day. Moreover there were other urgent matters which required attention: the intended kitchen re-development at Wharfegate had still not begun, and now new problems resulted from the house being closed up during the severe winter. This had caused water pipes to burst and flood the first floor with extensive damage to the dining room, hall and kitchen, all of which needed urgent repair and the house needed to be dried out thoroughly before any work could start.[15] Alfred then considered a move back to the house from his lodgings to act as a caretaker until the property could be fully restored, with a view to renting it temporarily until another suitable house could be found.

Meanwhile the news Alfred received from Blackpool hardly brought any comfort when it was found that Marie-Eugénie's close friend, Mildred Harper, who had been very ill for some time, had passed away suddenly at the age of only 35 years, leaving her husband Teddy and his children distraught.[15] Furthermore Marie-Eugénie herself, who had recently overcome a measles infection, was now treated by her doctor for continuing, severe abdominal pain, most likely as a result of a recent miscarriage, which not only left her with considerable physical discomfort, but also understandably in a state of severe depression.[15] As a result there was now an even more urgent need to reorganise the domestic arrangements, so that further temporary help was made available for the family, while Alfred moved back home and devoted his time to the repair and renovation of Wharfegate, with the hope of a return by the family in the near future.

All of these events took place against the backdrop of developments in the war both in England and France. Apart from the domestic and health problems the family had experienced in Blackpool, it was obvious that the threat posed by air raids appeared to be more extensive than previously imagined, and the children now underwent air raid practice at school on a regular basis.[15] As a result Marie-Eugénie came to the conclusion that she would rather be at Alfred's side in such circumstances and asked Alfred to speed up the work at Wharfegate and build an air raid shelter under the garage.[15] Furthermore the dreadful news from France, that the British Expeditionary Force's Battle for France was lost and a full retreat was underway, with the Dunkirk Evacuation at the end of May to early June, led to Marie-Eugénie's concern for her relatives in Calais. She had previously written to her cousins Jacques, Simone and Robert to suggest their children be evacuated to England if possible, but was unable to get any news of her relatives even via the Red Cross.[15] Moreover, the news that Paris had fallen to the Germans, and that England might even expect an invasion, was of such concern to her, that she not only wished to return to Wharfegate as soon as possible, but also considered the offer made to selected UK volunteers to be evacuated to Canada.[15] She had applied for guidance in this matter to the Children's Overseas Reception Board (CORB), and received the necessary application forms for the transfer of children abroad under a scheme whereby parents of children in fee-paying schools were required to pay part of the costs involved in the transfer to a suitable school overseas.[15]

Alfred and Marie-Eugénie considered the children's evacuation scheme as the best option for their children's future, and were anxious that they be placed in a similar Convent School to the one which the three young sisters attended in Blackpool. It was fortunate that they made contact with a school operated by the same order of Sisters of the Holy Child Jesus in upstate New York, USA, in the small town of Suffern, situated close to the state border of New York and New Jersey, about 30 miles north of New York City. Alfred and Marie-Eugénie received a most friendly letter of acceptance of their children into the Suffern School by the school's Head, Mother Superior Mary Gabriel,[15] who had been in contact with Mother Evangelista in Blackpool, with regard to the necessary financial terms of the arrangements. Since private education was somewhat more expensive in the USA than the UK, and because of the currency restrictions which operated in a time of war, it was generously proposed to continue the payment of fees via the Blackpool-based Order of Sisters. They were further reassured to learn that Mother Gabriel had been born and educated in England and also knew Mother Evangelista as well as well as several other nuns at the Blackpool School, and that she also shared the Brown's concerns about making the best educational choices for their children.

Everything now appeared to be in place for the transfer, but the formalities of applications to the American Consulate for passport and visa authorisation were still required, and the need for Marie-Eugénie to accompany the children on the journey to the USA, since they were not allowed to travel alone because they were to be sent privately, not as part a of government grant scheme. But important questions still remained: did the children want to go, and if so, was Marie-Eugénie willing to make the journey with them?[15] Alfred had heard of several children who had already been evacuated on a similar scheme and he was concerned that if there was any further escalation of bombing later in the summer as anticipated, this would increase the numbers seeking to secure this limited option. However the decision was almost made for them when the news that civilian shipping was now under threat, and two ships carrying children evacuees were attacked in the German U-boat campaign in the North Atlantic with child casualties aboard both 'The Volendum' and 'The City of Banares', which were sunk on 30th August and 17th September 1940 respectively. This terrible news probably finally dissuaded Alfred and Marie-Eugénie from going ahead with their planned evacuation scheme, and convinced them to find alternative ways of dealing with the threat of war which was being brought to these shores.

Alfred returned to Wharfegate in the spring of 1940 to oversee the repairs and modifications to the house which included an enlarged kitchen/dining room area, before Marie-Eugénie arrived with the children during the summer, accompanied by another child who needed temporary fostering. This latest addition to the Brown household occurred after the Headteacher of the school in Blackpool announced one day that a young girl who had escaped from Poland needed a place to stay until her parents could settle in England. Therefore young Zosia, who had been joined by her cousin Janek in England, returned with the family to Burley-in-Wharfedale, where they became good friends and playmates of the Brown children, and Janek lived with another family nearby, before their mothers eventually arrived from Poland.[1]

Nevertheless Felicity, Barbara and Rosemary returned to Blackpool in September to become weekly boarders at the Convent School, while Christopher remained at home with his mother. This new arrangement involved the three sisters travelling to and from Blackpool by bus each week, and they were initially placed together in a small bedroom dormitory, but had to be separated when the ceiling fell down upon them one night. This unfortunate incident was not the only time they were disturbed, since they were occasionally ordered out of bed and had to spend the rest of the night on the floor of the gymnasium which was below ground level, when there was the threat from nearby bombing.[1] The three sisters remained in Blackpool until alternative schooling arrangements were made in early 1941, this time at the Sisters of the Holy Child Jesus Convent School in Hookstone Drive, Harrogate, which is now the St. John Fisher Catholic High School. Although the school was about 15 miles away from Burley-in-Wharfedale, it was relatively easily accessible by public transport, and it provided the continuity of education in a system to which they had become accustomed, and where they were to remain for the rest of their schooldays.[1]

By now Alfred and Marie-Eugénie had given up any ideas about selling Wharfegate since house buying had virtually come to a standstill because of the threat of invasion. Furthermore because of the deteriorating war situation, for Alfred there was now only one decision to be made – a possible return to a branch of the armed services again in order to play his part in the defence of the country and the eventual defeat of Germany. He had already considered how he might serve his country once more in this new conflict, although Marie-Eugénie did not like his suggestion that he should take up a commission with the RAF and although he applied to join the Officers' Reserve for Active Service,[15] it was unlikely that he would be considered this time because of his age. Nevertheless, Alfred had been training with the Local Defence Volunteers or the LDV as they were known, an organisation which was later to become the 'Home Guard', but which at that time had been sarcastically described by its detractors as the 'Look, Duck and Vanish' Brigade. But this was unlikely to satisfy his desire to do something more useful in the war effort, and so in the New Year Alfred duly enlisted once more, this time in the RAF as an Intelligence Officer in the Second World War of the twentieth century.

References and Notes

1. Personal communication with Mrs. R. Sturrup (née Brown).

2. Baptismal Records, St. John Fisher and St. Thomas More RC Church, Burley-in-Wharfedale.

3. Alfred John Brown, Passport, 1ˢᵗ September, 1931 to 1ˢᵗ September 1936, Foreign Visa Stamps, AJB Personal File.

4. AJB Personal Correspondence File 1928-1929, Alfred John Brown letter to Marie-Eugénie Brown 17ᵗʰ April 1929.

5. 'Alan Dale', 'Needles and Pins', an unpublished manuscript written under Alfred John Brown's pseudonym about the trials and tribulations of early married life, 'Vaccinations', pp. 248-253.

6. 'Ramblers' Chief', the announcement of AJB's appointment in the *Bradford Telegraph and Argus*, 1933 (no date), Bradford Central Library, Local Studies Department, Yorkshire Authors Boxfile.

7. Alfred John Brown, 'In Memoriam', Halliwell Sutcliffe, The Yorkshire Tramper, pp. 15-17, 1932, Bradford Central Library, Local Studies Department, Yorkshire Authors Boxfile.

8. 'The Pathfinders', *Bradford Telegraph and Argus*, 22ⁿᵈ February 1933, Bradford Central Library, Local Studies Department, Yorkshire Authors Boxfile.

9. 'We Sing About Ilkla' Moor – But Don't Get Off The Beaten Track', *Yorkshire Observer*, 21ˢᵗ July 1933, Bradford Central Library, Local Studies Department, Yorkshire Authors Boxfile.

10. 'Rombalds Moor Rights', *Bradford Telegraph and Argus*, 19ᵗʰ September 1933, Bradford Central Library, Local Studies Department, Yorkshire Authors Boxfile.

11. **Note**: The biographer recalls holidays at Primrose Valley in the early 1950s, where mostly primitive touring caravans were the norm, with the odd converted single-decker bus or railway carriage, but only the most basic facilities were provided.

12. A.J. Brown, *Ground Staff* (A Personal Record), Eyre and Spottiswoode, London, 1943, Part 1: 'Prelude To War, 1938-1939' – 'Hitler Takes Vienna', pp. 7-24.

13. Ibid. In: Part 1, 'Prelude to War, 1938-1939' – 'Return from Riga', pp. 24-31.

14. Alfred John Brown Personal Correspondence File 1939, passim.

15. Alfred John Brown Personal Correspondence File 1940, passim.

16. 'Yorkshire News – Bradford Motorist Fined', *Yorkshire Post*, (no date) February, 1940.

CHAPTER 10

Alfred's Second Great War 1940-1945

Alfred's involvement in World War Two began when he enlisted on 29th July 1940 in the Royal Air Force Volunteer Reserve with the rank of Pilot Officer,[1] although he was not liable for conscription at any time during the war because of this age. He had completed nearly a year's service in the Officer Reserve of the Home Guard by this time, but at 46 he was considered too old for 'General Duties' (flying), and was commissioned in the 'Administration and Special Duties' Branch, or 'Ground Stooges' as they were known in RAF slang. His decision to enlist in this branch of the service was influenced by the recommendation of his close friend, George C. Heseltine, who had suggested Alfred write to the Air Ministry for a job in the Intelligence Branch.[2] George, like Alfred, had served in WW1 in the Royal Artillery, before he transferred into the Royal Flying Corps in 1917, which became the RAF in 1918, and he was now commissioned as a Squadron Leader in the RAF Intelligence Branch. Alfred was persuaded by George that his fluency in both German and French, and his extensive knowledge of Europe in general and Germany in particular, might lead to a post in the Special Duties Branch of RAF Intelligence.

Intelligence personnel had been included in a special branch of the RAF since its formation, but the role of RAF Intelligence was enhanced in 1939 following the out-break of WW2, when the 'General Duties' Branch consisted mainly of pilots who were on a 'ground tour', or those who for medical reasons were unable to fly. These men per-formed the duties of Squadron Intelligence Officers (SIOs) as part of the Air Ministry Intelligence Department, but by late 1939 there was a dedicated Air Intelligence Department (A&SD Branch) organised solely for intelligence duties. During the war further expansions included the Signal Intelligence Service at Bletchley Park, near Milton Keynes, and the Secret Air Intelligence Service, together with the Imagery Intelligence Service at RAF Medmenham, near High Wycombe. The distinctive badge of RAF Intelligence (1942-1969) consisted of a crown on top of a rounded laurel crest with the words: 'Intelligence School, Royal Air Force', inside of which a sphinx that denoted 'wisdom', was set against the background of a brilliant sun in 'splendour', that represented 'elucidation', with the scrolled motto beneath: *Praemonitus Praemunitus* or 'Forewarned is Forearmed'. RAF Intelligence thus became a vital asset in the air war against Germany during World War Two.

Alfred was enlisted into this prestigious branch of the armed services and served throughout the war, although his experiences within the different units of the service proved as demanding as they were varied. During his four and a half years of service, he was posted to no less than ten different RAF establishments which included: six Operational Stations of Bomber Command, but also unfortunately three RAF hospitals or convalescent centres, as well as the Head Quarters of Bomber Command, two RAF Training Command Operational Training Units (OTUs), and the Air Ministry Head Quarters in London. He was even billeted at home in Burley-in-Wharfedale for some considerable time. This somewhat itinerant role naturally placed a heavy physical burden on himself, but also emotional and financial ones on his family at the time. Nevertheless he was determined to fulfil the assigned roles to contribute in some small way to the war effort, which he, like many others, came to view with typical British stoicism, in the hope that a better future would ensue for everyone after the second major conflict of the century.

Alfred published a comprehensive account of his service during the first three years of the war,[3] and even before he joined the war effort he reflected upon the likely impact of the new conflict in an article written for the fledgling *Yorkshire Dalesman* monthly magazine after a brief tramping visit to the Yorkshire dales in October 1939.[4] He returned to one of his favourite stretches of upper Wharfedale, and having secured a room for the night at a farm beneath Buckden Pike, he took a stroll to the tiny hamlet of Hubberholme. He entered the George Inn, sat by a cosy fire and enjoyed listening to the familiar dialect and friendly banter of the local dalesmen and reported: 'The homely talk acted like a soothing balm. War seemed like a million miles away, until someone turned on the wireless and the BBC Home Service filled the air with a different kind of talk.' Then upon rising early next morning Alfred observed a peaceful Buckden:

> After the commotion in the city, it was a relief to find no evidence of ARP
> [*Air Raid Precautions*] in the village: no feverish work on air raid shelters
> seemed to be in progress, no gasmasks, sandbags, nothing... On the
> contrary, everything seemed to be perfectly normal and just how I wanted
> it to be... There was something satisfying about those grey stone farms and
> cottages; something reassuring about the way the blue smoke curled up
> from the chimneys; something solid and durable about the village that was
> singularly comforting. It was the best answer I had seen to the fulminations
> of the dictators and the vaunted strength of the Siegfried Line.[4]

Map 13. Service locations in WW2

Finally, Alfred was further reassured by how little Buckden had changed over the centuries of conflicts, although he conceded: 'This war may be different from all the preceding wars, but I fancy that Buckden will look precisely the same when the tumult dies again, and the men march back.' He also acknowledged the names of the dalesmen from this valley that were etched on the local church tablets which commemorated those who had fought and died for England at Flodden Field and in the last Great War, and while further additions would be needed when the present war had ended, he concluded: 'but still the dales life goes on unchanged, and will go on, I trust, when Hitler and Communism are long forgotten.' However, those scenes of seemingly unchanging tranquility were somewhat at odds with the events and changes that he, and many others like him, would experience during the course of the conflict.[4]

Initial Service with RAF Bomber Command

The RAF had undergone a huge expansion in the lead-up to WW2 to make up the deficiencies of this vital service during the early 20th century.[5] The earliest military aerodromes in the UK had been little more than areas of rough grassland close to Army garrisons, with some development in WW1 of new aerodromes for training pilots in the Royal Flying Corps in 1917. However soon after the war many airfields were abandoned, although a few were retained by the RAF from 1918 as bomber airfields in the 1920s, with a gradual build up towards the end of the decade. During 1935-1939 there was further development of airfields for Bomber Command with up to 100 bases established, and by 1939 all front line squadrons were based at airfields, often on sites of earlier aerodromes. But most of these lacked paved runways, so that in WW2 with the advent of heavy bombers, further airfields were urgently needed, which resulted in the construction of 444 RAF airfields during 1939-1945. This huge undertaking required a workforce of some 60,000 men, to build not only runways but all the necessary accommodation and support facilities for up to 2,000 officers and men at each of these large bomber stations, which were mainly sited in the eastern counties of the UK for strategic reasons.[5] It was into this vast network of Bomber Command that Alfred was inducted and worked as a Station Intelligence Officer (SIO) during his first three years of WW2 service.

RAF Marham, King's Lynn, Norfolk

In early August 1940 Alfred was posted to an operational RAF bomber station near Marham, about 8 miles southeast of King's Lynn in Norfolk, East Anglia.[6] The airfield was home to No. 115 Bomber Squadron, as part of 'B' Flight of No. 38 Squadron, RAF, flying Wellington Bombers. Alfred described his routine at the station as one of near 24 hour stretches of duty, and while he could not elaborate the details of his job, he confided that it involved planning night bombing raids, giving briefing instructions to pilots and crew and explaining maps of routes and targets. He also interrogated each pilot and crew member upon their return to obtain exact details of the bombing raid and wrote standard reports of the results achieved. All this took most of the rest of the night before he went to bed around 6.00 a.m. and then he was back on duty by 1.00 p.m. next day to plan the next night raid. In the first week of Alfred's service he had truly been 'thrown in at the deep end' with regard to the role that was expected of him, and he had to adapt quickly to the demands of the work involved. Then the grim reality of the situation dawned upon Alfred, when he reported that one of his pilots had gone missing on return from one of his first raids, and while the station staff hoped that he may have been lucky and would be found in the sea, this was acknowledged to be highly unlikely.[6]

Alfred's early experiences as SIO not only brought him into close contact with the operational aircrews, but with high ranking officials, such as the occasion when the Secretary of State for Air, Sir Archibald Sinclair (1890-1970), called unannounced into his office to have his role explained, which Alfred duly did and found his surprise visitor most friendly and unassuming,[6] much to Alfred's relief since he could not stand any kind of 'stand on' ceremony. Moreover there was even some respite from the arduous seven day week work schedule, when he got a few hours off duty in the hot summer of 1940 and cooled off with a swim in the huge lake in the park of nearby Narborough Hall. He also explored on foot the local villages and countryside, for which he had some affinity, since his father had been born not very far away in the county town of Norwich.[6] There was even the opportunity to visit one of the grandest Tudor houses in England, when Alfred and fellow servicemen were invited by Lady Beddingfield to attend Sunday mass in the private chapel of nearby Oxborough Hall, and afterwards to view this fine establishment which had been in the family since pre-Reformation days. However Alfred was also expected to accompany the fearless and dedicated aircrews on their Saturday evening jaunts to the local hostelries, which he gladly did to further the bonds of friendship with such a close knit group of comrades, even though most of them were less than half his age.

Alfred's new life was not without its day-to-day problems, since he had still not received any statutory pay, or his uniform allowance, which together with an ongoing dispute with his former employer about his outstanding financial commissions, meant that soon he and his family would be in financial difficulties.[6] The situation was compounded by the fact that Alfred's basic pay of £237 p.a. as a Pilot Officer was much less than his previous salary, which might preclude the payment of his children's school fees to balance the family budget. However he was not unduly worried since he expected a promotion soon, but what really concerned him was that the armed services were seriously undermanned. He expressed his displeasure about the lack of young men volunteering for the war effort in a very forthright manner: 'We will have to get more staff here, but young men still hang back and get themselves "reserved" [*occupational exemptions*], and enjoy life as usual while the fellows here are fighting the bloody blitzkrieg for them. It makes me sick!'[6] This strongly-expressed view may have been influenced by his recollection of the national fervour shown by volunteers in WW1, and while times had changed along with patriotic attitudes, Alfred's sense of duty had not been compromised by this new threat to the country, and his commitment to fulfil the responsibilities which it demanded was carried into his subsequent postings.

RAF Swinderby, Lincolnshire

A few weeks later, in September 1940, Alfred was posted to his second Operational Station near Swinderby in Lincolnshire. This RAF Bomber Command airfield was home to No. 300, the Masovian Squadron and No. 301, the Pomeranian Squadron of Polish airmen. Alfred was particularly pleased that there were so many Polish aircrews at the station, since he had spent much time in Poland before the war, and of all the countries he had visited, he had come to regard Poland and the Polish people with the highest regard. Alfred's empathy for the Poles' situation was summed up by his observation: 'Of all the nations of Europe, they have suffered most at the hands of the Hun.'[8] He was not alone in the expression of sentiment for the Polish cause, since in one of the first letters he received at RAF Swinderby addressed to: 'Spitfire Brown', was from the fellow author and poet, Dorothy Una Ratcliffe, who proclaimed her own affinity for the Poles. She suggested that they would enjoy Alfred's company because of his appreciation for their country and its traditions, and from her knowledge of their fighting potential she concluded that they were an 'unlickable lot.'[6] Furthermore while she admired the men on active service, she regretted that she could not be involved: 'I think I would give up my chance of a next incarnation to be on the sea in this scrap!' (WW2), although she was able to do her bit by the donation of her home Temple Sowerby Manor, near Penrith in Westmorland, for use as a temporary hospital when she moved into a nearby house for the duration of the war.

Alfred's admiration for the fighting spirit of Polish aircrews was only tempered by the excessive exuberance of their many parties, which celebrated anything from a birthday to a Polish Festival, or even the recent arrival of a new batch of 'refugee' airmen.[9] These squadron parties which involved music, singing, dancing and drinking were seen as a safety valve for the nostalgia of home and all their relatives left behind in the old country. On occasions however things got out of hand, such as when two visiting high-ranking officials from the Air Ministry almost became the objects of the wild but friendly game of 'throwing guests in the air', and had to beat a hasty retreat to the Operations Room, where Alfred was on sole duty and had to assure these startled impromptu 'guests' of the good intentions of the revellers. But Alfred's only real surprise with these boisterous events was how much hard liquor was consumed, how many glasses were smashed deliberately and how the participants afforded the mess bills involved.[6]

This lighter side of station life was not always uppermost in Alfred's mind, since he was constantly troubled not only by his ongoing personal financial predicament, but the renewed onset of recurrent health problems that threatened the continuance of his service career once more. He had still not received the outstanding financial bonuses from his former employer, and had not been credited with the previous month's pay and allowances by the RAF.[6] The situation was further compounded when Alfred learned of a scheme whereby servicemen like him, who had been former executives of trading companies, could receive full salaries, if their employers classified them as being 'on loan' to the Government, and while he did not expect this level of support, he tried to negotiate a 'make up' allowance of the salary differential from his previous employer, but to no avail. Instead he had been offered a 'generous allowance' of up to £400 p.a. by his former employer, which helped with the family's financial needs, provided that he managed on his RAF pay by 'living like a hermit', but since he had not even received any RAF dues yet he felt: 'I am fighting (serving) on nothing a day so far.'[6]

Meanwhile Alfred's other major concern was the recurrence of cold and influenza symptoms that had bedevilled his life since WW1, and now he became confined to bed and although his condition did not require hospitalisation, it was further compounded by a return of stomach trouble which had been another of his pre-war health concerns.[6] A further problem was that he had not completed his three months RAF probationary service, and these ongoing medical problems might have resulted in his early demobilisation yet again on health grounds. It was almost a case of '*déjà vu*'; in WW1 it was diphtheria, now in WW2 it was possible that this latest infection could have led to yet another inglorious war outcome.[6] However Alfred made a slow recovery, and although he was relieved to be back on duty after about ten days, he was highly disturbed by the recent news of the sinking of a children's evacuation ship by German U-boats in the North Atlantic on 17th September 1940. He recorded his horror at this aspect of the war, and resorted to strongly-worded and emotive language to express his anger at such a vile deed: 'My heart aches for the parents who have lost all their families on that terrible night. I hope they let us go to Germany and kill the whole pack of them, wipe them out of existence; they are not fit to live.'[6]

Nevertheless, it was not long before the demands of Alfred's job totally absorbed his attention in his new role with duties shared between 'Operations' and 'Intelligence', so that he was expected to become familiar with both aspects of the work and also to act as a liaison officer between the two sections, which had the benefit of more regular hours of duty.[6] His duties involved being responsible for daytime operations, which meant he was still required to prepare aircrews for their operational bombing missions and was required to conduct interrogations upon their return, as well as the completion of detailed reports about the raids. This was the sort of work he most enjoyed provided that his health stood up to the pace of the frenetic activity involved. The only alternative role for Alfred appeared to be a move to the Air Ministry Intelligence Branch, and although he preferred the more active life of a Bomber Command Operational Station,[6] his immediate future was decided by others when he received orders for his next posting to a unique RAF wartime institution.

RAF Bomber Command Head Quarters, High Wycombe, Buckinghamshire

In early October 1940 Alfred went south in response to a posting signal that was of the 'immediate' variety. He was summoned to proceed with all speed by the Adjutant at an obscure location to the West of London in rural Buckinghamshire. Unfortunately his journey was delayed due to the difficulties of road travel as night time fell because of the extensive 'black out' in force and he was stranded in Northampton. Here he received only frosty receptions at several hostelries, before he eventually found the friendly Fleece Inn which was prepared to take in an unannounced traveller for the night.[10] Indeed the welcome could not have been more hospitable, and when the landlord heard of his predicament he was provided with a hot supper and a telephone to call HQ to explain his delay, before he was bestowed with drinks 'on the house' and the opportunity to chat with locals until late into the night. The next morning after a very early but hearty breakfast, and a modest charge of only 5s/6d, Alfred was on his way again and arrived at the local police station where he had been told to report for further instructions. After the careful inspection of his credentials, the duty officer drew a map to the HQ of Bomber Command, since its precise location was supposed to be a closely guarded secret, even though most locals knew not only of its existence, but also the quickest way to get there. When Alfred finally arrived he reported to the Camp Commandant and received his temporary security pass, before being admitted through a mysterious entrance in the woods into the underground labyrinth of passageways to a door marked 'Intelligence'.[11]

RAF High Wycombe is currently situated in Naphill about 5 miles north of High Wycombe and serves as the Head Quarters of RAF Command. Prior to WW2 the Air Ministry required a safe location for Bomber Command HQ away from London, and a site was chosen hidden in the beech-wooded area of the Chiltern Hills near the village of Walters Ash, where trees provided natural camouflage from the air. All the buildings were designed to resemble rural structures and tunnels were dug to connect the various buildings and linked to the 'Operations' Block which was located 55 feet underground. To try to preserve the secrecy of the place the station was known as 'Southdown' and the postal address was simply 'GPO High Wycombe'.

Alfred's first impressions of his new location, this 'bomb-proof, fool-proof and sun-proof' place, together with its personnel, left him somewhat in awe to say the least, especially the long hours worked even by the most senior officers, with no evidence of the 'sinecures' held by high ranking staff appointments of the pre-war days.[11] He was quickly absorbed into the routine duty of the Intelligence Staff with 12 hour non-stop shifts both night and day and described the daunting experience of being in control of all the wireless telegraphy at night.[6] This included RAF Coastal Command, RAF Bomber Command, the Air Ministry and seven different Bomber Groups, as well as the coordination of information among each of these different divisions of the service. Alfred found the work demanding but enjoyable, although he thought that his new underground environment was very quiet after the roar of bomber aircraft at his previous operational station and he missed the opportunity of mixing with aircrews, but he acknowledged that his new post was likely to get him well-known to the 'powers that be', which was good for his prospects in the service.[6] However in spite of the friendly atmosphere, and without any evidence of snobbishness at the station, he remained concerned that his official appointment had not yet been confirmed, and together with having no official service number, nor identity disc, he felt that he was only 'half-in' the service, and it was not until these had been conferred, and he had received his permanent pass to Intelligence Quarters, that he truly felt part of the establishment.[6]

Soon Alfred was given a day off duty and he took the opportunity to visit London to see first hand some of the bomb damage that had resulted from the start of the Blitz, which had followed the 'Battle of Britain' and RAF Fighter Command's repulse of the Luftwaffe's attempts to gain control of the skies, before the enemy switched attention to bombing English cities. Inevitably he was shocked at the scale of the damage to central London although it was not as bad as the east end of the city, which was far worse due to the proximity of the docklands strategic port facilities. He was distressed to see mothers and young children queuing at tube stations in the late afternoon in order to get places of shelter for the night. Then, even though it appeared to him that London was carrying on as normal under this new onslaught, Alfred once again let loose his emotional reactions in another outburst: 'It makes my blood boil to see the damage done, and I hope that we blow the bastards to hell in Berlin.'[6]

It was perhaps important that Alfred found some relief from these feelings on other 'off-duty' occasions when he was able to walk in the Chilterns, although he found the gentle hills and valleys of the surrounding countryside not very demanding compared with his own county. One very popular walk for the staff at HQ was a two miles stroll to the village of Speen for a drink at the nearby famous Plough Inn, which was owned by Ishbel Macdonald,[6] the daughter of Britain's first Labour Prime Minister, Ramsay Macdonald (1866-1937). However since Alfred had far more ambitious walking habits, he preferred the numerous footpaths which stretched over the miles of landscape that often included access to private parks and woods, but he was surprised that, unlike his native Yorkshire, the local landowners were readily amenable to such access.[6] As a result of these walking exploits, it was not long before Alfred established a reputation as a prolific walker at HQ, much to the amazement of his staff colleagues, who could not believe that he actually walked so far just for fun.[6]

Towards the end of the year when Alfred had completed his probationary period of RAF service, he was disappointed to learn that there was no chance of promotion, since the Air Ministry had not yet agreed for him and several others to become permanent staff on the organisation's Establishment, so he would have to wait for a new posting before there was any chance of promotion to Flying Officer.[6] However, another more radical change of status suddenly appeared possible as a result of Alfred's ongoing dispute with his former employer, who had not been pleased about his decision to join the services. Now moves were afoot to tempt Alfred to leave the RAF and take up a position as their overseas representative in Athens where trade was still possible.[12]

Alfred had known about this post before he volunteered for service, but had considered it well below his previous position and rate of remuneration, and after he joined the RAF he was adamant that he did not wish to resign his commission and abandon the vital work in which he was engaged. Furthermore, the fact that there was also a possibility of involvement with the Intelligence Services in Greece seemed especially dubious to him, and he therefore politely but firmly declined the offer.[12]

In hindsight it seems likely that there would have been little chance of the approval needed for this post by Lord Swinton (David Cunliffe-Lister, 1884-1972), Chairman of the National Security Executive, since at that time there was a reluctance to release men from active service in any branch of the armed forces. Therefore Alfred was happy with his decision not to leave the RAF at such a critical phase of the war, and it now seemed probable that he would be based at HQ for some time to come. Instead he was resigned to the fact that until the Establishment staffing levels were increased, he would have to forgo any possible promotion in the near future, unless he was prepared to apply for a transfer to the Air Ministry Intelligence Group in London, which he seriously considered at the time.[12]

Unfortunately Alfred's health deteriorated and soon dictated the course of events of his war service once more, although this time to a lesser extent than the debilitating outcomes that rendered him unfit for service in WW1. He had already suffered one bad bout of influenza in September, but he was then struck down with tonsillitis and confined to bed before Christmas 1940, and regretted not having had his tonsils removed as a child, which was the common practice in those days. Nevertheless he recovered in time to get a 48 hour pass for Christmas Eve and Christmas Day and had returned to duty before the New Year.[12] Then towards the end of January 1941, Alfred's previous symptoms returned and it was suggested that he needed hospitalisation for a possible sinus operation to alleviate the condition. He was then referred to an ENT specialist at a nearby RAF Hospital in order to try to resolve the new problem which now threatened his war service once more.[12]

Active Service Breaks – Hospitalisation and Convalescence

RAF Halton Officers' Mess and Hospital, Wendover, Buckinghamshire[13]

The RAF Hospital at Halton between Wendover and Aylesbury, about 12 miles north of High Wycombe, had been opened in 1927 by Princess Mary (1897-1965), daughter of King George V and Queen Mary, and was known as Princess Mary's RAF Hospital. It had become one of the largest military hospitals in the country with over 700 beds, and during WW2 it treated over 20,000 casualties during the conflict. The hospital closed in 1995 and the buildings were demolished in 2007/2008 to build a housing development appropriately called 'Princess Mary Gate'. After spending almost four months in the underground labyrinthine HQ RAF Bomber Command, Alfred was hospitalised once more and cursed his latest condition: 'I seem fated to spend most of my war years in hospital with miserable illnesses when I would much prefer to be wounded (or killed) in battle and be done with it!'[13] But unlike the previous occasion, this time it was for a less serious condition, sinusitis, which required a simple operation and he expected to be discharged in a few days, then be back on duty after a short period of convalescence. In fact the whole process took over three months out of his active service.

Alfred was billeted at the RAF Officers' Mess in Rothschild House, named after the Rothschild family who had made the estate available for war service. He was examined by Squadron Leader John Simpson, a former Harley Street ENT specialist, who had to delay the operation because Alfred was still suffering from one of his interminable colds and his condition needed to improve before the procedure was carried out.[12] After the operation everything went normally at first and Alfred's gloom lifted as he looked forward to a period of convalescence in Devon, and he was cheerful enough to act as an 'unofficial orderly' to the more serious bed-cases.[12] However he felt something of an intruder in a ward in which many of the 24 beds were occupied by orthopaedic patients, including some seriously-injured young aircrew with multiple injuries resulting from crashes, who were destined for months of hospitalisation, years of disability or the likelihood of being crippled for life.[12]

Then just before Alfred was due to depart for his convalescence, he developed ear problems, which led to the onset of acute bilateral otitis media, an inflammation of the inner ear as a result of a viral or bacterial infection picked up after surgery, which had laid him low once again.[12] This setback led to deafness in both ears, delayed his convalescence, and resisted all attempts to clear the infection by syringing.[12] To make matters worse, Alfred had also received the distressing news of his father's serious illness due to gall bladder disease,[12] and following his own deterioration Alfred became almost resigned to the death of his father, but he hoped that his own condition might improve sufficiently for him to travel to see his father before his anticipated demise.[12] At the time it seemed to Alfred that both his life and that of his father had entered a temporary state of Limbo, and it was some time before he could rise to the challenge of travelling to be with his father, or even begin his own convalescence, whenever that might be.

RAF Officers' Hospital, Torquay, Devon

It was mid March 1941 before Alfred was able to take the opportunity of attempting to get his life back to normal after his latest health relapse, this time it was in the relatively luxurious surroundings of the Palace Hotel situated just over a mile outside Torquay in rolling countryside overlooking the sea. The hotel which was requisitioned by the Government in October 1939 opened as a convalescent hospital and training facility for RAF Officers and later developed into the 450 bed RAF Officers' Hospital. Unfortunately it was the target of German bombing on 24th October 1942, which resulted in the deaths of some 64 of the 203 patients and some staff at the time. It was abandoned after a further bombing raid on 8th January 1943, but after the war it was reopened in 1948 and developed into a large luxury hotel.

Alfred had arrived at this coastal convalescence centre on 17th March 1941, after he shared a train compartment with his new doctor, Squadron Leader Morris, who took over the ENT Section of the centre, and who, coincidentally, had been involved with Alfred's earlier treatment at RAF Halton.[12] Alfred found the relaxed, informal environment of the centre much better than the confined conditions which he experienced in RAF Halton, with the emphasis now on recreational activities in order to assist his rehabilitation, before he faced an RAF Medical Board to assess his suitability for continued service.[12] During his early days at the centre he received a visit from his wife and young son Christopher, which lifted his spirits enormously, and although he was making steady progress and spent as much time as possible outdoors taking short walks, it was obvious that his physical condition had declined during his previous hospitalisation, and that he would be kept at the centre for some time.[12]

Indeed, Alfred's physical state was so poor that he was excused the gym sessions which were almost compulsory for everyone and he was advised to take only gentle short walks.[12] Of course Alfred had brought about his own physical rehabilitation after his major affliction in the last war, so he knew only too well how to facilitate his recovery. To begin with though he could not even manage the walk of just over a mile into Torquay until he had been at the centre for some three weeks, and even then he had felt the strain.[12] However, always the optimist, Alfred reckoned that he would soon be on the mend, and with Easter approaching he obtained sick leave so that he could visit his family, although it turned out to be compassionate leave in order to attend his father's funeral following his recent demise on 5th April 1941.[12]

Subsequently Alfred was unable to obtain any further leave at Easter 1941, and instead he used his convalescent time to improve his strength and stamina with longer cliff-top walks to Torquay, where he enjoyed afternoon tea at the Grand Imperial Hotel and began to feel much better about his improved walking ability.[12] He was now confident that his convalescent discharge was imminent and looked forward to a return to HQ Bomber Command, High Wycombe, in a couple of weeks' time . Although he was still not quite feeling back to his usual state of robust health and had little reserve energy, he anticipated a return to active service very soon.[12] Unfortunately Alfred's expected return to High Wycombe did not come about and he was then posted to another Operational Bomber Command Station.

A Return to RAF Operational Bomber Command

RAF Wyton, St. Ives, Huntingdonshire

RAF Wyton which was situated about 3 miles northwest of St. Ives (formerly in Huntingdonshire, now in Cambridgeshire), had been a military airfield since 1916 but was upgraded in 1935 for WW2 use as an RAF Bomber Command Station, and was home to No. 15 and No. 40 Squadrons and No. 109, the Pathfinder Force. Alfred arrived at his new station in early May 1941 and took up the usual night duties again although he had some difficulty in adjusting to the night shift routine and sleeping, especially since the duties often extended into daytime to debrief other crews at nearby RAF stations. This added to the demands of his job and left him tired after his recent ill-health.[12] The work schedule was particularly heavy during the 'moon periods', whereby clear skies provided the ideal opportunity for night bombing raids which often led to continuous shifts. The situation was made even more demanding since 'Operations' and 'Intelligence' were combined at this station, so that Alfred also had to take his turn in control of the 'Ops' room when required.[12] As a result he needed medication to help with his sleeping difficulties, although he requested a prescription from his own doctor at home, rather than create any new health concerns for the MO at the station,[12] for fear perhaps that this might have an adverse effect on his service record so soon after his recent protracted illness. Even so he admitted that at this stage he was not only tired, but also depressed and struggled to cope with the demands of the job.[12] It was during this difficult period that Alfred contacted a local solicitor and instructed him to draw up a new simple will 'just in case' things did not work out in the future, which replaced the one that he had made in 1929, whereby his family would be taken care of in the event of his demise. He had designated his younger brother Tom Brown and Dr. Melvin, the family doctor, as executors, along with his close friend George C. Heseltine and author Dorothy Una Ratcliffe, as his literary executors.[12]

Fortunately it was not long before Alfred recovered from the demanding 24 hour shifts that had seen him fall asleep at his desk, and his sleep patterns improved with the help of the medication. He was also able to take advantage of the spring sunshine and shake off the heavy work load by taking the short walk into St. Ives through fields and a nearby bird sanctuary, along the river Great Ouse for the last part of the way, and he hoped to take out a punt on the river during some further time off-duty.[12] On other occasions he went into Cambridge about 15 miles away, to walk round the colleges which he had visited previously when he gave his 'Yorkshire' lecture to the Cambridge University Yorkshire Society. He relaxed by wandering over the 'backs', or former meadow lands behind the colleges which backed on to the River Cam, and delved into the town's bookshops in order to restock not only his own collection, but the station's library of books.

However Alfred surmised that his present posting was only a very temporary arrangement and soon, after a good report about his work from the station's Commanding Officer to his new Intelligence chief, he was needed by another station.[12] He believed that his record of volunteering for extra duties stood him in good stead for promotion soon to Flying Officer, albeit on not much more pay, and maybe to the next level of Flight Lieutenant, on substantially more pay, although he was concerned that any pay increase would inevitably result in the proportionate reduction of his 'generous allowance' by his former employer.[12] Nevertheless he did not dwell on circumstances that were beyond his control and participated fully in what time was left at this station. Then just prior to his next posting, he was affected again by the recurrent cold and influenza problems, which had not troubled him since his operation some three months previously, but he hoped that he could shake off the effects of this new bout before he reported fit and well at his new location.[12]

Finally, one of Alfred's most memorable moments at RAF Wyton was when he made a rare cross country training flight in a Wellington bomber to Carlisle and back, but it was not until after take-off that he discovered two disconcerting problems. Firstly, the ground visibility was almost nil due to haze, and secondly, the pilot and the navigator were both colonial 'freshmen' from Canada, and neither had any experience of flying in England. Shortly into the flight the navigator became lost and the crew was only able to pick out landmarks by flying at about 500 ft., such as the town of Peterborough, before groping their way further north to York, where the visibility temporarily improved, but the aircraft then entered low cloud as they took a north-westerly route towards their destination. Alfred, who was in the 'astro' hatch, then became aware of a further problem when he heard the pilot and the navigator argu-ing about their position over the intercom, and the pilot descended to 500 ft. once more to pick up visual landmarks as they left the plain of York and headed towards the moors and fells of northwest Yorkshire. At this point Alfred recognised the familiar countryside over which he had often tramped, and he intervened swiftly by urgently pointing out that they were rapidly approaching the high moorland areas of the north Pennines. Furthermore since Cross Fell and Mickle Fell were ahead at around 3,000 ft., he insisted that they gained height immediately, to which the pilot responded: 'Gee, thanks for that "gen", I thought all of this country was as flat as Yorkshire pud-ding!' Alfred was greatly relieved when he felt the aircraft nose upward suddenly towards the cloud tops at about 4,000 ft. and reflected afterwards: 'I have often walked over Cross Fell in "Helm" wind, and I didn't particularly want to be found there next morning!'[14,14a] This was Alfred's last flight experience at RAF Wyton as he was moved on yet again soon afterwards.

RAF Feltwell, Thetford, Norfolk

RAF Feltwell was located ten miles west of Thetford, Norfolk and was built in the late 1930s as part of the expansion of RAF airfields prior to WW2. It was home to a number of heavy bomber squadrons including No. 57 Squadron and No. 75 Squadron, a New Zealand Squadron, and both squadrons were part of No. 3 Group that operated from the station during 1940-1942. Alfred arrived at RAF Feltwell in late May 1941 with both an upset stomach and the remnants of one of his usual heavy colds, and imme-diately did not like the look of the place. It not only appeared to be miles away from the nearest towns of Newmarket (22 miles) Cambridge (40 miles) and Peterborough (30 miles), but in his opinion it was literally 'out of the blue.'[12] The station was com-manded by a New Zealander, with over half the officers from the Antipodes, whom he found a very matey bunch. Alfred had replaced a Squadron Leader Intelligence position and although he was still a Pilot Officer he hoped for a promotion to Flying Officer soon, then possibly Flight Lieutenant in a few months time, and in this regard he was greatly encouraged by his new Commanding Officer. There were two other SIOs already at the station, but he felt that the intelligence unit needed improvement and with his previous experience he believed this could be achieved, although he realised he would have to tread warily in his new post.[12] He was under no illusions about the job which meant a lot of night-shift work, but at least it was on site without the previous nocturnal journeys to other stations, and he anticipated that he would be there for some time.

Subsequently Alfred received news that his promotion to Flying Officer was scheduled for June, and that further enhancement to Flight Lieutenant could be as early as August unless the Establishment number was reduced. In fact his CO wanted to make him a Flight Lieutenant directly but the rules did not allow this, so he would have to wait a few months in order to get the second 'ring' on his sleeve.[12] Naturally Alfred was pleased with these promotional prospects since he hoped that his family would then be better able to manage on the increased pay, provided that his former employer's allowance continued. Meanwhile he had also been lucky enough to arrange a brief visit from his wife and son Christopher during the Whitsuntide weekend in lieu of not being able to arrange leave from his duties at the station for the holiday period.[12]

Alfred quickly settled into his new situation and it was not long before he accrued the extra responsibility of Mess Duties at the station. This was an additional job and he confidently expected to be able to make improvements on the arrangements in place, based on his past experiences of how a Mess should be organised at his former Bomber Command HQ in High Wycombe. He was put in charge of a kitchen staff of 23, including four cooks, with a Mess staff of 46 to look after in his 'spare time', as well as the organisation of all the social activities associated with this responsible position.[12] Alfred threw himself into this new challenge wholeheartedly but he was conscious that he had a hard act to follow. A former Mess Secretary had been the dynamic Lieutenant-Colonel Sir Arnold Talbot Wilson, KCIE, CSI, CMG, DSO (1884 – 1940), who had volunteered as a Pilot Officer air gunner at the advanced age of 55 and had been killed in action with the 37th Squadron while still the Member of Parliament for Hitchin, Hertfordshire.[15,15a] Although Alfred was not enamoured with all the office work associated with his new duties, he accepted the important responsibility the job entailed in a reflective mood:

> Being Mess Secretary of a large mess is a liberal education in itself. I held the office only once and the honour was thrust upon me against my inclination, but it is one of those burdens which some member of ground staff has to accept in addition to his normal duties – why, I do not know!... My own qualifications for this superhuman post were nil, but it gave me good insight into the running of a mess; the customs of service etc., and

it taught me quite a lot about human nature. I would have not missed the experience, but nothing could ever induce me to accept the office again![15]

Alfred's main intelligence duties also became more demanding as a result of the lengthy 'moon duty' periods at this time which were ideal for night-time bomber operations, and while the night shift work was continuous as long as this phase of the moon lasted, there was no let-up in his mess duties either, which meant that he was often busy both night and day.[12] After he had been formally appointed Mess Secretary he now had to tackle the difficult problems created by some of the 'wilder spirits' of the mess scene, particularly among the New Zealand Squadron and the damage often done by their boisterous parties in which glasses were smashed, tables and chairs wrecked and even the piano damaged, all of which had to be stopped and control regained of the rowdies who got roaring drunk on occasions. These actions not only required the disciplinary intervention by the President of the Mess Committee but also all the diplomatic skills that the Mess Secretary could muster, especially since Alfred partly understood the behaviour of those flight crew members involved, given that they lived on their nerves and never knew from one night to the next when they might be killed. Nevertheless things had got out of hand and an acceptable level of mess social behaviour had to be restored for the good of all concerned.[12]

It was soon after that Alfred received the promised good news that his promotion to Flying Officer had been confirmed and his salary was increased to £310 p.a. with an additional marriage allowance of £228 p.a., and he still had the prospect of further promotion to Flight Lieutenant to look forward to later in the year.[12] However, this piece of good news was accompanied by some bad news, in that his namesake, another Flying Officer Browne, whose mail was often mixed up with Alfred's, had been lost in action on a recent night bombing raid.[12] He was a young Australian who had made his maiden trip as the second pilot on an operational sortie and one of a crew of six in the only aircraft that failed to return. Alfred had got to know him well during his service training and had tea with him just before he went to the crew room in preparation for the flight. Yet even though he knew there was a only a slim chance of a crash survival at sea or over enemy territory, the blank space on the operations board looked ominous and to Alfred it seemed such a tragic waste of a young life.[16]

It may have been events such as this which stimulated Alfred to think about a revision of the necessary financial provisions for his wife and family in the event of his own death, even though he was not involved in the high risk activity of operational flying. Accordingly, Alfred completed a new will with a Warwick-based firm of solicitors, since one of the partners with whom he was now serving, Flight Lieutenant Gerald Hillman, had also been with Alfred at RAF Wyton,[12] where he had originally redrafted his former will, in which he had named both financial and literary executors. Alfred then sent an outline of the new will to his wife, along with his deep personal sentiments for the futures of Marie-Eugénie and his children should he not prevail in the conflict[12]. Alfred had also updated his life insurance policy recently, which together with his new will had been deposited with his branch of Barclays bank in Market Street, Bradford.[12] These actions seemed prudent given the uncertainties at this stage of the war, and in view of his health concerns at the time, and reflected his consideration for those left behind in the event of his demise.

Life at RAF Feltwell during the summer of 1941 had its lighter moments for Alfred and the rest of his comrades, and since most of the organisation of the social life at the station was the responsibility of the Mess Secretary, this time of year was very busy for him. There had not been a 'pukka' dance (proper dance) at the mess for about a year because the station was so isolated that it was almost impossible to get enough women to attend. Therefore Alfred undertook a series of visits to all the RAF hospitals in the surrounding areas and invited all the female nursing staff to attend as well as the usual WAAF officers, to provide partners for everyone. In total there were about 350 guests invited and afterwards everyone agreed that it had been the best dance ever held at the station.[12]

Sometimes though things went badly wrong with Alfred's best-intentioned mess arrangements, especially regarding the catering menu, and as usual the Mess Secretary got the blame. For example, when Alfred organised an important dinner in which one whiff from the speciality, 'Aylesbury Duck', had knocked everyone sideways, since it was 'high' and stank the place out much to the annoyance of everyone. Afterwards the suggestions box was filled with the most ribald remarks about the unfortunate fowl served and what to do with them, and some even suggested that the foul birds should be dropped on the next bombing raid, since in the opinion of the diners they were likely to be more effective than the ordnance they had been dropping on the enemy lately![12] In reply to these abusive comments, Alfred as the guilty person had to respond, and did so with a similar humorous retort, when he indicated that he had traced the aforesaid ducks back to the purveyor of the most famous ducks in the history of mankind; the immortal birds from the Yorkshire anthem '*Ilkla Moor baht 'at*'. He then publicly sang the poem and finished with the line: '*then we sall all be 'atin thee*',[12] which no doubt was received with widespread forgiveness and good faith for future fare.

The most memorable moment of the summer of 1941 for Alfred came during one of his usual stints of aircrew debriefing after a sortie, when it emerged that an incredible incident had occurred on the return flight from a raid over Germany, for which two members of the crew were likely to be to be decorated.[12] The Wellington bomber involved belonged to the New Zealand 75 Squadron but had landed at another airfield in a severely damaged state after barely making it back to England on the night of 7th July 1941. The aircraft had suffered cannon shell and incendiary bullet damage from a Luftwaffe night fighter over the Zuider Zee in Holland after a raid on Münster, and a fire had broken out near the starboard engine on the return flight across the North Sea. The captain, Squadron Leader Widdowson, prepared the crew to abandon the aircraft, but the second pilot, Sergeant Ward, volunteered to climb out onto the wing to put out the fire with a seat cover after repeated attempts had failed by the crew with fire extinguishers. This gallant action prevented the fire spreading to the engine fuel pipe and allowed the captain to bring the aircraft home successfully, and subsequently resulted in the award of a Victoria Cross for Sergeant Ward and a Distinguished Flying Cross for Captain Widdowson for their heroic actions that night.[17,18] There was tremendous excitement at the station when these awards were made known and a special dinner was held in the mess in honour of the occasion, at which both crew members were somewhat reluctantly regaled for their actions by their comrades. Moreover this brave action by Sergeant Ward may be judged in a wider context in that almost half of the all VCs awarded to airmen in WW2, i.e. 23 of 51 awards in total, went to men of RAF Bomber Command.[18]

After these celebrations Alfred turned his attentions once more to other duties which resulted in the redecoration of the mess, the development of a new library, the appointment of a nominated librarian, the introduction of new WAAF telephone orderlies and new waitresses, along with the organisation of sporting activities which became popular after some initial resistance to the changes. Even Alfred joined in the early morning PT sessions held every day in an attempt to encourage the staff to take more exercise.[12] Then on the first anniversary of his joining the RAF, Alfred was told by the station commander that he could soon expect his next 'ring' on his sleeve, although it depended upon Group HQ approval for his upgrade to Flight Lieutenant.[12] Unfortunately the anticipated promotion was ditched again as a result of newly-introduced Establishment staffing levels, and since there was unlikely to be any further vacancy for another Flight Lieutenant at the station, he considered a request for a move to another station in the hope of securing this next promotion.[12]

Meanwhile Alfred had pinned his financial hopes on a recent article in *The Times* which reported that in future, serving officers with families would be paid allowances based on the size of their families, instead of the flat rate of a married allowance. This would certainly have helped his family's financial situation, since he had almost given up any hope of further financial support from his former employer in Bradford, even though the firm had reported considerably increased profits at their latest AGM. Alfred had made up his mind that as long as his so-called 'generous allowance' from the company lasted, he was not going to beg any further assistance.[12] He was now resigned to the fact that there was little chance of a move to another operational station because of the range of his special duties involved in his present post, but as ever, the strange workings of those in charge of staff postings suggested otherwise, and a totally unexpected change of assignment occurred.

Redeployment: Operational Training Unit, RAF Pershore, Worcestershire

RAF Pershore was situated on the outskirts of Pershore, about five miles southwest of Throckmorton in Worcestershire and was built in 1940. During most of WW2 it was home to No. 23 Operational Training Unit (OTU) and was equipped with Wellington bombers for use by overseas aircrews in training for flight duties prior to their assignment with active bomber squadrons. Alfred had already spent a brief period at the station earlier in January 1941 following his time at Bomber Command HQ High Wycombe and before his admission to the RAF Halton Hospital for sinus surgery. This was when he had been newly assigned to give special lectures to aircrew in training after attending a short course for Station Intelligence Officers at Harrow.[12] However this new deployment did not last very long and was perhaps inappropriate for someone already suffering from a debilitating condition, especially when some of his duties required the supervision of snow clearing squads to remove deep snow from the runways during one of the worst winters of the war, which was the last thing he needed in his state of ill health.[12]

Alfred returned to RAF Pershore in November 1941 and soon found his new routine was quite unlike that of an Operational Station, and his new job now entailed giving orientation lectures to large groups of pilots and navigators training for their operational duties. The work involved lectures of up to four hours duration on most days of the week, which meant a lot of preparation work on top of the usual administrative duties. But Alfred found that there was little 'esprit de corps' at his new station, and he particularly missed the social side of life together with the lively mess duties of his former posting.[12] Moreover his new pay scale as Flying Officer had still not come into effect, even after a visit to his new Group HQ at Abingdon, near Oxford, to try to resolve the issue, although he knew that eventually his back pay would help alleviate this temporary inconvenience.[12]

Meanwhile Alfred was beginning to feel a little out of his depth with his new job since he attended only a brief one week training course for such demanding duties, so it was probably with some relief that he was once more temporarily assigned to further training at the RAF Intelligence School. This time he returned to the Fisher Road School in Harrow to attend a three week Advance Intelligence Course designed for Senior RAF Intelligence Officers from Operational Commands. This course covered such topics as air intelligence, escape and evasion procedures and basic intelligence analysis provided by visiting specialists from the Air Ministry, MI-6, MI-9, the Central Intelligence Unit at Medmenham and Station 'X' at Bletchley Park. Alfred found this particularly interesting and although at the time he could not reveal anything about it, he was desperately keen to complete the demanding training successfully, since it was not only important for his new role, but also for his future in the RAF.[12] The only problem was that Alfred's ill health problems continued, and the MO at RAF Pershore, who had consulted his notes from RAF Halton Hospital, considered sending him back there for further treatment. Naturally Alfred dreaded this outcome, not only because it might mean another operation, but also in his opinion it might result in the receipt of a 'bowler hat' at the end of it, in other words demobilisation from service yet again on health grounds.[12]

Fortunately Alfred's worst fears were not realised and he continued in his new challenging role at RAF Pershore, where he now had even more special lectures to provide as a result of his Harrow course. But he was also involved in keeping the men gainfully occupied when the station became snow-bound once more during severe weather, and they had to clear the snow from the runways of the aerodrome by hand which everyone detested since it was a huge task.[12] The only bright spot during these gloomy days occurred when Alfred was called upon to make another unexpected visit to his Group HQ, this time to meet his Group Intelligence Officer to discuss his rank of Flight Lieutenant in the complement of Station Intelligence Officers Establishment, along with the possibility of his post being upgraded to Squadron Leader. However it did not mean that Alfred would retain the post even if this new rank came about, since such posts in Intelligence were very rare, although he was encouraged by even the faintest chance of further promotion.[12]

Nevertheless this glimmer of hope seemed unlikely as Alfred reflected that, notwithstanding his successful completion of the Harrow course, together with the complete reorganisation of the chaotic state of training which he had inherited at his present OTU, further chances of his upgrade had been offset by his delayed promotion to Flight Lieutenant. This now made him a relatively junior officer among other more experienced senior officers, who would no doubt take precedence when the Air Ministry considered likely personnel for promotion to new postings.[12] As a result he was somewhat downhearted since he genuinely felt that he had demonstrated his capabilities, and yet it was likely in the circumstances that he would not even be considered as a senior Flight Lieutenant if posted to another Operational Station. It was not just the lack of rank which irked him, but the fact that he was his own boss at RAF Pershore, although as ever, he acknowledged he must accept this apparent injustice and get on with the job.[12]

Alfred put these promotion problems aside after he listened on the wireless to the live House of Commons debate on the current war situation that had taken place at the end of January 1942, in which the Coalition Government led by the Prime Minister Winston Churchill had called for, and eventually received, a vote of confidence in how the Government was handling this 'darkest hour' of the conflict.[12] While this had cleared the air to some degree, Alfred remained of the opinion that a more intensive effort was needed, and even though the war in the Far East looked all but lost, he was still optimistic that the country would win in the end, with the entry into the war by the USA following the Pearl Harbour débâcle of December 1941.[12] He continued his musings about the war situation at the time with the observation that although the news was grim, and he feared that it would be a much longer war now, and although he admitted that it was difficult to see an end at present, as ever the optimist he expressed the view: 'I think this is about the darkest hour, but we will see a big change in our favour before the end of the war.'[12]

In late February 1942 Alfred suffered yet another recurrence of his usual winter colds, although by now he was resigned to continue work since his special duties had to be performed, but he received little support from the station MO. On the contrary, when he presented himself on sick parade he was summarily examined for possible duty overseas, and like everyone else only his case notes were reviewed from the previous year without any further medical examination, before he was also added to the potential foreign posting list.[12] It was not surprising that Alfred considered February to be a fateful month for him in terms of ill-health, not only during the last war but the present one, and now just one year since his admission to hospital for his sinus operation he regretted the procedure as it appeared to have been a complete waste of time.[12]

He was also concerned about his continued prospects in the service, but he need not have worried since the Air Ministry apparently had no knowledge of his continued health setbacks, and soon Alfred received the news that he was to be posted yet again, this time back to another Bomber Command Operational Station in Lincolnshire not far from his former station at RAF Swinderby. His only other consolation was that having been promoted to Flight Lieutenant in October 1941 he would not be reduced in rank again to Flying Officer as a result of the new move, although he was amazed and disappointed to hear that his replacement at RAF Pershore would be automatically promoted to Squadron Leader.[12] Nevertheless Alfred stoically acknowledged that it paid to be on the move since it would prevent him from becoming stale, and in any case he was firmly of the opinion: 'it does not really matter, the only thing that matters is to win the war.'[12]

A Return to 'Ops' – RAF Elsham Wold, Lincolnshire

RAF Elsham Wold was situated about 6 miles south of Barton-upon-Humber and had been established during the first world war as an RFC training centre, but was greatly expanded in 1939-1940 and began operational activities in 1941 with the arrival of No. 103 Squadron. In 1942 it was further expanded to become one of the largest operational bomber stations in the country with around 2,500 airmen and women dispersed over a wide area. Alfred's first impressions of his new station were the most favourable of all his postings to date, and although it was a remote spot, he admitted that the ambience was appealing with the fresh sea air and the nearby rolling Lincolnshire Wolds, which reminded him of the family holidays spent at Filey on the east coast of Yorkshire before the war. He was also pleased to be nearer home so that short leave visits would be possible.[12] Soon after his arrival he received the good news that following his official appointment to Flight Lieutenant on 15th October 1941, he had now been credited with five months back pay of £370. He was also thankful that he had retained his status on return to 'Ops' when many others had been reduced in rank, and now his pay had increased to £456 with £228 married allowance.[12] However even though he had retained his rank, he was no longer a number one in seniority terms in this new posting, although he found all the staff very supportive in his new role, especially the M.O. who began a course of injections to try to improve his immunity to infections.[12]

Alfred's general outlook improved considerably with the onset of spring in 1942, which had arrived somewhat later than expected, after a period of hostile weather in which an east wind roared across the Wolds bringing daily rain, hail, snow, and cloudy conditions that seriously affected operational activities. Now suddenly the sun shone, the sky cleared and the air became milder,[12] and he took the opportunity of walking along the low 300 feet escarpment of the Wolds towards the Humber mouth. He felt as if he was walking on top of the world as he recited the line from the poem 'The West' by A.E. Housman (1851-1936): 'The son of heaven turns his brow West from forty countries now', although he admitted that instead he could only see forty miles across the Lincolnshire plain. Nevertheless, as he came to the end of a green track that ran due north, he took great delight as he neared the Humber estuary with the view of Yorkshire on the north bank, as he reflected on his county of origin and allegiance: 'I am, first and last, a Yorkshireman, no matter where I may be, but when I caught a distant prospect of Yorkshire from across the Humber like this, I felt strangely elated!' From where he stood on the Lincolnshire side of the estuary, Alfred could see the white cliffs of Hessle – the little 'Switzerland' – where he had played with his life-long friend George C. Heseltine, and the little East Riding Dales where he had walked over the Yorkshire Wolds, as the words of a Yorkshire dialect saying came to mind: '*Mi Hoame's Yorkshire, its accres brooad, ho'd moast mi kindred's boanes*"'[19] On the return walk he passed newly ploughed fields and saw lambs frolicking and the war seemed a thousand miles away, until a Spitfire and a Wellington roared overhead and brought him back to reality.[19]

On other occasions after coming off night shift on spring mornings, Alfred often took a path to the Wolds in the early sunlight and wandered for an hour or so before turning in to bed to forget about the frenzy of the previous night's duty. He often found a sheltered spot in a remote and quiet place where he could feel at peace even with a world at war, and dreamed his idle dreams, read a book of poems, or made plans for what he might do after the war was over.[20] Sometimes on his walks Alfred wandered further afield and revisited familiar local places such as Caistor where during WW1, he had spent the night as a young soldier in the RFA when his Brigade was on the move to their new quarters in Grimsby in 1915. He had been stationed there for some months before his illness, and he now linked together his two war experiences with some old memories of the past.[21]

Alfred's service at RAF Elsham Wold only lasted as long as the brief spring of 1942, before he was moved to a Personnel Reception Centre in Yorkshire within much easier reach of his home and family, although he had a further period of some three months service on the Wolds again one year later during April to July 1943. On this occasion Alfred was glad to be back in 'Ops' again after another prolonged period of OTU work, and found that his old station had undergone many changes needed to cope with the new intensive bombing effort that was now taking place, in which his old No. 103 Squadron was breaking all Group 1 service records. It had been re-supplied with many new aircraft including the new four-engined Lancaster Bomber that had replaced the old the twin-engined Vickers Armstrong Wellington. During one of his night-flying test experiences as a passenger, Alfred was astonished at the size of this new aircraft, which weighed about 30 tons fully laden with bombs, now had a crew of seven, and could fly faster, higher and with greater safety than ever before. In addition Alfred was also impressed by the enlargement of the whole place which had now made it one of the largest Bomber Command Operational Stations in the country. Finally, Alfred noted a more subtle change that had taken place in terms of the aircrew now based at the station, who appeared quieter, more serious and much younger than the old 'characters' with their outgoing personalities who had once occupied the place. But in spite of these personnel changes, Alfred still marvelled at the splendid qualities of courage, loyalty, comradeship and endurance of the average member of the RAF,[22] which was now in its Silver Jubilee year of existence having been formed from the former Royal Flying Corps on 1ˢᵗ April 1917.

A Final OTU Posting – RAF Hurn, Bournemouth, Dorset

RAF Hurn was a newly-opened station in August 1941, situated 4 miles north east of Bournemouth, and was a centre for paratroop training and a glider base for the North African landings in 1943. Then prior to 'D' Day in 1944, it was home to No. 507 Squadron that dropped supplies to the French Resistance. Following Alfred's brief first spell at RAF Elsham Wold, he received the shortest posting of his entire WW2 service to this south coast station. His new post was a return to an OTU role, and it appeared that he had been demoted in terms of his status, since he was not appointed to be the 'Officer in Charge' as he had been led to believe, and he fulfilled only a temporary substitute role until a further new posting could be arranged in Yorkshire.[12] However Alfred had very mixed feelings about this impending move, which may seem strange since it was back on home-ground, but the fact was that he was not looking forward to another instructional role even if it was closer to home. Nevertheless Alfred knew that his immediate future was entirely out of his own hands and he had to accept whatever the Air Ministry decided in their wisdom regarding the deployment of men in the Intelligence Service.

Air Ministry Personnel Reception Centre No. 7, Harrogate, Yorkshire

Alfred's penultimate posting of the war could not have been more of a contrast with the previous locations and it was one which would not only allow him easy access to home and family, but after six months he was able to live at home. His new place of work was the magnificent Majestic Hotel which had originally been opened in 1900 to accommodate the affluent visitors to the Spa Town of Harrogate. It is impressively situated off the A61 Ripon Road on rising ground overlooking the town centre, and was requisitioned by the Government on 8th September 1939 for administrative war purposes, since it was suspected that London would be subjected to immediate aerial bombardment and therefore it was considered to be a relatively safe haven.[23]

This assumption turned out to be false, when on 12th September 1940 the hotel was bombed by a Junkers 88, with one direct hit that failed to explode, and two others one of which exploded in the gardens and the third destroyed a nearby villa. Extensive damage was done by shrapnel to the hotel's Winter Garden and the blast severely damaged nearby homes and businesses causing many casualties, some of whom tragically died later. After the war it was discovered from captured documents that although the top target in the country had been British Fighter Command at High Wycombe, the hotel was number two on the list since it had been identified as Air Ministry Staff HQ Fortunately at the time of the bombing the hotel was not occupied by the Air Ministry, but it later became an Air Ministry Personnel Reception Centre, and was the location for hundreds of RAF non-commissioned staff, with as many as 850 pilots billeted there by 1943.

Alfred had spent two years being shuttled around the country according to the mysterious manipulations of the Air ministry, and now suddenly he was back in his native Yorkshire only 14 miles from home, and glad to be back in 'God's Own Country' once more, even if it did mean that he had returned to lecturing duties again which he least preferred. He was now billeted in the grand Queen's Hotel, which was a huge improvement on the austere dispersal hut where he had wintered during a previous posting. The Government had requisitioned 25 hotels in Harrogate, the grandest of which was the Majestic, where Alfred performed his daily duties that now included lectures of one hour's duration, with up to six lectures a day, delivered to as many as 500 pilots in the grand ballroom, where he had once 'tripped the light fantastic and talked all night to an audience of one.' This demanding schedule now became something of a chore to the extent that such performances became almost automatic, and while Alfred felt that he could go on all day like a gramophone, he admitted that he became tired of his own voice, and he found the experience shattering and had never worked so hard in his life, but it greatly increased his admiration for the work of schoolteachers.[24] Furthermore he felt guilty about his new nine to five existence and being at home in the middle of the war as he reflected: 'The Grand Hotel is all very well for a change, but it is too easy, too comfortable. I don't want to get soft and cling to my home like some of the chaps that I have met. When I joined the RAF I did so with my eyes open and I left home for the duration of the war.'[24]

Nevertheless he admitted that he enjoyed some of the compensations which his new posting permitted, and occasionally when he had a break in his duties, he was able to go on mini-tramping tours to some of his nearby favourite places in Yorkshire, such as York, which to him always seemed to be at the very heart of England and expressed the full glory of English history. But his favourite excursion was undoubtedly the journey home on foot for a weekend's leave, which gave him the most satisfaction of all and reminded him of his former pedestrian exploits in the area: 'I like the idea of tramping over the moors towards my home, and I was determined to walk from door to door – not to take a bus out of town or accept a lift halfway or any part of it. I like to feel completely independent of any transport when the walking mood is on me.'[25]

Alfred's route out of Harrogate went via Valley Gardens, over Oak Beck and along the quiet country road of Penny Pot Lane to the west of the town, then on past Beaver Dyke Reservoir, before he left the road towards Stainburn Moor by an ancient footpath between Nidderdale and Wharfedale. After he reached the low summit ridge of Sandwith Moor, he left the plateau and passed by the ancient ruins of John O'Gaunt's Castle and joined the Washburn Valley. In his opinion, even the extensive reservoir developments had not destroyed the lovely countryside, although now, since the valley had been declared a military training area, he needed a special pass to be able to enter this restricted zone. He then climbed the steep road towards Swinsty Moor and headed for the hamlet of Timble and the Timble Inn, which was a focal point for walkers and cyclists on weekend excursions. At this famous hostelry, he stopped midway on his journey to slake his thirst with a pint or two of the local brew, to accompany the traditional meal of Yorkshire pudding, roast lamb with mint sauce, roast potatoes and peas, with Wensleydale cheese to round off a very homely and satisfying meal, which in spite of widespread rationing was available. Beyond the Inn he headed straight for Wharfedale by way of Ellercar Pike, over Askwith Moor and Askwith village, then down from Weston Moor through pastures along a green track which led to the River

Wharfe. Here he reached the stepping stones below the weir to cross the river near the village of Burley-in-Wharfedale and arrived at the family home Wharfegate.[25,25a] This somewhat roundabout route of 18 miles was longer than the more direct road route of about 14 miles, by which Alfred returned by bus to his duties in Harrogate after a short break with his family.

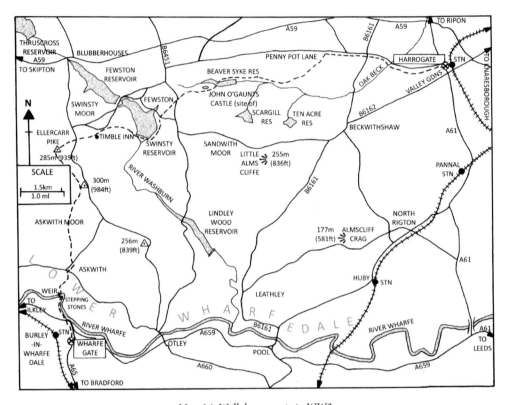

Map 14. Walk home route in WW2

By November 1942 Alfred was on the move again from his temporary billet in the Queen's Hotel, but rather than live in lodgings as other staff were requested to do, he was allowed to live at home.[26] This was particularly good news for Marie-Eugénie, who had experienced the loneliness of life at home without him, and especially for his four children who had enjoyed only the occasional brief visit by their father in the preceding two years. He hoped that they all understood his need to serve his country and that they were as proud as any other family whose husband and father was on active service. Moreover even the need to remove the three daughters from their boarding school in Blackpool due to financial pressures was overcome when another good Convent School was found in Harrogate.[27] The school also belonged to the same order of teaching nuns as those in Blackpool where they had been so happy for the last three years. Now they became day pupils and travelled daily by bus, which entailed an early morning start rising at 6.30 a.m. every day including Saturdays, although the fact that Alfred was often able to take them to the bus stop in the morning and meet them after school was compensation for their long school days. This situation was eased considerably when Alfred was provided with a petrol allowance for his own car and conveyed the girls to and from school each day much to their delight.[28]

Alfred spent a total of almost two years in his Harrogate post, during which time he was promoted to the rank of Squadron Leader and his pay increased to £639 p.a. with a married allowance of £228 p.a. This additional increment helped when the family celebrated a fifth but final addition with another son, Adrian Paul Quentin Fairfax Brown, who was born on 20th February 1944. Adrian like his brother and sister Rosemary was born at home with the services of the well-known local midwife, Mrs. Maufe, who was the granddaughter of one of the founders of the once famous Brown, Muff Co. departmental store in Bradford. The original Muff family was resident in Ilkley and had changed their name to 'Maufe' after founding the business in 1845. Adrian was duly baptised by Fr. Frederick Mawson at St. John Fisher and St. Thomas More RC Church in Burley-in-Wharfedale on 19th March 1944, where he became number 122 on the growing baptismal register, with godparents Mr. Richard and Mrs. Kathleen Carty, who were close friends of the family. Unfortunately Alfred did not have much time to appreciate his new son in these early days, since he was later posted in July to a final new service role in London, where he completed his time in the RAF before the war ended in 1945.

The Air Ministry Unit, Norfolk House, London

On the long train journey south to London, Alfred contemplated his past couple of years' service, and concluded that he had not been happy in his post at Harrogate, which was fine at first but was less appealing during the second year, when the novelty of his new situation had worn off and he felt he was out of touch with the war. He acknowledged that he could have remained at home and drifted along having a pleasant time like many others, but he felt he was going stale, instead of making the sacrifice by putting his whole self into the war effort.[29] He had been fortunate in this regard to have received the support from his sympathetic chief officer, who also longed to get back into action after having been shot down, but like Alfred had been sent to a Flight Training Command, and it was thanks to his help that Alfred had been able to influence the Air Ministry's Intelligence Postings Office to arrange an alternative position.

Even though it was difficult to leave his wife and family once more, he believed that the war would not last much longer now, and he envisaged that he would perhaps take up his old job in Bradford when it was over, buy a larger house in the country and settle down once more,[29] and no doubt with these prospects in mind he was looking forward to his new posting.

27. Squadron leader A.J. Brown

Alfred reported to the Air Ministry's Unit in Norfolk House, St. James Square, London, where his arrival had been eagerly awaited after some delay, and he was warmly received by his new chief of staff who showed him to his massive office which was almost empty, since there were none of the assistants in post yet who would eventually share the facility with him. At first he was unable to divulge much about his new role, except to describe it as very important, complicated and secret, and involved a 09.00 to 19.00 hours schedule, six days per week, with great responsibilities working alongside senior RAF planning officers, and with possibilities not only for early promotion, but working overseas in the near future.[29] It later emerged that Alfred had been posted to a group called the Control Commission for Management Strategy, which in liaison with other sections of the Armed Services, was to be responsible for the Allied Occupation of Germany subsequent to surrender at the end of the European Campaign. The CCMS was based in Norfolk House which was also the Supreme Head Quarters Allied Powers of Europe under General Dwight D. Eisenhower at this time.

On his first day at work, Alfred was given a lengthy document to read with the instruction: 'digest that for a start!' which Alfred discovered was the Draft Terms of Surrender for the German Armed Forces which was marked 'Top Secret', and was certainly the most exciting secret document he had ever seen.[30] Shortly afterwards his first assignment was to accompany several top brass RAF representatives at a joint meeting with their Army counterparts to discuss the imminent plans for the subsequent control of Germany, and as a lowly Squadron Leader at the time, he was a little over-awed by the presence of so many Brigadier Generals at the meeting. He was later more reassured when his role was further clarified, whereby he was responsible for devising a plan to set up a training school for senior officers intended to establish the advance elements of the overall CCMS in Berlin and elsewhere.[30]

Alfred's first three months in London were therefore occupied by the establishment of the infrastructure, staffing and resourcing of such an operation, along with planning the training schedules for those involved. He spent much of this time around Whitehall, visiting the offices of the War Cabinet, the Foreign Office, the Air Ministry at Adastral House, the Joint Intelligence Group and the Combined Operations Head Quarters. At planning meetings with a variety of Admirals, Generals, MPs, Peers, Economists, Health Officials and Technical Experts, he spent much time trying to persuade them to provide the benefit of their ideas and experiences of Germany to help formulate the plans needed to establish a training school for the first group of senior planning officers on the opening course which was to be operational soon.[30]

Initially Alfred was accommodated at the RAF Club in Piccadilly, in a small back bedroom on the third floor, hemmed in by walls on all sides and directly above the clamour of the kitchens below in the courtyard. But he often spent nights in the air raid shelter in the basement of Norfolk House because of the threat from the 'Doodlebugs' or 'V1' flying bombs which were launched as an attempt to retaliate in this later phase of the war.[29] It was because of disturbances to his sleep, and also the expense of living at the RAF Club, that Alfred tried an itinerant existence for part of the week, since he had friends around the London area who kindly offered alternative accommodation. His close friend George C. Heseltine and his wife Elsie who had a house in Fareham, Hampshire, suggested that Alfred could use a spare room, but this was too far to travel during the week, so he opted to spend occasional weekends there and tried to confine himself to the night shelter during the week.[29] Meanwhile the pace of work was beginning to increase considerably, and Alfred's intended plan to be able to get a weekend pass to celebrate his upcoming 50th birthday with his family at home was postponed.[29] He was not so much concerned about this significant milestone in his life as with the fact that he not only disliked the idea of ageing but the limitations that might be imposed on him as he lamented: 'It is so embarrassing to grow old. How I loathe it! I wanted so much to die young. I expect it is wrong of me, but life for me is over when I can't climb or walk over the moors with ease.'[29]

However Alfred's service life had some compensation, when it was confirmed that he had been promoted to the rank of Wing Commander with effect from 1st August 1944.[29] This sudden promotion surprised him since there were others who had expected upgrades, but he had been selected first even though he was almost last in post in his unit. Then before he knew it, a tailor had been called to change his 'rings' and sew the three impressive new broad blue bands to his sleeves, at a not so modest charge of 19s/6d, much to Alfred's consternation, since he was unsure about how long he would keep his new rank with the constant changes in the staffing 'Establishment'.[29] No doubt the resultant pay rise helped to offset the costs involved and he was rewarded with a salary of £867 p.a. with a married allowance of £274 p.a., which helped his family's growing financial expenditure and his additional costs of living in London.

Alfred continued to have a sleeping problem that affected his work, and although he had some respite at the weekends when stayed with his other friend and former book illustrator, William Littlewood and his wife Kathleen, at Canhurst Cottage, Knowl Hill, in Berkshire,[29] he now relied more and more on the medication to help him sleep prescribed by his friend from Ilkley, Dr. Jim Valentine. Even so he complained that he never felt well and did not look forward to another year or two with the RAF, since his workload was so demanding that, together with his interrupted sleep, it left him exhausted at the end of the day.[29] It seems likely that Alfred showed the effects of a form of 'war weariness' accumulated over the duration of his service, and for the first time he began to express an interest in the 'Demobilisation Plan' that had been established for men over 50 who to were be the first group to leave the armed services.[29] Alfred therefore considered an early discharge in the next few months, unless members of the CCMS were treated differently from other branches of the services, and the possibility of release by the summer of 1945. This prospect perhaps gave him the stimulus to continue to cope with his work load.

The outlook for Alfred's future remained very uncertain in the autumn of 1944, and even the possibility of demobilisation within a year was in doubt, since it was highly likely at the time that members of his unit would be earmarked for development work in Germany or Austria, and therefore he would not be released even when the surrender was achieved.[29] The prospect of a return to his old job in Bradford after the war also looked doubtful following Alfred's meeting in London with the senior partner in the business, at which he received little encouragement, and following his remuneration dispute, he did not relish the idea of returning to the company unless there was a senior position available to him. He had no intention of going back to fight yet another war for his rights in order to establish his position once more in the old firm.[29]

Eventually, after six months of intensive work and many sleepless nights, Alfred's health broke down again and instead of a much-needed weekend leave, he was admitted to a private ward at the Air Ministry Station Sickness Quarters in Hallam Street, Westminster, this time with an eruption of unpleasant carbuncles.[29] The infection had caused a swollen right hand, which required doses of strong medication and poultices to be applied every 2 to 3 hours that left him with a heavily bandaged arm in a sling, as well as wondering how he always seemed to contract some horrible kind of disease at this time of year.[29] Unfortunately Alfred had to dissuade his wife from visiting the hospital this time because of the danger of the random 'V2' rocket attacks on London, which were now at a peak of the retaliatory war period. When the inflammation had subsided, the Medical Officer informed him that he was to be discharged in about a week, after which he was then be entitled to extended sick leave to recover fully from this latest health setback.[29]

Later there was more bad news when Alfred returned from home sick leave and learned from his Group Commander that the future role of his unit was now in doubt, since the Army was to take over the major organisation of the CCMS in Germany, and that the RAF 'Establishment' had been cut as a result.[29] Moreover, since most of the unit staff needed would be the RAF 'Regular' rather than the 'Volunteer Reserve' category, Alfred was informed that he would be placed in the first group for demobilisation i.e. those servicemen in the 50 plus age range. He was very unhappy with this new development and consulted both the head of the RAF Intelligence Group and the Air Vice-Marshall to see if there was any chance of an alternative temporary posting in Germany in RAF Intelligence instead, but he was informed that this was highly unlikely, especially at the rank of Acting Wing Commander.[29] Some of Alfred's senior colleagues suggested that he should leave the service while he had the chance, and he came around to the idea that he should apply for a discharge for the sake of his wife and family. Alfred also had his doubts about whether his health could cope with the demands of a further period of service and came to the inevitable conclusion: 'I think my four and a half year's service is enough at my age as things have turned out. I don't like the atmosphere at NH [Norfolk House] and I like it even less now that I have experienced it again and see how things are. There is too much footling about and backscratching, before adding bitterly: Lord Douglas Hamilton has got the Austrian job – my job and he is a Regular [RAF].'[29]

Soon afterwards Alfred was examined by the MO again who concluded he had responded well to recover from a serious streptococcal infection and that his wound had fully healed although it had undoubtedly left him weaker than ever. Furthermore the MO also indicated that he would support Alfred's case for a medical discharge at a Medical Board if needed, but suggested that Alfred may not be considered as a serious enough case, since in the MO's opinion: 'they are passing old crocks as A1 fit for service these days.' Alfred would not have wished for another discharge on medical grounds even if it were possible, and in any case expressed the view: 'I dislike the idea of resigning before the end, but under the circumstances I feel that it is time to go home.'[29] Then in a final note to his wife towards the end of his service Alfred indicated that he was ill yet again with the usual compendium of winter cold symptoms and was confined to bed once more by the M.O., so he now acknowledged that after almost five years of war service perhaps, in his present state, he should consider being invalided out after all, but by then it was too late, since he had already written to resign his commission.[29]

In the New Year Alfred received the first official notification that the resignation of his commission in the RAF Volunteer Reserve was approved with effect from 3rd February 1945, and he was granted permission to retain the rank of Squadron Leader, without any emoluments, but with restrictions on the wearing of his uniform, and his pay ceased forthwith, but he was still subject to the Official Secrets Act.[31] Subsequently, in view of Alfred's further representations for the extension of his service record, he received a second official notification that his resignation was amended to 17th March 1945, and he was credited with a further 42 days of pay and allowances, but he did not qualify for any civilian clothing allowance or cash grant in lieu thereof until the final defeat of Germany.[32] Alfred's Second World War was finally over as he somewhat ruefully and ironically reflected:

> I have served in both World Wars, but I have not managed to get into Europe, I have not qualified for any campaign ribbons or medals, and I was only granted permission to wear my uniform for specially approved occasions.[29]

References and Notes

1. Alfred John Brown, West Riding Archive Service, Bradford Central Library, Document No. 69D90, Item 4.1.2., 'Ground Staff'.

2. AJB/MEB Personal Correspondence File 1940, passim.

3. A.J. Brown, *Ground Staff (A Personal Record)*, Eyre & Spottiswoode, London, 1943.

4. Alfred John Brown, 'All Quiet In The Dales', *The Yorkshire Dalesman* Magazine, December, 1939, pp. 7-9.

5. Bruce Barrymore Halpenny, *Bomber Aircrew in World War II*, 'The Development of the Bomber Airfield', pp. 1-39, Pen and Sword Aviation, Barnsley, 2004.

6. AJB/MEB Personal Correspondence File, 1940-1941, passim.

7. A.J. Brown, op. cit., Part IV: Off Duty, 'This England', pp. 100-104.

8. A.J. Brown, op. cit., Part III: Tonight's Target: 1941-1942, 'Poland', pp. 71-85.

9. A.J. Brown, op. cit., Part III: Tonight's Target: 1941-1942, 'Poland', pp. 83-85.

10. A.J. Brown, op. cit., Part II: Bomber Command: 1940-1941, 'The Road to HQ', pp. 32-35.

11. A.J. Brown, op. cit., Part II: Bomber Command: 1940-1941, 'Bomber Command', pp. 35-39.

12. AJB/MEB Personal Correspondence File, 1941-1942, passim.

13. A.J. Brown, op. cit., Part II: Bomber Command: 1940-1941, 'RAF Hospital', pp. 46-50.

14. A.J. Brown, op. cit., Part III: Tonight's Target: 1941-1942, 'Memorable Moments', pp. 98-99.
    14a. Note: There are various estimates that indicated about 15% of all Bomber Command aircrew fatalities occurred during non-operational flights as a result of training-related accidents due mechanical failures and pilot or navigational errors.

15. A.J. Brown, op. cit., Part IV: Off Duty, 'Mess Secretary', pp. 107-113.
    15a. Note: Sir Arnold Talbot Wilson was killed when his Vickers Wellington bomber crash-landed in northern France, near Dunkirk 31st May 1940. In *Time Magazine* 17th June 1940, he had famously stated: "I have no desire to shelter myself and live behind the ramparts of the bodies of millions of our young men."

16. A.J. Brown, op. cit., Part III: Tonight's Target: 1941-1942, 'Failed to Return', pp. 64-66.

17. A.J. Brown, op. cit., Part III: Tonight's Target: 1941-1942, 'Memorable Moments', p. 99.

18. Bruce Barrymore Halpenny, op. cit., 'Airmen of RAF Bomber Squadrons who were awarded the Victoria Cross', pp. 200-223.

19. A.J. Brown, op. cit., Part IV: Off Duty, 'Spr,ing Comes To The Wolds', pp. 127-128.

20. A.J. Brown, op. cit., Part IV: Off Duty, 'Dispersal Hut', pp. 128-129.

21. A.J. Brown, op. cit., Part IV: Off Duty, 'Two Campaigns', pp. 119-123.

22. A.J. Brown, op. cit., Part V: Air Crew, 'Back To Ops', pp. 159-164.

23. Malcolm Neesam, 'Hotel Majestic', Published by Paramount Hotels to Commemorate the Centenary of the Hotel Majestic and the New Millennium, 1ˢᵗ January 2000.

24. A.J. Brown, op. cit., Part V: Air Crew: 1943, 'In Yorkshire', pp. 148-149.

25. A.J. Brown, op. cit., Part IV: Off Duty, 'The Moors', pp.138-142.
   25a. **Note**: There is currently an ongoing plan to replace the stepping stones, which are often impassable when the river is high, to provide access to the footpaths on the north side of the river. (www.saveourstones.webs.com)

26. Alfred John Brown, West Yorkshire Archive Service, Bradford Central Library, Document No. 69D90, Section No. 7/9.

27. Alfred John Brown, ibid., Section No. 7/2.

28. Personal communication with Mrs. R. Sturrup (née Brown).

29. AJB/MEB Personal Correspondence File, 1942-1944, passim.

30. Alfred John Brown, West Yorkshire Archive Service, Bradford Central Library, Document No. 69D90, Section 7/9.

31. AJB Personal Correspondence File, 1945, Air Ministry letter to Acting Wing Commander A.J. Brown, 13ᵗʰ February 1945.

32. AJB Personal Correspondence File, 1945, Air Ministry Letter to Squadron Leader A.J. Brown, (no date) March 1945.

CHAPTER 11

Alfred's Wartime Writing

Alfred had enjoyed an exceptional period of published work in the decade leading up to WW2, but his level of productivity diminished after he joined the RAF in 1940, although he tried to maintain some output at least during the early part of the war. In particular he made contributions to the *Yorkshire Dalesman* Magazine which include a description of a journey through two lesser-known dales just before the war,[1] and his observations of dales life during the early phase of the war.[2] In 1940 he contributed two further articles, the first was an appreciation of Dorothy Wordsworth's account from her *Grasmere Journal* of the Yorkshire pilgrimages by William and Dorothy in 1800 and 1802, which included William's honeymoon journey to the county.[3] The second reviewed the many famous figures in English literature who found inspiration in the broad acres of Yorkshire for their writing, followed by an acknowledgement of the contribution made by Yorkshire authors to literature.[4] Alfred even made a contribution to his old school magazine with a short article, which, unusually for such a principled publication, extolled the virtues of beer in bringing about the inspiration sometimes required for writing.[5] Nevertheless these early war writings had mainly been completed before the start of the conflict when Alfred produced a wide variety of material, long before the weariness from the work, illnesses and financial worries associated with the war finally brought a halt to any further productive output.

However, during the early period of his RAF service Alfred also enjoyed continued support from his readership, and following a visit to his publishers, Country Life in London, while he was stationed at Bomber Command HQ, High Wycombe, he discovered that sales of *Striding Through Yorkshire* (1938) were still going reasonably well, even though the printers were now restricted to 33% of their former paper allowance.[6] This gave him some encouragement to continue his literary efforts, and he reminded the new manager of the firm that he had already completed a new manuscript entitled 'Broad Acres' when the war started, and that the draft had been provisionally accepted by the former manager, but it had been put on hold due to the conflict. While Alfred realised that no commitment could be made under the present circumstances, he was keen to publish this new piece of work and he resubmitted the manuscript for consideration when the situation improved.[6] He was further encouraged by the news that *Striding Through Yorkshire* continued to sell well, and his publisher planned to print and bind another 1,000 copies to meet anticipated future demand. This gave him new hope that 'Broad Acres' might be published after all, but it was not released until after the war in 1948.

The Struggle with Wartime Writing

Alfred had always enjoyed the twin passions of writing and walking which had sustained him in a symbiotic relationship until the war, but now these forms of escape from the relentless burdens of the wartime night and day work had virtually come to an end. His new lifestyle inevitably led to a reduction of both activities, especially since he was prone to suffer from regular infections, probably due to his weakened resistance as a result of his WW1 illness. While the cause of his health problems remained conjectural, the effect certainly was not, and his productivity was reduced when he was unable to fulfil his need to walk and write. But in spite of a depressive state brought on by health problems, he was determined get fit enough to be able to write effectively, and he needed to escape the lethargy of 'sedentariness' enforced by the war for his own sanity.[6] Unsurprisingly a reduction in both these vital aspects of his life resulted in a limited literary output during the war years. He often struggled to come to terms with, and was barely able to achieve, the limited outcomes that he eventually produced, although it seems likely that he was never really satisfied with his meagre output during this period.

Alfred reflected that there was little or no hope of writing or walking, even when he was posted to a non-operational RAF station, where he had more regular hours of work such as RAF Pershore, and that writing as such had become a source of self-amusement to counter the.boredom of routine[6]. During the early war years not only had his desire to write diminished, but worse still, he considered that this once important activity was now probably a waste of time anyway.[6] In such times of despondency, it was probably difficult for him to see a way forward and return to something like the level of written output that he had achieved previously. He even made an attempt to rationalise his restricted productivity with a tongue-in-cheek, self-deprecatory review of the circumstances that purportedly had led to his reduced literary output:

> I wish I were one of those writers who can write enormous novels on
> sixpenny Woolworth's writing-pads. One reads of how they decide to write
> a story and then sit down, without any further ado, and fill a succession of

writing-pads... For one thing, I never seem to have any such writing-pad... I doubt if I could even begin to write with such material, at least I must have a book of some sort and not just a writing-pad.

But even assuming I had the ideal sort of book, I should still feel handicapped by my surroundings. Anything I have previously written has been done in the same room, with the same surroundings, and with a particular lamp. My old lamp had an orange shade which cast a lovely orange tint all over the table and the room, and made me feel in the mood for writing.

Even so one or two other things were needed if I were to write freely. I liked a couple of red apples on my table to munch when I began, and a tankard of ale at my elbow when I had disposed of the apples. With these and a pipe to follow (and quantities of matches) and an equitable temperature, I might, with reasonable luck, write a thousand words, but not otherwise!

How can I be expected to write in the present circumstances, with the wrong sort of book, the wrong lamp, strange surroundings, a chilly room, no apples, no ale, and three matches? On the whole I think I will go to bed instead, because so far I have not written a word of what I intended: all I have achieved is one apology for not writing at all. Goodnight![6]

Influence of Renowned Writer Comrades?

In spite of Alfred's exasperation about not being able to write, he probably regained some incentive to write as the war progressed as a result of the association with other established writers with whom he came into contact during his time at various RAF stations. Early in his service he noted how impressed he was by the great variety of interesting fellow officers who served their country,[7] and perhaps none more so than a few who had written about their own war experiences and enjoyed publishing success. This may have provided him with the idea of formulating his war time jottings into some form of publishable work.

The first of these esteemed comrades was Wing Commander Peter Cooper (1919-2007), whom Alfred had met originally when he served at RAF Swinderby in Lincolnshire in late 1940. He was also stationed with Alfred at Bomber Command HQ at High Wycombe, and later the two of them were admitted to the RAF Halton Hospital in early 1941.[6] Under the pseudonym 'Colin Curzon', Cooper wrote two lively mystery stories entitled *The Case of the Eighteenth Ostrich* (1940) and later *The Body in the Barrage Balloon* (1942), but it was his morale-boosting book *Flying Wild* (1941) which described the humorous experiences of the author during his RAF service that captured the imagination of the public. Later in the war Cooper became Air Attaché at the British Embassy in Ankara, Turkey, and left the RAF after 22 year's service to follow a career in the Probation Service. Unfortunately he never pursued his writing talent further, although Alfred remained in contact with him after the war.

It was also while Alfred was at Bomber Command HQ that he became friends with Hugh George Durnford, MC (1886-1965), who had also served with the Royal Field Artillery during WW1.[6] Durnford had been captured on 5th August 1917 while acting as a forward observer for his Brigade, and was incarcerated at the Straslund prisoner of war camp before he escaped in September 1917, for which he was awarded the MC, but he was recaptured and sent to the officer prisoner of war camp at Holzminden, near Hanover. It was here that Durnford became Camp Adjutant and took overall charge of, but did not take part in, the tunnel escape on 24th July 1918, by 29 officers of whom 10 successfully made it back to England. Durnford subsequently wrote the classic escape book entitled: *The Tunnellers of Holzminden* (1920). Alfred enjoyed his 1940 reprinted Penguin edition and they regularly exchanged odd odes, although he much regretted not having kept such rhymes for posterity.[8]

Later in the war while stationed at RAF Feltwell, Thetford, Norfolk, Alfred became friends with yet another literary character, Alfred John Evans, MC and bar (1889-1960) who had also served during the Great War.[6] Evans had enjoyed a spasmodic first class cricketing career from 1908-1928, but he won greater distinction as a pilot with the Royal Flying Corps in WW1. During an early morning reconnaissance flight over the Somme on 16th July 1916, an engine failure at 4,000 ft. caused Evans and his observer to ditch the aircraft ten miles behind enemy lines, and they were both captured and taken prisoner to Clausthal Camp in Germany. Evans soon escaped but was recaptured at the Dutch border, before he made another escape and this time managed to reach Switzerland after 18 nights walking to avoid detection. Later in February 1918 he commanded No. 142 RAF Squadron in Palestine and was subsequently captured yet again, this time by the Turks, but he was returned to Egypt after the Armistice. He was awarded a bar to his MC for repeated escape attempts and wrote the very successful book *The Escaping Club* (1921) which was reprinted in 1936.[6]

It is difficult to estimate the influence of serving alongside other notable writers had upon Alfred's soon to be rekindled enthusiasm for writing. Undoubtedly his comrades' examples of successful writing about triumph over adversity during their war service inspired the public readership at the time and afterwards. However Alfred's own war service was unlikely to provide the kind of story to generate similar popular interest. It was therefore with a different objective in mind that Alfred began to sift through the random jottings that he had assembled during the course of his early years of service in the RAF, with a view to producing a different kind of publication.[9,9a]

A Return to Wartime Writing

While Alfred was stationed at RAF Pershore in Worcestershire in an OTU role, he drafted some rough working notes into a manuscript for an intended new book that he provisionally called: 'Ground Staff', but he had his doubts about whether it would be any good and even considered burning this early draft.[6] He was concerned that there were already a lot of 'flying books' due to be published in the spring of 1942 and that his own would be too late to make an impact. Nevertheless he considered that if the war was to be very protracted, some publisher might eventually take an interest in it, and he hoped that the later the book appeared, the more up to date it was likely to be.[6]

He acknowledged that the concept for the book was still premature and he had no idea if he would ever complete the work he had in mind, but he was also determined that if he did accomplish the task, he wanted a book that would be different from all the other 'flying books' which had begun to appear.[6] Unfortunately at this time he had to postpone further work on the manuscript since he was due to be transferred to another Operational Bomber Command station, where he would not have the evenings free to do any work. Even though he had already sent the first part of the manuscript for typing, he had reservations about the chances of ever finishing it because he had only completed about one quarter of the estimated work involved.[6] However since he had obtained the services of Miss Richardson, the secretary of his former Bradford employer, who had agreed to type the manuscript after working hours, he hoped that her work on the draft would encourage him to continue writing and complete the book.[6]

On arrival at his new posting at RAF Elsham Wold in Lincolnshire, Alfred realised that this return to night duties once more meant he had little chance of completing the work, and even though he had received the first few typed chapters of the book for editing and had plenty of new material assembled, he found that a combination of lack of motivation and insufficient time limited any further progress.[6] He therefore had to wait until his next posting to the Air Ministry Reception Centre in Harrogate in the summer of 1942, in order to complete the work involved. Finally just over three months later, he completed the draft manuscript of his book entitled *Ground Staff (A Personal Record)* for consideration and hopefully approval by officials at the Air Ministry.[10] Yet even at this stage he was full of doubts, not only about his own efforts but his lack of conviction about the likelihood of its publication when he confided to his wife:

> Darlingest,
>
> Here is the introduction I wrote for the book last winter in Pershore and here is the finished(?) book. In some inglorious fashion, I have contrived to overcome my disinclination to write in the wrong surroundings, and contrary to all precedent and prejudice, I have completed the task – after a fashion.
>
> I have written at Pershore, at Elsham, at Harrogate and at home. One chapter was written in a hospital. Some of it was written in lavatories on RAF toilet paper, which is certainly more suitable for writing than for wiping bottoms(!). Some of it was written at dawn after a long night duty and some at midnight when I couldn't sleep.
>
> I have posted the original to the Air Ministry today and have no great hopes that it will ever see the bookshops.
>
> But I have written it under such difficult circumstances and here it is for you... It is not worthy of you and your long-suffering devotion to me, but at the moment it is the best I can do in the midst of the war, and perhaps after the war I will write a better and more worthy book for you.
>
> Meanwhile, here it is, thank goodness! – my latest born; so don't be too severe on it – or me – weary from the throes of delivery,
>
> Yours devoted, Alfred John.[10] [He dedicated the book: 'For Marie-Eugénie']

Meanwhile, since Alfred was waiting for the Air Ministry's deliberations over the initial draft of his 'new born' book, he submitted three short sections from the draft text to a writing competition for RAF officers held by the RAF Journal in London.[11] The first, 'RAF Hospital' recounted his mixed experiences of the time spent in the RAF Hospital at Halton, the second 'The Colonials' described his observations of the quirky behaviour of Commonwealth Forces Officers in a popular West End London Hotel, and the third 'Memorable Moments' recollected the hectic activities in the 'Ops' room of an RAF Bomber Command Station. Unfortunately none of these was successful, nor were any printed in the journal, but this was not surprising given the numbers of other successful writers in the RAF who made submissions, and the sensitive material about which Alfred had chosen to write.

The Air Ministry's response to the draft manuscript appeared quite benign in terms of the content of the book, since the majority of the text portrayed the RAF most positively in the light of Alfred's personal record of service. With the exception of some censorship of certain aspects of restricted information, such as the locations of Operational Bomber Stations including the whereabouts of Bomber Command HQ, there was no major change recommended to the content.[12] However, in the case of other somewhat less sensitive information, the censor's red pencil had been firmly applied with the instruction: 'the whole of this section is to be omitted' and was crossed out by an Air Ministry official.[13] This was surprising given the topicality of the material, in which Alfred expressed his views concerning the absurd distinctions often made between flying and non-flying personnel, along with the ludicrous identification of 'Volunteer Reserve' and 'Active' status of service personnel by their respective 'VR' and 'A' lapel badges. Furthermore the illogical restriction of those 'Administrative & Special Duties' ranks, often referred to by the derogatory term 'Ground Stooges', meant that they were not entitled to wear any sort of 'wings' or other recognised RAF insignia on their uniforms or cap badges. In Alfred's opinion this vital group was in the same service, fighting the same war and should receive the same recognition because of their contribution to the total war effort.[14] But in this regard he had clearly touched a very sensitive nerve in the upper echelons of the RAF's hierarchical corporate constitution!

Following the revisions of the final manuscript required by the Air Ministry, Alfred submitted the approved draft to his publishers and signed a memorandum of agreement with Eyre & Spottiswoode in November 1942,[15] with an intended publication date early in the new year, although the wartime restrictions meant that publication was conditional upon circumstances over which the publishers had no control. Inevitably there were considerable delays in the publication process, so that Alfred could not complete the final proof-reading until September 1943,[10] and the book was eventually published in December 1943.[16] He received an advance of £164 and royalties of 12.5% of the published price of 10s/6d for the first 2,500 copies, rising to 15% between 2,500 to 7,500 copies and 17.5% on copies thereafter, with a further royalty of 10% of any sales abroad, along with the statutory six free copies, as well as an option to purchase any remaindered books at cost price.[15]

Impact of the Book

It is difficult to assess the overall impact of the book since there was a lack of sales figures and there were only limited local press reviews available, rather than the more widespread appraisals by the national press of some of Alfred's previous books.

Nevertheless the new work was no doubt most warmly welcomed by the large group of his loyal followers, who would have been among the readership of those Yorkshire-based newspapers and magazines that chose to comment on this new and very unusual piece of work by a local favourite author.

The critical commentary by the *Yorkshire Post and Leeds Mercury* was very limited in scope and mainly focused upon Alfred's return to his Yorkshire roots during his war service:

> Before the war A.J. Brown who is now a Squadron Leader in the RAF, wrote some good books on walking, and during the war he has managed to get down on paper in odd moments a book describing his ground staff experiences as an intelligence officer with Bomber Command... it is a readable kind of notebook, and in it I see that Brown, after two years' service in strange counties, found himself back in his beloved Yorkshire. They soon had him hard at work in a large hotel where he had often been a peace-time guest.[17]

On the other hand, the *Yorkshire Evening Post* critic, who paid tribute to Alfred's previous work, rather narrowly and dismissively highlighted the impact that the sound of a distant war made on his home ground:

> A.J. Brown whose books and articles on walking enjoyed a vogue, is now an officer with the rank of Squadron Leader with Bomber Command... By this time most of us are familiar with what goes on at aerodromes while our airmen are over Germany or preparing to fly there, the chief interest of this book lies in the reactions of the author to his native heath while on leave, or stationed temporarily on or near it... He touches on a fact that must have occurred to many people that however deeply they penetrate into the countryside, the sound of aircraft can nearly always be heard, even in the remote vastness of the Pennines.[18]

However a much more balanced and qualified review was presented in a lengthy appraisal by the founding editor of the fledgling *Yorkshire Dalesman* Magazine, Harry J. Scott, although he acknowledged the concerns which the magazine had about maintaining its distance from war-related topics:

> It has been the considered policy of this magazine to leave the war out of its pages, not because the war has ignored the Dales or that the Dales folk have no sense of responsibility, but because it seemed our special service

to keep alive and green the character of the unchanging Dales that outlives all wars and offers to both mind and spirit renewal and refreshment even in the greatest of the world's crises.

But an exception must be made when so notable and valued a Yorkshire lover as A.J. Brown is the author of book which in the main is about the war. *Ground Staff* is indeed more than a war book. Thus it begins with a picture of the German occupation of Vienna, as A.J. Brown witnessed on one of his many Continental journeys. It draws an intimate picture of the work of Bomber Command as observed by an officer of the ground staff, with all the stirring human life that can only be known by one living among it. It has an illuminating chapter on Poland and its tragedy told by one who has loved its ancient glory almost as much he loved the Yorkshire Dales. It contains innumerable rapidly sketched impressions of men, places, events, the intricacies of Bomber 'Ops', and life in an RAF Hospital. And inevitably, it has a great deal about Yorkshire slipped, pulled, dropped and sometimes dragged into its pages...

The editor then continued with several examples extracted from the book, together with a selection of some of Alfred's memorable experiences in the RAF, before recommending it to the readership:

I commend this book to all our readers because they will enjoy it. They will relish the freshness and vividness of it all as, I hope, they enjoyed some qualities of A.J. Brown's earlier Yorkshire books.[19]

Alfred's 'Different Kind of Flying Book'

Alfred sets out to write a book that is very different from the many 'flying books' which appear in the middle of WW2 and radically different from anything that he has written in the past, or would write in the future, and this difference is manifested by the subject matter. He deliberately chooses to write about the experience of serving in the RAF from a hitherto relatively unreported non-flying perspective, since he believes that the support of a plethora of ground staff personnel is vital to the successful operational capabilities of the only dedicated 'Offensive Command' i.e. Bomber Command, that takes the war directly to Germany in the early part of the war, when most of the armed services are largely engaged in 'Defensive Command' actions. In this regard he feels that his comrades on the ground deserve some recognition for their contribution to the total war effort, and not just the reflected glory which the

RAF aircrews gain from the other 'flying books' at the time.

Another interesting difference is the physical presentation of the book, which reflects the austerity of the period. In the words of the publisher on an inset page: 'This book is produced in complete conformity with the authorised economy standards' and is stamped: 'Book Production War Economy Standard', which might be considered as primitive recycled paper. The cover is made from a cheap, woven, fabric-covered black cardboard, and only the spinal lettering of title, author's name and publisher's initials in a faded 'Air Force' blue print is the least bit ostentatious. Even the dust cover suggests the limitations applied to the printing industry by its drab illustration of a silhouetted bomber with ground crew in attendance, beside a control tower, and the pale pink search-lit illumination of the title *Ground Crew* in the sky above. It is not surprising given these production limitations that not many copies of the book have survived the ravages of use with time.

However none of these limited physical manifestations of the book detracts from the inherent appeal of the material contained, which is written in a style that follows a narrative commentary from the point of view of both a passive observer and an active participant in the many RAF Bomber Command scenarios described in the text. In addition there is often a reflective analysis or interpretation of the events portrayed in terms of their historical significance in the progress made by the 'Offensive Command' during the early to mid periods of the war, albeit from a perspective of a member of the ground support staff personnel.

The scope of the book is not necessarily limited to the time-scale of Alfred's RAF service, but covers the period from 1938 in the lead-up to the war, as well as the projected progress of the war beyond the mid-point of the conflict when the writing ceases, although of course this was not known when the draft of the book was completed in late 1942 to early 1943. Within this time frame Alfred utilises his first hand knowledge to describe the range of activities which underpin the day to day duties of ground staff in general, together with the night time responsibilities of intelligence staff in particular, both of which often become blurred, especially in his own case when he often has to fulfil an odd combination of roles, for example Mess Secretary and Station Intelligence Officer. However this provides him with a unique understanding of the interactions between ground crews and air crews, and he uses this intimate knowledge of both groups to create an incisive understanding of their interdependency, as well to convey the vitally important roles carried out by a range of ground staff personnel which has not been widely acknowledged.

The structure of the book appears to follow the chronological time-scale set out according to the table of contents, with five major parts which cover the selected themes and time periods including: Part I: Prelude to War, 1938-1939; Part II: Bomber Command, 1940-1941; Part III: Tonight's Target, 1941-1942; Part IV: Off Duty (no dates); and Part V: Air Crew, 1943, followed by postscript speculation of the likely future of the war. However within each major part, a number of sub-sections describe the many characters, locations, routines and special events that contribute to the complexities of life at Bomber Command Operational Stations, Operational Training Units and RAF Hospitals, all of which Alfred experiences directly from time to time during his service. As a result the chronological 'thread' is often discontinuous in order to focus in more detail upon the topic most relevant to the story line at the time. In this way Alfred brings together a widespread collection of relevant RAF themes, each of which provides an insight into the constantly changing aspects of his life and that of others in the service. On other occasions Alfred often takes somewhat tangential turns away from the war directly, and relates the stories of people and places caught up in the wartime milieu to provide an appreciation of the impact that the conflict has upon the country as a whole. Furthermore there is an almost subliminal strand which runs through both the thematic and temporal dimensions of the book and this reflects Alfred's strongly-held values about sense of duty, service to society and the changing social order associated with the war, as well as the unwavering belief that winning the war is vital to preserve the democratic principles upon which our civilisation is based.

It is unsurprising therefore that none of the reviews of the book really did full justice to the essence of the work, which perhaps is best captured in the short introduction to the text by Alfred, and so the final short, abstracted overview of this unique publication is left to him:

Several books have been written about the RAF by pilots and others dealing with the thrills of flying and fighting in the air. This book can offer no such excitement. It deals with some of the writer's experiences on the ground staff as an intelligence officer with Bomber Command. Flying, naturally, is always in the forefront, since an intelligence officer sees a good deal of the excitement behind the scenes; but primarily it describes ground life at various Bomber Operational Stations.

It is a notebook – rather than a diary – in which I have set down a few experiences and reflections during my first three years' service with the Royal Air Force. If the resultant picture suggests more fun than fighting, I would point out that a good deal of one's work on the ground consists of rather dull routine and repetition which would make tedious reading, but which is none the less an essential part of the war effort. And on the other hand many of the essential aspects of intelligence work are, of necessity, of a secret nature and cannot be revealed at this stage of the war.

I am well aware that so far I have had an easy war – but not through any design of my own; and no doubt I shall see the other side of the picture in due course.

But while my experiences will not, I feel sure, increase anyone's knowledge of flying, they may help to reveal something of the drama of the work of the bomber crews and something of their light-hearted gaiety and fun in their leisure hours during the first period of the war.

And for my part, I look forward to the victorious final phase with considerable eagerness.[20]

Postscript to 'Ground Staff'

In a follow up to the book's publication Alfred suggested to Eyre & Spottiswoode that there might be a possibility for a reprint, since the book had found favour with the RAF in general, including the Commander-in-Chief of Bomber Command, Air Chief Marshal Sir Arthur Harris (1892-1984), the notoriously nick-named 'Bomber Harris', who commented on his copy of the book sent by Alfred: 'I have read it with great interest. It is excellent.'[21] Furthermore Alfred proposed that apart from a reprint, he was prepared to provide additional material to include his subsequent RAF experiences during the period 1943-1945. In addition he also suggested a sequel to the book which would cover the immediate post-war years, and the attendant problems of a return to 'civvy street' as seen through the eyes of an ex-RAF officer coming home after the war.[21] But after further consideration by the publisher, it was decided that because of market uncertainties, neither a reprint nor a sequel would be possible. Moreover, the publisher proposed to sever the link with Alfred in terms of any future work, since the continued limitations of the availability of paper meant that the company could not meet half of the demands made upon it from their list of well-established authors. Then to finalise the decision, the publisher indicated that the northern regional focus of Alfred's work would no longer fit easily into the company's portfolio of their nationally-based work as a London-based publisher.[21] As a result this was the end of the line for Alfred insofar as this particular publisher was concerned and he had to look elsewhere for future outlets for his work.

References and Notes

1. A.J. Brown, 'Coverdale to Colsterdale', *Yorkshire Dalesman* Magazine, April 1939, pp. 6-8.

2. A.J. Brown, 'All Quiet in the Dales', *Yorkshire Dalesman* Magazine, December 1939, pp. 7-9.

3. Alfred J. Brown, 'Wordsworth in Yorkshire', *Yorkshire Dalesman* Magazine, May 1940, pp. 9-10, 15-17.

4. Alfred J. Brown, 'Yorkshire in Literature' *Yorkshire Dalesman* Magazine, November,1940, pp. 9-10, 15-16.

5. 'Unascribed' author (Alfred John Brown), 'On Beer', St. Bede's School Magazine, Autumn, 1941, Vol. V, No.12. pp. 265-266.

6. AJB/MEB, Personal Correspondence File, 1940-1941, passim.

7. Alfred John Brown, letter to Fr. C. Tindall, 10th December 1940, Private Letters to Fr. C. Tindall, Box 9/3, St. Bede's Grammar School Archive, Hinsley Hall Pastoral and Conference Centre, Leeds.

8. A.J. Brown, *Ground Staff (A Personal Record)*, Eyre & Spottiswoode, London, 1943, Part II, 'Bomber Command: 1940-1941' pp. 35-39.

9. Alfred John Brown, West Yorkshire Archive Service, Bradford Central Library, Document 69D90, Section 5/1 (circa 1941-1944) RAF Service Book, and Section 5/2 (circa 5.xi.1945), RAF Notebook.
    9a. Note: Unfortunately both of these sections are almost illegible due to the damp-affected, hand-written ink script.

10. AJB/MEB Personal Correspondence File 1942-1944, passim.

11. Ibid., Alfred John Brown, Document No. 69D90, Section 7/5, letter to the Editor of the RAF Journal, 16th November, 1942.

12. Ibid., Alfred John Brown, Document No. 69D90, Section 4/1/2.

13. Ibid., Alfred John Brown, Document No. 69D90, Section 8/6 and Deed Box DB38, Case 4, Item 2.

14. Alfred John Brown, West Yorkshire Archive Service, Bradford Central Library, Deed Box DB38, Case 4, Item 2.

15. Memorandum of Agreement, Flight Lieutenant A.J. Brown and Eyre & Spottiswoode (Publishers), London, 27th November, 1942, AJB Literary Agreements File.

16. Squadron Leader A.J. Brown, R.A.F. *Ground Staff (A Personal Record)*, Eyre & Spottiswoode, London, 1943.

17. *Yorkshire Post and Leeds Mercury*, 'A.J. Brown's RAF Notebook', 10th December, 1943.

18. *Yorkshire Evening Post*, 'Sound That is Everywhere', 13th December, 1943.

19. *Yorkshire Dalesman* Magazine, 'A Yorkshireman's Diary', May 1943, pp. 182-183.

20. Op. cit., A.J. Brown, 'Introduction', p. 6.

21. Alfred John Brown, Eyre & Spottiswoode Correspondence File, 1944-1948, passim.

CHAPTER 12

A 'Happy Warrior' in a 'Brave New World'?

Return to 'Civvy Street'

Alfred's return to civilian life was not without its problems as he reflected on his new situation shortly after demobilisation in March 1945.[1] He found the excitement of his discharge from the RAF soon started to wear off and the feeling of anticlimax emerged after leaving the war before the final victory, so that his return, welcome as it was, also left something to be desired. His situation was compounded by his frustration at not seeing the 'other side' of the war since he had spent the duration of the conflict in England, and often enjoyed 'privilege' leave at home at regular intervals, although he had expected to be posted overseas to serve with some more direct involvement.

Alfred found his new civilian status before the end of the war was bewildering since he felt that he neither belonged to the Armed Forces nor the Home Front. In fact not wearing a uniform and saluting everyone in sight contrasted markedly with the daily need to dress appropriately for the occasion and deal with people more informally. He had even found the process of discharge to be somewhat dehumanising in the way it was carried out, in which the formalities seemed to be more concerned with the completion of all the petty forms required rather than the person who was being 'processed'. After almost three weeks he was now in 'limbo' having surrendered his 'Form 1250' and his Service Identity Card, but he still did not have a Civilian Identity Card, a ration card, any clothing coupons or even his pay from the previous month's service. He began to regard himself: 'technically, at least, a rogue and a vagabond, wandering about without any visible means of support or identification.'[1]

Nevertheless, these feelings of dispossession were strangely overshadowed by other feelings of personal guilt in terms of the experiences that he and his family had endured during the war period. From Alfred's point of view, as a married officer who had seen service only in England, he concluded that it was the wives who had stayed at home to look after the family who had experienced a far more gruelling time than the men in home-based forces. In the brief period of time he had been at home, he became aware of his wife's desperate struggle to provide meals for the family, deal with the endless household demands required to support the children in school and the baby at home, and all the 'make do and mending' that had to be accomplished, without any 'privilege' leave or other form of respite whatsoever. In Alfred's opinion, if anyone deserved a war gratuity and a victory ribbon, it was the hard-working housewives of Britain who had held the families together throughout the war.

In a wider context, Alfred reflected upon the changes in society that returning serviceman had to face, in which everything seemed to be much more depressed and dingy than before the war, in a civilian world which appeared to be full of older men, and even the roles of women had dramatically changed. Instead of returning to the supposed 'brave new world', there was the shock of the discovery that the old world was in ruins and far from having finished with the fighting, the real fight – for the future – had only just begun. There was little chance of picking up the threads of life from before the war, since they were no longer there, so that an ex-serviceman felt like a visitor from another planet and a stranger even in the once old familiar world.[1]

And yet in spite of these frustrations and disillusionments Alfred was naturally still glad to be home again, even though he had not had the kind of war that he expected at the outset; he had no medals and no ribbons, but he had the satisfaction of feeling that he had played a small part in laying the foundations for victory and counted himself fortunate to come home unscathed. It now seemed appropriate to set about trying to reshape the new world which he faced for the sake of his family, as soon as he had provided his wife with her first 'privilege' leave since the war had started, with a short break in the Yorkshire Dales, where else?

A Holiday from Hell

It had always been Alfred's intention to take a short holiday when he returned to civilian life before settling down to business again, so after a couple of weeks pottering about the garden, he decided to take Marie-Eugénie away for a well-earned break.[2] He decided that the Yorkshire Dales would make a convenient location and arranged to stay in a 'select' country inn before the Easter holiday of 1945.[2,2a] He booked a room for them and their son Adrian and made arrangements for the other children to be looked after at home, since they were now old enough to be left for a few days and were busy at school during term time. However the planned holiday was not without its problems, since Adrian was just over one year old and needed all the paraphernalia and foodstuffs to support an infant on holiday.

Alfred was used to transporting himself and his personal belongings around the country during his RAF years, but now he had to contend with an infant's large pram and the range of luggage for his wife and son. The pram was required not only for transport, but also for Adrian to sleep in, since the 'select' inn could not provide a baby cot, and this perhaps should have been a warning of the likely difficulties of taking a short break before the holiday season had started. The problems began immediately on arrival at the railway station at Hawes in Wensleydale, the nearest public transport link to the inn, when the taxi driver who arrived without the trailer which Alfred had requested to transport the pram, refused to take the pram, even unassembled, for fear of any damage to his paintwork or upholstery. As a result Marie-Eugénie and Adrian took the taxi, while Alfred foot-slogged the pram stacked with infant food, utensils and clothing, some five miles to the inn over the Buttertubs Pass into Swaledale. Then, if that was not bad enough, a lady who shared the taxi informed Marie-Eugénie that the 'select' inn had a poor reputation for hospitality. But there was a glimmer of hope to follow this grim news when she suggested that if the situation was unsatisfactory, she was more than willing to offer her own house and garden in the village for their respite.

Alfred caused quite a stir in the village on his arrival over two hours later, when a throng of children crowded around the childless pram and wanted to know what he had done with the baby, but at least these curious youngsters gave him a friendly welcome, unlike the frosty response of the landlady at the inn, who met him at the door and demanded to know where he proposed to put 'that' (the pram). She then refused to have the 'thing' inside since she said that there was no room for it and suggested he put it in the garage where it would be out of the way. Even after Alfred explained why it was it was needed in their room, she only agreed to have the pram inside at night, as it would be in the way of the maids, and would have to be garaged by day.

When Alfred joined Marie-Eugénie in their room his heart sank further, since there was no heat in the bedroom, nor hot water, and in the corner there was only a makeshift camp bed quite unsuitable for a young infant. In addition the window catch was broken, which made it impossible to close the window so that the room felt like a refrigerator, and while his wife tried to pacify the tired and hungry Adrian, Alfred was at a loss to explain their awful predicament. Marie-Eugénie tried to lift his spirits however with the good news of the kind offer of help from the local lady in the village, but this only confirmed their fears; what if the reputation of place turned out to be true? It was therefore with some trepidation that they went downstairs to a reasonable supper, and this gave them hope that things might not be so bad after all, especially when the landlady regaled them with stories of the ennobled people who had enjoyed staying at her 'select establishment'. But when Alfred and Marie-Eugénie failed to be suitably impressed by the gentry who supposedly frequented the place, her demeanour changed quickly, and she announced in an abrupt manner: 'breakfast at 9.30 a.m. alright!' and without further ado swiftly and dramatically departed for the night.

Adrian slept quite well until 6.00 a.m., then not liking the strange room, nor the makeshift camp bed, he sat up and began to whine even when given loving attention. The room was freezing cold, the pram and its contents were relegated to a dark passageway downstairs and Adrian had finished the remains of the milk in the thermos flask during the night, so the only way to try to pacify him and keep him warm was to put him in bed with them both. After a couple of hours Alfred decided to see if there was any signs of life in the inn, and to his surprise he saw a maid carrying a full breakfast tray to one of the bedrooms, so he returned to tell his wife of the possible good signs. But when he approached the same maid carrying another breakfast tray to yet another bedroom, she ignored him completely. Then Alfred went downstairs to a deserted sitting room where there was no fire and the place was still littered with empty glasses, newspapers and smelled of stale tobacco smoke. He found a surly maid in the kitchen lighting a fire and he asked her politely if breakfast could be served before 9.30 a.m. and perhaps some tea in their room beforehand. Her response was unequivocal: 'absolutely not, I'm far too busy', and even when Alfred recounted the scenes of breakfast trays being delivered upstairs and asked if they could be served earlier, he was told that those breakfasts were for the mistress of the house and her family, and that if he had any complaints he should see the landlady.

Alfred returned to the room where Adrian was raising the roof by now and related his failure to get an earlier breakfast, but he was determined to negotiate an earlier breakfast in future for the Adrian's sake. Unfortunately, 'Her Ladyship', as they had christened the landlady, did not appear for some time, then just as Alfred and Marie-Eugénie were about to take Adrian out in his pram for a walk and hopefully a sleep, she accosted Alfred about his 'complaint' to the maid. Furthermore when he requested an earlier breakfast to help with Adrian's needs, he was told firmly that breakfast was at 9.30 a.m. as stated, and not to upset the maids further with his demands, and that if he had any further complaints to see her directly, whereupon she swept away once more. This reaction seemed not only very rude but also totally inflexible since they were the only guests at the inn, and Marie-Eugénie was so upset by this treatment that she said she wanted to go home immediately. However Alfred suggested one more try to overcome the impasse, so that if they prepared an early morning hot drink for Adrian in the thermos flask, and if he still did not settle down, they would leave the following day.

That evening, after a long walk in the afternoon, Adrian went straight to sleep, and although Alfred and Marie-Eugénie had cheered up a little, 'Her Ladyship' caused them further distress when she admonished them about bringing up children correctly, as she had done so successfully herself. She then declared that she was tired out from the disturbance of the previous night and retired to bed early with a bottle of gin! Inevitably Adrian woke up later that evening, cried louder than before and could not be pacified, so Alfred and Marie-Eugénie took him out in his pram into the cold, frosty air where he became mesmerised by the starry night which had seemed to calm him down. They then decided to visit the kindly lady from the village and asked if they could sit with him in her house by the fire for a while. She was most pleased to see them and welcomed them heartily, sat them down, served them tea and commiserated with their circumstances, before she repeated her offer of further help if needed. They thanked her for her hospitality before they returned to the inn, hopefully for a more peaceful night, but it was not to be, and Adrian screamed almost all night long, and his distress was made worse by the fact that that his infected thumb, which he used to suck, had been bandaged and was unavailable for any self-comfort. Indeed, there seemed to be nothing that Alfred and Marie-Eugénie could do to pacify him, and in the depths of their despair they became convinced that apart from the hostile hostess, the malicious maid, the icy-cold rooms and the austere atmosphere, there was not only something odd but positively evil about the place, which left them despondent.

The next morning over another late breakfast, they debated whether to return home that day, but since Alfred had arranged to see a friend in the locality,[2b] together with the fact that they had arranged to stay for a whole week, they decided to give Adrian one more chance. But any remaining doubts about this decision were removed upon their return to the inn to be confronted once more by the histrionic hostess, who complained that she had been unable to sleep the previous night because of the awful screaming, and if there was any further disturbance she could not keep them any longer. This was the final insult, so on the third day, while the hostess and the rest of her family were being served their usual breakfasts in bed, Alfred and Marie-Eugénie packed their belongings, called a taxi, this time with a trailer, and departed to the station for the homeward journey. Much later, after an uncomfortably long trip, which took three changes of train and was over five hours duration, they were never so glad to have turned their backs on such a miserable inn and be in the comfort of their own home once more.

On his return home, Alfred reflected on their 'holiday' experiences, and in a rather more positive mood, came up with some important conclusions from their sad story:

(1) they should never have taken a young infant to such a place where they were not wanted, (2) nevertheless, having been accepted, they should have insisted on a more appropriate personal arrangements, (3) people who keep residential inns should be prepared to sacrifice some of their own 'comforts' for the sake of their guests, (4) surly maids were much worse than no maids at all and (5) a little touch of kindness would have made all the difference to the ambience of the inn. Furthermore Alfred believed that this 'holiday from hell' had not been his idea of what a country inn should be all about, and suggested to Marie-Eugénie that they could surely do a better job in the provision for discerning holiday makers. When she concurred wholeheartedly with this viewpoint, the absurdity of their desperately bad experience revived Alfred's latent longing to try his hand at running a residential inn, and perhaps provided the motivation needed for them to think seriously of buying such a place and making a fresh start in the post war era.[3]

Back to Business, Drudgery or Dream?

Alfred's immediate experience of a return to civilian life was perhaps similar to that of some other ex-service businessmen in that he found it difficult to return to the wool trade in his home city of Bradford. Initially, his old firm of D. Hamilton & Co. Ltd. had not welcomed him back as he might have expected, and instead 'recommended' him for a supposedly well-rewarded post in London which did not materialise. Subsequently the firm offered him a job 'of sorts', although not his old job of European Sales Director, but a more lowly position beneath younger, less experienced men, who had remained in post in so-called 'reserved occupations' during the war, which he found unacceptable.[4] Indeed, in a bid to resolve the matter, Alfred instituted proceedings against his former employer for re-instatement and/or compensation, since technically he was still a director of the company, and he would have been entitled to a mutually agreeable settlement of some sort.

This experience engendered in Alfred a somewhat jaundiced view of the changes that he detected among the city's businessmen whom he had known before the war, who had not only grown older, but in his opinion: 'they had grown harder, coarser, grimmer, fatter and more prosperous.'[5] He had never been happy working among such hard-faced men, whose very souls, in his opinion, had become atrophied along with their lives, and they appeared to have lost the quality of human kindness that he valued so much. Although Alfred acknowledged that there were exceptions, he suspected that all successful businessmen now seemed to have become embittered, cynical, pitiless and ruthless.[5] While he had once been caught up in the whirlwind of the business world and derived a certain amount of exhilaration from it, now it seemed to him that the struggle for supremacy in the commercial world did not bring happiness and served to make those involved more miserable and dissatisfied, while even the monetary rewards seemed only to make them meaner.

This general outlook contrasted markedly with that of Alfred's fellow officers in the RAF, who had been a happy-go-lucky lot whose last thought was one-upmanship. And yet in the face of extreme danger these individuals displayed the kind of character unique to their mission when he described their admirable quality: 'it is only in the services that one finds the "happy warrior" that I have in mind.'[5] Alfred's outlook on life as a result of his war experience had been transformed. Nearly five years of RAF service living a relatively care-free existence, where the chief qualities that counted were good fellowship, fair play and sportsmanship and a zest for the job, made him realise how much he would have to forfeit if he left this experience behind and returned to the life of a businessman. Alfred now had to decide upon a new career, although it was not going to be easy to make a vague, youthful dream come true at the age of 51, with growing family responsibilities.

In Search of a Salubrious Inn

While Alfred enjoyed the companionship of his wife and family at home after his demobilisation, he considered the possibilities of an alternative career that might allow for a home-based lifestyle. He began to write a little more but found himself woefully out of practice, and although he had often considered becoming a full-time rather than a spare-time writer, he recognised that this was unlikely now, even after his modest successes with published work over the last few years. But following serious discussions, Alfred and Marie-Eugénie considered whether or not together they might combine business with pleasure in some way. Eventually they came to the conclusion that if they could find a business which Marie-Eugénie could look after, with Alfred's supportive help, it may be possible to provide a basic living and leave Alfred with some time to pursue his writing.[6] The result was a fairly momentous decision: that they would turn their backs on their suburban existence and try an alternative rural lifestyle, and in order to do so, running a small country inn would be the ideal solution. After all, Marie-Eugénie was a first class French cook and always had a penchant for a small select hotel, and Alfred had the necessary business training to support such an endeavour, and since they both enjoyed meeting people they concluded: 'if we can't make a better job of it than the mistress of that snobby inn where we recently spent such an uncomfortable three days, we deserve all we get.'[6]

The more Alfred thought about the idea, the more attractive the role of an 'author-inn-keeper' seemed to be, and an inn would provide the 'bread and butter', while his books would provide the 'jam'. The sort of place that he had in mind would keep both of them occupied in the spring, summer and early autumn, but leave him free to write for the longer winter period during the 'off season'. However when Alfred consulted various country solicitors and estate agents for suitable inns or small hotels they seemed to be at a premium, so that when they came onto the market they were usually snapped up at once or were too expensive to consider, and there were waiting lists of potential clients. Clearly the boom in such properties had already started and Alfred was not the only ex-officer seeking an alternative lifestyle on the scent of a good country pub.[7] Undeterred, he began a series of excursions in the early spring to the Yorkshire Dales to try to investigate the possibilities himself, only to find the situation on the ground much more discouraging. Not only were the well-established old inns changing hands for highly inflated prices, but the standards of provision he found at various hostelries that he knew well had deteriorated during the intervening war years, often as a result of changes in ownership, with rooms and catering services often not available so early in the season. These changes, together with the somewhat unfriendly atmosphere that now appeared to pervade these once very hospitable institutions, left him to consider whether the heart and soul had disappeared from the once cosy, comfortable and convivial setting of a typical Yorkshire Dales inn, which he had so often enjoyed and had written about during his earlier tramping expeditions.

Then just when Alfred was beginning to become despondent about the prospect of finding a suitable place, he received news from an estate agent in Whitby to whom he had written, concerning the sale of a small hotel near Goathland on the North Yorkshire Moors, valued at the modest price of £3,500. While this seemed to be too good to be true, there were a few snags: the location was some 90 miles away and not in the district he had in mind, the price did not include any furnishings and fittings, and unfortunately it was classified as a 'private hotel' and not a licensed inn. Although Alfred did not particularly like the idea of a private hotel, he conceded that there were possibilities for such a place: it might be preferable for the children's sake, it would be possible to specialise in the catering and residential side of the trade, and perhaps it might be possible to obtain a drinks license later. The only major drawback was that it would have to be open throughout the year, which would limit his time for writing, but he and his wife decided to view the place quickly since others were interested in the sale, and they were keen not to let an opportunity slip away.

Alfred and Marie-Eugénie travelled by train to Whitby on a bright, sunny spring day in late March 1945 with no intention of buying the first property that they came to view. They were met at the station by the selling agent, who took them by taxi some 12 miles over the scenic Sleights Moor to the village of Goathland, situated in the upper Eskdale area of the North Yorkshire Moors overlooking the little valley of Murk Esk river, a tributary of the River Esk. After about half a mile they came to the sequestered hamlet of Darnholm, which is located above a deep fold in the moors overlooking Eller Beck, a tributary of the Murk Esk. Finally they arrived at a large property called Whitfield House Private Hotel, which had been closed during the war and not re-opened due to the illness of the owner. The place was unlike anything they had imagined, it was a solid, strongly built, 17th century farm house, with out-buildings and stood in its own large grounds that included a small paddock. It had been elegantly enlarged in the previous fifty years and therefore did not conform to any particular period. It was a mixture of several local moors styles of building which give it a most pleasing 'homely' presence, with bay windows, a pantile roof and sonsy chimney pots, which provided an unreal aura, almost like a fairy-tale image. Furthermore, the views beyond the house were magnificent, since the land fell away steeply at the end of the hamlet into the Eller Beck valley below, before giving way to views of the nearby moorlands. This gave the house the appearance of being almost surrounded by the moors and fells all the way to the remote horizons beyond.[8]

28. Whitfield House Hotel, c.1950

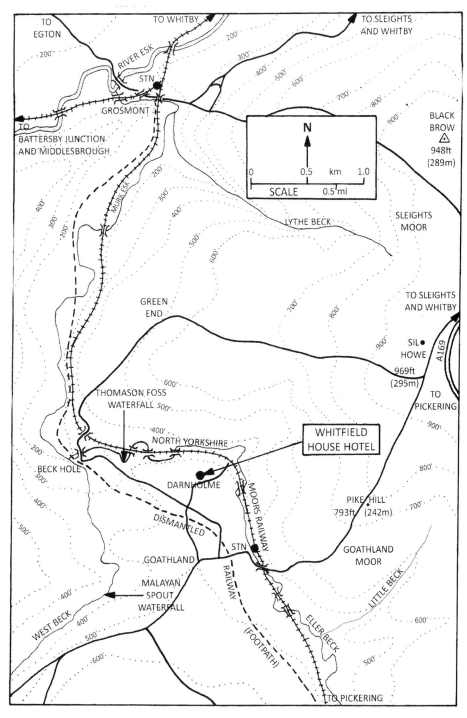

Map 15. The Whitfield House Hotel location

It was unsurprising that as Alfred and Marie-Eugénie approached the front door to be met by the owner, they were both most favourably impressed by the place, especially Alfred, whose hopes and expectations had been roused by the rural location and the splendid scenery. Upon entry they were even more impressed by the ambience of the place during their conducted tour of the interior. It included three low-beamed lounges on the ground floor, along with a dining room with an adjacent kitchen fitted with an Aga cooker, together with a scullery and large old-fashioned pantry, and outside a huge garage which could hold several cars. The first floor contained the larger double bedrooms, with single rooms and staff quarters on the second floor, and there were two additional wings added, one of which served as the owner's residential accommodation. But while the whole place had central heating there were a few immediate drawbacks in that there was only one bathroom for the 14 guest bedrooms, although there were several toilets, and while most of the bedrooms had wash basins with hot and cold water, planning permission had been given to install an additional bathroom. In addition there was no electrical supply in the hamlet as yet, since the planned installation had been postponed due to the war, but it was expected in the near future. Instead gas lighting was supplied to the property by a miniature gas plant, supplemented by oil lamps when needed, and the gas lighting source provided a wonderful Victorian-style soft light to the whole place.[8]

In spite of these obvious drawbacks, Alfred and Marie-Eugénie were impressed with what they saw as they returned to a lounge to discuss the terms of the sale with the agent, and Alfred, who now sat in one of the previously-admired, comfortable window seats, bathed in the warmth of spring sunshine, felt very happy and excited about the prospect of owning such a delightful place. In the opinion of the agent the asking price was relatively cheap at £3,500, and even with the extra costs of buying all the furnishings, fittings, and equipment needed to run the hotel, which was estimated to be in the order of about £2,000, the overall cost still seemed a bargain. Nevertheless, even though the place was in good repair, further expenditure was required to bring the hotel back into full operational order, since it had been closed for a few years, but this additional cost was not expected to be prohibitively expensive. So when the friendly former landlady returned to the lounge with tea, it was time for the would-be buyers to consider their next move, and they asked to delay a bid for a couple of days so they could deliberate further before making such a big decision. However they were told that this was not possible as another potential buyer had already asked for a similar option until the following day, when a final decision was to be made. So instead Alfred and Marie-Eugénie asked for a moment of privacy to allow them to make a decision.

Then after a brief stroll along the lane and a discussion of the many reasons why they should not buy the hotel, they settled on the only reason why they should: because they wanted it!

Hurriedly they returned to the hotel and wrote a cheque for the required 10% deposit, arranged for a second visit in order to settle details of the inventory costs, then dashed off again by taxi to the station in Whitby to catch the last available train that day. On the way home Alfred confided that his decision to buy the hotel had been sealed during his soporific experience on the window seat and although he would now have to assume the role of a reluctant 'hotelier', he relished the possibility of becoming a 'literary innkeeper' as well, subject of course to obtaining the necessary drinks license.[8] Furthermore Alfred summed up his expectations for his own and his wife's prospective roles in their new business venture:

> The general idea is that Marie will be the 'Resident Proprietor' and I will remain very much in the background, ostensibly writing best-sellers! However, I rather fancy that for the first season at least I shall have to be head cook and bottle-washer, handyman, office manager, taxi driver, shopper, 'Boots', gardener, and do any odd jobs that come along. In between whiles, I shall have to entertain the visitors, take old ladies for nice country walks and run errands for the missus.'[4]

At the time Alfred could not have guessed how prophetic his jocular description of his likely role would turn out to be, albeit without the ambitious literary outcome that he envisaged!

Another Family Upheaval

It was only when Alfred and Marie-Eugénie returned home that they realised the enormity of the task to which they had committed themselves, that involved not only getting down to the business of running a country hotel, but also the many arrangements that were needed to make possible the family's transition to a new life. The children had already experienced a good deal of change during the war years, but now they would have to make further adaptations in the immediate post-war period at critical times in their education.[4,9]

Felicity was nearly 17 years old and had left school after she passed her School Certificate, and planned to enrol at the Leeds School of Art, since she had shown some considerable talent for painting, but was not suited to the demands of a possible dancing career which would have been her preference. However her parents were still concerned about her lack of maturity to embark on a possible independent career in either field, but naturally supported her wishes to exploit her obvious ability. Barbara who was almost 16 years old, and Rosemary who was 13 years old, were both still at the Convent School in Harrogate. Barbara did not show any of her elder sister's artistic traits, nor was she particularly academically gifted, but she had domestic abilities and also had ambitions to follow a career in nursing. Rosemary, on the other hand, had shown a good deal of academic promise even in her early years, but she needed to remain in school until she had matriculated in order to allow her to pursue her talents in an appropriate field of her own choice.

Christopher who was now almost 11 years old had made the transition from junior to secondary school early and was probably the most academically gifted of all the children. Alfred had previously contacted Monsignor Charles Tindall, the Headmaster of his old school, St. Bede's RC Grammar School, in Bradford, with view to Christopher's attendance, since it had boarding facilities at that time.[10] Instead Alfred had subsequently decided upon nearby Otley Grammar School which also had an excellent reputation, although he would have preferred a Catholic school, since he hoped that Christopher would eventually attend Ampleforth College, the Benedictine Public School in North Yorkshire. Now a decision was urgently needed on Christopher's future schooling. There was no such choice required in the case of Adrian, who was just over a year old, but he needed some home care arrangements in place if his parents were to be able to devote the necessary amount of time to launch their new hotel business.

The Struggle into Business

It soon dawned on Alfred and Marie-Eugénie that it was easier to buy a hotel than it was to take it over, especially this one, and the preliminary formalities for the purchase were not straightforward, as Alfred discovered when he went to his bank for a start-up loan. He had to formulate written proposals giving plans and securities for the business, neither of which he had considered. At best he estimated the initial costs of the venture included: hotel purchase £3,500, furnishings £2,000, decorations and alterations £1,000, and a working capital of £1,500, for a total £8,000. This was balanced against his assets that included: the sale of his house at £2,500 and personal securities of £2,000, for a total of £4,500, which left a required total loan of £3,500. The bank also required an independent valuation of the business including its inventory, and the legal requirements needed lengthy exchanges between the solicitors and the estate agents, before a definitive go ahead could be obtained.[11] However all of these procedural issues had to be settled quickly if there was to be any hope of taking possession of the hotel before the looming summer holiday season of 1945. Furthermore another visit to the hotel was required to agree the value of the furnishings as well as the detailed inventory of the equipment needed to operate a successful enterprise from day one of the venture. In addition there was a need to renew the catering license that had lapsed during the war otherwise a start up would be impossible. So it was with some relief that the local food office quickly sanctioned the new business as a 'catering establishment', especially since six months later all such licenses were withdrawn due to the food shortages associated with rationing. Finally, there was the need to secure approval from the local Council for the new bathroom facilities and other minor internal alterations, which was likewise surprisingly quickly accomplished as soon as the surveyor's approval had been gained, although getting the workmen and materials needed to complete the jobs proved more difficult in the busy post-war period. The only remaining problems were to secure the necessary coal and coke fuel allowances for the central heating system, at a time of restriction of these essential supplies after the war, but these too were eventually forthcoming.

At last everything seemed to be in place for a completion of all these arrangements, with possession of the hotel planned for 15th May 1945, and that left only a matter of weeks to complete the family's removal to their new home and to plan for the first season of opening for their new hotel business. At this point Alfred worryingly reflected upon the biggest decision that he had made in his life as he conducted a soliloquy over the back gate of his new property, while smoking his pipe in order to try to calm his anxieties about this momentous move:

> Could we make a go of it? Was it going to be too hard on Marie-Eugénie? Was it fair to the children? Would the local people accept us for what we were, ordinary middle-class people trying to earn an honest living in a changing world, or write us off as 'common inn-keepers'? Was I too old at fifty, with five children to make a fresh start in a totally new profession about which I know next to nothing? Had I been too hasty and acted like a fool?'[12]

Perhaps the sensible thing to have done was for Alfred to return to the relatively reliable work of his former employment, but he had an uneasy feeling about the future of his former trade since his return from the war, and he wanted to break away and make a fresh start. He wanted to live in the countryside, especially near the moors and be his own master. Maybe this was just pure escapism, but whatever the urge, it was too late to back out now.

Undaunted by any last minute doubts, Marie-Eugénie and the baby went ahead by train and were followed the next day by Alfred and the rest of the children in his car, leading a procession of two removal vans, followed by a third one later, on the journey to their new life. On arrival at the hotel, the children were naturally delighted with their new home, since they had not seen it yet, but had heard all the stories about the place, and they were excited by the image that surpassed even their wildest expectations. They had moved from a modest-sized, semi-detached house in the growing village of Burley-in-Wharfedale, to a comparatively huge country residence in the sleepy little hamlet of Darnholm high on the North Yorkshire Moors. All that was needed now was for the removal men to somehow squeeze the family's household possessions into the hotel which was already largely full of furniture, and inevitably, to accommodate the excess. In fact most of the family's furniture was distributed throughout the hotel, which gave the whole place a more homely feel that was exactly what was intended. It was decided that Whitfield House Hotel was to be run on intimate, personal lines, just like a private house where guests could feel at home, not like a typical austere hotel, since it had not been that sort of establishment anyway and it would have spoiled the place if there had been any attempt to change its character.

There was still a great deal to sort out before the intended opening date only six weeks away, but unfortunately this 'settling in' period was accompanied by the urgent need to complete the many small jobs that came to light after the initial inspection of the place. As a result, partly due to Alfred's admitted inability as a handyman, and also the need to get specialist work done, there was a succession of plumbers, joiners, masons, painters and other odd job men recruited from the locality who were required to bring the hotel into acceptable working order. Then just when it seemed likely that the opening deadline at the beginning of July would be attained, it was discovered the hot-water and heating system required major attention due to the lack of use during the war years. The old iron hot-water pipes were so corroded that they all needed to be replaced with new copper pipes, which was a big expensive job just two weeks before the intended opening deadline. Finally, while Marie-Eugénie made the difficult arrangements to stock the larder and ensure future food supplies in times of food shortages due to rationing, Alfred tried to get to grips with the 'gasometer', or as he called it 'The Bloody Gasometer', [13] which was needed to provide the 'beautiful soft light' that was 'better than electricity' which had been promised by the former owner.

Alfred was filled with dread as he entered the outbuilding, through the door marked 'DANGER – NO SMOKING', where the 'Heath Robinson' contraption was housed.

The explanation of its workings had seemed so simple when he was shown the device by the previous owner, but now he had to contend with a detailed chart of instructions and complex diagrams that explained the operational intricacies of the infernal machine. Fortunately Alfred's memory served him well and he recalled the guiding principles of charging the gas engine with fresh calcium carbide, filling its feeder tanks with water to ensure a steady supply of acetylene gas into the gasometer and removing the spent calcium hydroxide from the retorts. The whole process was governed by the simple chemical equation: $CaC_2 + 2H_2O = C_2H_2 + Ca(OH)_2$, which ensured a steady supply of gas for the lights. However the device proved very temperamental to control, and because of Alfred's fear of a possible gas explosion, he wisely decided to use the alternative oil lamps for lighting until he could get further reassurance from the local plumber. Unfortunately, rather like the hot water system, it was discovered that the whole gas supply system needed to be replaced, although the plumber carried out some interim repairs that kept the system safe and operable until an expert from the gas company could be called to replace the whole thing as soon as possible. It was at this point that Alfred resolved to try to speed up the promised electricity supply to the hamlet as well as the hotel, but for now at least everything was ready for the opening day.[13]

Whitfield House Hotel Re-Opens

The official opening of the hotel was advertised in *The Times* for 1st July 1945,[4] since Alfred and Marie-Eugénie wanted to be sure that all the final preparations had been completed,[15] but in fact there were a few visitors who had already made reservations for June, while the very first 'customer' had been their old friend, George Heseltine, who paid a visit in mid May, probably to help out with the last minute jobs that needed to be done.[15] Even though Alfred and Marie-Eugénie had to forego the early start of their first season in business, there was some encouraging demand for accommodation from previous visitors to the hotel, who were contacted via details from the former owner's visitors book, which had been kindly left to help get the new venture underway. Furthermore, the nearby village of Goathland was a well-known moorland Spa with several successful establishments including: the Malayan Spout Hotel, the Goathland House Inn, the Goathland Hydro, and the Firs Hotel, as well as the Catalpa B&B next door in Darnholm, and these hotels also kindly offered to recommend any of their customers who could not be accommodated to the Whitfield House Hotel. Therefore the initial prospects appeared to augur well for this newly re-opened business, which had previously been ranked the third best hotel in the area, and had also been RAC and AA appointed in the past, although the start-up was not without teething troubles.

It was not easy to settle into the necessary well-established routine of running a hotel during the first three months, especially since the opening coincided with the brink of the high season and first major post-war holiday period. Moreover, Alfred and Marie-Eugénie began their tenure without all the necessary staff in place, and did not have enough time to prepare for the large influx of visitors that summer, when the demand for rooms outstripped the availability. Furthermore, they had not given much attention to the type of clientele they sought to attract to the hotel, but they soon realised that they had to balance the excessive personal demands made by some visitors with the need to provide the necessary high standards and good value for money, as well as charge competitive rates with other hotels in the locality. As a result they set their prices at one guinea a day (or 21 shillings) for full board, which made the charges slightly higher than some local hotels that charged between 8/6 and 12/6 per day, while those hotels on the coast nearby were almost double at £2 per day. However discounted rates were offered for children and young families were especially welcomed. Then based upon their own recent unfortunate 'holiday' experience, their *'modus operandi'* was that nothing within reason would be too much trouble, and that all services would be delivered cheerfully at all times.[14]

It was soon apparent that living up to these high ideals was very demanding and Alfred's perceived role as 'general factotum' became a reality. He quickly assumed the job of taxi driver to pick up and return guests at the nearest railway station at Grosmont some 3 miles away, since most visitors travelled by train rather than by private car as there were still considerable petrol shortages. In addition his support with the domestic chores was essential to keep the day-to-day hotel routine going, which not only involved late nights and early mornings, but included the constant maintenance of the Aga required for cooking as well as the attempts to get to grips with the temperamental gas lighting system, all of which taxed even Alfred's endurance. Even the simple jobs such as washing up after mealtimes proved to be an almost unending chore since it was done by hand, and the organisation of the old fashioned scullery and kitchen storage facilities for crockery was never designed for a busy hotel, and needed to be revamped to improve efficiency when time and resources permitted.[14]

As the high season in August approached, Alfred and Marie-Eugénie, who had been literally learning on the job, gradually began to get into their stride, and they employed a local woman to help out with the domestic chores. They soon developed a workable system that would just about keep the hotel going over the first busy period until they had time to plan their future organisational arrangements. At the time it was very much a 'make do and mend' approach, which hopefully hid from their guests any hint of how any impending chaos and catastrophe was kept at bay. So from the wild scramble of the delivery of punctual morning breakfasts, through the daytime service of either hot table or cold picnic lunches, followed by afternoon teas, to the sedate atmosphere of relaxed evening dining, Marie-Eugénie's culinary genius was always appreciated and much complimented. It also became a notable feature of the whole operation, which no doubt contributed to the growing reputation that the hotel generated in its first year. But it was necessary to introduce a weekly break in this demanding schedule, in which a 'cook's day off' came to be an accepted feature and an alternative cold table service was made available, since without this respite, Alfred doubted very much if Marie-Eugénie could survive the strain of the first season.[14]

Then as the season progressed, Alfred fulfilled another even more desirable role to which he had been looking forward, that of the genial hotel host, especially after breakfast time when guests planned their daily activities and often required assistance and advice about where to go, and what to see and do during the day.[16] Unlike guests at seaside hotels, most new visitors to Whitfield House came to enjoy the countryside, though many did not have transport, and therefore, except for elderly and infirm individuals who were often content to relax in the gardens, this meant exploration of the surrounding moors and dales on foot. In this regard Alfred was more than willing and able to provide suitable suggestions from his extensive knowledge of the locality, but of course it was the ardent walkers who often took up most of his time to avail themselves of his advice. Even so he felt that he should accommodate the needs of a range of the guests' walking abilities, and he found himself classifying his guests according to his own categories ranging from 'real walkers' to 'strollers and saunterers', which he described in his book *Striding Through Yorkshire*. Nevertheless even with his detailed instructions and use of maps for guidance, many people went astray on the myriad of footpaths, moorland tracks, green roads, pack horse trails and old Roman roads that were to be found in the area. But most people came back safely with stories of enjoyment, if a little blistered and bedraggled for their efforts, and all with renewed appetites from their rambles in the fresh air.

Alfred was never concerned about the experienced 'real walkers' who were always well-equipped and set out with map and compass to explore the remote, more demanding dales of the North Yorkshire Moors, or spent a day tramping across the moors to the sea and returned with tales of great achievement. Even the 'strollers and saunterers' he believed were relatively safe on a local walk across a packhorse bridge over the nearby Eller Beck, with a return via a circuitous route back to the hotel, which involved a gentle moorland meander. Sometimes though, these novices ignored the simple advice of turning left rather than right after the bridge, then followed the seemingly attractive beck path along the valley bottom , only to end up in a boggy, precipitous wood with no alternative but to retrace their steps in a mired state. On the other hand, Alfred's real worries were those he described as 'sublimely-oblivious-of-all-dangers-and-obstacles' types of walkers, who, although having no countryside awareness, knew exactly where they wanted to go – and went. An example of this type of intrepid walker was two charming elderly ladies who traversed a wild stretch of Fylingdales moorland to see one of the famous stone crosses. They wandered into an area under military control, having ignored the red danger warning flags, and picnicked amid the sights and sounds of live ordnance being shot from a nearby firing range, but returned safely, much exhilarated by their experience![16]

Mid-Season Problems and Solutions

Alfred's initial confidence that his business background would be sufficient for the management of a hotel was shaken by the day-to-day administrative load which took more and more of his time as the first season progressed. As a result he registered on a correspondence course in hotel management, which covered the many aspects of the business, but found that he had little time to read any of the guidance papers let alone complete the associated exercises, since he was fully occupied learning the job by hands-on practical experience.[16] He therefore put away the documents until he could give the material the necessary consideration during the 'off-season' winter months, but he suspected that he would never get around to completing the course due to the ever-increasing demands of the business, and indeed this was the case.

The problem of staffing had never been resolved from the outset, and even though Alfred and Marie-Eugénie had been able to persuade their experienced home help, Belinda, to move with them to the hotel, they risked a serious lack of kitchen and other general staff, so that during the first summer season they depended on help from family. This was only an interim measure, although Barbara, then 16 years old, had intended to go to domestic science college and would gain valuable hotel practical skills. Meanwhile Felicity, who was at Art College and Rosemary who was still at school, were both available during the busy holiday period to assist with domestic duties, for which they were all rewarded with appropriate wages. Whereas Christopher, now 11 years old, was happy to run errands to the village and local farms, as well as help in the allotment garden, and when he was not helping out he was more than happy to take his young toddler brother Adrian on forays and adventures around the local neighbourhood.

Nevertheless there was an urgent need to employ an assistant cook, but little progress was made until the Labour Exchange sent a stout, middle-aged woman, who looked more like a disreputable barmaid than a cook. Subsequently, after her late arrival on her first day in the job, reeking of gin, her inability to prepare food even up to the standard of basic NAAFI catering, together with her repeated hang-overs which prevented much useful work being done, meant she had to be released. When Alfred reported these problems to the Labour Exchange they had tried to make amends for this fiasco by sending a dour replacement, an ex-ATS cook, who at least stayed sober for the brief six week period of her employment. She was able to prepare good plain food of acceptable standards, without upsetting the rest of the household with the kind of ribald behaviour of her forerunner, but after her early departure the problem remained.[16]

However it was not just the lack of staff that caused problems, but the supplies of certain goods that would help the hotel to offer a more extensive range of provision to the clientele in the first season. The worsening state of food supplies because of post-war shortages tempted Alfred to organise some supplementary sources, including a small holding for the provision of eggs and poultry, although the availability of suitable hen-houses appeared non-existent locally. Then to Alfred's delight a solid 'Boulton Paul' henhouse, complete with a stock of hens, became available at a bargain price at a run-down farm north of Whitby, and only needed a hired a lorry and workmen to bring it to the hotel. Everything seemed to go to plan when the hens immediately started laying their eggs again in their newly-sited roost, and a steady, trouble-free supply of produce seemed to be in order – until the fleas appeared! On close inspection it was discovered that the source of the infestation was not the hens, but the henhouse woodwork, in which the fleas had taken up residence, and had been disturbed by the removal upheaval, although no amount of disinfectant eradicated the problem during the hot summer months. The danger of human transfer was not only to the staff who entered the henhouse, but even those who strayed too close, as evidenced by several unsuspecting visitors who left the hotel accompanied by some of these unwelcome insect 'guests'!

Alfred became desperate and considered wringing the necks of the whole stock to cut his losses, but after a reassuring visit from the local district Poultry Adviser, it was decided to let nature take its course, when the problem would be solved by the onset of colder autumn weather which would kill off the fleas. In any case by this time most of the previous stock had gone into the kitchen pot anyway and had been replaced by fresh pullets.[17]

Other potential problems in goods and services resulted from the lack of both the tobacco and alcohol licences needed to provide customers with these almost essential commodities that were expected in a good hotel. The tobacco licence had lapsed along with the catering licence, and there had never been a license to serve or supply drinks to customers at the hotel. But Alfred discovered there was no difficulty in renewing the licence to sell tobacco and cigarettes and the local Customs and Excise office readily granted a licence, which authorised him as a 'Dealer in and Seller of Tobacco and Snuff' at a modest charge of 5s/3d p.a. The real problem was getting the necessary supplies which seemed almost impossible given the post-war shortages. All the local suppliers were overstretched with orders from well-established shops and hotels in the area, and it was only after Alfred's direct approach to the Imperial Tobacco Company, that the subsidiary of Messrs. Wills and Players agreed to establish a supply quota through a local stockist, and Alfred was guaranteed his source of tobacco.[18]

The problem of the unlicensed Whitfield House Hotel however seemed insurmountable. While in theory it was possible to obtain a private supply of spirits, local suppliers told Alfred: 'you might as well try to find the magic elixir of life as a spare bottle of Scotch in Whitby'. Even after Alfred cajoled a local shopkeeper, through their mutual military interests and connections, and gained sympathy for this plight to supply him with a modest amount, the question of providing drinks in a private hotel remained a complicated issue. The only solutions according to the then legal requirements was that Alfred could act as an agent on behalf of his guests who ordered alcohol supplies, providing he did not profit from the transaction, or that guests could provide their own alcohol, for which he was then entitled to charge 'corkage'. Neither of these alternatives appealed to Alfred, who preferred to invite a guest to share a private drink with him without charge, or to dispense with any 'corkage' charge. But in terms of getting the premises licensed, Alfred concluded: 'it would be easier to open a house of ill-fame than to obtain a licence for the sale of intoxicating drinks in a respectable private hotel.'[17]

Undaunted, Alfred duly consulted the Local Constabulary and was directed to the Clerk to the Bench of the Local Magistrates' Court, who, after considerable deliberation, came to the sad conclusion that as far as a new liquor licence was concerned it was: 'Hopeless, I'm afraid. The Sessions would never grant it, and even if they did, it would be very costly'. Thus it seemed that Alfred's quest for this valuable permit was over, but in a last desperate effort he tried alternative approaches, and checked if it was possible to get a 'restaurant licence', or a 'table licence', or even a 'club licence'. In response he was informed that because of the complex licensing laws, the first two options were highly unlikely, and that his only hope was a 'club licence' at a modest registration fee of 5s. This option, even with the strict rules and regulations that were required, provided that there were no police objections, was the only way forward. In fact Alfred rather liked the idea of the 'Whitfield House Hotel Club', but he reckoned that until the present staffing problems were resolved, this little enterprise had to be postponed.[18]

The final service which Alfred wished to establish at the hotel was one that was not only very dear to his heart, but was also intended to be part of the ethos of the establishment. He intended to open a small bookshop, partly to give the place a literary dimension and partly to give guests an opportunity to buy new books, and he hoped to specialise in country books since most guests were likely be interested in country pursuits. Alfred also had grand designs on making the hotel a sort of Mecca for writers, poets and artists, and as an author he wanted to attract people with similar tastes – a sort of modern day equivalent of the pre-Fire of London's Mermaid Tavern in Cheapside, which attracted literary figures of the Elizabethan era – without the 'Sack' and 'Canary' wines of course.[18] However, once again Alfred experienced problems with 'officialdom', this time from the Board of Trade and the 'Location of Retail Business Order.' He was not allowed to open a bookshop, even if he had the agreement of the Joint Advisory Committee of the Publishers Association, which he had not, with the result that the idea was a non-starter. Instead Alfred provided reading material from his own large library, together with such periodicals that he could get his hands on during this period of paper shortages. He also offered a range of books, magazines and periodicals which were distributed throughout the hotel to stimulate interests, including guest bedrooms and even in the hotel's five toilets, since Alfred suggested:

Has anyone, I wonder, seriously considered the question of suitable lavatory literature? A lot has been devoted to Bedside Books, but after all one goes to bed primarily to sleep, whereas one goes to the other place to keep wide awake – yet in a contemplative mood and with a mind open to receive ideas among those brooding silences. I often feel that there are no other places where one is so much alone and so well disposed for improving one's mind. They remind me of monastic cells.'[18]

Away from the challenges of providing these important goods, services and facilities for guests, there was the problem of running the business part of the hotel, and Alfred was astounded by the amount of office work this entailed. One of the reasons why he had left city life behind was to get away from offices altogether. In his former job he had the full support of office staff at work and even during his extensive European travels. Now he found that he was virtually ignorant of general office administrative routines and knew nothing about book-keeping, account books, wages and especially National Insurance and PAYE procedures.[19] He had to come to terms quickly with these onerous activities which he had taken for granted, but did so with the help of an accountant, and also by making his office look as little like any normal office as possible. His new office was an eclectic mix of a writer's den, a cigarette shop and an *atelier*, with hint of a pub smoke-room about it, sporting an array of pipes, as well as tea pots, coffee pots and tankards for the night-shift writing sessions, and it was often occupied by a few welcome visitors who added life and vitality to the place. Even Marie-Eugénie had her own desk tucked away in the corner, and while Alfred got to grips with the anodyne activity of account books, she grappled gamely with the mass of forms related to the Food Office returns, but they still required the assistance of the PAYE Office and Food Office experts to complete all the necessary time-consuming procedures. However, unlike other folk engaged in similarly demanding office work, they could always get away from the drudgery when they had enough, but only to tackle a hundred other jobs which needed urgent attention![19]

The Autumnal Recess

After a hectic first summer season, Alfred and Marie-Eugénie were relieved to have most of the spacious hotel to themselves, and although a few guests stayed on, by the end of October, like most other local hotels, it was time to close for the 'off-season'. Whilst they had gone into the business with no illusions about the demanding nature of the work involved, they both found it harder than anticipated, with long 15-hour days, extra work on Saturdays and Sundays and virtually no respite, which was essential to operate a residential hotel with only limited staff. Towards the end of the season Alfred was concerned when Marie-Eugénie became exhausted by the strain involved, and he was determined that they would not remain fully open during the winter months, like some hotels on the coast in Whitby. They both decided that a break was needed to enjoy some of the benefits of living in the country. In Alfred's case this meant the opportunity to pursue his literary and walking interests, and for Marie-Eugénie it meant substituting the drudgery of the kitchen with some enjoyment of social life. The only remaining concern was whether this well-deserved break would be financially viable, but it was deemed so vital that they took the opportunity with alacrity, since they felt that they had never earned a holiday more than now.[20]

Following a few days of respite, while Marie-Eugénie took time off to visit friends and family in Bradford and Burley-in-Wharfedale, Alfred completed his remaining hotel administrative business arrears, tidied his office and converted it to his literary den for the writing season, although it was not long before the exhilarating autumnal days tempted him outdoors. Even though the fleeting full blooming colour of the luxuriant heather had passed in the late summer, Alfred enjoyed the moors in their seasonal splendour when the bracken turned to gold, then bronze and russet, and finally to pure wine-red, while the neighbouring valleys stood out like burnished gold in the brilliant autumn sunshine which emblazoned the landscape with an indescribable beauty.[21] These were the intoxicating images that Alfred had in mind when he set out to enjoy his recently-gained freedom. Although he was always delighted by moorlands in every season, the sharp nip in the air that spelled the turn of the year, the bejewelled morning rime on the fields, the dazzlingly low sunshine with splendid sunsets and the silver glory of the hunter's moon, drove him to take full advantage of the opportunities afforded by his new location.

Alfred had written about his experiences of the North Yorkshire Moors in *Tramping in Yorkshire – North and East* (1932), but now he explored the area more fully. He often wandered off the beaten tracks and followed the tops, along the ridges and the watersheds in as straight a line as possible. He revelled in the deep heather, peat hags and whams, that led him over hilltop ancient howes, or from stone currack to stone cross, and almost never met another soul along the way. He sometimes visited lonely, hidden moorland farms, or when walking alone for several days, slept in remote inns and farms scattered throughout the area. Here he was always welcomed with the same hospitality that he offered in his own hotel, and never refused a walker or anyone stranded a warm bed for the night with ample refreshment. On most occasions though he went back to the hotel each night where he was often still needed to supervise any out of season work in progress, but invariably he returned with revitalised vigour and renewed motivation to indulge his complementary literary interests.[21]

Festive Celebrations: A Traditional Christmas

The advent of Christmas at Whitfield House Hotel meant a potential conflict of interests with the problem of how to combine the time-honoured family Christmas at home and the sort of 'public' Christmas event that was expected at a hotel. Most local hotels remained open for the festive season, and as the winter expenses mounted up, Alfred and Marie-Eugénie decided to re-open for the holiday period, although they were determined not to let the hotel business interfere with the family's own important Christmas event. It was agreed therefore to limit the number of guests to a comfortable minimum, including any close relatives and friends, all of whom could be relied upon to enter into the Christmas spirit and join in with their family's traditional homely celebrations.[22]

Alfred and Marie-Eugénie had always taken a very traditional approach to this festive time of year with an emphasis on the symbolic rituals as well as the religious observances associated with the occasion. One ritual event focused on the Christmas tree and its decoration on Christmas Eve, with familiar emblems to make it both a thing of beauty by day and wonderment by night when the candles were lit. Family presents were placed under the tree on the Eve, never before, and never opened until after the King's Speech was broadcast on Christmas Day, followed by the family's rendition of 'God Save the King'. Furthermore, in keeping with the principle of giving at Christmas, the rule was that everyone gave a present to everyone else, without concern for how small or insignificant it may have been, just so long as it was properly wrapped and suitably labelled. The children's 'Christmas stockings' were another tradition in which there was always a range of token gifts including: an apple, an orange, a new penny, some nuts and a piece of coal, as well as the special surprise gift and a simple, inexpensive toy that matched their modest expectations during these times of austerity.

The observance of the religious foundation of Christmas was also of prime importance to the family, and the adults always attended midnight mass, while the children were taken care of until their own Christmas morning mass, both of which were held at St. Hedda's RC Church in Egton Bridge in the Esk valley, some three miles away over the moors. These holy ceremonies were seen as the joyous precursors for the festivities planned for the great day itself, which was invariably a time of feasting and fun-filled activities. The day began with an early traditional Yorkshire cooked breakfast, followed by a long vigorous walk to sharpen the appetite and enjoy the lunch time serving of the Yeoman Farmers dish of 'Frumety' i.e. creed or 'kibbled' (coarse ground) wheat, which had been simmered in milk for 12 hours, seasoned with nutmeg and cloves, with added currants, sugar, cream and rum, and sweetened with treacle. But before this concoction was devoured, the Yule Candle, which was set in a mistletoe 'kissing-bough', was lit by the master or the youngest daughter of the house, whoever won the toss of a coin, and this was lit using a piece of old Yule Candle saved from the previous year, which in turn had to be lit from the Yule Log burning in the hearth. A cross was then etched on the top of an uncut Wensleydale cheese, and the words 'A Merry Christmas' were uttered for the first time that season, before the repast was served with mulled ale. This was made from a gallon of strong beer heated in a large ale-warmer, with the addition of a table-spoonful of castor sugar, pinches of ground nutmeg, cloves and ginger, brought to near boiling point before being laced generously with rum or brandy, and served piping hot. It was only then, when these ancient rites had been duly performed, that the assembled mystified guests were allowed to taste the delights of the frumety and mulled ale.[22]

Immediately after lunch, the family and guests assembled in the big lounge of the hotel when all the children sang their favourite Christmas carols, before they set about their Christmas Stockings, surprise presents and toys with great whoops of delight, while the adults in turn exchanged their presents from under the Christmas tree. When all their excitement abated the children moved to the family lounge to enjoy their gifts, while the adults and their guests were invited for pre-dinner drinks in the private lounge, albeit with 'drinks on the house' since the hotel was not yet licensed. Subsequently the highlight of the day was the Christmas dinner served at 7.30 p.m. in the hotel dining room, which had been set up with a long high-table for the whole party, instead of separate tables, and this was illuminated with oil lamps and table candles, while the room glowed with a soft, warm, gas-lit ambience. Family, friends and guests enjoyed a splendid Christmas meal, which somehow had been conjured up in spite of all the Food Office regulations, with no expense spared in terms of the variety of the traditional fare served. Then all the children reluctantly retired to bed exhausted, while the adults continued with their boisterous parlour games, and finally finished off their celebrations with late night coffee and carols, which brought the first memorable Christmas at Whitfield House Hotel to a satisfactory conclusion.[22]

Hagmena (New Year) Celebrations

Some of the guests who enjoyed the family Christmas festivities stayed until the New Year and were joined by a few new guests who came to take part in the distinctive celebration of 'Hagmena', the North-Country name for New Year's Eve, and also the term for the offering for which children went to beg on that evening. Even then, the Christmas tree with its candles all aglow and its pungent aroma remained as a memory of the festive spirit which still pervaded the whole house, while other reminders also present included the remains of the still appetising Frumety which continued to be served as a snack, since traditionally no fresh Frumety was made until the following Christmas. New Year's Eve was the time for another special dinner celebration, but on this occasion goose rather than turkey was the main dish. The dining room once more was decked out and lit for a collective celebration, and in the time-honoured traditions of the frivolous New Year games, the risky but exciting Victorian parlour game of 'Snapdragon' was one of the highlights for Old Year's Night. This strictly adult yet almost naive game involved heating brandy or rum with raisins added in a shallow bowl, then the contents were set alight, and the aim was to pick out the red-hot raisins from the fiery mixture as the flames licked one's fingers and even the lips. Everyone tried to enjoy the spicy morsel by closing the mouth quickly to extinguish the flame without being burned, while chanting the words associated with this good luck toast: 'This year, next year...'[23]

Then as midnight approached the whole company assembled once more in the private lounge and waited for the first strike of Big Ben on the radio. This was the signal for the tallest, darkest male guest, who had slipped away earlier, to re-appear in a weird disguise and offer the party hosts the traditional symbolic items: a piece of coal (for warmth), a potato (for food), and some salt (for the spice of life or good luck) then wish the entire party a 'Happy New Year' as the 'first foot-in' the home that year, a ceremony referred to as 'first-footing'. As the midnight chimes continued to strike, kisses and embraces were shared all round, followed by rounds of 'drinks on the house' to toast the New Year, with 'God Save the King' and 'Auld Lang Syne' sung with solemn reverence, before a spirited rendition of the Yorkshire Anthem 'Ilka Moor baht'at' by the combined choir of all Yorkshiremen present. The last performance of the night was by the same group of Yorkshiremen, with the chanting of a fragment of the old North Yorkshire 'Hagmena Song', which was traditionally sung at Richmond in Swaledale on New Year's Eve by the Corporation Pinder. It was then left to those with enough stamina to continue the merriment until the early hours of the morning, when they retired to bed satisfied in the knowledge that they had done their best to bring in an even happier New Year than the one left behind.[23]

The Second Season

The lull after Christmas and New Year did not last long and although the new season's visitor numbers were low, the 1946 season started early with Easter and Whitsuntide bookings, while advanced bookings for the summer suggested a record year for the hotel. Alfred and Marie-Eugénie started the new season with more confidence based on their previous experience, and following reorganisation and planning during the winter months they looked forward to the challenge ahead.[24] Unfortunately some staff problems remained after the departure of Lena, their parlour maid, and although she was replaced by a local girl, along with an assistant cook and wife of the handy-man/driver, who had been hired in the first season, even with this extra help Alfred admitted that they would still have struggled in the busy season without the collective help of all the daughters during this demanding time.[24]

Unfortunately Alfred suffered an unforeseen long illness during this second season, which left him unable to fulfil his role for much of the year. He had experienced stomach problems for quite some time then suddenly became very ill, and the local doctor, John English, was called urgently. He arrived late at night on horseback, since the snowy conditions of February precluded any other form of transport, and he prided himself in attending his patients whatever the weather. He diagnosed Alfred's problem as acute 'cholecystitis', or an inflammation of the gall bladder caused by a gall stone that required surgical intervention. He administered morphine for the pain and arranged with the local hospital for the removal of the stone as soon as possible, followed by a period of convalescent recovery at a nursing home in Whitby.[25] It was some time before Alfred returned to the hotel to fully recover in the spring and summer, but even then he performed only light duties, and he used the time to draft notes for a possible book about the hotel. There was also another beneficial outcome of this event, when Alfred's daughter Barbara, who provided care for Alfred during his convalescence, became convinced that her own future would eventually be better fulfilled by a nursing career rather than in the hotel and catering business.[25]

Meanwhile guest numbers were not a problem in this second season, although guest 'types' gave some cause for concern, since the previous visitors book left by the former owners had selected names marked as 'undesirables' which suggested a sort of 'blacklist'. Alfred and Marie-Eugénie did not want to use this approach and instead instigated a new visitors book,[15] which had been presented by their long-time friend George Heseltine. Nevertheless they acknowledged that there were likely to be certain types of guests they also did not want to encourage including: (1) those with no consideration of staff, who showed no appreciation and took everything for granted, (2) those who left paltry tips for the staff, and (3) those with 'pampered pooches' who expected their dogs to be treated like people, which brought forth Alfred's comment: 'between dogs and children, we prefer children, and as we could not take both in the season, we excluded dogs.'[26] As a result of this unwritten guest policy, they tried to

WHITFIELD HOUSE

R.A.C. APPOINTED

MARIE-EUGÉNIE and ALFRED J. BROWN
PROPRIETORS
WHITFIELD HOUSE · GOATHLAND
N. YORKSHIRE
Tel. 215

ensure that guests were friendly, sociable and tolerant. Then in an attempt to attract this sort of people, Alfred designed a promotional brochure which was sent to potential guests, which not only outlined the essential information about the hotel, but also described the general ambience of the place, its setting, its scenic attractions and the kind of holiday experience that guests would find in a warm, friendly, family-run, small country hotel.[27] The brochure was illustrated with sketches by Alfred's book illustrator, William Littlewood, with the emblems of a white rose and a fleur-de-lis on the cover to indicate the combined spirits of Yorkshire tenacity and French flair of the proprietors, which reflected their endeavour to create a unique holiday experience for their guests. It was hardly surprising that the profile of guests invariably contained a balance of well-heeled, middle-class, professionals including: doctors, solicitors, bank managers, civil servants, vicars and school teachers, as well as businessmen, shop-keepers, retired armed forces officers and elderly single ladies and gentlemen, all of whom interacted in stimulating and often highly amusing ways, but of course there were occasionally eccentric exceptions who livened up the mix![27]

In addition to the staffing problems and the concerns of attracting a suitable clientele, Alfred also tried to appraise his own suitability for the role demanded by this new enterprise. While he admitted that he was not an authority on the operation of small hotels in only his second year of business, he had distinctive views on the attributes needed for those involved in the trade, whether they were amateurs like himself, or so-called professionals who often resented the intrusion of the former 'upstarts' into the business. Therefore concerning the pedigree of an ideal innkeeper, Alfred was of the opinion that the perfect host: 'should have a Swiss father, a French mother and an Irish smile,'[28] but he suggests other vital qualities that were essential:

> Sociabilty, hospitality, courtesy, savoir-faire, a sense of humour, bonhomie, an equitable disposition, a ready flow of conversation, long-sufferingness, benignity, unobtrusiveness, an encyclopaedic knowledge of the locale and things in general, with a wide range of interests. He should be all things to all men and should have a cast-iron constitution...

and if this was not enough he commented:

> These are only some of the attributes of a good innkeeper, but with these a man may at least try his 'prentice hand at this most difficult profession. Without most of them, he will fail.[28]

Moreover, Alfred wholeheartedly subscribed to the information on 'The obligations of an Innkeeper' which was later widely circulated by the Ramblers' Association and clearly stated:

> The innkeeper is one who, having the necessary facilities is prepared to receive and entertain travellers and provide accommodation for them. By Common Law, he is bound to provide at reasonable prices food and accommodation regardless of the hour which they may arrive. An innkeeper cannot pick and choose whom he will accept, provided they are willing to pay a reasonable price and arrive in a fit condition to be received.[29]

Towards the end of the second season, while Alfred convalesced from his latest illness, he considered the financial status of the business, in which, like most other hotels, there was little profit to be had under the conditions of post-war austerity and the slow return of the holiday habits of the nation. In the first season the hotel made a 'loss' of about £600, even though it had been fully occupied in the high season, although this 'loss' had been offset to some extent by the money spent on repairs and decorations needed to open the hotel. In the second season the turnover had doubled and a net 'profit' of about £750 was achieved, even after capital expenditure and living costs were taken into account. But even this small 'profit' was only realised by remaining open for most of the year and came at the cost of increased work load on the staff due to Alfred's illness. However he was optimistic that, with renewed health and with the possibility of a 'club' license in the third year, the turnover could be increased, but he was also realistic enough not to judge the future financial prospects for the business for another year or two at least.[30] Nevertheless after the short-lived busy season, and with the liberty of the 'off-season' to look forward to, Alfred and Marie-Eugénie had the satisfaction that they had achieved some initial success in this bold venture, and they were sustained in the knowledge that they had provided a valued service to others, and had enjoyed meeting people on holiday, and therefore they had fulfilled some of their ambitions for the enterprise.[31]

The Third Season

The start of this season was particularly memorable for the onset of a winter that was the worst in living memory. Indeed the winter of 1947 was one of the worst since daily meteorological records began in the seventeenth century, and snow fell somewhere in the UK on 55 consecutive days between 22nd January and 15th March, with temperatures that rarely rose more than a degree or two above freezing. Snow drifts halted food deliveries, and coal, gas, electricity and even water supplies were so severely affected that the whole country was brought to a near standstill. The North Yorkshire Moors suffered greater and more prolonged downfalls of snow than any other region, with some roads buried in drifts of up to 30 feet deep. Each morning Alfred dug his way out of the hotel, only to be snowed in again every night by another blizzard, so that the place was completely cut off for days on end. It was fortunate that the larder was well-stocked, but the antediluvian, temperamental gas plant froze solid, and as reserves of paraffin ran low, the only source of lighting was oil lamps and candles, but some heating was maintained by use of peat and log fires downstairs. Yet even under such dire circumstances Alfred happily reflected: 'I thoroughly enjoyed the experience of an old-fashioned winter that we had imagined had gone forever.'[32]

While the outdoor scene was one of entrancing beauty, the only modes of transport in the vicinity were by sledge or skis, and even the delivery of essential supplies by rail to Goathland was suspended when the railway line was blocked by snow drifts. Fortunately there were no guests staying at the hotel, so the only concern that Alfred and Marie-Eugénie had was for their own and Adrian's welfare, since Felicity and Rosemary were away at college and Christopher was at boarding school. Ironically Barbara had departed to Switzerland in early January to learn French cooking and language at a training school in Lausanne, where the winter was unusually mild, so that she could only indulge in winter sport in the very high Alps, and was envious when she heard of the conditions back home in North Yorkshire![32]

In contrast to this wintry start to the new season, just before Easter the weather changed rapidly and produced widespread flooding across the country due to melting snow, at the start of what was to be an equally unexpected, but remarkable summer. The hotel opened early and was almost full by the late May Whitsuntide holiday, at the start of one of the hottest and driest summers on record, with temperatures in the peak season of August in excess of 30°C and no rain at all. As a result the previously predicted fears among hoteliers that holiday makers would look to the continent after such an abysmal winter did not materialise, but even so the months of May, June and July were relatively slow, followed by the usual rush in August, which caused Alfred to lament the lack of action with regard to the often proposed 'staggered holiday' concept that was still a long way off.[32] In anticipation of the demands of the new season, Alfred had hired two maid/waitresses, but in the early part of the season there was little for them to do. Therefore he set out to attract new 'chance' trade by re-erecting the roadside signposts to the hotel that were removed during the war, and began to cater for coach parties of visitors in an attempt to make up the shortfall of the residential trade.[33] This enterprise initially produced mixed results;

on some occasions everything went well, but on others the driver failed to find the place and took his party elsewhere. Even when things went smoothly, with up to three or four coach parties per week, there was the additional demand to be considered, and perhaps more importantly, the fact that some regular residents resented the idea of coach loads of visitors, since in their opinion it spoiled the atmosphere of the hotel, and therefore Alfred reluctantly reviewed this initiative and subsequently put it into abeyance.[33]

Alfred then considered it was time to introduce an important extra service into the hotel that he had previously investigated, and just before Whitsuntide 1947, he registered the 'Whitfield House Country Club', which while simple in principle, in practice required much planning and preparation. He needed to gather a minimum of 25 people willing to become members – real people with names, addresses and occupations – who would undertake to abide by a set of Rules and Regulations. This list had to be submitted in the application approval request, and since there were no objections raised by the police and other local licensed hotels in the district, the registration was approved after the payment of the modest fee of five shillings. But this was only the beginning, a complicated system of committee management regulation, as well as a members' register, new membership application and approval procedures had to be instituted, and a separate set of book-keeping and accounting procedures had to be set up. Furthermore Alfred, as manager/secretary of the club, had to take responsibility for everything including any penalties for the infringement of any regulations which governed such an organisation.[34] It was fortunate that he had gained valuable experience of such matters as Mess Secretary during his RAF wartime service, but there were compensations for all his extra work. Alfred enjoyed the convivial camaraderie of local and guest members of the club, who often congregated in his office, which served as the club bar, while the private lounge of the hotel was turned into the club lounge, and together these created a whole new ambience about the place, that was pleasing to guest and host alike.

In contrast with this positive development, there were still day-to-day problems as a result of continued staff changes, since two of the locally-hired maids/waitresses who had found the work too demanding left, while a third walked out due to loneliness at the peak of the season in August. The situation became more difficult when Marie-Eugénie's health began to fail under the additional strain that this incurred. Even with the return of Barbara from Switzerland and the input of Felicity and Rosemary for the summer, Marie-Eugénie found it difficult to cope with the extra work of the 'chance trade'. Meanwhile Alfred took over the various duties of handyman, gardener and taxi driver once more when the general helper also left at the end of the season, having found the weekend and out-of-normal hours work too much for him.[35] And yet in spite of these difficulties, the turnover of the hotel grew substantially during the season, largely as a result of the new services offered, so that profits increased to around £2,500, and if only the staffing problems could be resolved, Alfred expected that the figure could be increased to £4,000 – £5,000 p.a., which he believed was the likely optimum attainable given the limited guest rooms available and without major expansion of the facilities.[35]

However he had more urgent matters than financial projections to deal with, and following the advice of his local doctor and now friend, John English, he decided that a complete change was needed to allow Marie-Eugénie's health to recover from the hectic schedule of the most demanding season so far. When autumn approached they packed the car, and together with Adrian, headed south for a ten day holiday which coincided with Christopher's half term break as a boarder at the Abbey School, in Hemingford Grey, near St. Ives in Huntingdonshire. They planned to enjoy the other side of hotel life, as paying guests, at some of the well-appointed hostelries that Alfred came across in East Anglia during his RAF service years.[36] The break also provided the opportunity to stay with their old friends George and Anne Heseltine in London, and while Marie-Eugénie also visited guest friends in Kent, Alfred had pursued potential agents and publishers in the City, in an attempt to provide further impetus to his continued literary endeavours, which had so far been somewhat limited by inn keeping.

It was during this break that Alfred reflected on the impact that the hotel business had on the family's disposition in general and his own aspirations in particular. Even after a month's rest, Dr. English formed the opinion that Marie-Eugénie could not carry on the burden of her input into the hotel without a complete and prolonged break. This might put the whole enterprise in jeopardy for the following season, since her reputation as an accomplished chef was a key factor in the success of the business. Moreover, both Alfred and Marie-Eugénie had come to realise over the past three years that no matter how attractive an old farmhouse hotel is to the guests, with all its quaint but primitive amenities, without electricity and the full range of labour-saving devices, the work was hard, notwithstanding the fact that it was now well-established and had begun to pay its way. They were left with the dilemma of whether to carry on with their amateurish approach, or try to upgrade the place to make life a little easier, or perhaps to turn into professional hoteliers and take on a larger, more modern hotel with modern facilities and a professional staff. But these alternatives would not solve the fundamental problem which they both felt most acutely, that of the loss of family life, since they only really had time to spend with their offspring when they were working in the hotel at holiday times, and even when they tried to merge family life with the hotel routine, such as at Christmas, it was not quite the same.[36]

Alfred came to the conclusion that, in spite of what he had believed at the outset, inn-keeping did not blend easily with his attempt at maintaining his literary output as he hoped it would. The combination was fine in theory, but the reality of running the hotel in a prolonged holiday season, and settling down to write in the winter months had only produced a modest output to date of two books: *Whitaker* (1946), which awaited publication for many years, and *Broad Acres* (1948), which had largely been prepared before the war, and even the present book *I Bought A Hotel* (1949) had been mainly drafted during Alfred's prolonged illness in the second season. Nevertheless, it was not the difficulty of writing that was uppermost in Alfred's mind concerning the possibility of leaving the hotel business, but Marie-Eugénie's health and the future of the family, especially the two boys who were at critical stages of their development.[37] Alfred and Marie-Eugénie concluded that they would be truly sorry if they had to leave the hotel, its surrounding countryside, and all the friends they had made, as well as their regular guests who had become friends, and they were unsure if they could bring themselves to sell the old place after all. In which case perhaps the only alternative to be considered was to install an electric plant, engage new staff, relieve the offspring of their burden of seasonal work and start all over again?[38] Meanwhile Alfred brooded as optimistically as ever:

> Peat and log fires are the order of the day in the old house, and by night the oil lamps are glowing brightly. The moors are arrayed in their lovely autumnal cloak of burnished gold; and I am walking in the old ways again.[38]

References and Notes

1. Alfred J. Brown, 'The Return', (undated) March 1945, Miscellaneous File: Articles and Short Stories, circa 1930s – 1950s.

2. Alfred John Brown, Journal, 'High Fell Hotel', 1945, pp. 7-19.
    2a. **Note**: Alfred did not identify the inn for obvious reasons. It was situated in Swaledale, where he and Marie-Eugénie spent part of their honeymoon.
    2b. **Note**: Alfred and Marie-Eugénie visited their friend and the author, Marie Hartley, who lived at 'Coleshouse' Cottage in Askrigg, Wensleydale. Her co-author, Ella Pontefract, had died recently on 23rd February, 1945.

3. A.J. Brown, *I Bought A Hotel*, Williams and Norgate Ltd., London, 1949, 'In Search Of An Inn', pp. 14-15.

4. AJB letter to Mr. and Mrs. B. Ratcliffe, 11th May 1945, AJB Personal Correspondence File, 1945-1954.

5. Op. cit., Journal, pp. 33-36.

6. Op. cit., Journal, pp. 43-44.

7. Op. cit., A.J. Brown, 'In Search Of An Inn', pp. 15-21.

8. Op. cit., Journal, pp. 20-35.

9. Op. cit., Journal, pp. 4-6.

10. AJB letter to Mgr. C. Tindall, 8th June 1944, Private Letters to Mgr. Charles Tindall, Box 9/3, St. Bede's R. C. Grammar School Archive, Hinsley Hall Pastoral Centre, Leeds.

11. Op. cit., A.J. Brown, 'The Big Five', pp. 37-39.

12. Op. cit., A.J. Brown, 'Soliloquy Over A Gate', pp. 49-50.

13. Op. cit., A.J. Brown, 'The Gasometer', pp. 71-76.

14. Op. cit., A.J. Brown, 'First Visitors', pp. 77-92.

15. Visitors Book, Whitfield House Hotel, 18th May 1945, George Heseltine, 706 Grenville House, Dolphin Square, London W. 1.

16. Op. cit., A .J. Brown, 'People,' pp. 93-99.

17. Op. cit., A.J. Brown, 'Problems' 'Starting from Scratch', pp. 109-137.

18. Op. cit., A.J. Brown, 'Books and Authorship', 'Bookshop', pp. 138-141.

19. Op. cit., A.J. Brown, 'Office Hours', pp. 132-135.

20. Op. cit., A.J. Brown, 'Autumn Days', pp. 153-155.

21. Op. cit., A.J. Brown, 'Exploring Farrdale', pp. 155-160.

22. Op. cit., A.J. Brown, 'Christmas at the High Fell', pp. 180-189.

23. Op. cit., A.J. Brown, 'Hagmena', pp. 189-191.

24. Op. cit., A.J. Brown, 'Staff Changes', pp. 193-196.

25. Personal communication, Miss Barbara Brown.

26. Op. cit., A.J. Brown, 'Black List', pp. 196-201.

27. Op. cit., A.J. Brown, 'Selecting Guests', pp. 218-221.

28. Op. cit., A.J. Brown, 'Qualities Of A Good Innkeeper', pp. 228-229.

29. The Ramblers' Association, London, Information Sheet No. 1, 'The Obligations of an Innkeeper', November 1949.

30. Op. cit., A.J. Brown, 'Finance', pp. 231-234.

31. Op. cit., A.J. Brown, 'Compensations', pp. 234-235.

32. Op. cit., A.J. Brown, 'Résumé', pp. 236-238.

33. Op. cit., A.J. Brown, 'Coach Parties', pp. 239-242.

34. Op. cit., A.J. Brown, 'Country Club', pp. 243-250.

35. Op. cit., A.J. Brown, 'Staff Changes', pp. 250-253.

36. Op. cit., A.J. Brown, 'We Go On Holiday', pp. 261-267

37. Op. cit., A.J. Brown, 'Farewell High Fell?', pp. 267-270.

38. Op. cit., A.J. Brown, 'Postscript', pp. 271-275

CHAPTER 13

The Hotel Venture: A Bold Endeavour or Business Enigma?

A Time for Reflection and Review

The fourth season in 1948 was a critical period in the venture which severely challenged the hotel enterprise.[1] The first year was launched successfully amid the excitement of taking possession of the hotel, when Alfred, Marie-Eugénie and family started a new life, and were rewarded with a post-war holiday rush of crowds of visitors in the first brief high season. In the second season they were more prepared for the onrush of summer guests, but it was tempered by Alfred's illness, which placed additional strains on Marie-Eugénie and the family. The third season was the most successful so far, when the hotel was inundated with guests, but it came at a price, when the extra strain took its toll on Marie-Eugénie's health, and resulted in a consideration of whether to sell the hotel. This was a great blow just as the business had taken off, but Alfred and Marie-Eugénie reluctantly agreed to carry on when there seemed to be better prospects of hiring more staff. In addition, following some modernisation of facilities, and the likelihood of the arrival of electricity, there was renewed stimulus to continue the venture. Now the question was whether the fourth season would see a continuation of the holiday boom, and if so, would their ambitions to firmly establish this business enterprise be realised?

Apart from these business concerns, Alfred and Marie-Eugénie had other important matters to consider in terms of their family situation, while Alfred had some very personal ambitions awaiting fulfilment. After the previous season there was a need to relieve the support provided by their three daughters who had worked hard during the busiest periods, and it was time for the girls to pursue their career ambitions. Felicity was at the Leeds College of Art and hoped for further experience in London, Barbara had changed her mind about the hotel trade and had applied for nurse training also in London, and Rosemary would take her School Certificate exams during the current year and had ambitions for a possible stage career. Christopher was near the end of his time at prep school and hoped to secure a scholarship place at a Catholic Public Boarding School, while Adrian was due to enter the local village school in the new year. Alfred had always placed great emphasis on his daughters' education in order to give them the best possible start in life, and he was equally committed to providing the same opportunities for both sons, even though he realised that it would be a financial struggle in the subsequent years.[2]

These immediate financial demands placed a further burden on Alfred's limited earning capacity, particularly in terms of his ability to derive any additional income from his literary work, which at best had been meagre to date. As a result he looked forward to some financial returns from his recently completed book *I Bought A Hotel*, together with his other book *Broad Acres – A Yorkshire Miscellany*, which were both due for publication in the near future. In addition, a revised edition of his book *Striding Through Yorkshire* was due to be reprinted in 1948, and the prospects of some extra income seemed to be reasonable, although it was uncertain whether this would even cover the costs of future school fees, but such earnings would help to redress the balance. Alfred's only other source of writing income was from the relatively poorly paid short story articles for periodicals and magazines which he loathed because of the inordinate effort involved for the trifling sums earned, but he also persisted with the idea of novel writing. He had several ongoing pieces of drafted work to which he occasionally returned in the hope that these might eventually be successful, even though the experience gained from his two previous novels suggested otherwise. While he recognised that these literary ambitions seemed like grasping at straws, if his literary income dried up completely, he would have to consider a return to the wool trade in order to fulfil his family financial commitments.[2]

Back to Reality

The 1948 season began with a slow start and a very disappointing Easter weekend, with only a handful of guests in residence, which made Alfred consider whether it was still worth the arrangement of Easter Mass at the hotel, even with a few extra guests from the nearby Mallyan Spout hotel in Goathland in the congregation.[3] However the gloomy situation was brightened by the arrival of Alfred and Marie-Eugénie's long-standing poet and writer friend, Dorothy Una Rafcliffe with her new husband, Alfred Charles Vowles, whom she had married just before Christmas.[3] They had not seen 'DUR' for almost ten years, but the reunion was most welcome even though their guests only stayed for afternoon tea, and expressed an interest in how the business was progressing, and particularly in Alfred's current writing projects. This welcomed interlude served to reinvigorate Alfred's flagging interest in his own literary endeavours once more at a time when the hotel was relatively slow in terms of trade.

It was also during this 'slack' time that Alfred took up one of his other passionate interests, namely the preservation of public access to the uplands of the North Yorkshire Moors, which had come under threat recently by the proposed requisitioning of nearby Fylingdales Moor by the military for army training purposes. There was to be a public enquiry into this serious threat to open access to the moor at the picturesque coastal village of Robin Hood's Bay, at which Alfred represented the interests of the Ramblers' Association (RA), led by his legal adviser and close friend George Heseltine.[3] The hearing in April was in front of a packed hall in which it turned out to be 'the Army versus the rest' with every possible Council and pressure group arrayed against the Army's need for more battle training areas. It was late afternoon when George had his chance to put the case on behalf of the RA, but instead of leading Alfred through a series of carefully prepared questions as other counsels had done, to Alfred's amazement and disappointment, he merely called on him as a witness for the RA, which left Alfred somewhat flustered. Consequently he embarked upon an impromptu, impassioned oration about the historical value of the moors, their tracks and ancient religious crosses, which only those with Alfred's intimate knowledge could possibly have appreciated. As a result Alfred felt that he had made a poor presentation until he received a thunderous round of applause with a standing ovation, and although he and George recognised that they had misfired completely, together with the other protagonists, they felt that they had won the day in the fight to preserve the established rights of access to the moor.

This temporary respite from the problems of the hotel could not alleviate the worries that Alfred had about the continued threat of a disastrous season, so he began discussions with his solicitor in Bradford about the possibilities of selling the hotel if the season turned out to be as bad as predicted by many in the trade.[3] The situation was further compounded by the return of severe migraine attacks that Marie-Eugénie suffered, which left her totally incapacitated, with no apparent relief from the long course of drugs over the winter period prescribed by Dr. English.[3] Alfred was concerned that even the modest demands of a mediocre season might be too much for her to tolerate, and began to devise alternative strategies to overcome the difficulties they might face, such as selling the hotel and returning to Bradford to seek other employment. Alternatively if a sale was not possible, he hoped to arrange for Marie-Eugénie and Adrian to go away for the season while he, his daughter Barbara and the remaining staff continued with the business until things improved.[3]

Nevertheless with the approach of what should have been the busy period of the Whitsuntide May holiday there was not a solitary guest at the hotel, staff were now largely redundant and the predicted disastrous year appeared to be unfolding as Alfred regretfully noted:

> This has not happened before, it is presumably due to the petrol restrictions not being lifted until June 1st, and as the continental holiday appeals, who would stay in England for the bleak summer of 1948 if they can manage to go abroad?[3]

Even with these pressing concerns, there was still important business to be done and none more so than the first AGM of the Whitfield House Hotel Country Club, which catered largely for locals during this depressed time of year.[3] In order to lift his own and his members' spirits on this occasion Alfred gladly served gin, brandy, whisky, madeira and port to the assembled group 'on the house' to ensure that the meeting went well, although it maintained a sense of sobriety when the local vicar, Dr. F.J. Mann, was elected as chairman for the coming year. There were also new members to enrol in the club and it seemed as if this one aspect of the innovations that Alfred had introduced was producing a beneficial if somewhat limited financial return, as well as a useful social service. He was also encouraged by his other fledgling services including the taxi business and catering provision for visiting coach parties.

The taxi business had grown from a 'pick-up and drop-off' service for guests who arrived and departed by public transport into a private hire service for locals, since there was a considerable demand from local residents for urgent transport needs in such an isolated area with only limited bus and train services. This convenient arrangement overcame the difficulties of obtaining a taxi licence as well as the need to secure a supplementary petrol allowance. Now Alfred was regularly called upon not only to provide essential transport services for locals, but residents of the hotel who wished to take sight-seeing tours of the moors and the coast, and even gained some business from neighbouring hotels whose proprietors were glad to use this valuable service for their own residents. The only problem now was that when Alfred lost the services of his general handyman/gardener/taxi-driver, he had to drive the taxi himself on top of all his other duties.[3]

The decision to re-instate catering provision for visiting coach parties had also been made out of necessity to generate more income. In view of the dearth of bookings for June which had been the worst so far, and with only a few secured for July, it was clear that the business was on the brink of failure that season. Even so Alfred was careful not to let the economic imperative override the sensitivities of the few residents who had previously objected to an influx of these 'hordes' as one guest had firmly put it!

The kind of boisterous parties of the 'club trip' variety, or 'Jolly Boys Outings', were avoided at all costs to preserve the reputation of the hotel as a haven of peace and tranquility. The extent to which this was achieved was judged by the occasional visits of a genteel party of nuns who sometimes arrived for afternoon tea and expressed the view that this was the most charming of places and they were the most appreciative of all casual visitors. Alfred only wished that all coach parties could be so kind and full of praise for the extra efforts involved in making such special arrangements.[3]

Nevertheless even the extra modest income from the Country Club, the taxi service and coach party catering could not hide the desperate reality of a business in crisis. The high season was supposedly in full swing at this time, but the low numbers of guests continued throughout August, and with no bookings confirmed beyond early September, it looked as if this would indeed be the worst season so far, but it also focused Alfred and Marie-Eugénie's attention on the need to sell the hotel.[3] However this solution might have proved problematical given that when Alfred completed his guest returns at the end of the season, they were nearly £800 down on the previous year, and in August alone the comparable deficit was £250. This would have made it very difficult to sell the hotel outright, and might even have forced its disposal at auction, whereby it was unlikely that a fair return could be made on their initial investment.[3]

Now Alfred also had to consider the immediate needs of his family as well as the problems of the hotel, which were to some extent intertwined. Marie-Eugénie found the strain of even a reduced season very demanding without sufficient staff to support the extra services offered, and she was almost at breaking point and would once more need a complete break from the hotel.[12] Meanwhile Felicity was determined to pursue her art career in London, while Barbara had opted for a nursing career also in London, and although Rosemary had passed her School Certificate, she put aside thoughts of training for the stage due to lack of finances. Financial considerations also determined Christopher's likely future education after he completed his final year at the Abbey Prep School in Hemingford Grey, near in St. Ives, Huntingdon, since he needed a scholarship to attend a senior Catholic Public School such as Ampleforth. Only Adrian's immediate need was secure when he started at the local village school in the New Year.[3]

The holiday season stuttered to a halt following the arrival of two parties of unexpected guests during late October, and a further small party in early November, which in view of the season's poor performance, the late trade could not be turned away.[3] Alfred and Marie-Eugénie were then faced with the problem of what to do about the upcoming Christmas and New Year Holiday periods. Marie-Eugénie had taken a much-needed break for a couple of weeks with friends in Ilkley,[3] but Alfred finally realised that they could no longer compete effectively with the larger hotels in nearby Goathland, even with all the supplementary services.[3] It was therefore inevitable that unlike previous years, they decided not to open for the end of year celebrations and instead to have a quiet family Christmas, since they were convinced that it was likely to be the last one at the hotel.[3] In addition Alfred let go a part-time handyman since he could now manage to do all the remaining odd jobs himself during the winter months.[3] The decision to close for Christmas seemed justified when all the children were at home to celebrate another traditional family occasion without the worries of what might lie ahead, although later Alfred confided: 'Christmas has come and gone, and another year has become a fateful one for us!'[4]

Worrying Prospects for the New Year

Alfred and Marie-Eugénie noted with little comfort and much dismay that they were not the only hotel owners in the country who anxiously waited to see what 1949 would bring, but Alfred had adopted the view: 'hope springs eternal in the hotelier's breast' or he would not have been in the business in the first place. In his opinion the main thing was to show a smiling face to the world, especially to guests and convince every-one that all was well.[4] The temptation to throw in the towel last year had been resisted since Alfred hated the thought of giving in, and he still liked the hotel life despite the disappointments, and to him there was always a chance that conditions would improve, so ever the optimist he decided to carry on. However there were some criti-cal questions as the new year began: would the 'slump' continue or not? Would turn-over return to previous levels and perhaps increase? Would staff be easier to recruit and retain? Would the long-promised electricity supply come to the locality at last? Finally, would they be able to reduce the overdraft of some £1800 by the end of the coming trading year?[4] It was to this financial burden that Alfred now turned his atten-tion and considered alternative means of income generation, including a possibility of a return to other forms of work.

After an extensive bout of spring cleaning, Alfred worked on another potential money-making strategy, and prepared public lectures for delivery to a number of audi-ences who had read his previous books and were keen to learn more about his tramp-ing exploits. He had given lectures to small audiences for some time, but his next one was delivered to a much larger audience at the City Museum in Leeds, where he spoke for an hour followed by a lengthy question time, and it seemed to have been well received by members of the public who were familiar with his published work.[4] Afterwards when Alfred stayed at the Great Northern Hotel in Leeds, he chanced to meet up with Wilfred Pickles (1904-1978), the well-known, Halifax-born actor and radio presenter, whose popular radio show, 'Have a Go', regularly attracted an audience of 20 million listeners. In discussion with Pickles, the possibility of some future radio broadcast work was suggested to Alfred, who already had some contacts at the BBC in Leeds. However Pickles suggested that Alfred should contact the BBC in Manchester and that he himself would be keen to promote some of Alfred's work, especially his novel stories, which might form the basis for a new series, although Alfred doubted whether this was likely to happen, given his past disappointing experiences with BBC Radio.[4] Nevertheless, undaunted, while he spent the weekend with an old RAF friend, Leslie Griffiths, at Barrowford in Lancashire, he arranged an interview with the Head of BBC Broadcasting in Manchester, then spent a couple of hours discussing future broadcasting possibilities with various people in the organisation. He left with only a suggestion of a possible contribution to a dialect programme, and although it was hardly his speciality he felt he ought to consider any chance of work for such a prestigious public broadcasting institution, but unfortunately nothing came of this initiative.[4]

On his return to the hotel, Alfred was troubled not only by the impact this ever demanding business continued to have on the family, but also by the growing discontent that was manifested by Marie-Eugénie and his daughters. His wife's health problem posed a real threat to the continuance of the business and was the main reason for him to consider the abandonment of the enterprise. But it was pronounced changes in his daughters' attitude and behaviour towards him that became a serious concern, as he reflected upon an apparent rift that he sensed had opened up between them in a discourse on the state of their relationships.[4] Alfred ruminated on what could be the cause of the apparent changes in his daughters, who had experienced a strict private Catholic education and subsequently endured demanding roles in the family business, but now pressed hard to follow their chosen careers and desperately tried to break away from protective parental influences.[4] To Alfred this response seemed a rebellious reaction, but in reality it was natural for these talented, ambitious, high-spirited young women of the age, who wanted to make their own way in the wider world. It was now clear to him that come what may, Felicity was determined to try to make a career in art, Barbara would pursue her call to nursing, and Rosemary intended to follow her sisters' examples of independence by enrolment at secretarial school with a view to a commercial career. This situation also left Alfred with the dutiful prospect of provision of the same educational opportunities for his sons to facilitate their future prospects and the need to meet the financial demands involved, so that some radical rethinking of the family's financial circumstances was required.

'Hotel for Sale'- By Auction

During Alfred's deliberations about his financial problems, he began to consider the prospect of a quick sale of the hotel, and was recommended by Bagshawe the Whitby solicitor to contact an auctioneer to discuss the possibility of a reasonably rapid sale.[4] Following a meeting with a representative of Giddings & Co., Auctioneers and Valuers of York, an inventory was made of the hotel's contents to prepare a catalogue for sale by auction which was fixed for the end of March 1949.[4] Alfred then started painting the front of the hotel in preparation for a possible sale, but was hampered by snow-storms and freezing conditions as he tried to complete the work before any potential buyers visited for a preliminary inspection.[4] Meanwhile the local advertisement of the auction in the Whitby Gazette newspaper astounded the villagers who were quite shocked at this sudden development.[4] All that was, except the Rev. Mann, Alfred's friend and chairman of the Whitfield House Country Club, with whom Alfred con-fided about the plan, and who expressed his surprise, sadness and some considerable disappointment at the news on behalf of the whole community, which he indicated held the hotel and its proprietors in high esteem.

Following the arrival of an impressively printed prospectus soon afterwards, Alfred and Marie-Eugénie considered the future plans they had made depending on the out-come of the auction.[4] Firstly, if the sale went ahead, they intended to put their fur-niture into storage and move to London to find temporary accommodation for the remaining family at home, so that Rosemary could attend a Commercial College and Adrian a day school, after which Alfred intended to return to Yorkshire to try his hand again at a full-time writing. Secondly, if the sale did not go ahead, the plan was for Marie-Eugénie to go to London with Rosemary and Adrian, while Alfred would carry on with the hotel, hopefully with new staff appointed, and attempt to continue writ-ing on a part-time basis as he had done before. Thirdly, if the sale not did meet the reserve price, they conceded that they would then be in the terrible situation of an unpalatable status quo, and that they would have to endure an indeterminate period until an alternative option could be devised. This last gloomy scenario unfortunately looked likely after Alfred had a depfessing meeting with the auctioneer, during which he was told that there had been no enquiries to view the property with only two weeks to go before the auction.[4] The only glimmers of hope came from a visit made by a family of potential buyers who viewed the hotel just a week before the auction, and an enquiry about the possible development of the hotel into a convalescent home by Brothertons, the large chemicals company in Leeds, but even these late interests seemed unlikely to be followed up.[4]

Finally Alfred and Marie-Eugénie nervously attended the auction which was held on 30th March 1949 at 3.00pm in the Station Hotel in York.[4] They arrived early and were greeted by Rawlinson, their solicitor friend from Bradford, the auctioneer from Giddings & Co., of York, and an agent from Bagshawe's solicitors of Whitby, but no members of the public were in evidence by the specified time. It seemed as if the auction would be called off until two men appeared together, an army major and a civilian. The auctioneer then proceeded with the conditions of sale legalities before he opened the bidding at £5,000, and slowly offers progressed to £7,500 towards the reserve price of £8,500. Here the bid remained stuck with no further offers, which was very disappointing since Alfred and Marie-Eugénie had paid the reserve price for the hotel in the first place. At this point the auctioneers called the various representatives together to confer, and announced to an astounded Alfred and his wife that most of the 'bids' had come from the 'plant' of a colleague in the audience, and that in reality nobody had made a bid at all, so that the whole thing had been a farce. Afterwards the apologetic auctioneer suggested to Alfred that the army might be persuaded to engage in further negotiations and that an arrangement might be possible to sell the hotel by private treaty. But by then Alfred had lost all faith in the process, and as he and his wife drove back over the desolate North Yorkshire Moors which were now shrouded in mist, they felt as gloomy as the surroundings which disappeared from view, just as their chances of a sale had done that afternoon. They later came to the conclusion that the auction had been too early to attract much genuine interest, since everywhere still looked very bleak, unlike when they originally viewed the place, and that summer time afforded the best chance of a sale when the hotel could be shown in all its glory, so for now it now meant they faced another hopefully busy season, or perhaps several more.[5]

A Distinguished Visitor Arrives for Lunch

A welcomed light relief to Alfred's problems came prior to the start of the new season when he received an enquiry on behalf of a very distinguished person following a telephone call from the Reverend Philip Wheeldon, the chaplain and private secretary to His Grace, the Archbishop of York, Dr. Cyril Foster Garbett (1875-1955), who wished to call at the hotel for lunch the following day.[4] Unfortunately Marie-Eugénie was away for a short break and Alfred was uncertain if he could cope with the request, but decided that with the help of Rosemary they would manage and confirmed the arrangement. Then to Alfred and Rosemary's relief Rev. Wheeldon indicated that the Archbishop was a man of simple tastes and that a modest lunch would suffice, and suggested an egg dish or a simple meat dish such as ham which His Grace liked. So Alfred settled on ham and eggs and decided to make use of the remaining Yorkshire Ham, a flitch of gammon, which had been hanging in the larder outside for some months. But to his horror, when he cut into the gammon joint it had traces of maggots or perhaps mites, and it resembled a ripe Gorgonzola cheese, so in his uncertainty he consulted the farmer who had supplied it to get a replacement. However the farmer had no hams left, but he came around to inspect the offending specimen, then immediately pronounced it 'perfect' and indicated that these little 'creturs' were always present in well-hung hams and that: 'it was just how a ripe ham should be'. Nevertheless Alfred was still in doubt when he proceeded with the ham and eggs which Rosemary cooked admirably, along with other complementary dishes. The meal passed without a hitch, and the menu of Scotch broth, Yorkshire ham and eggs, carrots, cabbage, and chipped potatoes, together with jam roll and custard, as well as Wensleydale cheese with coffee and biscuits, was complimented as being as absolutely delicious by the Archbishop and his chaplain,[4] which was a testament to Alfred and Rosemary's inventiveness and the ability to procure such a range of food during a time of post-war rationing.

After lunch, the Archbishop slept for half an hour in the quiet of the lounge, then took a stroll on the nearby old Roman road over the moor to the west of Goathland. Upon his return he chatted at some length with Alfred, who found him to be a very courtly, kind old man, with an intimate knowledge of Alfred's books and a keen interest in the moors, with the desire for a return visit as soon as possible. Before leaving, he signed the visitors book 'Cyril Ebor',[6] and also indicated that on his next visit he would like Alfred to map out a route west over the moors to Littlebeck and then to the coast towards Whitby. Alfred was not surprised to learn that 'Cyril Ebor' was then a vey popular figure in the English Church and was famed for trudging the length and breadth of his Diocese with his walking stick to visit his clergy and the laity alike. Subsequently, as he had indicated, he returned to the hotel later in the year, again for lunch, but this time not for the ham that was definitely 'off' by then, before he strode off once more over the moors on the Roman road towards Glaisdale this time, much to Alfred's appreciation and admiration.[4]

The 1949 Season

The first visitors of the new season arrived just before Easter when the hotel opened for its fifth season, and following a long cold spell, the weather had changed almost miraculously to fine warm sunshine just before the holiday weekend, which gave Alfred and other country inn-keepers faith in an upturn of visitor numbers.[7] But Alfred acknowledged that Easter was only a passing interlude in the year, a kind of false dawn to the real holiday season, which did not begin until the major May Bank Holiday weekend at Whitsuntide. As a result he was reluctant to hire any permanent staff at this time even though another cook, porter/handyman and chambermaid/waitress were needed, especially since his overdraft had now grown to over £2,000 with nearly two months of the so-called 'dead season' to go.[4] By his own estimation Alfred needed to raise another £1,000 just to carry on for the coming year, but he was concerned about whether the bank would agree to provide the necessary funds,[4] although after a meeting with the friendly manager he was assured that the bank would help him for the remainder of the season and then discuss the situation again in the light of the year's performance.[4] Moreover some staffing relief came in the form of another welcomed visitor, this time Mrs. Rene Dixon and her three children from Ilkley. Rene was a close friend of Marie-Eugénie and had earlier agreed to help out in the kitchen and perform other essential duties for the duration of the high season, which helped as a stop-gap measure to overcome the chronic staff shortage problem.[4]

While all this was good news, Alfred now struggled with two further personal problems, one new – his attempt to give up smoking, and one old – his continued bouts of ill health. He had given up smoking for Lent, appropriately enough on 'Ash Wednesday', and also to see if he could break the habit and he now found it very difficult to maintain the effort involved.[4] This was evident by a ten page long journal commentary on his reasons for, and problems with, giving up the addictive weed, then a further six page review of his temporary non-smoking status three weeks later, before his struggle finally ended in mid May, when he returned to his old ways, after another extended six page review of smoking, the behaviour of smokers, the sociability of the habit and his lack of esteem for non-smokers in general.[4] However Alfred was unable to come to terms with his struggle to manage the other long term problem of his recurrent bouts of illness, which were often associated with becoming run-down as a result of overwork. Apart from a sequence of hideous styes on his eyes that required him to wear an eye patch, he had never been able to shake off the cold and 'flu infections that appeared regularly.[4] These recurring ailments made him despair of ever overcoming the long-standing, weakened resistance problem that he attributed to the major illness that he had suffered in WW1. He also hated people to see him now in his present emaciated, out of condition state, which by his own standard certainly did not create the kind of image that he wished to portray as a healthy, robust country inn-keeper.[4]

Alfred put these trials and tribulations behind him quickly and steeled himself once more for the lead-up to the high season, although Whitsuntide was a lot like the Easter holiday period with only limited numbers of guests, including some of the now regular customers who often helped the newcomers settle into the hotel.[8] However this was only another short holiday and the hotel was soon empty again except for a few people who took advantage of the brilliant summer weather in June, and since the high season did not really begin until mid-July, Alfred and Marie-Eugénie looked forward to an improved uptake by residents which until now had been slow compared with previous years. Meanwhile they hoped that the installation of the electricity supply would have been finished by Whitsuntide as planned, but it was delayed until July, even though most of the external cable laying and internal wiring had been completed. This meant that the struggle to run a residential hotel for four years without an electrical supply would have to be tolerated a little longer, but now the prospect of electric lighting throughout the place and the benefits of all the modern devices such as a vacuum cleaner, iron, kettle, refrigerator, washing machine and even mains wireless seemed almost too good to be true.[9]

Furthermore, in anticipation of the electricity supply installation, Alfred renewed his efforts with the local Council to install a mains drainage system, because until then the hotel had been responsible for its own sewage disposal which went into a private sump in the fields below. Alfred had always detested this unhygienic and revolting arrangement, which may have been sufficient for the previous farmhouse, but it was completely inadequate for the numbers of people using the hotel's facilities and always gave problems during the busiest periods.[10] And yet this vitally important service was also delayed until the relative costs of the installation were calculated and the public and private liabilities were apportioned to the Council and the hotel respectively. As a result the final connections of both electricity and mains drainage services were not completed until the end of August.[11] By which time, although the busy season was nearing an end, Alfred and Marie-Eugénie were not only enlightened but also flushed with the success of putting the hotel on the map in so far as modern facilities and amenities were concerned, and could now compete more effectively with their neighbouring business rivals.

Unfortunately the high season had not lived up to expectations, although two further valuable additions were made to the permanent members of staff when a local married couple were hired who had experience of the roles needed by a small hotel.[12] Mrs. Scarth, or Sophie, had worked in the hotel trade before and was a good cook, an expert pastry chef, a trained waitress and an experienced chambermaid, which meant that she could cover the full range of duties required. She also had a most pleasant, friendly and outgoing personality, with an infectious good spirit and unflagging energy, and became the most reliable member of staff, which made a remarkable difference to the running of the hotel. Furthermore her husband, Isaac, also came to help out and covered a range of general duties when he was not busy with farming, and he could turn his hand to anything from taxi-driving, gardening and assistance with everything from kitchen chores to car maintenance. In addition to this most competent couple, further assistance was provided by a local girl, Connie Sykes, who was a next door neighbour of Mrs. Scarth, and she had experience as a kitchen maid and waitress, and became good friends with Rosemary who was about the same age. So after all the recent staffing problems it was of great comfort to Alfred and Marie-Eugénie to finally have a team who could work together, and they were now better staffed than they had ever been, but their chief worry still remained – whilst there was no the shortage of competent staff, there was a shortage of paying guests at the critical time of the holiday season.[12]

The struggle to maintain a healthy turnover continued throughout the rest of the summer season as guest numbers often dipped below those of previous years and forced Alfred and Marie-Eugénie to continue with coach party catering to maximise takings. But even these extra activities proved difficult especially on busy Bank Holiday weekends, when confusion often occurred due to the arrival of an unexpected coach party who sought afternoon tea.[13] Then there were problems due to late cancellation of bookings by inconsiderate guests on flimsy pretexts, which were sometimes offset by unscheduled guests who turned up late in the day in the hope of an evening meal, with bed and breakfast as well.[14] In such cases Alfred tried to accommodate them, and if not he called village friends to provide facilities for these 'sleepers out', which they often did with complementary service.[15] Alfred even let his own room to guests if Marie-Eugénie was away, and was more than happy to sleep on a camp bed in his office, but his wife was resolute that their room was sacrosanct while she was in residence.[16]

And yet, even with the hurly-burly with these additional requests, family life went on during the busiest times, and Alfred and Marie-Eugénie organised a formal 21st birthday party for their eldest daughter Felicity at the beginning of August.[17] It was fortunate at the time that the hotel was not too busy so that most of the family and friends who needed rooms could be accommodated. A sumptuous buffet supper was held in the extended Whitfield House Club Bar on a Saturday evening, and the celebrations continued on Sunday with an outdoor party, before guests slowly drifted away and left Alfred and Marie-Eugénie to their end of season hotel duties.[17]

From then on the remainder of the season followed a similar pattern to the unexpectedly low turn-out at its peak, and September was much quieter than usual, which, together with the poor holiday year overall, caused Alfred to conclude that the postwar holiday boom was finished.[18] Though guest numbers remained low, there were still occasional regular visitors who often came to stay at this quiet time of year, and Alfred always looked forward to their return and rewarded their loyalty with convivial evenings by the fireside. Moreover he found these autumnal days enchanting when there was a sparkle to the early mornings and a nip in the evening air, which brought a return of peat fires to give the hotel a cosy atmosphere, and when things were not so busy, he was often able to slip away over the moors. He always enjoyed these walks in solitude at this time of year, and he explored the deep valleys, forested slopes and moorland ridges dotted with their lonely Howes and Stone Crosses, around which he could wander for hours without seeing another living soul.[19] It was on one of these occasional tramping trips that he had come across a traditional wood carver who became a close friend, and who was eventually to be known widely for his craftsmanship in the region and well beyond.

Thomas E. Whittaker (1910-1991) was a traditional wood carver who lived at St. Hilda's Cottage in the little hamlet of Littlebeck situated in the deep wooded valley of Little Beck, about 3 miles north east of Goathland across Sleights Moor. He worked exclusively with English oak, seasoned outdoors for seven years, using a traditional adze tool to bring out the natural beauty of the wood, and specialised in commissioned ecclesiastical works and home furniture. He completed his apprenticeship with the famous wood carver Robert Thompson (1876-1850) at Kilburn in North Yorkshire, who was known as 'The Mouseman' for the emblematic mouse that adorned all his work. Tom adopted the mythical German Oak Spirit as the iconic emblem for all his work, which displayed a small gnome in a Gothic arch, and thus became known as the 'Gnome Man'. Alfred was keen to furnish the hotel with some of his work, but because of Tom's many commissions he had to settle for a large refectory table and some chairs,[4] but since no two pieces of work were identical, he proudly took possession of these unique pieces of furniture, which became treasured family heirlooms. Tom's work was continued by his sole apprentice, Chris Checkfield, and today both Tom's and Chris's work is highly desirable and much sought after by passionate collectors. Before Tom became so well-known, Alfred and his wife became close friends with Tom, his wife Kathleen and their daughters Faith and Claire, and Tom would often walk to the hotel from Littlebeck on a summer evening after work to share a pipe, a tankard of ale or an old Marsala or Madeira with Alfred and talk late into the night.[20]

As the year progressed towards the closed season Alfred enjoyed the peace and quiet that descended on the empty hotel, and not only pursued his outdoor interests but also turned his attention to spare-time writing. Although even these brief pleasures were often curtailed because there was always the need to complete the essential off-season work such as painting and decorating, as well as the many odd jobs needed to prepare the hotel for the next season.[21] It was also necessary to consider the upcoming Christmas and New Year festive holiday season which was traditionally a very busy time, but had been abandoned last year in favour of quiet family occasion. However in view of the worst year of trade so far, Alfred and Marie-Eugénie decided they could not afford to turn down the opportunity to redress some of the imbalance of their growing overdraft, and they planned another family occasion with their guests' requests for a traditional Whitfield House Hotel celebration.[22] By now the pattern was well established for the usual festivities to take place during this time, and no one, especially the guests, wanted to deviate from these family-oriented events, as it was uncertain for how long such a tradition could be maintained. Subsequently the hotel had a full complement of guests over the Christmas and New Year holidays, and although both occasions lived up to expectations, Alfred had the nagging suspicion that the dreaded overdraft would creep up to the limit of £2,500 by the start of the next season as he prayed for the future: 'So this is the end of 1949, and I hope for better things in 1950, the Holy Year – *Sursum Corda!* [*Lift up your hearts!*]'[4]

The Final Year

There was probably little doubt in the minds of Alfred and Marie-Eugénie that come what may, 1950 would be their last year of trying to make the Whitfield House Hotel the success they hoped that it might be when they embarked on this bold venture. At the start of the year Alfred focused his attention once more on the urgent problems posed by his family, that were to some extent linked to the problems of the business, and his own perennial problem of fulfilling his writing expectations.[23]

The hotel had not sold at auction and while the problem of a sale appeared to be no nearer a solution, selling now became an economic imperative for the family's future, and indeed Alfred's own writing prospects, since he had two new books which he hoped to complete in the coming year. With regard to the family, in Alfred's estimation, Marie-Eugénie would be hard pressed to sustain the effort needed to complete another season at the hotel. Meanwhile Felicity had settled down in London with bright prospects for her art career, Barbara was immersed in her nurse training course at Westminster Hospital in London and Rosemary had passed her School Certificate with credit and had embarked on a secretarial course at a Commercial College in York. Christopher had not been successful in obtaining a scholarship at Ampleforth or Downside, but was now happy to attend Ampleforth, although the fees continued to be a burden on the family's limited finances. Adrian was attending the village school in Goathland, but Alfred and Marie-Eugénie considered the possibility of moving him to the Ampleforth Prep School of St. Martins, at Gilling Castle, North Yorkshire.[23] Therefore it seemed that in order to continue to support the needs of his developing family, Alfred now had to make preparations for a radical review of the business so that it might have a chance of being sold in the coming year.

At the outset it was necessary for Alfred to complete his most detested chore, that of updating the book-keeping exercise for the inexorable 'annual returns'.[24] This was required not only for accounting purposes, but also to give any prospective buyer a chance to appraise the financial health of the business. However Alfred resented these procedures which reduced everything to a matter of cold figures for the assessment of the 'profit and loss' situation. In Alfred's mind this approach was all very well for the strictly commercial undertakings of large limited liability companies, in which money-making and dividends were all that mattered. In his view small country hotels were not run on such impersonal lines, and success and failure could not be judged solely on figures, and the real test was how far they succeeded in giving pleasure and satisfaction to their guests.[24] To Alfred these so-called 'imponderables' could not be assessed by a balance sheet, but were the true criteria of success in running a country hotel, and so it always depressed to him to have to translate these essential human factors into a bleak and misleading mercenary balance sheet. When he turned over the pages of the visitors book and remembered the season's residents, that rich cross section of humanity who gave such life and vitality to the place, whose names evoked the pleasure and enjoyment they experienced while on holiday, and the feeling that he and the staff had become part of their lives if only briefly, he lamented:

And now they are reduced to some miserable – and quite inadequate

– figures of pounds, shillings and pence! ... and when your accountant comes to do the books there is no column provided for romance – or sentiment – or memories.[24]

The hard fact of the matter was that the financial situation was dire and the overdraft was at the new limit of £2,500 with no sign of any real income for another four months, and Alfred would have to seek a further extension or perhaps a loan in order to keep going.[23] Even with the reassuring support of his very understanding local bank manager, who confided that this situation was to be expected in the hotel trade and that things would balance out with the onset of the new season, Alfred knew this could not continue. In reality they were now far worse off than they were when they started, after five years of hard work and that did not bode well for any prospective sale.

While this financial news was been bad enough, there was also serious concerns for two members of the family, namely Barbara who had suffered a serious accident[23] and shortly after Adrian became lost while out playing out.[25] Barbara fell while ice skating and sustained a head injury with concussion and was under close observation in a special ward at Westminster Hospital. She had suffered a similar accident two years previously while horse riding with Alfred, and this time Marie-Eugénie went to London to be with her. She returned later with the news that while Barbara was still bed-bound there was no sign of any brain damage, but she would need long term sick leave to help with her recovery. Subsequently Alfred also went to London to make arrangements for Barbara's convalescence and she was finally well enough to return home in the early spring, but could not resume her nurse training course until the summer.[23]

While Marie-Eugénie was away in London, Adrian went missing following an afternoon of snow sledging with friends and as dusk fell he was nowhere to be seen.[25] Alfred became desperately worried by 6.00 p.m. since Adrian, who was not quite seven years old, had never been out alone after dark before. He had a vision that the youngster had wandered off and maybe got lost in the snow, so he organised a search party with the help of the local grocer who turned up with a couple of his blood hounds. They set off over the nearby moor which was one of Adrian's favourite haunts in the hope that they might find him quickly. Then, to their astonishment, out of the dark gloomy, snow-laden skies, they saw the ghostly figures of another party of searchers trudging down the bleak moor road with an unconcerned Adrian dragging his sledge behind them. He was found at a farmhouse tucking into tea after he went to play with his friend, and was taken in by the farmer's wife who assumed that he was dropped off at the gate. He had dragged his heavy sledge up a steep moorland road that some of his would-be rescuers had struggled along in the deep snow, although he admitted to his much-relieved father: 'It was a bit hard Daddy, getting up that big mountainside, but once I was up, it was quite easy... There's nothing to worry about if you know the paths as well as I do!' Alfred considered this an understatement from one so young and was astonished at his achievement in such adverse conditions, although the incident remained a nightmare in Alfred's memory.[25]

It was during these testing times the decision was finally made to sell the hotel, although it was not due to any sudden impulse, but a course of action that had been forced upon Alfred and Marie-Eugénie by the worsening business situation and the demands made on the family which were now becoming intolerable[26]. Marie-Eugénie had been advised by her doctor two years before to give up the responsibility for catering when the strain had a serious effect on her health. The succeeding years had proved even more strenuous and on several occasions she had collapsed during a busy period, and since Alfred was unable to find a replacement the situation only became worse. He had been reluctant to give up the struggle, now it was obvious that not only the demands of the business, but the anxieties his wife had about their children's future were both contributing to her ill-health. It was now time to heed Dr. English's advice and sell out before the 'costs' became too high.[26]

Furthermore the effects of the business on the other members of the family had also become a serious cause for concern, since it was acknowledged that a gradual disintegration of family life was a problem that often affected many hotel proprietors. With the benefit of hindsight it was now clear to Alfred that the combination of 'normal' family life and running a small hotel was virtually impossible. Moreover, the daunting task of trying to run the business for profit had also proved impossible, and while the family lived reasonably comfortably on the business, there was no money available to save for retirement. Any 'profit' had to be ploughed back into the business to cover the ongoing costs of maintenance, repair, upgrading and the replacement of furnishings and fittings, not to mention the costs of hiring staff to operate the business. Alfred also concluded that the size of the hotel had been a contributory factor to their financial predicament. In order make a profit in a residential hotel, it was necessary to have either no more than 10 bedrooms which could be managed by the owners without the need for staff, or at least 25-30 bedrooms that would allow a full staffing complement, but with 14 bedrooms theirs had become a non economically viable entity.[27]

Alfred had also come to other profound conclusions with respect to the hotel business, in so far as he was now convinced more than ever that hotel-keeping was something akin to a vocation – like joining a religious order, and to do it properly he believed that 'One has to give one's whole life to it, body and soul – all the time.'[28] Then in spite of his previously held tenet, he was now convinced that he could not mix authorship with running a hotel and be successful at both, since the hotel business was far too exacting, and it was perhaps only surpassed by members of religious orders who worked harder and more unselfishly at their vocations. Furthermore he came to the decision that if a choice had to be made, he would now prefer to write books, whilst his only concern was whether he could now make a living by his literary efforts, but he was willing to give it a try.[28]

However before he could make such a choice there was the urgent matter of conducting the final year of hotel business until a buyer could be found, and with the start of another new season advance bookings began to accumulate more briskly than in the previous two slow years, possibly associated with the publicity received from the publication of his book *I Bought A Hotel* in 1949.[29] This year the hotel was full at Easter and Whitsuntide, and regular visitors turned up again between these holiday periods, and although the main influx of guests did not begin until late June, the place was very busy throughout the summer season until October. As ever August and September were the busiest periods, with residents being joined by inquisitive readers of the book, coach parties, chance visitors for meals, and touring motorists who often arrived unexpectedly hoping for bed and breakfast, and when this was not available they eagerly took advantage of the 'sleeping out' arrangements that were now quite commonplace.

Many old friends also returned during the high season and contributed to the reunion parties that became a feature of this busy summer, during which the now-established staff team maintained the unstinting support needed to offer the comprehensive services required. At this stage however, Alfred and Marie-Eugénie had not given any hint to staff, friends and regular guests that they planned to sell the hotel, since they decided to delay the announcement of their decision until later in the year, when they hoped to have secured the interests of a potential buyer.[29]

The sale of the hotel was again placed in the hands of the Whitby solicitor Bagshawe, who had been involved in the auction house's unsuccessful auction sale in the previous year, but now with the benefit of the high season it seemed like the prospect of a sale was much better. This time there were a number of prospective buyers who at least came to view the hotel, and among them was a married couple who arrived during a busy coach party visit, but they stayed long after the agent left, which indicated that they were perhaps more serious about making a possible bid.[30] Curiously they had heard about the hotel by chance when they were driving home one evening listening to the car radio which had broadcast a review of Alfred's latest book, and they were so interested in the story that they had bought the book, and having read it their desire to have a similar hotel was aroused. Afterwards they discovered the real name of the hotel and its location, and even found out about the auction sale, but had missed the event due to illness. Alfred, who had missed the broadcast but often courted BBC radio unsuccessfully with his work, acknowledged that they had done him a favour on this occasion. The couple visited again about a week later to look over the hotel once more and go through the inventory, and made up their minds to buy the place on the spot, just like Alfred had done on that sunny spring day in 1945.[30]

A few days later the agent telephoned to say that a firm offer had been made by the couple, although the only difficulty was that they would not be able to take possession until the new year since they had to wind up their own business, which suited Alfred and Marie-Eugénie admirably, as it allowed them to complete the current season and make all the necessary arrangements for their next move.[30] A contract of sale was duly drawn up and signed by the purchasers, Mr. and Mrs. H. Rippon of Moreton on the Wirral, Cheshire, on the 30th August 1950, for the sum of £8,000, which included all the furniture and fittings specified in the detailed inventory.[31] And so it was all settled, Alfred, Marie-Eugénie and family were soon to be on the move again, but where to this time?

While Alfred and Marie-Eugénie contemplated their next move, they had some three months during the autumn and early winter to plan for the move, but there was little time to relax. The season lingered on into mid October with visits by their regular late holiday guests and family friends, who, although they were sad and disappointed to learn of the news of the hotel sale, indicated that they would still like to return to the old place in future. It was during this period that Alfred and Marie-Eugénie decided to open again for one final Christmas season, since they had already taken a lot of bookings for this popular time of year, and it provided the opportunity to give a farewell party for all their friends in the neighbourhood.

Christmas saw a full house once more with over 26 loyal guests, as well as friends and family in residence,[32] and although it had a curious solemnity and significance associated with the occasion it was by popular vote the best one of all. But no sooner had the guests departed Alfred and Marie-Eugénie had to prepare for the farewell party on New Year's Day. This was one of the liveliest parties ever held at the hotel and provided an opportunity of thanking all the local residents who had got to know them so well during the previous six years,[32] with over 50 people in attendance including:

> Club members, neighbouring hoteliers, farmers, trades people, the local
> bank manager and solicitor, the butcher, the wood carver, the station master,
> the village school teacher, the vicar and his wife – all the interesting people
> who made up the life of the countryside. On the whole, it was perhaps the
> most representative party that Farrdale [*sic*] ever knew.[33]

The staff as ever rose marvellously to the occasion with Mrs. Scarth and her husband
Isaac, ably supported by Connie, scuttling around with sherry decanters and cocktail
shakers, filling up glasses and working hard to promote good cheer among everyone.
But the star of the show was undoubtedly Brother Oswald Vanhaus, a Benedictine
monk from Ampleforth Abbey, who astonished everybody with his skills of mixing
and dispensing the cocktails and liqueurs, and he stole the show!

Alfred's only regret on this happy occasion was that this living history of those
assembled was not recorded on film, and he had to be content with the signatures
of everyone present in the visitors book – the last entries of all.[33] Alfred and Marie-
Eugénie were sure that the farewell party was the high spot of their hotel careers since
it brought together most of the people they had lived amongst, worked with and made
friends in the neighbourhood, and even though it was sad to be leaving them, it was
good to know that they believed that they both had in some small measure achieved
what they had set out to do at the outset of this great adventure.[33]

Epilogue to the Hotel Saga

With hindsight, while the Whitfield House Hotel project may have seemed to be a very
risky enterprise at the time of post-war austerity, there appeared to have been some
good evidence that this bold endeavour was more than just a business 'black hole', as
suggested by a detailed analysis of the visitors book during the period of May 1945
and January 1951.[34] The 'signed in' visitor numbers during this period approached
some 1,800 guests, which included the first very short season of 1945 that nevertheless recorded a visitor total of over 200 guests during the summer months, which
no doubt gave Alfred and Marie-Eugénie great promise of future expected numbers.
Subsequently the second, third and fifth seasons realised guest numbers exceeding
350 per high season, but it was the fourth season that caused concern, when numbers
struggled to achieve 250 guests in high season. These occupancy totals could not have
come at a worse time when the financial situation was most precarious as a result of a
steadily growing bank overdraft following the investment needed to bring about the
modernisation of the facilities, together with the additional staffing costs needed to

maintain the high standards of services that had been necessary to operate the hotel effectively.

However the estimated core income derived from these guest numbers, based upon the 'bed and board' charges that were in operation, did not amount to an economically viable business, let alone a profitable return, during the periods in question. Undoubtedly the shortfall in income was made up from the additional financial returns derived from other related activities such as the coach party visitors, the taxi service and the Whitfield House Country Club, which together went some way towards making up for the losses of the hotel business. Even so, Alfred admitted that it was always a struggle to make the financial ends meet, and he always dreaded the annual financial returns drawn up by his accountant, which inevitably showed that the hotel was sliding irretrievably into greater debt as the years went by.

This gloomy scenario, together with Marie-Eugénie's steadily declining health due to the excessive demands of running the hotel, ultimately led to the decision to sell and seek an alternative livelihood. And yet, ironically, this decision came just before the early 1950s, when holiday visitor numbers began to increase in general throughout the country, and especially among the local hotels in Goathland and on the Whitby coast nearby. No doubt this changing situation led the subsequent owners of Whitfield House Hotel to thank Alfred and Marie-Eugénie for the foundation of the hotel's good reputation, as well as leaving them with a valuable guest list of established customers, and no doubt provided them with the opportunity to capitalise on the changing holiday habits of the nation during the subsequent post-rationing period after the war.

In addition to this business overview of the hotel, it is also worthwhile to consider the visitor profiles, as well as some of the interesting characters who either stayed at the hotel as guests or were casual visitors during Alfred and Marie-Eugénie's residency. Together these two aspects may provide some indication of the essence of the hotel, and the degree to which Alfred and Marie-Eugénie achieved their overall aim of making the Whitfield House 'a pleasant, family-friendly, "country house" sort of place, with as little fuss and formality as possible'.

The majority of guests came from the middle classes, who were often professional people, and were comprised mainly of business, clerical, medical and ex-military backgrounds, together with their families, although unusually about a third of all guests were single occupancy visitors, often retired professional people, who apparently found little difficulty in settling into the family atmosphere of the place. What was not surprising, given the travelling difficulties at that time, was that about 40% of guests were from the Yorkshire area, with only about 15% from London and the home-counties. Other areas that attracted up to 30% of visitor numbers included the relatively nearby counties of Durham, Northumberland and Lancashire, although guests from Scotland, Wales and Northern Ireland were not uncommon. There were also a surprising number of overseas visitors, who constituted about 5% of guest numbers and came from a total of 14 different countries which included: Canada, France, Greece, Hong Kong, Iraq, Malaysia, Netherlands, New Zealand, Northern Rhodesia, Norway, Republic of Ireland, Singapore, Sweden and the USA, which must have made for an interesting social mix on many occasions.

Perhaps unsurprisingly, the more regular guests, who often visited the hotel in successive seasons, and sometimes within the same season, included members of Alfred and Marie-Eugénie's families, as well as their friends from the Bradford, Burley-in-Wharfedale, Ilkley and Leeds areas of the West Riding of Yorkshire. Moreover, many of these groups formed the core of special guests who attended the famous Christmas and New Year celebrations at the hotel, for which there was keen competition to enjoy these special festive social gatherings.

Among the guests included in these visitor groups, there was also a number of interesting characters who either frequented the hotel as casual visitors, or sometimes as residents. In the former category, the Yorkshire poet and novelist, Dorothy Una Ratcliffe and her husband Alfred, who were friends of the Browns, often called when touring around the country with their caravan. Also the then Archbishop of York, Dr. Cyril Foster Garbett and his domestic Chaplain, Rev. Philip Wheeldon, of Bishopthorpe, York, sometimes called for lunch before enjoying a stroll on the nearby moors. Whilst among the latter category, another member of the clergy who stayed at the hotel was Alfred and Marie-Eugénie's close friend, and catholic priest celebrant at their wedding, Mgr. Charles Tindall, the retired Headmaster of St. Bede's Grammar School, Bradford, who was then Chaplain to the St. John of God Hospice for Incurables at Scorton, near Catterick, North Yorkshire.

There were also a few well-known, distinguished guest visitors to the hotel, such as the celebrated mountaineer, write and educationalist, Geoffrey Whinthrop-Young and his author wife Eleanor, as well as the BBC radio personalities of the day, Tommy Handley and Ted Kavanagh, of the then popular radio programme 'ITMA' (It's That Man Again) comedy series, who stayed there when they were performing at the regional theatre in Scarborough. Then, although not very well-known in their own right, Mr. and Mrs. Frederick L. Harry Attenborough, Principal of the then University College, Leicester were reclusive guests at the hotel, while their two sons, David and

Richard Attenborough, were becoming well-established in their respective acting and naturalist careers. Other well-known, and valued regular visitor friends included the artist, William Littlewood and his wife Kathleen and daughter Katie, of Knowl Hill, Berkshire, and the artisan, Tom Whittaker and his wife Joyce and daughters Faith and Claire, of nearby Littlebeck on the North Yorkshire Moors. William was the illustrator of most of Alfred's earlier tramping books, while Tom supplied some of his classical, hand-made oak furniture for the hotel.

Overall, the hotel experience proved an interesting challenge to Alfred, Marie-Eugénie and their family during their attempt to achieve their dream of running a successful country hotel in a manner in which they passionately believed. But in the end circumstances conspired against them and brought an end to the project before that dream was properly fulfilled. Meanwhile it remains a matter of conjecture as to whether the enterprise could have continued if Alfred had been more successful in his own ambition of making a profit from his writing at the time. In addition, if they had benefitted from the more profitable times which undoubtedly ensued, it might have been possible to overcome the excessive demands that exacerbated Marie-Eugénie's health problems, in which case they might not have sold the hotel and may have successfully fulfilled their dream after all.

29. Whitfield House, c.2010

References and Notes

1. A.J. Brown, *Farewell, 'High Fell'*, Williams and Norgate Ltd., London, 1949, 'Résumé', pp. 11-12.

2. Alfred John Brown, Journal, 1948-1950, 26th March, 1948.

3. Ibid., Journal, 1948, passim.

4. Alfred John Brown, Journal, 1949, passim.

5. Op.cit., A.J. Brown, 'The Auction', pp. 178-179.

6. The Whitfield House Hotel Visitors Book, 16th March, 1949, 'Cyril of Ebor' and Philip Wheeldon, Bishopthorpe, York.

7. Op. cit., A.J. Brown, 'Easter', pp. 18-19.

8. Op.cit., A.J. Brown, 'Whitsuntide', pp. 26-27.

9. Op. cit., A.J. Brown, 'Electricity', pp. 21-24.

10. Op. cit., A.J. Brown, 'Drains and Sumps', pp. 24-26.

11. Op. cit., A.J. Brown, 'Electricity at Last', pp. 56-58.

12. Op. cit., A.J. Brown, 'Mrs. Merryweather Arrives', pp. 38-40.

13. Op. cit., A.J. Brown, 'More Coach Parties', pp. 44-45.

14. Op. cit., A.J. Brown, 'Cancellations', pp. 49-50.

15. Op. cit., A.J. Brown, 'Bed and Breakfast', p. 51.

16. Op. cit., A.J. Brown, 'First Americans', pp. 51-53.

17. Op. cit., A.J. Brown, 'Twenty-First Birthday', pp. 45-47.

18. Op. cit., A.J. Brown, 'People', p. 59.

19. Op. cit., A.J. Brown, 'Winter Tasks and Diversions', p. 92.

20. Op. cit., A.J. Brown, 'People', pp. 61-63.

21. Op. cit., A.J. Brown, 'Winter Tasks and Diversions', pp. 85-93.

22. Op. cit., A.J. Brown, 'Christmas', pp. 102-106.

23. Op. cit., Journal, 1950, passim.

24. Op. cit. A.J. Brown, 'To Sell Or Not To Sell', pp. 143-144.

25. Op. cit., A.J. Brown, 'Peter Is Lost', pp. 106-108.

26. Op. cit., A.J. Brown, 'We Decide To Sell', pp. 146-147.

27. Op. cit., A.J. Brown, 'Profit And Loss', pp. 152-154.

28. Op. cit., A.J. Brown, 'Literary Problem', pp. 173-175.

29. Op. cit., A.J. Brown, 'Résumé', p. 184.

30. Op. cit., A.J. Brown, 'We Sell The Hotel', pp. 183-184.

31. Whitfield House Hotel Sale, Document of the Vendor's Solicitors, Seaton-Gray, Bell and Bagshawe, 38 Flowergate, Whitby, Yorkshire, AJB Legal Records File.

32. The Whitfield House Hotel Visitors Book, Christmas, 1950, and Farewell Sherry Party, 1st January, 1951.

33. Op. cit., A.J. Brown, 'Farewell Sherry Party' pp. 194-198.

34. The Whitfield House Hotel Visitors Book, 1945-1951.

CHAPTER 14

The 'Literary Innkeeper'

Preview of Post-War Writing

At the outset of the hotel venture, Alfred anticipated that he would have the opportunity to realise some of his literary ambitions, since he envisaged that Marie-Eugénie would assume the major role of resident proprietor, while he would fulfil a supportive role that would allow him to devote some time to his writing, especially during the 'off-season'.[1] However this arrangement proved to be virtually impossible because of the demands made by the establishment of the hotel as a viable business enterprise, which left little time for the equally demanding task of writing. Similarly, Alfred's expectation of providing a literary orientation to the hotel was also somewhat ambitious, since there was little hope at the time of attracting guests with writing and publishing interests, and even his plan to set up a bookshop to promote literary interests among other guests had fallen foul of the Board of Trade regulations. It would seem therefore, that far from being liberated from the overburdening demands of his former life in the RAF, Alfred was now facing further unprecedented obstacles to writing created by his newly-adopted innkeeper's lifestyle.

And yet in spite of these obvious drawbacks, Alfred was given some encouragement in pursuing his literary dream in the early hotel years, with the publication of two of his works that had been either under wraps or under preparation at the time of the hotel acquisition, namely *Whitaker* (1946) and *Broad Acres* (1948). Even the disappointment of not being able to complete the provisionally agreed follow-up to his RAF book *Ground Staff* (1943), due to the takeover of the publishers Eyre & Spottiswoode by Harrap & Co., had not dulled Alfred's interest in pursuing the opportunities for further possible publications when time permitted. Moreover, he was able to turn personal adversity into literary gain in the second year of the hotel enterprise during his illness and convalescence, when he was something of a passive participant in the day-to-day running of the hotel. He began to write the first of the two hotel books *I Bought A Hotel* (1949), which subsequently led to the follow up book about the winding down and sale of the hotel: *Farewell, 'High Fell'* (1952). In between these two volumes, he also completed a book of verse: *Poems & Songs* (1949), which was a long-cherished personal ambition, even though it was out of character with both his own literary profile and that of the genre of the era. Finally, he somehow found time to record the impressions of his six years of living in the North Yorkshire Moors area with his last topographical Yorkshire book: *Fair North Riding* (1952).

While this record of productivity seems remarkable given the circumstances, it should be seen in the light of the personal demands made upon Alfred in trying to balance his twin roles as innkeeper and author. This was achieved by his taking every opportunity to escape from the demands of the busy hotel season, by using the 'off-season' productively to refresh his writing by the enjoyment of moorland walking in some of the finest scenery in North Yorkshire. He was by nature a writer whose literary ideas came to him most readily when he was walking, since he was not the sort of person who could easily sit down at a desk each day and pour out chapter after chapter of a book,[2] but he would rather make copious notes in a pocket book during these inspirational wanderings. These excursions also provided the stimulus to overcome the lack of drive and motivation to write, following a long war period of relative non-productivity, after which he found it difficult to get back into the writing habit. Even a short walk helped to give Alfred the urge to maintain his daily journal, sometimes at the expense of more creative writing, but as he recalled: 'I walked over the moor this afternoon and felt much better for it. Merely to feel the heather under my feet seems to do me good, and the exercise and wind always clears my brain.'[3] However Alfred's problem of how to combine an active physical life with a writer's sedentary existence and the struggle to find the right balance would remain a constant source of concern.[4] Nevertheless, both of these aspects had to be given due consideration if he was to achieve a reasonably productive literary future, and so with this in mind he turned his attention to his immediate writing plans.

References and Notes: Preview

1. Alfred John Brown letter to Andrée and Bertie Ratcliffe, 11th May 1945, Family Letters File 1945-1954.

2. A.J. Brown, *I Bought A Hotel*, Williams and Norgate, London, 1949, 'Innkeeper to Author', pp. 160-164.

3. Alfred John Brown, 29th April 1948, Journal, 1948-1950.

4. Ibid., Journal, 22nd May 1948.

30. Alfred J. Brown, the 'Literary Innkeeper'

Alfred's Second Novel: Whitaker[1,1a]

Background to the Book

The original hand written manuscript for the novel had been drafted between 1924 and 1926, and Alfred had submitted a typed version to various London publishers after 1927 without success.[2] He had received positive interest in the work from Faber & Faber, but nothing had materialised largely due to the downturn in the economy that resulted from the 'Great Slump' of the 1930s, so he had shelved the work until times were more favourable. He had anticipated that the publication of his previous novel *The Lean Years* (1926), would have predicated an interest in another story which involved the Bradford wool trade, however this was not the case, and the work did not see the light of day again for almost twenty years. He had subsequently tried to interest his former publisher, Eyre & Spottiswoode, in this latent novel in an attempt to renew his novelist aspirations towards the end of WW2,[3] but the response to this new initiative was a frustratingly frank and adverse reaction by the publisher:

> We feel, quite frankly, that it *[the novel]* is more in the nature of a tour de force *[sic]* than anything else, that it is the work of someone who has set out to write a novel, but who is not a natural novelist. It will probably annoy you to be told this, particularly as I rather gather that you suspect it yourself. It does not mean that the novel might not sell – indeed in present circumstances it quite probably could – but I cannot help feeling that your best gifts as a writer lie elsewhere.[3]

Alfred's response to this very explicit summary of his apparent lack of potential as a novelist was understandably to be somewhat dejected, but he was not resigned to the fact that he had no future in this type of writing, and indeed he showed a remarkably resolute intent in a reply to this criticism:

> I am of course disappointed (though not 'annoyed') with your report on my novel. I appreciate your candid comments, even if I do not agree with them! Time will best show whether or not I can write a novel which you would care to publish. I can only say that I feel I have the germ in me, and I am certainly attracted by this form... while it is true that I do not profess to be a traditional story-teller, I think I have an eye for character and human nature and can create real people. I did not make any great claim for this particular novel, but I do feel that it is a good Regional novel, with some real people in it, and would be popular at least in Yorkshire.[3]

It was from this self-belief and confirmed conviction that his Yorkshire novel might be a success if he could find the support of another publisher in the near future, that Alfred was able to hold on, at least temporarily, to his ambitious dream of becoming a novelist of sorts, and so he tried his luck again with various London publishers.[4] In anticipation of an imminent medical discharge from the RAF, it appeared that he had considered a return to writing following his WW2 service, and this new attempt represented the first step in that direction, but as before it generated little or no interest among the well-known publishing companies.

In the past Alfred had always relied on his own negotiations with publishers in his attempts to get his work into print, but in early 1945 he decided it was time to consider the services of an agent to promote his work. He therefore made contact with the London Literary Agency of E.P.S. Lewin, and provided a profile of his previously published books, along with his ambitions for future work, as well as a copy of the

Whitaker novel for consideration.[5] Lewin's agency dealt with a range of literary work including novels, serials, short stories, films and plays, and was then being operated by Eileen Lewin, whose husband Peter was still on active war service and did not return to the business until the summer of 1945. Alfred received a speedy response from Mrs. Lewin who indicated that she would be glad to handle the book, along with other possible work, and initially offered the novel to MacDonald's Publishers who were on the look-out for new as well as established writers after the war,[5] although this first attempt was returned by the publishers as not suitable for their purpose.

But within a matter of a few weeks, Alfred's new literary agent confirmed that an offer had been secured from John Gifford Ltd., London,[5] and a memorandum of agreement followed shortly in which the detailed terms were set out.[6] The contract specified that the novel would published within twelve months, with royalty payments of 10% on the first 2,500 copies sold, 15% on the next 2,500 to 5,000 copies and 20% thereafter, with a price of seven shillings and six pence per copy, and Alfred would then receive a royalty advance fee of £35. In addition it was proposed that John Gifford and Company, which was a division of Foyles Books of London, would only undertake the work if they could also publish the book through their various book clubs. They proposed to distribute the book via the Woman's Book Club of London, at a reduced price of two shillings and six pence, twelve months after the publication of the ordinary edition, for which Alfred would receive an additional fixed royalty of £20.

Alfred was naturally quite happy with these arrangements and signed the agreement in May 1945, at which time he was settling into his new role at the Whitfield House Hotel and was very pleased to have the services of a literary agent just when life became very hectic indeed. Initially progress with the book went very smoothly and the early galley proofs were available in December 1945,[5] and final proofs were returned in February 1946,[7] with an anticipated publication date in August 1946. However there were problems later with the production of the book when it was held up by the binders, and the publication date was deferred until the end of October 1946,[7] but further unexpected delays meant that copies of the book were not ready for distribution for the important Christmas market,[7] and finally only became available in early 1947.[7]

Even after these difficulties, there was yet another problem with the distribution of copies of the book to the retailers, particularly in the North of England, such as those in Bradford and Leeds, where it was still unavailable and where sales had been anticipated being the highest. This was a particularly frustrating time for Alfred, since some favourable reviews of the book had already appeared in the local press,[7] and he pleaded with the publisher to overcome this potentially damaging delay and even offered to take copies of the book to the shops himself!

The Storyline of the Novel

The novel is set against the colourful background of the Bradford wool trade, with finely drawn Yorkshire characters from the trade in general, and in particular a young man of considerable idealism and determination, John Whitaker, who rises from humble beginnings to become a successful businessman in the wool trade. Whitaker then abandons his career for the sake of the woman he loves, Hesther Peacock of Swaledale, and takes up the equally challenging life of a sheep farmer in the Yorkshire dales.

The story of Whitaker's wool trade years is largely semi-autobiographical and is based upon the framework of Alfred's early work experience including his jobs as a 'teller' in the wholesale fruit market and a clerk with the railway company, before moving into the 'Millsborough' (Bradford) wool trade as a trainee manager. Furthermore, like Alfred, it is Whitaker's walking experiences which fire the young man's imagination as he explores the moorland surrounding his home town, by which he is both uplifted and downcast at the thought of what he has left behind in his dreary workaday world. Then at the age of 21, he is given the opportunity to work as an understudy to the chief buyer of his wool company, and begins to learn the business of dealing *'on't'change'*; the local wool exchange in Millsborough, the Mecca of the wool trade, as well as the chance to join other established wool buyers in their favourite haunt at the nearby Charles Dickens Café (Laycock's Café in Bradford), where it was often said that the other half of the wool business was done.

The story then takes a different tack with Whitaker's chance meeting again, this time on a train journey, with a young secretary, Rose Starling, whom he has met on a previous occasion some years before when they were both travelling to interview in 'Ledbridge' (Leeds). The narrative account takes on a new dimension, albeit one of a temporary diversion of a potential romantic encounter, until this budding relationship is thwarted by Whitaker's discovery that the young lady is already engaged. Following this romantic interlude, Whitaker applies himself once more to the more serious business of becoming a successful representative of his firm's foreign trade, in which he becomes the typical 'innocent abroad' when he is exposed to the high life of a travelling salesman in Europe with all its temptations, which he steadfastly resists.

Finally in a further twist to the story, following Whitaker's first major successful

European business trip, he is rewarded with time off with holiday pay to enjoy his passion for walking in the Yorkshire dales, where he meets up again with the Peacock family of Swaledale with whom he has previously become acquainted. On this occasion however, he is overawed by and becomes infatuated with Hesther Peacock, a shepherdess sheep farmer, and the realisation that he is in love with her and her lifestyle. Upon his return to the wool trade, the realities of the changing downward fortunes of the business, especially of the looming economic crisis in Europe at the time, convince Whitaker to make the radical decision about his own future by taking the financial commissions owed to him, and setting out on a new adventure with Hesther as a hill sheep farmer, with all the uncertainties that this risky move entails.

Impact of the Book

The reviews of Alfred's second novel, and the only other one he published, appeared to be very favourable across a range of local popular press including commentaries in the *Yorkshire Advertiser* and the *Yorkshire Dalesman* Magazine,[7] and subsequently in newspapers such as the *News Chronicle*, the *Star*, the *Daily Graphic*, the *Yorkshire Observer* and the *Newark Advertiser*,[7] as well as the *Catholic Herald Review*.[7] But it was the review in the *Yorkshire Observer*, which devoted two columns of praise to the book, that did most justice to the work in general and Alfred in particular:

> This is a novel about Bradford (though the author prefers to disguise it as Millsborough), about the wool trade, about Yorkshire people, and in particular about a rising young man of considerable idealism and great determination, who, to win the woman he loves, forsakes the wool trade for the farm... And it is a good book. Its mediocre dust cover cloaks as honest, as enthusiastic, as supremely simple a piece of writing as I have read for a long time...
>
> Mr. Laverack – the name hides the identity of one who served the city's main industry for a number of years – wrote *The Lean Years*, a novel published some two decades ago. His subsequent long silence in the realm of literary fiction is literature's loss. *Whitaker* will do a good deal to make amends for that silence, but for the sake of Yorkshire writing we hope that the present novel will be but the first of several... Other authors, some more famous, have written of the textile industry. There is room for all-comers, providing each new work is a sincere contribution. And Mr. Laverack's, without a shadow of a doubt, is that.[8]

This glowing review was followed up later in the year with another very positive appraisal in an editorial review in the popular *Yorkshire Dalesman* Magazine:

> It is several years since Mr. A.J. Brown gave us a new book... *The Lean Years* which I felt held the promise of things to come... Now Mr. Brown has returned to his novel writing with *Whitaker*, under the pseudonym Julian Laverack...
>
> There is no deep subtlety about the story, but it is a well-told, clean-cut tale, with plenty of grand Yorkshire characters in it. It has the characteristic atmosphere of the wool trade (by one who knows it from the inside), and the authentic tang of the moors. Whether the author sets his scene at a market stall, or in a sophisticated Hungarian hotel, or on a Swaledale fellside, there is a vividness and veracity about the telling which is satisfying.
>
> I must admit I enjoyed the earliest chapters the most. Mr. Brown gets under the skin of a boy's first jobs and conveys the minor thrills and excitements, the dashed hopes and rising ambitions of the fledgling in the wool trade. There is the clumsiness of a first love affair and the growing sophistication of a more serious romance, both well told. Into the later chapters creeps extraneous matter which, for me, lessened the interest – but other readers may have other views.
>
> However, I commend the book to our readers and hope that Mr. Brown will follow it up with another.[9]

It would appear that the novel sold reasonably well during the first year in print, albeit with little advertisement promotion, and Alfred received about £98 from the sale of some 2,350 standard copies, followed by a further return of about £42 from the sale of the book club copies in the second year.[7] And while Alfred was reasonably satisfied with an initial total sale volume of some 5,000 copies, with a return of around £150 including advances,[10] which meant that the book had sold more than his first novel *The Lean Years*, he was nevertheless disappointed with this performance.[7]

Alfred was especially concerned that the publishers had not advertised the book in spite of repeated requests by himself and his agent to do so.[7] In addition, he felt that the book's appearance, with a lurid book cover that depicted the hero of the novel attempting a rock face climb to reach his true love atop a cliff face, had not only misrepresented the true nature of the book, but had also put off potential readers.[7] Furthermore Alfred made some sound recommendations to remedy these problems, none of which were acted upon by the publishers, much to both his and Peter Lewin's dissatisfaction.[7] However it might be concluded that the publishers had fulfilled their obligations in terms of the contractual agreement, and that they were reluctant to commit further additional outlay on an expensive advertising campaign to promote the book when financial resources were limited. When the sales of the book declined significantly, Alfred and his agent both lost faith in the publishers and their likely lack of commitment to promote any future work, so their decision to look elsewhere for an outlet for Alfred's new Yorkshire book seemed entirely justified under the circumstances.

References and Notes: Whitaker

1. Julian Laverack (pseudonym of Alfred John Brown), Whitaker, John Gifford Limited, London. 1946.
    1a. Note: Alfred dedicated his second novel simply: 'For My Wife'.

2. Alfred John Brown, *Whitaker*, West Yorkshire Archive Service, Bradford Central Library, Document Number 69D90, Items 2/2/1 – 2/2/3.

3. AJB letters to/from Douglas Jerrold, Managing Editor, Eyre & Spottiswoode Correspondence File, 1944, passim.

4. AJB letter to MEB, 6th December, 1944, AJB Personal Correspondence File, 1942-1944.

5. AJB letters to/from E.P.S. Lewin, Literary Agent, Clun House, Surrey Street, London WC2, E.P.S. Lewin Correspondence File, 1945-1949, passim.

6. Memorandum of Agreement between E.P.S. Lewin/ Alfred John Brown and John Gifford Limited, 123 Charing Cross Road, London WC2, 26th April 1945, John Gifford Limited Correspondence File, 1945-1948.

7. AJB letters to/from the Editor, John Gifford Limited Correspondence File, 1945-1948, passim.

8. A review by 'R.D.C.' entitled: 'A Fine New Novel About Bradford', *Yorkshire Observer* Newspaper, 25th February, 1947.

9. Editorial Review, Yorkshire Dalesman Magazine, p. 15, Vol. 9, September 1947.

10. Alfred John Brown, 21st August 1948, Journal, 1948-1950.

Broad Acres – A Yorkshire Miscellany[1]

Broad Acres had an even longer gestation period than Alfred's novel *Whitaker* which had taken almost twenty years to be published. The material had been written intermittently over a period of some thirty years before it was compiled into a personal anthology of Yorkshire. It represented a collection of Alfred's impressions gathered over the period from 1918 to 1948, and was written as a selection of short articles, interspersed with verse, to express his feelings for the county of Yorkshire. The earliest contribution was a poem written during his convalescence period during WW1, which was followed by further poems shortly after the war. Then in the late 1920s Alfred started to write a series of short sketches and essays on his walking experiences in Yorkshire, and submitted these to various periodicals such as *Blackwood's*, *John O'London's Weekly*, *Punch*, *Tatler* and *The Spectator*, without much success.[2] Then in 1928 he sent a couple of articles to *Country Life* Magazine, which the founding editor, Mr. Edward Hudson, accepted with pleasure, and also requested further similar contributions, much to Alfred's surprise and joy.[3]

In view of this encouragement, Alfred then submitted similar material to other periodicals, journals and newspapers with a view to the establishment of an outlet for his observations regarding his Yorkshire excursions such as short stories,[4,5] a memorial to a well-known Yorkshire writer,[6] and further descriptive poems.[7,8,9] In addition, he abstracted material from his previously published 'Yorkshire Tramping' series of books,[10] and also drew upon similar items adapted from scripted work that had originally been used for a series of BBC Radio North broadcasts on 'Hidden Yorkshire'.[11] Then finally towards the end of the 1930s, and at the beginning of the Second World War, he published further articles about relatively unknown areas of Yorkshire[12] and his observations about the likely impact of the war on the dales,[13] as well as articles on Yorkshire's rich literary heritage.[14,15] Thus he began to draft a series of manuscripts for consideration by potential publishers,[16] however a final draft manuscript was rejected by McMillan & Co. Ltd. of London and J.M. Dent & Co. Ltd. of Letchworth during the war years.[17] Moreover, a tacit agreement with Country Life Ltd. to produce a Yorkshire anthology, had been abandoned due to the publication crisis in WW2.[18]

Then towards the end of the war he approached his former publishers, Country Life Ltd., London, who said that they would be willing accept a manuscript entitled: *Broad Acres – A Yorkshire Miscellany*,[19] and although he was requested to add several new chapters to update his collection of Yorkshire essays and adventures, the publisher also offered to have the book fully illustrated and include many of Alfred's original poems.[18] Later in 1945 Alfred signed a memorandum of agreement with Country Life for the publication of the book,[20] in which he agreed to provide the final typescript as soon as possible, and also to arrange for illustrations for the book to be undertaken by William Littlewood, the friend and artist who had illustrated Alfred's previous Yorkshire tramping book series. The royalties for the book were 10% of the published price of 18s/6d for the first 3,000 copies sold, rising to 12.5% thereafter, with an advance of £50 upon signing the agreement and a further advance of £50 on publication. Unusually, no proposed date was specified in the contract with regard to the actual date of intended publication, this was probably to give Alfred time to write the requested additional material necessary for the text. This included new chapters such as an account of ancient tracks in Yorkshire and a related poem, along with examples of traditional Yorkshire food available for the visitor to the county.[21] These additions, together with other newly-written material constituted about one third of the total number of twenty-six chapters, and about half of the twenty poems contained in the final version of the text, but it was over two years before the first edition of the book appeared in print.

A Broad Brush of 'Broad Acres'

The 'County of Broad Acres', as it has come to be known, is unique in terms of Shire County status of England, and is especially noted for both its size and variety of scenery. The sheer magnitude of the county can be summed up by the often-quoted facts that Yorkshire is not only the largest county in the country by far (and its subdivision, the West Riding of Yorkshire, is itself the second largest 'county' in terms of area), and that there are more acres in Yorkshire than there were words in the Bible.[22,22a] In addition it is recognised that one of its principal and uniquely distinguishing features, that of the 'Yorkshire Dales', number a staggering total of some 562 major and minor dales distributed throughout all three ridings of the county.[23] These figures give rise to speculation about one of the characteristics of the peculiar folk who inhabit this vast space, namely they testify to the tenacity of the 'Tyke' to take the trouble to 'tally' these totals. Moreover these facts and figures regarding the size of the county are matched by its perceived merits in relation to other English counties; Francis Fuller (1637-1701) noted: 'One may call and justify this to be the best Shire of all England.' Then with reference to the magnificent scenery, which was scarcely touched by man's defiling hand, the famous medical practitioner, Dr. R.W.S. Bishop (1864-1943) first describes the place as 'God's own Country.'[24]

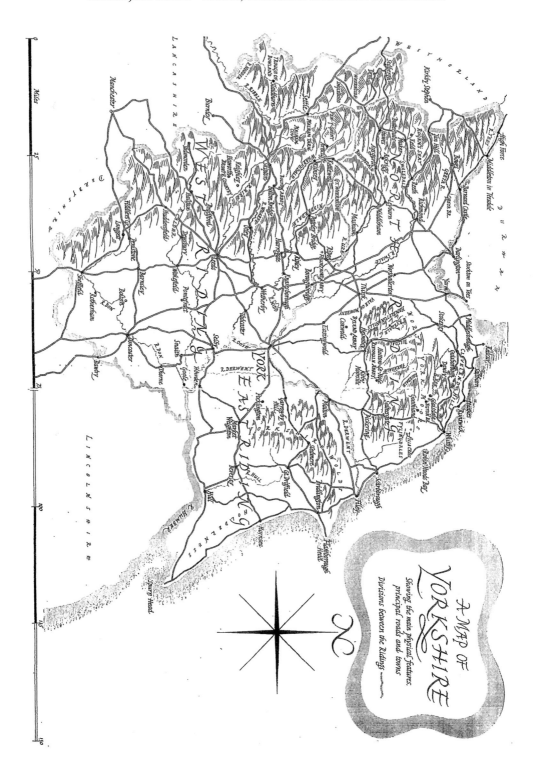

A MAP OF YORKSHIRE

Showing the main physical features, principal roads and towns. Divisions between the Ridings.

It may have been with these concepts in mind that Alfred came to his own conclusion about the landscape of the county when he stated: 'It is perhaps an exaggeration to say that if you took away all the best bits of the other English counties and shuffled them all together, the result would be something like Yorkshire; but it is certainly true that Yorkshire contains a greater variety of scenery than any other part of England.' Therefore Alfred approached his quest to compile an anthology that of necessity turns out to be a highly selective miscellany of Yorkshire-related material, whose scope is determined by his personal feelings for his beloved county, rather than the enormity of the potential subject matter that he could have included in such an ambitious proposal. In the preface he explains that the book follows no set plan, it is a personal miscellany with chapters dealing with places and people, encounters and adventures, together with historical and literary notes, and some related poems, which he hopes will make both a pleasant and informal selection. His main aim is to show the various aspects of the complex and inexhaustible county which constitutes the 'Broad Acres', while his secondary aim is to recall some of the places and things that made the most vivid impressions upon him during the course of some thirty years of wandering about his native shire.

In the first chapter of the book Alfred introduces the reader to the topic of the 'Broad Acres' with a general overview of the county in which he poses the question that often faces the perplexed visitor: 'Where shall I go to see the real Yorkshire?... for the real difficulty about Yorkshire is not where to go, but where not to go.'[25] He advises that the important thing to get clear in the visitor's mind is that Yorkshire is composed of the most diverse elements of scenery and that there is no short cut to the real Yorkshire. The many facets of the place suggest that it is not so much a county as a kingdom of its own, and he concedes that it is a bold man who singles out any one district and says that this is the real Yorkshire with the cautionary note:

> How difficult the problem is – and how simple? For Yorkshire is each and all of these widely different places; a great composite country... I for one sense there is no such thing as the real Yorkshire except the whole of it; but conversely, every little village, hamlet and town, every river and dale, every moor and mountain within the confines of the shire, is the real Yorkshire to the people who dwell there.

Therefore he concludes that he is no nearer to a solution to the problem he sets himself, and that the book is an attempt to help everyone find the 'real' Yorkshire for themselves.

Special Places and Features of Interest[26]

Alfred selects 'Moorland Farms' as places of particular interest and truly representative of upland areas of the county, where he is often treated with Yorkshire hospitality when in search of a meal and a bed for the night. And while he laments the desertion and dereliction of these historic upland dwellings, he relies on another ancient feature of the landscape, the 'Green Roads' to provide convenient pathways over remote moorland areas. In a review of these routes he traces the origin of these old tracks before he settles on his favourite, that of the 'Old Cam High Road', which offers one of the finest scenic walks in the county as he notes: 'this for me, is the green road of dreams'.

The most favoured stopping places for Alfred are the 'Village Inns' which contribute to the enjoyment of his tramps: '...spending a night at a strange inn is the crowning glory of a day's pilgrimage'. He had the temerity to mention some 150 Yorkshire inns in *Striding Through Yorkshire* and although he admits this is not a comprehensive list, he now laments their gradual closure and conversion into homes. It is the combination of remote farms, ancient tracks and village inns that provide Alfred with access to some of the most remote parts of the county. For example, the route from Coverdale to Colsterdale, or the secret valley of Raydaleside, while on the North Yorkshire Moors he extols the virtues of Goathland-Dale, before describing the miniature valleys 'In Whisperdales' near Scarborough as: 'the sort of place a man dreams of escaping to when the stress of life becomes too great.'

In a return to the western dales, Alfred describes with pleasure another favourite location that of Swaledale, with the remote upland village of Keld, surrounded by some of the wildest areas in Yorkshire, and he recalls many a hard-won respite taken at the former Cat Hole Inn in Keld. But he notes that it is 'The Unchanging Dales' such as Wharfedale, where he took his first long walks to the river's source before WW1, which impress him most. He also recalls returning there after WW2 to reflect on the subtle changes after the conflict, even though the Dales appear to be timeless. And yet it is the transient quality of places that entices Alfred to locations with such whimsical and alluring names as The Land of Nod in the Yorkshire Wolds of the East Riding. In a nearby inn he hears stories by the almost timeless 'vagabond woldsmen' who still peddle their wares, and he finds kinship with them as he peddles his own literary wares as a 'vagabond writer'. But of all the places that he prefers in the county, it is the lonely High Pennines where most rivers originate or 'The Way of the Watersheds', when he contemplates: 'Nothing disturbs the serenity of the mind as one wanders alone over the wastelands... and you are alone with nature – or with God.'

Finally Alfred acknowledges that his tramping adventures around the County of

Broad Acres are enhanced by good quality OS sheets 'In Praise of Maps'. In his view they are invaluable in discerning the beauty of the countryside by displaying the complex topography in a simple effective manner to help the walker interpret and appreciate the surroundings. It was the first map given to him by George Heseltine in 1915 that started Alfred's life-long Yorkshire tramping quest, and so he dedicates *Broad Acres* to his old friend using their respective nicknames: 'to OUSE (GCH) from WHARFE (AJB).'

Adventures, Encounters and Historical Notes[27]

Alfred's tramping adventures are mostly enjoyed alone, but he sometimes meets interesting characters along the way who add to the pleasure of his journeys. For example the lost cyclist 'Ixion on Whernside' in Nidderdale who, like his mythical counterpart, is tied to the tiresome task of transporting his wheels over the hills, and requires Alfred's help to rejoin his friends in Wharfedale. Or the elderly itinerant draper 'The Pinneyman', James Cowley (1854-1937), whom he engages in fascinating conversation on their eight miles return journey from Sunday mass in Pateley Bridge towards Middlesmoor. But sometimes Alfred is an inconvenience to those who do not accompany him, when he loses the view finder of a friend's expensive camera while taking photos for the book, only to redeem the piece by the saintly intervention for lost items, 'Adventure with St. Anthony'. Or, when he is alone, such as when he loses his precious gold hunter watch after a tumble on a wild moor, which also requires the help of the saint to find it.

But even when he is alone, Alfred does not always enjoy the solitude as undesirable 'guests' descend upon him in the form of an attack by vicious horse flies, 'A Swarm of Flies', on the North Yorkshire Moors. Whilst at other times he is accompanied by an army of young ramblers as President of the West Riding Ramblers Federation, and he is relieved to find that his committee members have arranged a splendid spread of afternoon grub for the youngsters who have devoured their own food on the day's tramp, 'The Ramblers Had Their Tea'. But even this catering cornucopia cannot compete with the classic cuisine served as the County's special course that Alfred extols in his review of Yorkshire's famous 'Ham and Eggs', along with the locations where such fare can be found on the popular walking routes.

Then turning his attention to the homely boarding houses of Yorkshire, Alfred registers his surprise to find that the provision of wholesome food, comfortable lodging and warm hospitality is available in these traditional B&Bs, which was once the preserve of village inns. He acknowledges the services offered by kindly landladies, 'Two

Ladies', whose doorstep always provides a welcome even to unexpected guests, and he then recounts the tale of an unusual assemblage of benighted fellow travellers at a remote country guest house, 'Any Port In A Storm'. Alfred reckons that these treasured landladies may even pass into the folklore of the Shire and receive recognition for the their support of other well-known characters who have also contributed to the cultural record of the County, such as his former friend, fellow writer and Dalesman, Halliwell Sutcliffe (1870-1932), about whom he elaborates in a detailed tribute.

But among the more sinister folklore legends Alfred relates the story of an evil old woman and her son who have robbed and killed unwary pedlars who stayed at their Woodale Cottage on the route from Coverdale to Nidderdale in 'Pedlars On Deadman's Hill'. Although he is bemused when his suggestion to popularise the tiny Thwaite Arms at nearby Horse House by renaming it 'Dead Man's Inn' receives short shrift from the landlord! On the other hand folklore neither sinister nor sanguine features in the historical tale that Alfred relates concerning the famous Yorkshire family from Wensleydale, 'The Metcalfes of Nappa Hall' and the Siege of Raydale, and their successful avoidance of penury in the 17th century.

Of course no Yorkshire anthology would be complete without mention of Yorkshire cricket, another fundamental feature of the County that Alfred admires immensely. For him this spectacle was personified by those great players during the inter-war years of 'Watching Cricket'. Like other young lads he recounts his early ambition to play for Yorkshire, but he only got as far as playing at the County ground of Bradford Park Avenue for a 'scratch eleven'. For the rest of his life he is content to recall the glorious days of Yorkshire cricket when no team in England could match them, and every member of the side was a Yorkshireman born and bred, so the team truly did represent the County of Broad Acres.

Finally to complete his Yorkshire miscellany Alfred devotes the largest chapter of the book to a topic as dear to him as the landscape itself, 'Yorkshire in Literature'. He presents an historical survey of well-known writers who had a close relationship with Yorkshire, or were residents of the County, or were born and bred in the Shire, and deals with the different phases and styles of writing from ancient to modern literature. He also documents the many famous poets and prose writers whose works have featured Yorkshire and acknowledges their contributions to the popularisation of the County. He makes special mention of the pioneers of the topographical genre of 'Picturesque Yorkshire', including the 19th century chroniclers who explored the County, as well as the band of more recent 'vagabond writers' who followed in their footsteps. Alfred summarises the purpose of his survey, which is not so much to show

Yorkshire's contribution to contemporary literature, as to identify those places that had special associations with English writers past and present. Therefore the last chapter provides an incentive for the reader to explore those aspects of the 'Broad Acres' which Alfred describes in his personal anthology of the Shire that he loves so much.

A 'Miscellany of Verse'[28]

Alfred chose to include a range of poems in the book to complement his feelings for, and observations about, the County of Broad Acres, gained from his wandering excursions around the Shire. While half of the poems had been published previously, the remainder had not appeared in print before, but few, if any, were written specifically for the book. Although almost every chapter of the book, 20 out of 26, contains a poem at the end, the themes are not necessarily related to the content of the preceding chapter, but to a more general theme that was often relevant to other topics contained within the book.

Among the poems that relate directly to their chapters of origin, some were included to accompany the new material written for the book, for example: 'The Green Road' for the chapter 'Green Roads', which describes Alfred's aesthetic delights in walking along these very ancient byways; 'Wanderlust', for the chapter 'The Way Of The Watersheds', which expresses Alfred's love of roaming in the remote uplands of the dales; and 'The Return', for the chapter 'The Unchanging Dales', which explains Alfred's affection for the landscape of his lost youth. In addition, two other poems relate to descriptive chapter topics including 'Lament', for the obituary chapter on Halliwell Sutcliffe, which expresses the grief associated with the passing of a close friend, and Emily Brontë's 'Grave', which appropriately ends the chapter 'Yorkshire In Literature', and portrays the image of Emily's liberated spirit wandering freely over the moors that she loved so well.

Other poems not related to their specific chapter locations, introduce new topics into the book, for example verses devoted to wildlife: 'Curlews', a bird often found in the upland areas of the preceding chapter 'Coverdale To Colsterdale', and 'Ring-Ousel', a bird often seen in the valley of the preceding chapter 'In Goathland-Dale'. Alternatively, natural phenomena feature in the poem about the rarely seen 'Hunter's Moon' at the end of the chapter 'In Praise Of Maps', whereas the poem about the farming landscape, 'These Fields', appears at the end of the chapter 'In Praise Of St. Anthony'. In contrast, the poem 'Interlude', although at the end of the chapter 'Ham And Eggs', might be seen as an introduction to the places in the following chapter 'In Whisperdales', since it describes a day-dream about the countryside during a busy office workday. A further new strand is also introduced by a few poems dealing with Yorkshire's famously unpredictable weather, such as 'Wind On The Face', describing battles with the elements to accompany the introductory chapter 'Broad Acres'; 'Rain' describes this feature of inclement weather, at the end of the chapter 'Moorland Farms'; and 'Fog on the Road', that is placed appropriately at the end of the eerie chapter about the 'Pedlars On Dead Man's Hill'.

In keeping with the spirit of the book, several poems describe Alfred's love of the various environments within his rural and urban homelands, including: 'Fain would I dally', a four line recollection of Alfred's pleasure in dawdling on high in his native uplands, in the accompanying chapter 'Ixion On Whernside'. Then in his most popular poem 'Dales In Paradise', Alfred describes his vision of wandering forever in the paradise of heavenly dales that awaited every true dalesman, who also dreams of such possibilities of life after death, such as the itinerant Dales packman described in the preceding chapter 'The Pinnyman'. Alternatively, even in the night life of the rain-dampened city streets, Alfred finds a glowing vitality in the short verse 'Street of Gold', that stands alone in splendid isolation between the chapters 'A Swarm of Flies' and 'The Way of the Watersheds'. Then he expresses his love of his native city in the poem 'Bradford', which offers a spirited defence against anyone who decries the town of his birth. This poem is strategically placed between the chapters that describe the rural idylls where groups of rambling Bradfordians roam: 'The Ramblers Had Their Tea' and his home in remote North Yorkshire 'In Goathland-Dale'.

Finally, under a miscellaneous category, Alfred includes the poem 'The Old Ladies', that might seem to relate to the preceding chapter 'Two Ladies', whereas it recounts a conversation overheard in a café between two genteel old ladies who praise their recent Yorkshire visit. By contrast 'To a Man reading a Book in a Busy Street', in four lines implores inattentive people to observe the world around them rather than focusing on bookish minutiae of their surroundings, and is located between the unrelated chapters: 'Watching Yorkshire' and 'Yorkshire In Literature'. The final poem 'Pigeon on a Window Sill' records Alfred's observations of man's conquest of the air, while still secretly harbouring the dream of flying naturally like a bird, and is also placed between the unrelated chapters: 'Any Port In A Storm' and 'Watching Yorkshire'.

In summary therefore, it appears that by including a range of old and new poems, Alfred adds yet another interesting dimension to his Yorkshire miscellany. In doing so he goes some way to the fulfilment of the twin aims stated in the preface, by providing the reader with sets of brief, occasional verses for a fuller appreciation of his personal anthology of the 'Broad Acres'.

Photographic Illustrations[29]

The publishers had agreed to illustrate the book with drawings by Alfred's close friend and artist William Littlewood, but this was rescinded and William's only contribution is the front dust cover sketch which depicts two of the loneliest farm houses in Yorkshire at Cam Houses, near the head of Littondale. But two outline sketch maps of Yorkshire by William were included to depict the main physical features, principal roads and towns of the county, along with the boundaries of the three Yorkshire Ridings, on the front and rear inside covers, but these maps only appear in the reprinted 1949 edition. It was perhaps inevitable that the former sketch-line drawings approach had been largely replaced by photographic illustrations in most topographical works by this time, and therefore *Broad Acres* includes a total of 49 impressive black and white images by some of the leading landscape photographers of the day. Each of the titled photographs had a brief note by Alfred about the image, except for three illustrations that had direct quotes upon the scenes depicted by the original distinguished observers, William and Dorothy Wordsworth, and Sir William Watson.

Among the talented group of photographers whose work appears was the Bradford photographer Walter Scott (1878-1947), who was famous for the production of pictorial postcards, as well as specialised views of Yorkshire scenery, and who contributed almost half of the total number of prints for the book. Further scenic views were also provided by the Harrogate-based photographer, Bertram Unne (1913-1986), who specialised in character studies but was particularly noted for his work on the scenery of the three Yorkshire Ridings. Additional material was supplied by R.W. Chaney, William Arthur Poucher (1891-1988), William F. Taylor and A.H. Robinson, along with other items supplied by the Crown Copyright Office, Country Life Publications and one unacknowledged source. These photographs provide an appealing display of carefully selected, Yorkshire-focused prints, which enrich the narrative of the book, and provide complementary images for the range of topics in Alfred's anthology, as well as generating a distinctive illustrative approach not seen in any of his published works before. In addition, Alfred provides a comprehensive eight page index to the book, which details all the major topics described in the text, and this is supported by lists of poems and illustrations in the table of contents, which makes the book very user friendly.

Impact of the Book

Following the publication of the book on 8th July 1948, it received a number of reviews that Alfred considered to be largely favourable with one or two exceptions:

The first review in the *Yorkshire Magazine* was good, and a fulsome notice in the *Whitby Gazette*, but the *Observer* dismissed it in a brief paragraph in the middle of a lot of 'Roundabout England' books. The reviewer seemed annoyed because it was not a 'Guide Book', though he explained that it was never intended as such!... while *John O'London's Weekly* gave it a puff *[a highly favourable notice]* and the *Manchester Guardian* was very favourable.[30]

He later noted that while he was pleased with the few generally positive reviews of the book he was disappointed with the response of *Country Life* Magazine: 'How maddening to get such a rebuff from one's own publisher!' Nevertheless, he was happy about the sales figures: 'It seems to be selling like hot cakes in Yorkshire at least.'[31] The book had sold 3,000 copies in the first month,[38] which was probably due to the promotion of the book especially in the north of England as Alfred noted: 'W.H. Smiths of Harrogate gave it a whole window with special photographs, and Brown Muff *[the departmental store]* of Bradford also did me proud.'[30]

Undoubtedly the book sales further benefitted from an especially supportive review that appeared in the *Yorkshire Dalesman* magazine that would have been eagerly received by many of the large band of Alfred's established readers:

I would like this month to commend a book which has long been awaited – it was begun before this magazine came into being (1939) and has been held up, like many others, by the war and its aftermath. Written by a contributor to these pages whose name is held in high esteem by all those who walk and enjoy our countryside, *Broad Acres* (Country Life, Ltd., 18s.) is an expression of Mr. A.J. Brown in his most felicitous vein.

Mr. Brown offers himself in this book as a companion, rather than a guide and for such an office, he is well equipped. He has many interests. He has a fine feeling for the country through which he rambles, and responds to every change in its atmosphere. His quick eye notes those salient features of form and colour which gives Yorkshire its infinite variety. He has that sense of the past which flames into enthusiasm over an ancient name or half-forgotten custom. And everywhere his human interest goes out to the lives lived, today as well as yesterday, by dwellers in upland villages and remote farmhouses and dales' inns.

This book is subtitled 'A Yorkshire Miscellany,' and it well describes its contents. Here are chapters on our county's wonderful variety, on moorland farms, on Yorkshire writers, on maps, on Halliwell Sutcliffe, on ham and eggs, interspersed with stories of particular walking adventures and with pleasant little poems. Some of the subject matter of these chapters has been contributed by A.J. Brown to our own pages and will be re-read with delight. The whole book is alive and stimulating and – in me, at any rate – created an intense desire to drop everything and set off and recapture forgotten days in Wensleydale and Eskdale and those rarely-mentioned 'little dales' of Yorkshire.

Broad Acres is a large volume to carry on a summer walking tour, though there are many things you might reasonably leave out of a rucksack to make room for it. But it will be an ideal book for the winter evening reading of those who have themselves followed the green roads and fells of the North Country and of older generations whose memories of similar ramblings will be quickened by the charm of its companionship. And when you have finished reading there are fifty beautiful photographs to gaze upon and linger over.[32]

It seemed more than likely that the book had also benefited as a result of the popularity of Alfred's previous 'tramping' book *Striding Through Yorkshire* (1938) which had been reprinted in 1943 and 1945, and was released again in 1949 around the time of the intended reprint of *Broad Acres*. The previous book had been Alfred's best seller to date, and there existed a loyal readership which no doubt ensured a sell-out of the full print run of both editions of the current book, but whether this momentum could be sustained was already in some doubt. In the post war years of austerity there were still considerable printing material constraints upon publishers which made them unable to satisfy the demands of a growing readership, as well as the expectations of established authors and new writers.

Furthermore at this time there was a marked shift in the orientation of the type of book that described the English county landscape. The 'County Book' series which was published by Robert Hale Ltd., London, was firmly established by 1950 and would have been a serious competitor to future editions of *Broad Acres* from a national perspective, since it had a regional focus that covered most of the English counties. This series was not seen as a set of guide books of the previous topographical variety, but rather as a very informative treatment of the life of a county, its past and present, and was very much geared toward the newly-expanding generation of the motoring public. Moreover the popularity of a regional topographical book such as *Broad Acres* would be further compromised by the three alternative books in the 1950 county series of publications by established writers: *Yorkshire: East Riding* by John

Fairfax-Blakeborough, *North Riding* by Oswald Harland and *West Riding* by Lettice Cooper. This new development may therefore have caused Alfred to consider seriously any further topographical treatment of 'God's Own Country'.

References and Notes: Broad Acres

1. Alfred J. Brown, *Broad Acres – A Yorkshire Miscellany*, Country Life Limited, London, 1948, reprinted 1949.

2. AJB, Journal, 'High Fell Hotel', 21st March, 1945, pp. 40-45.

3. Alfred John Brown, West Yorkshire Archive Service, Bradford Central Library, Document No. 69D90, Section 3/4/9, 'Biographical Notes'.

4. Alfred J. Brown, 'Adventures with St. Anthony', Journal 'The Month', February, 1931, pp. 117-121.

5. Alfred J. Brown, 'Ixion on Whernside', Yorkshire Weekly Post, 8th April 1933.

6. Alfred J. Brown, 'Halliwell Sutcliffe – In Memoriam', Yorkshire Tramper Magazine, 1932, p. 115-117.

7. Alfred John Brown, 'Wind on the Face' and 'Fog on the Road', *Yorkshire Tramper* Magazine, 1932, p. 22.

8. Alfred J. Brown, 'These Fields', *The Heaton Review*, 1933, Vol. vi, p. 9.

9. Alfred J. Brown, 'Bradford', *The Heaton Review*, 1933, Vol. vi, p. 54.

10. A.J. Brown, 'The Land of Nod', *Moorland Tramping in Yorkshire-North and East*, Country Life Ltd., London, 1932, pp. 54-57.

11. A.J. Brown, St. Bede's School Magazine, Vol. v, No. 39, p. 129, Summer 1932. A report on a BBC Radio North (Leeds) broadcast series on 'Hidden Yorkshire' (Moorland Farms, Village Inns, The Way of the Watersheds).

12. Alfred J. Brown, 'Coverdale to Colsterdale', *Yorkshire Dalesman* Magazine, Vol.2, No. 2, April 1939, pp. 6-8.

13. Alfred J. Brown, 'All Quiet in the Dales', *Yorkshire Dalesman* Magazine, Vol 1, No. 10, December 1940, pp. 7-9.

14. Alfred J. Brown, 'Wordsworth in Literature', *Yorkshire Dalesman* Magazine, Vol.2, No. 3, May 1940, pp. 9-10, 15-17.

15. Alfred J. Brown, 'Yorkshire in Literature', *Yorkshire Dalesman* Magazine, Vol. 2, No. 8, October 1940, pp. 9-10, 15-16.

16. Alfred John Brown, West Yorkshire Archive Service, Bradford Central Library, Document No. 69D90, Sections 3/4/1 to 3/4/10, 'Broad Acres' draft manuscripts.

17. Alfred John Brown, West Yorkshire Archive Service, Bradford Central Library, Document No. 69D90, Section 3/4/9, 'Broad Acres', letters 10th, 19th, 20th March 1943.

18. AJB letters to E.P.S. Lewin, E.P.S. Lewin Correspondence File, 1945-1949, passim.

19. Alfred John Brown, West Yorkshire Archive Service, Bradford Central Library, Ref. No. Deed Box DB 38, Case 4, Item No.2, Type-scripted manuscript draft of 'Broad Acres – A Yorkshire Miscellany', circa 1945.

20. Memorandum of Agreement between Alfred John Brown and Country Life Limited, London, 17th September 1945, AJB Literary Agreements File.

21. Alfred John Brown, West Yorkshire Archive Service, Bradford Central Library, Document No. 69D90, Section 3/4/5, circa 1946, Items: 'Green Roads' and poem entitled: 'The Green Road', 'The Ramblers Had Their Tea' and 'Ham And Eggs'.

22. John Mayall, *Annals of Yorkshire*, Vol. iii, p. 668, 1874.
22a. **Note**: Yorkshire Tourist Authority: Acres in Yorkshire: 3,923,359, Words in the Bible: 3,566,840

23. Editorial note, *Yorkshire Dalesman* Magazine, June, 2008, p. 48.

24. Dr. R.W.S. Bishop, *My Moorland Patients by a Yorkshire Doctor*, John Murray, London, 1926, p. 1.

25. Op. cit., Alfred J. Brown, *Broad Acres*, chapter 1, pp. 1-15.

26. Op. cit., Alfred J. Brown, *Broad Acres*, Special Places and Features of Interest; Chapters: 2. Moorland farms, 4. Green Roads, 9. Village Inns, 8. Coverdale to Colsterdale, 10. Raydaleside, 12. Goathland-Dale, 14. In Whisperdales, 20. Keld, 17, The Unchanging Dales, 23. The Land of Nod, 16. The Way of the Watersheds, 18. In Praise of Maps.

27. Op. cit., Alfred J. Brown, *Broad Acres*, Adventures, Encounters and Historical Notes; Chapters: 3 Ixion on Whernside, 5. The Pinnyman, 7. Adventures with St. Anthony, 15. A Swarm of Flies, 11. The Ramblers Had Their Tea, 13. Ham and Eggs, 21. Two Ladies, 22. Halliwell Sutcliffe, 6. Pedlars on Deadman's Hill, 19. The Metcalfes of Nappa Hall, 24. Any Port In A Storm, 25. Watching Cricket, 26. Yorkshire in Literature.

28. Op. cit., Alfred J. Brown, *Broad Acres*, A Miscellany of Verse; Chapter Related Poems: The Green Road, Wanderlust, The Return, Lament, Emily Brontë's Grave, Nature Related Poems: Curlews, Ring-Ousel, Hunter's Moon, These Fields, Interlude, Wind on the Face, Rain, Fog on the Road, Rural & Urban Related Poems: Fain would I dally, Dales in Paradise, Street of Gold, Bradford, Miscellaneous Poems: The Old Ladies, To a Man reading a Book in a Busy Street, Pigeon on a Window Sill.

29. Op. cit., Alfred J. Brown, *Broad Acres*, Photographic Illustrations; 49 black and white prints including: 16 villages and towns, 8 historic buildings, 4 mountains, peaks & fells, 3 each of ancient tracks, roads/passes, isolated farms, geographical features, rivers and waterfalls, 2 each of moorland and coastal scenery, and one lake view.

30. Alfred John Brown, 26th July 1948, Journal 1948-1950.

31. Ibid., Journal 2nd July 1948.

32. 'A Dalesman's Diary', editorial, Harry J. Scott, *Yorkshire Dalesman* Magazine, Vol. 9, September 1948, p. 169.

CHAPTER 15

The Poetic Publican

Alfred's Sole Book of Verse: *Poems & Songs*[1]

Alfred was encouraged to compile a book of verses partly because of the reception of selected poems which had been included in his previous book *Broad Acres – A Yorkshire Miscellany*. He also harboured an ambition to publish some poetic works that he had written for his own enjoyment, which had slowly accumulated over many years, even though he was told by some of his former publishers that poetry in general was not selling very well at this time, and that his style of poetry was out of date. Nevertheless, he wanted to please himself with the kind of book which until now he had admitted was outside his usual scope. In addition, Alfred had received very positive feedback from an experienced journalist, Mrs. Rayfield, a former literary columnist of the *Bradford Telegraph and Argus* newspaper under the pen name 'Isobel', who encouraged him to publish some of his poems after reading his selection of verses in *Broad Acres*.[2] Therefore with some trepidation Alfred drafted a manuscript of poems for possible publication, even though he realised his former limited vein of poetry had already been exhausted, and that he had lost the incentive to write such material for his own pleasure.[2]

However, during a meeting in May 1948 with Mr. Frank Horne, the proprietor of the Abbey Press in Whitby, who carried out the printing work for the Whitfield House Hotel, Alfred showed him the manuscript of poems and asked him about putting the collection of work together in a book and the likely cost of printing about 250 copies.[3] He had already hawked the manuscript around his usual publishers in London without a hint of interest or word of encouragement, and although he recognised the ignominy of having a book privately printed for sale, or even having to give the book away if there was insufficient interest, he considered that this was preferable to letting the collection of verses languish in obscurity.[3] Then after a discussion with the Abbey Press printer, Mr. Barker, in which Alfred indicated that he wanted a first class book produced and not a cheap paper back, he was asked to leave the manuscript, and an estimate of the costs would be made, and if agreeable, a book could be printed within six months and be ready for Christmas of that year![3]

This unexpected good news surprised Alfred as he reflected it had often taken his London publisher up to two to three years to publish his previous works. It was not surprising that when he left the printers he admitted to being 'tickled to death at having his previously despised book of poems' published at last and so soon.[3] At the same time he was also cautious about the venture and he decided to check with other printers for costs and production times, although he realised that he would be unlikely to find another firm who could do the job better, so quickly, and, based on his experience of the costs of previous printing work for the hotel, at a likely reasonable rate.

Subsequently Alfred received a quote from the printers of £72 for 500 copies of a book on a subscription basis,[4] which seemed relatively cheap by any standards at the time, so he prepared a copy of a draft manuscript ready for the press. He decided to have his book of poems printed privately and pay the costs himself, even though this meant raising the necessary funds required.[3] Then following a visit to Whitfield House Hotel by Mr. Barker, Alfred confirmed the order and arranged to deliver a revised manuscript as soon as possible, but he later expressed some mixed feelings about the project: 'It is rather fun publishing oneself... [although]... I suspect that this rash speculation is to satisfy my vanity, but at least it will fulfil a long-cherished idea.'[3] It was also at this time that Alfred prepared an advance notice with an order form about the forthcoming publication of his collection of poems and songs, on a printed leaflet distributed to all his friends and acquaintances, which informed them of the availability of a limited edition of 500 signed copies of a 'Foolscap Quarto' sized, 120 page book priced at 10 shillings and sixpence.[3]

Soon after, Alfred was present when the book went through the preparation stages at the Abbey Press and also enjoyed being directly involved in the printing process, although, as ever, he did not enjoy the tedious job of proof reading, and especially the task of deciding which poems to leave out of the finished book.[3] Nevertheless, he got great satisfaction from having the book printed according to his own requirements, rather than sending it to a London publisher and printer, and only seeing the final product after the proofs were returned. He especially enjoyed each stage of the process including discussion with the printer about the typeface, layout and paper selection, as well as watching the compositor set up the text in 'Gill-Sans type 3' linotype, and working closely with the firm's director, Mr. Frank Horne, who was still working at 92 years of age, and personally oversaw the whole process from start to finish.[3] When the book was taking shape, Alfred felt it really belonged to him, and believed that he might be able to sell the bulk of the first edition, with the help of this very obliging and cooperative firm of family printers, who optimistically expected it to be sold out. However, notwithstanding this rosy prediction, Alfred was perhaps more circumspect as he later mused: 'Whether I make a profit or loss on this book, I do not regret the experiment. It has been a great experience.'[3]

On the other hand, he thought that if the book really was a success, he would consider printing more of his own work in the future, especially while the adverse conditions in the world of publishing prevailed, and even speculated about producing a book of essays as his next possible literary venture.[3] But these ambitious intentions were probably made while Alfred was still in the euphoric state associated with his impressions gained from the standard and quality of the printing work that had been undertaken by his friendly local printers, and the fact that the production of his new book would be completed in record time, since he had only delivered his final manuscript on 1st October and yet was handed the last galley proofs on 26th October 1948.[9] All that remained was to check the revised proofs, arrange the final sequence and pagination of the book, and then it would be left to the binders to produce the final edition, hopefully before Christmas 1948 as planned.

Unfortunately this publication date proved a little optimistic, since the book was not available until early 1949, but this was not surprising, since Alfred was still writing new contributions late into the proposed production schedule. For example, and no doubt to the consternation of the printer, Alfred had included a couple of poems that had been written only in late October 1948, following his impressions gained from a walk over the North Yorkshire Moors entitled 'On Simon Houe', together with a further short lyric entitled 'The Wastelands', following another stroll on the same wild moors, just before he had delivered the final proofs to the publisher.[3]

In mid-November 1948, Alfred spent a day at the printers carrying out the final proof reading required by his late additions and arranging the final order of poems with the printer, but he came away somewhat deflated and despondent with the recurrent nagging question in his mind about his poems: 'Are they any good?', and was still in some doubt about whether or not he should have included the last section of the book entitled 'Love Lyrics', which seemed somewhat incongruous with the other themes.[3] But the following day he returned to the printers and gained renewed enthusiasm for the work as he was allowed to work the printing press under supervision, which he enjoyed so much that it dispelled some of the last minute misgivings he had about a few of the poems included, especially the Love Lyrics.[3] In any case it was too late to change his mind, since the book was going through the final printing stage, but he still had some residual concerns because he had only received some 20 pre-orders for the book from the circulation of the large number of pre-publishing notices that he had distributed.[3]

Finally a batch of *Poems & Songs* arrived at the Whitfield House Hotel just five days before Christmas, and Alfred spent a couple of days signing copies and dispatching the advance orders he had received, that only amounted to about 70, which he thought was a poor start to his new-style publishing adventure.[3] However there had been a problem at the printers, who had so far been most assiduous in their duties, but they had omitted to send the 'end papers' to the binders, so that there were no end papers at the front or back of the book, which Alfred felt spoiled its appearance somewhat. There were also problems with the uneven spacing of the text despite all his efforts, and he felt that he had made a mistake by rushing to have the book available before Christmas, since it was then too late for the bookshops anyway. He also regretted that he had not insisted upon a pocket-sized edition since the larger size was too big to carry about, otherwise he was pleased with the look of it and commented:

> It was bound in royal blue, with gold lettering (unavailable then in London!) with an attractive blue dust-jacket designed by an artist friend of mine, William Littlewood.[3]

Overview of the Book of Verses

Alfred's unusual little book of poems and songs was dedicated to his wife, 'For Marie-Eugénie', as might be expected, but on a preceding page he made a request to Caedmon (673-735), the earliest known English poet who lived in Whitby, and recognised as one of the most accomplished and inspirational Christian poets, for an intercession that the book of poems might be well-received:

> CÆDMON
>
> Cædmon! First poet of this rugged land,
> Divinely taught to sing Creation's story!
> Bless this last book of songs from your own strand
> That it may share the reflex of your glory.

This entreaty may have related to Alfred's own doubts about the likelihood of the book having an appeal to the public at large, if not to his personal friends and acquaintances, to whom it was primarily directed.

In a note of introduction rather than a preface, Alfred explains that the verses contained in this collection were written at widely scattered intervals in his life between the years 1921 and 1948, and are subdivided into six groups, with each group containing verses corresponding to specific sections including:

1. A total of 13 early poems related to his sickness years entitled 'Hospital Rhymes'.
2. A total of 17 lyrics about his outdoor life entitled 'Wind On The Face'.
3. A set of 10 verses about his working life entitled 'Office Rhymes'.
4. An odd group of 18 poems which covered a wide range of topics under the diffuse theme: 'Miscellaneous Verse'.
5. A group of 16 lyrics which were mainly songs rather than poems under the theme: 'Songs of Yorkshire Dales and Inns'.
6. The largest group of 28 poems written from the Alfred's emotional perspective entitled: 'Love Lyrics'.

In an introductory note Alfred also comments that the first two groups of poems belonged mainly to his early adulthood, some of which were included because of a pathological interest during his illness years, while others were written at various times in his life and were not intended to be in any chronological order. He also states that if it had been possible, he would have liked each group of poems printed separately because they were dissimilar in both mood and style, but this was not practicable and so they were produced in one collective edition of 102 poems.

In the brief introduction Alfred also acknowledges that some of the poems had already appeared in print in a variety of sources, including 8 poems that had been published in various Yorkshire magazines and anthologies, some 14 'songs' that were written for the book *Four Boon Fellows* (1928), while a selection of 20 lyrics had appeared in *Broad Acres* (1948). In total 42 of the 102 poems and songs in the first five groups had appeared in print, but none of those in the last group: 'Love Lyrics' had been published previously, and in the cases of those that had appeared in his former books, Alfred thanks the publishers J.M. Dent & Sons Ltd., and Country Life Ltd., respectively, for their kind permission to include the poems in the present book. Furthermore, Alfred chose not to include a further 9 poems from the original draft manuscript[4] and 7 more from earlier drafts.[5]

Finally, Alfred also indicates that it was largely because of the interest shown by readers of the lyrics contained in *Broad Acres* that he was encouraged to publish the larger collection of his poetic works, although he recognises the limitations of his lyrical ability: 'Inevitably, some of the poems are "old-fashioned", But – so am I! On the other hand some were written during the London Blitz, and after; so they, at least should be quite up-to-date.'[1]

Impressions of Poems & Songs

The overall impression gained from the book is how the style and content of the poems changes over the six sectional themes of the book, which not only reflect the time periods covered by the respective themes, but also the changes in Alfred's own influences and approaches to writing verse over the intervening period of some thirty years. Undoubtedly he was greatly influenced by the classical poetry with which he had become familiar during his long years of convalescence in WW1, so that in the early descriptive poems in the sections: 'Hospital Rhymes' and 'Wind On The Face', his style expresses romantic, introverted and melancholic approaches in which he appears to be consciously trying to be 'poetic', with distinct hints of Chaucer, Wordsworth, Coleridge, Auden, Masefield, Hardy and Yeats. Then although this style continues in the section 'Office Rhymes', in which his frustration with his work is often expressed, it is not so much influenced by his earlier interest in romantic poetry. Indeed the work is often characterised by more original approaches in which Alfred uses his poetry as an outlet to escape from his dull work environment and appears to indulge in the more calming influences derived from contemplating nature.

He also seems to become more confident, mature and expressive when he writes witty verses that involve the descriptive material contained in the subsequent section: Miscellany, rather than when he deals with the more conventional 'poetic' topics of the earlier sections, but even in this section there are discernible influences of other contemporary poets such as Frances Cornford and Hilaire Belloc. Nevertheless it is with increasing confidence that Alfred expresses his enjoyment in the theme: 'Songs of Yorkshire Dales and Inns', in which he exposes another more natural side to his nature, that of a jolly, imbibulous Yorkshireman, who loves to be in the company of other like-minded individuals. However this lighter mood contrasts markedly with the introspective aspect of Alfred's personality that is powerfully expressed in the final theme: 'Love Lyrics', in which he reveals a range of deep emotions from loving tenderness to regretful bitterness, along with self-conflict and self-pity in dealing with the complexities of the emotional side of life.

It becomes evident that during the various phases of his life which the sections in the book represent, Alfred had naturally undergone changes in his poetic expression, just as he did in his literary output. In the early period of formal education, he was not exposed to the systematic study of poetry, and only took an interest in reading classical poetry and literature as a result of joining a group of individuals who had formed 'The Shakespeare Club' at an Ilkley convalescent hospital where he had spent some time during WW1.[6] As a result Alfred never had the chance to learn the craft of writing poetry and become practised in its creation under the critical guidance of a qualified mentor, so that his early poems are necessarily limited by what he had read.

Even in the later stages of poetic writing, except perhaps for a couple of his published poems, and unlike his other literary works, he had not had any of his poetic works reviewed, assessed or critically appraised by expert judgment. He therefore relied on his own judgment in the form, content and style of the works he created, in which the maturity of expression and competence in handling the intricacies of verse construction, rhyme, rhythm and metre developed naturally, albeit somewhat inconsistently. Therefore his later poems tend to be of better quality, more refined, and expressed with greater confidence than his earlier work, and subsequently he was able to use poetry more readily as a medium for the expression of his thoughts, beliefs and feelings in a more intensely focused way than in his prose writing. Indeed he tried to relate the deep feeling that he had for his poetry with the euphoric feeling he derived from his passion for demanding moorland 'tramping' compared with leisurely walking, when he stated: 'Tramping is to Walking, as Poetry is to Prose.'

A Review of Themes and Poems

In a review of the general themes and specific poems contained in each section of the book, it is worthwhile to consider both the context and content of each of the sets of poems, since each represents a particular time in Alfred's life that had a direct influence not only on his poetic but also his prose work. Furthermore, it is also useful to appraise a representative selection of individual poems in terms of their strengths and weaknesses, as well as to comment on others within each theme, and thereby gain an impression of the overall merits of Alfred's book of poems and songs.

1. Hospital Rhymes

In the selection of these verses Alfred delves into his earliest attempts at writing poetry during his convalescent years of WW1, when he probably used written verse as a creative outlet to help him to come to terms with his debilitating condition, and this led to the creation of two journals of poetry,[7,8] from which two of the short poems included recalled some of Alfred's hospital experiences. The first, 'Dust to Dust', which was originally untitled,[8] conveys Alfred's feelings about the inevitability of death, but unfortunately the rhyming scheme changes in the last four lines, and the use of non-rhyming words, as well as arbitrary use of initial capital letters and clumsy construction - 'An Hundred', together with a perplexing ending, detracts from its intended impact, all of which might indicate the lack of maturity in Alfred's poetic skills at this stage:

DUST TO DUST

The banal shackles of this Earth,
Its Woes, its Cares, its specious Mirth:
When we attain our journey's end
We leave: and in the grave descend.

But in her contrariety
Earth piquantly decrees that we
Upon our tir'd frames shall bear
An hundredweight of earthly matter.
So taunting us with what we are:
And what avails our pompous chatter.

The second poem entitled 'Fain Would I Dally', which was also originally untitled,[8] and now includes the third verse of a four verse poem, was a sort of lament by Alfred to recover from his affliction and return 'home' in the figurative sense of freedom from the confines of his clinical condition, and yet despite being somewhat clichéd it shows some poetic development:

FAIN WOULD I DALLY

Before I die, I fain would gaze
For one glad, fleeting moment's space
Upon that most beloved place
My Home!

Fain would I dally in the sky
High as a cloud and as a kestrel high!
And peep deep down with flashing eye
Upon that spot – My Home!

I fain would for an instant climb
A peak as in the early time
And gaze as in my withered prime
Upon that spot – My Home!

So would I gaze with eager face
For one sad, fleeting moment's space
And then leave, for aye, that sacred place
My Home!

Other verses in 'Hospital Rhymes' often portray depressing images in such examples as the comparison of death from disease with death on the battlefield: 'Gateway To Hospital', death lurking around the patients: 'Hospital Night Scene' and a patient's deadly struggle with disease: 'Disease: The Wrestler'. In each case poetic devices are often used in a pretentious way to achieve the desired message, as well as the use of odd rhyming schemes and often the lack of rhyme, which could have been improved by the more careful selection of appropriate words. More positively however, images of Alfred's own psychological outlook are contained in a poem in which he expresses his appreciation of poetry itself: 'In the Company of Books: Unable to Read' and his desire for a return to health: 'More Than for Wealth', although in both cases the style is somewhat dated. Nevertheless, his desire to enjoy nature's wonders again is contained in several verses including: 'Lovely Moon', 'Clouds', 'Rose and Lily' and 'Easter Birds', although they represent a return to a pre-1900s style of poetry. Inevitably though, the overriding impression of the theme reflects Alfred's depressed state of mind at this time, with little positive outlook found in: 'Adversity' and with almost all hope abandoned for the foreseeable future expressed in 'Lament':

> LAMENT
>
> My tree has shed its every leaf:
> Now it sheds rain-drops for its grief;
> And for a spell its head will droop
> Till Spring returns the banished boon.
> But I have shed my every Hope
> And Hope will not return so soon...
> Would that man's grief were mild and brief
> As is this tree for its last leaf.

Finally it is worthwhile noting that Alfred did not appear to carry out much revision or reconstruction in his early poetry, which is evident from the hand-written drafts that still exist,[7,8] and therefore, in the absence of any expert critical review of early poems by others with more knowledge of poetic craft, there appears to be no attempt to improve the finished product of the verses presented for the book.

2. Wind On The Face

In this theme Alfred often reflects upon the experiences of his early lone tramping years, and he is clearly influenced by the range of natural phenomena that he observes during his outdoor activities. The tone is set in the first poem 'Wind on the Face' which attempts to bring together unusual elusive concepts among the forces of nature identified by the use of some unorthodox terminology:

Wind on the Face

I battled against the wind to-day	Savage and stern were the moors to-day:
In a lonely, moorland place;	And my fight was nearly vain;
Angrily over the hills it drave	Only the whip o' the wind in my face,
Arrows of rain into my face:	And the stinging steel of the rain.
Like a scourge of grace.	But I will go again!

The enjoyment of adverse weather conditions, along with its beneficial effects on an urban street scene, is also expressed in 'Rain', whereas in the poems 'Moors Again' and 'Remembrance' there is an acknowledgement of the underlying presence of God in nature in a style that is similar to that of the romantic poets. On the other hand heavenly wonders are romantically portrayed by other poems including: 'Starlight', 'Hunter's Moon', 'Street in Moonlight' and 'Full Moon', with the liberal use of alliteration. Alternatively, an admiration for a range of rural bird life is expressed in such poems as: 'Curlews', 'Hidden Birds' and 'Ring Ousel', whereas an appreciation of contrasting climatic conditions is portrayed in: 'Brief Summer' and 'Late Autumn', as well as a traditional English pastoral scene in 'These Fields'.

Then returning to the focus of the present theme, Alfred finds solace in an original description of his favourite mountain moorland, which nevertheless has metered overtones of John Masefield's poem 'Sea Fever', with some further similarity to W.B. Yeats' poem 'The Lake Isle of Innisfree', in the lamentation: 'The Waste-Lands':

The Waste-Lands

I will go far over the waste-lands,
To the lonely moorland tarn,
With only the sky for company
And the wind-swept mountain cairn.

And there I will refresh me,
And wash my wounds away,
Then, like a new-girt warrior,
Plunge back into the fray.

For there's healing in the mountains,
And solace in the sky,
And a man's soul needs revival
In a world so much awry!

Finally, to complete the theme, Alfred offers a vision of an escape from the boundaries of the human condition in which the eternal soul transcends into the joyful state of ultimate everlasting freedom with the poem: 'Emily Brontë's Grave':

EMILY BRONTË'S GRAVE

She is not buried here
Beneath this tomb:
Death could not pinion her
In such small room.

This is too strait a place
For her wild blood,
Only the dust of her
Rests in this rood.

Look for the soul of her
On the high Moor,
Where the wind wails for her
And the clouds low'r.

There the curlews cry
List for her voice!
Cage-free and glad – at last
Hear her rejoice!

3. Office Rhymes

The theme relates to a period in Alfred's life when he was working hard to establish himself in the wool trade in Bradford, and the poems often reflect his dream of escaping from the demands of the day to day drudgery associated with routine office work. The relief that Alfred feels when he is able to abandon his workplace for the freedom of the outdoors is expressed in the first poem: 'One Week' (see Chapter 1, p.13) and the last poem: 'Out of the Office' in which he finds comfort even in his working surroundings:

OUT OF THE OFFICE

Out of the office, as I step, I hear
A peal of bells, mellifluously clear:
The dulcet throbbing of Cathedral chimes –
Rising and falling, like majestic rhymes.

Straightway, the frenzied tumult of my brain
Quietens: my mind is calm again.
Beyond the traffic-roar, my spirit goes –
To the green precincts of a peaceful Close.

It is also apparent that Alfred regards office work with some degree of disdain, as evidenced by the poems: 'Pen Picture' and 'At the Office', in which work creates feelings that are in conflict with with those derived from his outdoor excursions, as he demonstrates in the poem 'On Beacon Lane':

ON BEACON LANE

There, in that city, I, by day, am mewed:
And sweat and swink in clerkly servitude.
Here, on this road, that climbs to cleave a cloud,
I live: I laugh: I sing: I shout aloud!

Furthermore, during Alfred's more abstract thoughts about his occupation, there is often a strong sense of poetic imagery, even before arriving at work: 'Going to the Office', as a diversion from his menial tasks at the office: 'Interlude', and ultimately the eventual escape to a better life from the perceived imprisonment by work of his poetic talents: 'Office Poet'. However, he acknowledges that there is no escape from the office work that demands dealing with the personal effects of the deceased: 'In a Solicitor's Office'.

Finally, Alfred's feelings about his business activities are probably best symbolised by the imagery created from the perspective of an imposing figure in the Bradford Wool Exchange in the poem 'Lines to the Statue of Cobden in the Bradford Exchange' (see Chapter 1, p.14). This highly original, well-crafted set of verses, with carefully chosen rhymes and polished metre, shows evidence of a maturing poetic talent, and succinctly encapsulates the fundamental premise that the great worsted industry of Bradford was built upon the backs of lowly sheep.

4. Miscellany

Unlike the other sections of the book, Miscellany represents an eclectic collection of work by Alfred, who was in the habit of jotting down ideas for pieces of prose or verse in a notebook whenever and wherever the urge came to him, and as a result the poems in this section are as diffuse as the circumstances underlying their origins.

Also unlike most of the other sections in the book, a majority of poems are of a comical nature, so that apart from overcoming any weakness in the verses, the inherent amusing aspects of the subject material can easily tolerate any less well-constructed features included, compared with those of more serious subjects in poetry. This results in such poems as the observational study: 'The Two Old Ladies' having a semi-humorous quality, while others: 'The Song of a Fat Cigar', 'November Apples', 'Fish Frier', 'Lady on a Train' and 'This Little Hog' all exemplify witticism in the treatment of the subjects, whereas some: 'Protection of a Foreign Traveller', 'Epitaph on a Youth', 'The Legal Lover' and 'Dust' display more satirical qualities.

In contrast with this light-hearted approach, Alfred also includes a selection of more scathingly sarcastic works such as: 'Elegy on a Thousand and One Articles' reflecting upon his often rejected written works, albeit perhaps deliberately based on the poem 'Lycidas' by Milton, while 'Signposts' states his disdain for the replacement of traditional old named road signs by new numbered versions, 'Prize Day' reflects a somewhat male chauvinistic view of the personal versus scholastic attributes of award recipients at a girls' school, 'To a Man Reading a Book in a Busy Street' comments on the need to be aware of the wider world outside of literature, as well as a spirited defence against attacks on his home city's image by those who should know better in 'Bradford' (see Chapter 8, p.167).

However the poem that makes a unique contribution to this section is one which Alfred opportunistically created following an inspiration he received while on duty as a look-out for 'flying bombs' on the Air Ministry roof during his RAF service in London during WW2: 'A Pigeon on a Window-Sill'.[9] Alfred's quirky set of verses records his thoughts on man's technological ingenuity in the achievement of flight while still dreaming of flying naturally like a bird (see facing page).

In order to bring this miscellany of verse to a conclusion, Alfred resorts to a parody of a quote by one of his favourite writer-poets, Hilaire Belloc: 'An Author's Hope', to express a similar hope in his own verse 'Epitaph':

EPITAPH

When I am dead, I hope my friends may say:
'He walked, head in the clouds – the poet's way.'
Far better this, when all is said and done.
Than walk with eyes on the ground - and miss the sun.

And finally he closes the section with a somewhat regretful wish that his own poetry might have been better expressed:

WORDS

With these same words which I now use,
Immortal stanzas have been made:
Ah! would that I might deftly choose
As they did – who so finely said!

A PIGEON ON A WINDOW-SILL

You –
Out of the blue,
strutting at will
on my window-sill,
And looking at me
Disdainfully...
Man, too, has
conquered the air
we are told everywhere.
and given a few
pre-requisites, 'tis true.

An aeroplane
(to sit in)
lots of gadgets
(to fit in)
An airscrew
(or two)
Tons of oil
and fuel,

A parachute
Harness to boot.
A mechanic
with aerodynamic.
An engine,
meticulously tuned-in,
with sufficient power
to do X hundred miles an hour
An 'R/T'
'Are you receiving me?'
Last, but not least,
(you insufferable beast!)
A Landing-Ground
With all found...

But on the edge
of my window-ledge
on the top floor
of a Departmental Store

You cock an eye
at the morning sky
And me
Superiorly:
And without a care,
Take the air!

* * *

Ah, what would I give
To live
As you –
Creature of earth
and heaven too!
To stand on Striding Edge
As on a window-ledge,
Admiring the view
with You –
And then, without a thing,
Take wing!

5. Songs of Yorkshire Dales and Inns

It is likely that this theme is the one dearest to Alfred's heart, since it represents the sharing of many happy social occasions during his Dales tramping adventures with a few close friends and other acquaintances in the landscape that he loves so much. Some of the poems are rollicking pub songs dedicated to the enjoyable times that he has in the various inns for which he has some special affinity including: 'The Withins' Inn' which was on Ovenden Moor west of Bradford (now a private house), 'The Pineberry Inn' in the village of Mountain, near Queensbury, Bradford, 'Old Raggalds' Inn' on the Queensbury to Haworth Road near Bradford, and 'The Rose and Crown' in Bainbridge, North Yorkshire. However Alfred reserves some wrath for the lack of traditional service at a Durham hostelry in Darlington: 'O Miserable Boot and Shoe', and the occasional niggardly reception received at some other inns elsewhere: 'Malediction'. In contrast, two songs are dedicated to the sociable characteristics that Alfred associates with his Yorkshire kinsfolk whom he holds in high esteem: 'Song of the Yorkshireman' and 'In Praise of Lads'. He also demonstrates his great regard for a life-long friend and walking companion in verse: 'Dedication (To Ouse – G. C. Heseltine)', and acknowledges the praise-worthy places where he finds nourishment for both body and soul respectively: 'Song: Appletreewick' and 'Mountain Manna'.

The theme also provides examples of the solace of soul and mirth of mind that Alfred derives from the exploration of the Yorkshire landscape in general, and in particular the benefits of the ancient tracks that allow him to enjoy his beloved upland retreats:

THE GREEN ROAD

The green road pulls at my heartstrings,   I will follow the feet of my forbears
I know why it is so;   Wherever the green roads run;
But the voice of my forbears calls me   Over the shivering mountain
And cheerily I will go –   Till my journey shall be done.

I will go where the green roads wander   I will go to the ultimate haven
High up the steep fellside,   Where all the green roads end,
To the far horizons yonder –   And there, perchance, find comfort,
Where the Legion marched and died.   And there, perchance, a Friend.

Alfred's love of the Yorkshire Dales is also conveyed by an urge to make the most of the opportunity to enjoy its landscape while he is still young enough to be able to appreciate the experience in the poem 'Wanderlust', which has some of the hallmarks of Yeats' poem 'When You Are Old'. Furthermore, Alfred finds some affinity with the ancients of the desolate upland moors,whose spirits are all that remain of the now-desecrated tumuli: 'On Simon Houe'. But the poem which best sums up Alfred's feelings for the Dales, and all that they represent in terms of their eternal spiritual importance, is the one that most people would deem to be one of his best, and the one from which he would select two lines for inscription on his own gravestone, 'Dales in Paradise':

Dales in Paradise

There must be dales in Paradise,
Where Wharfe and Aire and Swale
Fulfil their several destinies
And tell their various tale;
Flinging themselves just when they choose
Into the honest arms of Ouse!

There must be dales in Paradise,
With noble tops atween:
Swart fells uprearing to the skies
And stretching to the green –
And ower t'tops we two shall go,
Knee-deep in ling and broom or snow!

There must be dales in Paradise,
Else what will dalesmen do
Throughout the long eternities,
And none to wander through!
Where walk and sing and laugh and laik
Before the rest of heaven's awake?

There must be inns in Paradise,
Where nappy ale is sold,
And beef and pickles – even pies
Such as we've known of old!
And we will find a parlour there,
And call for pints for all to share!

There must be dales in Paradise,
Which you and I will find,
And walk together dalesman-wise,
And smile (since God is kind)
At all the foreign peoples there
Enchanted by our blesséd air!

O we will walk with stalwart tread
Through the eternal day,
And waken all the lately-dead
With ditties loud and gay!
Inciting the angelic choirs
To twang the chorus on their lyres!

6. Love Lyrics

Many of the poems within this last section are something of an enigma, since it is almost impossible to envisage the contextual source of them without resorting to speculation. It is likely therefore that this collection represents the spectrum of Alfred's life-long romantic experiences, beginning with his youthful, casual affectionate interludes, progressing through the more serious relationships of his early adulthood, to the later enduring commitment of his mature years. However a few poems fall outside this framework of personal experience and Alfred portrays the affective domain of love as a powerful human emotion. None of the 28 poems included in this largest section of the book had been published before, and therefore this is the first time that Alfred's personal romantic thoughts and feelings have been displayed in a public way, so that caution has been exercised in any critical analysis of the content. Furthermore, because of the speculative nature of the contextual classification outlined, and the underlying sentiments portrayed, only a few poems have been selected to represent the overall nature of the various love lyrics contained in this section, in the hope that these will provide a useful synopsis.

One of the earliest poems written during Alfred's recovery from his WW1 illness was the sonnet: 'Epithalamium', to celebrate the intended marriage of his close friend George Heseltine.[10] However at this time Alfred suffered not only from physical debilitation but also from social isolation, and perhaps he relies upon his imagination to express his feelings regarding the normal affectionate views that any young man might harbour in 'Song: 'Tis Astonishing':

SONG: 'TIS ASTONISHING

When the lamps are alight, and the moon's aloft
And Night her jewelled cloak unfurls,
And the gallant stars their caps have doff'd,
And Man walks abroad with a roving eye:
'Tis astonishing how many beautiful girls
Go by!

And whether it is – as some assever it is,
Merely the wild moon's witchery,
Working a tricksy alchemy,
On powder and paint: or whatever it is –
(Powder and paint can't account for curls!)
'Tis astonishing how many beautiful girls
Go by!

Then following Alfred's return to work after his enforced isolation, he was once again able to take the opportunity to enjoy the female social company that he has been deprived of for so long, and perhaps the renewed thrills of infatuation as expressed in 'Love's Power':

LOVE'S POWER

There is such courage in her face,   There is such goodness in her soul,
Her eyes they shine so clear: She is so fair within:
I need but look on her to be   I need but think of her to be
Disarm'd of every fear.   Clean-wash'd of ev'ry sin.

There is such valour in her hand,
I need but touch to be
Arm'd with the keen and flashing steel
Of noblest chivalry.

There is such magic in her mouth,
Her lips they have such power:
I need but kiss them to be free
Of all the ills that lour.

There is love within her breast,
It brimmeth with such measure:
I need but touch her heart to be
Enrich'd with heavenly treasure.

Moreover there is some indirect evidence in Alfred's second semi-biographical novel *Whitaker* (1946) that he had entered into a more loving relationship during the years of becoming established in the wool trade, but the fact that this early romantic encounter was not successful and may have led to some rueful resentment, is suggested by the poem, 'Willow':

WILLOW

I kissed my little sweetheart,
Under a willow-tree
There, then, her name I carvèd
Proudly, for all to see!

I lost my little sweetheart
How weeps the willow-tree!
The kiss for which I starvèd
Sweet name! I give it thee!

Alas , my little sweetheart!
How cold the willow tree!

Alternatively, an involvement that Alfred described in his first auto-biographical novel *The Lean Years* (1926), was a more serious matter which he felt, perhaps with some justification, was an unrequited relationship, that ultimately led to the bitterness and regret as expressed in the verses 'She Will Not Come Again':

SHE WILL NOT COME AGAIN

She will not come again,
I shall not see her more:
I strain my eyes in vain
Hope dupes me as before.

I listen for her feet
In many a secret place,
Where I was wont to meet
And greet her face to face.

I wait: she does not come
I strain my ears in vain:
The silence speaks my doom
She will not come again.

However these initial romantic disappointments were eventually replaced by the choice of a lifetime partner that Alfred subsequently made by his engagement and marriage to his wife Marie-Eugénie, and while his pre-engagement present to her was the subject of a poem to her radiant beauty: 'To a Lady with a Gift of a Miniature Mirror', and his subsequent poem acknowledges that the unforgiving advancement of the years upon her beauty, would not diminish his love for her with time: Furrows:

FURROWS

Love, when the fierce team of the years
Shall plough across thy lovely face,
And I, abreast of Age who steers,
Survey the furrows he doth trace:

Love, if my foolish heart should droop
To see such beauty so o'erlain,
And I should lose my certain hope
That precious soil will yield again:

Love, let me look into thine eyes
And spie the granaries of thy soul,
And see them with that first surprise
Teem with their wondrous harvest-full!

And finally Alfred's eternal love for Marie-Eugénie was summarised in the verse 'The Flame of Love':

THE FLAME OF LOVE

Love's like a fire, men say; and like all fires
Love must be tended else the flame expires:
But we, my Dear, whose love knows no such doubt,
Touch hands and burn; and talk men's fires out!

Responses to the Book of Poems and Songs

There appears to be little evidence available for how Alfred's book was received, but since it was produced primarily for circulation among his family, friends and acquaintances, rather than for the general public, it was likely that any feedback that Alfred received was largely personal and no doubt politely proffered by those who had enjoyed his previous foray into poetry with his earlier book *Broad Acres* (1948).

The only public acclamation of the book was made by the local Whitby newspaper which provided a short but positive review of the attributes of the work:[21]

> Alfred J. Brown, author of *Broad Acres*, *Four Boon Fellows* and *Striding Through Yorkshire* has had a collection of *Poems and Songs* published by Messrs. Horne and Son Ltd., at 10s. 6d. The verses were written between 1921-1948, and it is interesting to observe the variation which followed experience. There are six groups, including early poems in sickness, lyrics out of doors, office rhymes, miscellaneous verse, songs of Yorkshire dales and inns, and love lyrics. The majority have not been previously published, and all have an appeal of their own. The author says that some of the poems are old fashioned, but this does not detract from their charm, and the lover of Yorkshire will find in the verse much to admire, and conjure up visions of various aspects of the county for Mr. Brown has the knack of drawing a facile scene by the use of words.[11]

It is interesting that the same newspaper article also included a review of Dorothy Una Ratcliffe's recent book of verse for children 'Little Gypsy in the Wood', since Alfred had received encouragement from this author and poet friend of his in the preparation of *Poems & Songs*, and she had ordered two copies of the book in advance of publication.[12] Subsequently she also wrote to Alfred after the publication of the book to convey some of her views about its contents:

> No need to tell you that it is unequal. Every poet knows that about his work without telling, but there are some (poems) that should be in every Northern Anthology: 'The Wasteland', 'Dales in Paradise' (top note), 'Old Raggalds' Inn', 'Wanderlust'. Your best work is about the county you know and love so deeply... I hope that the book has found its way to the shelves of other poets and to lovers of your dales.[12]

However it was only after receiving these largely supportive comments that Alfred, in reply to Dorothy, expressed his regret in not having someone else go through the collection of his poems before final selection, but he felt that this was too much to ask of anyone, and in any case he stated that he would prefer to stand or fall in his own choice.[12] He also indicated that since it was highly unlikely that he would ever publish another volume of poems, he wanted the book to be as representative as possible, but he acknowledged that he was surprised how the different lyrics had appealed to different readers of the book.[12]

Finally, in summary of *Poems & Songs*, it might be argued that the book added a poetic string to Alfred's literary bow, which perhaps produced a more positive result when powered by a prose string, and that while Alfred had admitted that his poetry was not only out of date but also out of style, it might might be added out of character with his more well-established literary offerings to date. Nevertheless, it should be acknowledged that the interpretation of poetry is made in the mind of the reader, and that the appreciative worth is largely judged subjectively, which perhaps is all that Alfred expected from his readership.

References and Notes

1. Alfred J. Brown, *Poems & Songs*, Horne and Son, Ltd., The Abbey Press, Bridge Street, Whitby, 1949.

2. Alfred John Brown, 20th May 1948, Journal, 1948-1950.

3. Ibid. AJB Journal, passim.

4. A.J.B., A file of type scripted drafts for Poems & Songs, 1948.

5. Alfred John Brown, A Draft Manuscript of Poems & Songs, 1948.

6. Julian Laverack, (Alfred John Brown pseudonym), Prologue: 'The Shakespeare Club', *The Lean Years*, Methuen & Co. Ltd., London, pp. 1-4.

7. A.J. Brown, Journal of Poems, 1917.

8. A.J. Brown, Journal of Poems, 1917 - 1918.

9. A.J. Brown, 'A Pigeon on a Window Ledge', a handwritten poem on the reverse side of a schedule: 'Duty Roster: Roof Spotting for Flying Bombs', 2nd October 1944, File 'Some War Letters', 1940-1944.

10. A.J. Brown, Epithalamium, Journal of Poems, 1917-1918.

11. 'Poetical Works', A review of Poems & Songs, *Whitby Gazette*, 23rd December 1948.

12. Dorothy Una Ratcliffe letters to/from Alfred John Brown, A.J.B. – D.U.R. Correspondence File, 1948-1952, passim.

CHAPTER 16

The Hotelier's Chronicles

Part I: *I Bought A Hotel*[1]

An Original Idea?

The book came about as a result of an unfortunate indisposition when Alfred had time on his hands due to an attack of a prolonged illness. He had never let an opportunity to write go amiss, and he used this latest bout of ill health to start another book with an entirely new orientation – a chronicle of his hotel experiences. While *Broad Acres* was in production and with *Poems & Songs* needing minimal attention, Alfred utilised his journal notes as a source of material to develop a narrative story for what would become his first hotel book.[2] If he had been searching for a new subject to write about, he had a ready-made topic to hand, provided that he and a potential publisher felt that a book about hotel-keeping might have a general appeal to a wide audience.

Alfred recognised that from a literary point of view the advantages of hotel keeping seemed obvious, because during the busy holiday seasons he was surrounded by the best material that any author could desire – human nature. Then when all the guests had departed, he thought that he could retire to his den in the evenings and settle down to write.[3] Although he had completed the final draft of *Broad Acres* during the second season of the hotel's activities, it was a difficult book to write since it abounded in great detail, but he intended a follow-up with a similar text, had it not been for the onset of a serious gallstones problem that intervened in his plans:

> Once I had exchanged the comforts of my pub for the rigours of a nursing home, I realised that I could only hope to write an easy book in such circumstances, a book which would provide a congenial distraction rather than a burden. Hence this book, which so far has been written almost entirely in bed, and though it suffers from this handicap, it may perhaps appeal to some readers and country-pub-ites as a bedside book and send them to sleep if nothing else.[3]

While the consequences of this latest illness were distressing because of his incapac-itation during the busy spring and summer of the 1946 hotel season, he was able to draft notes for his 'hotel book' as he referred to it at the time. But he may also have had another motive for this new book, since he had enjoyed reading about other estab-lished writers who had not only been reasonably successful hotel keepers, but had also benefitted from publishing their experiences of the hotel trade. The novel *Poet's Pub* by Eric Linklater (1929) about a young man who managed an old inn where he spent most of his time writing poems, and the largely autobiographical work *An Innkeeper's Diary* by John Fothergill (1931), had both entertained Alfred and appealed to his own latent desire to run a country inn.[4] Moreover, it seems likely that he had first hand knowledge of the successful redevelopment of an old run-down Victorian rail-way hotel, 'The Stanhope', near Horsforth, Leeds, that eventually resulted in the suc-cessful publication *Welcome Inn* (1952) by the flamboyant amateur, John G. Showers. Thus there appeared to be an established foundation for the likely popularity of a book which told the story of how Alfred and his wife bought an old-fashioned coun-try hotel and operated the business during the post war years of austerity, so all that remained was to convince a publisher of the merit of such a book.

Therefore Alfred sought a new publisher for his hotel book, since his previous pub-lisher, Country Life, was unlikely to be interested because the subject matter was out-side their portfolio. So with the help of his London agent, E.P.S. Lewin, he searched for another outlet for his proposed new book. In 1945 he wrote to Peter Lewin and suggested the confidential idea of a hotel book soon after taking over the Whitfield House Hotel:

> I propose to write a brief, cheerful sort of book about this new venture
> of ours in buying an hotel and setting up as amateur hoteliers... I think
> I will write it in a straight forward narrative style, not as fiction. A lot of
> ex-Colonels and Wing Commanders etc., seem to be looking to hotels for
> their living and I would like to do this book before someone else pinches
> the idea (which please keep in the dark!) Do you think it is a saleable
> proposition?[5]

And soon after he was pleased to receive the positive reply from Peter: 'The story of a "Yorkshire Hotel" (whatever it shall be called!) is definitely a suitable proposition.'[5]

In response Alfred confirmed that he would concentrate on his 'Country Pub' book during the winter of 1945/1946, but his illness interrupted this plan,[5] and it was over a year later in 1947 when Peter contacted him again to enquire about progress with the book.[5] By then Alfred had made good progress with the work and provided Peter with a draft manuscript with the provisional title of 'Country Pub'.[6] He indicated that he had drafted a text full of fun, philosophy and human interest, which he hoped would appeal to lovers of country inns, strangely though he wished to remain an anonymous author, and did not want to seem to advertise the hotel, so even the names of places and people were disguised. He also requested Peter's view of the manuscript, and advice about the title since, although he felt that 'Country Hotel' might be better, 'Country Pub' might best catch the eye.[6]

Author and Agent Conflicts

In a reply Peter indicated he thought the draft told a most interesting story that would appeal to many buyers, but the excessive use of bracketed material held up the story's continuity. This was not only annoying, since most of the information was relatively unimportant, whereas if it were germane to the story it should be included in the narrative.[5] Upon receipt of this mild criticism Alfred appeared to over-react and responded with a very tetchy reply by defending the use of parentheses as a legitimate literary device. He suggested that the draft should not be condemned on this fault alone, with the explicit caveat that if the story had not come across effectively, then it should be returned forthwith![5] While Alfred had not wished to make excuses for the draft, he recounted the difficulties under which it had been written and resigned the book's fate to his agent's advice.

To placate Alfred and provide him with encouragement Peter responded with a sensitive reply of understanding, support and positive action. He expressed his professional judgment that there was excellent material for a book, but resolutely defended his own candid opinion of every author's work for the betterment of the product. However he indicated he would offer the draft immediately to a publisher for consideration.[5] But within a month Peter informed Alfred that Collins Publishers had rejected it and indicated that their objection was not the subject material but the way it was written. Peter was still of the opinion there was too much extraneous material, substantial revisions were needed and small uninteresting sections as well as repetitious material needed removal.[5] Nevertheless he was prepared to offer the draft to other publishers to see how it fared, and suggested that if it was returned with similar comments, then suitable modifications would have to be made.[5] While Alfred agreed that the story might benefit from some reductions and revisions, he did not think it needed drastic reconstruction, but conceded that if it was returned by other publishers, it would have to be revised substantially, even if it meant a long delay in the process.[5]

Delays, Disappointments and Despair

In the late summer of 1947 Peter informed Alfred that the draft had not received a favourable response from two further publishers, Hodder & Stoughton and Warner Lauries, although he planned to approach others before he suggested revisions.[5] But with no indication of interest by early autumn, Alfred concluded it was probably time to make the necessary revisions, since he did not want to spoil the chance of a favourable response by sending the work to other publishers in its present form.[5] He then had time to recast the work during the 1947/1948 hotel 'off season' and also agreed to publish it under his own name as suggested, but still insisted on fictional names for the hotel, his family and surrounding places.[5] In early 1948 he informed Peter that he had revised the story with the proposed new title 'Country Pub' and had drastically pruned the text of the offending bracketed and repetitious material, with whole paragraphs and odd small chapters scrapped, along with all the redundant items.[5]

After a further long delay in the spring of 1948, Alfred became impatient about the lack of news from publishers, and questioned Peter if he had been able to find a suitable outlet for his book.[5] Unfortunately Peter reported the bad news that of five publishers contacted, it was rejected by Longmans, Collins, Sampson Low and Hodder & Stoughton, but it was still under consideration by Herbert Jenkins.[5] However Alfred was not keen on the latter publishers and ventured to suggest a range of other publishers to be approached, presumptiously perhaps telling his agent how to do his job! Clearly this did not help their relationship, but it indicated the depth of Alfred's despair at this point. This situation did not improve following news from Peter that the book had also been declined by Herbert Jenkins and George Bell, although he had contacted half a dozen other firms in the hope of attracting some interest.[5] Alfred was also disappointed that the book had been misinterpreted as a work on 'hotel management', even though the preface made it clear that this was not the case , but he agreed to wait for further views by other publishers before he considered any other changes.[5]

Success at last

Then, after yet another rejection this time by Faber, Peter indicated that Williams & Norgate had shown some interest in the 'Country Hotel'.[5] Their report suggested that after a quick read of the manuscript by the managing director, Mr. Edgar L. Skinner, it was felt that the company would make a proposal for its publication, and that the manuscript was in the hands of the company's reader.[5] Furthermore Mr. Skinner had asked if was possible to meet with Alfred in London to discuss a number of points.[5] Needless to say that Alfred was delighted with this news and a meeting was arranged in September 1948.[5] Subsequently Alfred received an agreement via Peter for a book with the newly-agreed title: *I Bought A Hotel*, with many appended comments in order to clarify several clauses in a somewhat archaic contract to protect Alfred's interests.[5] He duly signed the contract and returned it with pleasure in the knowledge that his new book would now be published in the New Year.[5]

The contractual agreement was completed for the delivery of the manuscript of 110,000 words or thereabouts by 30th September 1948, and Williams & Norgate Ltd. undertook to publish the book within six months.[6,6a] The price was 12s/6d per copy, with a royalty paid to Alfred of 12.5% rising to 15% after the sale of 4,000 copies, plus a further royalty of 10% for any overseas sales and an advance of £100. The publishers reserved the right to publish a cheaper edition if and when the current edition ceased, while Alfred was entitled to receive six free copies and the right to purchase further copies for personal use at 33% discount rate, and he would have all the rights to the book referred to him after five years if the publishers decided not to issue further reprints. Unfortunately when Alfred followed up this agreement after some seven months to expedite the date of publication, he was saddened to hear that Mr. Skinner had died suddenly, although the company continued to fulfil their contractual obligations, and he was assured that the book would finally appear later than agreed on 14th September 1949.[5] It then remained for Peter to arrange advance publicity and reviews to promote the book to try to ensure that the anticipated sales would be forthcoming.[5]

The 'High Fell Hotel' Story: *I Bought A Hotel*[1]

*No, Sir, there is nothing which has yet been contrived by man by which
so much happiness is produced as by a good tavern or inn.*
– Boswell's 'Johnson'

This is one of four similar well-known quotations which Alfred includes in the frontispiece to express his own sentiments for the conviviality conveyed in such hostelries. It is followed by a poignant dedication, which acknowledges the special people in the story of the hotel adventure: 'For my Wife and the Children who made this possible.'

In the Preface Alfred provides an overview of how he came to buy a residential hotel, and why, against his inclination, he bought a private hotel rather than a licensed house, how he turned it into a sort of 'Country Club', and the relative success of the venture. He suggests that his experience is not typical, nor is he a born inn-keeper, and that the reasons he went into hotel-keeping were complicated, and how, like others, he found it difficult to take the plunge into the hotel trade after a life in the business world.[7]

He explains that the book tells a true story, although he disguises the location, appearance and the name of 'High Fell Hotel', and while he uses his imagination here and there, all the salient facts are correct. He also states that while it is not true to say: 'no reference to any living person is intended', he hopes that he does not give offence to anyone who may recognise themselves in the composite characters mentioned in the story, and that all the names used are fictitious.[7]

He also cautions that just as any hotel may appeal to some and not to others, so this book may appeal to some but not everyone. Moreover, the circumstances in which it was written make it somewhat disjointed, and that it is not intended to be a consecutive narrative about hotel keeping alone, but essentially it is a story of how he and his wife bought and developed an old fashioned country hotel and the outcome of this venture.[7]

The story line follows a chronological timescale of the first three years of the hotel's operation, written in a somewhat journal style, in which 10 thematic chapters are further subdivided into some 79 topical sections which embellish the 10 major themes contained in the book.

At the outset, Alfred relates how he went 'In Search Of An Inn'[8] and recounts with black humour the disastrous holiday experience at a 'select' country inn in early 1945 that leads him and his wife to consider buying an inn of their own. But this proves almost impossible and he is relieved when he finally discovers a suitable place. at last. However unlike their intended plan, it is an hotel, not an inn, and it is on the North Yorkshire Moors, not in the Dales. Then after a spring time visit to The High Fell Hotel[9] in Farrdale (Goathland Dale), near Seacombe (Whitby), Alfred describes how he and Suzanne (his wife Marie-Eugénie) become enchanted by the small country hotel. On return home to Hillside (Wharfegate) they realise the scale of the problems they face trying to get the place ready for the upcoming holiday season. In an intriguing account he details the how they achieve the almost impossible transition to a new life style for themselves and their family. Even before the official opening of the hotel in the 'First Season'[10] there is the arrival of early guests who are only too keen to help with the many minor chores while the workmen are still finishing off the major alterations to the place. However they face many teething problems before the start of the main season, and they have to adjust to the shock of their new seven day week roles as hoteliers.

The storyline then focuses on the 'Problems'[11] associated with the hotel business during its first season, and the difficulties of recruiting staff since Alfred and his wife cannot cope alone. Even with the help of a domestic assistant who moved with them, and their daughters: Colette (Felicity), Sally (Barbara) and Marlene (Rosemary), they still need additional staff which proves both hard to recruit and retain. Moreover there are supply problems with the most essential foodstuff during post-war austerity years, but help is on hand from local farmers who provide the basic needs for hotel catering, albeit sometimes from black market sources. However supplies of luxury items such as tobacco and alcohol remain elusive, and when a drinks license is with-held, Alfred establishes a residents' 'Country Club' scheme to overcome the problem. At this point he realises how much behind the scenes work is needed to run even a small hotel without administrative support and he has to work even longer hours than he ever did before. Meanwhile his wife is also overworked by the official food office and ration book returns on top of her catering duties, and it becomes necessary to increase guest numbers in future to meet the growing running costs of the hotel.

In another shift of theme Alfred elaborates on his ongoing literary interests in 'Books and Authorship'[12] and his hopes of establishing a sort of 'Literary Inn', which proves less than successful since the intended attraction of literary figures to the hotel is somewhat over ambitious. While his attempt to operate a small bookshop is thwarted by governmental regulations, he has more success in establishing himself as a kind of 'Literary Innkeeper', even though the demands of the hotel restrict his lit-erary output. But he vents his frustrations with the publishing business and the lack of support for struggling writers, before providing an interesting insight into his own literary profile so far, with the only autobiographical account of his personal history in any of his works.

The storyline then reverts to the hotel once more after the summer season when fam-ily life returns to 'normal' in the 'Autumn'.[13] For Alfred this means exploring Farrdale and the surrounding moors, and having time to write in the evenings, while his wife gets away to visit relatives and friends. But neither of them can escape their worries about the precarious financial position of the hotel which runs at a deficit during the 'off' season. Therefore the need to generate extra income is helped by the licensed taxi trade that Alfred starts with the help of the newly-hired handyman, Mr. Parker, for both guests and local residents of the village. The end of the year is then brought to a glorious close with an account of the traditional celebrations of 'Christmas'[14] and the New Year, which become an established feature of the hotel whereby the family and guests join together in a series of well-planned festivities.

The New Year of 1946 is expected to bring better prospects for the business in the 'Second Season'[15] since advance bookings for the holidays have increased substantially. However Alfred's unexpected long illness reduces his input into the hotel, although it allows him to work on the present book. He also has to come to terms with 'difficult guests', the 'undesirable element' and whether or not to operate a 'black list' to avoid problem people. But he has few qualms about the restriction of owners of 'pampered pooches' with their child substitutes, although he is more tolerant with regard to children (well-behaved of course!), and he eventually abandons the idea of a pre-booking questionnaire that he planned to use to get the right sort of guests.

Towards the end of the second season Alfred carefully considers the hotel's performance and assesses the situation after the accountant's review in terms of 'Profit and Loss'.[16] He reflects on how well things have gone for them as relatively raw amateurs in the hotel world which is run almost exclusively by professionals. Furthermore he even states his views quite categorically on what he believes to be a 'good innkeeper', an 'ideal inn' and a 'perfect guest'. But in spite of this levity he recognises the financial uncertainties that lie ahead even after a relatively successful season.

The 'Third Season'[17] of 1947 does not start well with the onset of the most severe winter in living memory, but when the snow eventually clears by Easter, trade picks up, new staff are appointed and Alfred plans more income generating schemes. These include attracting coach parties and an ambitious general 'Country Club' facility, which proves difficult and can only be achieved by a less pretentious 'Club Bar'. This not only appeals to guests and locals alike, but also gives Alfred some credibility as an 'innkeeper' of sorts. Nevertheless there is still the near constant problem of staff turnover to solve, but with some valuable replacements and the return of Sally (Barbara) from hotel training in Switzerland, Suzanne (Marie-Eugénie) is relieved of some catering duties and Alfred enjoys his new innkeeper's role.

After another busy season Alfred and his wife take time off from the hotel with a visit to London and he then reflects on the level of demand placed on his wife which is beginning to affect her health adversely. He further regrets the loss of 'normal' family life and also realizes the incompatibility of running an hotel with his literary ambitions, and concludes that he may have to seek another career very soon.

Finally in the 'Postcript',[18] Alfred reviews the performance of the hotel and highlights the successes but also the problems facing owners of small country hotels, but he recognizes there is no alternative than to carry on and hope for better times, while he ruefully reflects on the future prospects for the present book: 'With the publication of this book, the "High Fell" throws its doors wide-open to the world – and its critics.'

Impact of the Book

The book received a collection of very positive opinions from a variety of local and national press sources which have been briefly summarised by the following selected items:

'It has humour, commonsense, a gift of describing others to themselves and much practical commentary on the difficulties and frustrations – both economic and bureaucratic – which beset the hotelkeeper of post-war Britain.' – *Liverpool Daily Post*

'A thoroughly enjoyable description of his first three years in the adventure of innkeeping'. – *News Chronicle*

'This book is written with tremendous zest and fun, and reads much better than most novels.' – *Catholic Herald*

'Brown himself clearly belongs to the literary tradition of the late G.K. Chesterton.' – *News Review*

'Told with modesty and humour, and while practical details are not excluded, it never bores and leaves a most pleasant impression in the reader's mind.' – *Times Literary Supplement*

'Mr Brown always writes with distinction, and tells the story of the trials and triumphs of an innkeeper's life, with a shrewd eye for significant detail and a quiet humour that make excellent reading.' – *Yorkshire Post*

'More than a chronicle about hotel-keeping – an intimate personal story of a family man who turned his back on security at fifty and made a success of his new business.' – *Yorkshire Observer*

'Beneath the light-hearted manner there is a tale of difficulties overcome, successful improvisation and family partnership which is peculiarly heartening and English.' – *Books of Today*

In addition to these brief press opinions there were two complimentary and detailed reviews that appeared in two of the most influential press sources of the time, the first in *John O'London's Weekly*:

> ...The author is a Yorkshireman and a business-man. His prose as one would expect, is robust and forthright. He had various reasons for embarking on this career. Ranking high among them was his own experience based on the belief that he could do better than most... The two hundred and fifty pages of this most enlightening book tell the story of Mr. Brown's venture. He was fortunate in having a very highly qualified cook for his wife; in lighting on a house of real character and charm in a district ideal for tramping.
>
> He was less fortunate in that he could only expect a short season, from Whitsuntide to October at best, since 'High Fell' was situated in a district of Yorkshire off the beaten track and liable to severe weather. He had thus to keep open throughout the long wintry months storing food, burning coal and oil, to pay wages, with only the smallest hope of a return for his outlay. Had it not been for his own pluck, and the sterling loyalty of his wife and daughters, the venture might have failed almost as soon as it began...
>
> I could meet Mr. Brown much more than half way, for I too once bought a small country hotel, and for much the same reasons as his. I ran it for about as long as he had done when he wrote the book, and I made all the same discoveries. There are cranky, obstreperous visitors; but the great majority blossom like flowers to reasonable treatment. Free access to books, bowls of fruit in the bedrooms, to one's expert knowledge of the district, to one's maps and sticks, and to one's sympathetic attention at all times: all this thaws out the most diffident guest...
>
> The tone of the book is warm, mellow; but he can be acid. As for example when he encounters the Licensing Authorities... But there is the stuff of the poet in Mr. Brown too. As when he draws the book to a close... A good note on which to end a book crowded with interest, revealing the author as the sort of man whose personality one would wish to find pervading every inn and hotel, large and small, at which one paused to take one's ease.[19]

In the second lengthy, but equally incisive review, the focus was as much on the author's own characteristics as the relative merits of the book, in the *News Review*, London:

Brown, formerly in the export trade in the West Riding, and a WW II intelligence officer, dreamed of owning a country inn. Finding it impossible to acquire one, he bought a 14 bedroom private hotel, 'High Fell', in a picturesque position on the Yorkshire Moors.

Accompanied by his French-born wife, with a genius for cooking, and their five children, he had to overcome many obstacles. His capital was small, and he had a serious illness just after opening. But with good will and good humour he seems to have made a modest success out of his venture.

But it is doubtful whether Brown's ideals are typical of his profession. The worst kind of boarding-house owner (whom Brown describes devastatingly and exactly) probably has no ideals at all. Brown himself clearly belongs to the literary tradition of the late G.K. Chesterton, a fellow Catholic. He adores the British inn. His heart instinctively goes out to children. He loves the countryside, has a kind of sentimental love of drinkers and conviviality, is interested in eccentric individuals, and is drawn towards things ancient and traditional.

On the other hand, he instinctively dislikes regulations and officials, though he gets on with them as soon as he knows them as individuals. He has little love for big cities and no use for the masses. In fact, like fellow-author, John Fothergill, he is a bit of a snob.

But Brown is a good-hearted snob, and is always willing to admit his mistakes. Thus, when financial circumstances forced him to open his hotel to charabanc parties, he frankly recognises that they were well-behaved and much nicer than he and his staff had expected.

Hotels have become a vital part of Britain's economic survival. The foreign tourists and British holiday-makers whom they accommodate sometimes praise and sometimes blame them. Only rarely does the public learn the inside story, from the hotel-keeper's viewpoint. Alfred J. Brown, Yorkshire writer turned to hotel-keeping at the age of 50, now helps to fill in the gap.[20]

It might have been expected that along with many other wide ranging, comprehensive and complimentary press notices and reviews, there was a strong possibility that the book would not only sell very well, but might even become one of those rare entities – a 'best seller' – but that was now out of the control of Alfred and his agent and firmly in the hands of the publisher.

Outcomes of the Book

There appeared little doubt about the impact the book made, and while Alfred was naturally pleased with the press opinions and reviews, which he hoped would get the sales off to a flying start, he was concerned about the effects they might produce. In particular he expressed his worry as to whether Williams & Norgate would be able to meet the anticipated demands.[5] However his agent Peter Lewin cautioned that good reviews did not necessarily mean good sales, and in some cases even where abominable reviews had been received a book had sold out within a week.[5] Nevertheless Alfred's fears were borne out when some 2,000 copies were sold in the first couple of months, and yet the company had only printed 3,500 copies and initially only 1500 copies were bound, so they quickly had to bind the rest.[21] Alfred also persuaded Williams & Norgate to print a second impression of 1500 copies at once, while Peter had pressed the company to consider a third impression as well, since sales were around 200 copies per week. At this stage Alfred was convinced that the book might sell up to 10,000 copies, and may even become a 'best seller' with a sale over 20,000 copies possible, so that Peter suggested a big reprint to the company along with a national advertising campaign before Christmas 1949.[21]

These suggestions appeared to have the backing of the chairman of the company, Lord Inman (1892 -1987), who was a self-made man of humble origins, born and bred in Knaresborough, Yorkshire, with public service, business and political interests. Inman had indicated that a national advertising strategy was being considered and that the printers, Unwin Brothers, would be encouraged to produce a third print run of 6,000 copies.[5] In addition, he also suggested that if a broadcast talk could be arranged with the BBC it might stimulate sales to that magic figure of 20,000 thus becoming a 'best seller', and there was also the possibility of selling a serialised version of the book to a newspaper, although perhaps complacently he had also stated that the book was selling on its own merit at present. In response to this good news, Peter Lewin discussed further marketing and reprinting of the book, but the company made this dependent upon a successful BBC talk to stimulate sales.[5]

Meanwhile at a local level Alfred had noted that book sales were going very well with not a single copy available in Whitby and Scarborough, but somewhat disturbingly the booksellers were kept waiting for the delivery of new supplies.[5] Furthermore in a subsequent visit to give a public lecture in Leeds, he noted that he had called at three of the major bookshops, none of whom could produce a single copy of the book, and all had reported that it had been in great demand but they continued to be kept waiting for new stock.[5] At this point Alfred became frustrated with Williams & Norgate's poor response to the book's demand, since it appeared that they could not cope with the problem of distribution let alone the reprint situation, even though they planned to make a further 2,000 copies available to meet the anticipated 1949 'Christmas rush', and he suggested that the entire new print run could be sold in Yorkshire alone![5] Unfortunately there was also the bad news that the BBC in London had rejected Alfred's draft script prepared for a possible radio talk, and with it went the chance of any likely serialisation of the book, so that Peter could now only suggest that he would approach BBC Northern Region BBC in Manchester for a possible short broadcast talk in order to promote sales of the book.[5]

Meanwhile on another broadcasting front, Alfred had received an approach in early 1950 from Mr. Larry Henderson, a Canadian Broadcasting Company producer who was on holiday but looking for material on English country pubs, and having read the book, wanted to broadcast a talk about the work and the hotel, which Alfred thought might influence sales in Canada and the USA.[22] This was followed by a weekend visit to the hotel by Mr. Henderson and his wife, during which two interviews with Alfred were made on a portable recorder, one on his reasons for taking the hotel and its beautiful location on the moors, and the second on his dual role as an author/innkeeper. Furthermore two additional interviews were conducted with Marie-Eugénie in French for use in the Quebec region of Canada, and even young Adrian got into the act by saying a few words too![22] This new development pipped Northern Region BBC which had not shown the same enterprise and originality, but they managed to arrange a radio talk in Leeds by Alfred for subsequent broadcast in 1950, and the Canadian broadcasts also went out later that year. Unfortunately the offer of further work with the BBC in Leeds was abandoned because of the termination of its 'Yorkshire Series', which disappointed Alfred especially since his broadcast talk had attracted the interest of listeners who had written to him via the BBC for more of the same.[2]

Negotiations with Williams & Norgate to resolve the issue of reprinting the book did not go well either with no further commitment by the publisher. Alfred now believed that the book had been 'buried under a wall of silence' and the company had also fallen behind on the agreed schedule of royalty payments.[22] He suspected that because the company was only a small firm, with limited capital reserves, they did not intend to reprint a third impression, let alone renew the advertising until the second impression was sold out, and that his efforts to get the company to promote the book had been in vain. He was especially concerned that a potential 'best seller' now looked as if it was being suppressed, and he regretted letting Williams & Norgate handle the book in the first place.[22] However Peter defended the company and bluntly reminded Alfred that it was too late now for recriminations since the book had been turned down by many other publishers, and that Alfred had been only too glad to take up the offer of the now sadly-demised Mr. Skinner on behalf of a relatively small firm with limited resources.[22]

Further difficulties loomed when Alfred received the company's updated figures for the end of year sales as of 31st December 1949, which reported 3,500 copies sold, with 1,500 copies still in hand, and that there was no justification for spending more on advertising, while the BBC talk appeared to have no impact on sales in the North of England.[22] Soon after matters came to a head with the news that Williams & Norgate were only prepared to spend more on advertising provided that two conditions were met: firstly, a new edition was to be prepared with updates and amendments where required, and secondly, the company was to be given the option of another book to be agreed on new terms.[22] However Alfred was totally against this so-called 'offer' and indicated that he had no intention whatsoever of offering a new book, let alone making any alterations in the present book, and that if the company insisted on a reprint on these terms, he would ask for a return of the copyright immediately. As for a new book, he declared that he intended to write a sequel, but would not offer it to Williams & Norgate unless they could make a much bigger success of the present one.[22]

In order to overcome the impasse, Peter cautioned that while the present book should be treated on its own merits and not be dependent on another book, and even though the company had not fully exploited the first one, it would be extremely difficult to withdraw the book from Williams & Norgate, even if they agreed, let alone to try to interest another firm to take it over under the present circumstances. Subsequently Peter reported that after long and tedious discussions with Inman, it was agreed that no conditions would be laid down regarding the reprinting of the book, and that it would feature in all future advertisements by the company, and it was hoped to continue to publish Alfred's future work, but he left the decision to Alfred concerning the outlet for a possible sequel.[22]

It was almost three months before the outstanding issues were resolved when Williams & Norgate called Alfred's bluff, threatened that a reprint would not happen, and he was asked to consider a new book as a kind of sequel.[22] It was then confirmed that a new arrangement was dependent on a suitable contract as well as an agreement to reprint the book, subject to Alfred's undertaking to write a sequel, and also subject to the new terms being acceptable, such that a reprint would be published before Christmas 1950.[22] Alfred finally acquiesced, since there would be no reprint without a signed contract for the sequel, and he had no option than to submit to a new contract of agreement with a suitable set of terms agreed.[22] Finally, following these prolonged, often bitter, sometimes acrimonious exchanges, the second impression of *I Bought A Hotel* was on sale by mid February 1951[23], no doubt to the relief of all concerned.

General Appeal of the Book

Soon after the publication it was apparent from various press opinions and reviews that this new hotel story appealed to a wide audience and struck a chord with the general public, and even among those in the hotel trade, and not just the established group of Alfred's readers.[24] He received numerous letters not only in about the book itself, but also regarding the hotel in general, as well as an interest in his Northern Radio BBC broadcast, and where possible he replied to all correspondence received.

The book generated many letters which expressed everything from admiration for the work, requests for autographed photos of Alfred, and even for additional recipes from Marie-Eugénie. Moreover the book was well received by those working in the hotel business, who wrote letters to express their admiration for what Alfred and Marie-Eugénie had achieved and recognised the hard work needed to be successful in this demanding business.[24]

A few owners and operators of small guest houses or bed and breakfast facilities identified with the problems of starting a business with all the difficulties that Alfred and Marie-Eugénie had faced. Other people who owned larger hotels recognised their aspirations as amateurs who tried to compete with professionals in the business, but applauded their attempts to do so, and there was encouragement and support from someone who struggled to operate a similar 'Country Club'. There were even some who indicated they were interested in taking an hotel and requested advice on getting into the business.[24]

In most cases the correspondence Alfred received about the hotel was passed on via Alfred's publishers, or merely addressed to 'High Fell', Farrdale, N. Yorks Moors, since he had disguised its whereabouts. There were numerous requests for the hotel's precise location along with further details about the place, often followed up by requests for brochures and booking information, since it was considered as an ideal place for a holiday.[24] There were also examples of those who completed Alfred's customer profile questionnaire, and even one from an established hotelier who sympathised with the need to screen potential guests.

Naturally, there were many letters received from people who had stayed at the hotel and having read the book wrote to express their delight in both instances, sometimes passing on personal regards to Alfred and his family members, or occasionally to apologise for having left some personal item at the hotel such as ration books, clothes, shoes etc., with requests to forward the return of the same. There were even offers by former guests to work at the hotel, and sometimes requests from potential guests who, like Alfred and Marie-Eugénie, had previous experiences of poor standard hotels, with eager anticipation of staying in the well-run establishment of 'High Fell'.

Alfred also received numerous letters after his Northern Radio BBC Leeds broadcast at 6.15 p.m. on 20th February 1950, in which he gave a live 15 minute talk entitled: 'On Taking a Country Hotel'.[24] In most cases listeners had written via the BBC for information about the location of the hotel since Alfred did had not give details in the broadcast. Finally, the hotel received further broadcasting exposure when Alfred received confirmation from the programme producer, Mr. Larry Henderson, of the Canadian Broadcasting Company, that the recorded interviews conducted with Alfred and Marie-Eugénie had been widely enjoyed in Canada, especially in Ontario, where there was a large number of English expatriates.[24]

It was apparent that the range of Alfred's correspondents and their topics of enquiry were evidence of an alternative, independent testimony to the overall impact and outcomes that the book had achieved. This must have provided Alfred with considerable satisfaction in terms of the success gained from this alternative approach to his literary endeavours. Perhaps his only regret was that if the book had been properly promoted by a publisher with sufficient financial assets to ensure more sustained and comprehensive promotional advertising, it might have indeed become the 'best seller' that he suggested possible from the outset. All that remained now was the need to concentrate upon the sequel in order to complete the hotel saga and fulfil his new contractual obligations with Williams & Norgate.

References and Notes

1. A.J. Brown, *I Bought A Hotel*, Williams & Norgate Ltd., London, 1949.

2. Alfred John Brown, Journal, 1948-1950.

3. Op. cit., A. J. Brown, p. 235.

4. Op. cit., A. J. Brown, p. 11.

5. AJB/E. P. S. Lewin Correspondence File, 1945-1949, passim.

6. A Memorandum of Agreement, Alfred John Brown/ E.P.S. Lewin and E.L. Skinner on behalf of Williams & Norgate Ltd., London, for a book entitled: I Bought A Hotel, 27th September 1948, AJB Literary Agreements File, 1923-1959.
6a. Note: The West Yorkshire Archive Service, Bradford Central Library, Catalogue No. 69D90, Section 4, Items 4/2/1-4/2/2, Draft manuscripts.

7. Op. cit., A.J. Brown, Preface, pp. 9-10.

8. Op. cit., A.J. Brown, Chapter 1, In Search of an Inn, pp. 11-21.

9. Op. cit., A.J. Brown, Chapter 2, The 'High Fell' Hotel, pp. 22-76.

10. Op.cit., A.J. Brown, Chapter 3, First Season, pp. 77-108.

11. Op. cit., A.J. Brown, Chapter 4, Problems, pp. 109-137.

12. Op. cit., A.J. Brown, Chapter 5, Books and Authorship, pp. 138-152.

13. Op. cit., A.J. Brown, Chapter 6, Autumn, pp. 153-179).

14. Op. cit., . A.J. Brown, Chapter 7, Christmas, pp. 180-191.

15. Op. cit., A.J. Brown, Chapter 8, Second Season, pp. 192-223.

16. Op. cit., A.J. Brown, Chapter 9, Profit and Loss, pp. 224-235.

17. Op. cit., A.J. Brown, Chapter 19, Third Season, pp. 236-270.

18. Op. cit., A.J. Brown, Postscript, p. 271.

19. Garry Hogg, 'Literary Man's Hotel', *John O'London's London Weekly*, 30th September 1949, p. 601.

20. Unnamed Reviewer, 'Buying An Hotel', *News Review*, Travel Section, London, 1st December 1949, p. 22.

21. Op. cit., Alfred John Brown Journal 26th October 1949.

22. AJB/E.P.S. Lewin Correspondence File, 1950-1954, passim.

23. Alfred J. Brown, 'I Bought A Hotel', Williams & Norgate Ltd., London, 1950, Reprinted Edition.

24. AJB Fan Mail Correspondence File, 1945-1951.

Part II: *Farewell, 'High Fell'*[1]

Background to the Sequel

Alfred agreed to write the sequel as a precondition for reprinting the first book *I Bought A Hotel* and he had continued to draft new material for the follow-up story while the new terms and conditions were drawn up. The new agreement for a book originally entitled 'I Sold My Hotel' was signed by Alfred and Philip Inman, on behalf of Williams & Norgate, on 21st October, 1950.[2] Alfred was required to deliver a manuscript by 30th September 1951, and the publishers undertook to publish the book within six months of receipt of the final draft. The price was 12s/6p per copy with royalties to Alfred of 12.5% per copy, rising to 15% after the sale of 3,000 copies, and 17.5% after the sale of the next 4,500 copies and thereafter, along with 10% on all overseas sales, and Alfred received an advance of £150. The publisher retained the right to publish a further edition or a cheaper edition with Alfred's permission subject to future demands, and the rights of the book reverted to Alfred five years after the book went out of print. In addition Alfred was entitled to receive the usual six free presentation copies of the book with the right to buy further copies for personal use at a one third discounted price.[2]

While Alfred was satisfied with the new contract, he was concerned that there was no mention of the costs for promotion of the book, but he thanked his agent, Peter Lewin, for dealing with the problems surrounding the sequel.[3] He felt the right decision had been made to overcome all the difficulties involved with the previous negotiations, and felt that Williams & Norgate would do their best from now on to ensure the sales of both hotel books.[3] However Alfred's completion schedule was compromised because having sold the hotel in late 1950, he and his family moved in early 1951, first for a short time to Bradford, then temporarily to a flat in West London, before finally to a house in York.[4] He also took time off in the late summer of 1951 to spend time with his family in France on their first holiday in several years.[4] Therefore after the upheavals of moving he had little chance to complete the sequel by the agreed deadline and he asked Peter Lewin to intervene with the publishers on his behalf about the unforeseen delays.[3] After he had settled in York he concentrated on drafting the sequel and hoped to complete it by early January 1952, and the publishers then agreed to delay publication until September 1952, but Alfred completed the draft earlier than expected and delivered it before Christmas 1951.[5]

Early in the New Year, while Alfred heard that Inman had enjoyed reading the draft sequel, he was concerned that Inman had also made some critical observations including: a title change from 'I Sold My Hotel', and suggested a few dubious alternatives such as: 'I Ran A Hotel', 'I Had An Hotel' or 'I Owned An Hotel' for consideration.[5] In addition Inman was concerned that Alfred's attack on hotel critics was too sweeping and unjustified, and should be toned down, while the section that dealt with the arbitrary and unfair system of 'starred' hotel classification by the RAC should be eliminated altogether. Alfred's response was that he would come up with a suitable alternative title, but he and his agent considered the attack on critics to be a good thing and wanted to retain the material concerning hotel classification, furthermore he requested a meeting with Inman as soon as possible to discuss these matters.[5]

Unfortunately, after a lunch meeting with Inman was cancelled because he was 'indisposed due to a chill', Noel Ranns, the managing director deputised for him to resolve the outstanding issues, but Inman passed on assurances that he would do all he could to promote the book. However Ranns also gave Alfred a gloomy report about the company which had made financial losses recently, and confirmed that they were prepared to print only 3,500 copies of the sequel.[5] Now after Alfred's optimism about the first book, he dared not hope for a similar success with the sequel and remained uncertain about its chances of having the same impact as its forerunner.[5] In spite of these misgivings he made the final modifications to the draft manuscript now entitled *Farewell, 'High Fell'*, and returned it for consideration in late January 1952,[5a] and then received acknowledgement that both Inman and Ranns were satisfied with the manuscript. However he was keen to discuss the advertising details and suggested a meeting during his visit to London at the beginning of February, but once again it was not possible to meet with Inman, who was due to leave on a business trip. At this point Alfred felt that the company was not interested in the promotion of the sequel, and he was being given a polite 'brush off' again as he had been during the procrastinated dealings over the first hotel book.

Alfred tried yet again to arrange a meeting in London in May, this time with plenty of advance notice, and also indicated that he had recently received a copy of Inman's autobiography: *No Going Back* (Williams & Norgate, 1952) to review for the *Yorkshire Observer* newspaper.[5] It had given him greater insight into the character of the man, and tellingly perhaps, he now knew more about what to expect in his dealings with the person who represented the publishing company. Meanwhile Ranns commented on the curious coincidence of Alfred's review of the chairman's book, and presumptuously intimated that the work would now receive a good notice in at least one newspaper.[5] He also informed Alfred that the composition of *Farewell, 'High Fell'* was now completed, with the proofs due to be printed soon, then confirmed that a lunch meeting had finally been arranged in early May with Inman at his flat in St. James's Court, West London,[21] which Alfred was only too glad to attend.

This meeting was probably no more than a polite gesture by Inman since there were no details reported about any discussions of the book's prospects, promotion or publicity. Even so Alfred appeared to be satisfied with the outcome because he returned the gesture with an invitation to Inman and his wife to call at York to see him during their forthcoming northern holiday.[5] Unfortunately Inman's response was once more non-committal when he indicated that the planned trip to the 'North' was postponed because so many matters claimed his attention in London that it was impossible for him to travel 'so far away'.[4] Perhaps this 'Northcountryman', as he described himself, had lost some affinity for his northern roots and personified the title of his autobiography: No Going Back? Or, more likely, there was much more behind the change of plan, since later Alfred learned that one of the matters which required Inman's attention was the sale of Williams & Norgate.[4]

Meanwhile Alfred busied himself reading the book's galley proofs and returned them with a few additions and insertions, together with the corrections, and indicated he hoped for a successful sales outcome. He conceded that the sequel was more controversial than the first book, since it raised some other important issues, such as the criticisms levelled at the hotel business, the problems of hotel classification and the publishing industry in general as well as 'best-seller' dominance in particular.[5] He then turned his attention to the final production and promotion of the book including: why the frontispiece did not contain a photograph of the author this time and the lack of dust cover reviews of the first hotel book, as well as the need for a promotional leaflet to help sell the book, the advertising required to give the book the best chance of success and the expected publication date, so that all these matters could be organised accordingly.[5]

In response to these concerns the managing director, Ranns, could only provide a publication date of 'late October sometime', and while he included Alfred's latest additions and insertions, he explained that a frontispiece author photograph would not be included to save production costs, although it was proposed to make mention of the previous book and include the author notes which Alfred had drafted.[5] The production of a promotional leaflet however had to wait until nearer the publication date, whenever that was, and with regard to advertising promotion the company 'would do what we can'.[5] Clearly the sequel was not going to enjoy the generous support that the company had provided for the chairman's recently published book.

Shortly after this Alfred concluded that with a dwindling income and ongoing family expenses he could no longer afford the valuable services of his agent Peter Lewin, and he wrote to him and suggested that they should terminate their agreement from the end of the year.[3] Peter replied with his usual friendly and generous advice but suggested that they terminate their agreement immediately rather than at the end of the year since the Williams & Norgate contract would continue until then anyway. He also gave Alfred some parting wisdom by warning him that he must adapt and change his approach in order to keep up with the times, and end his continued recriminations with the publishing business which did not help his cause. He encouraged Alfred to make his own arrangements for future publications, but assured him that he would be available if required.[5] It was with some relief and but much regret that Alfred received this most positive response and confirmed that he had enjoyed Peter's friendly association and enduring support during the last few years.

Later that summer Alfred received news that advance copies of the book were expected in late September, with a publication date of 23rd October 1952, and he considered it time to prepare a special promotional leaflet. Once again he took the initiative and proposed some strategic moves for the publisher to consider including: the production of an A4 folded promotional leaflet to provide details of both hotel books with supporting press notes and author information, a leaflet distribution address list which included all the people from his extensive hotel 'fan mail' files, together with the hotel's visitor book addresses which numbered many hundreds of former residents, and a selection of popular press and special periodicals lists for the supply of complimentary review copies of the book.[5] Furthermore he also requested sufficient copies of the book to be ready for the Christmas period and suggested that the company should have the full print run available to meet the expected demand. Finally in a cautionary note he identified a possible rival book that had just been published: *Welcome Inn* by John G. Showers (Pilgrim Press Ltd., Derby) which had been given a great deal of publicity and the need to match the promotion enjoyed by this competing text.[5] If this seemed like he was trying to do the publisher's job, it was because he had experienced the lack of promotion for his previous book, allied with the suspicion that the company was still not fully committed to the present book.

In late September Alfred received his six advance copies of the book and the confirmed publication date, but only the weak assurance that the company would do all they could about publicity. However Ranns cautioned that while the original print run would not be large there was a possibility of a reprint if and when it was required.[5] Alfred was disappointed with this response and suggested that the publicity campaign should target the hotel industry directly by supplying the promotional leaflets to all the major hotel groups in the country. These latest suggestions met with yet another lukewarm response by Inman who confirmed that a reprint would only be considered if demand warranted a second edition, while the hotel industry would be better served by postcard notifications rather than promotional leaflets.[5] Clearly this was someone with little knowledge and understanding of the hotel business, who was reluctant to promote the work among the representatives of a service industry of which he had little or no experience. No doubt by then Alfred was totally exasperated with the company's performance but the outcome was now out of the hands of all concerned and rested with the overall response of the book-buying public.

The Sequel Story – *Farewell, 'High Fell'*

There were no introductory quotations in the sequel, only a dedication to the nation's hostelries and their owners for the provision of vital services to the country: 'To the long-suffering, much maligned and officially "inspected" Hotels, Inns and Innkeepers of England, this book is respectfully dedicated'.

In the foreword[6] Alfred briefly explains that many readers asked him to write a sequel to the original book and bring the story up-to-date. So much has happened since he wrote the first volume, he has agreed to do another one, and hopes if he has to eat his own words as a result, it is poetic justice for an author-innkeeper. He explains to any new readers who want to know more about buying and operating a small residential country hotel that they must read the first book: *I Bought a Hotel*. He indicates that although the book is a story of what happened next, it is always more difficult to tell a tale of failure than success, and while this is undoubtedly a story of failure in a sense, he has stuck to the task for six years and sells the hotel only with great reluctance and states: 'The reader will be in a better position to judge why we sold it, when he has read this story'.

The book is in four parts and each part is sub-divided into generic chapters, which in turn have further thematic subsections, and ends with the short reflective postscript. It is a much more eclectic piece of work than *I Bought A Hotel*, in which Alfred includes a wide range of subject matter over a broader perspective. This explains why the text contains such a variety of topics which are detailed in a highly structured format of 20 chapters and 110 itemised subheadings in which there is something new on almost every page.

Part One continues the story of the hotel by setting the scene for the planned new developments for 1949,[7] in which Alfred reviews the first four years of the operation and the struggle to establish the business. To increase turnover he tries to offset the decline in bookings by attracting day visitors, but by the end of the year income dwindles with fewer guests, less food available and more trade restrictions, plus higher costs and increased wages. He is anxious about the new season,[8] but like others in the trade, he always takes the optimistic view that things will improve. After a long cold spell the season opens with only a trickle of guests, but special events such as weddings bring some extra income. Fortunately the future installation of electric power will bring all the benefits of domestic 'mod cons' and the connection of main drains and sewers means modernisation at last.

With the approach of the main season there is an urgent need for new staff,[9] since until now Alfred has been reliant on help from his daughters who must now pursue their own careers, and there have been excessive demands made on his wife at the expense of her health. Unfortunately the searches for a suitable chef, porter/handyman and chambermaid/waitress are unsuccessful. Then with huge relief Alfred finds a local married couple, who together with the young girl next door to them have the experience to make up the full compliment needed to solve the staffing problems. And yet at the start of the high season guest numbers are still worryingly low,[10] so Alfred tries to attract more custom from passing motorists but coach parties are a more obvious target. These large groups place extra demand on staff and care has to be taken not alienate residents who feel the hotel is being invaded. On the other hand special guest groups are most welcome, such as those attending the coming of age party held for Colette (Felicity), to which all the guest are invited. Even so Alfred worries constantly about the conflict of interest between running an hotel and the need to maintain a normal family life.

The high season also brings extra long days of service, but when the work is done Alfred enjoys serving drinks and chatting with guests, which for him is reward in itself. But worries remain especially when guests suddenly cancel bookings, and when this happens sometimes passing motorists and their families take the rooms, or rarely if the hotel is full, rooms are found for unexpected visitors in the village. Alfred even gives up his own room and sleeps on a camp bed in his office when his wife is away. Following the disappointing late summer trade,[11] Alfred and his wife have more time to enjoy the company of some special visitors such as the Archbishop of York and other clerical guests, along with a honeymoon couple on their way to Scotland. Others can be tiresome, such as the eccentric lady who arrives on horseback in the early morning hours and causes many problems for other guests who christen her

'Lady Godiva' on account of her equine mode of transport. Then Alfred discovers that she has absconded from a secure nursing home and he makes swift arrangements for her safe return to the institution.

Meanwhile Alfred's new taxi service raises additional income and needs another car to meet the demands of guest transport to and from the railway station, weddings and funerals, and the now popular tours of the district.[12] For Alfred this is the fun side of the job, although there are some unusual fares including lost drunken passengers, emergency hospital dashes and even a car dealer who wants to buy his taxi on the spot. Extra income also comes from wedding receptions and traditional Yorkshire funeral teas or 'arvals', but the Country Club scheme yields greater returns.[13] It provides members with special events, as well as artistic and literary functions, and these often attract well-known literary figures. Other special visitors include popular BBC radio entertainers who stay at the hotel when their shows move to Scarborough for the summer season.

During the 'off season'[14] there are numerous jobs requiring attention and Alfred needs help to carry out internal and external decorating work to maintain the hotel and make it presentable for next year. All this is a far cry from guests' view of what is perceived to be a long winter rest period. And yet there are the compensations of invigorating walks on the North Yorkshire Moors or attending local animal fairs, but Alfred avoids the local hunts on principle. Then there are other features of interest including a variety of social functions with a round of evening activities in the village, while important services are provided by interesting local characters, such as the friendly postman, the newspaper lady and the man who runs a mobile library, which all add to the community spirit of the village.[15] But Alfred's greatest admiration is for some of the disappearing sorts like the 80 year old drystone waller plying his trade alone whatever the weather. Nevertheless this rural idyll is sometimes disturbed by dangerous moorland fires and all hands are needed to overcome the devastating effects.

At the end of 1949 Alfred describes the traditional Christmas festivities at the hotel that are now well-established celebrations by family and guests alike.[16] He also relates the alarming story of how his six year old son Peter (Adrian) causes a full scale search when seemingly lost on the moor after sledging with friends, but turns up unharmed after going to a friend's farmhouse for tea on the way home. He then rounds off with two amusing anecdotes: one about the burial of a dead hen that is disturbed by his youngest son's need to see if has really gone to heaven by digging it up, the other about the egg laying habits of its live counterparts that prefer the comfort of the hotel lounge for the delivery of their important contributions to breakfast.

Part Two concerns Alfred's literary and broadcasting endeavours, along with readers' correspondence received about the previous hotel book. He reminds the reader that the hotel venture includes writing in his spare time,[17] and although the business is a full time job he has completed two books: *Broad Acres* (1948) and *Poems & Songs* (1949). But it is the poetry book that gives him more pleasure than anything else he has written. He also considers his first hotel book: *I Bought A Hotel* (1949) without the same sense of satisfaction, and yet he cannot disguise the pleasure he derives from the enthusiastic reviews it has enjoyed, but he is rightly cautious about whether it will be a best seller.

He then devotes attention to the letters received from readers of his previous hotel book which helped to stimulate the writing of the sequel.[18] The response to his earlier 'Yorkshire' books was nothing like the avalanche he received about this latest book. He is astonished by the correspondence from all parts of the world and not just the UK, and all this to an author at an unknown address due his disguise of the hotel's location. The most unusual comments refer to Alfred's recommendations for suitable reading matter for toilets, which brought one suggestion from a London reviewer for him to compile an anthology of lavatory literature entitled: 'Privy Counsel'. While on the subject of the library availability of books, Alfred supports a proposal from the Society of Authors that readers should be charged a small nominal fee on books loaned from public libraries, to be paid to struggling writers like himself.

To complete this part of the sequel Alfred considers radio broadcasting as means of promoting his books, and gives an amusing account of the untold difficulties of getting work accepted by the BBC.[19] Unlike his early experiences when he gave short talks on the radio with little interference from broadcasting staff, it is now a highly structured, complex technical affair dominated by 'media experts'. Since he has been unsuccessful in this new style of broadcasting and has abandoned further attempts and remains convinced that writing talks for broadcasting is an arduous task requiring immense time with little reward. However he does not deny the benefits that radio broadcasting may bring to would-be authors who are prepared to conquer this medium, but he remains cautious about the effect that radio is having upon the public's reading habits. Nevertheless he acknowledges the benefit gained from a recent radio programme about his first hotel book, albeit by an enterprising producer from the Canadian Broadcasting Company.

Part Three is almost exclusively devoted to the hotel business, along with the English hotel scene in terms of the standards and classifications applied to the trade. Alfred reviews the difficulties of his hotel at the start of 1950 and the problems facing similar hotels around the country.[20] He regards performance assessments as inadequate in judging the success of a small hotel when imponderables such as guest satisfaction are important, but recognises that accounts and annual returns are an evil but necessary legal requirement. He laments the adverse influence of the 1948 Wages and Catering Act on the trade, which bedevils small hotels with visits by inspectors and food standards officers, and appears to legislate for everyone except the proprietor and guests. Subsequently he focuses on the quality of hotels in the country,[21] and admits that when he bought the hotel in 1945, the standard of food, comfort and services was poor, with the hotel trade suffering from a bad reputation. But he contends that conditions improved marginally after the war before a decline set in once more in with prolonged austerity. Now he believes a revolution has taken place in spite of continued shortages of food and properly trained staff, but even so the trade still suffers from widespread public criticism. Then in a riposte to these critics he documents many first rate hotels that he has experienced lately, no doubt to the complete satisfaction of their proud proprietors.

Alfred then embarks on a criticism of the classification and method for selection and 'starring' of hotels having frequently received 'inspections' by 'snoopers' as he calls them.[22] Often judgment is made after a cursory review, sometimes without the presence of the proprietor. His concern is that the traveller expects a 'starred' or 'appointed' hotel to be superior to a place that is not recognised by these dubious designations, which is not always the case. Unsurprisingly he prefers the official guide by the British Hotels and Restaurants Association. He also suggests that the selection of hotels for recommendation needs revision, and proposes a fair, true and clear assessment process for recommending hotels to the public. He has no time for the so-called professional groups' representatives who select and recommend hotels on their supposed merits but charge for the privilege. Instead he favours the French system of the 'Club des Sans-Club' which publishes the annual *Auberges de France*, which lists all hotels and restaurants with the emphasis on the services and food available that provides a useful guide for what to expect.

Finally on the subject of his own hotel, Alfred considers how his previous hotel book has put the place 'on the map' in a way that advertising, word of mouth and signposts have failed to do, but it has brought some unforeseen outcomes too.[22] Readers search out the place and while he enjoys meeting them he is embarrassed to be the subject of such pilgrimages. People call at inconvenient times, and although they are invariably friendly and charming, most just want to look around, some stay for a meal, and many say nothing about the book until leaving when they proffer a copy for signing.

Yet as much as these unexpected visitors are welcome, Alfred feels the time has come to leave and start all over again, since the double harness of hotelier and author has become too much, even for someone with his undoubtedly robust constitution.

Part Four concludes the story of the hotel with its sale during the busy final year and the need to find another livelihood and place to live, and while the decision is hard, the process is far from easy.[23] Potential buyers like the look of the place for the same reasons that attracted Alfred and his wife but most cannot raise the capital. The selling agent suggests a sale by auction in late 1949 which turns out to be a sham event with no genuine bidder making an offer. Following this fiasco Alfred and his wife have no choice but to carry on during the upcoming season.[24] By the spring of 1950 Alfred has to inform the loyal staff about the plan to sell the hotel and take on temporary staff to cover the work for those who find work elsewhere. Meanwhile the agent sends interested parties to view the hotel, but on one occasion Alfred is too preoccupied with a group of disabled visitors, and he turns away both agent and prospective buyers. This is nearly a disaster since upon their return the clients are genuinely interested in buying the hotel and make a reasonable offer with the only proviso that they are unable to take possession until early 1951. In the interim Alfred and his wife adjust to thought of leaving and have time to make plans for a move to London in the near future.

The proposed move presents new problems,[25] so Alfred decides to seek a furnished flat 'pro tem' and luckily finds a place through an old WW2 contact. On returning home his wife is so pleased that they both go to London for a few days to make arrangements for the move. All that remains is to transfer the hotel to its new owners before they leave the cherished old house that has provided so much more than a business adventure. However one of the hardest parts of leaving is breaking the news to local people who have become good friends during almost six years of residency in the tight knit community of the village. But there is the opportunity to celebrate one more traditional 'High Fell' Christmas which takes on a curious solemnity and significance as it is realised that this the last time for everyone. Then a farewell party is arranged for family, friends and villagers to say goodbye. Later Alfred reflects on both his hotel books which portray an insider's view of life behind the scenes of a small country hotel, and concludes that even though he and his wife are only amateurs in the business, they will sadly miss the social life of busy hoteliers.[26] Finally in the postscript,[27] Alfred summarises his personal thoughts about leaving, albeit with the expectation of returning occasionally to breathe the fresh moorland air, for he doubts whether he can exist very long without its invigorating effects.

The Impact of the Sequel

Farewell, 'High Fell', like its forerunner, received very positive reviews from a range of press sources which included both local and regional papers such as the *Manchester Guardian*, the *Yorkshire Observer*, the *Yorkshire Post* and the *Liverpool Daily Post*, as well as national papers such as the *Sunday Times* and the *Times Literary Supplement*, and some monthly magazines including the *Yorkshire Dalesman* and *Sport & Country*.[5]

In addition there were two very complimentary reviews which appeared perhaps unusually in the most influential hotel journals of the time, the first focused on Alfred's honest attempts at hotel keeping:

> Mr. Brown is extremely honest about his professional claims and is the first to admit he is an enthusiastic amateur who took to hotel-keeping shortly after the last war. He has the trained eye and pen of an author to offset his lack of early training in the industry, which means he grasped the ideas, atmosphere and conditions far more quickly than a person who enters it with the fond belief that all you need is the ability to be a good mixer and your future is assured...

> He should in turn be respectfully thanked for the gauntlet he flings down on behalf of the small hotel keeper and the industry. Seldom can the public have received such an insight into the day to day running of an establishment nor can it often have seen so resolute a champion.

> Throughout the book runs a vein of humour of the rare brand today that makes the reader chuckle... On the more serious side, Mr. Brown pulls no punches – his Yorkshire bluntness would not permit it anyway...

> ...after six years the Brown family gave up hotel keeping. In the eyes of the industry they may rank only as amateurs, but there is no doubt that the most hard-bitten of professional men on reading *Farewell, 'High Fell'*, will agree it was the industry's loss. Mr. Brown was a 'natural' – we should thank whatever gods watch over hotelkeepers that he recorded those six years.[28]

In the second review the emphasis was on the insider's view of various aspects of the hotel business:

> In his new book, A.J. Brown, who wrote *I Bought A Hotel*, ends the story of his hotel on the Yorkshire moors with an account of the last two seasons and how he eventually sold the hotel...

Everyone should find something of interest in this book for, apart from the tale of the day-to-day running of the hotel, there are descriptions of Yorkshire country scenes, local characters and events. The Catering and Wages Act is shrewdly attacked, together with the critics of the British hotel industry...

Although humorously written, the book does not conceal from the reader the hard struggle the country innkeeper has for survival...

But it was not all hard work and tears. Mr. Brown describes some of the many pleasant times he and his wife, Suzanne, had at 'High Fell'; the happy Christmas parties; the interesting, and often amusing, visitors; and the marvellous glow of pride and satisfaction it gave them when they were thanked for their hospitality and complimented on the cooking...

Then after six years at 'High Fell', came the reluctant decision to sell – and Mr. Brown tells of the factors that combined to make them reach this decision.[29]

In view of these most favourable notices, Alfred no doubt hoped that the sequel would be a success and maybe sell even better than its forerunner, but this would depend upon further promotion by the publishing company, although on past evidence there was little to suggest that this would happen.

Outcomes of the Sequel

Although there was little doubt about the initial impact of the book, Alfred was again worried about the availability and promotion of the work by Williams & Norgate. He raised these concerns even before the book went on sale in October 1952, when he discovered that their representative had not yet called on his friend and local book-seller, E.A. Holman of Whitby, who was unaware that the book was ready for sale. In response Noel Ranns reassured Alfred that the company's representatives tried to cover the whole country as far as this was humanly possible with only two men, but he was only now beginning to distribute the leaflets that Alfred had designed earlier in order to promote sales of the book.[5] While not wishing to tell the publisher how to do his job, Alfred nevertheless took the initiative again and asked Ranns to send complimentary review copies of the book to a comprehensive list of the Catholic press and a range of women's magazines which might ensure further coverage in the press promotion of the book. But Ranns replied that over 70 review copies had already been distributed and this circulation must cease unless a further request was made by a specific newspaper whereby a review was assured.[5] Even when Alfred requested more copies of the leaflet to distribute personally, he was informed that only a few copies of the 1500 printed remained and these would now have to suffice. At this point Alfred then asked for another meeting with Inman, when he planned to be in London again in early November to resolve these problems, but again only received the curt reply that Inman was too busy to see him so soon.[5]

In view of this intransigence it was not surprising that Alfred felt his latest book had been smothered by the recent avalanche of Christmas books in 1952, but he requested further advertising to try to promote sales in the New Year.[5] His earlier fears about the plethora of publications may have been borne out, since there had not been a single London review of the book in the lead up to Christmas except for the two excellent reviews in the hotel press. Moreover Williams & Norgate informed him that they had only sold about 1500 copies out of an initial print run of 3000, but hoped to sell more by Christmas, although Alfred received no further good news about sales in telephone conversations with the company at this time.[5]

It was not until early 1953 that Alfred heard from the company again to say that Inman had not been too well lately and had not had time to discuss the book's present situation. However it became evident that Inman was not too indisposed to deal with the sale of the company.[5] Alfred was informed that an agreement had been reached with the London publishers, Ernest Benn Ltd., for the sale of the company which would occur very soon, but until such time all further issues with regard to his book and any future work by him would have to wait until everything was settled.[5] Soon afterward Ranns confirmed that Benn Ltd., had obtained the controlling interest in Williams & Norgate, and that the chairman, Mr. Glanville Benn had been appraised of Alfred's situation and would contact him, meanwhile Ranns departed to a new job with Hulton Press.[5]

Upon receipt of this news Alfred responded somewhat magnanimously that he appreciated the relief on behalf of the company in finding a buyer, although he was apprehensive about his future dealings with a new company, and he wrote directly to Glanville Benn and requested an opportunity to meet to discuss his situation.[5] In response Benn apologised for the delay in replying since the new firm had to deal with many books and authors as a result of the Williams & Norgate takeover, and while he was pleased with the sales of Alfred's first hotel book and hoped for similar success with the sequel, he could not give any undertaking about any future work.[5] Finally Alfred received news from the publications manager of Benn Ltd., who agreed to fulfil the obligations of the previous publisher with respect to the sequel,[5] but in reality this was the end of any possible follow up to the hotel story that Alfred may have had in mind with this company.

The Appeal of the Sequel

In the same way that the first hotel book had caught the imagination of a general readership, the sequel produced a similar flow of letters of appreciation, and many readers who had now read both books wrote to Alfred, via the publishers, to express their enjoyment of the continuation of the story of the hotel years.[30] Most commonly there were still enquiries about the location of the hotel and requests for brochures, terms and possible holiday bookings, even up to 1953, long after Alfred had sold the hotel[30] Many others wanted to buy further copies of *Farewell, 'High Fell'* directly from Alfred, which indicated that because there was no reprint of the book it was difficult to obtain, and some even went to the trouble of sending their copies to him for his autograph.[30]

There were also some intriguing personal aspects that were evident, such as the letter from the widow of the former chairman of Williams & Norgate, Mr. E.L. Skinner, for Alfred's very kind comments made about her late husband in the book.[30] On a happier note, Alfred received a letter from the lady who acknowledged with great delight Alfred's mention of her honeymoon stay at the hotel.[30] Other letters requested possible summer employment at the hotel on behalf of two female students attending a Liverpool Catholic Teacher Training College.

Finally there were a number of letters which dealt with specific issues relating to the hotel business including: requests for Alfred's assistance in finding a partner for a proposed country hotel enterprise[30] and complimentary letters from a country club owner and a hotelier, who recognised and applauded the family's struggle to make their business a success in the difficult post war years.[30] Then there was a request for the final 'profit and loss' status of the hotel, to which Alfred responded that 'on paper' a small profit had been made, but since much investment was needed, and property values had only risen marginally during the years of operation, in reality there was little gained except the satisfaction of the belief that a good job had been done well.[30]

In summary it was apparent that *Farewell, 'High Fell'* enjoyed widespread general appeal which suggested that Alfred had brought the hotel story to a satisfactory conclusion. And yet he was probably still haunted by the feeling that if the publishers had given the book more sustained promotion and publicity it could have achieved greater sales success, which was also the case with *I Bought A Hotel*. However no doubt Alfred's thoughts now turned to the next book he intended to write with a return to the lifestyle of a non-publican author once more.

31. Alfred J. Brown, proprietor, the Whitfield House Hotel

References and Notes

1. A.J. Brown, *Farewell, 'High Fell'*, Williams & Norgate, London, Ltd., 1952.

2. A Memorandum of Agreement between Alfred John Brown, C/O E.P.S. Lewin, and Philip

Inman, Chairman of Williams & Norgate Ltd., London, 21st October, 1950, AJB Literary Agreements File.

3. AJB/E.P.S. Lewin Correspondence File, 1950-1953, passim.

4. Alfred John Brown, Journal, 1950-1954, passim.

5. AJB/Williams & Norgate Correspondence File, 1951-1953, passim.
   5a. Note: The West Riding Archive Service, Bradford Central Library, Catalogue No. 69D90, Section 4, Items 4.3.1 – 4.3.2, Draft manuscripts.

6. Op. cit., A.J. Brown, Forward, pp. 9-10.

7. Op. cit., A.J. Brown, Chapter 1, Taking Stock, pp. 11-16.

8. Op. cit., A.J. Brown, Chapter 2, Fifth Season, pp. 17-27.

9. Op. cit., A.J. Brown, Chapter 3, Staff Problems, pp. 28-40.

10. Op. cit., A.J. Brown, Chapter 4, High Season, pp. 41-58.

11. Op. cit., A.J. Brown, Chapter 5, Autumn, pp. 59-68.

12. Op. cit., A.J. Brown, Chapter 6, Taxi Sir? pp. 69-75.

13. Op. cit., A.J. Brown, Chapter 7, pp. 76-84.

14. Op. cit., A.J. Brown, Chapter 8, Winter Tasks and Diversions, pp. 85-93.

15. Op. cit., A.J. Brown, Chapter 9, Village Life and Characters, pp. 94-101.

16. Op. cit., A.J. Brown, Chapter 10, Christmas, pp. 102-108.

17. Op. cit., A.J. Brown, Chapter 11, Books and Authorship, pp. 109-117.

18. Op. cit., A.J. Brown, Chapter 12, Letters from Readers, pp. 118-134.

19. Op. cit., A.J. Brown, Chapter 13, BBC, pp. 135-142.

20. Op. cit., A.J. Brown, Chapters 14, New Year, pp. 143-154

21. Op. cit., A.J. Brown, Chapter 15, English Hotel Standards, pp. 155-164.

22. Op. cit., A.J. Brown, Chapter 16, Hotel Classification, pp. 165-175

23. Op. cit., A.J. Brown, Chapter 17, Prospective Buyers, pp. 176-179.

24. Op. cit., A.J. Brown, Chapter 18, Sixth Season, pp. 180-184.

25. Op. cit., A.J. Brown, Chapter 19, In Search of a Flat, pp. 185-193.

26. Op. cit, A.J. Brown, Chapter 20, Closing Scenes, pp. 194-198.

27. Op. cit., A.J. Brown, Postscript, pp. 199-200.

28. Unnamed reviewer, 'Farewell, High Fell', the British Hotels and Restaurants Association Journal, November 1952, p. 511.

29. Unnamed reviewer, 'He Sold A Hotel', Hotel Management Journal, November 1952, p. 51.

30. AJB Fan Mail Correspondence File, 1952-1957, passim.

CHAPTER 17

The Taverner's Travelogue

A Topographical Tour: *Fair North Riding*[1,1a]

Background to the Book

This latest book originated quite fortuitously after Alfred made a visit to London in late October 1949 to meet his publisher and agent about the promotion and development of his books *I Bought A Hotel* and *Farewell, 'High Fell'*. During the visit he was invited to lunch at the Reform Club with Mr. Francis Whitaker, the director of Country Life Books, the publishers of his previous 'Tramping' book series, and was persuaded to consider writing another 'Yorkshire' book about a region that was relatively unknown at the time, with the possible title: 'The North Riding'. Alfred somewhat reluctantly agreed to this request even though he was busy with the hotel books, and planned to write a follow-up hotel book in the coming winter of 1950.[2]

On 9th November 1949 he signed an agreement for a book provisionally entitled: 'The North Riding of Yorkshire' and to deliver a typescript of approximately 60,000 words by 30th September 1950.[3] The book was to be priced at 15 shillings, with a royalty paid to Alfred of 12.5% for up to 3,000 copies sold, rising to 15% thereafter, with a royalty of 10% on overseas sales and an advance payment of £100, with a further payment of £50 after the delivery of the typescript. The publishers reserved the right to publish a cheaper edition in future, and Alfred was entitled to receive the usual six free copies of the book, with the right to purchase further copies for personal use at a one third discounted price.

Alfred set to work immediately with an ambitious writing schedule of up to 5,000 words per week,[2] but was unlikely to maintain this output and submit the typescript by 1950 because of his many other commitments. He soon despaired when the book came to a virtual standstill in early 1950, since his enthusiasm had waned with the worries of trying to sell the hotel and his wife's illness.[4] Moreover he was concerned about rival books in preparation at this time by other London publishers namely the 'County Book Series' by Robert Hale Ltd., and the 'Vision of England Series' by Flek Ltd.[5] Furthermore his attention was also diverted by pursuit of a proposal for a reprint of his book *Moorland Tramping in West Yorkshire* (1931), which was rejected by Francis Whitaker in favour of an alternative book entitled: 'On Walking and Other Essays', using previously discarded material from 'Moorland Tramping' as a basis for a short work on walking in general.[5]

Not surprisingly these diversions interrupted Alfred's writing schedule and he informed Country Life that the deadline would be delayed, but assured Whitaker that most of the groundwork had been done and he would take a break from the hotel to complete the writing.[5] Whitaker confirmed that he would not insist on the deadline if there was good reason for any delay, and this would not compromise the planned publication date of Christmas 1951.[5] Soon after Alfred stayed at the Bumble Bee Hotel in Harwood Dale to try to complete the draft, since part of the delay was due to the preparation of his commissioned article entitled 'North Yorks Moors State Forests' published by Country Life Magazine, 30th June 1950.[4]

Unfortunately Alfred incurred further delays due to the busy hotel summer season and his wife's continued ill health, and even the good news of the sale of the hotel was mitigated by the fact that the new owners could not take possession until early 1951, so Alfred informed Whitaker that he now hoped to finish the manuscript by Christmas 1950.[5] Meanwhile Whitaker continued to be sympathetic and indicated that Country Life's planned production of the book would not be compromised.[5] However Alfred revised the completion date by a further three months, when the task of writing about the vast area of the North Riding was greater than he estimated.[5] Even then Whitaker remained understanding, but emphasised the need for the agreed 65,000 – 70,000 word maximum to keep the price down to 15 shillings, although he accepted Alfred's suggested new title: 'The Fair North Riding'.[5]

Subsequently, after his move to London in early 1951, Alfred delivered the completed typescript to Country Life some six months later than planned and ruefully reflected:

> How I sweated at it! It seemed never ending. I must have travelled thousands of miles getting the new material and freshening up my memories. In the end the manuscript is about 120,000 words instead of the 60,000 required. Inevitably it will have to be cut, but it will spoil it. As it stands, I think that it looks fine but C.L. [Country Life] are sticky about costs and length, and they will never print it all. However, I have got rid of it and can lunch with Frank Whitaker at the Reform Club next week to discuss it.[4]

Alfred also sent a meek apology with the manuscript to say because of the size of the North Riding, he could not cover the subject within the agreed word limit.[5]

Whereupon, while Whitaker complimented Alfred on the presentation of the manuscript, he was astounded that it was nearly double the size agreed, which would increase the book's price prohibitively, and it needed to be drastically cut down.[5] Unfortunately Alfred was not convinced especially when Whitaker sent him a review copy of the competitor book by Oswald Harland (*Yorkshire – North Riding*, Robert Hale, London, 1951), with the comment that it was a shame it had appeared before Alfred's book.[5] However Alfred responded that this competitor book was 150,000 words in length and priced at only 18 shillings, and hoped that Country Life would print his own work as it stood.[5] This response almost resulted in a major impasse, when Whitaker firmly stated that if the agreed word limit had been kept, a drastic cut would not be necessary and that Hale's book had been produced before recent price increases. Moreover, he intimated that any other publisher would take the same stance, and ominously suggested that if Alfred did not accept this, then he should offer the book elsewhere![5] Clearly Whitaker's sympathy for Alfred's reticence to revise the work had come to an end.

At this point the editor of Country Life Books, Mr. W.R. Birt, intervened to defuse the situation and suggested ways of making cuts of 18,000 words, with detailed but sensitive modifications to achieve the desired outcome.[5] Alfred's bluff had been called once more in a conflict with yet another publisher, so he agreed to all the cuts and suggestions by Birt and he proceeded with the required task without delay.[5] He then made required reductions, but defended his position on the major sections of the book to be retained and the sequence of presentation to preserve the coherent picture of the North Riding that he had intended to convey.[5] In response Birt thanked him for completing the onerous task of revisions and promised he would check it personally before it was sent to the printers, and assured Alfred that unless there were any residual points to clarify, no further changes would be required.[5]

It was nearly two months later when Birt reported that the printer had started work on the book now entitled *Fair North Riding*, with the final changes incorporated and confirmed that Alfred's cut of 16,500 words was sufficient.[5] Unfortunately while Birt was busy assembling a set of illustrations from various professional photographers, Whitaker was unable to complete the necessary changes required due to the pressure of work with the end of year publication deadlines.[5] This meant that Alfred's book would not be completed until late 1951, and he was requested to carry out the proof reading, along with final selection of photographs over the Christmas period which he completed in early 1952.[5]

In the early new year he was also asked to write a short article for *Country Life*

Magazine about the new National Park in the North Riding, The North Yorkshire Moors National Park[5] which was due to be officially designated on 28th November 1952. While Alfred was happy to do so, he also suggested that his book should contain brief details about this important development and an outline map of the National Park be included on the map of Fair North Riding by the book's illustrator, Mr. Leo Vernon.[5] While these important additions did not interrupt the production schedule, there were other issues that still needed to be resolved, including a reduction in the number of photographs and the size of the index before the final proofs were ready for Alfred to read and approve.[5]

In view of the imminent printing of the book, Alfred now turned his attention to the likely sources for its review and suggested a range of editors and critics of various press outlets that may not have been on the standard review list of Country Life Books, including a list of Yorkshire newspapers and periodicals, as well as various Catholic press sources.[5] Meanwhile other outstanding issues concerned the design and content for the dust jacket of the book, and after a lunch meeting with Birt at the Reform Club, Alfred made detailed suggestions for both the descriptive material about the book's contents, together with the author's biography for inclusion on the book cover.[5] Soon after he also urged Birt to expedite the publication date of the book, since there was now even more competition in the field from a recently-launched new series of works by 'The Regional Books' Group, which was a companion series to the well-established 'County Books' series by Robert Hale publishers of London.[5]

Unfortunately Birt later informed Alfred that the final publication date had been delayed yet again, this time due to the technical difficulties associated with the printing of the attractive, glossy dust jacket, although advance copies of the printed and bound book were now ready.[5] When Alfred received this frustrating news he expressed his concerns to Whitaker about the publication delays after he had sent the final manuscript some 15 months earlier, and even after reassurances that things were going to plan, a further 6 months passed, which meant that the critical summer sales season would be missed.[5] Moreover Alfred was disturbed by the news that yet another direct competitor book: *A Companion to the North Riding* from Methuen of London had been published recently, and he suggested that a bold advertising campaign would now be needed to regain some of the ground lost to all the competitor books published during the last few months.[5] Whitaker once more apologised for the unforeseen delays and indicated that copies of the book were now ready at last, but promised to promote the book vigorously during the upcoming summer season.[5]

When Alfred received three advance copies of the book from Mr. W.J. Tate, the sales manager of Country Life Books, he responded with great relief and satisfaction about the final quality of its production, binding and dust cover, which he considered to be the most attractive volume of all his books to date.[5] Finally Alfred was informed that the publication date for his new book: Fair North Riding would be 30th July 1952, and that a wide distribution of copies was to be made to all the agreed press sources, as well as bookseller promotional displays.[5] Furthermore he was requested to suggest possible additional press outlets for the circulation of review copies, since the company was anxious to gain the maximum publicity for the book in view of the intense competition now in the market for books on Yorkshire.[5]

Yorkshire's 'Fair North Riding'

The book is undoubtedly the best presented of all Alfred's work. It has an attractive glossy jacket with a photograph of a scenic North Riding landscape on the front cover, emboldened with the title above and Alfred's name below. On the rear cover is a portrait photograph of Alfred with a biographical summary of his life, works and interests. The inside front cover provides an account of what the reader will find most interesting about the region and captures the essence of the friendly character of both the place and especially its people. Alfred dedicates his last Yorkshire topographical book to his friend, writer and Yorkshire dialect poet: 'For Dorothy Una Ratcliffe, Singer of the Dales.'

In an unusually lengthy feature Alfred includes a page of acknowledgements thanking the many people in the North Riding from all walks of life who helped in the preparation of the book. He also thanks the many unknown people who have provided valuable information in another personal dedication:

> My best thanks are due to all those country innkeepers (and their wives), who have stayed me with flagons and regaled me with true Yorkshire hospitality during my tour of the North Riding. Without their help, this book would never have been written![6]

Alfred's appreciation of the North Riding of Yorkshire was gained from his previous book *Tramping in Yorkshire – North and East*, but now having lived there some years, he is able to draw upon a wealth of additional knowledge about the region. The book returns to a broad theme of topographical writing more typical of his earlier 'Yorkshire' books for which he is noted, but now with a very distinctive 'travelogue' theme. As a result it differs from his earlier 'Yorkshire' books since it is intended as a practical guide for the holiday traveller who plans to explore the area irrespective of how the journey is made, whether on foot, on two or four wheels, or on public transport. In this sense Alfred has modified his approach to the changing interests of the potential readership, whilst trying to provide a well-founded, comprehensive guide to another part of his beloved County of Yorkshire, and thus takes the reader on his own personal tour of the North Riding.

In the Foreword Alfred indicates there are various ways of presenting a picture of such a large and diverse area as the North Riding of Yorkshire, but his chosen method is to let the countryside and the people speak for themselves.[7] Alfred starts his tour at the most northerly point of the Riding, but since each part of the book is complete in itself, the starting point is left to the reader to decide upon. The endpapers map shows the boundaries of this vast area and all of the different regions which according to Alfred demonstrate a greater variety of scenery and interest than anywhere else in the whole of England. The book is illustrated with 25 full-page, black and white annotated prints by a number of well-known photographers of the time, with a range of scenic views: seven from the Pennine Dales, seven from the North Yorkshire Moors, three of the Cleveland Hills, and one each from the Howardian Hills, Hambleton Hills, the Vale of Mowbray and the vale of Pickering, as well as four views of the North Riding Coastline.

Alfred notes that York seems an obvious starting point to the tour since it stands at the gateway of the North Riding and is the hub around which all three Ridings revolve, and it also provides the correct historical background and perspective for the tour. However in a disclaimer Alfred indicates that space does not allow a detailed description of York in its own county of 'Ainsty', and that while there is more than enough to see in the extensive North Riding itself, he hopes that anyone beginning the tour in York will spare time to see this beautiful ancient city.

He also explains that the reason for the title *Fair North Riding* is because this is how he regards this part of Yorkshire, and it is impossible to exaggerate its richness and variety, or the beauty of its landscapes throughout the seasons. Moreover it is primarily concerned with scenery, history and people; with moors, dales and rivers, with market towns, moorland farms, villages and inns; with historic castles, abbeys and churches; with old customs, stories and legends; and with famous literary figures, sporting squires and country clergymen. Therefore he takes the broadest topographical approach to describe the region which is truly a mammoth task when the impressive size of the North Riding is considered. At the time it covers an area almost twice as big as the East Riding, and although not quite as big as the West Riding, it is larger than almost all of the other shire counties of England.

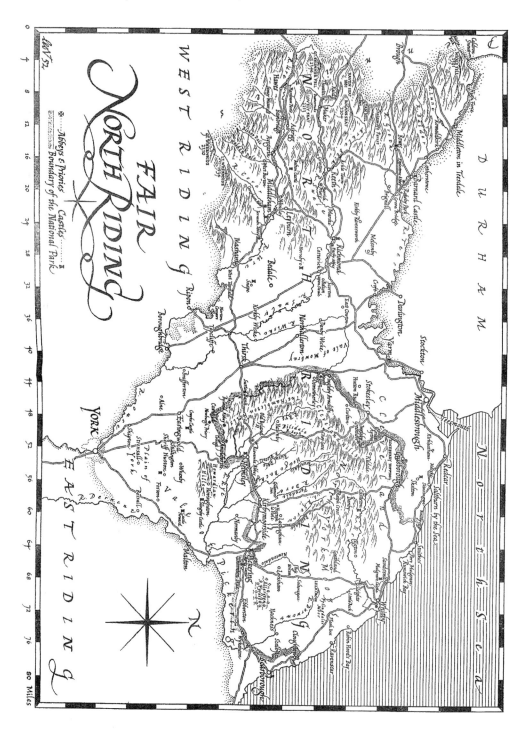

Map 17. the Fair North Riding

Finally Alfred notes that the recently signed order by the National Park Commission designates an area of nearly 600 square miles of the north-eastern part of the Riding as a new National Park. He hopes that when the order is confirmed, thousands of tourists will take the opportunity of visiting the district for the first time. While The North Yorkshire Moors National Park Order of Confirmation came into effect on 28th November, 1952, he concludes the Foreword with a cautionary note:

> All this new parkland – and the rest of the region – is described in this book, but I should be the last to claim that I have given more than a hint of the richness and beauty of this fair North Riding in these few, crowded pages.[7]

The book is divided into seven main parts that encompass each of the broad geographical areas of the North Riding including: (1) The Dales, (2) Rydale, (3) The Hambleton Hills, (4) The Plain of York and The Howardian Hills, (5) The Goathland Country and the North-East Moors, (6) The Cleveland Country and (7) Towards the Coast. Each part contains a number of discrete chapters which correspond to separate areas, townships, villages, farms and geographical features, and additional material describes the North Riding from the human, historical, land-use, industrial and literary perspectives that are essential to gain a proper understanding of the North Riding as a whole. Although Alfred presents a step by step geographical approach to his tour, the text is interwoven with details of the historical antecedents that created the landscape and provides an insight into the way in which ordinary men and women go about their business today. However behind this image of normality Alfred alludes to the changes taking place, even in the apparently timeless North Riding, as the traditional English country scene disappears slowly before the observer's eyes.

The following overview of the book is a generalised account of the journey on which Alfred takes the reader along the North Riding roads and over moors and dales to describe the countryside, with frequent pauses on the way using timely changes of subject to enrich the experience. Furthermore, to convey Alfred's own perspectives, the overview relies heavily on Alfred's narrative storyline and his style of presentation to capture the descriptive approach to 'topographical' writing in his own inimitable way.

Part 1. The Dales

The first part encompasses the western dales and Alfred begins his tour in Teesdale.[8] He considers this the most romantic approach to the North Riding of Yorkshire, and although he acknowledges that the River Tees is a Border River, which shares its banks with Durham and Westmorland, there are plenty of places along the Yorkshire side to claim attention. He advocates the classic approach to Teesdale via Scotch Corner and the old A1 or 'Great North Road' then on to Greta Bridge. Travelling along the route of the Romano-British road he suggests stopping at an old coaching inn, the Unicorn Hotel, in Bowes. Here he recommends a visit to the ruins of the Norman Castle, which together with the church of the same period, bears witness to the long and chequered history of this ancient settlement.

At this point Alfred advises backtracking along the A66 to Rokeby to see the ruins of Egglestone Abbey which overlooks the River Tees which is best approached from Abbey Bridge. While he concedes that crossing this former toll bridge results in a brief excursion into County Durham, he summarises some of the features that attract the visitor to this High Tees area. He then recommends the road on the Yorkshire side of the river to the walking country around the High Force waterfall in upper Teesdale, where the counties of Yorkshire, Westmorland and Durham meet, and concludes with some regret: 'But this is outside the Yorkshire boundary and I have no right to be wandering there at all – at least not in this book!'[8]

Alfred completes his coverage of lower Teesdale with a review of two interesting but contrasting places, the township of Yarm and the village of Croft. Yarm[9] stands at the northern border of the Riding on the banks of the River Tees. The high street is lined with Georgian houses and numerous inns, the most famous being the old George and Dragon Inn, where the promoters of the Stockton-Darlington Railway met in 1820, and he reflects on how such a world-shaking event took place in such a sleepy old town. On the other hand Croft,[10] near Darlington, straddles both banks of the river, and this remote place was where Lewis Carroll (1832-1898) spent his early years when his father, Rev. Charles Dodgson was the incumbent at the local church.

Moving south to Swaledale,[11] Alfred indicates that it is much more secluded than Teesdale and in his view: 'Of all the great dales, Swaledale seems to come closest to one's ideal of a pure, unsullied dale – a shepherd's dale'. In his opinion High Swale offers some of the most enchanting moorland tramping in the whole county with tracks over the high watersheds of Teesdale, Swaledale and Uredale; while the motorist can derive pleasure from driving through the dale and over its high passes. Keld is recommended as the best centre for exploring the dale, where the Cat Hole Inn (now no longer an inn) was the base for many of Alfred's former tramps and for part of his honeymoon, while other villages such as Muker and Thwaite also typify Swaledale.

However Alfred suggests that no trip to the North Riding would be complete without a visit to the most famous inn, Tan Hill, the highest pub in England (1,732 ft.), where he also spent part of his honeymoon. Then follows the descent into the former lead mining valley of Arkengarthdale, and on via the Muker to Reeth road, Muker being one of the most striking of all Swaledale villages. Then the Reeth to Richmond road offers a change of scenery as it passes through Grinton, before the choice of either the lower Swale-side road or the higher road towards Marske, passing the 12th century Priory and the remains of Ellerton Abbey. Richmond is reckoned to be one of the finest examples of any old market town in England although it does not conform to the North Riding style, except for the numerous inns around the market square. Here Alfred recommends the riverside walk to the ruins of Easby Abbey close by, along with a visit to the mansion of Aske Hall just north of the town.

To continue his guide to lower Swaledale, Alfred describes the area Around Catterick,[12] or rather the three 'Cattericks': the attractive old village of Catterick, Catterick Bridge nearby and some way off, the army town of Catterick Camp, and he refers to the ancient Roman Camp of 'Cateractonium' on Swale, which provides the common name and refers to the nearby river feature. Then following a visit to the derelict Hornby Castle nearby, he suggests crossing the river to complete a tour of lower Swaledale.

At Bolton-on-Swale[13] Alfred recalls the life of the Patriarchal Henry Jenkins (1500-1670), reputed to have been the oldest man in England, and just beyond Henry's village, he recommends a stop at Kiplin Hall, home of the first Lord Baltimore, whose son founded the city of Baltimore in Maryland, USA. Alfred's final sortie in lower Swaledale is to Scorton to visit a Catholic Hospital-Monastery, which though forbidding without is a revelation within.[13a] Founded in 1850 by the Order of Hospitaller Brothers of St. John of God, it cares for those with chronic incurable infirmities, yet despite its grim mission it radiates peaceful acceptance among its patients. He is shown round by the Chaplain, Rev. Monsignor Charles Tindall, former head master of St. Bede's RC Grammar School in Bradford, who was also chief celebrant at Alfred's wedding and has been a special guest of the Browns at the Whitfield House Hotel. Unsurprisingly Alfred leaves the hospice with great admiration for the work of the Brothers who devote their lives to the sick and dying and remain dedicated to their vocation.

Moving into Wensleydale,[14] Alfred considers this to be the fair sister of rugged Swaledale and is both scenically and historically, with its Wensleydale Pageantry, one of the most interesting of the great Yorkshire Dales. This spacious dale with good roads lets travellers explore all the main beauty spots and its subsidiary dales. He favours the approach from Swaledale over the Buttertubs Pass, from Thwaite to Hawes, that reveals views of both dales en route. But all roads seem to converge on Hawes and trail over the surrounding hills to join this town, while the main road from here goes on to Bainbridge. To appreciate this landscape, Alfred encourages a walk along the old Cam High Road using the broad green road adapted by the Romans from an older British track, while for the less ambitious he advocates a visit to another striking dales village, Askrigg. Beyond here stands Nappa Hall, the ancestral home of the Metcalfes, where Mary Queen of Scots spent some days during her captivity at nearby Bolton Castle, which Alfred suggests as the starting point for the portion of the tour through Wensleydale that resembles a journey through English history of the period. Visits to the subsidiary dales of Bishopdale and Waldendale are also recommended before going to the village of Wensley, which gives its name to the dale, and continuing to the old market town of Leyburn overlooking the River Ure, passing through Spennythorne, before arriving at Middleham the ancient capital of Wensleydale with its ruined castle. Then after a brief consideration of Coverdale, Alfred returns to the local historical theme and the famous Scropes of Danby, one of the greatest families of Yorkshire and indeed of England who lived at Danby hall, and from here via East Witton to see the ancient Cistercian Abbey of Jervaux, where the monks originated Wensleydale cheese and bred the famous horses.

Alfred comes to the end of his guided tour of Wensleydale proper after passing through the village of Masham, where the scenery changes distinctly even though the River Ure flows on its way for some miles, before he travels to West Tanfield which marks the North Riding boundary. However the route continues with a visit to Snape Castle, sometime home to the last wife of Henry VIII, Catherine Parr, before arriving at the elegant market town of Bedale. Finally Alfred's historical overview is completed by exploring the connections between the villages of Well and Wath with the Neville and Latimer families associated with the former, and Norton and Graham families with the latter, before paying tribute to the great Tudor House of 'Norton Conyers'.

At this point Alfred turns his attention to the old market towns of the Riding, which act as focal points of the countryside and the importance of 'Three Market Towns'[15] as centres which characterise the North Riding rural scene. He summarises the main features of most towns of the district as being built along a broad main street or around a square, lined with solid stone houses, a generous sprinkling of inns, with an ancient church nearby. He also contends that the best place to appraise the character of the North Riding populace is by meeting local people in one of the old inns on the market square especially on market day. Here you can rub shoulders with farmers and townsfolk, and listen to the rich musical rhythm of their folk-speech, especially in three typical market towns, Northallerton, Thirsk and Easingwold.

Part 2. Ryedale

The second part focuses on Ryedale,[16] and Alfred takes the traveller to the 'Heart of the Riding' which he considers to be the richest and most varied countryside in the North Riding. The little River Rye runs through a landscape of deep wooded valleys and hills, with ever-changing moorlands, meandering rivers, little becks and secret dales, together with monastic ruins, ancient churches and picturesque villages, which together he considers as a kind of Yorkshire in miniature.

He advocates Helmsley as the gateway to Ryedale with its vast square, ancient market cross, and the old coaching inn, the Black Swan, where Wordsworth halted on his honeymoon. Three miles south is Rievaulx Abbey, the first large Cistercian Abbey built in England (1131-1175), constructed unusually in a north-south rather than the normal east-west orientation due to the terrain. Six miles away, Byland Abbey may not have the impressive setting of Rievaulx, but it has a beauty of its own, and Alfred relates details of the historic rivalry between the two abbeys.

Among local villages that he contends make an interesting tour, Alfred cites Coxwold as one of the jewels of the North Riding, with its old inn, The Fauconberg Arms, furnished with oak tables and chairs by 'Mouseman' Robert Thompson (1876-1955). While 'Shandy Hall' at the top of the village is where Lawrence Sterne (1713-1768) spent seven years and wrote some of his literary masterpieces. Less than a mile south is Newburgh Priory and nearby the great hillside white horse of Kilburn, where in the village Thompson established his workshop that produced hand-made oak furniture with the iconic mouse emblem on every piece, after his first major commission for the nearby Ampleforth College. The chief glory of Ampleforth village is the Benedictine Ampleforth Abbey and College, which Alfred recommends to those who tire of ruined ecclesiastical sites and wonder what a monastery looked like in its prime.

Alfred's tour then moves deeper into Ryedale via the village of Old Byland following a bye-road that leads into the secluded valley of Caydale or 'Yolassdale', which is flanked by woods that become a paradise of wild flowers in the spring. The route continues to the hill-top village of Hawnby in a unique setting, and beyond to the 17th century Arden Hall built on the site of a Benedictine Nunnery said to have sheltered Mary Queen of Scots on one occasion. To complete the Ryedale village tour Alfred advises taking the 'Sneck Yat' from Hawnby road over the Hambleton Hills to the village of Boltby, and into the heart of the Hambletons, with visits to Morton and Cold Kirby for fine views of the hills and dales of the area prior to exploring the sister dales of Ryedale.

Moving from east to west through The Dales of Ryedale,[17] Bilsdale with the River Seph stretches down from the Cleveland Hills and although a great sprawling dale, is easily seen by road. Riccaldale also begins on the high moors, but becomes a gentle, tree-covered dale lower down, while Bransdale has magnificent moorland scenery at the dale head, before changing into a green dale flanked by moorland ridges. In its lower reaches it continues as 'Sleightholmedale', 'Skiplamdale' and finally Kirkdale, where Hodge Beck leaves the wooded valley at Kirkmoorside. The next parallel dale, Farndale with its pretty River Dove, is most famous for its profusion of wild daffodils in the spring, and is one of the highlights of the Ryedale area. Finally a little further east, Rosedale watered by the River Leven passes through bare, bleak country in its upper reaches before it broadens into a green and fertile valley at the heart of the dale at the village of Rosedale Abbey.

Alfred completes the account of Ryedale Around Kirkbymoorside[18] by reviewing the towns and villages that lie along the southern edge of district, beginning at Kirkbymoorside. Further along the main Pickering to Kirkbymoorside road other villages that make a worthwhile tour include: Cropton, the birthplace of the navigator and Arctic explorer, William Scoresby (1789-1857), Wrelton, Crowthorn, Sinnington and Middleton. Then just north of the main west-east road are examples of other interesting old villages such as: Appleton-le-Moors, Lastingham and Hutton-le-Hole, which is more reminiscent of a Cotswold village, while perched on a ridge is Gillamoor with its 'surprise view' of the valley of the River Dove.

Part 3. The Hambleton Hills

In this part Alfred takes the visitor westward on the Helmsley to Thirsk road and the ridge of the Hambleton Hills, where one of the most spectacular views in Yorkshire is to be seen from the top of Sutton Bank.[19] To the left is Roulston Scar, to the right is the dramatic Whitestonecliff with lake Gormire below. Over the vast plain to the west, the shadowy Pennine hills can be seen from the Bank, and the great panorama unfolds from the River Ouse to the River Tees from the top of the cliff. But at this point he urges the reader to leave the road behind and take the Old Drove Road north towards Yarm, and follow on foot the kind of broad green route that only a true walker dreams about.

Alternatively the tour continues to 'Some Hambleton Villages'[20] situated on the western flanks of the Hambletons in the Vale of Mowbray, with an approach from Thirsk by the main Helmsley road, for fine views of the Hambletons. These include: Sutton-under-Whitestonecliff, Felixkirk, Boltby, Kirkby Knowle, Cowesby Kepwith, Nether Silton, Over Silton and Osmotherley, with others that have an almost musical sound: Thirlby, Thimbleby and Thirkelby. From the hill village of Osmotherley Alfred prefers the steep road over Snilesworth Moor for views of the surrounding countryside, and he also recommends the road from Osmotherley to Hawnby-in-Ryedale for views of the scenery of the 'Snilesworth Country'. An additional route visits Mount Grace Priory to view the most complete example of a Carthusian Order Charterhouse in the country containing the 'cells' where isolated monks once lived in silent prayer and contemplation.

Close by this relic of religious reflection Alfred carried out some contemplative cogitation of his own, when stranded one cold winter's night while preparing this book. The Tontine Cleveland Inn near the Priory gave him much needed shelter and sustenance, and stimulated the survey of Some North Riding Inns and Hotels for inclusion in the text. Alfred then reflects on these examples of numerous old coaching inns that serve the modern traveller, and also notes many hostelries off the main roads that provide traditional Yorkshire hospitality to the travelling public.[20a]

Part 4. The Plain of York and the Howardian Hills

This part covers the Southern North Riding[21] which Alfred describes as being shaped like an inverted triangle with York at its upturned apex, and Easingwold and Malton at the west and east points respectively. It is comprised of part of the plain of York and the Howardian Hills, and although it is not as spectacular as other hill regions, it is of historical interest with many notable views and villages. While The Plain is flat and does not impress Alfred, he acknowledges that the area has some of the best farming country of the Riding with fields and pastures bounded by trees, as well as gracious halls and manor houses. One break in these flatlands is the hilltop village of Crake, where the body of St. Cuthbert may have rested during his monks' long flight from the Viking invaders. Further eastwards across the plain, Sherriff Hutton is noted for its ruined castle, one of Yorkshire's strongholds associated with many confrontations in the Wars of the Roses.

Rising from the plain in its northerly aspect, the rolling country of the Howardian Hills contains the great park of Castle Howard, one of the great 18th century treasures of Yorkshire and one of the stateliest homes in England. Across the park is the never-completed castle in the 'street' village of Slingsby, which together with the other 'street' villages of Barton-le-Street and Appleton-le-Street afford fine views over the Howardian Hills.[21a] Beyond Slingsby and a further 'street' village of Hovingham is Hovingham Hall, another of Yorkshire's famous houses with its renowned Riding School and within its grounds one of the finest cricket fields in the country.

Next on Alfred's route, on the coast road to Scarborough, the town of Malton,[22] both 'Old' and 'New' Malton, lie on the banks of the River Derwent, the boundary of the East Riding, and mark the gateway to the Yorkshire Wolds to the south. This country opens out to reveal views of the Howardian Hills to the left and the Yorkshire Wolds to the right, with the river and Kirkham Abbey deep below. He indicates the importance of Malton's position as an agricultural centre that serves all three Ridings and although it may not be picturesque, he suggests that it has an honest, hard working look about it, and is often full of farmers and racing men from the famous Malton Stables, and was famous for the old brewery that once produced fine ales.

To complete the account of the area Alfred notes that Pickering,[23] which lies eight flat miles beyond Malton, is unique among the market towns of the North Riding towns and indeed of Yorkshire. It is full of narrow streets and odd corners, and cut in two by the railway and the beck, but it is the higgledy-piggledy arrangement that gives the town its distinct character. Its chief attractions are the rugged, battlemented exterior with a spired church, and its ruined hilltop Norman castle which was besieged and badly damaged by the Roundheads during the English Civil War. It was also the home of many famous men including: Dr. John L. Kirk, the country doctor and antiquarian, Mr. Austin Hyde, the Yorkshire dialect poet and John Castillo, the Cleveland poet.

Part 5. The Goathland Country and the North East Moors

In this part Alfred describes the scenery from Pickering to Whitby,[24] especially the views on the Moorland Road of 21 miles, as one of the most spectacular areas of the North Riding, with Fylingdales Moor on one side and Goathland Moors of the other. This journey offers magnificent views above Saltersgate, on the edge of the Ice Age gouged deep ravine of the Hole of Horcum, a green oasis in the midst of the wild moorlands around. The route also affords views of Newtondale to the west, the wooded valley of Littlebeck to the east, along with a stretch of coastline to the north and south of Whitby, while the Pickering to Whitby railway runs through Newtondale, one of the most picturesque in the country. Halfway along this road, the old fish track to Robin Hood's Bay cuts across the moors towards Lilla Cross on Lilla Howe, the oldest stone cross in the Riding. Of the many old tracks in this region Alfred again encourages following one on foot from Saltersgate to Hackness, which dips down into the hidden valley of Langdale beneath the curiously pudding-shaped hill of Blakey Topping. Another recommended dale is Staintondale, which also lies just off the Pickering-Whitby road, and extends into the secluded valley of Dovedale Griff, a tiny offshoot enclosed by moorland riggs, dominated by the gaunt High Bridestones, and one of several 'Dovedales' known locally as the 'Doodle'.

To the west of the main road about 9 miles south of Whitby is the village of Goathland,[25] close to Darnholm, where Alfred was living when he wrote most of the book. Alfred describes how Goathland changed from a quiet North Riding village to a popular Moorland Spa with hotels and boarding houses, although farming is still the main occupation. It is surrounded by moorlands with wooded valleys, watered by streams broken by waterfalls, and displays fine landscape colours in the late autumn. He indicates that it is also an anomalous Yorkshire village that belongs to the Duchy of Lancaster with Crown Property moorlands and farms, and is one of the few places with Sword Dancers and 'Plough Stots', as well as the famous Goathland Hunt with one of the oldest packs in the country.

Goathland also lies on a section of the North York Moors railway between Pickering and Whitby that once included an Incline Railway between Beckhole and Goathland. The earliest railway coaches were drawn by horses, except on the steep hill between these locations, where they were hauled by a rope counterbalanced by a four ton water tank, but this was abandoned after a serious accident in 1864 and an alternative route was devised. Today the old route offers a pleasant valley walk along the abandoned railway, and Alfred entices the reader to sample this and other gentle walks around Goathland to the waterfalls of Mallyan Spout, Nelly Ayre and Keld Scar Foss. Whereas he proposes the challenge of more demanding walking country found on encircling Moors that often display Bronze Age howes and barrows, along with the preserved stretch of Roman road on Wheeldale moor. Alternatively the nearby hamlet of Beck Hole remains a quiet moorland valley gem, consisting of a few cottages with the tiny inn of Birch Hall, and retains the old custom of playing Quoits on the green. But it is the walks Around Beck Hole that inspire Alfred, especially the number of green tracks, ancient monk 'trods' or pack horse trails that cross the unforgiving moors in all directions.

Before leaving this area, Alfred devotes a small chapter to The Lost Valley of Littlebeck[26] and describes separate approaches for the walker and the motorist into this most secluded valley of all. It is flanked by precipitous wooded slopes and has one of the loveliest waterfalls in this land of waterfalls, the Falling Foss. At the head of the valley the hamlet of Littlebeck has a few cottages and farm houses, with a small chapel, but seems to have little communication with the outside world. But this 'lost valley' is full of strange stories and odd goings-on, such as the 82 year old, Nicholas Postgate (1597-1679), who was executed for baptising a local infant, while the informer, John Reeves, drowned himself in a fit of remorse in the beck at 'Devil's Hole', which remains cursed with no fish caught there ever since. On a happier note Alfred notes that this sleepy-looking hamlet contains the workshop of his close friend and traditional oak woodcarver, Thomas E. Whittaker (1910-1981).

At this point Alfred's description of the North Riding deviates somewhat with a description of the North Yorkshire State Forests.[27,27a] He elaborates on the conflicting opinions about the intrusion of state forests into the landscape, but concedes that in the vast county of Yorkshire many of the older forests have been denuded of trees during two world wars. Hence he advocates that there is room for these developments if they are carefully managed. Concerns were expressed about smaller dales but in such places most farms and grazing lands have been left undisturbed, with only the upper slopes planted, which were largely non-productive lean moorland or rough marginal land. But on the vexed question of conifers versus hardwoods, he points out that the moors only produce carefully selected conifers, while hardwoods are grown in the more sheltered valleys and lower slopes.

In a return to the main theme, Alfred highlights the motorists' drive along the Pickering-Scarborough Road,[28] which passes through several pleasant villages and provides striking views of the hills to the north and the Wolds to the south. Beyond Pickering, Thornton Dale is considered to be one of Yorkshire's prettiest villages with cottages and a beck that run parallel to the main street, while the attractive villages of Allerston and Ebberston are just off the main road, before reaching Stainton. Next, Brompton interests tourists, since Wordsworth courted his future wife Mary Hutchinson at Gallows farm and they were married in the church in 1802. The continuing road bypasses Hutton Buschel, but worth a detour, before going on to East and West Ayton and across the Forge valley to the upper Derwent country, where the road forks towards the nearby coast.

In another aside, Alfred notes just one of The Old Squires[29] that Yorkshire produced, a unique character who became the most famous Sporting Squire in England, George Osbaldeston, of Hutton Buschel (1786-1866). He excelled at all forms of sport, but cricket was his passion, and he was the first of the great Yorkshire cricketers to foster the game nationally. He was also a top tennis player, a first class marksman, a dead shot with a duelling pistol and equally handy with his 'daddles' in any fisticuffs. His posthumously discovered autobiography is more exciting and amusing than many thrillers, with tales of prodigious feats of strength, wagers, duels, jests, amours, prize-fights, hunts, quarrels, lawsuits and racing triumphs and disasters. Alfred intimates that no one enjoyed life more than '*T'owd Squire*', as he was known, and was arguably one of the finest and loveable sports icons that Yorkshire ever produced.

Part 6. The Cleveland Country

In this section Alfred contends that Cleveland[30] extends far beyond the range of hills and includes the flat country south of the River Tees and the north-east moors. He intimates that it is a kingdom within a kingdom, and although integrated with the Riding, it is a self-contained community with strong traditions and customs of its own. In view of its richness and variety, he finds it impossible to do full justice to it, and instead provides only personal impressions and suggests ways of exploring the district.

He divides Cleveland into two parts: rural Cleveland with Stokesley at its centre, and ironstone Cleveland around Guisborough and Middlesbrough, but since the latter is only important from an industrial perspective, it is of little interest to the tourist. The 'other' Cleveland, the country of hills and dales, market towns and villages and hill sheep farms as well as its lore and legends thus becomes the focus. To see Cleveland Hills in perspective, Alfred suggests travelling along the northern fringe where the chain of hills ends and plunges down to the plain that stretches to the Tees. The Hills are much bleaker than others with 'rigg' roads over the fells and ridges, with moors that are tinged with a melancholy that numerous ancient howes emphasise. The 21 mile long Whitby-Guisborough Road that cuts across the northern tip of the Cleveland Moors reveals something of this wild unforgiving landscape with scarcely a village, and it contrasts markedly with the scenic moorland road from Whitby to Pickering.

Alfred maintains that the Cleveland country cannot be fully understood without recognising the strange quality of mystery imbedded in the remote valleys and high moors such as Baysdale, Westerdale, Kildale and the Danby Moors which all reveal aspects of the Cleveland Superstitions. These lonely moors have spawned powerful dialect poems such as 'The Cleveland Lyke Wake Dirge' and 'A Dree Neet', which allude to the transport of a corpse over the moors for burial and passing from life to the 'other side' respectively. The home of witchcraft was the North Riding, especially in Cleveland, which was well known for tales of witches and sorcerers, familiars and wisemen, as well as hobs, boggarts and fairies. The area was full of superstitions and traditions associated with these malevolent and mischievous spirits that still linger on, but beneath these dispositions there was also deep religious belief that found expression in folk songs and dialect poems. While a less daunting symbol of the area is that of the Cleveland Bay horse, a pure-bred farm animal but now mainly valued for exhibition roles.

The two prominent townships feature in Alfred's tour. Stokesley, (pronounced 'Stowlsa'), is the administrative centre of west Cleveland, and many roads converge on this market town with the little River Leven hidden behind the façade of shops and Georgian houses. The nearby town of Great Ayton with the Leven flowing through it is quieter but has an impressive setting under the Cleveland Hills with the peak of Roseberry Topping in the background. The town also contains the little school attended by the great navigator and explorer, Captain James Cook (1728-1779), but the cottage where he lived was dismantled and rebuilt in Australia, an act which Alfred regards as unforgivable civic vandalism! Other 'Cleveland Villages'[31] are noted including Carlton-in-Cleveland off the main Stokesley-Thirsk road in the foothills of the 'Cleveland Chain', and leaving the village two interesting routes are recommended: one over the Cleveland Hills to Chop Gate (pronounced 'Yat') in Bilsdale with impressive views of the hills and the plain, the other via Faceby to the valley of Scugdale. Meanwhile the Three Ingleby Villages: Ingleby Arncliffe, Ingleby Cross and Ingleby Greenhow on the main Stokesley road have some of the finest scenery in the Clevelands. But Alfred is not impressed by an Ancient Church that always appears locked, so he can only gain entry after searching for the elusive key holder of Locked Churches and even then he is regarded with suspicion for wanting an out of service hours visit.

After this grumble Alfred recommends Roseberry Topping and Guisborough[32] by taking the Great Ayton to Guisborough road which allows close views of Roseberry Topping, Easby Hall and Cook's Monument. While the view after a walk to the monument is impressive, he favours the one from the summit of the peculiar sugar loaf-shaped hill of Roseberry Topping (1,057 ft.), isolated on the fringe of the Cleveland Hills, which makes it conspicuous from all over north-east Yorkshire. He also intimates that there is something peculiarly 'Cleveland' about this strange peak, since it figures in so many old legends and seems to express the very spirit of this mysterious part of the world. Then after such topographical delights he implies that Gisborough is an anticlimax, even though it was once the capital of Cleveland.

The tour then moves around the northern perimeter of the Cleveland Hills south of Redcar to Kirkleatham and Upleatham.[33] The former was once a remarkable village, but sadly without much of its former glory it now stands like a memorial to a vanished age. A few miles south Upleatham is distinguished by one of the tiniest churches in England and a remnant of the 12th century original. While nearby Skelton-in-Cleveland is perhaps worth a visit for Skelton Castle, a rebuilt 18th century edifice surrounded by extensive parkland. In contrast Alfred encourages viewing the delights of Eskdale[34] by following the Esk which rises in Westerdale and flows through the dale to the coast at Whitby, even though the river is often hidden deep in the valley. He recommends the route from Whitby to Ruswarp and Sleights, and along Eskdale to Grosmont and Egton Bridge, before continuing over the hill to Lealholm, Danby, Castleton, Westerdale and on to Commondale. But he acknowledges that even this tour misses many of the highlights of Eskdale which can only be seen on foot.

Further along Eskdale the village of Danby-in-Cleveland allows another foray into the hills via the twisting road to Castleton, Westerdale and the wild moors beyond. It was in the parish of Danby that the famous 'Walking Canon' John Christopher Atkinson (1814-1900) ministered for 53 years and wrote the classic book about the history and folklore of the dale: 'Forty Years in a Moorland Parish'. Two miles beyond Danby, Castleton is also surrounded by magnificent scenery with challenging roads that climb over the moors northwards to Commondale, and southwards to Westerdale and Bilsdale. A further recommended route is from Castleton over Castleton Rigg to Ralph Cross, one of the roads that cuts across the high moors and commands panoramic views of the surrounding dales and moors. Then on the subject of Stone Crosses Alfred provides a discourse on these ancient monuments which are such a notable feature of the north-east Yorkshire moors, as are the numerous howes or barrows. The crosses often stand on a moor near a howe, sited on high ground, usually on an old track or near a junction of several old paths, and some of their many functions were to guide wayfarers over the moors, bless the journey of travellers and to foster the Christian faith during the Dark Ages.

Rural activities have been mentioned by Alfred throughout the book and now he focuses on North Yorkshire Sheep Farms,[35] which are small with only about 50-60 acres of mixed land, but the right of 'stray' over many more acres of moorland which is used to graze mainly Blackface sheep. They are 'heafed' or bred to the moors and spend their lives on the bleak uplands except for lambing, shearing, dipping or during severe snowstorms, when they are brought down. When farms change hands the flock remains on the moors and passes to the new owner, with each farmer having his own 'stint' or 'stray' that is covered on foot, and the sheep recognise the 'stint' instinctively and rarely wander beyond their boundaries. Sheep are integral to the moors and are as hardy as any animal, like the farmers who work from dawn to dusk, and often longer in some of the worst wintry weather, to feed their stock, Alfred expresses his admiration for this remarkable breed of men who keep their flocks for meagre return but great personal reward.

Finally while Alfred also makes reference to villages in the book, he now chooses two examples of individuals who play key roles in 'Village Life',[36] namely the doctor and the parson. Notwithstanding the changes after the NHS came about, in some areas of the Riding the doctor's practice still extends over miles of countryside, and in addition to towns and villages, he has to serve scattered hamlets and isolated farms. Apart from the arduous round of visits, the doctor is liable to be called out at any hour of day or night to attend a patient in all seasons, and in Alfred's view no praise can be too high for the difficult work of these dedicated professionals, like his own GP, Dr. John English. Alternatively he suggests that the rural parson has a more crucial role than his urban counterpart, and is expected to be at the call of parishioners throughout the week for many social services that play a bigger part in village communities than in towns. He acts as friend and counsellor for personal problems and times of difficulty, and officiates at the formal wedding and funeral and a range of other services which are more solemn and intimate occasions than their equivalent urban ceremonies. If an incumbent at one of many ancient churches, he also has to be an authority on the history and architecture of the building, the archeology of the district and be able to answer almost any question from visitors to his parish. Alfred acknowledges his debt of gratitude to these men of the cloth from whom he received much help whilst gathering information for the book.

Part 7. Towards the Coast

In the final part Alfred's tour follows a route along the North Riding's Yorkshire coast beginning just inland from the Whitby-Scarborough road at Harwood-dale,[37] where he stayed at a cottage on the small-holding of Bumble Bee Hole while he was drafting the manuscript for the book. But much has changed since he first stumbled into this unsullied paradise of miniature dales, deep-set valleys, 'lost' villages and moorland becks. The War Department has acquired the Fylingdales Moor and the noise of the army firing range disturbs the peace and tranquility of the place. The Forestry Commission is also planting swathes of saplings cutting across strips of moorland, however Harwood-dale has retained much of its essential beauty, with the moors bearing the brunt of the invasion by the military. To avoid this turmoil Alfred advises the visitor to move down the dale to the 'Whisper Dales' around Hackness, and explore these miniature dales on foot. From Hackness he recommends the minor road over the heights of Silpho and Broxa, and on through the Forge Valley to Ayton and Scarborough with a stop in Langdale End. He reminds the visitor that this is walking country and in order to appreciate it best it is necessary to walk over the steep ridges and follow the wild moorland streams to the heart of these hills and dales.

Before starting the coast tour proper, Alfred apologetically offers an account of the once important industrial city of Middlesbrough,[38] which rose from an obscure village on the mudflats of the Tees estuary in 1805, to become one of the great iron and steel cities of the world. Indeed it may have remained just a name on the river bank, if the right men had not appeared at the right time, and developed a range of industries from iron and steel production, machinery manufacture, bridge building, chemicals, ship building and other support industries, along with an important sea port. However since this is not the remit of the book, he advises journeying from north to south along 'The Yorkshire Coast',[39] which visits twelve towns that have become popular holiday resorts. However he suggests that the only way to see the coast properly is to walk along the cliffs and seashore, since the 'coast road' often deviates inland and misses many spectacular features, although he offers short-cuts off the main road to see the most interesting places en route.

The popular part of the coast begins at Redcar which is a playground for Teesside, and features the long promenade and a stretch of magnificent sands that are typical of this coastline. A little further south Saltburn-by-the-Sea occupies a dominant position on a high terrace above the shore with a 5 miles stretch of sands and the Cleveland Hills beyond which makes a fine backcloth to this dignified resort. Then following the twisty road to Skinningrove and its harbour, the route allows an easy walk to Boulby Cliff (666 ft.) and magnificent sea views. The coastal scenery gets even better with the approach to Staithes (pronounced 'Steers') where the old fishing village lies far below between cliffs in a narrow coomb. The steep main street plunges down to the sea with little stone houses huddled on either side, while at the foot of the hill is the Cod and Lobster Inn, with an incomparable harbour wall sea front and great towering cliffs all around. Alfred then recommends a visit to the deserted harbour of Port Mulgrave for an entrancing view from a cliff path vantage point as good as any on this coast, while a quiet bay provides a place of solitude.

Continuing down the 'coast road' Alfred endorses Runswick Bay as the perfect place for a picnic with a great arc of sea far below the village and cliffs to the north and south culminating in the headland of Kettleness. Runswick has been transformed from an old fishing village into a holiday resort with special appeal for children, and further along the coast at another isolated village of Kettleness, impressive views of

Runswick Bay can be seen from the headland. Then he proceeds to Sandsend, another small resort built around an old village, towards Lythe and Mulgrave Castle, which together with other villages en route provide an interesting end to this part of the tour of the coastal countryside.

Now the traveller is recommended to join the main road again and to enter Whitby from the West Cliff high above the sea. At the far end stands a fine statue of Captain Cook gazing over Old Whitby and the sea, while just around the corner of 'Khyber Pass' the best view of the old town and its harbour is seen, with red pantile-roofed houses huddled together against the background of the East Cliff and the estuary of the River Esk in between. There is also Georgian Whitby to be seen, with its terraced houses built when the old ship owners, bankers and sea captains spent part of their fortunes on fine properties by the sea. But the outstanding feature of Whitby is the Abbey, as Alfred contends: 'The Abbey is Whitby: certainly it makes Whitby what it is, for, wherever one turns, the ruined Abbey dominates the scene'. However he considers the real charm of Whitby to be the friendliness of the close knit local community, and when its quaint streets are invaded by visitors wearing strange 'Gothic' costumes, it still preserves its characteristic dignity and charm.

South of Whitby the road leads to Robin Hood's Bay where a steep road drops down to the old village, once a secluded fishing hamlet, which is a medley of cottages, shops, inns and cafés, and much favoured by artists. Although it resembles Staithes and Runswick it is more compact, hemmed in and rugged, every nook and cranny on the cliffs is built upon. On leaving the 'Bay' Alfred once more indulges in a favourite topic with an appreciation of The Flask and The Falcon Inns on the way to Scarborough, although he names another 90 in the North Riding as worth a visit! Three twisting miles south, the cliff top village of Ravenscar overlooks the great sweep of Robin Hood's Bay, but the best view is from the Raven Hotel, which stands atop the impressive rugged Scar that soars 600 ft. out of the sea. Pressing on southwards, the village of Staintondale reveals the distant white cliffs of Flamborough Head, passing Hayburn Wyke to approach Scarborough from the North Bay foreshore, and along marine Drive with the great cliff of Scarborough Castle on the headland. At the end of the beach area the splendid Spa and Grand Hotel are seen, before turning towards the Valley Gardens and the dignified Crescent and the Esplanade, from where the most striking view of the fine old castle can be had. While Scarborough may not be the exclusive resort it was during its heyday, Alfred maintains that there is still an air about this popular resort that distinguishes it from other similar holiday townships, and it is often still called 'The Queen of the Watering Places' because of the historic

Spa waters.

The tour of this part of the coast ends at Filey, which marks the boundary of the North and East Ridings of Yorkshire, and this old Victorian resort is located on a sweep of the perfect arc of Filey Bay, with the Brigg to the north and Flamborough Head to the south. Filey may be less impressive than Scarborough, but with its seven miles long sandy beach, it was once the most exclusive of all holiday resorts on this coastline. Finally Alfred sums up his personal feelings for this extensive tour of the Fair North Riding:

> So much – or so little – about this fair Riding. There is much else I should like to have said about its people, its customs and its beauties; but my space is exhausted while the country itself is inexhaustible. But perhaps I have said enough to send some reader off on his own pilgrimage of discovery – and that is the only way to appreciate this rich and fair North Riding ... Good Luck – and God-speed![40]

Impact of the Book

The book received widespread reviews, particularly in the north regional press, and especially in the Yorkshire-based newspapers and magazines such as: the *Yorkshire Gazette*, the *Yorkshire Evening Gazette*, the *Yorkshire Post*, the *Yorkshire Herald*, the *Northern Echo*, the *York Star*, the *Beverley Guardian*, and the *Sheffield Telegraph*,[5] along with the following positive acknowledgements about its merits:

> 'Mr. Brown unerringly picks out the heart of the Riding... the importance of the book, quite apart from its charm, will be heightened by the designation of 600 square miles of the Riding as a National Park.' – *Yorkshire Evening Post*

> 'Mr. Brown knows how much, and how little, to tell us, which is what a good topographical writer ought to do... he has the eye for the past, an appreciation of the good inn, the lovely church, the stately hall... and a downright loathing for the Planners.' – *Yorkshire Observer*

> 'The value of the book can scarcely be over estimated... more than a guide book, it is the epitome of the County written by a shrewd pen.' – *Whitby Gazette*

> 'The best book yet on the North Riding... it is likely to become a standard work.' – *Malton Gazette*

In addition to these brief press opinions there was a particularly rigorous and detailed review which appeared in the leading *Catholic Yorkshire Monthly* Magazine:

> This review should, in theory, be either a complete failure or nothing less than perfect, for it is an attempt by a native of the East Riding, to criticise a book on the North Riding, by an author of the West Riding! ...he has also tramped the North Riding many times and has frequently written of it *passim* in his books for hikers and tourists...

> This book on the North Riding is by one who cannot even by a few year's residence claim to be one of us. We who have spent most of our adult years in the North Riding have a deep resentment of the fact that most Englishmen think that the West Riding is Yorkshire... How we glow with indignation when the Editor of a West Riding magazine calls it 'The Yorkshire Catholic Weekly'. How unbearable is it when the same Editor asks one to review thirty-two chapters in which a West Riding author explains our scenery on our behalf. And how indescribably painful is it to discover that the chapters are not such that one can tear to pieces but must truthfully declare to be very good indeed.

> With considerable ill-temper, therefore, one read Mr. Brown's latest book... with a feeling of rare virtue one has decided to be honest and call it excellent. It parcels the North Riding into seven sections, such as Teesdale or the Hambleton Hills, and we are allowed to ramble round each section at leisure. There is no straining of lungs, nor stretching of muscles to complete a day's walking. We may take our time; we pause to walk round a church, or watch a quoits match in the cool of the evening. Occasionally we take a whole afternoon off, to lie peacefully in the sun and listen to Mr. Brown talking to us about the Old Squires, or the venerable ancient, Henry Jenkins. Even for those of us who know this Riding and love it, there is much pleasure in being in the company of a writer who discourses agreeably and never forces the pace.

> It would be possible, of course, to make a list of grumbles about things the author has omitted or to administer a series of pats-on-the-back for points which pleased us... again Mr. Brown gives to ale-drinking a semi-sacramental value... Admittedly there were years when Catholic writers made frequent tankard raising a test on one's orthodoxy or moral soundness, but surely this is an out-dated survival of an unfortunate adjunct of the Belloc cult.

It happens that this notice is being written after a four hours' tour through Ryedale and Bilsdale. Many of one's companions saw this glorious countryside for the first time; others went through it nostalgically. When we returned to the picturesque High Street of Yarm, not a few asked for another, more leisurely outing. One was happy to say, 'Tomorrow go along to your bookseller or lending library, and bring home a copy of Fair North Riding. Tell your friends to read it. You'll get hours of enjoyment out of it, and its photographs are really magnificent. Now I am going home to read the book again. Good-night.'

– Reverend David Quinlan[41]

In another National Catholic newspaper, the book received a further extremely favourable review in the arts and literature section:

Those who found pleasure in the author's previous books on Yorkshire may confidently expect some enjoyable hours awaiting them in turning the pages of his new book, and they certainly will not be disappointed. In it he takes us pleasantly and easily through the North Riding – the real Yorkshire, whose fair countryside is unspoilt by mountainous piles of slag and pit detritus or by wens of roofs and chimneys, and whose people are Yorkshiremen of John Browdie's type, lacking the aggressive stridency of their more southern kinsmen.

It is a land of moor and dale, and the author's knowledge of the moorland tracks and his love of the land is apparent on every page. The feudal market town of Thirsk, with its sixteen inns around the square; the Cleveland moors, where witches and warlocks were still flourishing little more than a generation ago; the stone crosses beside the moorland pathways, erected by contemporaries and successors of St. Aidan and used as churches; the village life, the upland sheep-farms, the rural postmen, the forestry workers in the State forests, the lifeboatmen on the rocky coast are but few of the interwoven aspects of life and landscape he touches upon.

Perhaps the greatest interest of the book lies in the author's almost casual introduction of anecdotes of the history or traditions of inn, abbey or local celebrity. At Bowes, for instance, he spent the night at 'Dotheboys Hall – Original Proprietor Wackford Squeers' now a transport café and hotel. At Rievaulx he recalls how St. Aelred, when a young novice, stayed a panic on the outbreak of a fire in the refectory by seizing a great flagon of ale and extinguishing the flames with its contents. One of the best stories is that of an old woman in Littlebeck who, when gold was rising in price during the last war, agreed to sell her hoard of golden sovereigns which, with superb understatement, she described as '*twoathri*'.

A delightful book, finely illustrated and produced in the high standards usual to Country Life Publications.

– J.C. Marsh-Edward[42]

On a personal level Alfred confided that the press reviews of the book were mixed and fewer than his previous books,[5] and in his opinion not as good as usual with a few exceptions that he noted including the *Yorkshire Herald* and the *Malton Gazette* which gave a splendid review, and the *Yorkshire Observer* and *Yorkshire Evening Post* were in his view both excellent. On the other hand he felt the *Yorkshire Post* was patronising and critical of minor points, and he believed that the reviewer had not read the book thoroughly, like so many of the reviewers of that time. Nevertheless he acknowledged that Country Life seemed satisfied with the press responses and planned a special promotional campaign in order to promote the book.[4]

Outcomes of the Book

Country Life were very keen to get as much exposure for the book as possible to promote sales, and to this end a comprehensive list of some 40 national newspapers and magazines had been sent review copies of the book to coincide with the publication date of 30th July 1952.[5] In addition a further 24 North of England and Yorkshire-based newspapers and magazines were also targeted with review copies,[5] and Alfred was encouraged to arrange for personal appearances at some of the larger bookshops in Yorkshire in order to sign copies of the book, to which Alfred responded by making calls on some of the booksellers in the region notably in Bradford, Leeds and York.[5]

Furthermore, as planned, Country Life had put together a short descriptive promotional leaflet from reviews gained and distributed these widely to encourage sales.[5] At first Alfred was not keen on this idea and was opposed to what he considered to be this modern vulgar style of cheap publicity, but he admitted that it was inevitable and certainly cheaper than advertising in the press which Country Life never did in any significant quantity, and he was also reluctant about the attractive window displays provided in bookshops which he found embarrassing when he walked past.[5] However he was persuaded to go along with these initiatives and had a close hand in the preparation of the biographical and review material for inclusion in the final promotional leaflets before their distribution.[5]

Soon afterwards a supply of these leaflets was sent to Alfred for his personal use, together with the note on their mass distribution that included: 12,000 inserted into the magazine *Ramblers' News*, 1,200 for insertion into the Association of Yorkshire Bookmen's Broadsheet, 1,200 to the Society of Yorkshiremen in London for distribution among members as well as to another 37 various associated Societies of Yorkshire.[5] Copies were also sent to the Fell Walkers Association and the Fellowship of Fell Walkers, and further copies to all the places mentioned in the book including hotels, inns, village halls etc.[5]

Naturally Alfred responded with great appreciation for the excellent work regarding these promotional leaflets and hoped they would promote sales.[5] He also indicated that the editor of the *Yorkshire Dalesman* Magazine had suggested that an advertisement would be inserted into the magazine which then had a monthly circulation of over 20,000.[5] Country Life responded immediately to confirm these arrangements, since there was some disappointment that despite all the efforts to date, the sales of the book had only been about 2,000 copies, although this may have been due to the current surfeit of Yorkshire books that were then on the market.[5]

The sales situation had not improved much towards the end of the year with the plethora of Yorkshire books published in the lead-up to Christmas and end of year sales, and it became increasingly difficult to advertise and promote the book, even in local press outlets such as the Yorkshire Post's special 'Christmas Book Number', which was unable to take further advertisements.[5] As a result it was increasingly likely that although 3,000 copies might be sold by the end of 1952, out of a total of 5,000 printed copies, there was no evidence that there would be a demand to warrant a further print run, nor that of a second edition in the foreseeable future.[5]

In the new year Alfred suggested the possibility of selling a cheaper version of the book, but this was not considered since it was no longer possible to produce 'cheap editions',[43] although as sales dwindled it was suggested to Alfred that it might help to clear stocks if the price of the book was reduced from 21 shillings to 10 shillings and 6 pence to which Alfred readily agreed.[43] Even then sales remained slow over the next few years and totalled no more than 350-450 per year until 1957 when the book was finally withdrawn after selling approximately 5,000 copies,[43] which was as good as most of Alfred's earlier books except *Striding Through Yorkshire* which sold over 20,000 copies over four editions between 1938-1949.

Moreover Alfred's 20 year long and reasonably successful association with Country Life came to an end the following year when Frank Whitaker announced he was to relinquish the editorship of the book company, to which Alfred responded with grati-tude and appreciation for all the help and support he had received from him over the years.[43] In an honest Yorkshireman's reply, Frank indicated that nothwithstanding all their 'ups and downs' in the past, he was glad that even during difficult circumstances, there was a feeling of friendship that had endured above all, and he hoped to meet Alfred again during a visit to his home town of Keighley, whence they might walk together in their native land.[43]

The Lack of Appeal of the Book?

Unlike his former hotel books which generated scores of fan mail letters, *Fair North Riding* produced only a handful of responses from the general public, although in every case readers wrote about how much they enjoyed his latest book, and in most instances Alfred wrote thanking them for their kind words.[44] Even one from a native of the North Riding who pointed out the glaring 'blunder' of a photographic mistake, still recorded the pleasure from reading the book, and Alfred replied to assure him that the error was acknowledged and that erratum slips had been inserted into every copy.[44]

The general lack of appeal of the book, as evidenced by an unusually low fan mail response, does not explain the relatively low sales figures and prompts the question – what went wrong? The book had potentially promised so much but it seemed to slip away into relative oblivion. This time it could not be blamed on parsimony on behalf his publishers, since unlike Williams & Norgate's ambivalent attempts to promote the hotel books, Country Life had done their best to promote, advertise and distribute the book widely, but perhaps not with the same vigour as some of their competitors. In this regard there had been intense competition from other authors and publishers in the so-called 'Yorkshire' market with the growth of the successful regional series of books, such as the 'County Book Series' by Robert Hale publishers of London.

There was also the possibility that other influences could have been factors in the book's lack of success, such as the rapidly changing interests of the reading public of the early 1950s, even among Alfred's former long-standing loyal readership who may have moved on from this broad topographical approach, albeit a modified one that Alfred used in Fair North Riding. Moreover there were dramatic changes in the type of popular literature available at this time with the growth of new types of novel aimed particularly at the younger end of the market whose interests were also changing rap-idly with the times.

Finally maybe Alfred had misjudged the changing reading interests of the general population, or had begun to lose his affinity for writing, and perhaps even lost belief in himself as a writer, during a period when he struggled to come to terms with his rapidly changing personal circumstances and those of his family. After his apparent success as a 'literary innkeeper', what was there now to look forward to concerning his future as a writer? It was clearly a time for making the decision about whether to try to become the full-time writer that he had always wanted to be, or to revert to the safer but still insecure career of his former business years.

References and Notes

1. Alfred J. Brown, *Fair North Riding*, Country Life Ltd., London, 1952.
   1a. Note: The West Yorkshire Archive Service, Bradford Central Library, Catalogue 69D90, Section 3, Items 3.5.1-3.5.3, Draft manuscripts.

2. Alfred John Brown, Journal, 1948-1950, passim.

3. Memorandum of Agreement between Alfred John Brown and Francis Whitaker, Country Life Ltd., London, 9th November 1949, AJB Literary Agreements File, 1925-1959.

4. Alfred John Brown, Journal, 1950-1954, passim.

5. AJB/Country Life Correspondence File, 1950-1952, passim.

6. Op. cit., AJB, Acknowledgements, p. 10.

7. Op. cit., AJB, Foreword, pp. 11-13.

   1. THE DALES.

8. Op. cit., AJB, Chapter 1: Teesdale; Border River – Bowes – High Tees, pp. 15-30.

9. Op.cit., AJB, Chapter 2: Yarm, pp. 28-30.

10. Op. cit., AJB, Chapter 3: Croft and Lewis Carroll, pp. 31-32.

11. Op. cit., AJB, Chapter 4: Swaledale; High Swale – Keld – Thwaite – Tan Hill – Arkengarthdale – Muker to Reeth – Reeth to Richmond – Richmond – Easby Abbey – Aske Hall, pp. 33-41.

12. Op. cit., AJB, Chapter 5: Around Catterick; Catterick Bridge – Catterick Camp – Hornby Castle, pp. 42-44.

13. Op. cit., AJB, Chapter 6: Bolton-upon-Swale; Patriarchal Henry Jenkins – Kiplin Hall – Scorton, pp. 45-48.
    13a. Note: The hospital care services transferred to Bowood Care in 2004 and the brothers relocated to Richmond.

14. Op cit., AJB, Chapter 7: Wensleydale; Wensleydale Pageantry – Hawes – Bainbridge and Askrigg – Nappa – Bolton Castle – Bishopdale and Waldendale – Wensley – Leyburn – Spennithorne – Middleham – The Scropes of Danby – East Witton and Jervaulx – Masham – West Tanfield – Snape Castle – Bedale – Well and Wath – Norton Conyers, pp. 49-62.

15. Op. cit., AJB, Chapter 8: Three Market Towns; Northallerton – Thirsk – Easingwold, pp. 63-70.

2. RYEDALE

16. Op. cit., AJB, Chapter 9: Ryedale; Heart of the Riding – Helmsley – Rievaulx Abbey – Byland Abbey – Coxwold – Newburgh Priory – Kilburn – Ampleforth Abbey and College – Old Byland and Caydale – Hawnby – Murton and Cold Kirby, pp. 71-82.

17. Op. cit., AJB, Chapter 10: The Dales of Rydale; Bilsdale – Riccaldale & Bransdale – Kirkdale – Farndale – Rosedale, pp. 83-86.

18. Op. cit., AJB, Chapter 11: Around Kirbymoorside; Kirkbymoorside – Pickering to Kirkbymoorside – Appleton-Le-Moors and Lastingham – Hutton-Le-Hole – Gillamoor, pp. 87-92.

3. THE HAMBLETON HILLS

19. Op. cit., AJB, Chapter 12: Sutton Bank, Old Drove Road, pp. 93-94.

20. Op. cit., AJB, Chapter 13: Some Hambleton Villages; In The Vale Of Mowbray – Osmotherley – The Snilesworth Country – Mount Grace Priory – Some North Riding Inns And Hotels, pp. 95-102.
    20a. Note: A total of over 90 hostelries are mentioned in the book with many others identified but not named.

4. THE PLAIN OF YORK AND THE HOWARDIAN HILLS

21. Op. cit., AJB, Chapter 14; Southern North Riding; The Plain – Crayke – Sheriff Hutton – Castle Howard – Slingsby – Hovingham Hall, pp. 103-108.
    21a. Note: The so-called 'street' villages stand on the old Roman Road or 'Street' which once ran through the district.

22. Op. cit., AJB, Chapter 15: Malton, pp. 109-110.

23. Op. cit., AJB, Chapter 16: Pickering, pp. 111-112.

5. THE GOATHLAND COUNTRY AND THE NORTH-EAST MOORS

24. Op. cit., AJB, Chapter 17: From Pickering to Whitby; The Moorland Road – Lilla Cross – Saltersgate to Hackness – In Staindale, pp. 113-117.

25. Op. cit., AJB, Chapter 18: Goathland; Moorland Spa – Sword Dancers and Witchcraft

– Goathland Hunt – Incline Railway – The Moors – Quoits at Beck Hole – Around Beck Hole – The Duchy Of Lancaster, pp. 118-126.

26. Op. cit., AJB, Chapter 19: The Lost Valley Of Littlebeck, pp. 127-130.

27. Op. cit., AJB, Chapter 20: North Yorkshire State Forests, pp. 131-134.
   27a. Note: Most of this chapter appeared as a publication in the *Country Life* Magazine, 30th June 1950, pp. 1972-1973.

28. Op. cit., AJB, Chapter 21: The Pickering-Scarborough Road, pp. 135-136.

29. Op. cit., AJB, Chapter 22: The Old Squires, pp. 137-139.

6. THE CLEVELAND COUNTRY

30. Op. cit., AJB, Chapter 23: On Cleveland; The Cleveland Hills – The Whitby-Guisborough Road – Cleveland Superstitions – The Cleveland Bay – Stokesley – Great Ayton, pp. 140-146.

31. Op.cit., AJB, Chapter 24: Some Cleveland Villages; Carlton-in-Cleveland and Others – On Locked Churches – Three Inglebys And An Ancient Church, pp. 147-149.

32. Op. cit., AJB, Chapter 25: Roseberry Topping and Guisborough, pp. 150-152.

33. Op. cit., AJB, Chapter 26: Kirkleatham and Upleatham, Skelton Castle, pp. 153-154.

34. Op. cit., AJB, Chapter 27: Eskdale; The Esk – Danby-In-Cleveland – Castleton And The Moors – Castleton Rigg – Stone Crosses Of The North Yorkshire Moors – Ralph Cross, pp. 156-158.

35. Op.cit., AJB, Chapter 28: North Yorkshire Sheep Farms, pp. 164-168.

36. Op. cit., AJB, Chapter 29: Village Life, pp. 169-174.

7. TOWARDS THE COAST

37. Op. cit., AJB, Chapter 30: In Harwood-dale; At Bumble Bee – War Department – Hackness – Langdale End, pp. 175-179.

38. Op. cit., AJB, Chapter 31: Middlesbrough, pp. 180-182.

39. Op. cit., AJB, Chapter 32: The Yorkshire Coast; Redcar – Saltburn – Skinningrove – Staithes – Port Mulgrave – Runswick Bay – Towards Kettleness Lythe and Mulgrave Castle – Sandsend – Whitby – Robin Hood's Bay – The 'Flask' and 'Falcon' – Ravenscar – Scarborough – Filey, pp. 183-199.

40. Op. cit., AJB, Envoi, p. 200.

41. Reverend David Quinlan, Reviews of Recent Books; North Yorkshire: 'Fair North Riding' by Alfred J. Brown, *Yorkshire Catholic Monthly*, September 1952, Vol. I, No. 8, pp. 152-153.

42. J.C. Marsh-Edwards, 'North of Ilkley', 'Fair North Riding' by Alfred J. Brown, *The Tablet*, 11th October 1952, p. 20.

43. AJB/Country Life Correspondence File, 1953-1964, passim.

44. AJB Fan Mail Correspondence File, 1950-1954.

CHAPTER 18

'Going Private' to 'Go Public'

The Move to London

After the sale of the Whitfield House Hotel in late 1950, Alfred attempted to real-ise his long-cherished dream of becoming a full-time writer, and provide Marie-Eugénie with respite from the demands of running a busy hotel. They were both glad to leave the hectic business behind, and since Alfred had been moderately success-ful as a 'literary innkeeper', he was hopeful that a new career in writing beckoned. When innkeepers retired from public life it was termed: 'going private' and he looked forward to 'going public' with an increase in his literary output.[1] The decision was made to move to London and find temporary accommodation so that Alfred could be closer to his literary agent and the centre of the publishing business, while Marie-Eugénie would benefit from the social and cultural opportunities afforded by the cap-ital.[2] Moreover they would be close to the family since all three daughters were based in London, Felicity as an artist, Barbara in nurse training and Rosemary as a secre-tary with a publishing company. Meanwhile Christopher was a boarder at Ampleforth School in North Yorkshire, and Adrian was able to continue his early education locally.

Just before the end of 1950 Alfred had spent a few days in London and met his agent Peter Lewin to discuss his ongoing commitments and also to find a suitable flat as a temporary residence until he could search for a house to buy later.[3] While he stayed at the RAF Club in Piccadilly he became aware of the difficulties of finding any kind of reasonable rented accommodation. Fortunately Alfred was recommended to a let-ting agency by the cashier of the bank which he used during the war and where he still had an account. He visited the agency and was shown a furnished flat nearby, a large roomy place on the third floor of a small block of apartments just off Kensington High Street. He was impressed by its size and spaciousness, and although it had a shabby-genteel air as if it had seen better days, it was large enough for a family, and at 8 guineas per week inclusive of utilities, it was much better than others he had seen at twice the cost, so he took it on the spot.[3]

Alfred and his family moved into their newly-rented flat at 10 Avonmore Mansions, Avonmore Road, West Kensington, on 8th January 1951,[4] but he returned to the hotel to oversee the transfer of the property to the new owners and then moved all their household goods and furniture into storage in York. The Brown family members were all together again on occasions and settled into a new life in the metropolis. Initially it was good to wake up in the new flat without the worry of daily hotel chores; no residents to serve, no staff to organise, no scramble for daily provisions, no coach parties to cater for – nothing to do but think about themselves. It was also a great feeling to call one's place, even a rented flat, one's own home again, after being at the beck and call of the general public for almost six years, as Alfred commented: 'We were back in the paradise of private life again, which is what the term "going private" means.'[2]

Nevertheless, all was not idyllic since they were often kept awake by the interminable noise of London traffic and there was still the problem of the family food supply during the prolonged post-war rationing period. Standard family rations in London came as a blow after they had enjoyed relatively plentiful supplies in the country, where they were not short of the essentials such as, butter, eggs, bacon, ham, poultry etc., and often had other supplies that were considered luxuries from sometimes illicit sources in the close-knit farming community. Marie-Eugénie now faced the same problems as other Londoners and had to re-register with the Food Office and negotiate for basic supplies with the local grocer, milkman, coal merchant etc., who all seemed so impersonal and indifferent to the requirements of these 'newcomers', after the overt friendliness of their previous local shop keepers and farmers.[2]

However, the family's finances improved marginally following the move, since the bank overdraft was paid off with the proceeds of the hotel sale along with other outstanding bills. Even so there was not much capital left over, but enough to face the coming year without anxiety, although Alfred had to finish the two books in hand in order to earn some small additional income. Furthermore it was his intention as a full-time writer to use some of the family's present and future experiences in a follow up to the two hotel books,[2] and he envisaged that the family could pass the time most agreeably in London over the next few months. During their previous time in North Yorkshire they had made the most of the little free time available to explore only the nearby countryside and coast with an occasional family holiday. Now they were in London, they intended not only to see as much of the capital and its surroundings as possible, but even to enjoy a holiday abroad as well.[2]

The most urgent problem was to find a suitable school for Adrian who was nearly seven years old and had spent the last couple of years at a local village mixed school of about 60 pupils aged 5-15 years. While he had enjoyed this early school experience he was now behind hand in reading and writing, but ahead of his peers in physical development as a robust, outdoor-living youngster. Now he needed to catch up academically if he was to benefit from the educational advantages of his siblings, all of whom had attended selective boarding schools. The difficulty was finding a local Catholic primary school that would take him during the academic year, since most were full and had long waiting lists as a result of the post-war 'baby boom'. The only alternative was to find a private school reasonably close, but these also had no vacancies until the autumn term. Fortunately there was a Convent School in Cavendish Square run by the Sisters of the Holy Child Jesus, the same order of nuns as the school which his sisters had attended, and while it was also full, the Reverend Mother Head Teacher agreed to find a place immediately for Adrian. The school was a delightful, spacious, beautifully-kept and well-managed establishment, and Adrian settled down happily after he adjusted to the changes from an informal rural school, to the strict confines of a religious boys' preparatory school in central London, and a bus ride of some three miles across the busy capital, which was all quite a contrast for him.[2]

A New Life in London

Life in a London flat was a strange experience for the Browns after a roomy old house on the North Yorkshire Moors and even though it was a large family dwelling, it was in a gloomy block of other flats with only a tiny balcony overlooking the street below. Other residents of the building were very reclusive and hardly spoke when met on the stairs, before they rapidly retreated to mysterious lives behind closed doors. Only the resident caretaker who serviced the building's ten flats was friendly, and being an ex-guardsman named Darling, who lived up to his name, he was only too willing to help with any little job needed. He and his wife befriended the Browns since they had common interests with Marie-Eugénie's appreciation of the Royal Family and Alfred's love of sport, and Mr. Darling also became friends with young Adrian who delighted in doing the caretaker's rounds of duty with him. Nevertheless Alfred and Marie-Eugénie found life in the flat very impersonal. Even the delivery of essential goods and services was done without making contact with the milkman, the postman, the coalman and the newspaper man, unlike their country counterparts who always seemed to have time for a chat and kept them up to date with all the village news.[2]

The day-to-day business of shopping also presented challenges for these 'out-of-towners' who had lived in a small village with only two shops, whereas they were now confronted by a multiplicity of small shops all selling the same items, as well as large general stores which sold everything, although this novelty soon wore off as they were considered too big, too casual and too expensive. But Alfred and Marie-Eugénie found the larger stores on the well-known London streets a source of fascination, as well as the many parks, squares and large open spaces which always seemed to be thronged with people from all over the world. They also enjoyed their own separate interests; for her there were always plenty of royal processions and celebrations to be seen, for him there were the famous London houses where many literary, arts, polit- ical and other notables were acknowledged by the blue plaques on the homes of for- mer residents.

In the evenings they found the night life equally interesting and although they did most entertaining at home, the night life of London provided a plethora of possibil- ities in terms of intellectual, artistic, theatrical, operatic and musical attractions. It was necessary however to restrict attendances at these entertainments to special cel- ebrations because of the cost of such activities. Alternatively, there were times when they were invited to the occasional literary dinner but more often to cocktail parties, where the norm was formal dress which they did not mind, though they often found them decorous and dull affairs. Alfred hoped on such occasions he might have the opportunity to get to know other more successful writers, but often found that, with the exception of a well-known individual, the majority were struggling writers like him with the same unrealistic expectations. While these literary events were largely disappointing, this was not the case with musical evenings which Alfred and his wife attended as guests of their friends, which often created an enjoyably relaxed social outlet that provided respite for Marie-Eugénie in particular, which was one of the reasons for the move to London.[2]

At the weekends, after the hectic weekday life of the city, the family sometimes explored outer London and the Thames Valley with occasional trips to the coast. These excursions were aided by having a car, and on Sundays they went en famille to venues such as Richmond, Windsor, Maidenhead, Marlow, Henley and especially Knowl Hill where their old friends the Littlewoods lived in a delightful country cottage. On other occasions the seaside beckoned with Hastings and Eastbourne being favourite resorts on the south coast. Inevitably though, the countryside around London never quite came up to expectations after the more expansive and wilder moorland scenery of North Yorkshire. But they enjoyed these outings enormously because they gave time for the family to be together which had often been so sadly lacking during the busy hotel years. However while life had become so much more relaxed in London, during the spring and early summer of 1951, there was now the urgent need to establish a home base if the move was going to become more permanent.[2]

House Hunting Again

Finding a suitable house in London proved far more difficult than finding a flat, not that there was any lack of houses for sale, at a price, so that Alfred and Marie- Eugénie spent a great deal of time hunting for their 'ideal home'. The big problem was that while houses in the north of England were largely freehold properties, the majority in central London were leasehold, often with very short leases. Moreover, in the areas in which they were particularly interested, such as Kensington, Notting Hill Gate and Hammersmith, houses were mainly out of their price range. They were also conscious of not spending too much of their shrinking 'nest egg' of some £5,000 from the sale of the hotel, since they had to be self-sufficient until Alfred could hopefully derive enough income from his writing.[2]

After extensive searches they were attracted to a large house in King Henry's Road, between St. John's Wood and Hampstead, priced at only £1,300 on a 13 year lease.[4] At first sight it was very tempting since it matched most of their requirements, even though it was in a very dilapidated state and required extensive costly renovation. They decided to have the place surveyed with a view to purchase and consulted a contractor to carry out the upgrading work needed, but when the extent and cost of the renovation was made gloomily clear, the initial glamour faded, and they regretted their impulsive decision. Fortunately they were relieved of their commitment to proceed when their solicitor discovered from the deeds that the lease had only 10 not 13 years to run and as a result they were free to renounce the purchase.

Alfred and Marie-Eugénie then viewed dozens more houses and had tentatively 'bought' three more after this disappointment, each one with some similar hitch attached, before they decided that perhaps their chances of finding something suitable were hopeless. More frustratingly, when an 'ideal home' was discovered it had been sold by the time they viewed it, since most of the attractive, reasonably-priced houses were being snapped up quickly, often on the same day of the sale. It was hardly surprising that their keenness to remain in London began to wane even in a short time, and after a couple of months of the exhausting business of searching desirable areas of London, they both began to despair. Alfred in particular regretted time spent on the maddening yet admittedly tantalising search for their impossible 'dream home' that could have been devoted to his writing, which so far he had found impossible.[4]

Eventually, although they were prepared to remain in London for up to two years to get re-established, the first few months had convinced them they could not afford to continue to live there on Alfred's meagre income as a writer, with the cost of living being much higher even if they found somewhere cheaper in the outer suburbs. Moreover the need to be near their daughters receded, since Felicity intended to go to Italy as a governess, Barbara was resident at the nurses' home and Rosemary had found accommodation with friends. Furthermore, Christopher was mostly away at boarding school and Adrian would leave his convent preparatory school in the summer. Therefore it was with some reluctance and regret, but considerable relief that the decision was made to move on once more.[4]

Alfred's Unresolved Writing Problems

It was also during this transient London phase that Alfred began to have concerns about his future writing prospects even though he was now relatively free to pursue his passion on a full-time basis. He had always wanted to be a professional writer, but he acknowledged that he had left it rather late and conditions in the publishing market were now more difficult than ever, so it seemed like an inappropriate time to have taken this literary plunge.[4] On the other hand he had tried for so long to attain independence by spare time writing without success, perhaps it was time to embark on a full-time effort. As a writer he was reasonably well established, he had a dozen books to his name, and while this was the main justification for this bold step, he was under no illusions about the risks involved.

Unfortunately Alfred was acutely conscious of his environment when writing and had always found inspiration when surrounded by the great outdoors, and now his London flat looked out onto a brick wall which he found extremely depressing. Furthermore he was not sure if he could endure the loneliness of a professional writer after the excitement of his former hotel existence which was such a stimulus to his writing. One of the first things he had to do was to discipline himself to write during the daytime when he longed to be out and about, and if he tried to work at night he found sleeping by day abnormal and disturbed the household routine. Since much of his previous work had been topographical in nature, a great deal of the time had been spent walking and gathering material which he found most agreeable. However he knew that topographical books rarely became best sellers and he could no longer afford the time for this type of work in return for the inadequate rewards. But with plenty of time at his disposal, he now had the chance to write that elusive novel which he so craved. The only thing he was not prepared to do was to put his family through penury to achieve his desired aim, so he would either try to make a comfortable living by his pen or try something else.[4]

Alfred was nevertheless worried about the commitment to the creative writing that he had envisaged. He had recently experienced another health set back following his gall stones operation almost two years previously, and was now unable to do any sustained writing as he was feeling tired, torpid and despondent, at a time when he probably had the best chance of making the most of the full-time writing opportunity he had been looking for most of his life.[4] A subsequent visit to Westminster Hospital to try to diagnose this recent malaise did nothing to alleviate his latest health concerns and he questioned himself: 'Is this a phase I am going through, or am I finished?' and as a result of the current deleterious situation in which he found himself: 'There seems to be no future for me as a writer today with things as they are, but I don't like to confess failure – yet.'[4] Perhaps therefore this lack of motivational drive for literary progress, together with the accumulated frustrations of the London experience itself, finally prompted the decision to make a move away from the capital to an environment more conducive to the achievement of his ambitious plan.

The Return to Yorkshire

Alfred never intended to stay in London permanently, nor did he want to swell the ranks of Yorkshiremen who had migrated to London and wrote nostalgically about the County they had left behind. On the other hand, although Marie-Eugénie was Yorkshire born, she was half French and had spent much of her early years living in London and France and therefore could not be expected to be drawn back to Yorkshire in the same way. This led to a problem in the choice of an appropriate place for their resettlement. Since Marie-Eugénie ruled out the whole of the West Riding with which she was not enamoured, and Alfred's preferred choice was to live in or near a sizeable Yorkshire town or city, the compromise was reached by the selection of the historic city of York.[2] It was an obvious choice, since it stood at the heart of the greatest County in the country and it had fascinated Alfred for years. He had often dreamed of living in the old city surrounded by its walls, albeit with miles of the flat countryside of the plain of York around, but still near enough to the moors which forever held him in thrall. Marie-Eugénie was also greatly attracted by York, both for its beauty as a city and the more practical considerations of shops, churches, libraries and schools as well as its cultural attractions. In addition there were the added advantages that Christopher's school was located not far away at Ampleforth, while all the household furniture had been stored in the city.[2] All that remained was to find a suitable property for sale, retrieve their furniture and set up house once more.

   With the decision made Alfred and Marie-Eugénie had no intention of wasting time house hunting as they had done in London and intended to buy the first suitable family home that came along, and with the added benefits that most properties were freehold, there was plenty of choice and all were relatively cheaper than those in the capital. Nevertheless they had some preferences: a small Georgian house within the city walls if possible, somewhere with character, space and a modest garden, although in the end they had to settle for something less exclusive since such properties were at a premium in the highly desirable centre of York.[2] The choice came down to two houses outside the city walls; a detached superior modern brick residence, or a substantial Georgian house with Victorian additions, and although they preferred the former, both properties were being auctioned by different agents on the same day within 15 minutes of each other. But their choice was reduced when the modern property exceeded £5,000 which was beyond their means and they hurried across the street to the other agents and entered into the bidding until the sale was withdrawn for private negotiation.[2] Fortunately, unlike the fiasco of their attempted hotel auction sale, this time the outcome of the event went favourably for them and they bought the property for £2,950. The whole process took less than an hour to complete, and only seven weeks later, on 20th July 1951, they gained possession of 'Ivy Bank', at 11 Acomb Road, in the Holgate district of York, just over a mile west of York Minster.

32. Front & 33. Rear (with Alfred) of 11 Acomb Road, York

The London experience had lasted just over six months but Alfred and Marie-Eugénie had both appreciated the time in the capital even if it had not come up to their expectations. While Felicity and Barbara remained in London temporarily, Christopher was at school nearby and Rosemary who had taken a job in York, and Adrian, both returned north, so that Marie-Eugénie was most contented with the move and settled into her new home. Alfred was also very happy with the idea of returning to

Yorkshire, especially York, in order to get to know better the city he greatly admired, and expressed his satisfaction with the new location: 'For the moment it was enough to know that we were coming back to the bosom of our County – coming home.'[2] However after the hectic move and a brief settling in process was completed, their priority then was to take a much-needed summer holiday, since it had been many years since they had enjoyed the experience in the pre-war days and they decided on a long vacation abroad.

A Holiday In France

Marie-Eugénie still had many relatives living in France and Alfred had a strong affinity for the country having spent some time in France in his younger days, and this led to the choice of Brittany and Normandy for the holiday, together with visits to Calais, Tours and Paris to give the family a chance to meet their French relatives. But the vacation was a little unconventional since they travelled in a relatively new Ford Prefect saloon car, fitted with a roof rack fully loaded, including camping and cooking gear, and the belongings of a family of five, soon to become six en-route with the addition Barbara. Felicity could not travel due to work commitments in Italy, thus the happy band of travellers set out in late August for a tour of northern France with the expectation that the 'girls' would stay in hotels while the 'boys' would camp nearby, but the reality turned out somewhat differently.

Following an overnight stay in Dover, they crossed the channel and were met in Calais by Simone West, a cousin of Marie-Eugénie's, and were entertained at a local restaurant to celebrate their arrival. But Marie-Eugénie was disappointed to see the still bomb-damaged town and to discover that her Aunt Elise Marie Messe's house had gone. Furthermore, following the privations of the war, in which the family had lost almost everything, her aunt and cousin were the only family members left in the area, where they lived in an impoverished state in a small apartment and awaited resettlement in a new municipal development.[2] The Browns remained in Calais for a few days, where Marie-Eugénie had spent part of her youth as well as in Versailles, before they headed off through Picardy into Normandy and on to St. Malo, where they picked up Barbara who had sailed from Southampton to join the family during her annual leave from nursing at Westminster Hospital.[2]

While the family was in the St. Malo area they visited St. Servan, deep in the countryside near Rennes, including the Château de Bourg, where Marie-Eugénie had spent some time during early family holidays. The château had been owned by an aristocratic friend of her mother, who had been a governess to the family's children, and the dignified building was set in a beautiful park with ornamental gardens with a lake, as well as a chapel that served the local villages, and where Marie-Eugénie had been baptised. The estate was now owned by a retired army colonel who showed them around the chapel with the memorial tablets to her mother's family friends, and although Marie-Eugénie had not visited since she was seven years old, when she was introduced to an elderly woman in a nearby farm house, she was remembered with great affection by the former housekeeper at the château. She was disappointed not to view the château itself, but she enjoyed the reminiscences with the friendly old lady, as well as stories told by the charming, elderly colonel, who displayed all the courtesy of the old French aristocracy, but seemed to live in a dream world that had gone forever.[2]

The family then headed to the Brittany coast via Dinan and made directly for a ten miles long peninsula that led to Quiberon, where Alfred had spent part of a walking holiday with his cousin Lawrence Geoghegan in the 1920s. Quiberon was selected because it had grown from an old fishing village into a small holiday resort on the southern tip of what is almost an island, connected to the mainland by a narrow strip of causeway and surrounded by sandy beaches. Unfortunately the choice of this idyllic spot seemed a mistake when it was discovered that their reservations, albeit at a rather seedy looking hotel, had been let to others without apology, regret or offer of any other rooms, but they soon found alternative accommodation at a large well-appointed hotel. Apart from this instance, the Breton experience was only spoiled towards the end of their stay by stormy weather, but they enjoyed the place so much that they stayed for the following week and explored the locality, before they departed just as the holiday season came to an end.[2]

When they left the coast behind the next stage of the family holiday was spent in the northern Loire valley and the château country, travelling to Nantes and Angers. At this point Adrian's constant demands for a camping adventure had to be fulfilled, so instead of pressing on to St. Georges-sur-Loire, Alfred turned off route to find an hotel in the small village of Ingrandes where a local auberge, the Lion d'Or, sported the reliable 'Club des Sans-Club' sign. The ladies of the party were happy to stay at the auberge, while Alfred and the boys chanced their luck to find a campsite nearby at a suitable spot on the edge of the village in a field by the Loire, where Christopher cooked supper before they spent the night in the tent. However following this solitary night's camp, the boys expressed no further desire to repeat the experience, and all the camping gear was consigned again to the car's roof rack for the rest of the trip. Subsequently the family enjoyed their journey via Anjou through the Loire valley to Tours and Touraine, where they were reacquainted with another of Marie-Eugénie's cousins and family and Barbara left the group to return to England, while the rest of the family continued on to their final destination, Paris.[2]

Originally they had not intended to visit Paris, but for the sake of the children and for Marie-Eugénie's fondness for the place, it was decided to detour and spend a few days there before they left for home. So after a brief visit to Chârtres they headed for Versailles which had been second home to Marie-Eugénie's family and where she had spent some of her youth, before they found a suitable hotel in Paris to spend their last weekend in France.[2] This was something of a whistle-stop tour of the major tourist sites, although it impressed the family and pleased Marie-Eugénie who was able to make a brief visit with yet more cousins who lived in Colombes. Then they completed the three week circular tour of Northern France with a return to the coast, where they spent their last night with friends in Calais before they sailed home with fond memories of their French tour, but sadly perhaps the last family holiday for the foreseeable future.[2]

Life In York

The Browns looked forward to their new home in the ancient city of York and a return to a private house once more. It had been redecorated during their absence, but Alfred faced the task of sorting out the large rear garden, and although he disliked gardening, he acknowledged the need for a large open space to provide Adrian with a safe place to play, and more practically, for a vegetable garden which would supply some of the family's needs. Meanwhile Marie-Eugénie was more than happy with the cluster of shops in the neighbourhood, which provided almost everything that they required without going into the city, since the Holgate area was a self-contained suburb that retained much of its character since its former 'Holdgate' days. Alfred was also particularly pleased with his new study which overlooked the rear garden and hoped that this would provide not only the stimulus needed to complete his ongoing work, but also the inspiration to embark on new literary enterprises.[2]

The family soon settled into their new situation as Christopher returned to Ampleforth in late September 1951 and entered the sixth form with the intention of gaining a place at university. Adrian made another fresh start in a large mixed class at the English Martyrs primary school located nearby in a shabby-looking condemned building, which came as quite a shock compared with his former rather exclusive Convent School in central London. He was too young for a residential preparatory school, but his parents were determined that he should have the private education of his siblings and attend one of Ampleforth's prep schools as soon as possible. Rosemary also made a new start after she left the London publisher's office and found a secretarial post in York, where she had attended secretarial school earlier, unlike her elder sisters Felicity and Barbara who remained in London but returned to the new home from time to time. Therefore the family's circumstances stabilised after their recent upheavals as they spent their first real family Christmas since the war alone together at home. And yet while Alfred was happy with their new life, he was anxious about what the New Year might bring[4] and he summarised their still precarious financial position:

> In 1951, therefore – an expensive year involving the flat in London, the holiday in France, and the move to York – I had lived largely on my capital, my total income from royalties, lectures and articles amounting to very little.[2]

It was soon obvious that 1952 was going to be the most critical year since Alfred had embarked on the hotel venture, and crucially he began to feel that he had lost confidence in his own future as a writer so that he might have to consider some other job just to survive.[5] Since buying the house the bank balance had been spent and was now in the red once more, and although the house was mortgage free, Alfred had to deposit the deeds as security for a prospective overdraft of £1,000 to keep the family going in the coming year. He was thus confronted with the stark choice of whether to continue to write or return to a commercial job, neither of which appeared to be particularly likely at this stage. In the former case he had perhaps arrived at a point which was known as 'writer's block', while in the latter case he was now 57 years old and he had been out of the business world for over 12 years, so that even Marie-Eugénie considered taking a job to help out with the family finances.

On top of this dilemma Alfred also faced a recurrence of a health problem that had caused him to seek the help of Mr. Pyrah, the Leeds surgeon who had performed the earlier gall stones operation.[5] Following a further consultation and a three day stay in hospital for tests and X-rays, Pyrah had reported that Alfred's gall bladder was not functioning and he advised an operation for its removal. However under the circumstances Alfred was reluctant to go ahead immediately and asked for a delay as long as possible unless it was considered that the operation was urgent. Although this news came at a bad time, Alfred appeared to have acted somewhat rashly in the belief that he could not afford the time out of action that a long period of convalescence would bring, especially when personal circumstances were so critical. Meanwhile he struggled on with other attempts to try to offset the lack of income caused by both of his recently commissioned books not having achieved their expected sales.

'Going Public': Lectures, Reviews and Press Articles

In his earlier days Alfred was always keen to talk to local interest groups about his life and work, and he often gave public lectures, along with writing book reviews and occasional press and magazine articles concurrently with his other writing in order to supplement the meagre income from his literary activities.[2] Then after the publication of his first hotel book, he was accepted by the Foyles Lecture Agency of London on their registered list of speakers to provide a succession of lectures around the country, mostly to women's clubs and organisations.[6] This new outlet proved to be a little more rewarding since until then he only received expenses or perhaps occasionally up to 2-3 guineas per lecture, whereas now he received as much as 10-20 guineas. Although he had to pay his own expenses and any accommodation costs, the sessions were often arranged in groups of two or more a week in neighbouring towns and cities, so this part-time work offered reasonable rewards even if it detracted from his writing time. In the first year of this engagement he delivered about 20 lectures to various societies, but this declined by half in the following year, which was a disappointment since the earnings then hardly made up for the short fall in royalties resulting from the mediocre sales of books.[2]

In the entry of Alfred's profile and current lectures available through 'The Lecture Agency' of Foyles of London, a biographical synopsis noted that he was: 'a well-known authority on the Yorkshire Moors and Dales, and author of twelve books' which were listed with the comments that: 'he had walked himself better after a long illness..., served in both wars..., and after the last war took a country hotel.' This was followed by a list of 'not too serious lectures' on offer including: 'The Enchanting County of Yorkshire, The Best of Yorkshire, Literary Yorkshire, Walking Was My Salvation, Foreign Adventures and The Funny Side of Hotel Life' with the cautionary note: 'No Slides'.[6] Alfred had always detested the use of 'lantern slides' since he invariably got them mixed up, and even when he used an 'epidiascope' during the war, he admitted his errors sometimes left the unfortunate briefing squads of RAF crews somewhat confused about their intended targets.[7]

Alfred always felt more at ease when he gave a friendly talk to a group of strangers rather than delivering a formal lecture and his casual informal approach was more conducive to the subject he favoured most, namely his beloved Yorkshire. He believed that if he demonstrated how much he enjoyed talking about the 'Broad Acres', the audience would respond appropriately. However he invariably returned home tired by the demands of these presentations, and the journeys involved, and often had to sit through the lengthy, tedious business meetings of the group or society that preceded his talk. Furthermore the rewards of the demanding schedule expected by the Lecture Agency were diminished by the time lost from any literary work.

In an alternative attempt to supplement his income Alfred reviewed books on behalf of the local press whenever the opportunity arose but this returned little financial reward. Most newspapers and magazines expected the work to be done for the sake of the receipt of the book and sometimes for a small fee, nevertheless Alfred carried out regular reviews for the *Yorkshire Observer* newspaper for which he often received the generous sum of 2-3 guineas on behalf of the editor.[8] But he was always assiduous in this task and read each book thoroughly before he wrote a carefully considered opinion, then provided a detailed account of its merits and deficiencies, without attempting to influence the likely reader. As a writer he was conscious of being on the receiving end of some cursory reviews by others who had at best merely skimmed the contents of his book, and often only reflected the publisher's publicity material on the dust cover, or at worst, had damned the book out of hand. His efforts in this type of supplementary work also detracted from his writing and although it helped to keep him in touch with a range of current literature, it did not alleviate his financial problems.[2]

Similarly Alfred spent only a limited amount of time on his attempts to publish short articles in newspapers and magazines which produced meagre financial returns. Over the years he had reasonable success with this type of writing in which he was able to adapt material from his published books to serve the interests of the popular press and its readers. Now, however, he found that the work often entailed commissioned topics that demanded much more work to assemble the required material, which hardly provided a fair return on the outlay of time, effort and expense. For example, in an article written for *Country Life* magazine on the development of the new Yorkshire Dales National Park, he had travelled extensively by car to gather the information required, and although he had received 8 guineas this did not compensate for all the work needed.[9] Clearly in view of his now ever more precarious financial position, he needed to consider finding a job and perhaps to relinquish his dream of being able to support himself and his family by writing alone.

In Search of a Job

Alfred had begun to sound out the possibilities of alternative employment and used a short curriculum vitae to promote his prospects with potential employers in which he described himself as an author, journalist and Foyles Agency Lecturer, who had recently served in WW2 as an RAF Intelligence Officer. He outlined his business experience before the war as a successful export manager and later director of a Yorkshire firm of wool exporters, who had travelled extensively in Europe and was also fluent in German and French. Following the war years he referred to the successful operation of a country hotel for six years, and stated that he now sought a suitable travelling sales post in any appropriate field of commercial activity.

Alfred had also made contact with a former business colleague, Eric Baker, who advised him to consider a return to the wool trade in which he had most experience, but he was reluctant to do so unless there was no alternative.[5] However he continued to search for job opportunities via box numbers in the national press, but he became depressed when he was often considered too old for the posts advertised, and yet he continued to bombard the situations vacant columns and hoped for the best.[5] However it became clear that the possibility of a job through personal introduction was more likely than by speculative application, whereby at 57 his age was a disadvantage, notwithstanding his obvious experience. Then following a new offer of a European sales post with the Norton Motorcycle Company of Birmingham, via his contact Eric Baker, the self doubt re-emerged about his ability to stand the demanding pace of overseas travel while he suffered recurrent health problems.[5]

However there now loomed another serious financial crisis in which Alfred's overdraft exceeded £800, with an unpaid tax bill of £255 which needed to be settled on the sale of the hotel, while the earnings from his attempted literary efforts in the last two years had only amounted to £450.[5] He therefore concluded that while he had wasted so much time chasing elusive sales jobs in the press, it was now time to swallow his pride and try to get back into the wool trade once more.[5] To this end he met with former business colleagues in Bradford who advised him to advertise in the 'Wool Review' trade journal and the local press in search of a post in Bradford's export markets in which he had spent more than half his working life. In doing so he consoled himself with the notion: 'It seems sad to have to quit writing and start again at my time of life – but what else can I do? ...it will be something not to be ashamed of if I can succeed in making another "fresh start".' [5]

Subsequently Alfred had two interviews in Bradford just before Christmas 1952, the first with Schunck & Company, wool merchants founded by one of many émigré German businessmen in the late 19th century, and the second with Pool, Lorimer & Tibbener, a Leicester wool firm who also owned a mill in Bradford.[5] Then just after Christmas he had a further interview with a former close contact, Joseph Clay, who was seeking his own replacement as the manager when he retired from Alfred's old firm of David Hamilton & Co. Ltd., Bradford. He then reflected speculatively: 'So there it is. I seem to be on the brink of returning to Bradford for a late second innings after all. Hateful as the prospect is in many ways, I don't care as long as it provides me with a four figure income and marks an end of this awful penury, for now all my reserves are exhausted, and I must get a job somehow'.[10] Nevertheless, in spite if this expectation, Alfred had no success with any of the firms which had expressed an interest in him.

While Alfred was depressed by his unsuccessful attempts to find a job, he did not direct his efforts to the commercial world alone, since he was willing to consider alternative work for which he had some talent. To this end he contacted his older brother Edwin Brown, who was then Bursar at Leeds University about the possibility of any suitable posts that might be available.[11] Naturally, as his brother had indicated, any academic post was out of the question and although Alfred had previously had the opportunity of extra-mural teaching through the WEA (Workers' Educational Association) organised by the university, such part-time work was unlikely to interest him now. Furthermore, it was also unlikely that any suitable administrative post would be available to him, since most senior staff members were graduates with experience of other universities. Nevertheless there was the possibility that a hall of residence steward's post might become available with accommodation and a modest salary which might suit Alfred's situation.[11] In view of the experience he had gained as a Mess Secretary in charge of catering and social activities at a large RAF station during the war, this type of post would have been worthwhile, but unfortunately such a post was never forthcoming. Therefore the prospects for the New Year looked very bleak indeed, until a completely unexpected job became available in early 1953.

A New Job At Last!

In late February Alfred received the unexpected news that he had been offered a job with Brotherton & Co. Ltd., the chemical manufacturing group in Leeds, and perhaps even more unlikely, that if he was willing he would be assigned to the post of Personnel Manager.[12] The offer came from Bertie Ratcliffe, chairman of the company, who was a friend of Alfred's, while Marie-Eugénie was a close friend of Bertie's wife, since their school days together, and with whom they had both continued to socialise regularly during their brief stay in London. Bertie's nephew, George Brotherton-Ratcliffe, who was the only family member left in the business, had been promoted from Personnel Manager to Managing Director of the company, and his former post was available for Alfred. But even he found this somewhat difficult to comprehend, since he had no experience of personnel management other than during his WW2 RAF experience. On his appointment Alfred had to work closely with George and took a training course to learn the role, but he was encouraged to create a more informal atmosphere in the firm and had a free hand to implement the changes needed to bring this about. Alfred was also surprised at the relatively low salary for such an important role of £750 rising to £1,000 p.a., and although he would have preferred a role as foreign traveller selling the company's valuable dyestuffs to the textile trade abroad, he acknowledged it was a great opportunity and that the prospects appeared to be very good.[12]

Alfred started his new job in Leeds on 2nd March 1953, which meant an easy commute by train from York and so obviated any necessity to move house and family. From the outset however he realised that he was up against a very hostile MD, George Ratcliffe, who resented his appointment, although he had a good working relationship with the rest of the staff, and even enjoyed the full support of George's uncle Bertie, the chairman, who unfortunately took no active part in the running the company. Then following the engagement of a group of consultants to advise about the reorganisation of the company, Alfred had requested to be considered for the Foreign Sales Department, a move that was backed by the consultants, but not by George, nor the Board of Directors who had been influenced by George. Then after a recommendation by George that he should be replaced as Personnel Manager, followed by a very unpleasant meeting with him, Alfred had no option but to resign his post.[10] The job had lasted just six months and by September 1953 he had to consider his future employment plans carefully, but first there were other equally important decisions to be made in terms of the recurrence of his ongoing health problems, as well as mounting financial pressures that needed to be resolved.

Health and Financial Problems Prevail

Alfred was no stranger to health and financial pressures, but the collective problems he now faced were among the most critical of his life and also had serious implications for his family. He had a long history of recurrent health setbacks dating back to his demobilisation during WW1 and he had often rescued some difficult economic circumstances with deft financial moves during his career. However he now had to deal with the twin problems of another health crisis and the rapid deterioration of his financial status since he had resigned his position at Brothertons with no likely job prospects.

Much earlier he had suffered from 'the old problem' as he put it, with numbness in the side and base of the spine that lasted for some weeks, which coincided with a general malaise of lassitude and listlessness, and subsequently by severe influenza which confined him to bed.[5] Then during the winter of 1952 he had suffered one of the worst colds in years, followed by what he described as a 'deep-seated and vile condition' that resulted in a return to his surgeon Mr. Pyrah, and he was advised that his dysfunctional gall bladder should be removed.[5] But Alfred deferred a decision when the painful attacks subsided, although he had continued to suffer the old feeling of semi-paralysis of his lower limbs and lower spine during the summer which greatly depressed him once more.[5]

In search of some respite in the summer of 1952, Alfred had taken his family on a much-needed but ill-afforded short holiday to Beckhole, near Goathland on the North Yorkshire Moors. They had the use of 'The White House', a friend's cottage which overlooked the picturesque Eller Beck, and the break allowed them to meet old friends from their hotel days and enjoy the surrounding countryside once more. But even this idyllic sojourn had its health downside, since Alfred ruptured a finger tendon during a ball game and also suffered badly bruised ribs after he was hit by the hasp of a heavy farm gate. The former required an operation to repair the damage, while the latter caused severe chest pain for weeks, which contributed to the already distressful symptoms of his non-functioning gall bladder.[5]

Inevitably almost a year later Alfred suffered further attacks of severe gall bladder pain and was confined to bed. His family doctor strongly advised him to go ahead with the postponed operation as soon as possible and he realised that he could no longer safely put off the surgery.[5] But even at this stage he delayed the event until after Felicity's wedding on 12th October 1953 to Colin Millward, a creative artist with a London advertising company. Soon after the wedding urgent arrangements were made with Mr. Pyrah at Leeds General Infirmary, and on 20th October Alfred underwent a successful operation for the removal of both his gall bladder and an offending appendix without complications. He was then required to comply with a lengthy but painful convalescence before he returned to normal and then slowly began to increase his walking activity once more in the long-held belief that this was always the way to remedy his health problems.[5]

Meanwhile during this long process of recovery Alfred brooded over the family's financial burdens while he was receiving a meagre sickness benefit of £2.10s.0d. to £3.0.0. per week. Then the reality of his desperate financial position was made explicitly clear after a gruelling interview with the bank manager in which Alfred now faced an overdraft that had exceeded the agreed extended limit of £1,300, and he had to off-set this debt against the security of the house. As a result a decision was made to try to sell the property to clear off the remaining mortgage and raise money to pay off other outstanding debts. In addition Marie-Eugénie tried to help by taking a job as the man-ageress of a nearby dairy shop at a weekly pay of £4.10s.0d. Naturally, while Alfred detested this arrangement, he admired her efforts to alleviate their plight, although she appeared to enjoy the novelty of the work and was only too willing to help out with the family's finances. Furthermore Barbara left her London post at Westminster Hospital and returned to become a staff nurse at the nearby Purey Cust Nursing Home opposite York Minster, and also contributed to the house-keeping costs while she kept a close eye on her father to make sure that he adhered to his convalescent routine.[5]

Alfred was finally 'signed off' sickness benefit by his doctor just before Christmas 1953, but he still felt weak and had none of his usual drive and motivation, while Marie-Eugénie became tired with the demands of the shop work.[5] Alfred pleaded with her to give up the job before Christmas, but she declined even though it was beginning to take its toll just as the hotel routine had done. She was determined to shoulder the extra responsibility rather than face further financial difficulties, and if necessary she was prepared to work until Alfred found another job, whenever that might be. Meanwhile Alfred sold his car in order to help meet some of the bank's demands and hoped that this would ease their financial difficulties over the coming Christmas period.[5]

In the New Year Alfred began to feel much better as his vigour slowly returned, even though he continued to have discomfort after the operation and still displayed signs of being rundown, such as a pernicious cold and recurrent conjunctivitis, but he hoped that he was on the way to a full recovery. He nevertheless pondered what 1954 would bring, and whether in his 60th year he would still be able to rise to the challenges ahead.[9] Marie-Eugénie was still at work in early spring and for Alfred there seemed to be no prospect of finding employment, so that he despaired of ever mak-ing another new start to his working career at his time of life.[9] Unfortunately, the likelihood of him making a success of the intended fresh start to a writing career now seemed an equally remote possibility since he appeared to have almost come to the end of his literary endeavours.

Writing Stalled by Literary Stalemate

Alfred's hopes of becoming a full-time writer remained unfulfilled in spite of his brave, bold, but belated quest to achieve this ambition so late in his life, and his most recent attempts to turn around his languishing literary career remained as remote as ever. He tried to retrieve an apparent writing impasse by the resurrection of some pieces of unfinished work that were sidelined as a result of the time needed to complete his two hotel books. Moreover, both his health and financial problems, together with the need to earn some income from lectures, book reviews and occasional press articles, all conspired to create distractions from any further constructive literary output during the three years spent in York. As a result he was faced with the prospects of either trying to concoct a long-awaited but elusive novel from the remnants of material he had drafted much earlier, or attempting to have the sequel to the hotel books published. In either case it now seemed too late to bring about any revival in his literary fortunes.

Alfred had a number of pieces of unfinished work at various stages of preparation at this time, as well as the completed draft of a follow-up story to his hotel books, but with the exception of trying to get this published, he remained undecided about which one he should concentrate his rapidly diminishing energies upon. This was understandable given the dire financial circumstances that he and his family faced, but had their situation been more favourable, there appeared to have been a real possibility that, given time, one or more of these works could have provided him with a way out of his predicament, and maybe even led to his desired full-time writing career success after all.

The most promising novel in preparation was a story entitled 'Erratic Journey' or 'Viennese Rhapsody',[13] a story set in Vienna just before WW2. It had its origins in Alfred's travels in Europe at that time and was probably based upon characters with whom he came into contact via his commercial connections in the city. Two sections entitled: 'Viennese Rhapsody' and 'Rumanian Interlude' [sic] of the type-scripted draft of some 84 pages, describe how the hero of the story, Crawfurd, who is a commercial traveller, meets and falls in love with Sylvia, the secretary of one of his agents in Vienna. The love affair develops in secret because she is engaged to an up-and-coming young police officer, chosen for her by her family. At one point the affair is almost discovered, but soon after Crawfurd leaves Vienna for Bucarest [sic], where he meets Graberstein, his Rumanian [sic] agent, and Dennison, a fellow commercial traveller, both of whom know about his affair with Sylvia, much to his surprise. Both sections of the draft novel describe the febrile atmosphere in Eastern Europe in the late 1930s just before Hitler's annexation of Austria and the invasion of Poland, and the account of the lifestyle of British and European commercial agents is particularly interesting. However the reader is left to speculate on how the story might have continued – would the affair be discovered? would Sylvia's fiancé have a part to play in the looming Austrian crisis? and so on. Moreover, Alfred's storyline may have been influenced by the classic mystery genre 1949 film noir *The Third Man*, as well as his own personal experiences, which intriguingly might have made the novel's appeal more likely had it been completed.

A further unfinished novel that also had its origins in Alfred's early life experiences in WW1 was entitled: 'Kershaw's Cure',[14] and consists of a 76 page type-scripted draft that was begun as early as 1934, with later additions in the 1940s. It was a semi-autobiographical story about Anthony Kershaw, who joins the Royal Field Artillery as a gunner in the First World War, but is incapacitated by injury in France and sent home to 'Broadstones' (Bradford). After attempted but unsuccessful treatments at various military hospitals, he is invalided out of further service and spends time at a Catholic nursing home run by an order of Hospitaller Brothers (St. John of God), where he takes up an interest in poetry and prose, as well as writing. But during his residency there he also struggles with his incapacity and impulsive thoughts about a girl who lives opposite the care home. However with the support of some of the home's priestly brothers he undergoes a spiritual reconciliation, and makes a near miraculous recovery from his invalidity during the receipt of the sacrament of Holy Communion. He eventually returns home, settles down and meets a girl who becomes his sweetheart, so the reader is left with the impression that his life will now return to normal, although whether this was Alfred's intention is uncertain, since the story remained unfinished.

Other incomplete novels were also grounded in Alfred's personal experiences, or developed out of his interest in his antecedent family's background, together with the continuation of his own family story. In a follow-up to his book *Ground Staff* (1943), he began a sequel about the latter half of his WW2 years and his return to civilian life, this time in the form of a novel entitled: 'Green and Pleasant Land'.[15] It was started in the late 1940s and emerged as a 50 page type scripted introduction in the 1950s, but received no further attention. On the other hand, Alfred had attempted to create an historical novel dealing with the 19th century Irish Catholic immigration into the West Riding,[16] which focuses upon the Carroll family who had risen to pre-eminence in 'Millsborough' (Bradford), and was reminiscent of his own family's background through his maternal line of the Geoghegans. He had also made a start to a novel about his own family experience during his early married life in the 1930s, although this never proceeded beyond a hand-written document of some 30 pages in notebook form.[17]

It seems likely that Alfred's failure to give his undivided attention to one of these possible alternative novels created such an impasse as to cause him to turn to the one piece of work that he had completed at this time, namely 'Going Private'[1] in the hope of extricating himself from this predicament. Therefore he was probably relying on this story as a potential stop-gap measure in the hope that resulting publication returns would enable him to complete one or more of his unfinished novels to continue his dream of a full-time literary career. However it is unlikely even if this draft book had been published and resulted in modest sales, that it would have made any difference to his overall financial situation, since the lead time to get any new novel into print would still have left him in a precarious position and unable to support himself and his family on any literary income alone.

Nevertheless Alfred hoped that the completed draft would attract the attention of a suitable publisher, but the proposed book was perhaps both too wide-ranging and too much of a miscellany of unrelated topics to have any real appeal to either publisher or reader alike. It was intended as a sequel to the hotel books, and in this respect it initially continued the family's story with their moves to London and then York to begin a new life. But it soon turned into a travelogue of an extended family holiday to Northern France that occupied almost half of the book, which maybe should have been published as a separate story. It was only Alfred's descriptions of ancient and modern York that has any real merit, in which he returns to his topographically-gifted writing style at its best, and even then this was perhaps more suitable for a magazine where it might have had more appeal. Towards the end of the draft book Alfred focuses on aspects of literary York and his own literary efforts, and in a short, terse postscript, he faces up to the reality of his literary problems, in which he proposes a likely return to the business world.

It was not surprising that Alfred's former literary agent, Peter Lewin, confided his considerable doubts about the possibility of getting this latest draft into print.[18] He was concerned that, regardless of the storyline, a sequel to the hotel books would not find favour with any new publisher, since it had been rejected by Earnest Benn & Co., London, who took over Williams & Norgate, the publishers of the previous hotel books, and it would be too much of a gamble for another firm to take as a single book. But undeterred, Alfred persisted with further attempts to try to interest other publishers by dealing directly with them including: J.M. Dent & Sons Ltd.,

George Harrap & Co. Ltd., Hulton Press Ltd., Methuen & Co. Ltd., Robert Hale Ltd. as well as the Manchester firm André Deutsch Ltd., all of whom rejected the manuscript in early 1954.[19] This series of refusals could not have come at a worse time so soon after Alfred's latest health and financial crises had left him vulnerable and dispirited, and he noted in his copy of the manuscript that this 'unpublished sequel to *Farewell, 'High Fell' [was]* Despised and Rejected!'

It now seemed that there was no obvious way out of Alfred's present problems after almost three years had elapsed since he set about the task of writing for a living, and now all he had to show for his efforts was his near bankruptcy. Of course there were reasons for this lack of achievement, especially the short time scale that he had set for himself to write a successful novel, even though he admitted that he was not a natural novelist. Moreover he had spent most of his writing career in the time-consuming process of assembling material for his topographical works rather than concentrating on the more popular types of fictional writing, but he had neither talent for this type of work, nor would it have satisfied his temperament.

Furthermore his health had deteriorated markedly, and he had little opportunity to indulge in his favourite pastime of walking neither for his personal enjoyment, nor for the purpose of gathering material for his usual topographical works that had virtually ceased. In fact Alfred only ever produced one more piece of work that was typical of the former glory days of descriptive writing about his beloved Yorkshire. This was a guide to the North York Moors National Park specially commissioned by the North Riding County Council.[20] It was a handy, fully-illustrated, pocket-sized book, complete with detailed fold-out map to show the setting, scenery and places of interest that enabled visitors to enjoy the many attractions of some of the most beautiful country in Yorkshire and it proved to be a very popular edition.[20a]

Notwithstanding this last testimony to Alfred's ongoing love of writing about one of his favourite topics, he had effectively come to the end of his would-be writing career. What now remained was to turn his attention to the demands of making yet another fresh start, this time with a return to the commercial world of business from which he had struggled for so long to free himself. Now his dream of a successful literary career had gone forever, and there was no alternative but to try to pick up the threads of his earlier wool-trade activity that he had abandoned almost fifteen years previously.

References and Notes

1. A.J. Brown, 'Going Private' (A Family Story), 1953, an unpublished 400 pp. sequel to *Farewell, 'High Fell'*, West Yorkshire Archive Service, Bradford Central Library, Document No. 69D90, Item 7/11/1/.

2. Ibid., A.J. Brown, Book 1, 'Going Private', passim.

3. A.J. Brown, *Farewell, 'High Fell'*, Williams & Norgate Ltd., London, 1952, 'In Search of a Flat', pp. 185-193.

4. Alfred John Brown, Journal, 1950-1954, (1951), passim.

5. Ibid., Alfred John Brown, Journal, (1952), passim.

6. A.J. Brown/E.P.S. Lewin (Literary Agent) Correspondence File, 1945-1949, passim.

7. Alfred J. Brown, *Broad Acres* Lectures File, late 1940s – early 1950s.

8. Alfred J. Brown, *Yorkshire Observer* Correspondence File, 1952-1954.

9. Op. cit., Alfred John Brown, Journal, (1954), passim.

10. Op. cit., Alfred John Brown, Journal, (1953), passim.

11. Alfred John Brown/Edwin Joseph Brown, Correspondence File, 1948-1953.

12. AJB letters to Eric Baker, Alfred J. Brown, Family and Friends Correspondence File, 1945-1954

13. A.J. Brown, 'Erratic Journey' (or Viennese Rhapsody), an incomplete draft novel, West Yorkshire Archive Service, Bradford Central Library, Document No. 69D90, Item 7/7, circa 1940s-1950s.

14. A.J.Brown, 'Kershaw's Cure', an incomplete draft novel, West Yorkshire Archive Service, Bradford Central Library, Document No. 69D90, Items 7/2, 7/3 and 7/15, circa 1930s – 1940s.

15. A.J. Brown, 'Green and Pleasant Land', an incomplete draft novel, West Yorkshire Archive Service, Bradford Central Library, Document No. 69D90, Items 7/9 and 7/12, 1940s-1950s.

16. A.J. Brown, Untitled, incomplete, handwritten and type-scripted manuscripts, West Yorkshire Archive Service, Bradford Central Library, Document No. 69D90, Items 7/9 and 10/1, circa 1940s-1950s.

17. A.J. Brown, 'Early Family Life', incomplete handwritten manuscript, circa 1940s-1950s.

18. AJB – E.P.S. Lewin Correspondence File, 1952-1954.

19. A.J. Brown, 'Going Private' (A Family Story), Publisher Correspondence File, 1953-1954.

20. A.J. Brown, *The North Yorks Moors National Park Guide Book*, The Home Publishing Company, Croydon, 1958.
    20a. **Note**: Further editions of this modestly-priced 2s/6d guide book were reprinted by The County Publications Publishers, C. & D. Constaple Ltd., London, 1959, 1963, 1965 and 1967, which indicated an enduring appeal for visitors to the area.

CHAPTER 19

Back to Bradford - 'Labor Omnia Vincit'

Introduction

The return to Bradford was just as difficult for Alfred as the many moves he made during his long and varied career, and while the affinity for his home city had perhaps waned over the years since his pre-war days, no doubt there still lingered some affection for the place of his birth. Now out of necessity he returned to his occupational roots, although the city had changed immeasurably since his former employment in the one-time, world-renowned, wool trade centre. It had all but lost its former epithet of 'Worstedopolis', and yet despite its decline it remained the UK's international centre of the worsted trade with almost 40% of the city's working population still employed in textiles.[1]

The post-war recovery of Bradford's textile trade had been especially difficult since there was a shortage of labour with pay levels in the trade often less than in other employment and there was fierce competition in the wool trade from overseas. Bradford's primary industry continued to decline and many small family-run firms either went out of business or had to amalgamate in order to survive, with the result that the number of woollen and worsted mills declined from 1,123 in 1950, to 825 in 1967, and by 1975 over half of the industry was controlled by only fifteen large companies. These changes, together with new methods of working, new machinery and new business practices, produced the necessary economies of scale that kept Bradford's textile industry alive.[2]

It was in this rapidly-changing business era that Alfred picked up the threads once more of a trade that had been shaken to its foundations since the time, almost 45 years previously, when he entered the worsted wool trade as a trainee, and his subsequent departure from it some 15 years ago as a highly successful overseas sales director. He found a job with a Bradford-based wool agency,[3,3a] and he had to adapt quickly to the highly competitive world of the Bradford textile business, which had made up for the loss of its former unchallenged status by traditional dogged determination to strive, survive and succeed; the same qualities which Alfred needed at a critical stage of a new career in his 60th year.

Alfred Rejoins the Wool Trade

Alfred's initial return to the wool trade was not directly to Bradford since he secured a job as a foreign sales agent in London for a Bradford-based company. He was extremely fortunate to get a foothold in an organisation which had become successful in representing the interests of large textile manufacturers, both in Bradford and other parts of the UK, whose products were directed at the export trade. The Bradford International Cloth Supply Agency Limited, known by its acronym 'BICSA', had registered offices in Bradford, although the company maintained offices in London, Paris and Cairo. It had an international profile of business activity with contacts in the Middle East, all of the then UK Dominions and Colonies, North Africa, West Germany, Scandinavia, South America and the USA. It was to the BICSA's London office that Alfred was appointed in the spring of 1954, at Grafton House, 2-3 Golden Square on the fringe of the Soho district of West London., and the only square in London to be devoted to the textile business.[4]

The appointment necessitated a return to the capital after Alfred and Marie-Eugénie had departed only two years previously. This time however their relocation was only temporary and they took a rented furnished flat at 15 Mortimer Street, near Oxford Circus in late 1954, having placed their furniture in storage after selling the house in York.[3] In this latest move there was almost a reciprocal arrangement among some Brown family members; Christopher started National Service with the West Riding Regiment at Fulford Barracks in York, having deferred his entry place at Lincoln College, Oxford to study modern languages. Adrian moved southwards to attend St. Augustine's Benedictine College in the preparatory Abbey School at Madeley Court in Hemingford Grey, near Huntingdon, and thus followed in the footsteps of his brother Christopher who attended the same school before going to Ampleforth College. Meanwhile their daughters were now well-established in London; Felicity settled down with husband Colin Millward, Barbara returned to her nursing career at Westminster Hospital and Rosemary pursued a career in publishing with Country Life magazine. Therefore Marie-Eugénie was glad to be near her daughters again, while Alfred was satisfied with his new job back in the wool trade and able to support his family once more.

The rented flat was most convenient for Alfred's new job, since he could walk to his office in Golden Square in just a few minutes, but it was only a stop-gap arrangement until he could find a suitable house to rent, so that he and his wife could bring their furniture out of storage and set up a home again where family and friends could be entertained. In the spring of 1955 they rented a roomy, three-storey terraced house and eagerly moved into a family home again at 38 Melrose Gardens, just off the Shepherds Bush Road in West London.[3] Alfred then settled into a radically different work routine after the relative freedom of his last attempt to become a full-time writer, which had left him in the doldrums and brought the family's financial circumstances to an all-time low point, so that now he grasped the chance to bring about a turn round in the family's fortunes.

The new job was similar in a way to his previous hotel business, since there was a seasonal pattern to the European market cloth supply business. The majority of the company offices in Golden Square were only used for the few weeks of the year when the foreign buyers came to town, so that during the 'buying seasons' of spring and autumn, the offices became hives of activity in preparation for the assembly of goods to be delivered some months later. These buyers took residence in the West End hotels and spent days reviewing all the products, designs and cloths available from manufacturers from around the UK, and normally placed sample orders for supply in subsequent weeks. Then when the buyers departed, English sales agents such as Alfred assembled their clients' sample collections and pursued their potential customers back to Europe. This was when the real work began and Alfred spent some four to six weeks, usually in May/June and November/December, travelling to see all the buyers who had visited London, to try to secure block orders for a range of products to be supplied in future.[4] This became the pattern of Alfred's commercial life in the years to come as a sales agent acting on behalf of individual and collective groups of British clothing manufacturers, which meant that he was away on prolonged European trips at least twice a year, as well as numerous visits to the manufacturer clients within the UK regions of production. However it was not long before he left the capital and finally made his way back to Bradford.

A Bradfordian Returns Home

The London move was a short term arrangement with the new company until Alfred became more familiar with their working practices. He needed to be available to the West Riding and other UK clients he represented in Europe, but then he needed to be available to foreign buyers during their biannual London buying seasons, and he took temporary accommodation at the RAF Club in Piccadilly. Therefore in the autumn of 1955 Alfred joined the staff at the headquarters of BICSA Limited in Bradford, which was located at 46 Peckover Street, situated among the many warehouses of the former German wool businesses in an area known as 'Little Germany'.[5,5a] The district was composed of impressive buildings dating back to the mid 19th century and was largely the legacy of the mainly German-Jewish merchants who built imposing warehouses in the Italianate style for the storage and sale of textile goods for export. During the period 1855-1890 some 85 buildings were constructed of which 55 are now listed, and it remains an area of particular historical and architectural interest in the centre of Bradford in which many new commercial enterprises are now located.

34. 'BICSA' Offices, 46 Peckover Street, Bradford

Alfred's priority now was a suitable family home and he quickly found a large Victorian house in the Manningham district of Bradford, and he negotiated with the solicitor and the Building Society for an advance of half the purchase price of £1,000, although he needed a further loan from his new employer and the bank for the remainder of the costs.[3] The house was old and needed considerable repairs, upgrading and decorating, and it was in a poor condition having been empty for almost a year. But they had to act quickly to guarantee the sale, so Alfred secured the deal with a £100 deposit at his bidding price offer and informed Marie-Eugénie: 'At least we have a house – unless there is a last minute hitch again!'[3] However there were still the formalities to complete before they gained possession in late November 1955, and Marie-Eugénie, perhaps somewhat reluctantly, moved back to Bradford to a house which was only about half a mile from her childhood home in Peel Square, Manningham.

The house at 2 Mornington Villas was at the corner of this quiet road and Manningham Lane and at one time belonged to Mr. Claude Taylor, a former boss of Alfred's in his earlier Bradford days. It was a fine three storey, end terrace family dwelling, built in the late 1800s, but it required a lot of attention to make it a comfortable residence once more. It had large, high-ceilinged rooms on the ground and first floors, together with a top floor flat which had letting potential to offset the mortgage and loan costs of the purchase. There was a separate lock-up garage in the back yard off a narrow back street, with small side and front gardens which required little attention. The house was conveniently located about a mile from Alfred's city centre office, so that when he was not away on his travels, he could walk home for lunch. Its only drawback, apart from its dilapidated state, was the noise of the traffic along the busy thoroughfare of Manningham Lane which was a major road,[3] although it enjoyed close proximity to the largest municipal open space in the city, namely Lister Park which was donated by the wool magnate Samuel Cunliffe Lister, later 1st Baron Masham (1815-1906).

Alfred and Marie-Eugénie had chosen an attractive location in which to live, since by 1870 the Manningham district became one of the first middle-class suburbs just to the north-west of the central industrial heart of the city. It was settled by many émigré German wool merchants who arrived in Bradford in the mid to late 1800s, and had also acquired the epithet 'Little Germany' – the residential district as distinct from its namesake where their business premises were located in the centre of the city. Many fine houses had been built by these German merchants, such as the families of Humbert Wolfe (1885-1940), poet, writer and civil servant, and Frederick Delius (1862-1934), composer and musician, and were large detached or semi-detached villas designed in both the Italianate and Gothic Revival styles by the architects who had designed the ornate warehouses of these same merchants in the city centre.[6]

The houses provided spacious accommodation that the successful mercantile middle-class Bradfordians desired, and it was into one of these properties that the Browns moved in 1955, although the area had undergone a transformation since these earlier days. Many former businessmen had moved away from Bradford to the more desirable areas of Ilkley in Wharfedale, but there was renewed interest in these properties by new professional classes because of their proximity to the centre of Bradford.[7,7a] This trend has continued today, but only no. 2 Mornington Villas remains residential, although now converted into a number of flats while business premises occupy the remainder of the street.

Nothing was ever straight-forward about the house moves that the Browns made and this was no exception, since unfortunately when the time came to take possession Alfred was away on business in Germany, so Marie-Eugénie had to organise the move on 26th November 1955.[3] However members of the family helped with the installation of all the furniture and personal belongings when the removal men arrived, but even with the help of her two sisters-in-law and their husbands, Gertie and Dick Hynes and Vera and Frank Schmitt, together with her youngest daughter Rosemary, the task was impossible to complete over a weekend and it took many weeks before they settled-in properly. Meanwhile Alfred was relieved to learn that the move was accomplished, although he regretted not being there to help, but he looked forward to seeing the house again, this time with their personal possessions installed, instead of the empty, soulless place that he remembered from his earlier viewings of the deserted dwelling. Nevertheless he had to wait until almost Christmas before he saw his new abode, since his business in Germany kept him away until mid-December. Even then he did not return to Bradford directly, since he attended the wedding of his life-long friend George Heseltine whose second marriage to Isobel took place in London on 17th December. However the family were together again in their new home for Christmas, which was made even more special by the arrival of their first grandchild, Sophie to Felicity and Colin Millward, during the festive season on Boxing Day.[3]

35. 2 Mornington Villas, Manningham, Bradford

A.J. Brown: Foreign Sales Agent

In early 1956 Alfred planned a spring business trip to Germany and Austria to establish a sales link between the British cloth manufacturers that he represented and the potential foreign customers most likely to buy the products available. This meant he had not only to keep up-to-date with the demands for different types of cloth and changing designs, but also gauge new trends in styles and fashions of clothing in forthcoming seasons, to advise manufacturers about the types of product that would be in demand in the near future.[8] Then loaded with a range of 10-20 sets of cloth samples bound in large heavy 9 x 6 inches pattern books, he arranged a series of appointments with likely customers to show examples of the materials available in model lengths for the manufacture of garments. This involved a busy schedule of daily meetings starting early in the morning, since German clothing factories started at 7.00 a.m. with offices open from 8.00 a.m. for appointments. This required Alfred to stay at a local hotel the night before, often having travelled 100-250 miles on the previous day, in order to be available to visit four to six customers per day, with each appointment lasting 1-2 hours. These meetings were highly structured events in which Alfred was expected to arrive punctually and presentably, often attired in clothing which reflected his clients' products. Customers were represented by buying teams which often included principals of the company, financiers and male and female fashion advisers who worked rapidly but thoroughly in the assessment of the materials and designs on offer. Alfred was required to present his collections speedily in German, with a minimum of 'sales talk', in which his own presentational skills counted as much as his technical knowledge, since most foreign buyers took pride in their expert judgment having been trained in technical schools and factories.[9]

After a busy round of presentations there was little or no time for socialising as Alfred typed his own reports of meetings and wrote letters during the evenings before he prepared for the next day's visits, or travelled to his next destination with a large collection of heavy baggage items and personal effects needed for a 4-6 week business trip. It was only occasionally at the weekend that Alfred was likely to have any time off, and he often took advantage of a stroll in the countryside to try to recuperate from the demands of his weekly schedule of work and travel. Moreover it was only at the end of a prolonged business trip that he would have any idea of how successful he had been, when the numbers of guaranteed orders of model lengths were received by the cloth manufacturers some two to three months later, with further bulk orders often not being placed with the suppliers until the approach of the next sales/buying season.[9]

It was after meticulous planning and preparation that Alfred set off expectantly in 1956 on his spring sales trip by air to Austria and Germany.[10] But when he arrived his main contact in Vienna was still away for the long Whitsuntide weekend, which was celebrated in Europe by an extended holiday, so he took advantage of having time at the beginning of a long trip to go for walk in the woods around the city. After Vienna Alfred continued to Stuttgart, Munich and Berlin in June, and while he found business became more difficult to conduct, with fierce competition and an unrelenting pace, he anticipated some decent orders along the way and a good start to his new job. But following the initial air travel, he found transport of the heavy cases with all his samples by train very demanding, with a return of the old 'dead feeling' in his side and legs which became worse when he was tired. In addition he found the demanding schedule that he had set himself left him in very low spirits at times and led him to consider whether he had made the right choice of a return to this type of work.[10]

Furthermore these introspective thoughts were compounded when Alfred discovered that there were problems within the BICSA Agency. While in Bremen he received a telephone call from Mr. Ross, a director of BICSA, who had sold one of his textile businesses and was due to take charge of the Agency in Bradford. There were concerns about the cost of maintaining the Agency's London office, which meant the likelihood of staff cuts and a reduction in business for Alfred to manage, as well as in his commissions associated with this branch of the Agency's business, that might have serious financial implications for his future.[10] In spite of this disturbing news Alfred continued to conduct business for BICSA during the remainder of his trip to Hamburg, Berlin, Munich and Hannover until he returned in June.[10]

Alfred realised that any reorganisation of the Agency was out of his control and he consoled himself with thoughts about the upcoming 21st birthday of his son Christopher and the family summer holiday which they had planned in a cottage on the North Yorkshire Moors.[10] During that summer holiday of 1956 Alfred also renewed acquaintanceship with his old friend George Heseltine and his new wife Isobel, when they met the rest of the Brown family on holiday in Goathland.[11] The holiday helped to re-establish the close bond that had existed between two old comrades, which would become invaluable in the testing times ahead for Alfred. George's career had blossomed at the age of 57 after he studied law before being called to the Bar in London in 1951, and joined the Chambers of D.N. Pitts at The Cloisters in Temple, London EC4, where he now practised as a defence barrister in criminal law. He also held a position as Counsel involved in Military Courts Martial both in England and Germany, and retained a Commission as one of the oldest RAF Volunteer Reserve Officers in the country.[11]

Crisis at the 'BICSA' Agency

In late September 1956 Alfred contacted George for some legal advice concerning the ongoing problems at the BICSA organisation. The Agency represented cloth manufacturers, some of whom had definitive written agreements, while others had no specific written agreements. Ross maintained that in the latter case, provided that the Agency did its job, the directors could not terminate posts in the Agency. The London office, which was now in a financial crisis, employed two representative agents without written agreements, and according to Ross and the Agency's solicitor, their posts could not be terminated, and therefore the necessary cost savings could not be implemented.[11] In response George suggested that the London representative agents must be working on some sort of terms however loosely expressed, and the view that the Agency was bound to them was nonsense whatever the solicitor's advice.[11]

The problem of agent retention was further complicated by the fact that both London agents were appointed without detailed terms and conditions, under arrangements made by Ross on a trial basis, with only sketchy details of any termination date by the Agency in letters of appointment.[11] Moreover, since employees were also regarded as 'agents' for the manufacturers they represented, even these arrangements suffered from the lack of written agreements. This included Alfred's own arrangement as the representative 'agent' for the major firm of Moxon's Worsteds of Huddersfield, which had also been arranged by Ross, with only a letter of his appointment to represent Moxon's interests abroad. In this regard George was of the opinion that these arrangements were highly dubious, based on unsound legal advice and detrimental to good working practices.[11] This reinforced Alfred's view of the need to draw up detailed future written agreements for the agents concerned, with specified termination clauses, along with compensation arrangements, and to insist that his own personal arrangements were similarly endorsed.[11] But this would put him in conflict with Ross, which could have adverse consequences in terms of his already tenuous position in the Agency, and possibly jeopardise his future as a dependent agent.

Meanwhile Alfred's other major concern was the private education of Adrian who was now 12 years old. He had recently started a new school in the Junior House of the Ampleforth College, but in view of the financial uncertainties about his future, Alfred wondered if he could continue to meet the costs of the fees involved, since he wanted to provide Adrian the same educational opportunity as that of his siblings.[11] Subsequently Alfred was able to discuss both his occupational problems and educational matters with George during a two week visit to London at the end of October, when the foreign buyers arrived, before he left on another autumn sales trip to Austria and Germany that kept him away until Christmas 1956.[11] He was glad to have personal support and legal advice from George at a time of conflict and he valued the input from his trusted old friend to help with the resolution of his problems.

Business and Life, as Usual, Alas!

Alfred's business trips to Europe now settled into a regular pattern of extended sales visits to customers in the spring and autumn of the year, with intervening visits to the clients he represented abroad, as well as the London-based work when the foreign buyers came to town to review the products that were available from the major cloth producing areas of the UK. This regular round of routine business activity meant that he spent almost half the year 'on the road', which was not only very demanding for him, but was also very depressing for Marie-Eugénie, even though she had nearby relatives and friends on whom she could rely for company. However in the spring of 1957 she joined Alfred briefly during his trip to Germany and saw how hard he worked on his travels.[12] But even when Alfred was at home in Bradford, he often had to put in extra time in the office at the weekend, which naturally Marie-Eugénie resented, especially at holiday times, and she felt that Ross expected far too much of Alfred, whose position in the organisation was not being properly acknowledged, nor his valuable contribution reasonably rewarded.[12]

Alfred's intercession with Ross about new terms and conditions for the agents did not produce any changes, nor did it help their working relationship, and the previous questions about the future reorganisation of the Agency remained unresolved.[11] The only respite Alfred got from his ever-demanding business role was the annual family summer holiday at a rented cottage on the North Yorkshire Moors. In 1957 however the family rented a cottage in Sleights, near Whitby, which belonged to a friend from their Whitfield House Hotel days, Ralph Taylor, a retired joiner who had carried out much work at the hotel during their years of occupancy. Alfred and Marie-Eugénie still had many friends in the surrounding area, including Tom and Joyce Whittaker and their daughter Faith in Littlebeck, as well as others in Goathland. At this time it seemed that in the event of a turn around in the family's fortunes, Alfred and Marie-Eugénie started to consider living in this area once more, but next time it might be a place of possible retirement when circumstances permitted.[11]

Unfortunately this brief, speculative, future dream was soon replaced by the reality of another autumn business trip to Germany and Austria, where Alfred represented a number of important clients who constituted his portfolio in the European cloth export market. Of primary importance was the firm of B.H. Moxon & Sons Ltd., one of Yorkshire's oldest family-run businesses, which was then part of the Tulketh Group of Companies. The firm was known for its high grade fine worsted cloths which were unsurpassed in quality and design, and had recently invested in the large new Southfield Mills in Kirkburton, Huddersfield, and became the leading exporter of cloth to European and other markets around the world. In addition Alfred also represented other UK specialist cloth producers including William Watson and Sons of Hawick and Arthur Bell of Langholm, both based in the Scottish Borders. On the autumn schedule Alfred visited many of his now regular German customers in Munich, Stuttgart, Goslar, Berlin, Hamburg, Dusseldorf, Bremen and Cologne, and then went on to Austria and one of his favourite cities, Vienna, before he returned home just in time for Christmas in 1957. It was another long, busy and very demanding trip that left Marie-Eugénie echoing Alfred's own sentiments about their current lifestyle: 'All this travelling and constant worry and I hate this separate existence. We have got to the time of life for a quiet more regular going on – but what can we do? It seems to be a battle and hard work whatever we do. If only we could find something much easier in England, (signed) a "grass widow", Marie-Eugénie'[12] But their concerns were even more intensified by news that the scale of Alfred's business activities was to be extended the following year to new countries in the Middle East.[12]

36. Alfred J. Brown at Berlin Airport, 1957

New Challenges at Home and Abroad

The year 1958 presented quite different problems for Alfred and Marie-Eugénie, each with a unique set of circumstances which had to be faced alone, and each with quite different demands which taxed their capabilities, but with potentially serious consequences for both of them. Marie-Eugénie dealt with a development threat to their residential situation at home, while Alfred had to accommodate to the new increased demands of an expansion of his sales duties overseas with the unforeseen difficulties and dangers that this entailed.

Alfred began his first trip to the Middle East in January with an initial stop in Athens, before he moved on to Beirut, Baghdad and Tehran in February. While in Athens he conducted business through his close contact Ioannidis, and he secured small orders for Moxon's, but had no luck with the Scottish Tweeds and Twists of Watson's and Bell's of Hawick and Langholm respectively, but he hoped for better luck in the Middle East.[13] On arrival in Baghdad he found not only the heat oppressive, but the competition equally taxing, with many other English sales representatives who pursued the newly expanding markets vigorously, although he was fortunate to receive good orders for Moxon's, but again had no luck with the Scottish products.[13] However he struggled to come to terms with the laissez-faire attitudes of potential customers, since Arab businessmen had a different 'modus operandi' from the highly formalised practices of their German counterparts to which he had become accustomed, as it appeared that time meant very little to them, with appointments often delayed and sometimes never kept. In addition he suffered from stomach problems with the so-called 'Middle East Complaint', otherwise known vulgarly to the British as the 'Bagdad sh***s', but he struggled on to Tehran through a much delayed schedule and returned to England a week later than planned.[13]

If this new experience was not demanding enough, Alfred faced one of his busiest European travel schedules so far with another spring business trip, after he had completed the usual London-based round of meetings with foreign buyers in March and April, which involved an ambitious six week, 29 city tour of Germany and Austria during May and June.[13] This was also at the time when there was speculation about his proposed move back to London to restore the office's cost-effectiveness. Naturally he was very dubious about such a move given his present unresolved arrangements with the BICSA Agency, and he lost confidence in Mr. Ross and his fellow director Mr. Kinder. He was determined not to consider the move unless he could obtain firm agreements in writing about his position, his commissions and his future arrangements with the Agency, since the strain of the trips abroad was such that unless he was adequately rewarded the effort involved was simply not worth the return.[13]

Meanwhile Alfred's European travels were eased by the use of a car after the arrival of Mr. Watson from Hawick, who shared some of the long distance driving needed to meet the customers. Unfortunately not many big orders were secured, as business in Germany was difficult at this time, and with the exception of the new designs of Watson's, the cloth sample sets supplied by Moxon's were relatively poor, and customers were reluctant to order while the price of wool continued to fall.[13] Furthermore while the business outlook did not look promising, the prospects of driving through the frontier into the Russian sector of the eastern zone to Berlin also filled Alfred with some apprehension. Indeed he sought reassurances about the situation from the British Embassy in Hannover, and if the travelling pair was detained for any reason he had taken the precaution of seeking help from the Foreign Office.[13]

When Alfred began the Austrian section of his trip he was nearly a week behind schedule, but the delays had given him time to consider his employment arrangements,[13] and he wrote to Ross and Kinder to make his demands known and was prepared to stand by his terms in order to negotiate a better deal. His demands included: a written contract of agreement with full terms and conditions specified, agreed levels of commissions paid on sales performance, with BICSA rates for agency work of 5% in Europe and 7.5% in the Middle East, not the variable 1 – 3% on top of basic salary currently paid for overseas work, and that travelling expenses were not be deducted from commissions, which was the existing iniquitous practice.[13] He received full support for this bold stance in discussions with his close friend and now legal adviser, George Heseltine,[11] and he decided that unless the agreed commissions were repaid in full without deductions of necessary business expenses, he would refuse to make the next proposed Middle East trip, even if this meant leaving the Agency.[13] Moreover, he also began to seriously consider becoming an independent agent and representing those companies around the UK with which he had established good working relationships as a possible viable alternative to his present situation.[13]

Development Disturbance Threat at Home

While Alfred was on his travels in Germany, Marie-Eugénie had an unusual problem to deal with at home, when it was discovered plans were being considered to convert some neighbouring residential properties into business premises which might have had detrimental effects upon homes in the locality. The controversy centred upon a terrace of three substantial early Victorian houses on Manningham Lane, less than 50 yards away from 2 Mornington Villas. At a Public Enquiry it was reported that these large properties stood empty but Bradford Corporation was reluctant to approve their conversion for office usage.[13] Furthermore planning permission for a garage proposed by a property developer was also refused by a government minister on the grounds that there was significant loss of housing accommodation and encroachment of business into a residential area. The developer then appealed against the Council's refusal to allow the alternative office conversion, and proposed that conversion to business use offered the only effective solution.

It was also reported that Mrs. Mary [sic, Marie-Eugénie] Brown objected to these proposals on the grounds that further encroachment of commercial premises would result in the deterioration of a respectable residential district. She argued that businesses would increase the parking pressures on local residents, who already had problems of access to their properties due to the advancement of commercial premises along Manningham Lane.[14] Indeed she was supported by the City Engineer and Surveyor, who confirmed that the properties concerned presented an attractive and dignified residential feature, which was important given that Bradford had a substantial housing waiting list, and that poorly-planned commercial developments along the main busy road had seriously reduced the local amenities for occupiers of residences in the area.[15]

Arguments and counter arguments were presented by the protagonists concerning the relative quality of life and status of the neighbourhood. The developers portrayed the area as being adversely affected by the presence of regular, noisy disturbances by inebriated members of a local Lithuanian Club. However Marie-Eugénie countered that this was not a true reflection of the social order, in which perfectly respectable people lived in the area, many of whom were members of the local Jewish Club, which gave a genteel ambience to a quiet residential district. Then in a personal attack the developer's solicitor suggested that the Browns had taken advantage of buying relatively cheap property in a run-down less than desirable area, which was bitterly rejected by Marie-Eugénie. She vigorously defended their choice of the locality as a desirable place to live, and that most residents like themselves had made significant improvements to their properties by the investment of substantial sums to modernise the formerly elegant houses of the area. Furthermore she indicated that any commercially-related development which took place was tastefully carried out mainly by professional people, such as two doctors in Mornington Villas who had incorporated surgeries into their residences, and thereby provided valuable health amenities to other local residents.

Unfortunately Marie-Eugénie had to leave the Public Enquiry before the end of the proceedings, but not before she had requested the City Solicitor to formally register her support for the rejection of the appeal for development. Afterwards she recounted all the events that had taken place in a long letter to Alfred,[13] who congratulated her on her fine performance and indicated that the monstrous proposal for the development for such elegant houses should never have been considered in the first place.[13] Subsequently the appeal was rejected and the future development of business premises in the area was thwarted, at least in the interim, since the house at 2 Mornington Villas today remains almost the sole property not transformed into professional business premises, but it is converted into a number of self-contained flats.

Mayhem in the Middle East – The Baghdad Debacle

Alfred reversed his decision about the summer business trip to the Middle East and went ahead with the planned schedule to visit Iraq, Lebanon and Iran because he did not want to jeopardise the negotiations about his employment arrangements, and he did not want to be seen as 'letting the side down' by a refusal to carry out his duties. Nevertheless he was concerned about the disturbing news of conflicts in the region in the summer of 1958, and Marie-Eugénie expressed her concern about the trip, as well as young Adrian, who was worried for his father's safety in view of the dangerous situation in Lebanon with a civil war in progress.[13]

Alfred began the first stage of the trip in late June in Athens, where once more he found the heat overpowering even in his tropical attire, especially since he carried the heavy books of cloth samples to show to customers in the usual demanding series of appointments.[13] Unfortunately business was especially bad from the outset, and he felt that he should never have agreed to make the trip, but he had failed to convince Ross of the unlikely success of doing business especially in this region at this time of year, when trade in general was depressed. After Athens he was due to fly to Baghdad, then on to Beirut and Teheran, which promised even more difficulties under the present circumstances, but even Alfred could not have predicted the near disastrous outcome of this Middle East adventure.

When he arrived in Baghdad the temperature was 116°F but business was not so hot, in fact it was quite disastrous owing to the conflict in Lebanon, which required military intervention by the USA to prevent the overthrow of the government in a conflict that could spread within the region. Alfred was now convinced that he should not be there and he reported the bad news of the near impossible sales situation in a telephone conversation to Ross, who seemed quite unperturbed, unfriendly and unsympathetic, even though he had insisted that the trip went ahead.[13] Regardless of the political crisis, there was also a product crisis since the collection of cloth samples were regarded as 'old and stale' instead of the new designs which the customers expected, but Kinder had refused to authorise special Middle East sample sets of cloth by Moxon's, which other firms had taken trouble to arrange, so that the present trip seemed a waste of time.[13] This reinforced Alfred's idea that he should get out of his present situation and take on other agency representation since he doubted if he could continue with Moxon's much longer, but he was now more concerned about completing this trip as soon and as safely as possible.

All Alfred's carefully laid plans were suddenly interrupted by the revolution in Iraq that took place over the night of 13th/14th July 1958, which resulted in the overthrow of King Faisal and the government by an army-led coup d'état, and he found himself a virtual prisoner confined to his hotel along with a group of other foreign guests. He was unable to get a flight out of Baghdad since all public services were suspended, including planes, trains and even telephone links with the outside world, and visitors looked on helplessly as mobs of young men rushed through the streets shouting and holding up pictures of Nasser of Egypt.[13] Nasser had been a source of inspiration to 'Free Officers' after the overthrow of King Farouk, but he had no practical role in the 1958 Iraqi Revolution. Nevertheless the mayhem reminded Alfred of the scenes of the Nazi take over that he had witnessed in Vienna in 1938, but these crowds looked far more menacing, undisciplined and wild. He was concerned that anything might happen, and although the hotel was not targeted by the mob which mingled with the Army units, the situation looked very dangerous. Moreover, the local news reported that the Regent Faisal II, the Crown Prince Abd-al-Ilah together with some members of their families, and the Prime Minister, Nuri Al-Said, had all been assassinated during the coup, with others hanged in the streets, and all foreigners were advised to remain in their hotels.[13]

While Alfred contemplated his present predicament he set down some thoughts and feelings about the current situation:

> Of course it's another exciting experience in my life and providing things go smoothly it will mean only a slight delay – but will they? I shall be content if the mobs don't get out of hand and break in on us! However I am not afraid or worried: this sort of danger never bothered me and I shall fight to the end if need be.[13]

As he continued his letter to Marie-Eugénie he indicated that it might only be a short-lived uprising or the revolution might even fail, but it appeared to be a dark conspiracy and that he should be prepared for the worst if necessary, before he reminded his wife about the provisions he had made for her and the family in his will, as he heard more shots fired in the street outside.[13]

Two days later Alfred wrote to Marie-Eugénie again, although he had no idea whether this or the previous letter would reach its destination, and indicated that he and other guests had been kept imprisoned in the hotel as the streets were too dangerous for foreigners, and that there was no possibility of escape from the country.[13] He was staying at the old Sinbad Hotel in 'Haroum El Rashid', the main street of the old city of Baghdad, which overlooked the River Tigris in which he swam only a couple of days previously. The situation was quite desperate even with the hotel gates and doors locked, and guests were withdrawn to the gardens on the banks of the river behind the hotel. It was from there that Alfred heard shots fired on the nearby bridge and saw a large fire across the river in the vicinity of the British Embassy where he had called recently. He saw figures in the Embassy garden throwing papers into the river, and guessed that the Embassy had been sacked and burned by the mob as the Union Flag disappeared from view. However by early evening the violent and menacing crowds outside the hotel had dispersed under a curfew imposed by the military authority, and as a result the hotel guests were now somewhat relieved.[13]

Later Alfred heard news that the British Ambassador and his staff had been safely evacuated to the new Baghdad Hotel further up the river, so he telephoned the British Delegation to find out more about the ongoing situation. To his surprise he found himself speaking to the British Ambassador, Sir Michael Wright, who appeared most kind and anxious to help, although he was also in something of a predicament having escaped from the burning Embassy with no more than the clothes that he and his wife were wearing! Nevertheless he gave Alfred an update about the current state of affairs which he passed on to his fellow guests as well as those hotel staff who still remained at their posts.[13]

During this temporary incarceration Alfred befriended a small group of individuals who were anxious to get out of their hotel as soon as possible, and together they decided it would be better if they moved to the relative safety of the Baghdad Hotel upriver, out of the congested Rashid.Street, which by day was still full of hostile crowds who might yet break into their hotel. Therefore Alfred and this small group were moved under escort to the new hotel only to discover that a faction of the army had entered this supposedly safe haven the previous day, and rounded up and taken away some innocent guests, several of whom had been executed. But one of this captive group who had been bundled into a car at gunpoint was a Swiss contact known to Alfred, and had then calmly asked his captors to stop at the roadside in order to relieve himself, and being allowed to get out, he simply disappeared into the crowd, then made his way back to the hotel and regaled his fellow guests with his remarkable escape story over a drink in the bar. Afterwards the British Ambassador negotiated for an armed guard to be placed outside the hotel and reassured the guests that they would then be safe from any further intrusions by hostile groups.[13]

There were now some 80 guests who had taken refuge in the new Baghdad Hotel and many were still quite shaken by the previous violent incident so the atmosphere remained very tense, although things calmed down with the night curfew in place, but the airport was still closed so there was no chance of leaving the country just yet. Some guests then settled into a typically British routine of eating their communal meals together, with the British Ambassador, his wife and their English guests seated at high table, while the appointed Army Liaison Officer in charge of security occasionally updated them with more reassuring local news, supplemented by gatherings round the radio to listen to broadcasts of home news on the BBC world service.[13]

Most guests were content to endure the present situation until some post-revolutionary order was established, which happened a few days later, when everyone was able to leave peacefully. Alfred then flew home having cancelled the Tehran and Beirut stages of his business trip, after which a short article about his safe return appeared in the local press under the title: 'A.J. Brown Back From Baghdad'.[16] Earlier in an interview broadcast on the ITV Television 6.00 p.m. evening news programme when Alfred was asked about the ordeal he simply replied: 'it was just another one of life's adventures', which gave much relief and enjoyment to his family and friends who learned of his recent Baghdad escapade.

Following the near disastrous Middle East trip that was a total business failure, Alfred took some time off his overcrowded work schedule for a while, and enjoyed another sojourn in Sleights together with his family, where he celebrated his 64th birthday in the peace and quiet of the North Yorkshire Moors. But he was reminded of his ongoing work predicament by his friend George, who was keen to help him resolve his employment problems.[11] George encouraged Alfred to give more serious consideration to a break with Ross and Kinder, even if it proved temporarily less financially rewarding, and encouraged him to try to substitute his Moxon's agency representation with other more supportive companies for whom he acted as a primary agent. Soon after Alfred met with Watson's of Hawick on a regular visit to his client, and although they could not totally replace his agency work with Moxon's, they supported the expansion of his representation. This reassured George that although his old friend needed to make some financial sacrifice, it might reduce the physical demands and nervous strain associated with the work, which if unchecked could have serious consequences for a man of his age.[11]

In spite of these concerns Alfred embarked on another demanding business trip in the first week of November, which involved a mammoth six week tour of three countries, when he visited some 34 cities in Germany, Holland and Austria, and did not return home until the week before Christmas.[13] Moreover on leaving he suffered from a throat infection which needed two penicillin injections and he was supplied with tablets for the trip, for which he had been declared fit to travel.[13] But the pace of his job increased with more English sales agents than ever who competed for limited business opportunities, some of whom enjoyed the support of an assistant with a car to transport their baggage. Meanwhile Alfred continued to struggle with public transport and his own baggage which included up to 5 bags of samples, his personal luggage, a large dispatch case, a small brief case and a portable typewriter, but he was worried about being overwhelmed by the demand and expressed his concern to his wife for the future: 'If only I could get out of this now and settle down at home! There seems to be no end to it and no future in it for us, it is no life for me or you. But unless a miracle happens I expect I shall have to keep on until I drop.'[13]

Alfred's Role, Range and Remuneration Conflicts

If the previous year had been difficult in terms of the new challenges which Alfred faced in an increasingly competitive business market abroad, there was further expansion of both his agency role and range of his sales territories in the coming year, and continued difficulties about his remuneration arrangements. In 1959 Moxon's became his primary representative company, but not at the expense of the other companies with whom he was expected to increase his representational role. Furthermore Alfred also added new countries to his expanding Middle-East territory including Jordan, Israel and Egypt. These extra commitments required him to increase the length of his business trips abroad whilst maintaining close contacts with his UK suppliers and the foreign buyers who visited London each year in the buying seasons, which resulted in him being away for more than half the year in total. Moreover there was still no resolution to his terms of agreement and commission payment problems. This situation not only placed extra pressure on Alfred but it had further detrimental effects on his family life at a time when most men at his age anticipated retirement and a more relaxed way of life.

In spite of a previous threat not to accept extra agency responsibilities without written terms of agreement and an associated commission package, Alfred began another trip to the Middle-East in early 1959 without such undertakings on the part of his employer. He left London in late January and intended to go back to Lebanon since last year's conflict had passed and the country had settled down.[17] This time he used Athens as a base of operations between visits to Lebanon, Jordan, Egypt and Israel, since it was easier to travel to and from Greece for destinations in the eastern Mediterranean, but this added to the time and costs involved although he had also important customers in Athens and Rhodes.[17]

Alfred's sales activity in Beirut was slow because business was almost at a standstill after the earlier Lebanon conflict with most firms badly affected, but he secured reasonable orders for his Scottish manufacturers Watson's and Bell's without much success for Moxon's. Then on arrival in Jerusalem he visited potential new customers, but found many were only interested in cheaper cloths, with Moxon's products regarded as too expensive. However he secured some orders for the Scottish products, although he attributed his limited success to the rapport he established with a group of Arab-Christian anglophile customers who had sons at universities in England. Moreover the Jerusalem visit also gave Alfred great personal satisfaction when his hosts took him to visit all the holy places and historic sites in and around the city, which had such an impact on him as a deeply religious person that he vowed to take Marie-Eugénie on a tour of the Holy Land as soon as possible.[17]

Following a return to Athens Alfred was frustrated by the poor state of business in Greece which was also almost stagnant, so that he had little success even among his well-established customers and found the situation similar in Rhodes.[17] At this point he became concerned about the prospects for the remainder of the trip, but with time on his hands he wrote to Kinder again to clarify his position. He had only received one offensive letter and an unpleasant cable from Kinder during the trip in reply to 20 long reports he had filed so far.[17] Now Alfred's feelings of despair set in once more after Kinder's refusal to accede to his demands for adequate commissions, as well as the complaints about the cost of the trip which had largely been Kinder's idea anyway.[17] Nevertheless Alfred had secured enough orders to cover the costs of the expenses involved and he intended to pursue his claims until he received a fair deal, with the added threat of leaving the company if his demands were not met.[17]

The final stages of this Middle-East trip also proved problematical since Alfred had to abandon his visit to Kuwait since it was too far off route and too expensive, and even his visit to Jordan was only possible as a result of a generous arrangement by a customer to travel to Amman and return to Jerusalem by car. Finally after he secured the delayed visa, Alfred left Athens and completed the last stage of his trip with a visit to Egypt.[17] On arrival in Cairo he was overwhelmed by a series of official meetings with Government officials, representatives of the British Embassy and some of the country's most important customers, and then he almost succumbed to an equally demanding round of social activities. These included a traditional meal at the prestigious Nile Hotel, which Alfred's sensitive digestion found hard to take, then dubious entertainment at the 'Auberge des Pyramides' club which involved a traditional belly dancer that he quite loathed, before he made his excuse of tiredness and retired for what was left of the night.Unfortunately Alfred later developed another throat problem from a tonsil infection and spent 36 hours in bed, which resulted in the postponement of his trip to Alexandria and extended this already lengthy, sometimes frustrating and often demanding journey, which meant that he did not arrive home until late March just before Easter that year.[17]

Alfred was able to take only a short break from his travels at Easter but managed to meet with his old friend George again who continued to provide support and advice for his ongoing employment problems.[11] Alfred also regretted that he was unable to enjoy the short family break in the Yorkshire Dales when Marie-Eugénie, their daughter Felicity and her young children stayed at the Manor House in Burnsall which was operated by some friends. Marie-Eugénie also expressed her deep concerns over Alfred's continued long absences: 'I spend so little time with you these days and life is shortening and the years fly by. We must make the use of what is left.'[17] No doubt Alfred reflected bitterly on these words since he was unable to see neither his two daughters, nor his young grandchildren, during recent busy meetings in London before he departed once more for his next European trip.[17]

Alfred became further downhearted when he received retirement papers as he approached 65 years of age, but remained adamant that he would not complete the forms nor raise the matter with his employer, who might see this as an opportunity to replace him. But the prospect of the continuation of his demanding job also filled him with foreboding: 'I suppose I shall have to continue trailing around Europe and the Middle-East for another five years – if they will let me! There seems to be no alternative. What a prospect!'[17] Indeed the prospect of having to work until he was 70 or longer and still have an inadequate pension seemed unrealistic, since he doubted if he could stand the physical and mental strain of many more business trips. He acknowledged that the job got harder all the time as the agency work increased, while the Moxon situation was not only unsatisfactory but humiliating. But he did not intend to give in just yet, and hoped to hold on to the end of the year then bring about a change in his circumstances.[17]

In the late spring of 1959 Alfred undertook another extended business trip which not only included established customers in Germany and Austria, but potential new customers in Holland. He began his trip in Germany with visits to four cities in northern Germany, before he took the night train to Holland to visit Gröningen, Rotterdam and Amsterdam.[17] This was followed by a return to Germany and the possibility of not being allowed into Berlin due to the impending end of May deadline imposed by the Soviets for the withdrawal of Western powers from the city, but fortunately the Soviet ultimatum passed with discussions to resolve the latest Berlin crisis and Alfred kept to his overstretched schedule.[17] He then continued with the remainder of the German stage of a seven city tour to southern Germany before he finally completed the Austrian stage with visits to Innsbruck, Graz and Vienna, then returned home again after another epic two month trip thoroughly exhausted.[17]

That summer Alfred enjoyed the annual summer holiday at Sleights in early August since, with the exception of Christmas, it was the only time that he had the opportunity to be with his family. He and Marie-Eugénie, Barbara and Adrian were joined by Rosemary and Felicity and her two young children, with only Christopher absent due to his summer employment in Spain.[17] He also felt some trepidation with the approach of his 65th birthday especially since he preferred to forget the passage of his own annual milestones. And if he needed something to take his mind off this one, his good friend and now quasi-legal adviser George provided it. In response to the receipt of a copy of Alfred's latest letter to Kinder, George was brutally critical of Alfred's meek approach to his work problems.[11] He criticised Alfred's lack of insistence on clearly defined terms of agreement, which included salary and travelling expenses, particularly when Alfred's nominal 1% commission was swamped by expenses and was far below the 5% norm for other representative agents. Moreover he was not even paid any follow-on commissions for repeat orders which often formed a large part of his sales.

Alfred indicated that he had not received even the courtesy of a written response from Kinder, nor was he able to meet with him to discuss the matter before went on holiday, and only had a brief conversation with Ross about his situation, who indicated that nothing would change the present arrangements.[11] He also suggested that Kinder and Ross had a reputation for meanness towards employees, who were undervalued and underpaid, and they resented any demands made by rebellious staff such as Alfred, to whom they could be quite vindictive. However in spite of this he was still prepared to make one final attempt to reach a fair settlement before he threatened action.[11] But he was also aware that the unscrupulous pair might risk losing his services rather than agree to new terms or commission payments, and since he was nearly 65 they probably expected him to retire anyway.[11] This did not satisfy George who suggested that Ross's statement of no change was ominous, and that Alfred had got nowhere with the two directors, so it was time the broke he away from Moxon's to find new agency work elsewhere, and then promised legal action on behalf of Alfred if any attempt was made at dismissal without fair notice and compensation.[11]

Alfred kept in close contact with George on another extended two month tour of Germany and Holland, during which further serious conflicts developed in the ongoing dispute with his employer. While in Holland he received a telephone call from Kinder who instructed him to abandon his scheduled meetings with the remaining customers in Holland.[17] Kinder was unable to manage with the large orders already received from German customers and suggested Alfred should cut short his trip and focus exclusively on Germany. But this presented an impossible situation since he had commitments to pursue agency work on Watson's behalf in Holland.[17] Under the circumstances Alfred decided not to accede to Kinder's request since all the necessary arrangements were in place and he could not ruin the plans already made as well as perhaps Watson's and his own reputation in Holland. Furthermore in view of this conflict of interests, Alfred had no option but to resign with effect from 1st January 1960 and make some interim arrangements with both Watson's and Bell's, his Scottish suppliers, until he could secure a third major agency, then take the risk to become an independent agent in the new year.[17]

This news was naturally received with concern by Marie-Eugénie who nevertheless supported Alfred's position with Moxon's as being untenable and suggested that the sooner he became independent the better. She believed that he deserved to be happy in his work at his time of life and not be subjected to the intolerable pressures imposed by others.[17] George was also adamant that it was time for Alfred to part with Moxon's and make the most of his other agency contacts, especially since he could take with him many of his Moxon customers free of any obligation to the firm, and without any concern for feelings of personal loyalty, once he had made the break with the company.[11] All that remained now was for Alfred to consider carefully this radical change to his working life and take the necessary action, before he returned home just before Christmas after another exasperating trip, but hopefully one that would lead to a positive change in his future personal circumstances.

References and Notes

1. Alan Hall, *The Story of Bradford*, The History Press, Stroud, Gloucestershire, 2013, Chapter 11, 'Start of a Long Decline', pp. 154-159.

2. Bob Ducket, and John Waddinton-Feather, *Bradford History and Guide*, Tempus Books, Stroud, Gloucestershire, 2005, Chapter 7, 'From City to Metropolis: Twentieth Century Bradford', pp. 107-134.

3. AJB/MEB (and others) Correspondence File, 1954-1955, passim.
    3a. **Note**: AJB did not keep journals after 1954, therefore most subsequent information was abstracted from personal, family and business correspondence, or in personal communication with family members.

4. Adrian Paul Brown, 'Exporting British Cloth to Europe', 'Golden Square, London', pp. 29-39. A draft of an unpublished thesis in partial fulfilment of a Diploma in Textile Industries, Leeds University, 1964.

5. AJB letter to MEB, 15th August, 1957, Personal, Family and Business Correspondence Files, 1955-1957, passim.
    5a. **Note**: The biographer had a summer vacation job in 1963 on Peckover Street with a textile company and assembled the types of sample books of cloth which Alfred used to show to customers when he travelled on business trips abroad.

6. George Sheeran, *The Building of Bradford: An Illustrated Architectural History*, Tempus Books, Stroud, Gloucestershire, 2005, Chapter 1, 'Bradford: A City Defined', pp. 1-30.

7. Ibid., George Sheeran, Chapter 5, 'Building a Victorian City 1850-1914', pp. 74-106.
    7a. **Note**: As a youth, the biographer passed the house on his daily bus journey to/from St. Bede's Grammar School for 7 years (1957-1964), then spent another 7 years in later life investigating the life story of one of its former illustrious residents!

8. Op. cit., Adrian Paul Brown, 'The Agent's Role', chapter 7, p. 40.

9. Op. cit., Adrian Paul Brown, 'An Agent's Day', chapter 8, pp. 41-48.

10. AJB Personal, Family Business Correspondence File, 1956, passim.

11. AJB/GCH Correspondence File, 1951-1959, passim.

12. AJB Personal, Family and Business Correspondence File, 1957, passim.

13. AJB Personal, Family and Business Correspondence File, 1958, passim.

14. Newspaper article: 'A Little Germany Property Appeal', The *Yorkshire Post*, 7th May 1958.

15. Newspaper article: 'Bradford Parking Problem: Demand for Offices out of the Centre Enquiry Told', *Bradford Telegraph & Argus*, 8th May, 1958.

16. 'A.J. Brown Back From Baghdad', *Bradford Telegraph & Argus*, 31st July, 1958.

17. AJB Personal, Family and Business Correspondence File, 1959, passim.

CHAPTER 20

A.J. Brown – Independent Textile Agent

The Move to Independence

Despite Alfred's determination to break away from his odious ties to Moxon's it was several months before he established an independent agency by taking on additional clients in a risky new venture to represent customers in Europe. Until then he continued his present role and after another short period in London for the spring buying season of 1960, he began the long boat-train journey from Harwich to the Hook of Holland bound for his annual spring trip to Germany, Holland and Austria in early May.[1] On arrival in Munich he was not only apprehensive about this particular trip, but also regretted not having brought his car, since he struggled with his many items of baggage on public transport because of a hernia problem, and it convinced him to use his own vehicle to make these journeys in future.

However he was shocked to hear disturbing news from several of his German customers who were furious about Kinder's appointment of a new German agent, Herr Rohe, in his place.[1] They resented this unannounced change and intensely disliked the new man whom they regarded as arrogant, conceited and unbearable, while they regarded Kinder's action as beyond contempt.[1] His customers were also concerned about Alfred's position in future, and his own feelings about the situation were only ameliorated by the thought that this would bring things to a head, together with the fact that many of his customers supported him in this conflict. Meanwhile business sales on behalf of Moxon's were poor since customers were disappointed with the new range of samples because Kinder had not produced a specific German collection. To compound these problems Alfred also suffered from a sore throat caused by infected tonsils, and was in such a poor state that he had to remain in bed, miss several appointments and delay his schedule by at least a day.[1]

This already desperate situation was further aggravated when Alfred received a tersely offensive letter from Kinder which threatened that there was no future for him at Moxon's:

Dear Mr. Brown,

Once again you have taken the opportunity of writing to me a personal letter whilst in Germany. This happens every time and I will just not stand it any more.

You are endeavouring to 'make a mountain out of a molehill' as far as Rohe is concerned. In my opinion you are overpaid, and if you do not wish to work for us then you can take whatever attitude you like.

Again I say that if you do not like the set up we have then there is always an answer to it. You are definitely not an agent of ours, but just an employee and you are paid as an employee

S. Kinder.[1]

Alfred received this letter while he was delayed in Berlin where he was attended at his hotel by a doctor who prescribed medication for his infected throat. As a result his planned schedule was disrupted and he sent apologetic telegrams to his customers in Hanover and Goslar for the appointments he had missed but hoped to rearrange them, but it gave him some time to consider his current position.[1]

This letter from Kinder was one of the very few replies that Alfred had ever received on his trips, and it was in response to his report of the dissatisfaction of the German customers to Rohe's appointment. Alfred felt that he had endured a lot of humiliation at the hands of Kinder for the sake of a peaceful solution to his ongoing employment problems, but he had had enough and it was the end. He now believed that the only thing to do was to resign and risk the consequences, and although he was in despair about the situation and unable to work or sleep, he believed that his only salvation was to leave the firm and take a chance with his other agency work.[1]

In order to plan his next move Alfred returned home for the Whitsuntide week-end of 5th and 6th June after the brief Holland stage of his trip,[1] so that he could discuss his options with Marie-Eugénie and hopefully George Heseltine, before trying to arrange a potentially difficult face to face meeting with Kinder. While he was at home he also visited Watson's in Scotland and discussed his future arrangements with the firm and investigated possible alternative firms to replace his Moxon agency work.[1] But Alfred returned to Germany without being able to confront Kinder and any meeting had to wait until his return in July. While Kinder's note had spoiled his trip to Germany, Alfred at least had the support of the Watson Company, and he now considered that he had unofficially finished representing Moxon's interests and would travel on Watson's behalf for the rest of his current trip.[1]

During the summer Alfred made all the necessary arrangements to become an independent agent from the 1st October 1960, and he sent a specially printed letter to that effect to all his customers in Europe to inform them of his new status as: 'A.J. Brown – Textile Agent'. In it he listed the companies for which had representational interests abroad, along with their main products, in the hope that he would continue to enjoy the productive relationship that he had developed with his established customers over the last five years, and politely informed everyone that he would no longer be representing Moxon's of Huddersfield for personal reasons.

A. J. BROWN

𝕮extile 𝕬gent

Telephone } BRADFORD 46665
Telegrams

2 MORNINGTON VILLAS,

MANNINGHAM LANE,

BRADFORD 8.

October, 1960

Messrs.

Dear Sirs,

I beg to inform you that I have made arrangements to represent the undermentioned firms in Germany and Austria as from October 1st, viz :—

Wm. Thomson (Fine Cloths) Ltd. Woodhouse Mills, Huddersfield.	(Fine Worsteds)
Odersfelt Worsteds Ltd., Lloyds Bank Chambers, Huddersfield.	(Fine Worsteds)
Spamount Woollen Co. Ltd., Castleberg, N. Ireland.	(Irish Tweeds, Sports cloths, Twists, coatings)
Broadhead & Graves Ltd., Riverside Mills, Galashiels, Scotland.	(Ladies fabrics)

I shall continue to represent as before, my friends :—
William Watson & Sons (Hawick) Ltd.
Dangerfield Mills, Hawick.
for the sale of their Scottish Worsted Twists, Cheviots, Saxonies, Cashmeres and Novelty fabrics.

For personal reasons I have relinquished my position with Messrs. B. H. Moxon & Sons Ltd., of Kirkburton.

May I take this opportunity of thanking you most warmly for your past support, and of expressing the hope that you will continue to favour me with your valued orders and enquiries which will receive my prompt, personal attention.

I hope to have the pleasure of calling on you, at your convenience, with the new Autumn/Winter collections in November/December this year.

Should any of your gentlemen be coming to London during the forthcoming season, I shall be very happy to be of service to them in any way possible.

Yours sincerely,

A. J. Brown.

Before Alfred embarked on his autumn business trip he visited Adrian at Ampleforth and consulted his tutor, Fr. Oswald, about Adrian's application for a university place in the coming year, since it was unlikely that he would be back in England until Christmas. Alfred then left for Germany immediately after visiting London after meetings with foreign buyers at the autumn buying season in late October, this time on his first trip as an independent agent. Now he was the master of his own destiny and after a long and tiring boat-train journey to Goslar he took time out briefly before starting the usual busy schedule of meetings. He relaxed by walking in the Hartz Mountains and ascended the Steinweg peak then returned via an easy stroll through forested valleys to prepare for his upcoming initiation – 'the first on my own!', about which he was very apprehensive even though he had done everything possible to try to ensure the best outcome.[1]

Alfred's initial worries about his first foray proved unfounded because he recorded a splendid first day's performance in Goslar when he sold 21 pieces for Spamount's and 8 pieces for Watson's (a piece equaled 230 ft. X 4.9 ft. of woven cloth, enough to 'make-up' 20 suits from one piece of cloth) and he had made a very acceptable £100 on his first call.[1] He then moved on to nearby Bad Harzburg where he had similar success with an order for 11 pieces for Thomson's and 6 pieces for Odersfelt's, with orders for Spamount's and Watson's to follow in March of the following year, that would yield another £80 which could mean up to £250 when all the orders were received. While Alfred was somewhat relieved with this start, he was cautious about whether he could sustain this performance, hoped that he would not be dogged by the bad luck associated with a return of his throat infection again which had affected his last trip, as well as the niggling problem of his hernia.[1]

At this rate, by the half-way point, Alfred was able to cover the entire expenses of the whole trip so that the remaining returns constituted earned income and he still had some of his biggest buyers to visit. However things slowed down after this outstanding start, and he was aware that he was working as hard as ever and did not expect to be so lucky as to make up to £300, which he had done in his most successful week so far, even with a lot of hard work.[1] He continued to have moderate sales success even though some of his customers were still 'tied' to commitments with Moxon's, ironically largely through his own previous efforts, and only benefitted later when these 'ties' were finally over.[1] Unfortunately he continued to have problems with the throat infection which could have jeopardised the remainder of the trip, and he consulted another doctor to help him keep to his visits schedule. To further complicate matters Alfred was also plagued by an attack of colic, which necessitated the cancellation of further appointments in spite of taking enteric tablets, and this gave him further concerns about whether he could sustain the pace of work that he had set for himself.[1]

His other major concern at this time was to pursue his ongoing claim with Moxon's to recover the money to which he was entitled, since he refused to accept the 'expenses' figures that the company had provided.[1] He disputed their claim that he actually owed them £200, because on his miserly 1% commission he had not covered his total incurred expenses of £4,800, when in fact the company had placed a 5% charge on his prices to customers which would have netted them some £25,000. Indeed he speculated how these figures would be interpreted in a court of law ,when he could demonstrate that his total sales over the last four years was nearly a half million pounds. He now intended to take legal action with the help of his advocate George Heseltine.[1] After all Moxon's could easily afford a rightful settlement, since they were part of the Tulketh Group of Companies that had posted an annual group profit for the year ending 31st March 1959 of £204,356, with current assets of £428,404 and an 18% dividend paid to shareholders.[2]

Unfortunately Alfred received two rather lukewarm responses from George about his claim against Moxon's and wondered if he was dragging his feet over the issue as it was nearly six months since they discussed a proposal to seek compensation.[1] But George countered that he had presented the case with the utmost vigour, and Alfred apologised for putting pressure on him, but could not hide his frustration that the case had become so drawn out. Furthermore he considered that it might have been a mistake to impose on his close friend in this way, and maybe he should have engaged a local solicitor instead, but it was too late now and he would have to be patient enough to see how everything worked out.

As Alfred neared the end of his first trip as an independent agent he acknowledged that it had been his hardest so far. He found the routine was getting harder as he grew older and it was exacerbated by his ill-health during the trip, as well as worries over the Moxon claim which caused additional anxieties. Although business had only been moderate, the income derived indicated that his first independent trip would pay dividends in due course. As to the future, he vowed to pursue the Moxon claim, but doubted if he would return to the Middle-East and instead he proposed to concentrate on the German and the perhaps the UK markets for the new companies that he now must devote more time to in England.

Alfred's First Solo Business Year

At the start of his first year as an independent agent in 1961, Alfred was able to organise his working life for a change. This meant he could devote a little more time to his family life which had suffered because of the demands others made upon him previously, which now afforded some freedom to choose his scheduled pattern of work. He therefore deferred his spring season trip abroad until after Easter 1961, and remained in Bradford to take care of family matters, as well as to plan the first of his two major sales trips during the coming year. As Adrian approached his 17th birthday Alfred was keen to provide support and advice for his application to university, and he accompanied Adrian on a visit to Leeds University where he intended to apply for a course of studies in the Textiles Department with a view to future employment in a related industry.[3] Then having spent the Easter holiday with members of his family at home in Bradford Alfred left for Germany during the third week of April.[3]

As usual Alfred travelled via London where he not only met with foreign buyers again, but also with George to advance his claim against Moxon's in the hope of getting the best possible outcome.[3] He was very apprehensive about this trip during which he needed to sell about 100 pieces of cloth before he made a profit, although he had eight weeks to make it pay. Everything depended on the state of trade and his customers' reactions to the various new sets of sample materials that he had selected.[3] However he wished he could lead a more normal life since he detested the long periods of separation from Marie-Eugénie, the hectic rounds of customer visits, the nights of dealing with correspondence and particularly the transport of his heavy baggage. He was now convinced that using his own car for future transport would make travelling a lot easier and cheaper, which together with staying in cheaper hotels would reduce the overall costs involved.[3]

Then during this trip in early May Alfred received the disturbing news that Marie-Eugénie awaited news about a gynaecological condition which had manifested itself the day Alfred left for Germany, and following a visit to her GP she was referred to a specialist who had confirmed the original diagnosis.[3] He indicated that surgical intervention was needed to correct the problem, followed by a three month convalescence period, when help would be required from her husband, family and possibly a home-help to assist with the lengthy recovery process. When Marie-Eugénie was placed on a hospital waiting list, she requested that the operation be delayed until Alfred returned home at the end of June, so he would be able to care for her along with other members of the family.[3] Subsequently the operation was postponed until early July when all the arrangements for a short period of clinical care and a more prolonged period of convalescence were organised, along with the assistance required at home for Marie-Eugénie's later care needs.[3]

During the lead up to Marie-Eugénie's operation Alfred continued with his busy sales trip since it would have been difficult to cut short his visit without incurring major problems, although he had offered to abandon the remaining portion of his trip in view of Marie-Eugénie's ill-health. He acknowledged that he did not have the heart for the present trip when he received Marie-Eugénie's bad news, and only enjoyed his work when business was good enough to make provision for her and the family, otherwise it could be very depressing. However this gloom was temporarily lifted after he received news from George who had prepared a detailed account of his claim against Moxon's and had given them 14 days to respond before a writ was to be issued, so it seemed as if some progress was made at last. In the interim the acting solicitor had received a cheque for £475 from Moxon's in respect of commission owed so that was a start at least.[3]

Meanwhile Alfred's schedule of sales visits in Germany produced mixed results in which some days he sold nothing at all, while on a good day he earned orders up to £200, but he needed three types of daily medication to alleviate his throat symptoms in order to keep to his busy schedule.[3] However he was now reassured that Marie-Eugénie received daily home help from friends and support from Rosemary and Barbara.[3] When Alfred had completed the remaining portion of his trip in Austria he then made the long return journey by train to Ostend and boat to Dover to be home with Marie-Eugénie.[3] He was at her bedside before and after the operation, and made visits to the Waddilove Hospital for Women in Queens Road, Bradford, near their home during her recovery. After this he took her to the Elmleigh Convent, a nursing home operated by the Cross and Passion Sisters in Kings Road Ilkley, for a more pronged period of convalescence.[3] Then a further period of recuperation followed in early August when Alfred and Marie-Eugénie enjoyed a summer holiday in Sleights, where they were joined at various times by members of the family. Finally they returned to Bradford at the end of the month for Marie-Eugénie to continue her recovery to full health, since Alfred had not planned another lengthy business trip until late October.[3]

While Alfred was at home in Bradford he visited some of the firms that he represented in Scotland, especially Watson's of Hawick, a company that was now of special importance to his agency work in Europe.[3] He was also able to advise Adrian about his proposed studies at Leeds University, and suggested that while a textiles career involved a lengthy training period, it had some advantages including the possibility of joining his father's business one day, but the decision was entirely his own.[3] Alfred then arranged for Mrs. Helliwell, an experienced home-helper, to take care of all the day-to-day domestic chores needed so that Marie-Eugénie could complete her recovery. Meanwhile he planned the schedule for his second lengthy trip of the year to Germany, Holland and Austria, in the knowledge that he needed to work hard to try to establish a sound economic base for his business and the future financial security of his family.

Alfred's autumn sales trip began with the usual ten days of foreign sales meetings in London before he caught the Harwich-Hook of Holland boat-train and an overnight train to Bavaria in early November.[3] On arrival he made another promising start with a very successful first day of sales which gave him great encouragement. He was also pleased when Marie-Eugénie began to help in the business by processing orders received and keeping track of his sales by the maintenance of an order book and so had a record of his business transactions.[3] In addition she began to learn German at evening classes, as Alfred had done all those years ago when he was a trainee in the wool trade. This eventually helped her to deal with correspondence from customers, although she had some difficulty coming to terms with a new language.[3] Following her return to health Marie-Eugénie was keen to provide further support for Alfred's fledgling agency which operated from the study that was now his home-based office. She now took care of all correspondence, orders, invoices and receipts, and maintained business ledgers for each country where Alfred worked in Europe.[3] This new 'partnership' arrangement was similar to their former hotel business but in role-reversal whereby Alfred delivered the services and Marie-Eugénie provided the administrative support for the business.

While Marie-Eugénie had recovered from her previous ordeal her doctor cautioned that a complete recovery would take some time, and advised her to continue to take things easy.[3] Fortunately as well as her domestic help, Adrian now lived at home after he took the offer of a place at Leeds University and was able to help out, whereas Barbara had left for Hyderabad in India to take up a new nursing post in a private hospital.[3] Adrian had settled into his textiles course but was also involved in various student activities including the Catholic Society at the University Chaplaincy, although Alfred advised that he should focus on his studies and not be distracted by other interests.[3] Nevertheless he was not surprised to learn that Adrian had befriended Fr. Adrian Smith who had joined the White Fathers, and had expressed an interest in his own 'calling to the cloth'. Indeed Alfred recalled as a young man he was very active in the

St. Vincent de Paul Society but refrained from any formal religious commitments. Even so he did not discourage Adrian and indicated would be happy if he found a true vocation, but suggested he carefully considered his future options.[3]

When Alfred had almost completed the German section of his autumn business trip he reported buoyant sales which now totalled over 50 pieces and he expected this to increase to well over 100 pieces by the new year when all the orders were received.[3] He was also immensely grateful for Marie-Eugénie's splendid efforts to organise the home business office activities so efficiently which would help the agency in future. His only concern was that he was unable to take up a business colleague's offer for additional agency work on behalf of the textile firm of Broadhead and Graves of Galashiels in Scotland, since he was already fully committed with his other clients.[3] But he became concerned when George informed him that a formal claim and a writ for a large financial settlement had been sent to Moxon's to try to expedite some action, since he remained dubious about the outcome because this nasty affair had gone on for so long.[3]

Development of the A.J. Brown Textile Agency

Alfred had worked hard since he established his new agency and he continued to consolidate and to develop the business, while he tried to achieve a more equitable balance between his work activities and his family commitments. Nevertheless there was no let-up in the demands of his spring and autumn sales trips to Europe, although he made special efforts to return home regularly to take time off from his busy schedule. However there remained the ongoing problem of his case for financial compensation against Moxon's of Huddersfield to be resolved. Moreover the need to establish a firm financial base for his new business took such a toll on his physical and psychological well-being that he often doubted his efforts to continue with the agency. Furthermore while Marie-Eugénie had recovered from her recent health problems, she began to feel more isolated as members of the family pursued their own lives, and felt the depressive loneliness associated with Alfred's long absences. The only respite for both of them was the occasional family holiday and special family events such as another family wedding and the arrival of grandchildren.

Alfred delayed his 1962 spring business trip to Europe until the end of May, but found things more difficult than on his last visit, not only in terms of business sales, but also due to feeling the pace harder to sustain with the continued hernia problem and the usual strain of trying to manage his heavy bags of samples.[4] On arrival in Munich he was disconcerted to receive a visit at his hotel from a director of the

Scottish firm of Wilson & Glennie which had recently taken over Watson's of Hawick. The new owners already had an English agent who represented them in Germany, and Alfred discovered that his services were no longer required for Watson's after this trip, although he continued to receive earned commissions for six months. This turned out to be something of a mixed blessing, since Alfred found the Watson cloth samples difficult to sell, and although he found this turn of events distasteful, he now concentrated his efforts on other firms, which were as much as he could cope with under the present difficult business circumstances.

Meanwhile he received the other startling but more pleasant news from Marie-Eugénie that their daughter Rosemary had announced her forthcoming marriage to James Sturrup,[4] although she was somewhat concerned that it was to be a London rather than a Bradford based wedding. She felt that traditionally it was the bride's parents' responsibility to chose the location and arrangements for the event. But Alfred persuasively suggested that Marie-Eugénie was still not well enough to undertake such a big social occasion in her present nervous state of health and with a continued migraine problem, so he was pleased when she agreed to be relieved of the strain of trying to cope with all the arrangements.[4] Furthermore he was pleased to learn that the new in-laws proposed to host an engagement cocktail party at their home in Wimbledon for the happy couple at the beginning of July, and that he was able to complete his trip in good time to meet up with the Sturrups and their friends prior to the proposed wedding date of early September 1962.[4]

Other events did not however make smooth nor speedy progress, in particular Alfred's case against Moxon's had made no further progress while George had been in hospital but he assured Alfred that the case was being handled by a colleague and that he would return to it soon.[4] But when Alfred received no further update from George after another month, he began to think that this was something of a hopeless cause and wished he had never instigated the action in the first place.[4] Furthermore he had very mixed results on his present business trip insofar as difficulties were being experienced even by his normally good customers who complained about the poor state of trade. Nevertheless he added another agency and now represented Broadhead & Graves of Galashiels in Scotland with only one week left of his German trip, and when the Austrian portion of the trip was completed he reckoned the overall returns would be quite favourable.[4]

Later Alfred was relieved to know that Marie-Eugénie had overcome some of her lonely isolation in the early summer with a visit to their eldest daughter Felicity and her husband Colin Millward in London, followed by a visit from their youngest daughter and her intended James Sturrup to Bradford.[4] In addition she had made arrangements for their annual summer holiday together in Sleights once more, when members of the whole family would join them during August, and even Barbara was to take annual leave from her job in India to be there, along with Adrian.[4] This was not the only happy occasion when the family were together this summer, since they all gathered again to celebrate the wedding of Rosemary and James in London in September. But it was not long after that they reassembled for a more sombre funeral occasion in Bradford, after the sudden death of Alfred's former school friend, brother-in-law and husband of his sister Gertrude, Richard Hynes.[4] Unfortunately Alfred could not attend this since he left on his autumn sales trip to Europe after being advised to continue his journey by Marie-Eugénie, who ruefully reflected on these recent contrasting occasions: 'a wedding one week and a funeral the next'.[4]

When Alfred began another arduous 25-city autumn sales tour of Germany, Holland and Austria, he was worried about his ability to stand up to the rigours of the trip from the outset in which he lugged 225 lbs of samples around with a troublesome hernia, so that when he reached Austria he was concerned about the likelihood of completing the trip: 'so much to do, so many journeys – hotels, porters, taxis, visits, correspondence and expenses to contend with – I wish I could drop it all soon, I have had enough now.'[4] Things became much worse after he was crippled by pain from the hernia and he wondered if he would even finish the trip, and yet he could ill-afford to curtail it.[4] His tight schedule also meant that he had little or no time to see a doctor, but eventually he was forced to consult one in Karlsruhe who prescribed medication that relieved the painful symptoms sufficiently for him to carry on.[4]

However his elder son Christopher was so concerned about his father's state, that he offered to take two or three weeks leave from his job in London to join his father to help him complete the trip. Although this generous offer was not needed, it caused Alfred to think about the possibility of Adrian joining him in the agency when he completed his Diploma in Textile Industries at Leeds University, although he suspected that Adrian had hopes of a clerical vocation.[4]

It seemed ironic that while Alfred struggled to cope with the demands of the new business, there were opportunities for the addition of more firms to his portfolio and sufficient work for his younger son to join him as a junior partner in the near future, after he was approached by Mallinson's Worsteds of Huddersfield about taking on agency work for the firm.[4] But Alfred was unsure about representing an unknown firm in Germany and it might have caused a conflict with his other Huddersfield agency work such as Thompson's. Likewise there was interest from other West Riding worsted firms such as Peter Wilson's and Gillespie's, so that Alfred was tempted by these other potential clients, but Adrian was far from the completion of his studies and gaining any experience for a partnership just yet. Therefore Alfred gave no further consideration to this future prospect, and with almost three weeks left of his current trip, he planned to complete it early the week before Christmas 1962 to enjoy another festive family occasion at home in Bradford.[4]

Increased Demands of European Business Travel

By 1963 Alfred had an established pattern for his biannual business trips to Europe which involved travelling around Holland, Germany and Austria along progressive straight lines or occasionally in circular directions in order to save time and minimise travelling expenses. These trips often caused problems, not only in terms of the time and costs involved since he travelled on long distance trains and used taxi services for local visits, but also because of the amount of baggage he needed. He had previously tried using hire cars for some local visits, but now at last he decided to use his own car for transport to ease the strain of the journeys, especially in view of his recent bouts of debility due to his persistent hernia problem which was exacerbated by lifting heavy bags.[5]

This new arrangement had another advantage in that Marie-Eugénie was able to join him occasionally on some parts of his visits, which together with her family visits, would help to ameliorate her sense of isolation and loneliness while he was away on long business trips. Furthermore, since she was now acting as his paid personal assistant/secretary at his home-based office, it was permissible to claim the expenses involved against the tax on the business. Accordingly, in the spring of 1963, Marie-Eugénie joined Alfred in Munich, while Adrian took care of correspondence received at the office.[5] While Alfred went about his business locally, she enjoyed the company of the Lumper family, who were customers and close friends of Alfred, before they left together to visit Goslar and the Harz Mountains, which was one of his favourite spots on his visits to southern Germany. Then on her way home Marie-Eugénie visited her cousins Colette and Simone in Paris, before she stopped in London to see her eldest daughter Felicity, and arrived back in Bradford with renewed vigour at the end of May.[5]

It was also about this time that Alfred provided Adrian with some hands-on experience of foreign travel in the textile business and got some assistance with the long daily driving when he joined his father for the Austrian part of the trip after his end of year examinations. Adrian met his father in Saltzsburg, appropriately enough on 'Vater Tag' or Fathers Day, Sunday 9th June 1963,[5] and they enjoyed the local festival that was taking place before taking the famous 'Salzkammergut' route over the mountains to Graz. Then after Alfred's planned visits to customers in the area, they left for Vienna for a further week of business appointments, although they took time off during the Corpus Christi holiday festival to go walking in the Vienna woods.[5] Alfred was pleased to have Adrian's company and found him helpful with the work involved, while Adrian impressed his father's customers with his limited spoken German, and looked forward to sharing the long drive back to Amsterdam and their return to Bradford.[5]

While Alfred and Adrian were away the summer holiday arrangements had not gone too well when Marie-Eugénie found that St. Joseph's cottage in Sleights was not available, since the wife of cottage owner, Mr. Harrison, was very ill and the cottage was not free for the usual Brown family holiday this year. Other enquiries for holiday lettings in the Sleights and Goathland areas were not successful either.[5] Marie-Eugénie had also called to see the Whittakers, their friends in Littlebeck, to find anything suitable in the little hamlet but again without success. Even their former Whitfield House Hotel in Darnholm could not oblige, since the owners had struggled to continue the business after Mr. Rippon suffered heart problems.[5] Then just when a summer of disappointment seemed likely, Marie-Eugénie rented 'Lynton Cottage' in Sleights and saved the situation. It was probably this scramble for holiday accommodation which gave the Browns the idea of buying a property for future use since Marie-Eugénie's searches indicated a number of letting cottages were also for sale, although at that time such places were beyond their means even for possible retirement.[5]

Before Alfred left on his autumn sales trip in October he had a few urgent problems to resolve. He was asked to take over part of the agency of the Scottish firm of Wilson & Glennie, whose overseas representative had retired through ill health, but he was reluctant to consider this offer since it might have caused a conflict with his established agencies. He was also asked to take on the new London office for Spamount's of Northern Ireland after they planned to break away from Broadhead & Graves of Galashiels in Scotland, but again he was reluctant to take on more work at the time and perhaps put his own agency in jeopardy.[5] Then other problems arose unexpectedly when he arrived at Harwich for the Hook of Holland ferry, and had his textile bags inspected by the Special Branch of the Customs and Excise Department. They suspected anyone with such a large amount of baggage because of the Great Train Robbery that had recently taken place, and considered he might be smuggling the stolen cash out of the country![5] Then all his bags went missing when he arrived in Munich by train and did not reappear for a couple of days, at which point they were thoroughly searched again, this time by the German Customs Department who had impounded them. He then regretted not bringing his car on this trip but had decided against it because of the difficulty of travelling in adverse weather conditions during the latter part of his last autumn trip to Austria.[5]

Alfred's autumn trip covered most of the usual territory in Germany and Austria, but he regretted not having any assistance this time, especially since he was almost overwhelmed by the demands of report and letter writing necessary on behalf of the six firms he now represented.[5] He could barely keep up with the administrative load and clearly needed the support of a travelling secretary or an assistant, roles that Marie-Eugénie and Adrian had partly fulfilled during the spring sales trip. However he was glad not to have agreed to take on the additional agency representation which was offered earlier, and even considered giving up some of his established agency work unless he could appoint an assistant in the near future.[4] Furthermore he only enjoyed one brief break in this trip in Goslar on the German public holiday of the 'Day of Mourning and Recollection', when he took the coach into the Harz Mountains to relax and then returned by a 9 miles walk through the wooded slopes in only a couple of hours and concluded that he must still be in reasonable shape on this showing.[5]

Finally, on his arrival in Austria, Alfred reflected on the excessive demands of this trip: 'it has been the toughest trip I have ever done and I have not been able to "spare" myself at all – no time off, no weekends (with one exception) – nothing but a mad stampede from start to finish.'[5] Even sales in Vienna were poor this time, whereas he was usually guaranteed good orders from very reliable customers. However he took comfort from the fact that he had completed most of his visits and was hopeful that the results would turn out favourably when all the orders arrived in the new year. When he left on the overnight Vienna – Ostende Express, he reserved a 'Wagon Lit' compartment since he felt that he deserved a little luxury after such a demanding trip. He then spent a couple of nights at the RAF Club in London to see some of the family, and also George to get an update on what seemed his forlorn case for compensation, after which he was more than relieved to arrive back in Bradford in good time for Christmas, and the anticipated arrival of the family en masse over the festive season.[5]

Conflicts of Business, Family and Personal Life

The new year of 1964 raised new personal and professional challenges for Alfred and his family to over-come, as well as old problems to face as their fortunes changed, not the least of which were the ongoing health problems of both Alfred and Marie-Eugénie, the possibility of retirement and a possible further house move in the near future. Alfred's agency faced new threats to its economic stability, while the demands of his travels abroad continued to take a toll on his health and well-being. Likewise, Marie-Eugénie suffered further bouts of depressive loneliness, as well as other physical ailments, but reduced the adverse effect of these setbacks by her involvement with her extended family. Meanwhile Alfred had no resolution to his case for financial compensation from his old employer, but he freed himself from additional agency responsibilities and involvement with the reorganisation of the London offices of those companies he continued to represent.

Alfred spent some time in London dealing with residual work problems before he set off on his annual spring sales trip, this time using his own car, but he had a disturbed sleep on his last night in the capital due to his swollen septic tonsil again, and had almost missed the boat from Harwich.[6] Then on arrival in Holland his car became stuck in the air when the unloading crane jammed and it was stranded aloft until an engineer came to fix the problem. The delay meant he had to find a hotel for the night, which proved almost impossible since most places were full due to the national holiday and the celebrations of Queen Juliana's birthday.[6] When he eventually found accommodation he suffered another interrupted night's sleep due to a noisy gathering of young people whose disco dance went on until 4.00 a.m.! The next day while wearily trying to find the Hague-Arnhem road, he luckily chanced to ask the Dutch Harbour Master for directions and found he was going the same route and offered to lead the way.[6] As they made their way in a heavy rain storm the brakes on Alfred's car began to jam and caused him to swerve violently whenever he applied them, but driving carefully he was guided to the Dutch-German border, where he joined the autobahn and completed the 350 mile journey to Hamburg.[6] After his brake problem was fixed next morning, Alfred called to see Dr. Hoffman again, who had previously treated his troublesome tonsil. Once more he received a penicillin injection, then left somewhat relieved both in body and mind, and continued his way to Kiel on the Baltic coast after the most eventful start to any of his trips to Europe so far.[6]

But even this inauspicious start was marred on Alfred's arrival in Hamburg by the news of the sudden death of his sister Vera's husband, Fred Schmitt, but once again he was advised by the family not to break from his trip to attend the funeral.[6] Soon after he also learned of his elder brother Edwin's hospitalisation after suffering from an internal haemorrhage and that his condition was critical with little expectation of survival.[6] Alfred was so shocked by this news he prepared to abandon his trip and return home in the event of his brother's demise, since he believed that family ties were all that mattered. Fortunately Edwin made a surprising but slow recovery from his life-threatening condition, but Alfred now considered that his plans for this trip were all going wrong and that somehow it was an ill-fated time for him to be away.[6]

It was against this background of unfortunate events that Alfred's and Marie-Eugénie's thoughts turned towards their future lives and the need to make provision for the time they had left together. Alfred was concerned about Marie-Eugénie's recent bouts of ill health and questioned his own ability to sustain his present work load, when he posed the question to her: 'What do you think about my retirement and when should I plan for it?'[6] although the prospect of retirement seemed a remote dream at the time. However Marie-Eugénie was more realistic after she visited Goathland and viewed a little house in Whitby, which although she considered expensive at £2,400, it indicated her consideration of Alfred's prospective retirement.[6] Meanwhile, she found a cottage to rent in Goathland for a week in July, and suggested a short break to look around the area for suitable properties for sale. But the prospect of any imminent retirement received a severe jolt when later in the year Alfred received his first pension payment for a period of 12 weeks of £53, and he doubted if they could live on this meagre amount since it was much less than the commission on one good week's orders at present.[6]

Alfred ——————

Marie-Eugénie ——→

Felicity ——————

———— Adrian

←—— Barbara

———— Rosemary

37. The Brown family at 2 Mornington Villas, Bradford

It was clear that he needed to continue earning and saving for some time yet before they could think of his retirement. However his business prospects did not look good later that year when a 15% import levy was applied to all British goods by the six EC countries, which significantly affected all Alfred's European customers.[6] Local and national newspapers reported dramatic headlines at the time: 'Firms at Trade Fair Return Empty Handed' about a 'British Sales Week' that had been held in November in Amsterdam. British businessmen also reported that their goods were being boycotted as a result of the import surcharge which effectively gave European companies a 15% sales advantage over their British counterparts. Subsequently Alfred found business very difficult under the circumstances, since most of his customers were furious about the import duty levy and threatened not to buy from his British suppliers.[6] While he could only apologise profusely for the surcharge, he hoped that he could rely on the good will of his customers for the supply of some of his superior quality products.[6]

Nevertheless Alfred now carefully considered the future of his agency, and the possible expansion of the business to include a partner who would continue the agency after his eventual retirement. It was logical to think of his younger son Adrian as the 'heir apparent' for this role, since he was shortly to complete his Diploma in Textile Industries at Leeds University. Alfred had given his son full support during his studies and was keen for him to succeed in whatever career he had in mind. Adrian for his part expected a favourable outcome to his studies and to join his father in the business, having gained some insight about the work on his recent trip to Austria with his father. However Alfred wanted Adrian to be under no illusions of what the day-to-day job of an overseas sales agent demanded, and accordingly he described a typical day he spent in Munich during the fifth week of his spring trip to Germany. His short account provided the details of one day's meetings in the context of a multi-city schedule of business appointments that lasted for up to two months duration in total:

> My day began at 05.30 hrs. when I arose, took coffee in my hotel room and prepared myself for the work ahead. I loaded my sample baggage and drove 90 miles on the autobahn from Munich to Regensburg for an 08.00 appointment, the first of three that were scheduled at hourly intervals to show collections of cloth samples to three separate minor customers, and completed my morning meetings at 12.00 noon. After a short lunch break, I drove a further 120 miles to Ingoldstat alongside the River Danube to arrive at 14.30 for a meeting with a major customer, which included a formal reception as well as a lengthy presentation of cloth samples to a selection of company representatives. I eventually left Ingoldstat at 16.30 and drove back to Munich, this time via the autobahn, and arrived at 18.00 during the peak rush hour traffic. After I unloaded my samples, I returned to my hotel room to begin the evening's administrative work of report writing and dealt with orders and correspondence, before I took a light supper at 20.30. Then after a short period of reading to try to relax, I retired to bed at 21.30 after a demanding 16 hour day, in order to rise early, pack the car with all my baggage again and drive to Salzburg to following day.[6]

No doubt this punishing daily schedule of appointments and travel would have dissuaded even the most enthusiastic young would-be salesman, let alone even a successful sales agent of almost 70 years of age. Perhaps it was Alfred's intention to challenge his young son's sincerity about a textile sales career?

While Alfred was on his autumn sales trip of 1964, Marie-Eugénie visited Christopher and her daughter-in-law Brenda in Brussels, where they had recently moved after Christopher's appointment as a general manager of a UK subsidiary company. Brenda had just given birth to baby daughter Nicola, and Marie-Eugénie went to help with domestic matters and prepare for the forthcoming christening.[6] This was a busy time grand-parenting for her since her daughter Rosemary had also earlier given birth to daughter Louise, and she spent some time with Rosemary and James in Wimbledon on her way home and also visited Felicity and Colin in Barnet before she returned to Bradford.[6] Unfortunately Alfred missed yet another family christening when he was unable to re-arrange his busy schedule, but he hoped to get to see his new granddaughter on his return home via Brussels for Christmas.[6] Meanwhile on her return home, Marie-Eugénie's elation of her family visits wore off as a new depressive state took hold as a result of her relative incapacity after a fall at Felicity's house in which she injured her back.[6] Furthermore she worried about Alfred's safety during the final part of his trip to Austria during the early onset of winter when the roads became treacherous. But she was reassured when Alfred left his car in Germany rather than make the 900 miles round trip by road, and instead he travelled on the Vienna Express to complete the Austrian portion of his trip.[6] In addition she was pleased by the news that he intended to return home about two weeks before Christmas this year so that they could spend more time together, with only Barbara and Adrian at home, since other members of the family were busy with their young children and delayed their visits until the new year.

Only one issue now caused Alfred continued consternation; the unresolved case of his financial compensation from Moxon's which languished in its fourth year of relative inaction. Earlier in 1963 he received an apology from George who had been too busy to deal with the ongoing case, but having reviewed all the papers with their solicitor, he prepared to press ahead with the proceedings.[6] But after almost another year Alfred was disappointed with the lack of further progress and felt the case had been neglected when there was a chance of a possible settlement. Meanwhile George and the solicitor wrote to Moxon's again to demand action on compensation and requested that an independent accountant be allowed to inspect the firm's financial accounts related to this matter, if an out of court settlement greater than the amount offered so far of £1,330 was not forthcoming.[6] By the end of 1964 Alfred had no further update about his case, but he expected to receive an increased offer from Moxon's rather than allow any inspection of their finances. He also indicated that if and when such an offer was made, he would accept it to conclude this lengthy distasteful debacle. He would then use whatever money received to make some provision for his future retirement.[6]

Retirement on the Horizon – At Last

Alfred's case for financial compensation was finally settled in 1965, but not without a further protracted period to resolve the problems which continued for almost the whole year. The first good news came in May with a marginally increased offer from Moxon's of £1,500, but without mention of costs that had been incurred during the nearly five year settlement process. George advised Alfred to reject this latest offer again and instruct his solicitors to proceed with the demand to inspect the company's books in the hope this would improve the offer.[7] While Alfred was minded to accept this offer, George advised against it, since he considered there was only a small risk of the offer being withdrawn, and he hoped for a higher settlement of between £2,000 and £3,000.[6] Subsequently, Moxon's made a further increased offer and Alfred considered it was best to accept a figure of £2,000 with costs, rather than risk everything by further haggling.[7] At last it meant that he and his wife could begin to plan seriously for their future retirement.

Alfred now became more concerned about the need to make his retirement decision soon since he feared that he might be imprisoned by his agency work until he was past the point where he and Marie-Eugénie could enjoy the benefits of retirement.[7] While he considered it was too late to pick up the threads of his writing interests, he looked forward to a few less strenuous years with a relatively care-free life whilst he could still enjoy walking in the countryside once more. When he finally received the compensation payment with substantial costs added in late November 1965 he hoped that he and Marie-Eugénie could now buy the little cottage that they had dreamed of for their retirement. But first they celebrated the settlement with an extended trip to London for Christmas and spent time with their family and grandchildren and asked Barbara and Adrian to join them for the festive season.[7]

Meanwhile Marie-Eugénie had some retirement plans of her own. She had already gained a City and Guilds qualification for her cookery expertise and with the advent of her 60th birthday the following year she proposed to undertake some part-time teaching of the subject to have an interest outside the home and family life, as well as have some financial independence.[7] Moreover she embarked on a Teachers' Certificate in Cookery to be able to instruct in her favourite subject via Further Education Courses by studying for the award at the Bolton Royd Institute in Bradford,[7] and wanted the opportunity to teach others about a subject for which she had natural flair and enthusiasm. Furthermore, with a growing interest in the subject in the expanding Further Education sector at that time, she felt that she would be able to teach wherever she and Alfred decided to settle down in their retirement.[7]

While these new developments held the promise of the realisation of some of Alfred's and Marie-Eugénie's future dreams, there was still much to be achieved to fulfil their expectations, and Alfred's need to consider how and when he might divest himself of his business interests.[7] As time went on he saw little or no prospect of his sons following him into the business. Christopher had taken a new managerial job with an American company in Spain and relocated with his wife and daughter to Madrid, while Adrian was uncertain about his career prospects. He had to re-sit some exams to qualify for his Diploma in Textile Studies in Leeds, but in the interim he pursued his previous interest of a religious vocation. He was accepted as a novice with 'The White Fathers', a society for the training of the Catholic Missionary Congregation of priests and brothers for service in Africa, and he now studied at their seminary in Black Lion, County Cavan in Ireland.[7] He was encouraged to follow his call to the cloth by his parents, who hoped he would fulfil his vocation, but only time would tell if this was the right course of action. Meanwhile Alfred searched for a likely candidate to join him in the agency and discussed the possibility with Jörg Lumper, the son of his loyal customer and good friend from Munich.[7] Jörg had considerable experience in the business already, and Alfred proposed that he take over part of the agency work if his UK clients agreed, but the prospect never materialised after Jörg was tempted by a career move to Australia.

Alfred had coped reasonably well with the demands of his European travels during the year, and he was very successful in both his biannual sales trips to Germany and Austria. During the spring trip he had earned commissions of £1,266 from one company alone,[7] while his autumn trip had produced the single biggest order that he ever obtained with 200 pieces of cloth worth about £1,000 in commission.[7] Furthermore he had sold over 400 pieces of cloth on this trip alone and hoped for sales of 750-1,000 pieces in total, which would net commissions of some £3,850 and £5,000 when all the final orders were received by the new year.[7] This was good news for Alfred's 'retirement kitty' as he called it, although it was not the business of selling that was a problem, but that of travelling which was making life more difficult for him. For example he began his spring trip in Munich, which meant he travelled the length and breadth of Germany and Austria in four long stretches; south to Munich from the Hook of Holland, then returned north to cover the Hamburg and Baltic coast areas, before he headed south again to Munich and Vienna, then the final journey to Ostend and home. This involved driving long distances that often amounted to over 400 miles in a day.[7]

However there was some respite on one of these long journeys when Alfred arranged for Marie-Eugénie to accompany him again on part of his spring sales trip and they enjoyed a brief albeit semi-working holiday together in the early summer of 1965.[7] Marie-Eugénie looked forward to this working holiday since it was unlikely that they would have time to take a holiday later in the year, and after all the costs were partly covered again as legitimate business expenses since she travelled as Alfred's secretary on this occasion.[7] Towards the end of May she flew from Yeadon Airport (Leeds-Bradford Airport) to London, then on to join Alfred in Düsseldorf, after which they drove to Cologne where he had a couple of appointments, before they continued to Munich and on to Graz in Austria where he had to visit more customers. By the time they arrived in Vienna in early June, Alfred's work schedule was virtually over, and they then enjoyed an extended weekend in his favourite city at the Sacher Hotel opposite the great Opera House. Although there was not a great deal of time for sightseeing, they returned via Salzburg and drove through the Austrian Tyrol on a leisurely scenic route before starting the long road trip to Ostend and the return home.

This pleasant summer sojourn contrasted markedly with Alfred's autumn trip in which the onset of wintry conditions caused him to abandon his car in favour of the train. On the long drive from Munich to Goslar he was delayed by snow and ice which caused chaos on the roads and when he arrived hours late at his hotel he was greeted with great warmth and relief by the friendly staff who had given up hope of his arrival that evening.[7] Later in the trip he garaged the car in Cologne and took the train to Vienna since it was unsafe to tackle the high Austrian passes due to the adverse road conditions.[7] Hence it was of great relief to him when he returned to Cologne to find the roads free of snow and ice for his long journey to back to Ostend. This time he arrived home in mid December to get ready for the planned end of year extravaganza that he and Marie-Eugénie had arranged as a result of their windfall settlement. He then reflected on the exceptionally good returns from his current sales year and concluded that they were very fortunate to be blessed with earnings in what he described as an 'annus mirabilis' which had left them with no immediate financial worries for a change.[7]

It was also about this time when unfortunate circumstances appeared to be working to their advantage, when they heard the sad news of the death of their close friend Mr. Harrison, from whom they had rented St. Joseph's cottage in Sleights for so many happy summer holidays, and that his family were keen for them to have first refusal on the purchase of the property.[7] This was fortunate since Marie-Eugénie had been searching the local newspapers for suitable cottages around the Whitby area for a possible place to retire and this seemed like the perfect opportunity to acquire a much-loved house to make this happen.[7] Alfred was dismayed to receive the news of their friend's demise, but he suggested that if the property was not required by any members of the Harrison family, it was in their mutual interests to make a fair offer on the place in which they had enjoyed so many good times with their family. Even though it required considerable modification, it would make an ideal home for their eventual retirement.[7] So the scene was set for yet another significant change of location, although at the time they did not know that this was to be their final move together.

References and Notes

1. AJB Personal, Family and Business Correspondence File 1960, passim.

2. 'Company Affairs': 'Tulketh Results', The *Yorkshire Post*, 17th October 1959.

3. AJB Personal, Family and Business Correspondence File, 1961, passim.

4. AJB Personal, Family and Business Correspondence File, 1962, passim

5. AJB Personal, Family and Business Correspondence File, 1963, passim.

6. AJB Personal, Family and Business Correspondence File, 1964, passim.

7. AJB Personal, Family and Business Correspondence File 1965, passim.

CHAPTER 21

Semi-Retirement in Sleights

Moving Delays

Alfred and Marie-Eugénie's move to semi-retirement was not immediately possible and suffered from the usual frustrating delays and complications which had always bedevilled their many moves in the past. There were problems with the sale of their house at Mornington Villas in Bradford and the need to make changes to St. Joseph's cottage in Sleights to make it more habitable. In addition Alfred had to reorganise his textile agency business, and there remained the problem of Barbara and Adrian, who still depended on the family home in Bradford. Therefore it was the late summer of 1965 before the move could be considered, and even then delays in the sale of the house in Bradford caused further problems, which meant running two households until satisfactory arrangements were made.

Alfred was beyond the normal age of retirement of a self-employed person and in his 71st year he intended to relinquish his agency business within a year,[1] but this proved to be more of an ambition than a realisable goal. The windfall which he received from his compensation settlement with Moxon's was put to good use with the bid accepted for the purchase of the cottage, while Alfred also invested in two new cars to provide more reliable transport for him and his family. He bought a Triumph Herald for his daughter Barbara, who now commuted daily to a GP surgery in Brighouse where she worked as the general practice nurse, and he replaced his own car with an updated version of the Wolseley which had served him so well. While he reflected on his unusual and atypical extravagance: 'with the purchase of the cottage and two new cars it has been a very expensive week', the Brown household rejoiced in the news of the arrival of Alfred and Marie-Eugénie's first and only grandson, Paul Duncan Brown, to Christopher and Brenda in Spain.[1]

These exciting new developments did not deter Alfred from making his usual spring sales trip to Europe at the end of April, but first he had to help prepare for the move to Sleights.[1] Alfred and Marie-Eugénie took possession of St. Joseph's cottage on 19th March, 1966, the Feast Day of St. Joseph, which Alfred took to be a good omen: Joseph was his confirmation name, he had attended St. Joseph's RC Junior School and had worshipped at St. Joseph's RC Church, so for him it had great significance.[1] Alfred and Marie-Eugénie visited the cottage at the end of March to measure up for carpets then took their first load of furniture in an old Bedford van which Alfred borrowed from his friendly Lithuanian grocer, Mr. Kutka, over the Easter weekend of April.[1] While they endured something of a camping weekend in the cottage, they made plans for the necessary alterations needed, arranged for the installation of central heating and for redecoration during Alfred's spring trip. After all this was completed they hoped to move the remainder of their furniture to the cottage in mid-June after Alfred's return from his trip, before they spent their first holiday there as residents in the summer.[1]

In the interim Alfred still had to prepare for his eventual retirement hopefully in the following year, meanwhile his business had been going very well lately and he was sometimes in the galling position of occasionally having to delay the orders received to keep pace with the demand for the materials.[1] Nevertheless he was concerned that his work still kept him fully occupied and that he might have no time to enjoy retirement unless he found a way of withdrawing from the demands of business, even though he would miss the monetary rewards. But he was adamant that he wanted to make the most of future freedom from the demands of work: 'I should like a few active years of retirement to write a bit and walk a lot; to read and to think',[1] so with this in mind he decided to sample this longed-for freedom.

A Nostalgic Adventure

In a letter to his old friend George, Alfred recounted a return to activity with a day's walk over the moors near Bradford, where together with George he had developed his love of moorland tramping:

> My Dear Ouse,
>
> I set off for a walk on my own. Foolishly, I took my car to get out of the city and drove to Queensbury – Old Raggalds *[Raggalds Inn]* – Causeway Foot, via Mountain *[the village]* and that old cottage *[where he and George stayed on their youthful tramps]* – Ogden Reservoir, where I left the car and started my walk to Withens *['The Withens Inn stands high and dry Atop o'the moors!' ...etc. (Poems & Songs, 1949)]*
>
> It was a cold, sombre day for a start, but I soon warmed up and climbed the moors to Withens, where I called for a pint. It is sadly changed (as an Inn), all tarted up and modernized, and yet the atmosphere around it is

unchanged and I felt something of the old fire. It was almost deserted and I continued in the direction of Haworth. I intended to walk another few miles and then return to my car and be home for tea as promised. But once I sniffed the air of those moors and felt the eerie atmosphere, I got the bit between my teeth and went on and on until I came high above Oxenhope and crossed the main road and resolved, against my better judgement, to be hanged with the car and continue to Haworth and beyond to Wuthering Heights – a hell of a long way for me today!

From Shaws *[the village]*, the road climbed fiercely, almost perpendicularly for a good two miles, until you reach part of the moors where there is an old (oak) seat inscribed: 'In honour of Tom Stell who loved these moors'. I sat down and remembered him *[Tom Stell, 1861-1932, was a 'delver' or quarryman who worked in Crow Hill Quarry, one of the Penistone Hill Quarries nearby]*.

But I had a long way to go – the hardest part of the walk; first across the rough moorland shoulder and then dropping gradually towards the valley that leads to the Brontë Waterfalls. I was beyond Haworth by now and beginning to feel the strain for the first time, but I scrambled through bog and boulders to the waterfalls and then sat down for a few minutes and debated whether I should or could do the extra couple of miles or so – very up and down, steep at first – over the wild moors to the remote, derelict farm of 'Top Withens'.

It meant another four or five miles back to Haworth, but I had every intention of entering the threshold of 'Wuthering Heights' again – and did! It is still quite unspoilt up there – apart from the tablet on the outer wall (which displeased me with its doctrinal tone). I touched the walls again, and stamped in the kitchen and felt glorious again for a brief moment. I have such memories of that spot and I felt full of excitement and gratitude that I had been permitted to walk all that way again; that my body was still so strong and my heart full of fire.

The mists which seem inseparable from that part of the moors were rolling up rarely and the horizon vanishing, so I started my long return tramp towards Haworth; but this time I kept on the high moor and took the fork to Stanbury (a lovely little hill village perched on top of a ridge overlooking two valleys). All I wanted was a cup of tea, since I had walked all day without food.

I clomped into Stanbury at almost six o'clock and looked around hopefully for a tea room, a farm, a pub where I might have tea before going any further, but my luck was out. In any case, I discovered that I could get a bus back from Stanbury to Keighley (through Haworth) at 6.00 p.m. so there was no time. I telephoned home and arranged for Barbara to bring her car to Keighley and pick me up; then drive me to Ogden where my car was standing forlornly by the reservoir. We were home at 7.00 p.m. and Marie had prepared a wonderful meal, and I opened a bottle of Fleurie and how I relished the supper!

Footnote: There is much more to it than this – a mere outline – but I may start to write it up when I retire. Still not bad for a ... year old, what do you think? Why don't you get rid of those onions and start shadowing me again?

Love to you both, Ever, Wharfe.[1]

At 71 years old, Alfred could be forgiven for the somewhat self-congratulatory tone of his final comments, since he had covered a total distance of some 16 miles in about 8 hours, over some demanding terrain, which took him up to 1500 ft. over Oxenhope Moor. In addition the conditions were not the best for moorland tramping and he was fortunate not to be caught out by some very inclement weather at that time of year, when the moors are noted for sudden squalls of rain, often with sleet and snow showers, as well as blanket mists or dense fog. Nevertheless the walk had taken him over the same range of moors that he had explored with his friend George more than 50 years before during their youthful tramping days prior to the WW1. He knew that when he moved to Sleights there would be little time for another nostalgic experience like this one, but he probably wanted to reassure himself that he was still capable of a full day's vigorous activity in readiness for the walks he planned on the North York Moors during his retirement.

With these thoughts in mind Alfred's began his spring sales trip to Germany and Austria in late April, after he spent the usual pre-trip meetings with overseas buyers in London, which gave him time to visit his daughters and their families, Felicity in Barnet and Rosemary in Wargrave.[1] Meanwhile Marie-Eugénie had her own travel plans, since no further progress could be made with the cottage until Alfred returned in June. She arranged to go back to Spain with Christopher, Brenda and their family after their recent visit to Bradford, and made the long trip with them by car to Madrid, where she stayed for the duration of Alfred's spring trip before she joined him in London on his return.[1]

The St. Joseph's Statue Saga

Alfred enjoyed driving his new car through Germany and in between his business appointments he took time off to search for a suitable souvenir for the cottage as a permanent reminder of his travels in Germany in the form of a statue of 'St. Josef: Der Zimmermann' (St. Joseph: The Carpenter). Before he left Munich he visited many studios and shops which displayed various carvings of St. Joseph from Oberammagau, which was noted for its wood-carving tradition, but he was unable to find one of the carpenter with the boy Jesus that he preferred. He was even undecided about buying a statue since he hoped that he might get his friend Tom Whittaker, the wood-carver from Littlebeck, to produce a bespoke version. While it would not be the same as a German souvenir, it would be much cheaper than the 300 Deutschmarks that was the average price for a traditional statue.

Although the Munich statues did not fully meet his requirements, he felt that Marie-Eugénie would be disappointed if he returned empty-handed, so he returned to the shop where he saw the first examples a week before. There was an image of 'St. Joseph: The Worker', alas with no child, but it was one that he liked most as a 20 inch statue carved from a solid piece of Limewood, and although it was pale in colour, it had an alive, almost human, if not divine countenance, and to his chagrin it was the most expensive of all the Oberammagau examples in the shop.

He was still unsure about the statue which he favoured, so he asked for reassurance that the wooden carving would stand up to the rigours of the North York Moors weather. The elderly lady proprietor suggested that it would survive best if was placed in a little niche in an exterior wall, but it still needed to be painted with 'Luftlack' or lacquer. Since he could not bear to leave without this souvenir, and with the thought of this lonely sentinel outside the cottage, he risked the purchase. He hoped it would be a success with Marie-Eugénie, paid the exorbitant price and as he left the shop a happy man, he promised the shop owner a photograph of the statue 'in situ' outside the cottage, where it became the family's favourite figurine.[1]

A Few Unforeseen Difficulties

Alfred faced unexpected problems on his spring sales trip when his business was suddenly disrupted by two sets of industrial action. A national seamen's strike in the UK delayed all shipments abroad including his backlog of orders, while a strike by the Irish banks meant one of his most important suppliers, Spamounts, could not remit any money transfers on the orders received, so that the combined effect of both actions was likely to adversely affect Alfred's subsequent commissions.[1] This was a particularly difficult time with ongoing delivery problems, the strikes and the higher price of exported goods, and Alfred feared that unless Britain joined the Common Market soon, it would be increasingly difficult to sell his goods abroad. However since he hoped to retire soon these adverse circumstances might not be so critical to his future,[1] but first he had to make the necessary arrangements for the move to Sleights and the sale of the house in Bradford.

There were other family problems which had to be faced after Adrian returned from Ireland ostensibly to re-sit examinations for his Textile Industries Diploma, and while Alfred welcomed Adrian's help to prepare for the move to Sleights, he was concerned for his son's success in qualifying for the award.[1] He was also worried about Adrian's future with the White Fathers, since they had encouraged him to complete his studies before a return to the seminary, in case his vocation did not become a reality.[1] Meanwhile Alfred's return journey from his business trip was delayed due to the Seamen's strike so he did not arrive home until late June. He and Marie-Eugénie then visited the cottage every weekend to oversee the alterations including the installation of a new kitchen. Unfortunately when Marie-Eugénie eventually moved in the major alterations were still in progress at the cottage, and she had to take temporary accommodation in a local B&B, so that the work could be completed as soon as possible, while Alfred remained in Bradford to take care of the house sale.[1]

By way of some light relief, he gave some less than serious thoughts about how they would dispose of the Bradford house when he drafted a light-hearted notice which took the form of a parody of a horse race event, namely: 'The Mornington Villas Plate (value £10,000) for likely "winners" [i.e. buyers] Open to Doctors, Dental Surgeons, Chiropodists, Psychiatrists and other ranks to be run on 1st July 1966'.[1] While this might have been a frivolous approach, it was based on his expectations of what the property might realise on the open market, as he tried to justify this stance:

> Not that I am a grasping, hard-headed screw, but simply because I need the money for our retirement and I regard the home (and its position) as worth every penny I ask. I am not a charitable organisation or a St. Vincent de Paul Society, but inviting impoverished Chiropodists, Catholic Marriage Councils, Child Welfare Societies, or property racketeers looking for an easy 'conversion' into flats etc. etc. I am not interested in what a half-baked surveyor thinks about the cash value of the house and the district, I know it is a fine house in a first class position and worth a lot more than I am asking to the right sort of buyer.[1]

Even so, Alfred had grossly over-estimated the value of the property to the professional clients that he had in mind, as he would soon find out, much to his dismay.

While the linked problems of the move to Sleights and the sale of the Bradford home continued over the summer, Alfred and Marie-Eugénie also dealt with the serious matter of Adrian's change of vocation. While his academic supervisor at the seminary recommended a return home to qualify for his diploma award as a future safeguard in case he left the Order, the Superior of the Order had a more fundamental concern.[1] He was satisfied with Adrian's intellectual ability and spiritual motivation, but was concerned about whether he would meet the rigorous tenets required by the vocational training programme, which might preclude his acceptance by the Order, and recommended that he should withdraw from the seminary.[1] Understandably this left him at a low point and on his return home Marie-Eugénie became very worried about Adrian's state of mind after the pressures of re-sitting his exams in June. However his condition improved with the help of family support and counselling therapy, but he could not pursue his vocation and he was advised to seek an alternative career.[1] Therefore later that year he took a temporary post as a textile laboratory technician at Leeds University,[1] which allowed him to return to secular life once more, regain his independence and eventually led him to join Alfred in his textile agency.

Future Prospects On Hold

In the autumn of 1966 Alfred made another sales trip to Germany and Austria, but he found other extraneous factors conspired to make his job more difficult, especially the collapse of the German Coalition Government which adversely affected the trade markets.[1] As a result he found business very difficult to conduct and the prospects for the trip seemed bleak, partly because of the serious political and economic crisis in Germany, but also that of Europe in general.[1] In addition his commissions suffered from the late delivery of goods to some of his clients, as well as the adverse reactions of some customers who became dissatisfied and threatened not to tolerate future delays. In response Alfred concluded: 'If the final results are bad, it seems a good time to retire next January or in spring. In any case I think we should now try to sell No. 2 (Mornington Villas) and get things moving. We can't afford to run two homes, the sooner we settle in one place the better. I begin to long for some peaceful days at St. Joseph's, but will it ever happen?'[1]

Meanwhile Marie-Eugénie became tired, depressed and downhearted by the matter, especially since she kept the two homes going, and found solace only by spending more time in Sleights, leaving Barbara and Adrian to look after the house in Bradford.[1]

However she was given some hope of a possible sale of the house after visits from the Marriage Guidance Council, who were interested in the property, as well as from a Catholic Society who wanted to use the building as a residential centre, and she tentatively suggested a price of £6,000, but needed to consult Alfred about any agreed sale price. In addition she contacted the accommodations office at the recently-created Bradford University to see if the Bursar was interested in buying the house for use as student accommodation. She desperately hoped for a solution to the house sale problem, especially since she began to enjoy life more at the cottage and wanted to share the new lifestyle with Alfred in retirement as soon as possible.[1]

In order to try to expedite the move, Marie-Eugénie encouraged Alfred to endorse their daughter Barbara's intention to buy a small flat to have an independent lifestyle and enjoy the company of friends of her own age.[1] Barbara had viewed a suitable place in Brighouse near the general practice where she worked, and Adrian had suggested that he was willing to share the place with her from the start of the new year.[1] This would solve the problem of the maintenance of the family home for their resident offspring and would allow Alfred and Marie-Eugénie to transfer their remaining belongings to Sleights, where Alfred could still continue his business for a while, until he could implement his retirement plans. However the problem of the house sale remained and required renewed efforts to dispose of it in a market that proved to be very difficult at that time.

When Alfred was well into his autumn sales trip, the atrocious weather conditions caused him to abandon his car again in southern Germany, and he completed the Austrian portion of the trip by train, since at one point he was lucky to have spent a night at a wayside inn after the road became impassable.[1] Later, even though he had kept to his schedule of business meetings, he was concerned that this was the most disappointing and difficult trip that he had made since he started the agency.[1] The depressed economic situation in Germany and the rest of Europe did not help, and his turnover was likely to be greatly reduced compared with previous occasions. Therefore he concluded that if another general slump set in, as he feared it might, this would be an additional inducement to opt out of this ever more demanding business and enjoy the benefits of retirement at last.

Selling and Moving, with Retirement in Mind

The year of 1967 turned out to be a significant year in which the solutions to a number of inter-related problems were found. These culminated in changes to the lifestyle of Alfred and Marie-Eugénie, which they hoped would lead to them become a happily retired couple together at last. However this would only come about after a series of events had taken place including: the sale of the house, the move to Sleights and the implementation of Alfred's retirement plan, along with the support for Barbara's and Adrian's plans for independence.

Alfred delayed his usual spring sales trip to set the sale of the house in motion, but he was disappointed with the response of the estate agents who provisionally set the value at £5,250. Furthermore the agents suggested only a limited advertisement of the property to potential buyers, such as the medical profession, since it was difficult to obtain permission to sell the property for business purposes.[2] But Marie-Eugénie was keen to sell the house to any potential buyer as soon as possible, since she could not sustain the running two of houses for much longer. Indeed she was reluctant to stay in Bradford while Alfred was away on business and often spent time with Felicty's and Rosemary's families during his absence. Furthermore she did not look forward to the upheaval of moving again as soon as Alfred returned in May, even if the proposed sale went smoothly.[2] However she was pleased about Barbara and Adrian's move to their new flat in Brighouse, and although they did not take possession until April, they worked on the place at weekends to make it ready for occupancy. Subsequently Barbara continued her nursing career in general practice in Brighouse and Adrian took the post of a quality control technician at Smith, Bulmer & Co., Textiles in Halifax.[2]

Other developments in Alfred's retirement plans caused Marie-Eugénie some alarm in view of her eager anticipation of their spending more time together at Sleights. Alfred met with representatives of Spamount's in Huddersfield and informed them of his impending retirement, although he agreed to complete his planned spring sales trip before setting a firm date.[2] Nevertheless the directors were astounded by the news since they had not suspected that he was considering the move in the near future, and they suggested a semi-retirement arrangement to begin with so that there was time to find a suitable replacement. This seemed reasonable to Alfred, although he was worried about whether an eager young successor would have the experience to fulfil the role, but he agreed to defer his final decision until after his next trip and to discuss his plans further with Spamount's and other companies that he represented on his return.[2]

By April the delays in the house sale caused even more concern for Marie-Eugénie, especially after a surveyor's report valued the property at only £4,500 for use as professional premises, but less than half that at £2,000 for conversion into flats, since there had been a decline in property values in the area. She also despaired about Alfred's insistence on asking more for the house, since 12 years previously they had only paid around £1,000 for it, even though they had carried out many improvements to the place.[2] The problem resulted from changes in the demographics of the Manningham area in which nearby Lumb Lane became a focus of settlement for Asian immigrants. Many of the more affluent local residents had moved away and their large houses were ideal for multiple occupancy or conversion into cheaper flats.[3] As a result there was then a restricted market for the sale of their property and Alfred and Marie-Eugénie only had very a limited number of offers. These included a chiropodist and a dentist who were both interested in the premises for professional use, as well as the Soroptimist Club who wished to use it for their meetings, and even their own milkman, a speculator, who was keen to buy the property as an investment.[2] However only the chiropodist had sufficient capital for the asking price, and the estate agent recommended that they accept this offer which represented a good return on their initial investment. Therefore to facilitate their move to Sleights in the summer, Alfred quickly agreed to the offer and they finally planned to leave Bradford by the end of June.[2]

38. Alfred John Brown at St. Joseph's Cottage, Sleights

Whilst their move to Sleights was completed in the summer of 1967 there was still a considerable amount of work needed to make their new home comfortable, but this could be accomplished without any disturbance to their settling-in period, and Alfred even found the time, energy and patience to renew his interest in gardening along with the establishment of a vegetable patch. During this time they got to know their new neighbours and renewed acquaintanceships with old friends in nearby Darnholm and Goathland, as well as received visits from the family, which brought back happy memories of the cottage when they rented it for their summer holidays. However the only unresolved problem resulted from Alfred's decision to defer his retirement once more. He had planned another autumn business trip and began to operate the agency from a small new office tucked away in an upstairs room of the cottage, much to the chagrin of Marie-Eugénie. But at least he had begun to make arrangements to extricate himself from the business, although this would not be completed before other events took over what remained of their lives together.

New Agency Arrangements

In February 1968 Alfred took a step closer to retirement when Adrian joined him in the business which then became the 'A.J. Brown & Son Textile Export Agency'.[4] Adrian's first task was to find new worsted and woollen manufacturers to represent on a commission basis in Germany and Austria, in order to increase the income to support the additional business costs. In this respect he was successful and added Barry Worsteds of Bingley, the producers of fine worsted and mohair cloths, to the portfolio, before he accompanied Alfred to London to present the new spring collection of materials to visiting overseas buyers. As a junior partner Adrian then began to learn the business under the tutelage of his father which started with the improvement of his German language competency during the four weeks of the London spring sales season.

At the end of April Alfred and Adrian left London by car for the usual spring sales trip, and Adrian was introduced to all Alfred's well-established customers in Germany, before he was left in Aschaffenburg in northern Bavaria, where he took a temporary post as a 'Volontäre' in the men's clothier company of August Vordenfelde KG. He then had the chance to learn more about the manufacturing side of the textile business and continue with his German language improvement while he stayed with Alfred's good friends, the Vordenfelde family, and he helped to teach the daughter and nephew English in return for his board and lodgings and pocket money.[5] In the meantime Alfred continued with the rest of his trip to Germany and Austria alone, before he eventually returned in October to collect Adrian, who then joined him again for the autumn sales trip and so he began his formal training in sales techniques.

In the junior partnership arrangements, Alfred also intended to place Adrian with major supplier clients in Halifax and Huddersfield in between the spring and autumn sales trips, in the hope that after a suitable training period he would eventually take over the business entirely.[4] But first he would have to get the agreement of his major clients, such as Spamount's of Northern Ireland, to approve the takeover of the agency when he retired. Therefore he decided to continue his agency work for another year in order to give Adrian a chance to prove himself, and he had set the deadline of his 75th birthday in 1969 for the long-awaited exit from the world of business.[4] He then planned to fulfil his cherished dream of walking, writing and enjoying life together with Marie-Eugénie once more – a dream that would tragically never be realised.

39. Marie-Eugénie and Alfred J. Brown at St. Joseph's Cottage

During the long last summer of 1968 there was a final get-together of most of the family members at St. Joseph's cottage when a series of visits took place which included joint birthday celebrations for Alfred, his son-in-law Jimmy and Rosemary, with only Barbara and Adrian missing the occasion. This was followed later with holiday visits by Felicity, Colin and family, as well Christopher, Brenda and family soon after.[4] In the remainder of the summer Alfred busied himself with the many unfinished jobs that still needed to be done around the cottage, and even though they would require months to complete, he looked forward to these chores when at last he finally had the time. But with yet another autumn trip to organise in conjunction with the ongoing training of his junior partner Adrian, he had to postpone this work until a later date.[4]

The Final Business Trip

Alfred began his last business trip with a short visit to London in early October, then set out on his usual planned schedule of visits to Germany and Austria during October and November 1968.[4] He met Adrian as planned in late October in Aschaffenburg and looked forward to his help on this and perhaps one more business trip before he handed over to Adrian after he had completed his training to take over the business.[4] But this last trip was not completely taken up by business matters, since Alfred and Adrian took a couple of short breaks to walk around the Black Forest resort of Herrenberg and the Harz Mountians near Goslar.[4] But as they picnicked on a warm, sunny late October day in the forest of the Harzburg range of hills, Alfred reported not feeling too well. He had complained about having a sore stomach for a few days and thought it was a digestive problem, since he was also constipated. Nevertheless they continued with the trip and Alfred tried to remedy the problem with his old-stand by cure of castor oil.[4]

At the time Marie-Eugénie was in Spain for a short break with Christopher and his family who now lived in Barcelona. When she learned of Alfred's problem she admonished him for relying on one of his usual self-medicated 'purges' for such conditions, and strongly advised him to visit a doctor or at least a chemist to try to overcome the problem.[4] Likewise his daughter Felicity also learned of Alfred's ill-health and became worried about his ongoing stomach pain, and she advised him to return home to find the cause of the problem, which Adrian fully endorsed since he had seen a marked deterioration in his father's condition.[4] By then Alfred was feeling so ill that he just wanted to fly home as soon as possible and seek medical help for his deteriorating condition and he returned later in November. Meanwhile Adrian remained to complete the rest of the business schedule in Austria but he was relieved that his father had returned to England for treatment.[4]

Alfred's Decline and Demise[6]

On his return home Alfred was briefly hospitalised in Scarborough while he underwent treatment for his digestive disorder, while the cause of his gastro-intestinal problems was investigated, before he was discharged to await the results of these clinical assessments and further proposed follow-up procedures. However he was up and about again when Adrian returned from Austria in mid-December, and he was keen to know how his son had coped with his first solo efforts, and especially pleased to hear that the trip had yielded greater returns than the previous disappointing spring trip. Indeed he was in such a buoyant mood, that he and Adrian visited some of their major clients in Huddersfield and Bingley later in December to reassure them that his son would be a satisfactory replacement for him in the business in the coming year.

But after spending Christmas and New Year at home Alfred was hospitalized once more in late January 1969, and the results of the clinical investigations revealed that he was suffering from terminal pancreatic cancer, which had progressed so far that he only had a few weeks to live. Even today this type of cancer remains one of the most difficult to diagnose early, resistant to management by surgical and chemotherapy interventions, with the highest mortality rates and lowest survival times among those affected. In Alfred's case the tumour cells had spread to other organs which resulted in secondary carcinomatosis of the liver, and it could only be managed by palliative care directed towards pain relief and maintenance of some tolerable quality of life.

In early February Alfred was transferred to the Chubb Hill Nursing Home in Whitby which was run by an order of nursing sisters who specialised in the care of terminally ill patients. Here the patients' pain relief and personal requirements were of paramount importance, and Alfred was administered sedative doses of morphine by the nuns, as well as a tot of his favourite whisky every evening at 6.00 p.m. prompt, in a friendly, supportive and devout environment which was important to him. However in late February he requested to be allowed to return home in order to die and returned to St. Joseph's cottage, where he was then attended by his daughter Barbara, who obtained compassionate leave from her general practice duties to care for him during his final days. She had experience of the end-stage palliative care of cancer patients, having treated a senior partner from her general practice and others who had suffered from the same condition, and she was able to administer doses of morphine in accordance with the prescribed limits to help alleviate Alfred's pain.

During the last week of February Marie-Eugénie, Barbara and Adrian were joined by Christopher, his wife and family, who had flown from Spain to be there at the end. Alfred now occupied a bed downstairs, and as well as the sedation provided by Barbara, the family took turns to provide a 24 hour vigil at his bedside in the sitting room during his rapidly deteriorating state. He also received visits from the local Catholic priest, Fr. J. O'Rourke, who heard his confession, gave him Holy Communion and administered the sacrament of 'Extreme Unction' or 'Last Rites', now known as the 'Anointing of the Sick' with holy oils, in preparation for his imminent death. Finally, while other members of the family were out walking in nearby Darnholm for a brief respite from their vigils, and with Marie-Eugénie and Rosemary at his bedside, Alfred died peacefully early on Saturday afternoon 1st March, 1969.

This was not the ending that Alfred had perceived nor hoped for himself. In his younger days he had reflected on his own imagined and even desired form of death in a passage of prose entitled: 'Dying In A Blaze Of Glory', which contained a short, uncanny, but unfortunately in terms of Alfred's wishes, an undesirable prescience that declared:

Few men – I make bold to claim – have so lusted after a fine death as I. Few if any, of the more heroic ways of dying have not – at some time or other – aroused my enthusiasm, setting my pulse racing, and my heart on fire. Active death: that is what appeals to me, rather than the ceremonial common death shuffling into bedrooms with all his pomp. Death to be abhorred! I should hate to pass away peacefully in my bed surrounded by weeping friends. I should hate to sink inch by inch under the pressure of his very hand. Life is too magnificent for that. And when the time comes, let me lose it in a flash. Not for me, I trust, the melancholy anticlimax of a city funeral! Not for me the weeping and gnashing of teeth, the solemn parade of mourning. Let death take me suddenly, gloriously, and let me go with a laugh.[7]

Alfred supported a view espoused by one of his favourite writers, James Joyce: 'Better pass boldly into that other world in the full glory of some passion, than fade and wither dismally'. Alas this was not to be.

Alfred's Final Farewell

Alfred was received into the RC Church of the English Martyrs in Sleights where he had worshipped on the evening of Monday 3rd March at 7.00 p.m. for the short traditional 'Lying in Vigil'. His funeral took place the following day Tuesday 4th March at 12 noon, with a Requiem Mass offered by Fr. O'Rourke, and a eulogy delivered by his close friend George Heseltine, followed by burial in the nearby graveyard of the Anglican Church of St. John the Evangelist. The funeral cortège made the short journey across the Pickering to Whitby road at the bottom of Blue Bank, since the Catholic Church did not have its own consecrated graveyard, but there was an arrangement with the Anglican Church to provide a communal graveyard for both denominations. An impressive headstone was later installed on the grave situated in the south-east aspect of the graveyard with views over the moors that Alfred loved so much. It has an emblematic carving of an open book overlain by a quill pen to signify Alfred's writing achievements, and is inscribed with the words from one of his own favourite poems: 'Dales in Paradise' that reflected the eternal tramping hopes for his friends and himself: 'There must be Dales in Paradise, Which you and I will find...'

Marie-Eugénie made all the funeral arrangements with Alfred's wishes in mind, and the reception that was held at St. Joseph's cottage was carried out in the true Yorkshire tradition of being 'buried with a ham tea' when a delicious ham repast prepared by Marie-Eugénie was served. Then unlike the church and funeral services that had been very formal, in which Christopher and Adrian dressed in morning suits as Alfred requested, the reception was quite an informal gathering and had quite a jolly atmosphere in which a small group of family, close friends and some business acquaintances enjoyed convivial reminiscent exchanges about Alfred's life and time past.

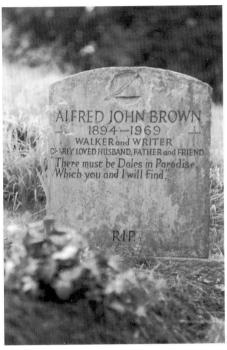

40. Alfred John Brown's Gravestone

Alfred's Obituary Notices

Subsequently a number of obituaries appeared in both the local and national press about Alfred's life and works that commented with varying degrees of similarity and difference, as well as some errors in reporting the salient details of his biography. Perhaps the one with the most widespread impact was provided by Alfred's closest friend, George Coulehan Heseltine,[8,8a] tramping companion, former best man, confidant, fellow author and life-long friend of Alfred and the Brown family who paid the following tribute to him in *The Times*:

Mr. A.J. Brown, Walker and Writer
G.C.H. writes:-

Mr. Alfred John Brown, who died on Saturday, was the author of popular books for walkers. Born in Bradford in 1894, educated at St. Bede's Grammar

School, he served as a gunner in the 1914-18 War, but contracted fever which left him totally incapacitated, with 100 per cent pension, for several years. The story of his recovery inspired his first novel, The Lean Years. Against all medical predictions and warnings, he became a great walker, exploring Belgium and France, the Alps and the Pyrenees. 'Rough walking was my salvation' as he said himself.

His main enthusiasm however, was the moors and dales of his native Yorkshire, which he explored from end to end. He became a champion of moorland freedom, president of the Yorkshire Ramblers' Federation for many years, and an indomitable fighter for the preservation of footpaths and open spaces – (Fylingdales in particular until national defence decreed otherwise).

He wrote a series of exciting walking books (he detested the world 'hiking'): *Moorland Tramping* and *Striding Through Yorkshire* were in every walker's rucksack. His other works included *Poems & Songs*; a picaresque *Four Boon Fellows*; *A Joyous Entry* (travel); *Whitaker* (novel); *Ground Staff* (he became a Wing Commander in RAF Intelligence); *National Parks Guide Book to the North York Moors*; *Broad Acres* – his tribute to the county, and *Fair North Riding*. He was a frequent contributor to *Country life* and *G.K.'s Weekly*, the BBC and local periodicals.

Alongside all this he had a successful business career in textile exports, becoming (from scratch) director of a Yorkshire textile export company, travelling and 'selling British' extensively on the Continent.[8]

Alfred's home town newspaper, the Bradford *Telegraph & Argus* gave particular attention to his origins, his Yorkshire affiliations and his writing:

Yorkshire Author dies at Sleights

Mr. Alfred John Brown, the Bradford-born author best known for his writings about Yorkshire, died at his home in Sleights, near Whitby on Saturday.

His knowledge of Yorkshire was described as encyclopaedic and he lived in different parts of the county, including Bradford, Burley-in-Wharfedale and Sleights.

A member of the Yorkshire Dales (North Riding) National Park Committee and former president of the West Riding Ramblers' Federation, Mr. Brown wrote many articles about Yorkshire outdoors. Among his publications were

Striding Through Yorkshire, *Tramping in Yorkshire* and *Moorland Tramping*.

He published a Yorkshire miscellany *Broad Acres* and a novel about Bradford called *Whitaker*, which he wrote under the pen-name Julian Laverack.

Experience as a Yorkshire hotelier provided him with material for another book, and his work as an RAF Intelligence Officer in the 1939-45 war gave him background for another.

Mr. Brown, who was educated at St. Bede's Grammar School, Bradford, was in the wool trade for many years and he travelled abroad widely. He was in Baghdad during the 1958 revolution and was virtually a prisoner for two weeks while mobs roamed the streets and burned the British Embassy. Three Americans were taken hostage from the same hotel and murdered.

Mr. Brown leaves a widow, three daughters and two sons.[9]

Another provincial newspaper, the *Whitby Gazette*, also paid tribute to Alfred's life and works and emphasised his connections with the local district:

The death occurred on Saturday, at his home, St. Joseph's, Main Street, Sleights, of Mr. Alfred John Brown. Well known as a writer in Yorkshire, Mr. Brown was a Bradford man. His publications included: *Moorland Tramping*, *Tramping in West Yorkshire*, *Striding Through Yorkshire* and *Fair North Riding*.

In addition he wrote two novels, the first was *The Lean Years*, also a book of poems, largely about the Yorkshire Dales.

In the last war he served in RAF Bomber Command, attaining the rank of Wing Commander. As a Squadron Leader he published a further book *Ground Staff*, which described his experiences as an intelligence officer. Later after six years at the Whitfield Hotel, Goathland, he published his best selling book *I Bought An Hotel*.

For the last three years Mr. and Mrs. Brown had lived in Sleights. In addition to writing, Mr. Brown was an export textile agent, and travelled a good deal abroad, particularly in Germany and Austria.

As his books about Yorkshire indicate, Mr. Brown who was a member of the London Branch (The Keys) of the Catholic Writers' Guild, loved the dales country, particularly Wensleydale and Swaledale. At one time he and his family lived in Burley-in-Wharfedale.

Mr. Brown was a member of the North Riding's Yorkshire Dales National Park Committee. He advocated the establishment at Semerwater in Wensleydale of an open-air encampment with facilities for boating on the lake, picnics and car-parking.

He is survived by his wife Marie-Eugénie, three daughters and two sons. The funeral took place on Tuesday following a Requiem Mass at the Church of the English Martyrs in Sleights where Mr. Brown worshipped.[10]

However one of the most personable obituaries was written in the *Middlesbrough Evening Gazette* by the reporter Harry Mead, who also wrote about Alfred long after his death, and he gave a very complimentary critique of the appeal of Alfred's literary works:

The Magic of Alfred Brown

The death of Alfred John Brown, of Sleights, near Whitby, has robbed North Yorkshire of one of its most enjoyable authors. North Yorkshire, unlike the Lake District, does not prompt an unquenchable flow of words from the presses. But the few books it has inspired are mainly good, written by authors who know the area and understand its people. A.J. Brown's works hold their place among the best.

Many people who may never have heard of Mr. Brown are nevertheless indebted to him. The most popular guide to the North York Moors, published by Constaple with the assistance of the North Riding County Council, is based on Mr. Brown's most notable work, *Fair North Riding*. This latter book published by Country Life in 1952, is perhaps the best general guide to the North Riding yet published.

It does not stop at county things. One chapter, for instance, does admirable justice to the tremendous story of the growth of Middlesbrough. Mr. Brown is also enthusiastic about the night view of Teesside from the high land around its fringes – perhaps as dramatic as anything of which hills can boast. But what Mr. Brown liked best was to clatter down the cobbles of some market town after a long day in the hills and enjoy the company around the fire of some hospitable inn. His great gift was being able to convey the pleasure of these occasions.

The last time I saw one of these books on the the open market was at a knock down price in a rather old fashioned newsagent's shop in a North

Yorkshire County town. I browsed agreeably through it, but decided to put off the purchase until another day. When I returned it had gone. A.J. Brown was not short of admirers – and anyone who picked up one of his books was likely to come under the spell.[11]

It is likely that Alfred would have been agreeably satisfied with all these tributes to his life and works, and particularly pleased that he had not been referred to as 'a writer of books on rambling in Yorkshire'. He detested the terms 'hiker' or 'hiking', since he regarded himself as a walker, which in his terms was a different thing altogether.

Postscript

The 'A.J. Brown & Son Textile Export Agency', operated by Adrian and his mother, continued to trade until 1972, when it was finally terminated while it still showed a profitable return and had no debts.

Marie-Eugénie lived alone at St. Joseph's cottage in Sleights until 1983, when she unexpectedly remarried a neighbour and friend, the widower Mr. George Albert Taplin. He was her companion during her later years after she became incapacitated by a series of minor strokes. Latterly they moved into a care home in Whitby, where she died on 22nd September 1988 aged 82 years, and was buried with Alfred and her name was added to the original headstone.

41. Alfred John Brown and Marie-Eugénie Brown's Headstone

Of the five Brown family offspring, the three daughters continue to live in England, while the two sons live abroad. Felicity is widowed and lives in Barnet, Barbara, a spinster, lives in a care home in Huddersfield, while Rosemary is also widowed and lives in Henley-on-Thames. Christopher is retired and lives with his wife in Torreblanca, Spain, while Adrian, a bachelor, lives in Murrhardt, Germany, where he runs an English Language business enterprise. Alfred and Marie-Eugénie also had six grandchildren, only one of whom has the Brown surname, while among their great-grand children, none now bears the family name made famous by the passionate Yorkshireman, Alfred John Brown, whose spirit lives on through this biographical account of his life and literary works.

References and Notes

1. AJB Personal, Family and Business Correspondence File, 1966, passim.

2. AJB Personal, Family and Business Correspondence File, 1967, passim.

3. Allan Hall, *The Story of Bradford*, The History Press, 2013, chapter 12, 'Towards a Multi-Ethnic City', pp. 174-178.

4. AJB Personal, Family and Business Correspondence File, 1968, passim.

5. Personal communication, Adrian Paul Brown.

6. Personal communications, Felicity Millward, Barbara Brown, Rosemary Sturrup, Christopher Brown and Adrian Brown.

7. Alfred John Brown, Diary Journal, May 1925 – November 1927, abstract from: 'Dying In A Blaze Of Glory', 10th November 1925, pp. 90-98.

8. George Coulehan Heseltine, *The Times*, Early Edition Newspaper, London, Wednesday 5th March 1969.
   8a. Note: George Coulehan Heseltine died in 1980 aged 86 years old.

9. *Telegraph & Argus*, Monday 3rd March 1969.

10. *Whitby Gazette*, Friday 7th March 1969.

11. Harry Mead, *Middlesbrough Evening Gazette*, Wednesday 5th March 1969.

Epilogue

Alfred John Brown Remembered

There have been a number of published articles that have documented the life and literary works of Alfred since his demise, which has helped to maintain an interest in his memorable accomplishments. One of the first was by David Rubinstein, who paid sincere tributes to him in his book *The Wolds Way*.[1] He acknowledged that while others often walked their own versions of the 'Wolds Way', Alfred had used the term in a rather different context some 70 years previously, before the definitive 67 miles route from Filey to North Ferriby was established. Rubinstein also expressed his gratitude to Alfred's account of walking in the Wolds in his early tramping book *Tramping in Yorkshire – North and East* (1932), and indicated that his own book followed in Alfred's pioneering footsteps. Moreover Rubinstein was convinced of the influence of Alfred's work: '...that all ramblers in North and East Yorkshire owed him a great deal whether they realised it or not'.[1a]

In a later newspaper article by the *Northern Echo* reporter, Harry Mead, was a short piece that sought to bring the public's attention to what he termed: 'the forgotten giant of Northern Countryside writing – Alfred John Brown'.[2] He commented that it had been astonishing how 'A.J.' as he was fondly known, had fallen into obscurity since his death in 1969. He went on to acknowledge the popularity of his works which were distinguished by his warmth of personality and the breadth of his interests, both of which he claimed shone through his writing, and suggested that his books were like huge, refreshing gulps of fresh air. But he also admitted that he was surprised to discover that Alfred had also written poetry and he quoted a couple of poems from his classic work *Fair North Riding*, before he welcomed the news that a local man, Tom Burns, was preparing a biography of Alfred.

Subsequently, there followed a more detailed article by Tom Scott Burns, a potential biographer of Alfred. This provided a framework of his life and literary achievements, in a short four page biographical article in the popular Yorkshire *Dalesman* magazine.[3] Tom, a resident of Nunthorpe in Cleveland, had come to know Marie-Eugénie and some members of the Brown family and had started to assemble material for a biography of Alfred based on archive sources available from the family. Tom was an accomplished author who wrote several books on walking in North Yorkshire in

the 1980s and 1990s, however he suffered from the early onset of a degenerative ageing disorder before he could fully develop a biography. Nevertheless it was his initial
efforts to re-popularise Alfred's life and works that laid the foundation for others to
follow, including the present biographer.

Then some considerable time later, a further article by Tom Scott Burns featured
Alfred in a short review about his life and times for the *Voice of the Moors*, the magazine for the North York Moors Association.[4] In it he lamented the loss from the ranks
of the 'North Country Chroniclers' of the jaunty writer and moorland tramper Alfred
John Brown, and drew attention to the special features of Alfred's prose and poetry,
whose spirit lived on through his superb books. Sadly this was one of Tom's last contributions to the memory of Alfred, since he became debilitated by early dementia
and died in 2011, aged 65 years old.

Alfred's contribution to the fledgling *Yorkshire Dalesman* was also acknowledged
by the inclusion of one of his articles in a book by David Joy, the former editor of the
magazine from 1988-1994, which celebrated the 50th anniversary of the best-selling
regional magazine in the UK.[5] Joy recalled the most dramatic change in the *Dalesman*
occurred when the magazine was just six months old and the country was plunged
into war: '...the atmosphere in the higher Dales was beautifully captured by Alfred J.
Brown'. This was then illustrated by Alfred's article: 'All Quiet in the Dales', originally
published in 1939, but included in its entirety in Joy's book which features contributions from well-known writers over the intervening years.

In a another reference to Alfred's contributions to the development of long distance
walking paths, Malcolm Boyes and Hazel Chesters, proposed the route: 'A.J. Brown's
Derwent Way'.[6,6a] This was based on the last four days of Alfred's walking holiday
in the early 1930s from Robin Hood's Bay to York, using the River Derwent as an
approximate guide. The route was described earlier in his book *Tramping in Yorkshire
– North and East* (1932), in which he chose the best scenery and the most interesting places to visit along the way, which Chester and Boyes suggest takes the walker to
the less-frequented locations away from the bustle of the 1990s. But in order to avoid
the last 7 miles into York, which even Alfred found annoying because of the traffic,
they suggest today's walkers follow the pleasant route of the 'Minster Way' between
Stamford Bridge and York.

By way of contrast, a near full page article by the reporter Harry Mead again, not
only documented Alfred's life and works, but intriguingly explored the possibility of
using the story from Alfred's hotel books for the production of a new television series,
to rival the then current ITV programme *Heartbeat*.[7] He suggested that the Whitfield

House Hotel was really the hidden gem of the fictitious village of 'Adensfield', and commented that while television had made the village of Goathland famous through fiction, the real local story would make an even better subject for the small screen, and allow the then desperate BBC to counter both ITV's *Heartbeat* and *Peak Practice* to have a moors-based success on the scale of the dales-based 'Herriot' series. However it remains unknown whether or not Mead made any overtures to the BBC in this regard, although the possibility remains an interesting prospect.

After the turn of the century a number of further articles began to appear which continued to renew interest in Alfred's life and works, such as the challenge laid down by the editor of the *Voice of the Moors* magazine that required the readers to solve an 'AJB' problem.[8] The short article again paid tribute to Alfred as one of the most enthusiastic and hardy walkers of the 20th century, the irrepressible author, adventurer and lover of all things Yorkshire, then challenged readers to find Alfred's last resting place which was illustrated only by his headstone marker.

In the following year an amusingly-titled article by the Yorkshire *Dalesman* writer, Steve Goodier, suggested that readers should follow in Alfred's footsteps by 'Following the Ale Trail'.[9] Strangely enough, while the article reviewed much of Alfred's life story and his published books, there is only a fleeting mention of Alfred's propensity to mention the many inns frequented on his Yorkshire tramping excursions (for example there are 147 named in *Striding Through Yorkshire*). However the author noted Alfred's attraction for such hostelries: 'My inclination when I enter any of the Dales villages is to spend a week in each to drink my fill – not only of ale, but of the lore and legend and friendliness in which they all abound.'

But perhaps one of the most moving memories of Alfred came from a reader of the *Dalesman*, Roy Richards in 2001, when he recounted an interesting day out under the regular end piece item of the magazine entitled: 'My Best Day Out', from which the following is abstracted:

When I was in my mid teens, 40 years ago, I spent weekends walking, always going alone as I am partially deaf. My teacher who introduced me to walking in the Dales, told me of a 'Ramblers Special' train and was leading a party from Dent over Whernside to Ribblehead. Wishing to be on my own, I got off at the next station, Garsdale, aiming to walk the seven miles to Dent station and follow behind.

I set off from Garsdale with one other walker, a tall man in his early 60s ahead of me. As we toiled up the hill, we began to chat, in spite of the difference in our ages we had one thing in common, a love of the Yorkshire Dales and Moors. The miles went by and my new friend pointed out hills, villages, even farms. He knew the names of them all.

I was fascinated by his knowledge of the area and in no time at all, we reached the Sun Inn. He suggested lunch but, having never been in a pub before, I said I was quite happy to stay outside and eat my sandwiches. He would have none of it and ushered me inside. Soon we were sitting at a table, him with a pint of 'old', and me with a pint of shandy, and the biggest plateful of ham and eggs I have ever seen in front of us. Apple pie with cream followed, making it a meal to remember. He insisted on paying for it all, and we then made our way down the cobbled street and back up the riverside, leaving Whernside Manor and following the Craven Way, before striking up the shoulder of Whernside to the summit cairn.

We got around to talking about authors. We talked about the old generation of Frank Elgee, Edmund Bogg and Harry Speight, finding we shared an admiration for Halliwell Sutcliffe, but that my favourite author was a comparatively modern one, called Alfred John Brown. I spent the next half hour reeling off everything I had read from his books, while we shared my sandwiches and a flask of tea.

We took the shortest way to Ribblehead, straight down the slope, then strode past the farm, under the viaduct to the Station Inn, with time to spare for a drink before the last train. As we sat in the bar, the party who should have been ahead of us arrived – we had overtaken them by going directly down the slope!

My teacher knew my friend and was interested in all we had done that day. I mentioned all we had talked about – including authors – and, when my teacher asked me if I knew who I had been walking with all day, I was thunderstruck to find it was my hero – Alfred John Brown himself.

I never met him again, but it was a day I shall never forget. I have collected all his books and even now, after 40 years, I still think him the best author on Yorkshire, simply because he did he didn't just write about Yorkshire, he loved Yorkshire. Whenever I am in the area I visit his grave at the side of the little church at Sleights, near Whitby, sit awhile, and recall that wonderful day and, especially, his kindness to a very unsure and lonely young boy.[10,10a]

Most recently there have been a number of short biographical articles about Alfred in various Yorkshire journals by the biographer to raise awareness of his life and works in anticipation of the publication of this biography. These include: the Journal of the Yorkshire Dales Association,[11] the online magazine of the North York Moors Association,[12], the local press[13] and the most widely circulated monthly magazine in the UK, the *Dalesman*.[14] In addition an entry has been secured in the prestigious Oxford Dictionary of National Biography in the near future.[15]

Furthermore there have been two Alfred John Brown walking trails established which include routes around two of his previous home locations in Burley-in-Wharfedale[16] and Sleights.[17] Finally the installation of two memorial plaques are planned at Alfred's former homes of 'Wharfegate' in Burley-in-Wharfedale and 'St. Joseph's Cottage' in Sleights to commemorate his residences at these locations.

Alfred John Brown – A Biographer's Tribute

This biography of Alfred has detailed the major themes that contributed to his life story, and although these have been elaborated in the usual chronological order, it should be recognised that they were largely influenced by a variety of historical events which took place during his lifetime.

He was born in the late Victorian era, and his early childhood and youth were heavily influenced by his strict, middle class, Catholic family upbringing, reinforced by religious principles imparted through formal church and school experiences. Together these undoubtedly shaped Alfred's beliefs and values that persisted through-out his life, and yet within these constraints, he was able to develop a sense of per-sonal freedom that led to an interest in the world around him. This was manifested in early childhood experiences of moorland walks with his father and elder brother to Ilkley, with moonlit returns at dusk, and his apparent rejection of formal education as a youth of 14 years of age to try his luck in the world of work, much to the disapproval of his parents. However it was not long before he discovered the error of his ways, and with help he was able to take up a traineeship in the wool trade, which would eventu-ally provide the basis for his long term employment.

When Alfred's first test of duty came, he followed the urge to serve his country's needs in WW1, even though he was in a reserved occupation. Unfortunately his dis-appointment at not being able to take an active part in the war was overshadowed by the appalling realisation that the dreadful affliction from which he suffered left him a virtual invalid, unable to walk or work for several years. But it was only out of this adversity that he was able to rise to the challenge of learning to walk again, and establish a life-long interest in the world of literature that led to the development of a secondary writing career.

Alfred's subsequent challenge was then to return to the reality of normal life and work, which was only achieved through the sympathetic support of family and friends, together with the patient understanding of his caring employer. This allowed him to readjust to a changed post-war situation which had left many servicemen adrift from society, but in his case allowed him to progress rapidly in his chosen career. This liberation from his previously weakened state also provided him with a renewed impetus for embarking on a new lifestyle, which saw the production of his first published works. It also allowed him the opportunity of travelling throughout Europe, with only 'Mother Russia' being absent from his extensive business travels.

The stabilisation of personal circumstances was crucial to the next phase of Alfred's life when he married his half-French wife Marie-Eugénie, and together they settled into a new life in Burley-in-Wharfedale, one of Alfred's favourite dales, where they brought up their family of five children. While this in itself was not particularly remarkable, his ability to conduct a normal family life and a demanding business life, and still have time to engage in his twin passions of walking and writing, suggests that he had a remarkable degree of reserve energy to pursue a potentially attractive, if elusive, alternative writing career, but only at the expense of attempting to be a business man by day and a writer by night.

These early attempts to become a writer during the interwar years produced some impressive results with the publication of the widely-acknowledged series of three Yorkshire tramping books. And yet while Alfred was happy to receive the acclaim of reviewers for some of his best-selling work that had established him as a leading Yorkshire topographical writer, he was especially pleased to be recognised as a 'Moorpoke', that is someone who is completely at ease with wild moorlands and is able to find the way in these desolate landscapes. He regarded this term as one of the best compliments he was ever paid, especially since this came from a true native of the moors, an old shepherd friend.

In spite of the call of the wild moors, Alfred continued his extensive travels in Europe as WW2 loomed, and he reacted angrily to the threat posed by the expansion of Germany under Nazi rule. He witnessed the annexation of Austria in Vienna, the propaganda attempts to woo Greece into a pro-German alliance in Athens and the arrest of Jewish business colleagues attempting to flee Austria. Then after he and his wife were almost detained in Germany on business just before the war started, he took the deliberate step of evacuating his family from the likely effects of the German bombing offensive on strategic targets in England. He had seen the build-up of German military power and was critical of England's apparent lack of concern for the threat that this posed.

Once more historical events produced an urge in Alfred to join the King's colours again in WW2, only this time he was thwarted by age rather than incapacity for active service. Instead he was assigned to the RAF Intelligence Branch and served at RAF Bomber Command HQ, as well as numerous Bomber Command Stations around the country, planning operational missions by British, Commonwealth and Allied Foreign air raids over Germany. It was during this period that he developed a close affinity not only with aircrews on dangerous bombing sorties, but also the support crews who made the bombing offensive possible. It was these experiences that allowed him to write a sensitive tribute to all those involved in this vital aspect of the war in his memoirs of his service during the war.

If Alfred's return to 'Civvy Street' was a little easier after this conflict, it was brought into sharp reality when he turned his back on the wool trade and began life in the brave new world with an hotel adventure, which proved to be one of his greatest challenges. Once more he showed great resilience and reserves in adapting to a new role, ably abetted by his wife's culinary expertise, in the rejuvenation of a war-closed hotel during a time of post war austerity. With no prior experience of running such a business, they were only able to make a success of this bold enterprise by sheer hard work and blind faith in their own ability to succeed in this demanding enterprise. But eventually after years of toil, which took its toll on family life, his wife's health and financial stability, they were forced to sell the business and seek a new life.

In spite of the demands of the hotel business, Alfred had some other significant successes as the landlord hotelier with his wife as the resident proprietor. In what little spare time he had to write in the 'off-season', he had published a couple of books about his hotel experiences, along with further works about his favourite topic, Yorkshire, as well as a book of verse, which found an outlet for his latent poetic talents. Thus on the strength of this limited success as a 'Literary Innkeeper', he made one last desperate attempt to fulfil his long-held dream of becoming a full time writer.

After selling the hotel, Alfred moved to London, then York, in order to devote a couple of years to try to rejuvenate his penchant for fictional writing. In his two earlier semi-autobiographical novels, he had demonstrated a flair for the development of a sound storyline, along with the creation of credible fictional characters, and an ability to produce entertaining dialogue that explored their relationships within the context of an interesting plot. But he was unable to capitalise on this former ability to create the elusive successful novel that he wished to produce as a true fiction writer and hopefully launch a career as a novelist.

In the end Alfred's career went full circle when he returned to Bradford and rejoined the wool trade as an export sales director of a West Riding worsted company. Later he established his own freelance enterprise as the 'A.J. Brown Textile Export Agency' to represent the overseas sales interests of various UK worsted and woollen manufacturers and travelled extensively in Europe and the Middle East. This was a truly remarkable achievement since he had been absent from the business for several years, and it was a testament to his considerable talents as a salesman and to his linguistic abilities that he was able to make a success of promoting the sales of products overseas from an industry that was already in the throes of a severe decline at home.

It had been Alfred's intention to retire as soon as he could hand over the business to his youngest son, then a junior partner, who needed the opportunity of an entry into the commercial sales world. Alfred had then planned to indulge in his favourite pastimes of walking and writing once more, but sadly this final freedom of retirement with his wife was denied him after a sudden dramatic decline in his health.

On his return home due to illness from a business trip to Europe, he was diagnosed with terminal cancer, but faced the prospects of his imminent demise with typical stoicism and fortitude, and opted to die at home with his family on hand. His funeral service and interment were carried out according to his wishes and he was laid to rest in the tranquility of a churchyard overlooked by moorland, with views of the sea and the ruins of Whitby Abbey in the distance. Appropriately a headstone was installed inscribed with his own words which included a line from his poem 'Dales in Paradise' and his grave is now often visited by those who enjoyed his works.

Alfred John Brown – In His Own Words

In keeping with the major underlying strands of his biography, it is perhaps fitting to allow Alfred to comment in his own words on those aspects that underpinned his life and works, namely his reflections of a life lived as a prodigious walker, a prolific writer and a passionate Yorkshireman.

AJB: 'On Walking'

Alfred's recovery from the incapacity suffered in his early life had been largely due to self-rehabilitation when he learned to walk again:

I knew in my heart that walking – rough walking – was my real salvation. Sitting around only made me miserable and weak. All I needed was fresh air and exercise, and I had developed a passion for both. I walked miles. On every weekend and holiday I was off over the hills and far away.[18]

He also described the inherent joy of being able to walk again and the unbridled pleasure that he derived from this simplest of activities:

To me, so long silenced by sickness, it is a lovely thing to be able to walk at any time: to me, so long abed, it is a supreme joy to walk at all. No wonder I lose my head and feet and fail to walk steadily and slowly and circumspectly as do the rest of my kind; no wonder I try now and again to tread a cloud and ape the lark; no wonder I come an occasional cropper and kiss – yet never curse – the road". Now that I too can walk the road, is it any wonder that I am almost beside myself with joy when I tread this Appian way?

Later Alfred developed a skilful dexterity in the description of his footloose wanderings that perhaps could only be fully appreciated by those accustomed to the art of what he termed 'tramping', and he was careful to point out: 'Rest assured, you will not experience the ecstasies in an easy chair by the fireside! Tramping is an active delight that only those who practise can rightly apprehend',[19] while the following graphic extracts, describe in vivid detail the physical and mental stimulation that he experienced during his tramping activities:

A stiff twenty miles yesterday over the moors, pelted by icy rain and lashed by the flail of the wind has greatly chastened me. Nothing, I think so knocks the conceit out of a man as a gruelling walk over moor and fell. It is as if body and mind alike have been flogged by an Omnipotent Power; and the effect is humbling in the extreme. My own body, like a foolish colt pawing an impatient foot in the stable, charges furiously over the savannahs the moment it slips the postern. But at night, panting and steaming, it comes back with a good deal of the nonsense – and all the energy – stamped out of it.

The mind too, luxuriating in on an overplus of oats in the study, is apt to give itself airs and notions, and image vain things. How vain they are, it only realises when it is confronted with the vast and inscrutable moors. For perhaps nowhere else in the world does a man realise how small and inarticulate he is on a high and lonely moor. It strips him naked, before those old, wise, eloquent and searching monitors, he stands abashed and silent.[20]

But what are the elusive joys that only stout members of the tramping fraternity so generously pour forth on those who are uninitiated?

> The joy of free movement; the bluff assault and repulse of the wind; the feeling of fighting one's way forward in the teeth of the elements; of contesting every yard of the way; of being beaten back and still struggling on. To cross a stretch of moor like this in a gale is something like sailing a yacht single-handedly over an angry sea. There is the sense of absolute dependence on one's own vigilance and strength, with the added satisfaction of making one's own pace. One lays a course and attempts to steer by it, tempest-tossed and buffeted for hours on end. One looks out over a wide and sombre waste of heath unbroken by a shelter of any kind.

> And always one must keep one's eye fixed sharply on some directing point on the horizon, and reach it, or risk being benighted in the high secret places. In these wild delectable places, the difficulty is not where to go, but where not to go, once you are in the high places. As like as not, you will find yourself torn asunder with doubts and conflicting desires; like me, you will want to walk north, south, east and west at the same moment, and in such crisis the best way out is to shut your eyes and let your legs decide.[21]

AJB: 'On Writing'

While Alfred had spent a good deal of his youth exploring the local moors, his first long walking tour through Nidderdale made such an impression on him that 'I remembered writing a long poem in blank verse about it – forty rapturous stanzas which, fortunately, I have since lost'.[18] However it was another not so pleasant experience of being incapacitated that stimulated his literary interests:

> It was during my illness that I began to write. I developed an intense love and appreciation of poetry, especially short lyrics and sonnets, and words in general. I began to write a little verse myself, and then prose sketches. They were of no importance, but I experienced for the first time the essential joy of creation that is sufficient reward.

> I had never any special intention to write about Yorkshire. I enjoyed walking for its own sake too much. I would write poetry, essays and fiction, and in between my walking and my working, I was writing hard.[18]

But it was another different tour that further stimulated Alfred's drive to write about his excursions:

> My next venture was a short walking tour of Belgium, and I enjoyed it so much that I wrote my first book on the strength of it. It was only a little book and nobody paid the least attention to it anyhow. I paid for its production, but that little book was a landmark in my life; it commemorated entry into literature and it was worth every penny it cost me, but being a Yorkshireman I didn't intend to pay for any more books being printed.

> Two years later, I gave expression to my love of Yorkshire and walking in my first book, Four Boon Fellows. I wrote this book to please myself and thoroughly enjoyed the task. It has the faults and high spirits of youth. Later on, as one gets older and more cunning, one writes with more restraint, if only to please publishers; but I doubt if one ever recaptures the joy and freshness of one's early work.[18]

Even so, Alfred commented about the frustration he often suffered by being unable to achieve the desired outcome in his writings:

> Words, words, words! What are these to ensnare that strange, elusive, glamorous bog o'lanthorn that haunts me from the first milestone to the last? And always beyond reach of my clutching hands! Here I am – poor fool! driving my leaden pen page after page – and the revelation as far off as ever![19]

Over the years Alfred accumulated an extensive collection of written material, both published and unpublished, in typescript and handwritten form, but found it hard to dispose of superfluous items:

> I am one of those people who find it difficult to destroy anything. Under the quite mistaken idea that somebody, some day, may be interested in my original writings. It is not perhaps just the faint chance that someone else may be interested in them when I am gone, but that I like to glance myself at early manuscripts from time to time, to recapture past moments of creation; and they always seem better than my more recent efforts.

> Manuscripts and articles which countless editors have firmly rejected, poems which publishers have serenely but emphatically refused: they are all lying in their respective catacombs awaiting the crack of doom. Not for me – or rather not for my pursuers – that tantalising occultation: that baffling eclipse. Where I walk look for foot prints, where I write look for thumb marks.

No, it is not pride: not cocksure confidence in ultimate recognition: I am long past that. At the beginning perhaps, but not now. I have knocked too long on and too loudly at too many doors to hope anyone will knock at my coffin, I have littered my path with too much lumber to tempt any posthumous scavenger to look for hidden jewels.[22]

Towards to end of his life Alfred's writing took on a more reflective tone and although he did not have the time to engage in much more of his favourite poetic expression, he did summarise his feelings for the stimulating tramping experiences of his younger days. This was in the form of a lengthy five page ode by Alfred ('Wharfe') to celebrate the 70th birthday of his life long-friend, George Coulehan Heseltine ('Ouse'),[23] which has been abstracted and given a generic title to describe the main theme contained in its stanzas:

A Lament for Lost Youth

O give us back our Youth Dear Lord!
And give us back our fire:
We only ask the grace Dear Lord
To climb a little higher!
The peaks which then eluded us,
The dales we did not see
These were the most mysterious
And there we long to be!

They said that growing old was grand
The best was yet to be:
A fig for what they said my 'Ouse',
I'd rather have the world we knew
In nineteen twenty-three.
O give us back our Legs Dear Lord! etc.,

Do you remember the Dales, my lad,
When we first walked together
Singing our litanies of praise,
Knee deep in Yorkshire heather?
O give us back our Dales Dear Lord! etc.,

Do you remember the Peaks we climbed
From dawn to dusk like gods together

Three in a day and one for luck
In the wild Dales weather?
O give us back our Peaks Dear Lord! etc.,

Do you remember the Inns, my friend
The sturdy inns of the Dales countree?
The pints o' nights we drank by the fire?
The Ham & Eggs and the Pies for tea?
O give us back our Inns Dear Lord! etc.

Envoi

Well done, my Ouse! I am most proud
To have so staunch, so true a friend
You scaled the Heights through storm and cloud
You struggled on to Journey's End.
O give us back our Strength Dear Lord! etc.,

Who knows perchance we will walk again
Together in the Heavenly Dales
And climb the peaks we failed to climb
And sip the Ambrosial Ales...
O give us back our Youth Dear Lord! etc.,

Happy Birthday and God Bless! – 'Wharfe'.

AJB: 'On Yorkshire Dales'

Alfred regarded 'God's Own Country' of Yorkshire as more of a kingdom than a just a county, and was of the opinion that: 'If you took all the best parts of every county in England, and put them together, you would have something resembling Yorkshire.' He was the most robust of walkers and covered almost the entire length and breadth of his beloved county on foot, but it was his love for the Yorkshire Dales that probably inspired him more than any other part of the county. When he gave public talks about his favourite Yorkshire topic, he would often summarise his feelings for those aspects that he found most rewarding during his tramping activities.[24] The following is an itemised collection of Alfred's own 'Great Moments' that epitomised his experiences of being in unison with the Yorkshire Dales, which for the sake of convenience have been classified into four categories:

GREAT MOMENTS IN THE YORKSHIRE DALES

'Demanding Moments'

- Tramping across a high ridge between two great Dales.
- Climbing several peaks in a day over miles of rough moor and mountain.
- Following a Green Road from end to end over a great divide
- The happiness and well-being that comes from a hard day's tramping.
- Making a new map come alive by striding across the countryside it portrays.

'Stirring Moments'

- Feeling on your face the chill of the wind, the sting of the rain or the burn of the sun.
- Sprawling on your back in the deep heather on the tops under a clear blue sky.
- Seeing the first upland lambs, finding the first violets and viewing the heather in its prime.
- Singing a cheerful song on the tops or making one up as you go along.
- Descending from the tops at dusk to a friendly inn, with a ravenous appetite and a raging thirst.

'Sensory Moments'

- Listening to a moorland beck.
- Bathing in a moorland tarn.
- Having a nice tea at a remote moorland farm.
- Bird watching on the tops.
- Talking to chance wayfarers, shepherds or famers.

'Contemplative Moments'

- Setting out at dawn before the rest of the world is awake.
- Being in a remote secret little Dale with nothing to spoil the solitude.
- Standing alone atop a remote 'Man', 'Cairn' or 'Howe' with a vista of hills and dales below.
- Times when you feel the influence of bygone Ages and feel the presence of the 'Ancients'.
- Times when it seems your senses depart, your spirit leaves the body and you enter 'paradise'.

'These are a few of my favourite moments, but they may suggest others to you' – AJB.

Envoi

In writing this biography I have been privileged to get to know, understand and appreciate more about this unique individual, and indeed the intriguing but complex character of the man himself, to the extent that I feel that I have almost got to know him personally. It is therefore my sincere hope and wish that readers of this tome may also feel that they have come close to knowing the prodigious walker, prolific writer and passionate Yorkshireman, that was Alfred John Brown.

42. Alfred John Brown

References and Notes

1. David Rubinstein, *The Wolds Way*, Dalesman Books, 1972, pp. 7, 15-16, and 38-39.
    1a. Note: Personal Communication, 2nd January 2016.

2. Harry Mead, 'The tramper who mastered the metre', The *Northern Echo*, 7th May 1981.

3. Tom Scott Burns, 'Alfred John Brown: Yorkshire's Tramping Author', The Yorkshire *Dalesman*, August 1981, pp. 358-361.

4. Tom Scott Burns, 'A.J. Brown – The Prince of Walkers'. *Voice of the Moors*, Spring Issue 1996, p. 3.

5. David Joy (Editor), *The Dalesman: A Celebration of 50 years*, Pelham Books, London, 1989, chapter 12, 'Half a Century of Change' – 'All Quiet in the Dales', pp. 184-196.

6. Malcolm Boyes and Hazel Chesters, 'A.J. Brown's Derwent Way', The *Yorkshire Journal*, 1990, vol. ii, pp. 73-79.

   6a. Note: The printed journal has since been replaced by www.theyorkshirejournal.com

7. Harry Mead, 'Heartbeat village's real hidden gem', *The Yorkshire Post*, 24th December 1995.

8. Editorial, 'Where On Earth?' *Voice of the Moors* magazine, Summer Issue, 2007, p. 9.

9. Steve Goodier, 'Following the Ale Trail', The *Dalesman*, November 2008, pp. 69-71.

10. Roy Richards, 'My Best Day Out', The *Dalesman*, May 2001, p. 96.

    10a. Note: Roy became a member of the West Riding Ramblers and served on the Committee of the Ramblers' Association.

11. John A. White, 'A.J. Brown, Walker, Writer and Passionate Dalesman', *Yorkshire Dales Review*, Winter 2015, Issue 129, pp. 14-15.

12. John A. White, 'Alfred John Brown, Walker, Writer and Moorsman', *Voice of the Moors* Online Magazine, Issue 122, Winter 2015, pp. 10-11.

13. Colin Speakman, 'Dales were a Paradise for Writer', *The Craven Herald & Pioneer* Newspaper, 31st December 2015, p. 26.

14. John A. White, 'A.J. Brown – Walker, Writer and Passionate Yorkshireman', *Dalesman* Magazine, (In press).

15. John A. White, Alfred John Brown Biographical Summary, The *Oxford Dictionary of National Biography*, (In press).

16. Burley-in-Wharfedale, 'The Alfred John Brown Trail', 'Rambles from the Roundhouse Series', 'Walkers Are Welcome' Programme (In preparation).

17. Harry Whitehouse, 'Tramping in A.J. Brown Country', 'The Classic Walks – Northern Yorkshire Coast and Moors', Peaksoft Media Publications, 2015, pp. 27-29.

18. A.J. Brown, *I Bought A Hotel*, Williams & Norgate Ltd., London, 1949, chapter: 'Books and Authorship, III Autobiographical' pp. 144-152.

19. A.J. Brown, *Moorland Tramping in West Yorkshire*, Country Life Ltd., London, 1931, Part One, 'Moorland Tramping', Section VIII, 'Ower T'Tops', pp. 27-31.

20. Alfred John Brown, 'The Moors' (no date, circa 1920s - 1950s), West Yorkshire Archive Service, Bradford Central Library, Document No. 69D90, Section 10/1, Item B, typescript of the draft: 'Brevities and Levities' from the 'Journal of a Curious Scribe'; 'His Walking Book'.

21. Ibid., Alfred John Brown, 'Twin Joys'.

22. Alfred John Brown, op.cit., 'On Cobwebs and Literary Corpses' (no date, circa 1920s - 1930s), West Yorkshire Archive Service, Bradford Central Library, 'Document No. 69D90, Section 10/2, typescript of the draft: 'Loose Leaves from the Journal of a Literary Clerk'.

23. AJB letter to GCH, 14th January 1965, AJB Personal, Business and Family Correspondence File, 1965.

24. Alfred John Brown, extracted from a 'Broad Acres' talk on 'Yorkshire Themes', Foyles Public Lecture Series File, 1951-1953.

Appendix

Alfred John Brown – List of Published Work

Yorkshire Books

Alfred J. Brown, *Four Boon Fellows – A Yorkshire Tramping Odyssey*, J.M. Dent & Sons, Ltd., London & Toronto, 1928, re-issued 1930.

Alfred J. Brown, *Moorland Tramping in West Yorkshire*, Country Life Ltd., London, 1931.

Alfred J. Brown, *Tramping in Yorkshire (North and East)*, Country Life Ltd., London, 1932.

Alfred J. Brown, *Striding Through Yorkshire*, Country Life Ltd., London, 1938, revised edition 1943, reprinted 1945, revised edition 1949.

Alfred J. Brown, *Broad Acres – A Yorkshire Miscellany*, Country Life Ltd., London, 1948, reprinted, 1949.

Alfred J. Brown, *Fair North Riding*, Country Life Ltd., London, 1952.

A.J. Brown, *The North York Moors National Park Guide Book*, The Home Publishing Co., Croydon, 1958, 1959, 1963, 1965 and 1967.

Novels

Julian Laverack (pseudonym), *The Lean Years*, Methuen & Co. Ltd., London, 1926, reprinted for the Woman's Book Club, London, 1947.

Julian Laverack (pseudonym), *Whitaker*, John Gifford Limited, London, 1946.

Personal Stories

Alfred J. Brown, *A Joyous Entry into Brighter Belgium*, Simpkin, Marshall, Hamilton, Kent & Co. Ltd., London, 1923.

Squadron-Leader A.J. Brown, *Ground Staff* (A Personal Record), Eyre & Spottiswoode, London, 1943.

A.J. Brown, *I Bought a Hotel*, Williams & Norgate Ltd., London, first impression September 1949, second impression October 1949, third impression (reprinted) 1950.

A.J. Brown, *Farewell, 'High Fell'*, Williams & Norgate Ltd., London, 1952.

Verse

Alfred J. Brown, *Poems & Songs*, Abbey Press, Horne & Son Ltd., Whitby, 1949.

ODE TO ALFRED JOHN BROWN

When striding through dale or over moor,
I recall a 'tramper' who's been there before,
A renowned writer from bygone days,
Whose works all hail these hallowed ways.
He stirs a reader with his winsome written word,
And rouses every rustic rambler who has heard,
His call to 'tramp ower t'tops' of each majestic Yorkshire Dale,
To savour the splendid scenes that one and all avail,
And take pleasure in pacing ancient path and droving road,
Or sward green track, that all abound in his beloved abode.
And though he's gone, his words remain and help me exude,
His joys of tramping in 'God's Own Country's' solitude.
When rambling in this Arcadian place I find,
Those rich rewards, solace of soul and mirth of mind.

John A. White, 1st August 2014 (Yorkshire Day)